Polo in the
United States

Polo in the United States

A History

HORACE A. LAFFAYE

FOREWORD BY DENNIS J. AMATO

UNIVERSITY OF ROCHESTER

McFarland & Company, Inc., Publishers
Jefferson, North Carolina

Except as noted, all the illustrations are courtesy of and with permission by the National Museum of Polo and Hall of Fame, Lake Worth, Florida.

The present work is a reprint of the illustrated case bound edition of Polo in the United States: A History, first published in 2011 by McFarland.

LIBRARY OF CONGRESS CATALOGUING-IN-PUBLICATION DATA

Laffaye, Horace A., 1935–
Polo in the United States : a history / Horace A. Laffaye ;
foreword by Dennis J. Amato.
p.   cm.
Includes bibliographical references and index.

ISBN 978-1-4766-6790-4
softcover : acid free paper ∞

1. Polo—United States—History.   I. Title.
GV1011.6.U6L34   2016   796.35'30973—dc22   2011002276

BRITISH LIBRARY CATALOGUING DATA ARE AVAILABLE

Front cover: "Mallet Work" by Sam Savitt. The scene is the Fairfield County Hunt Club in Westport, Connecticut, where Savitt was a frequent visitor sketching his polo art (private collection, Alex Pacheco photograph).

Printed in the United States of America

McFarland & Company, Inc., Publishers
Box 611, Jefferson, North Carolina 28640
www.mcfarlandpub.com

To my family:
Martha, Patrick, Gisèle, Ann, Trent,
Martina, Derek, Grace, Mark and Todd,
and to my friends in the world of polo

Table of Contents

Part IV. American Contemporary Polo

Acknowledgments

Many people helped me to write this book — so many that it would be impossible for me to name all who contributed their knowledge of polo in America.

In the first place, I wish to record my appreciation to the selection committee that honored me with the John H. Daniels Fellowship in 2009. This fellowship allowed me to conduct my initial research for this work within the friendly confines of the National Sporting Library in Middleburg, Virginia.

I am particularly indebted to Dennis Amato for writing the Foreword and going over the complete manuscript.

Henry Anderson, Jr., guided me in new research at the Newport Reading Room and gave me a book tracing that old club's history.

Robert Beveridge talked about his journey to Buenos Aires for the Cup of the Americas and the 30-goal Copa Sesquicentenario.

Thomas J. Biddle, Sr., chairman of the U.S. Polo Association, provided photographs and discussed some of the current challenges facing the Association.

George "Pete" Bostwick and Alan L. Corey, Jr., related many facts about their participation in international matches against Argentina.

Many thanks to Maureen Brennan for her invitation to visit Llangollen in Upperville and her loan of photographs.

Melinda Brewer loaned her painting of the polo pony Tobiano.

Mike Bucci related his memories of the Myopia Hunt Club and the F.I.P. Centennial Cup.

A special word of recognition to Frank Butterworth, Jr., Frank "Butch" Butterworth, III, George Haas, Craig Heatley, Kent Logan, Peter Orthwein, Adalbert von Gontard, Jr., Adalbert von Gontard, III, and William Whitehead, some of my teammates on Fairfield teams.

Elizabeth Day, director of memberships and handicaps in the U.S.P.A. office, provided important data.

Reuben DeGani, manager of the Cheyenne Mountain Country Club, took us on a tour of the club, including the site of the long gone polo fields, and showed us the polo memorabilia, including the handsome Foxhall Keene Cup.

George and Brenda DuPont at the Museum of Polo were, as always, a constant source of support during my innumerable visits to that unique institution searching for information and the photographs that illustrate this book.

Tylor Field, II, president of the Newport Reading Room, honored me with an invitation to speak at a dinner party on the occasion of the polo matches between Buck's Club from London and the Reading Room polo teams.

Fred Fortugno shared many delightful stories about American polo.

A heartfelt thank you to my dear friend Tommy Glynn, who for many years provided wonderful company while talking about his seven decades of involvement in polo.

In the course of a lengthy interview, Carlos Gracida talked about his extraordinary career and offered a kaleidoscopic view of the current situation in world polo. Regrettably, the conversation was never published.

Guillermo "Memo" Gracida reminisced about his father and uncles, and candidly expressed his views on polo today from a top professional player's point of view.

Debbie Gracy and Brent Holbert gave much information from Boerne about early polo in Texas.

James M. Healey, the St. Louis Country Club historian, clarified several aspects of polo at that old club.

Julian Hipwood shared his thoughts on many aspects of the game and his assessment of the current state of polo in America.

Ambassador Glen Holden loaned photographs and talked about the Federation of International Polo, where he served as President and the World Cup in Santa Barbara.

Stewart Iglehart gave freely of his time, giving not only information about his sporting career, but also acute observations on the state of contemporary polo.

S.K. Johnston, Jr., has always greeted my endless questions with a smile and plenty of savvy in his appreciation of many issues confronting polo in the United States.

Seymour H. Knox, Jr., gave me some of his books and described in great detail his recollections of several journeys to Argentina and England.

Robert Lubash talked at length about his experience while learning polo with Bob Skene and allowed me to research his extensive polo library.

Robert Mountford reviewed part of the manuscript and offered several worthy suggestions.

Thanks to Stephen A. Orthwein, Sr., for his gift of a book on the history of polo at the St. Louis Country Club, and his unflinching support of research at the Museum of Polo.

My appreciation to my friend Alex Pacheco for providing wonderful photographs.

F. Turner Reuter, Jr., and his wife Dana were marvelous hosts at their Red Fox Inn in Middleburg and adjacent fine art gallery. Turner spent hours educating me on many aspects of sporting art.

I wish to thank Frederic Roy, editor and publisher of *The Morning Line*, for providing photographs. Polo aficionados have contracted a huge debt with mon cher ami Frederic for his tremendous effort in bringing extensive coverage of the game in a daily basis.

The gifted artist Sam Savitt talked about his painting and gave us a beautiful work depicting the Kentucky Derby. One of his paintings adorns this book's cover.

In Santa Barbara, Bob Skene reminisced about his polo life, especially his three journeys to Argentina, his participation in the Westchester Cup and his subsequent career as a professional player in America.

Charles Smith talked at length about his father, the legendary Cecil Smith, and his own high-goal and international polo career.

Bobbie Stribling helped secure some illustrations for the book.

Boone Stribling related interesting facets about his polo endeavors and the South African tours.

I wish to thank Chris Vining for her invitation to give lectures at the International Polo Club Palm Beach, her loan of newspaper clips and for sharing her expertise in sporting art.

Tommy and Rosey Wayman talked about Hap Sharp's polo and automobile racing careers, Tommy's own exploits in polo and related stories about their favorite polo ponies. Rosey also loaned photographs from her family album.

Alex Webbe provided material on polo in Colorado, besides being a great pal in the press box at International Polo Club.

Paul and Sheldon Withers (née Gerry) talked at length about their life-long involvement with polo.

Several libraries provided bibliographical help. I wish to particularly thank the wonderfully helpful staff at the National Sporting Library, especially head librarian Lisa Campbell and Dr. Elizabeth Tobey, director of research and publications.

Jody Jones guided me through the Rare Book Room at the Penrose Public Library, Colorado Springs, and searched for obscure data about early polo in Colorado.

Daniel J. Linke, University Archivist and Curator of Public Policy Papers, Seeley G. Mudd Manuscript Library at Princeton University; Marilee Meyer at the U.S. Military Academy, West Point; Sean B. O'Brien from the Princeton University Alumni Association, the staff of the Palm Beach County Library System, Wellington Branch, and the staff at the Pequot Library in Southport, Connecticut, were particularly helpful in my searches.

Also, I wish to thank many individuals who along several decades taught me many things about the game:

In Argentina: Mariano Aguerre, José M. Azumendi, Dr. Enrique Braun Estrugamou, Roberto Cavanagh, Carlos de la Serna, Francisco Dorignac, Gastón Dorignac, Heriberto Duggan, Roberto Fernández Llanos, Tommy Garrahan, Juan Carlos Harriott, Jr., Dr. Alberto P. Heguy, Horacio A. Heguy, Alberto Laffaye, Roberto Laffaye, Luis E. Lalor, David M. Miles, Alejandro Moy, Miguel Novillo Astrada, Ernesto Pinto, Alfredo Podestá, Jorge Torres Zavaleta and Marcos Uranga, all of whom helped bring me closer to the world of polo.

In Australia: Chris Ashton and Sinclair Hill, for extensive correspondence and for sharing their thoughts on the game.

In England: Nigel à Brassard, Nicholas Colquhoun–Denvers, Brigadier Arthur Douglas-Nugent, Tony Emerson, Peter Grace, Edward Horswell, Claire Lucas Tomlinson, John Tinsley, John Tylor, Roderick Vere Nicholl, Mary Ann Wingfield and David Woodd.

In Canada: John Benitz, who provided the scrapbooks of the Argentine tour to California, and Frank Vlahovic, who talked about Canada's involvement in the World Cup.

Last, but certainly not least, many thanks to Mrs. Margaret Hickey for her solid judgment and dedication in reviewing the final draft of this book. Marge has corrected my writing far longer than I care to admit.

Foreword by Dennis J. Amato

Despite the long and illustrious history of polo in the United States, surprisingly there has been a dearth of books published on the subject. That is not to say that there are not a lot of books covering various aspects of American polo. In fact, the bibliography on the sport in this country is quite extensive but is mainly populated by club histories, biographies, regional accounts of the game and the like. A quick sampling would include such admirable pieces as Benjamin Allison's *The Rockaway Hunting Club* (1932), Nelson Aldrich Jr.'s *Tommy Hitchcock, an American Hero* (1984), and Harry Worcester Smith's *Life and Sport in Aiken* (1935). However, these and other books typically focus on polo only in the narrower contexts of their subject matter.

Histories devoted strictly to tracing on a systematic basis the origins and the development of the game of polo in the United States are very rare. In fact, to date there really have been only two principal books produced: Newell Bent's *American Polo* (1929) and Ami Shinitzky and Don Follmer's *The Endless Chukker: 101 Years of American Polo* (1978).

Bent's book has now acquired almost iconic status among polo bibliophiles. Bent wrote his tract a mere half century after polo was first imported from England into the United States by James Gordon Bennett in 1876. Consequently, he was able to speak with or to correspond with some of the key principals who played a major role in promoting polo during its infancy and formative stages. In addition, he could utilize what was the equivalent of oral histories among the polo populace at the time as well as written accounts from a wide variety of media such as magazine articles and club directories. Although the book may have been more journalistic than scholarly in its methodology, it nevertheless continues to rank as the accepted standard on the introduction and the early years of polo in this country.

Endless Chukker's debut occurred around the centenary of the game in the United States. It was and remains a highly entertaining and an informative, if not a bit breezy, recounting of polo's beginnings and evolution in America. Further, it is profusely illustrated throughout which further add to its appeal.

Dr. Horace Laffaye's newest book, *Polo in the United States: A History,* however, represents a major milestone in the annals of polo publishing. First and foremost, it is written by the pre-eminent polo historian in the world today — an individual who has numerous articles and several books to his credit, including *The Evolution of Polo* (2009) and the monumental opus, *The Encyclopedia of Polo* (2004). Also as a polo player himself, Dr. Laffaye has a thorough understanding of all aspects and nuances of the game, which further enhances his carefully crafted and extremely well-documented manuscript. Moreover, he has taken a multi-disciplined approach to his research whereby he is able to leverage not only a vast amount of primary and secondary source materials, much of which come from his personal collection, but also his very large network of personal relationships within the polo community.

Any attempt to write a history of American polo in itself would clearly be a daunting as well as a risky undertaking and could easily result in a very high-level, if not a superficial rendition. Much to his credit, Dr. Laffaye is highly successful in achieving that delicate balance of surveying in a most readable fashion an enormous number of topics in a level of detail that can only be described as extraordinary, while still providing a continuous thread and a broad perspective of polo's rise, decline and renaissance in the United States over more than a century and quarter.

The reader can follow the game's initial arrival in its rudimentary form at Dickel's Riding Academy in New York in 1876 (or perhaps earlier as Laffaye's prodigious sleuthing suggests) all the way to present-day high-goal play in Palm Beach and elsewhere. Also at the macro level, the book provides considerable color on such important national events as the Open Championship, the Junior Championship (later renamed the Twenty-Goal Championship and subsequently the Silver Cup), and the East-West Games as well as such legendary international tournaments as the Westchester Cup, the Cup of the Americas, and the Avila Camacho Cup. Similarly, the development of the Polo Association and its transformation into the United States Polo Association, the origins and changes to the handicap system, depression-era polo, the postwar recovery, contemporary play and other "big picture" topics are all given ample treatment.

For those seeking more in-depth coverage of more specific areas, they will not be disappointed. For example, a substantial portion of the book covers regional polo (e.g., New England, Upstate New York, Long Island, the Southeast, the Southwest, the Pacific Coast and the Northwest) as well as polo in individual states (e.g., Massachusetts, South Carolina, Florida, Texas, Colorado and California). These various geographic surveys are supplemented by a number of short essays and thumbnail sketches on many of the more famous clubs (e.g., the Myopia Hunt Club, the Meadow Brook Club, the Chagrin Valley Hunt Club, the Oak Brook Polo Club, the St. Louis Country Club, the San Antonio Polo Club, the Santa Monica Polo Club and the Hawaii Polo Club). Additionally, there are some very specialized subjects interspersed within the book (e.g., American players in the Olympics, polo in the military, intercollegiate polo, indoor polo and women's polo).

In many respects, an updated and comprehensive chronicling of American polo has been long overdue but with Horace Laffaye's *The History of Polo in the United States*, the wait has been well worth it! Undoubtedly, the author's epic effort is likely to be viewed as one of the most important books ever published on the sport of polo and is destined to become a major reference work for decades to come.

Long Island resident Dennis J. Amato is a respected polo historian with a large number of publications to his credit and one of the world's largest private collections of polo art, memorabilia, books and other printed materials. He was the club historian for the legendary Meadow Brook. He earned a Ph.D. from Johns Hopkins University College of Advanced International Studies.

Introduction

When I suggested the idea of this book to Robert Franklin, the founder of McFarland & Company, my publisher, his reply was: "What? Another book on polo?" To his credit, Robbie once more sent me a signed contract without even looking at one word of *Polo in the United States: A History*. Such an unconditional mark of confidence places a tremendous burden upon the author because the game of polo, so immensely enjoyable to play and watch, is very difficult to write about.

The main reason for taking up this challenge was my urge to research, elucidate and explain facts and stories about this absorbing pastime. Whether the result of this investigative research will end the reign of some myths is another matter. History abounds with instances showing that revisionism is a slow process. This is not to infer that the demise of a legend is an earth-shaking fact or crucial to the survival of the game. But truth is truth, and for all seasons. Nor do I pretend to absolute objectivity, which historian C.W. Wedgwood called "that alluring but unattainable goal." This work describes polo in America as I see it; quite simply, it is a personal view.

At the onset it should be pointed out that there was just not enough room for everything and everyone in this book. Therefore, many happenings are either not mentioned at all or just briefly touched upon. As an example, aficionados of indoor polo will find pertinent information in only one chapter. The reason is quite simple: it is a different game. The ground is different; so are the ball, the goals and the number of players. Polo player Robert Lubash got it right when he wrote in *Polo Wisdom*: "Not that arena, bicycle, cowboy polo aren't great sports, but there is nothing like grace under pressure and the thrill of a chase down a long, wide open field of outdoor polo."

Early practice games in a riding arena hardly qualify for prominence of the indoor game in the United States because as soon as the balmy spring weather of 1876 made its appearance in New York City, the small polo contingent moved on to a field in the Bronx, and the game remained a totally outdoors endeavor until the early 1900s. Each version of the game of polo was under totally separated governing bodies, which finally merged in the middle of the twentieth century.

Those who expect to find in this book results such as what club took the Coronado (California) All America Champion Cup, or the players on the teams that participated in the 1976 Centenary Match, will be disappointed. To obtain such information they should consult other sources, the best and most comprehensive being the National Museum of Polo and Hall of Fame's complete collection of U.S. Polo Association's Year Books. The present work is more of a painting of polo in America, not a stroke by stroke tale of the game from 1876 to 2010.

It has been said that history is made by great players, the game's superstars. It may be so; however, there is much in this book about average and below average players. They are representatives of the nameless, faceless polo players who toil mostly on Sunday afternoons. They are the salt of the earth in the game of polo. So I would occasionally like to recognize them as they so deserve. Without those players, this wonderful world of polo would be the poorer. May the salt never lose its flavor.

This game of polo is part of the twentieth-century phenomenal growth of sports in these more or less United States. Tinged by the public at large with an aura of snobbism, thought of as a diversion for the super-rich, and watched only by the elite from Palm Beach to Palm Springs, in reality it is a magnificent spectacle of beautiful horses and skilled horsemen — a game that, in spite of some enormous sums collected by the top professionals, is mostly played just for the fun of it.

Polo is also a family game. The records of tournaments are replete with the names of fathers, sons, daughters, uncles, nephews and nieces, as well as in-laws. This family involvement in the game is also perceived while walking along the sidelines, or in the pony lines, when one often meets parents and grandparents who talk with fluency and much technical knowledge of past glories and present failures.

In comparison with other vigorous games and sports, polo shows unique characteristics: the formal dress, the impeccable manners (by and large), the unblemished turf, the restrained audience and the unobtrusive officials. Frederick Ayer, sometime Myopia Hunt's Captain of Polo, touched the right chord when he stated: "Some players swear at the world in general, and some swear when they miss the ball, and some swear at their horses, and nobody minds much. But some people swear at somebody else, and that is one of the things we don't like in polo." This show of sportsmanship has been a pattern of behavior since the very beginnings of the game and, hopefully, will remain as a distinctive quality of everyone associated with the most elegant of games.

A final thought. Polo may not build character, but it certainly goes a long way to reveal it. Perhaps not so much as the game of golf, but playing a single match against previously unknown opponents, both flaws and sterling qualities of sportsmanship appear on the surface, long before the final bell is rung.

Wellington, Florida
February 2011

PART I

The Herbert Era, 1876–1921

CHAPTER 1

The Beginnings of All Things
Polo in America

Sometime in the winter of 1875-1876 a group of New Yorkers, all members of the metropolitan *jeunesse dorée*, decided that the newly rediscovered pastime of polo should become the latest fashion in town, as it was rapidly expanding in England. This group of trend setters — and they were pretty fast — was led by none other than Leonard Jerome. His beautiful and witty daughter, Jenny, had married a younger brother of the Duke of Marlborough and was the mother of Winston Leonard Spencer-Churchill, one of the towering figures in the history of the world.

The group's daily life was centered at the celebrated Delmonico's restaurant for lunch and they spent much of their leisure time at the Jockey Club, an institution that had a theater and offered many conveniences of the good life. Another institution that catered to what a century later would be called the jet-set was the Union Club. This citadel of the metropolitan aristocracy was open all night, offering refuge to those revelers who did not care to go home. Among the members were the Jeromes, the Heckschers, the Howlands, the Oelrichs, the Osgoods, Gunnig Bedford, William Proctor Douglas, Arthur Leary, Lloyd Phoenix, Pierre Lorillard, Jr., William Travers, Frank Work and, most conspicuously, James G. Bennett, Jr.

James Gordon Bennett, the younger, was born in New York City in 1841 with the proverbial silver spoon his mouth, a spoon that Bennett eventually turned into a golden one. One of his biographers, Oliver Carlson, described his early days thus:

> Young Bennett had been raised in the lap of luxury. He was spoiled, self-centered, and high-spirited. His education had been largely acquired abroad, under private tutors. He was tall, like his father; handsome, like his mother; and seemed destined to become notorious only as a sportsman and play-boy.[1]

Next to Commodore Cornelius Vanderbilt and William B. Astor, the younger Bennett, after his father's death in 1872, enjoyed the largest personal income in America. This certainty of resource made him a good spender. He had no desire for piling up millions and never tried to do so.[2]

Bennett became the most notorious and uncouth millionaire of his times, both in Newport and New York City. Perhaps he was the first American to revel in the cult of instant gratification. As an example, the Newport Casino, now the home of the International Tennis Hall of Fame,[3] was commissioned by Bennett in a fit of pique following a vote of censure by The Reading Room, a club restricted to gentlemen only, in 1879. The vote of censure was the result of a bizarre incident involving Capt. Henry Augustus "Sugar" Candy, an officer and a gentleman in the 9th Lancers, one of the cavalry regiments that participated in the first polo match in England.[4] For a bet, probably quite substantial, Captain Candy rode his horse into the sacred confines of The Reading Room, the most exclusive social club in Newport. There are three versions of the escapade. Nevertheless, whether Capt. Henry Candy guided his mount onto the club's porch, into the salon, or up the stairs, was totally immaterial to the powers that be at the club. Thus came about the vote of censure against Mr. Bennett, who had introduced Capt. Candy to The Reading Room membership.

That is the party line. Documents recently made known to the author during a visit to The Newport Reading Room and the Clambake Club tell a different story.[5] From the minutes of The Newport Reading Room:

James Gordon Bennett standing next to a true pony. This photograph illustrates the difference between the sizes of ponies today and at the beginning of polo in this country.

Resolved that Captain Augustus Candy having conducted himself in an Unbecoming manner in the Newport Reading Room, the privileges of the Club are hereby withdrawn from him & the Secretary is directed to furnish him with a copy of this resolution, & to return to him his subscription to the Club.[6]

The facts of the matter are that Gordon Bennett never was a member of the Reading Room, while Captain Candy was a temporary member. Negotiations for the purchase of Sydney Brook's estate on Bellevue Avenue had started many months before the Candy incident. The Newport Reading Room historian Alan T. Schumacher, members R. Campbell James and Henry Anderson, Jr., confirm that there was no cause and effect connection between the concept of the Casino and the "Captain Candy calamity."[7] End of the myth.

The young man was difficult to approach and hard to deal with. His social escapades and bizarre behavior were the talk of the town. Some defied description and one particular incident led to a duel between Bennett and Frederick May, the brother of Miss Caroline May. James G. Bennett had engaged in the courtship of Caroline; however, his extravagance and recklessness while paying a visit at Dr. May's home on New Year's Day 1877 was such that one of his biographers stated that it could not be told politely. As a result, Frederick May — his fiancée's brother — horsewhipped Bennett in front of the Union Club, which led to the duel. Fred May purposely shot in the air and Bennett missed his mark. Bennett's vagaries also brought him into frequent and unwanted contact with the New York police.

In 1878, just two years after the game started in America, Bennett sold his ponies at auction. His best mount, Sultan, was sold for 85 dollars. Eventually, James Gordon Bennett moved to France, spending much of his time in Paris, and also in Pau, a provincial town in southern France noted for its superb climate and affinity for British sports, games and gardens. A large British colony, as well as North and South American vacationers, made Pau their winter retreat. True to form, Bennett also became obnoxious in the quiet town at the foot of the Pyrenees.[8]

The British brought with them to Pau their sports and games: polo, rugby, steeplechasing and foxhunting which became their pastimes. As entertainment, these were added to golf, which had started on the Plain de Billère — later the site of a polo ground — towards the end of the Napoleonic Wars, when Scottish officers played the royal and ancient game. The Pau Golf Club is the oldest golf club in continental Europe, dating back to 1856. It is interesting that several American polo players became Masters of the Pau Fox Hounds. Among them were William K. Thorn, Jr., Henry Ridgeway, Frederick H. Prince, Jr., and, of course, James Gordon Bennett, Jr.

Probably no other individual in the nineteenth and twentieth centuries did more to generate attention and provide financial backing in sports and games than James G. Bennett the younger.[9] An avid yachtsman, Bennett participated in races for the America Cup and traveled extensively aboard his many vessels. Today, there is even a Gordon Bennett Cup offered in competition by the Royal Bombay Yacht Club, on the shores of the Indian Ocean. The Gordon Bennett balloon competition is still held in Europe. The Gordon Bennett airplane races were a feature in the early days of aviation. And, finally, although the donor was a lukewarm automobilist and never attended any of the races, the Gordon Bennett trophy, run from 1900 until 1905, is considered the precursor of international motor racing and the forefather of the now formidable successful Formula One World Championship.[10]

Even though Bennett owned several homes in New York and Newport, it was the one in Paris, the city of lights, which became his main base while overseeing the tremendously successful *New York Herald*, inherited from his father. He had a palace in the Avenue d'Iena and an apartment on the Avenue des Champs Elysées, from where he oversaw the operations of the Parisian *Herald*, with his typical tyrannical methods.

A confirmed bachelor, with a well-established fondness for stage girls, in 1914 Bennett married an American woman, the former Maud Parker, widow of the Baron de Reuter, a scion of the famous news agency. In September 1918, towards the end of World War I, a childless James Gordon Bennett passed away at his residence in Beaulieu, near the Cote d'Azur. Bennett wished to rest on French soil; accordingly, he was buried in the Père Lachaise cemetery in Paris.

Thus the man.

The Myth

Established dogma is that James Gordon Bennett, Jr., brought polo to these United States. The party line states that Bennett saw a game of polo in England, purchased mallets, balls, a set of the Hurlingham Club's rules, and sailed the ocean blue to America.

Frank Gray Griswold, a contemporary of James Gordon Bennett, who played with him on the initial practice games at Dickel's Riding Academy, gives a slightly different view: "He had been playing polo in France with Messrs. Ridgway, Brincant [sic], Hennessy and others and was full of enthusiasm."[11]

In a later interview, Hermann Oelrichs further clarified the story. An article in *The San Francisco Call* states:

James Gordon Bennett and friends concluded that polo ought to be introduced to America. As Mr. Herman [sic] Oelrichs was going to Europe, he was commissioned to bring back from England the necessary paraphernalia. When Mr. Oelrichs returned with the outfit necessary the practicing began at Dickel's. Mr. Bennett and Mr. Oelrichs were the main movers.[12]

The occasion for the interview was a report on a game to be held in Burlingame between the 4th U.S. Cavalry and the local team. At the time, Mr. Hermann Oelrichs, the man who brought the first mallets, polo balls and shirts into the United States, was in San Francisco. As a bachelor in his forties, while playing tennis at the Newport Casino he met, and soon married, the heiress Tessie Fair. The Oelrichs commissioned architect Stanford White — whose firm McKim, Mead and White was responsible for the Newport Casino — to design Rosecliff, one of the grand houses on Bellevue Avenue. It is now owned by the Preservation Society of Newport.[13]

The New York Times in his obituary states, "He [Oelrichs] introduced the game of polo into America."[14] Oelrichs, the American agent for the North German Lloyd shipping line, was one of the richest men in the country. He was also a multi-talented sportsman, reputed to be the best swimmer — he swam in the Atlantic Ocean among sharks — amateur baseball player, hammer-thrower and boxer. A bout was considered pitting Oelrichs at six feet and over 200 pounds, against John L. Sullivan, the world boxing champion; however, it never came to be. A multi-faceted sportsman, Hermann Oelrichs was the first president of the U.S. Lacrosse Association.

However, as Michael Capuzzo wrote in *Close to Shore*,

Yet there was about Hermann Oelrichs, too, the ache of promise unrealized. He remained aloof, declining offers to run for both mayor of New York City and president of the New York Athletic Club. "Hermann Oelrichs was so richly endowed by nature and so perfectly equipped both mentally and physically," opined *The New York Times*, "that his friends have been almost unanimous in declaring that had he so chosen he might have made for himself a much larger place in life."[15]

Perhaps this reticence, quite the opposite of James Gordon Bennett's flamboyant style, has prevented the recognition of Hermann Oelrichs' role in bringing polo to the United States. The fact that Oelrichs brought over the polo equipment from England is further corroborated by Frank Gray Griswold:

In 1876 he [James G. Bennett] had mallets and balls brought from England and started playing polo in New York, indoors, in what was then Dickel's Riding Academy at Fifth Avenue and 39th Street, today the very heart of the Metropolis's fashionable shopping center.[16]

The fact that Bennett had played or at least witnessed polo in France is confirmed by the doyen of American polo editors, Peter Vischer:

James Gordon Bennett's early essay is believed by most historians of the sport to have been the first polo played in the United States. Whether it actually was or not I do not know, but, 2,000 miles from Mr. Dickel's now famous riding academy, I was once shown a field in the town of Boerne, outside of San Antonio, Texas, a settlement founded in 1546 which had grown to a city of 100,000 by 1877, when the first train came through. There a group of sport-loving Englishmen is supposed to have played the first polo in America, years before Mr. Bennett saw it in Paris or brought it to New York. Certainly San Antonio had the game in 1885, when an enterprising dealer from Iowa named Pat Jones started shipping ponies to New York.[17]

Now Mr. Vischer throws a new item into the equation, that is, the possibility that polo in the United States began in Texas. More about that anon.

There is no question that John G. Bennett was the guiding spirit in bringing polo to

America. Writing in 1902, Eben Willard Roby, Harvard graduate, lawyer and Meadow Brook Club player, states that in 1876 Bennett gave a dinner at his home on 5th Avenue and 38th Street to the following gentlemen: William Douglas, William Jay, Charles Franklyn, William Thorn, Perry Belmont, Lord George Mandeville, John Mott, and Samuel Howland.[18] It was at this gathering of notables that a decision was made to bring polo into the United States.

Dickel's Riding Academy

In the northeast corner of 5th Avenue and East 39th Street there stood a wooden building which was the home of Dickel's Riding Academy. The structure was considered, for the period, quite colossal and magnificent. Col. Christian Frederick Dickel, who had been in the Prussian army, was the proprietor. Colonel Dickel had been in command of the 4th New York Volunteer Cavalry in the Civil War. When the first polo practices took place in the arena, his son, Charles, owned Dickel's Academy.

The games were a version of the indoor game, a variant that would not take hold in America until almost half-a-century later. The indoor ring was used as a convenience during the period in which construction of an outdoor field was in progress. Associated with James G. Bennett in this endeavor were such well-known men as Hermann Oelrichs, Colonel William Jay, Frank Gray Griswold, Hollis Honnewell, Sir Bache Cunard and others. With some ponies procured through Harry Blasson — an Englishman riding master who rode to hounds with the Queen's County Hunt — they commenced practice games at Dickel's Academy.[19]

Harry Blasson was dispatched to Texas with a carte blanche order to buy mustangs particularly suited and selected for polo. Blasson executed his commission with great fidelity and expert judgment, and greatly to the fancy of those who were establishing polo. After the arrival of the ponies, Harry Blasson was commanded to put them in good form.[20]

As to Dickel's Riding Academy, three years later, in 1879, the wooden structure was torn down to make way, ironically, for the Union League Club building, where so many of the polo pioneers in this country passed many hours of enjoyment. By 1886, the academy was located at 124-136 West 56th Street; the building's back was on 7th Avenue, between 56th and 57th Streets.[21] At the time, the streets were unpaved and the location, at the edge of Goat Hill near Central Park, was so far uptown that it was considered out in the sticks.

The Westchester Polo Club at Jerome Park

In March of 1876 the Westchester Polo Club was formed by James G. Bennett and 14 of his friends. They were Sir Bache Cunard, Frederick Bronson, William P. Douglas, George R. Fearing, Charles G. Francklyn, Frank Gray Griswold, Samuel S. Howland, Hollis Hunnewell, Col. William Jay, Lord Mandeville, John Mott, Hermann Oelrichs, Fairman Rogers, and William K. Thorn, Jr. A ground was laid out and a clubhouse and stables put up in Westchester County, near Fordham station, directly north of the old Jerome Park.[22] The clubhouse merited an illustration and a detailed description in the *Daily Graphic*.[23]

The first game at Jerome Park was for a saddle, offered as a prize by Mr. Bennett. The players were James G. Bennett, Harry and Hermann Oelrichs, Dick Peters, John Mott, Fairman Rogers, Lord Mandeville (later Duke of Manchester), William Douglas and Col. William Jay.

Polo at Jerome Park on 10 June 1876. This was one of the earliest matches of the new game of polo. All the players except one are identified: Unknown umpire, Frank Griswold, Harry Oelrichs, William Jay (Back), William Douglas (Back), James Gordon Bennett (front), Howland Robbins, John Mott (Back), Samuel Howland, Hermann Oelrichs, Fairman Rogers and William Thorn.

The Westchester Polo Club original attire was described as blue and cardinal, and blue and orange; riding breeches, either buckskins or cords.[24] The new game met with such success that next year the Club made its headquarters at fashionable Newport. The first game in Newport took place on 10 July 1876, with only four players: James Gordon Bennett, Frederic Kane, Howland Robbins and Lord Mandeville.[25]

From then on success was rapid. At some time between the move to Rhode Island and 1886 the shirts were changed to yellow. The Westchester Polo Club was the only club until polo at the Buffalo Country Club came into existence. With the Westchester Polo Club settled in Rhode Island, the location of the ground was on Earl, Meikle and Vaughn Avenues, adjacent to Morton Park's east side. After part of the property was sold for development, it was moved to Bateman's Point.

Then the New York polo group moved to a parcel of land delimited by 110th and 112th streets and from 5th to 6th avenues. This was the Manhattan Polo Association, whose officers were August Belmont, Jr., president; Frank T. Iselin, treasurer; and Henry L. Herbert, secretary. The first polo games took place in the spring of 1880, the grounds being formally opened to the public on 25 September 1880 at the start of the fall season.

The initial field was described as bare, with the ponies raising clouds of dust that enveloped players and spectators alike. During the summer, turf was planted, a grandstand for 2,000 people was erected, refreshment booths were added, and a cinder track suitable for athletic events, one-third of a mile in length, was constructed around the polo field. The match was a friendly contest, all players being Westchester members. About 200 spec-

1969

Augustus Belmont was one of the pioneers of polo in America.

tators witnessed the event, which pitted the Reds, captained by August Belmont, Jr., assisted by Lloyd Bryce, against the Blues, led by Frank Iselin, with Henry Herbert and Frederick Beach. A brass band entertained the public during the intervals between bouts (goals). Belmont and Iselin made the charge to start the first bout, which lasted 20 minutes before the first goal was scored. The rest of the bouts lasted from one-and-a-half minutes to 13 minutes. At the end of the fourth bout Lloyd Bryce retired from the contest, Iselin changing shirts for the Reds to make the teams even, two-a-side.

The contest, which was reported in great detail, was described as: "the struggle was a long and severe one. Six bouts were played before the setting of the sun put an end to the match."[26] The final score, 4–2, favored the Blues.

Polo continued, but the grass refused to grow and players became so dilatory in their engagements that spectators, who initially had came in good numbers, soon enough dwindled to such an extent that public games ceased and the property was sold, with a good profit being obtained.[27] Subsequently, the facility was leased out to the New York Giants baseball team. When the Giants moved uptown to new premises around 1890, they renamed the field "Polo Grounds," although no polo was played at this location.[28]

The Match at Prospect Park and Other Early Clubs

With the closing of the Manhattan Polo Association, Henry L. Herbert, who years later would achieve everlasting fame as the creator of the individual handicap system, started the Brighton Polo Club in Long Branch, New Jersey, together with George W. Elder, Adolph Ladenburg, Henry J. Montague, Clarence H. Robbins, W. Ward Robbins, Arthur Sewell,

Howard Stokes and a Captain Wilson. This club lasted only some three seasons, after the first matches in 1877. Then some members of the Narragansett Gun Club gave polo a go, among them being Carroll Bryce, Edward W. Davis and Pierre Lorillard, Jr.

A match that engendered much publicity was the one held at Prospect Park in Brooklyn, between Westchester and Queens County Hunt on 11 June 1879. Other sources give the date as 13 May 1879. In reality, all the players belonged to the Westchester Polo Club. Clad in blue and yellow, the winning Westchester squad presented August Belmont, Jr., Carroll Bryce, Henry Herbert, Harry Oelrichs and William W. Stanford, with Adolph Ladenburg and William Oothout as substitutes. The blue and cardinal Queens County Hunt team was Frank Gray Griswold, Frank T. Iselin, Pierre Lorillard, Jr., and Hermann Oelrichs. Henry W. Hallock and Center Hitchcock were named as substitutes. It was reported that 10,000 people watched the game.

Among the polo players and hard-riding members of the Queens County Hunt was the colorful figure of William Eliot Zborowski. Born in Elizabethtown, New Jersey, in 1858, the son of Martin and Emma Morris Zabriskie, he years later changed his surname. Eliot was a colorful and popular member of the social set, but also a very shrewd businessman. Zborowski had done very well in Wall Street before he married Margaret Astor Carey, great granddaughter of John Jacob Astor. Zborowski divided his time between New York City and Newport, where he distinguished himself as one of the pioneers of polo in the United States, and also suffering several spills as a results of his daring equitation. Then he took up residence in England as a Polish member of the nobility, having styled himself as Count Zborowski. Eliot Zborowski lived as befitted his station: a palatial home in Melton Mowbray in Leicestershire, England's premier foxhunting country; riding with the County Carlow Hunt in Ireland; and maintaining a suite in the Elysée Palace Hotel in Paris and a chateau in Nice.

As one of the most glamorous and promising racing drivers of his times, Eliot was nominated by the Mercedes factory — as was another American polo player, Foxie Keene — to race in the Gordon Bennett race to take place in Ireland in July 1903. It was not to be. Zborowski was killed while competing in the hill climb at La Turbie on 1 April 1903. One of the Zborowski legends began in the aftermath of the accident. Fastidious in his personal habits, Eliot was wearing stiff cuffs with gold links. According to the myth, just before he crashed his cuff was caught in the accelerator handle, pushing it to full speed. The driver lost control of the car and crashed head-on into a stone wall.[29]

The tragic theme in the Zborowski legend continues. His only son, Louis, was 8 years old at the time. He went on to become a racing driver and the force behind the large Chitty-Bang-Bang cars that raced at Brooklands in the 1920s. In 1924, while competing in the Italian Grand Prix at the Monza Autodrome, Louis Zborowski crashed in the notorious Lesmo curve and was killed. He was driving a Mercedes automobile, just like his father, and was wearing his father's gold cufflinks. Another coincidence is that Louis Zborowski's riding mechanic, Martin, survived the accident; his father's riding companion, the Marquis de Pollange, although injured, also was a survivor.

The First Inter-Club Match

The first real match between clubs took place in Newport, Rhode Island, in 1878, between the Westchester Polo Club and the Buffalo Country Club teams. The winner was

Westchester, with August Belmont, James Gordon Bennett, Frank Gray Griswold and Hermann Oelrichs. Playing for Buffalo Country Club were Lawrence Rumsey — brother-in-law of the Carys — Dr. Charles Cary, Thomas Cary and John Newton Scatcherd. Writing on his reminiscences of the match, Griswold noted that

> The ball was placed in the center of the field and was charged for from a white line about five yards in front of the goal-posts, which were of wood and driven well home. I, being the lightweight, had the hair-raising experience of always leading the charge for my side. After each goal sides were changed and the ball was charged for again. When the ball was out of bounds, over the sidelines, there being no boards at the time, the umpire or a spectator threw the ball in. I say a spectator, because the umpire was on foot in those days and had to be a good pedestrian.
>
> The return match of that first encounter was played at Buffalo the following year according to the rules of the Buffalo club.
>
> The ground was the infield of a trotting track with hardly a blade of grass on hard baked clay, and the ball we had to play was small, unpainted and difficult to see. The size of their ponies was unlimited and some were fully 16 hands.
>
> We had a hard fight in that match at Buffalo, the first period lasting sixty minutes before a goal was scored, ponies being changed at knockouts. We finally lost the goal and the match because Buffalo had a supply of fresh ponies and ours were done.
>
> It was here that we saw the first round or cigar-headed mallets. They were invented in Buffalo. The English mallets and ours were all square-headed at that time. They also used hickory sticks instead of cane. These did not break, but became badly bent.
>
> The match was a great social event in Buffalo but we were not introduced to any of the lovely maidens we saw about, because "we had failed to present the Buffalo team to our lady friends in Newport the year before. We had not appreciated that they were ladies' men as well as warriors."[30]

Early Polo in Texas

There is a strong oral tradition that the game of polo was started in Texas by English settlers. There is ample documentation that polo was played in the Lone Star State early on; however, there is no confirmatory evidence indicating that it took place prior to the practice matches in New York City.

The first notice about the game in Texas appeared in the Thursday 6 April 1876 issue of the *Galveston Daily News*:

> Mr. Harry Blasson from New York has been in the region (Bexar County, Texas) as agent of *The New York Herald*'s owner, Mr. James Gordon Bennett, to purchase twenty small ponies for a Polo Club of which he is president. This institution requires particularly small and active nags... The New York Club is first to introduce it into this country. Texas cow-boys and rangers would make admirable players... One great advantage to be derived from the game of polo, we are convinced, will be that it will make all who practice it good horsemen, and give an impetus to equestrianism that has long been needed in this section of country....

Two days later the same periodical reports that "James Gordon Bennett's twenty Polo ponies passed through Luling (Texas) on Wednesday. They are beautiful little creatures and active as young leopards...."

And on Tuesday, 2 May 1876, there is a notice in the *Galveston Daily News* that polo had been played in Grayson County, near Dallas, also stating that "Denison has a polo club."

Something is known about the pioneers: they were retired British Army officers.

Capt. William Michael Glynn Turquand was commissioned as an ensign in the Coldstream Guards on 22 May 1866 and was eventually promoted to lieutenant — in 1868 — and then captain, before resigning his commission on 6 January 1875.[31] Glynn Turquand purchased the Balcones Ranch in Boerne, in 1878.[32] Apparently, the original polo field is still visible. Capt. Turquand married Eleanor Duff, from Fetteresso Castle, Scotland; they had a daughter, Ann, who died in infancy, and a son, William, who eventually was manager of the Coronado Hotel near San Diego, when it was a mecca of polo in California. Capt. Turquand died, age 41, on 14 September 1887, in Green Spring, Ohio, and is buried in Bexar County Cemetery, San Antonio, next to his children.

Another pioneer polo player was Capt. Egremont Eadon Shearburn, who was commissioned into the 3rd Regiment (Light Infantry) West York Militia, in 1871.[33] Later, on 1 January 1880, he transferred to the 9th Lancers and on 10 November of the same year, by then a captain, resigned from the service. Capt. Shearburn carried the dubious reputation of being the most extravagant officer in the British Army. He was born in Manstead House, Goldaming, county of Surrey, in 1853, the son of Capt. Thomas and Sarah Shearburn, and was educated at Marlborough College. He served in the Afghan War with the 9th Lancers before his retirement. The 9th Lancers, one of the regiments to play the first polo match in England, was obviously his polo school. His name is mentioned in criminal warrants, indictments and complaints by the State of Wyoming in 1882. Capt. Shearburn had asked the Frewens, one of whom, Moreton, was manager of the vast Powder River Cattle Co., to introduce him at the elite Cheyenne Club and at the Stebbins & Post Bank, and to endorse his notes. Shearburn then proceeded to gamble away the cash and default the repayment.[34] By 1891, he was back in England, married and living in Hammersmith.

There is a paucity of polo news in the papers until 1883, when the *San Antonio Light* reported several games. On 9 July 1883 there appears a report of a match at San Pedro Springs where the Texas Polo Club introduced polo to San Antonio on Saturday the 7th.

The Blues—captained by C. Williams, with H.G. Mitchell, A. Russ, and a Mr. Mosely — faced the Reds, R.M. Glazbrook, A.S. Stanuel, O. Fitzpatrick and S. Wheatley. The Blues won, but the score was not reported. The players were attired in white flannel costumes, having belts, caps and scarves of appropriate colors. The umpire was Capt. Turquand, who placed the ball in the center of the field and then dropped a flag to signal the start of the game. Fitzpatrick led the charge for the Blues and Williams for the Reds. Regrettably,

> They collided with such force that both riders and horses were thrown to the ground. This incident created great excitement among the spectators, and fear was entertained for the safety of these energetic players but they rallied, and in a few minutes remounted, apparently none the worse for the contretemps. After 15 minutes of strong contest in which both goals were well guarded, the Blues, by a clever stroke of Captain Williams, secured the first goal. No further advantage was gained by either side until the innings closed in the 20 minutes allotted for it. After an interval of 10 minutes, during which the Reds were esteemed first favorites and considerable money wagered on the success, the second inning commenced. The Reds turned the tide and by the clever play of Glazbrook scored their first goal.

The chronicle also mentions that several accidents occurred, which should have been prevented. A few days later, the *San Antonio Light* reported a match for $100 between Texas Cowboys and Englishmen, which perhaps merits some consideration as both the first professional match as well as the first American-English international polo contest. The venue was, again, San Pedro Springs, and the teams were the Texas Polo Club, with Capt. Egremont Shearburn, U.M. Glazbrook, C. Mitchell and Howie Glazbrook; and the Texas Cowboys, with Fred Parker, as non-playing captain, Sam Bennett, George Maltzberger, Manuel Rentour and Joe Davis.

The Cowboys protested the first goal scored by the Texas Polo Club because a horse's hoof had sent the ball through the goal. The English gave up what would now be a pony goal; however, they easily ended the contest by winning three goals to nil.

In August of that year, there is notice of a game at the Texas Polo Club in Boerne, in which O. Fitzpatrick, John Molesworth, A. Aue, N. King, L. King, H.G. Mitchell and A. Russ took part, with the comment that some very good playing was exhibited.

On 23 October 1883, the Texas Polo Club celebrated the end of the season with a dinner prepared by Mrs. Pearlman. The *San Antonio Light* reported that after a toast to the Queen, the President, and the United States, "drink, laughter and songs were indulged in, and not until the sun had tipped the eastern hills with light did the party break up."[35]

The Texas Polo Club Challenge to New York

On 12 September 1883 the *Galveston Daily News* published a notice indicating that the Boerne, Texas, Polo Club had challenged James Gordon Bennett's club, of New York, for a match game. John Molesworth, one of the players selected, wrote that the idea was to travel to New Orleans, play some exhibition games there, and use the proceeds to continue their sea journey. Arriving to New Orleans, players and their mounts were accommodated at the local racetrack. The problem was that polo did not awaken any interest in New Orleans and the promised promotion of the game did not materialize. The racetrack action and the social life of the city appealed to most of the players, with the sad result that their carefully trained ponies had to be sold to a pony express line operating in Florida, forcing the players to head back to San Antonio, their ambition of playing against the Westchester Polo Club unfulfilled and their pockets empty.

Polo in California

Buried deep on the shelves of Yale University's rare book collection in the Beinecke Library there is a four-page pamphlet with the title *California Polo Club 1876*. This written proof of early polo in the Golden State was discovered by historian Dennis J. Amato some years ago. The publication is an advertisement for an event to be held at Charter Oak Park on 17 October 1876, offering feats of horsemanship, buck-jumping and three games of polo. The pamphlet states that over 200,000 spectators have watched such polo events at Boston, Long Branch, Newport, Providence and Saratoga. Also included are the rules of the California Polo Club, the earliest known written rules of the game of polo in the United States. (See Appendix 1.)

The announced teams were Red, with Capt. Mowry, Ballard and Jordan, against Blues, with Capt. Morgan, Carillo and Figuero. Capt. Nell Mowry had a reputation as a well-known long distance rider, having recorded a 300-mile ride in 14 hours, 9 minutes. In the course of this trial he rode 200 miles in 8 hours, 2 minutes, thus bettering the legendary George Osbaldeston, the much celebrated Squire of England, who rode the same distance in 8 hours and 42 minutes. Ballard, Carillo, Figuero and Jordan are listed in the program as buck-riding untamed Mexican horses.

Dennis Amato's assessment of these matches is that "it was at best a fad that lasted several months and then quickly died out."[36] However, the fact remains that the game of polo was played in California in the same year as in New York.

More lasting were the pioneering efforts in Southern California. According to Ingersoll's book *History of Santa Monica Bay Cities*, a polo club was established in Santa Monica in 1877 and the following year the club played a match against "Manuel Marquez and four other Mexicans from the canyon — and was beaten. Apparently, it did not survive the shock."[37]

After a futile attempt in the early 1880s by Mr. C.A. Summer, his brother Cecil and Capt. Hutcheson to start the game in Los Angeles — an enterprise that netted only five players, all Englishmen — nothing happened until the winter of 1888, when Dr. J.A. Edmonds, who had learned the game on Long Island, gathered a group of Englishmen promptly joined by some Americans led by Mr. John B. Procter. The Santa Monica Polo Club was the result of their endeavors. Senator John Percival Jones was president; Mr. W.H. Young was vice-president; Dr. Edmonds, secretary; and Mr. Robert Payton Carter, treasurer. Senator Jones (R-Nevada), who had gone West during the Gold Rush and was co-founder of the town of Santa Monica, donated a polo grounds, in conjunction with Col. Robert S. Baker. Colonel Baker was from Rhode Island; with his wife Arcadia Bandini they purchased large tracts of land, including what is now Pacific Palisades.

The first match was held in the summer of 1889, married men taking on the bachelors. The teams were "Singles," James Parker, Cullum Birch, Jack Machell, and R. Payson Carter at Back; and "Married," E. Templar Allen, J.A. Edmonds, John B. Procter, and playing Back, W.H. Young. The bachelors rose up to the occasion, scoring 8 goals against 6 by the married men. There were no polo mallets to be had, so billiard cues were purchased, the heads were turned from maple wood, and the balls from willow. They had to do until canes and bamboo roots balls were obtained from the Far East by the Tufts-Lyon Arms Co.[38]

The club staged an exhibition game at the Los Angeles Fairgrounds, which resulted in a financial disaster, leaving the club facing bankruptcy. A benefit performance organized by club member Payson Carter, who was an actor, saved the day.[39] The club continued on, with the support of George L. Waring, to become the main center of polo in California. The polo field, described as "charmingly situated with a west boundary shade of gum and pepper trees," was dusty and only 190 yards in length.[40] Many matches were played with only three-a-side, under the theory that, unless a top player, the Number 1 was an expensive luxury, more likely to impede rather than to assist in the game. Hooking mallets and the off-side rule were in effect, reflecting the strong British influence in Southern California Polo. The Association also required "guards," in practice 30-inch planks along the sidelines. In 1897, the Santa Monica Polo Club, also known as Southern California Polo Club, hosted a team from Burlingame.

The next polo club was the Riverside, started in April 1892 by Mr. Robert Lee Bettner when he returned from an extended journey to the eastern states. Charter members were G. Allen, R. Allen, C.E. Maud, J. McConnochie, and C. Walton, with Mr. Arnold Hatson later as president.[41] Several Englishmen who had played in their native country became players at the Riverside Polo Club. The British influence upon southern California polo was prominent until the advent of World War I.

The Game as Played in the 1870s

Polo in the United States was an adaptation of the game as played in England and, perhaps, France. The rules adopted were those of the Hurlingham Club promulgated in 1874:

a game was two goals out of three, or three out of five, with no time limit. Because the ball was placed in the center of the field and charged for, not only at the start of the match, but after each goal, the game was very severe on the ponies. The only chance to change mounts was at knock-ins and after a goal had been scored. However, plenty of time was allowed between goals for liquid refreshment.

Each team captain decided who should lead the charge and named the goalkeeper who remained in front of his goal most of the time. In practice games, it was not unusual to have five or more players on each team. On the other hands, matches between pairs became quite popular and several tournaments, such as the Turnure Cups, were hotly contested.

The ball was made of wood, painted white, about three inches in diameter. The best mallets were made of Malacca cane, although others adopted the less expensive hickory.

Before long the American players changed the rules of the game to adapt it to evolving local custom. The off-side rule was abolished, the hooking of mallets was banned, and the backstroke at first looked upon with a dose of scorn, was then also prohibited. American polo suffered, as in England and India, from the power of the super-star. The modifications to Hurlingham's code favored individual brilliance, at the expense of combination play. The game, as it developed from that time, was a pretty game to look at, and a pleasant one for the individual player. It was, however, a poor team-game and caused the loss of the first international match against England, because John Watson and his confreres demonstrated that team-play would invariably win against individual play, no matter how brilliant that might be.

After the 1886 Westchester Cup match in Newport, Rhode Island, the American polo players adopted the backhander, as a complement to the under-the-neck shot. However, to their credit, they did not legalize the offside rule, making the game more fluid and allowing the Number 1 to become a more active participant in the game.

As far as bodily protection, knee-guards were far away in the future. This was the time of a pleasant pastime, best exemplified by the "pill-box" cap, cocked over one ear. For some unknown reason, caps were cast away and the great majority of players went bareheaded while the game kept developing. In his quaint manner, James Cooley described the change in custom as, "the baby wore the fetching little cap, but the boy wore none."[42] In spite of a number of accidents, a few fatal, players waited until the turn of the century to adopt the protection of a polo helmet.

CHAPTER 2

The First International Games

The last week of August 1886 in Newport, Rhode Island, witnessed two international matches between teams representing England's Hurlingham Club and America's Westchester Polo Club. None other than 10-goaler John Elliott Cowdin called this series the most important games in the history of polo in this country.[1]

The genesis of polo's oldest international competition took place in the spring of 1886 at a dinner in the Hurlingham Club in Fulham, a London suburb, attended by the American player Nathaniel Griswold Lorillard, an heir to the tobacco fortune. Mr. Lorillard's comment that polo was played in the United States aroused interest among his hosts, and the possibility of a challenge series was raised. Lorillard sent a cable to Frank Gray Griswold, secretary of the Westchester Polo Club, stating that the Hurlingham Club would send a representative team if the players' expenses and the freight for the ponies were paid. This was agreed to, and the show was on.[2]

The Hurlingham team made the North Atlantic crossing aboard the Cunard Line *Servia* in early August and endured rough weather. On the other hand, their fifteen ponies on the National Line *Erin* had a clear sail earlier. Upon arriving in Newport, the team was lodged at the Ocean House Hotel, reputed the best in the summer resort. They quickly became the season's sensation and hostesses vied with each other to invite the members of the British team to parties and dinners.

The Hurlingham team was led by Irishman John Henry Watson, the dominant figure in British polo in the late nineteenth century. With him came Capt. Thomas Hone, 7th Hussars, Capt. the Hon. Richard T. Lawley, later Lord Wenlock, also an officer in the 7th Hussars, and Malcolm O. Little, 9th Lancers. Mr. Thomas Shaw Safe, a British national who spent the summers in Newport, was the spare man.

To withstand the British challenge, the Westchester Polo Club players went into a caucus to select the defending team, eventually becoming a matter for a ballot. Everybody voted, and when the smoke had cleared away the challengers named were Foxhall P. Keene, Raymond R. Belmont, Jr., Thomas Hitchcock, and Edwin D. Morgan. An undisclosed illness in the Morgan family prevented Edwin for participating and William K. Thorn, Jr., took his place on the team.[3] It is perhaps the only time that a democratic process was followed in the selection of a national team.

The first polo match was scheduled for Wednesday, August 24, at 4 P.M. By 3 o'clock the three main roads to Izzard's Field — a parcel of land now next to Morton Park — were jammed with all manner of conveyance: at least a dozen four-in-hand coaches, many park phaetons, barouches, buggies, curricles, carryalls, jumpers of every style, men and women on horseback and even mobs on foot. Most of the last were off for the Dead Head Hill, which overlooked Izzard's Field on Halidon Hill. The matches were played on the old Westchester Polo Club's ground there, at the bottom of Thames Street, on Earl, Meikle and Vaughn Avenues, adjacent to Morton Park.

Pomp and circumstance permeated the ambience. The British and American flags were flying, alongside the club flags, yellow for Westchester, light blue for Hurlingham. Mullaly's Orchestra was playing, the clubhouse was overflowing and the spectators' coaches were drawn up to five and six rows deep. Newport had never seen anything like it.

The Hon. Charles Lambton was umpire for the British team and Mr. Egerton L. Winthrop, Jr., for the Americans. Mr. S. Howland Robbins, Jr., was the referee in the first match; then he resigned and Mr. Frederick O. Beach took his place for the second match on Saturday. Mr. Samuel Stevens Sands, Jr., acted as time-keeper.

Before the match had even started, team captain John Watson showed his mettle. Watson insisted that the referee, Howland Robbins, should not be mounted, as was the custom, but should stand on a platform at the edge of the ground. To the Americans, it seemed a small point; however, Watson informed the committee that his team would refuse to play if the change was not made.[4] *The New York Times* reported, "The referee was perched on a stand, as the visitors refused to play with him mounted."[5] This small unpleasantness was dealt with by erecting a small stand and placing Mr. Robbins therein. Probably, this argument was the motive for his refusal to referee the second match.

The big moment came. The shorter than regulation ground on Halidon Hill was on a slope and the Americans were hitting down hill. The ball was put in the center of the field, and the two designated hitters dashed out from behind the backlines and headed face to face. Up the gentle slope galloped Capt. Little (*The New York Times* says Lawley), down galloped Foxie Keene, whose mount was a little faster, got the ball first, hit it and missed demolishing Capt. Little by inches, followed up his first shot with another, and the ball went through the British goal-posts. First blood went to the American team.[6]

After such a propitious beginning, the match became one-sided in favor of the Hurlingham squad. As the unequal contest developed, it became a learning experience for the Americans. The folly of banning the backhander stroke became apparent rather quickly, for John Watson's powerful defensive shots—always on the off-side of the pony — quickly convinced the Americans that it was a most powerful offensive tactic as well. While pony power was about equal, and so was dash by the players, the visitors proved that combination play would always beat individual prowess, no matter how brilliant it might be. The final result, 10 goals to four, tells the story. The second game was more of the same, with Hurlingham cantering to a 14–2 win.

For the second game on Saturday the crowd far surpassed that of Wednesday's, with carriages twice as numerous. Dead Head Hill was more crowded, with spectators pressing against the wire fence. At game time a light fog hung on the field and, as play progressed, became denser, until at the end it interfered with both view and comfort and caused many to leave before the finish.

The Americans took the lesson to heart. Mr. Cochran Sanford, one of the guiding lights of Newport, said after the series was over:

The result of the thrashing the Hurlingham team gave us will be a good thing, because there will be now a reorganization of our system. Our fellows are all right as individuals, but we have enjoyed playing to the galleries, so to speak, too well, and have had more regard for personal than for team brilliancy and success. We can never bring back the cup until we meet the

Hurlingham players with their own system, and the sooner we go about to obtain the system the better will be our future chances.[7]

Mr. Sanford proved to be an accurate soothsayer. Following two unsuccessful attempts on English soil to regain the Westchester Cup, it took the organizational skills and financial resources of Harry Payne Whitney to recover the trophy.

Gracious in victory, John Watson remarked: "I have played polo in all parts of the world, and I have never met fairer or better intending opponents that those of to-day."[8]

After the series was over, the British players—following the practice started by the Manipuri players in Calcutta—sold their ponies at advantageous prices.

The British players did not linger overly long at Newport, but they did take part in one final social and financial coup. They put up at auction their ponies, complete with saddles, bridles and, in a few cases, even blankets. The polo pony sale, as with everything else connected with the visiting team, was a social occasion. Carriages lined the street in the vicinity of the auction site, Keene's Riding Academy, and everyone who was anyone was in attendance, including all members of the English team except Captain Hone. Eleven of the 15 ponies were purchased, with miscellaneous equipment, and the lot was knocked down for $5,476, not including one horse taken off the list and later sold to Augustus Belmont, Jr., for an undisclosed sum.

With the exception of *The New York Times* reports, the Westchester Cup matches received little attention in the American press. Lt. Col. Edward Miller, who was in the United States with a cricket team — the "Gentlemen of England"—was not even aware that there was an international series offered for competition.[9]

The Trophy

Shortly after the competition's terms had been agreed to by the Hurlingham and Westchester clubs—the organization of the Polo Association was still in the future—the issue of an appropriate trophy came up. There are two versions regarding who paid for the trophy. James Calvin Coolidge states that "the kindly Mr. William Waldorf Astor presented a challenge cup."[10] The second version is that Frederick Gebhard put $1,000 towards the trophy, whereupon other enthusiasts insisted they should be counted in. These gentlemen were Frederick Beach, Raymond Belmont, Oliver William Bird, Nathaniel Griswold Lorillard, Edwin Denison "Alty" Morgan, Elliott Roosevelt, John Sanford, William Thorn, Jr., Cornelius Vanderbilt, and Egerton Leigh Winthrop.[11]

As secretary of the Westchester Polo Club, F. Gray Griswold was charged with obtaining an appropriate prize. This he accomplished with some difficulty, because Mr. Griswold wished the cup to be emblematic of the game of polo and the designer responsible for the trophy had never seen a match and there was no opportunity for him to witness one.[12]

Tiffany & Co. was commissioned to manufacture the trophy. A London silversmith described the cup as "comprising a base of series of twelve shields, interlaced with a design of laurel leaves. Above this, some boldly chased scrollwork, with six figures of polo players, mounted, springing there from, the whole being surmounted by a massive three-handled egg-shaped cup, with three panels on it. The first panel contains the inscription, *International Polo Cup USA*; the second bears the arms of England and America; while the third is a representation of a couple of players passing each other in opposite directions."[13]

Mr. Nigel à Brassard is of the opinion that the origins of the stylized representations of the players are clearly open to debate. Gray Griswold believed that the polo player with the forage cap was himself, while the one with the peaked cap was Lord Leesthorp, and that the ponies' heads were from sketches of Griswold's celebrated pony, Tommy.[14]

It appears that the players are Capt. John Fielden Brocklehurst and Capt. Francis "Tip" Herbert, as depicted in George Earl's monumental picture of a polo match between the Royal Horse Guards and the Monmouthshire Club that was decided at Hurlingham on 7 July 1877.[15]

The cup is said to have cost $1,200; the Tiffany archives show the cup was made from 396.3 ounces of sterling and the manufacturing cost was $840.[16] Although considered by many to be the most impressive international polo trophy, as in many art objects, there is room for a difference of opinion. James Calvin Cooley called the ornate cup "that dreadful example of the silversmith's art."[17]

Nevertheless, the Westchester Cup, last played for in 2009 at International Polo Club Palm Beach, remains the most coveted trophy in international competition.

CHAPTER 3

Polo Across the Land

After the introduction of the game of polo to the United States in 1876, the next fifteen years was an organizational period for the early polo clubs. They were mainly located in the Northeast, but stretching as far south as Aiken and Camden in South Carolina, westward to San Francisco and Santa Monica in California, north to Wyoming and Montana, in the Midwest centering in Iowa, later in Chicago, and in the Southwest in Texas.

Newport, Philadelphia, suburban towns of Boston such as Dedham, Hamilton and Hingham, and the New York metropolitan area were at the beginning the hubs of the game, a pre-eminence that lasted for many decades. It was in New York City where the Polo Association — as it was originally named — was organized in 1890. The new entity amalgamated the majority of the initial polo clubs and their successors, incorporating them into an organization that has fostered the sport ever since and into our days.

Aiken Polo Club, Camden Polo Club, Chicago Polo Club, the Country Club of Westchester in Pelham — sometimes mistakenly spoken of as the Westchester team — Dedham Polo Club, Essex County Country Club, Meadow Brook Club, Myopia Hunt Club, Philadelphia Country Club, Point Judith Country Club, Rockaway Club, and the Westchester Polo Club in Newport were the principal centers of activity.

The California clubs, such as Burlingame, Coronado and Santa Monica, played under the rules of the Hurlingham Polo Committee and did not join the Polo Association until the 1910s.

Polo in Saratoga

The origins of Saratoga Springs polo date back to the start of the game in the United States. Historian Dennis J. Amato found a document in Yale University's library in which it is stated that the game was played at the upstate New York spa in 1876, instigated by no other than James Gordon Bennett.[1]

In all probability, the event took place in the month of August, coincidentally with the thoroughbred racing season. Nevertheless, polo was formally organized in Saratoga in 1900, when the Saratoga Polo Club was started by William Collins Whitney, Harry Payne's father. Other players included John A. Manning, John Sanford, E.L. Smith and Roland W. Smith.

William C. Whitney donated the polo field, which is still in use, its original location rediscovered by Thomas B. Glynn in 1977. The initial trophies were the Saratoga Polo Cup, the Hitchcock Cup, and the Sanford Cup. There is also notice of the Ballston Cup, played for in 1902 between Meadow Brook and the local team, the Long Islanders being victorious by a score of 14–11, in a match that went on into darkness. Meadow Brook had in its lineup Henry S. Page, Archibald Alexander, Harry Payne Whitney and Robert L. Stevens. Saratoga presented Augustus Belmont, Seward Cary, Charles C. Rumsey and E.L. Smith.[2]

The Game in Buffalo

In 1877, Dr. Charles Cary gathered about him his brother Thomas Cary, John Cowing, Dr. Henry R. Hopkins, Edward Mov-

Clubhouse at the Saratoga Polo Club, circa 1900. Polo is still going strong at the spa town in upstate New York.

ius, Bronson Rumsey, Lawrence Rumsey, John N. Scatcherd, and others interested in horses and the new pastime and they formed the Buffalo Polo Club. Addison Geary Smith, writing under his *nom de plume* Addison Geary, recorded that

> Enthusiasm ran high, in spite of skepticism of some of the horse lovers, who could not comprehend what they called "shinny on horseback." It was considered a wild, reckless sport in a day whose concept of speed was the bicycle and the fast-stepping trotter. Conservatives shook their heads in dismay over the "latest fad" of the young bloods and made solemn predictions concerning the result of such folly.[3]

There were obstacles to be surmounted, mainly securing an adequate field and suitable ponies. Attempts to play in an apple orchard on the Rumsey estate failed because of the difficulty in hitting the ball between rows of apple trees. Therefore, a flat space inside the race track at Driving Park proved to be a reasonable solution, although the playing surface was hard and dry.

As to ponies, a carload of Western ponies, small, wiry and alert, was secured, the ponies being drawn by lot. This first summer of 1877 was spent in practice games. As mentioned previously, the following summer the Buffalonians received an invitation from the Westchester Polo Club to play two matches in Newport. This invitation was gladly accepted and careful preparations were undertaken. The five men selected to represent Buffalo's colors, Dr. Charles Cary, Thomas Cary, Bronson Rumsey, Lawrence Rumsey and John N. Scatcherd, practiced hard for weeks before the engagement.

The ponies were shipped by railway one week ahead of the scheduled match, but the 500-mile journey took longer than expected and the ponies arrived on the afternoon of the day prior to the first match. The crack ponies of the Westchester players were in top form and ran circles around the visitors' outnumbered and unfit ponies. The smooth turf made play much faster than it had been possible on the Driving Park surface and it was no surprise that the local squad won both games.

More embarrassing to the visiting team was that it rained during one of the matches. The Buffalo players wore white riding breeches and cherry-colored yarn sweaters. Flannel shrinks when wet, as the Buffalonians discovered to their regret and the spectators laughter when the players realized that the breeches crept well up to their knees as the match progressed. Nevertheless, this was the first true inter-club match in the United States.

Embarrassment added to defeat left a bitter taste in the Buffalo players. They planned their revenge even more carefully than the expedition to Rhode Island. Several extra ponies were secured, allowing the players to change mounts more often during the game. The playing surface at Driving Park was improved and the players themselves practiced assiduously.

August Belmont, Lloyd Bryce, Maj. Gen. Daniel Butterfield, F. Gray Griswold, Lawrence Jerome, Hermann Oelrichs, Charles Palmer and Dr. Charles Phelps, captained by James Gordon Bennett, were among those from Westchester who made the journey upstate. Bennett, Belmont, Bryce and Oelrichs made up the team; James Wadsworth was the referee. Dr. Charles Cary, the Rumseys and Scatcherd played for Buffalo, which, somewhat surprisingly, took both games. In the second match, Dr. Henry Hopkins replaced Lawrence Rumsey, who had been injured in a collision with his own teammate Charles Cary, in the first match. Some 5,000 people watched the matches.

Those early successes increased the interest in the novel game. The old ground inside the Driving Park racetrack was discarded in favor on a new field on Park Meadow, within the confines of the Rumsey estate. In 1889, another Cary, George, returned after studying architecture overseas, and joined the club.

Seward Cary played polo for 58 consecutive seasons. Of Seward's generation there were six brothers and one sister. Trumbull Cary was combination of banker and horse dealer. It was said about him that he was so much a part of the horse that he thought like one. Thomas "Whistling Tom" Cary was a Buffalo lawyer who never found time to hang his shingle because his work as executor of the Cary estate took up all his time. Tom and Charles helped to start polo in Buffalo with their brother-in-law Laurence Rumsey. Charles Cary was a prominent physician.

An amusing incident occurred one day that shows the sporting proclivities of the Cary family. The Cary boys were playing in a match at the Country Club of Buffalo and their delightful, elderly mother was sitting in her great barouche, watching the game. Dr. Charles Cary was hurt during a mad dash down the field — being knocked out cold. Many minutes passed with Mrs. Cary tapping her fan nervously and her son remaining inert. After much delay, a stretcher was finally brought, but Mrs. Cary could not stand it any longer. Rising to her full height in the carriage, she exclaimed, "Why don't they go on with the game? Surely there must be another Cary to take his place." Whereupon Tom Cary came forth, removed the boots from the unconscious Charles, jumped on a pony and continued the game. Mother Cary brought up her family to be absolutely fearless.[4] Allan Forbes tells the same story but gives the setting as Myopia Hunt Club.[5]

Other Buffalo players included H. Townsend Davis, Harry Hamlin, Arthur E. Headstreet, J. Herbert Moffatt, Robert K. Root, and Lawrence D. Rumsey

The Country Club of Buffalo remained a very active member of the polo community until the onset of World War II. After that conflict, the Knox family continued the polo tradition and their Ess Kay Farm, named after Seymour Knox's initials, was the home of the Aurora team, winners of the U.S. Open Championship and Hurlingham's Championship Cup.

The Beginnings of Polo in New England

The first polo in Massachusetts was played in Watertown in 1883, when Harvard College students started hitting a ball on a makeshift ground.[6, 7] Raymond Rodgers Belmont, Class of '86, was the guiding light. In August 1883, in Newport, Belmont, who had been playing on his brother Augustus' ponies at Meadow Brook, started hitting a ball with some of his friends on an empty field on Bellevue Avenue, near the Havemeyers' cottage. Those friends were Oliver Bird, Hugh Dickey, Egerton Winthrop, Jr., and Amos French, who soon purchased one pony each and shipped the lot to Cambridge in October.

Raymond Belmont found a field for lease near the Alva Mansion in Watertown, as well as a stable, both some three miles from the college. Then Winthrop Cowdin was the first to join the initial group of players. In the spring on 1884 a new, regulation size grass field was cut and rolled on the south side of the Cambridge-Watertown Highway.

No club records were kept from 1883 until 1886; however, the *Harvard Index* lists the names of the Executive Committee: Robert Dumont Foote, Chairman; Hugh T. Dickey, Secretary; and Raymond R. Belmont, Treasurer. Additional members were Oliver Amos, II, Oliver W. Bird, Stephen Chase, Winthrop Cowdin, Amos T. French, José Victorio Oñativia, Herbert Timmins and J.S. Wright, the latter a "special student." Winthrop Chanler, familiarly known as Winty, also played at Watertown. Amos French, who knew him well, referred to Winty as being "as careless of his bones as a jellyfish."[8]

In 1885, a Harvard team — Raymond Belmont (Capt.), Oliver Bird, Amos French and "Egg" Winthrop — took the Newport Championship Cups, first defeating the Westchester Polo Club squad, and then, in the finals, the Meadow Brook team, with William K. Thorn, Jr. (Capt.), Henry L. Herbert, Stanley Mortimer and Elliott Roosevelt. Thus, the club won its first tournament and the "Harvard Boys" became the toast of Newport's holiday colony.

The Harvard Polo Club became in the course of time associated with the genial Ted O'Hara, who was not exactly the beau ideal of a polo player. One of the delegates to the Polo Association was Rodolphe Louis Agassiz, then an undergraduate and later to become one of the most celebrated figures in the game, an Internationalist handicapped at 10 goals.

Dedham Polo Club

The Dedham Polo Club was formed in 1887, the charter members being Samuel Dennis Warren, Herbert Maynard, Frederick J. Stimson, later ambassador to Argentina, the famous astronomer Percival Lowell, and William F. Weld. Joining the club soon were George A. Nickerson, Reginald Gray, Louis D. Brandeis,[9] and Dr. Arthur Tracy Cabot, a surgeon. Other members joined the ranks along the next four years: Charles Henry Wheelwright Foster, A.B. Harvard *cum laude*, capitalist and banker; Dr. John Wheelock Elliot, another Harvard man and a surgeon at the Massachusetts General Hospital; Augustus Hemenway, who presented the Hemenway Gymnasium to Harvard College; Henry Lee Morse, ENT surgeon at the Massachusetts Eye & Ear Infirmary; Arthur Rotch; George G. Shaw; and Capt. John FitzHerbert Vernon Ruxton, Royal Artillery, an Irishman married to a Bostonian, Mary Chickering. It is sad to record that in 1892, Capt. Ruxton was killed in the course of a polo pony race at The Country Club.

Some of the polo members besides the above were Frank Seabury, Master of the Myopia Fox Hound and a renowned steeplechaser; George Lee Peabody; George von L. Meyer[10]; and Congressman Augustus Peabody Gardner. The first captain of the team was Percival Lowell, later succeeded by Samuel D. Warren, who served until 1901. The members first leased the rooms in the westerly part of the present house. The original purchase of the building and grounds was made in 1891, and the final purchase was in 1894.

The club had not yet joined the Polo Association, although regular practice games were held on the Nickerson Field up to 1890. This field had a tree in the center of it, and players used to play around it, but no one seemed to be bothered by having it there. It was a sort of direction post, as in golf.[11]

From October 1889 until 1895, the Rodman Field was used as the polo ground, and Karlstein, another field, was first played on in 1891. For some obscure reason, Karlstein was named after the Charles River, which ran adjacent to the polo ground.

The Club's early records were kept in a book marked "Register of Vaccinations in Dedham," dated 1809, and in this book may be found some of the early history of the Club.

The first regular practice match was on June 7, 1888, the sides being

Percival Lowell	William Weld
Frederick Stimson	Herbert Maynard
Reginald Gray	Augustus Hemenway

The first match was played on September 17 of the same year at Myopia, the players on the Dedham side being Maynard, Weld, Lowell, and Samuel Warren. Dedham was badly beaten; however, the main incident was a tremendous collision at the start of the game between Percival Lowell and George Meyer. Both players were removed by ambulance, their destination being Myopia's bar, rather than a hospital. Both victims had uneventful recoveries.

The price of the first carload of ponies brought up in 1889 was about $100 a pony, which — the unknown scribe noted in 1906 — it "would not much more than buy a sound hind leg at the present time."[12]

In 1892 the first practice game took place as early as April 7, the new players being Winslow Clark, Charles Foster, and Charles Putnam. In 1893 the team was Maynard, Ned Weld, George Osborn, and Warren. The team once during the year beat a very strong Myopia team.

The Dedham Polo Club had its share of humorous incidents. Gardner Perry, a graduate of Harvard Law School, played once, and during the game he was asked to ride the experienced Herbert Maynard off. A beginner, Perry presumed his orders were to ride him off the field, so he went charging at Maynard, and the latter took to the woods for safety.

The club joined the Polo Association in 1894. The first team won all the games played that year. Some said it was by a lucky combination, some said it was because of their low handicaps, and some said it was by skill. The team was Allan Forbes, Dr. Charles G. Weld, Charles Foster, and Samuel Warren. Foster and several others of the Club's heavy gamblers were believed to have reaped a vast sum of money from these early games; however, the reporter notes that it apparently has been returned since and probably a great deal more.

Eighteen ninety-five was an off year for Dedham. Some said they lost because of poor health, others said the team was not well mounted, while the wise ones said very little.

The Club Tournament was won by Cushing, Maynard, Foster and Cabot, and besides the players named above the club had Alfred Weld, Moses Williams, Jr., W. Cameron Forbes, Dr. Elliot, and Frederick Stimson.

Playing on home turf, Dedham won the Polo Association Cups in 1898, although, oddly enough, it was done by the second team, instead of the first team. Alfred R. Weld, Elton Clark, William H. Goodwin, and Joshua Crane, Jr., were the heroes of the day, because it was the first national tournament taken by the club. Two years later, Allan Forbes, Edward M. Weld, William Goodwin and Joshua Crane, Jr., took the Championship and Added Cups at Prospect Park in Brooklyn. Thus, the Dedham Polo Club had its name inscribed on the two most prestigious Polo Association tournaments.

In August 1898, the Polo Club struck its tents, and started for a week's outing at Narragansett Pier, for polo and fun. The Dedham people flocked together in whole families, but the chronicle states that those who left the families behind probably had the best time.

On 19 May 1910, the Dedham Polo Club and the Norfolk Country Club merged to form the current Dedham Country and Polo Club.

The Country Club at Brookline

In 1882, a member of one of Boston's wealthiest families, J. Murray Forbes—father of the polo players Cameron and Allan — organized a group of his friends in his dining room at 107 Commonwealth Avenue, with the purpose of purchasing a rolling expanse of land in Brookline.[13] They renovated the farmhouse into an elegant clubhouse with dining, card and billiard rooms, and accommodations for those who wished to sleep over. A racetrack was constructed for horse and polo pony racing, lawn tennis courts, a bowling alley, and polo fields. They organized a variety of activities—from skeet shooting to afternoon concerts— and then invited prospective members to join them in their pastoral paradise, after, of course, paying an initiation fee and membership dues of $50 a year.

The early days of The Country Club at Brookline were marked by conflict as well as congeniality. Devotees of the new game of golf defied the state's blue laws to play on Sundays, generating complaints that the game was corrupting public morals. One Sunday, over 30 members were arrested and hauled off to court. Soon afterwards, the club's influential members helped persuade the legislature to lift the Sunday ban.

It should be pointed out that polo players started golf in Massachusetts in the summer of 1892. Robert Shaw and Arthur and Hollis Hunnewell, Jr., played a makeshift game on the Hunnewell estate in Wellesley. Some friends joined the fun and Laurence Curtis realized at once the potential enjoyment that the new game could provide, and followed with a letter to the executive committee of The Country Club. The rest is history. The Country Club became one of the most celebrated venues in the world of golf, thanks to the extensive publicity surrounding the historic victory of a local amateur, Francis Ouimet, in the 1913 U.S. Open in a play-off with Ted Ray and Harry Vardon, two of the best British professionals; the triumph of Curtis Strange in the 1987 Open, also in a play-off against Nick Faldo, and regrettably, as the venue of the 1999 Ryder Cup, where the crowd's shocking behavior marred the incredible victory achieved by the American team.

There was also friction between the equestrians and the growing number of golfers. Because land was limited, the original course overlapped the horse track. The horse lovers were incensed when golf balls whizzed over their heads. They called the golfers "idiots intent on chasing a quinine pill around a cow pasture." When the course was expanded to 18 holes in 1899, the club's horseracing, polo, and trapshooting enthusiasts objected to the "ruthless cutting down of fine trees to satisfy the whim of the Golf Committee."

The Country Club affiliated with the Polo Association on 1 March 1892. The initial players were members of other polo clubs: George A. Nickerson, Robert Gould Shaw, II, Samuel D. Warren, and William F. Weld. The polo field was constructed within the race track.

One of the earliest games was against Dedham — Maynard, Ned Weld, Osborn and

Warren — in June 1893. The Country Club presented Maxwell Norman, Bob Shaw, F. Black-wood Fay and Dolph Agassiz, a powerful combination that was unexpectedly defeated by the visitors. A newspaper reported that "the field was vocal during exciting periods of the play with picturesque, unmistakable, and energetic language."[14] Vociferous language has been part of the game of polo since the early days. The return match held on Karlstein Field a few days later saw the result reversed.

The Country Club resigned its membership in the Polo Association on 15 April 1902.

Myopia Hunt Club

The Myopia Club was established in 1880 in Winchester, Massachusetts, with Marshall K. Abbott as president. The Myopia Fox Hounds was the third polo club to be formed, in 1883. Probably the first practice games at Myopia took place in the summer of 1887 on the Gibney Farm field.[15] The public, however, was not invited to witness the prowess of the players until the following summer. These practice games encouraged the club members to challenge Dedham to a match, which was held on 17 September 1888 at Gibney Field. The Myopians won by the lopsided score of 13 goals to nil, a result that Herbert Maynard of Dedham called a "glorious defeat." Play was ragged, which caused Jack Wheelwright to remark that the best playing that day was performed by the band. Francis R. Appleton, Jr., officiated as umpire and the teams were

Myopia	Dedham
George von L. Meyer	Herbert Maynard
George L. Peabody	William F. Weld
Randolph M. "Bud" Appleton	Percival Lowell, captain
Archibald Rogers, captain	Samuel D. Warren

In fairness to the Dedhamites it should be pointed out that they lost the services of their best player, Lowell, as soon as the game started. Lowell and Meyer charged at the ball, collided head on and both ponies and players were hurled on the ground. As mentioned above, both men were taken by horse ambulance, not to a hospital, but to the Myopia bar's hospitality.

Percival Lowell was a famous astronomer, and one of the wags Myopia was— and still remains— notorious for said that he must have seen stars after the accident.

Budd Appleton was one of the first polo players in the area and became captain of Myopia from 1889 until 1894. He also was Master of the Myopia Fox Hounds.

Archibald Rogers, a New Yorker who had a summer home in Beverly, was a great sports-man on land and water. He owned a cutter, "Bedouin," had a pack of foxhounds in Virginia, and the fastest iceboat on the Hudson River. Rogers was killed as the result of a car accident while trying to save his dog from jumping out of an open window.

George Meyer's string of polo ponies always called attention because of their unusual colors. One would be white, one a flea-bitten grey, other a piebald, another an albino with pink eyes, and yet another a black or chestnut with white legs and a large blaze.

George Lee Peabody, who scored the first goal in the historic match, was the "baby" on the field; unfortunately, he died at an early age without fully filling his promising polo career.

The following autumn the Myopia team, formed by Bud Appleton, Augustus P. Gard-ner, Robert G. Shaw, II, and George P. Eustis, ventured to Newport, where the Freebooters team — Foxhall Keene, Stanley Mortimer, Winthrop Rutherford, Joseph Stevens — a powerful squad from Long Island, defeated Myopia. Another game was played against a team that included Thomas Hitchcock, Egerton Winthrop, Jr., and Edward C. Potter. Although the Myopians lost both games, it was a learning experience for the true beginners at the game.[16]

The most important tournament win for Myopia before the turn of the century was the Championship Cup and Added Cups, held at Prospect Park in Brooklyn in 1895. The team — Augustus P. Gardner, Robert G. Shaw, II, Rodolphe L. Agassiz, and Frank Blackwood Fay — took the tournament. Bob Shaw would eventually reach a 9-goal handicap and Dolph Agassiz the maximum rating, in addition to representing his country in the Westchester Cup of 1902.

Hingham Polo Club

The Hingham Polo Club, in that preppy town south of Boston, was represented by the burly F. Blackwood Fay, who invariably played at Back, and who was ideal for the position, being so robust and steady and solid that to get through his defense was like battering down the walls of a fortress. Other players included Adelbert H. Alden, Hammond Braman, Peter Butler Bradley, George D. Clapp, Roscoe L. Coe, Frederic Cunningham, F.B. Daniels, F.D. Hussey and S. Downer Pope. They were a small group that played for years on the old Bradley Field and most of the time did not venture beyond those friendly confines, limiting their matches to contests with Dedham, the Country Club and Myopia, and Rumford in Rhode Island. The Hingham Polo Club affiliated early with the Polo Association, in 1891, and resigned in 1897.

The Game of Polo in South Carolina

Polo began in Aiken in 1880. The ponies came all the way from Texas and were driven up through the different states with the poor ones sold off for keep of the better ones, so by the time the drove reached South Carolina they were pretty well weeded out and only the better class remained.[17]

The guiding spirit was Mr. George Custis, who was joined by three other Northerners, such as George Hellen, Richard MacCreery and Col. Clarence S. Wallace, a New Yorker who was connected with the polo-playing Havemeyers, the sugar magnates.[18] They were joined by some locals, among them Buck and Halt Buckwalter, Bob Chaffee, Judge William Quitman Davis, Wade Lamar, B. MacWilliams, and others. They were all excellent riders and soon became very handy with the mallet.

In a recollection by Mrs. Louise Hitchcock, the participants in the first official game were William Chaffee, Quitman Davis, her two brothers, George and William Eustis, a Hostetter, a Lincoln (W.R.), James Oakley and Colonel Wallace.[19]

The first field they used was sandy, with soft spots where the tufts of scrub grass had been removed, and also hard spots where the ball went very fast. The dirt and sand raised by the ponies' feet made the playing dusty. Nevertheless, it was good practice for the players because they got used to playing under adverse conditions, which turned to their advantage when they played on better grounds.

The polo mallets were made by the local carpenter, from hickory, 40 inches long and about three-quarter of an inch in diameter, with a thickness for the handle. They used cylindrical heads about eight inches long and about two inches in diameter. These were made of hard pine, inserted at a right angle to the sticks. There being no such thing as adhesive tape in those days, the players used rosin to keep the smooth handles from slipping, which was particularly hard on the hands and generally took some skin off when two mallets came together, unless one of them lost its head, which it generally did. Later on, they wrapped the mallet about six inches up from the head with strong waxed twine, which saved the mallet-heads and incidentally the expense of new sticks, and then they thought of putting loops on the handles, which saved a great deal of time lost in getting off the ponies to pick up the mallets. The balls were made of soft pine and were unpainted.

The matches were started in the old-fashioned way of both sides retiring behind the goal posts and charging down one after the other at the ball, which was usually placed in the center of the field by an individual who then gave the signal to start the game — and ran for his life. However, as the opposing players with the fastest ponies were always chosen for the charge and as these gentlemen's one idea was to get to the ball first and if necessary, bluff the on-coming out, there were many near-accidents, as expected. After one real accident occurred in which the two opposing players plus their ponies met head-on with dire results to all, the picturesque old-fashioned charge was abandoned and the present custom of the umpire throwing in the ball at the center of the field was adopted.

Other early players were Captain R.B. Barber, of Englewood, New Jersey; Mr. Peterkin, of the Manhattan Club; W.R. Lincoln, prominent in Baltimore society; and Edward Tuttle, of Boston.

The current Whitney Field near the center of town claims, alongside several others, to be one of the oldest in America. Betty Babcock casts some doubts on the matter. In her own words, "At that time there was an unsatisfactory polo field and Mr. Hitchcock decided to build a good one. From Mr. Williams, one of the few remaining Charleston owners, he leased a large tract of land, built a polo field and surrounded it with a race course. This proved so satisfactory that some years later Mr. William C. Whitney bought the land from Mr. Williams and presented it to the Aiken Association."[20] So, it appears that Aiken's first polo field location is unknown.

Though polo began at Aiken very early, in 1880, and the club celebrated its 50th anniversary in 1932, it did not become a member of the Polo Association until 1899.

Camden Polo Club was started in 1898 by a dropout from Harvard College, Rogers Lewis Barstow, Jr., class of 1897. He was a wealthy young man who came as a winter visitor and set roots by building a mansion in town. He left in 1906, almost broke, and died in retirement in Florida, an unknown pioneer, in 1961. Who were Barstow's polo companions? The oldest was Clem C. Brown, from Minnesota. Brown's brother-in-law was K. Gerald Whistler, an Army brat born in West Point.[21] Another player was Alexander "Dal" Kennedy, Jr., a local youth. William Courtney Salmond, who played in the first match against Aiken in 1900, recollected that the final score was 28 to 0 in favor of Aiken.[22] The next year the Camdenites achieved a form of revenge when they defeated their tormentors 11 goals to 8½. Kennedy, Salmond, Boyken and Whistler played for Camden, while Aiken was represented by Charles N. Welsh, Reginald Brooks, T.L. Stevens and E.L. Smith.

Other early players included Alexander H. Boyken, Jr., Lewis C. Clyburn, James Teane the younger, and George F. Woodman. A player of interest was Sydney Smith, who played polo for Camden and professional baseball for the Philadelphia Athletics, the St. Louis

Browns, and the Cleveland Indians. Sydney Smith is probably the only man to achieve such distinction.[23]

At the end of the 1902 winter season, the Camden team was invited to play at Lakewood, the Gould's club in New Jersey. Ponies and players—Rogers Barstow, Dal Kennedy, Bill Salmond and J.E.D. Woodman—undertook the long journey north. The team also played a match against powerhouse Country Club of Westchester, losing the game by only one goal.

The polo grounds used in 1898 was that same as in 1993. Initially a sandy field, it was sod within two years and became a very good surface. An interesting match was played versus New Orleans in 1904, with a final score described as "shameful," 23¾ goals to 1¼ in favor of Camden.[24]

The British Colony in Iowa

Frederick Brooks Close believed himself to be the first polo player in the United States.[25] When he immigrated to Virginia in 1874, Fred already possessed knowledge of the game, which he had learned from Army officers that had played in India. One of four brothers in a well-connected aristocratic family, Fred elected to forgo the opportunity of the Cambridge education obtained by his siblings in order to seek his fortune in America.

William Brooks Close, Fred's older brother—all four shared the middle name Brooks, after their mother—also came to America and became associated with Daniel Paullin, a land agent. They jointly owned the Iowa Land Company that by 1882 was offering half-a-million acres for sale in Illinois and Iowa. Wealthy British families invested heavily in real estate in America, mainly in Colorado, Iowa, Texas and Wyoming. They send their younger sons—the remittance men—to learn the ropes of managing ranching and agricultural endeavors, and in some cases, just to get the youngsters out of the way.

The baggage taken by British settlers was as much cultural as physical; sport being one of it basic components. Golf, steeplechasing, racing, riding to the hounds, cricket, tennis and tobogganing were some of the pastimes indulged by the "pups," as they were called.

Also, the settlers played the ancient game of polo. Early in the summer of 1885, the Le Mars Polo Club was formed in Iowa. Although entirely isolated at the beginning, the club managed to thrive. The charter members, all British, were G.C. Maclagan, who had played at forward for the Calcutta Polo Club in India, Jack S. Watson, J.H. Grayson, Henry J. Moreton, Francis J. Moreton, O.T. Pardoe and H. O'K. Richards.[26]

In 1887 the Le Mars Polo Club team traveled to St. Louis and helped that city's polo players organize, playing in a demonstration game. After Le Mars had achieved a win at Sportsman's Park at a subsequent contest, one player was heard to remark that his pony "is even aware of the distinction between on and off side."[27] The polo ponies in the Close Colony were cowponies—quick, smart and easily trained. Wearing uniforms made in England, the Le Mars polo team was a major attraction at county fairs throughout the Middle West and a featured event at the St. Louis Exposition of 1893.[28]

In 1886, Cecil F. Benson; Matthew Blaney Smith-Dodsworth, later Sir Matthew; Julian Walter Orde, later Sir Julian, for 30 years the secretary of the Royal Automobile Club; G.B. Gray; and Frederick Cadwallader Smith-Dodsworth—all members of the British colony— started a club at Sibley. Interestingly, there is a polo link between the Smith-Dodsworth and the Tetley families in Argentina. Elizabeth Smith Dodsworth, a cousin, married Joseph

D. Tetley; their son Cadwallader James Tetley, was a winner of the Argentine Open Championship in 1893 and 1895.

In 1888, Frederick Close started the Sioux City Polo Club with William H. Dinsmore, William T. Humble, R.T. Patrick, W.H. Statter, C. Statter, Arthur F. Statter, G. Perry Statter, and Floyd Tappan, the only American.

The official date of the beginning of polo in Iowa is also 1888, with the formation of the Northwestern Polo League, including clubs at Omaha, Blair, Yankton, and Sioux Falls. That same year the North Western Polo Association was formed by the union of the Sibley, Le Mars, Sioux City and Larchwood clubs. Larchwood, in Lyon County, close to the South Dakota state line, boasted of good polo grounds and also had a race track to which the British colonists sent their best horseflesh. In 1881 Jesse W. Fell, the lawyer who had started the Larchwood Colony — a farming development where he had planted over 100,000 trees and cuttings — sold his interests in Lyon County to the Close brothers, who in turn later sold the tract at about $1 per acre to Richard Sykes of Manchester, England.

The Larchwood Polo Club's grounds was situated on a farm east of town owned by Peter and Sigri Rulland, immigrants from Norway by way of Wisconsin. Sigri spent much of her time baking pies and doughnuts to serve with milk, fresh from the cows, to the Englishmen who gathered in the Rulland home before and after the games.

Interestingly enough, the North Western Polo Association championship trophy was a copy of the Westchester Cup, first played for in 1886. Three successive victories for the Le Mars team gained the club permanent possession of the cup.

The First Polo Casualty in the United States

While hunting in England, Frederick Close had a bad fall and injured his arm. Fred had a photograph taken: his arm in a sling, an amused look in his eyes. He had only limited use of that arm when he participated in a polo match between Le Mars and Sioux City on 18 June 1890 in Crescent Park, the Sioux City polo field. Fred's team had scored three goals, and during a pause between chukkers he congratulated his men on how well they were doing. As play resumed, Jack Watson of the Le Mars team "was making a splendid run down the field, when for some unaccountable reason, Fred attempted to cross in front of him, and to the spectators it was evident that the two would cannon."[29] Just before the horses collided, Fred swayed in his saddle. When the horses collided, he was thrown, falling under his mount, which rolled on top of him. As Fred's horse struggled to retain his footing, Watson's pony went down and also rolled over Fred Close. Watson was thrown clear and escaped injury but Fred was completely knocked out.

In the past ten years audiences had frequently seen Fred take a bad fall, but he always got up and laughed it off. Reckless as he was in horsemanship, he was aware of some of the physical dangers involved. His groom, T.J. Maxwell — who was still alive in 1953 — once said, "Fred was expecting it. He was always saying to me, if I get it, Jack, you tend to the mare."[30]

A young Norwegian doctor in the crowd of polo spectators came on the field and tried to revive Fred. Margaret Close, although she repeatedly tried to reach her husband, was kept away from him. Two additional doctors were summoned by telephone. When they arrived and examined Fred they discovered that the right upper part of the chest had caved in. Worst of all there were unmistakable indications of cerebral hemorrhage. The attending physicians decided against moving Fred from the playing field and a tent was erected over the spot where Fred lay. Frederick Brooks Close, a pioneer of the game in America, died on the polo field a few hours after the accident, without regaining consciousness.

Polo Starts in Missouri

The St. Louis Country Club was started as a polo club on 15 April 1892, by twelve members, of which some had learned the game while going to eastern colleges. On that date, a 5-year lease was signed for a 235-acre parcel of land known as Collier's Farm, in Bridgeton, near what is now Lambert International Airport.[31] The club's by-laws were adopted on that day.

There followed a move to Hanley Road, Clayton, where 200 acres were leased from the Davis family in 1895. A clubhouse, polo ground, golf course and tennis courts were built. Among the early players were Dwight Davis, donor of the world-wide renowned Davis Cup in tennis, and George Herbert "Bert" Walker, who presented the trophy to be played between American and British golf amateurs. The final move to the club's present location in Ladue took place in 1913.

A polo ground located at Sportsman's Park, on the divide of the Mississippi and Missouri rivers, was the venue for a first match against the Le Mars Polo Club from Iowa on 21 October 1893. Otto Lewis Mersman, forward, Allerton S. Cushman[32] and Hugh McKittrick, Jr., half-backs, and Charles W. Scudder, Back and team captain, were the players. St. Louis also had two substitutes, J. Reginald Frost and Irwin Z. Smith. Every player listed two ponies each, bearing names such as Jack Horner, Dick Swiveller, and Bobby Shafto. The visiting team presented G.C. Maclagan, the team captain; Ed Dalton; and the Sammis brothers, J.M. and Payson. The Le Mars team, reputed to be the best in the Midwest, easily defeated the rank beginners from St. Louis. The final score, 9½ to ½, tells the story without further words. In those days, half-a-goal was deleted from each team's total tally if a foul was committed in the course of action.[33]

The St. Louis Country Club's official colors were lilac shirt, with white cap. Later, in 1898, they were changed to red with a white sash, white cap. The great majority of the players were also members of the Noonday, St. Louis, Mercantile, and Jockey clubs. Among the initial list of polo players—in addition to the ones mentioned above—were Alfred Lee Shapleigh and John Foster Shepley, members of the club's Board; Wayman C. Cushman, George P. Doane, Jr., Charles Hodgman, Lindell Gordon, Clifton R. Scudder, James W. Scudder, C.F. Simon and J. Sidney Walker.

In 1896, a St. Louis team — Charles Scudder (captain), Otto Mersman, George Doane, Bert Walker and one of the Davis boys, brother of the then Secretary of War — traveled to Fort Riley in Kansas to face the local army team. The Fort Riley team was Price Adams, Sam Sturgis, Brook Payne and Lt. (later Brig. Gen.) Charles G. Treat. The St. Louis team won the contest.[34]

Chicago

The Chicago Polo Club was started during the 1893 World's Fair. James Carey Evans and Capt. Francis Michler were the organizers, play being carried out on the lawns of a house in Brookline, near Chicago. William T. Carrington, Ellicott Evans, S.H. Hubbard, Col. William V. Jacobs, F.W. Lamport and Arthur J. Whipple were the other participants in those early bouts, on ponies brought from the Indian Territory.

From this small beginning, the Chicago Polo Club was established in the winter of 1893–94. The initial membership list included Urban H. Broughton, William T. Carrington, James C. Evans, Walter Farwell, R.B. Fort, Edward C. Green, James O. Heyworth, Lawrence Heyworth, H.M. Higginbotham, Col. Jacobs, Walter W. Keith, Frank Jay Mackey, Capt. Marion P. Maus, Charles P. McAvoy, Capt. Francis Michler, J. Henry Norton, Vernon Shaw-Kennedy, George Henry Wheeler, and Arthur Whipple. A Board of Governors was elected, with James Carey Evans as Chairman; Messrs. McAvoy, Norton, Wheeler and Capt. Michler. All were members of the Washington Park Club; therefore, a polo grounds was easily secured in the Park.

The first match was played at the Washington Park grounds on 17 June 1894 and society gave its approval of the new game by showing up in droves, and, after the game was over, by proclaiming polo "quite the thing."[35] The players were "Blues," James Evans, Capt. Michler, Farwell and Shaw-Kennedy; and the "Reds," Ellicott Evans, Whipple, Carrington and Lawrence Heyworth.

A prominent player was Marion Perry Maus (pronounced "Moss"), a lieutenant colonel on the staff of Gen. Nelson A. Miles. Maus was a West Point graduate, famed as a fighter in the Indian Wars. He had, in fact, been awarded the Congressional Medal of Honor for bravery.

Onwentsia

The Onwentsia Club was established on 25 October 1895 as an outgrowth of a golf club started when Hobart C. Chatfield-Taylor laid out a seven-hole golf course on the Lake Forest estate of his father-in-law, Senator Charles B. Farwell.[36] Mr. Chatfield-Taylor, Henry N. Tuttle and Robert A. Waller reorganized the club with the intention of adding several games to golf, a true country club. Thus, the chosen name, Onwentsia, Iroquois language for "country."[37]

The club affiliated with the Polo Association on 9 March 1897, replacing the Chicago Polo Club. In addition to the latter members, new players included W.V. Booth, J.E. Doane, Stanley Field, H.M. McIntosh, William W. Rathborne, G.A.H. Scott and H. Gordon Strong.

Onwentsia was the host for the 1907 Senior Championship, a portent of things to come, because in 1933 it became the battleground for the first East-West series, the most publicized polo event in the United States up to that time.

Glen View Golf and Polo Club

Incorporated on March 29, 1897, the Glen View Golf and Polo Club has remained on its original site in the tiny village of Golf as an 18-hole layout. By 1900, polo was dropped from the club's activities, as was the designated game within the club's name. Another nine holes were built, primarily for women, on the former polo field. Early founders were from Evanston, several being on the faculty of Northwestern University.

The Beginnings of Polo in Colorado

In the state of Colorado, polo began in 1886, with Colorado Springs being the main center of the game.[38] This game of well-bred gentlemen fits right in with the concept of Colorado Springs being referred to as Little London. Mr. Joseph S. Stevens, from the Rockaway Club on Long Island, was the instigator and coach.

The Gazette reported that "a brisk game of polo was played at Templeton Gap" on January 12, 1887. The English citizens of Colorado Springs organized a polo club in the 1890s, and the sport was played regularly until the outbreak of World War I.

Prominent among the players were Arthur M. Baker, François Braggiotti, Horace K. Devereux, Thomas Edsall, Frank Gilpin, Percy Hagerman, Harry Leonard, and Hervey Lyle. Hervey Lyle, a handsome Irishman, has been cited by Percy Hagerman as "the father of polo in Colorado, wielding a mallet that was a veritable war club." His death in 1912 was a tragedy. Though in pain with appendicitis, he insisted on playing a match against his doctor's orders and died that night on the operating table.[39]

The Cheyenne Mountain Country Club was formed on 18 February 1891 by Dr. B.F.D. Adams, Arthur Baker, Thomas W. Edsall, Richard Hutton, Godfrey Kissel, William A. Otis, Thomas C. Parrish, Count James Pourtales, E.C.G. Robinson, William H. Sanford, William R. Varker, C.H. White, William J. Willcox, and Henry Le B. Wills, near the Casino in Broadmoor. William Sanford, a scion of a wealthy family from Brooklyn, was elected president.[40]

The founding fathers came from widely different backgrounds. The majority were health-seekers, persuaded that the climate and high altitude of Pike's Peak would cure anything that ailed the human body. Among them, Dr. Adams had studied medicine at Harvard and Europe; Edsall was a lawyer with degrees from Brown and Columbia, and a member of New York's Union Club; Kissel came from a family prominent on Staten Island; Otis was from the Cleveland banking and steel family; Robinson had designed many of the mansions in Broadmoor's North End; Willcox was a wealthy Philadelphian; and Wills had sailed around the world before settling near Pike's Peak.

As to the other members, Tom Parrish was an artist and a miner. Hutton, an Englishman, was in business with Count Pourtales, who hailed from Silesia and had come to Pike's Peak in an effort to restore the family estate to its former glory.

President William Sanford recovered from tuberculosis, and although not a polo player, was the head of the Polo Committee.

In 1896, Foxhall Keene joined the club as a non-resident member. In 1905 he presented to the Club the Foxhall Keene Cup, to be played for by visiting teams. The visitors were many and varied. From Glenwood Springs came Walter Devereux and his sons, with Hervey Lyle and Alec Thomson; from Philadelphia, publisher Jay Lippincott. Harry Payne Whitney came to play, as did Malcolm Moncreiffe, one of the pioneers in Wyoming. To cap it all, Theodore Roosevelt played in a practice game, which was probably arranged by his former Rough Riders friend, Horace Devereux.

Capt. Ashton Potter, who had served in the Philippines, came to Broadmoor to play polo and marry Grace Goodyear, whose divorce from Ganson DePew had occupied the nation's gossip columnists, who referred to her as the richest woman in the U.S. Other polo players included Percy Hagerman — who in 1947 would write a club's history — and Charles A. Baldwin, who built the magnificent Claremont, modeled after Louis XIV's Trianon palace in Versailles. The building now houses the Colorado Springs School.

An interesting character in Colorado Springs polo was Spencer Penrose. "Spec," as he was nicknamed, was introduced to the Cheyenne Mountain Country Club by Charles Leaming Tutt, a rancher in Black Forest, originally from Philadelphia and later a realtor and mining investor. Penrose had come from Las Cruces, New Mexico, where his fruit business had failed, leaving him destitute. To give him a hand, Tutt offered Penrose half his interest in the Cripple Creek gold mine for $500. Penrose never paid the debt.[41] It did not bother Tutt too much, because the two men developed a mining empire that became the U.S. Reduction and Refining Company, and a phenomenal fortune in Utah's copper mines, eventually sold to the Kennecott Copper Co.

Spencer Penrose joined the club as a monthly member in 1893. Initially, his conduct was perfect, as expected from a Philadelphia blue-blood and a Harvard graduate. However, within days, Penrose embarrassed his introducer by participating in a brawl in the card room with Harry P. McKean and Dan D. Casement. Quite a bit of furniture was damaged during the fracas. The Board, shocked by such unseemly behavior at their civilized club, suspended the trio, although later the sanction was lifted. In 1917, Penrose built the Broadmoor Hotel, a Colorado landmark still in existence as a premier golfing resort.

Just like the honorable Hurlingham Club in London, the Cheyenne Mountain C.C. ran into trouble because of the practice of using live birds for target shooting. Actually, it was the club's women who raised the issue, which the Board politely tabled. The Colorado Humane Society then entered the fray in the person of Francis B. Hill. After a protracted lawsuit, the club was fined and forced to use clay pigeons. For his troubles, the polo players also came under scrutiny because of the practice of docking the ponies' tails. The Polo Committee also lost this legal battle, and the barbaric custom came to an end.

In the early 1900s, the Cheyenne Mountain was a thriving center for polo. Dr. Gerald B. Webb, an Englishman who came to Colorado Springs in 1899, was an all-round sportsman who excelled at cricket and polo. The club took the Rocky Mountain Polo Championship, with Dr. Webb as captain, Charles Baldwin, Harold J. Bryant and Horace Devereux.[42] In 1905, Lawrence C. Phipps presented the Interstate Polo Cup to be played in Denver. The Cheyenne Mountain team took the trophy in 1906, with Webb, Bryant, Frank Gilpin and Hervey Lyle; they repeated the conquest the following year, with William Ruston replacing Lyle.

Polo in Denver was started by D. Bryant Turner in 1897, who raised polo ponies at his Trinchera Ranch south of Colorado Springs.

Wyoming

According to the book *British Gentlemen in the Wild West* the first polo grounds in Wyoming was a parcel of land used by the Powder River Cattle Company, a corporation established by British capitalists in 1882.[43] The company's manager was the controversial Mr. Moreton Frewen — Sir Winston Churchill's uncle by his marriage to Miss Clara Jerome. Those were the days of the free range, during which large companies, many with investments of British capitalists, owned hundreds of thousands head of cattle that grazed on federal lands, free of charge, but with no title to the land.

Overcrowding of the range by huge herds of cattle and the disastrous winter of 1886-87 brought hard times to the cattlemen in Wyoming. Most of the British in the area cut their losses and left, seeking other venues to invest their money. Therefore, whatever polo was played in the Powder River basin, nowadays the largest coal-producing area in the

United States, was short-lived and, most likely, was only an amusement for the British contingent.

Nevertheless, the seeds had been planted in Wyoming and the Sheridan Polo Club was started by Capt. Frank D. Grissell and Capt. G.G. "Pete" Stockwell, both British Army officers, in June 1893. Frank Grissell had participated in the first organized polo match played in England in June 1870 at Hounslow Heath, as a subaltern in the 9th Lancers. Capt. Grissell had his ranch near the Tongue River, in Dayton.[44] The new club members were, in addition to Grissell and Stockwell, George T. Beck, George Bentley, Robert H. Brown, W.C. Burnet, S. Corolett, P.H. Jones, David Lee, Dr. Marcus A. Newell, Robert Nix, S. Peeler, and A. Sickler.

The formation of the polo club in Sheridan was followed shortly after by new clubs in Beckton, founded by George Beck: Big Horn and Buffalo. All these polo clubs played by the Hurlingham Rules.

On the 4th of July, 1893, at the Sheridan Fairgrounds, two polo teams calling themselves Sheridan and Beckton squared off in what editor Joe Debarthe described as a wild scramble. Army scout and former Sioux tribesman Frank Grouard umpired the game. Mike Evans, founder of Tepee Lodge, George Beck, founder of Beckton, and Captain Pete Stockwell, a British officer formerly stationed in India, were among the players for Beckton. Bob Brown, Estes Polk, and Robert Nix played for Sheridan. Over one thousand spectators witnessed the event.

In 1898 Scotsman Malcolm Moncreiffe moved from Powder River to Big Horn and built a polo field and started a cattle breeding operation. Moncreiffe exported Wyoming-bred polo horses and foxhunters to England and organized local horsemen to play polo in Big Horn. Early rosters included the names Spear, Cover, Sackett, Skinner, Wood, Roberts, Burnet and Bard.

At the turn of the century, Malcolm Moncreiffe, Bob Walsh, John Cover and Lee Bullington won a tournament on the lawn of the Broadmoor Hotel in Colorado Springs that featured several Army teams, a Denver team and a team from Kansas City. During this tournament, local cowboy John Cover was hailed as one of the top players in the United States.

The Moncreiffe and Wallop surnames are intimately associated with polo in Wyoming. Malcolm Moncreiffe was the fifteenth of sixteen children born to Sir Thomas Moncreiffe and his wife, Lady Louisa. Malcolm went to America, first to Miles City, Montana, where William Lindsay had started polo, and then settled in the area north of Gillette, starting a cattle operation. Malcolm purchased the land that was known for many years by the name of The Polo Ranch. His older brother William, a Cambridge University graduate, stopped in Wyoming along a round-the-world journey. He liked the area and purchased the Charles Becker Ranch. The brothers formed a partnership; their ranch is now the Gallatin and Brinton ranches.[45]

Oliver Henry Wallop, the other polo pioneer in the Big Horn country, was the second son of the Earl of Portsmouth. After graduating from Oxford University, he immigrated to the United States, and after the mandatory stop in Miles City, he purchased land on Otter Creek in southeast Montana. Oliver Wallop sold some horses to a settler in Wyoming, the Big Horn's area beautiful scenery caught his eye, and in 1891 he purchased the Oliver Hanna homestead. The Wallop and Oliver families became not only business partners providing thousands of horses to the British Army, but also developed family ties: Oliver Wallop married Marguerite Walker and Malcolm Moncreiffe in turn married her sister Amy.[46]

CHAPTER 4

The Founding Clubs and the Organization of the Polo Association

After 16 years of polo in the United States it became clear that creating a central organization was paramount for the game to grow and expand across the continent. On 21 March 1890, John Elliott Cowdin gave a dinner at his home to a number of prominent polo personalities to discuss the formation of a polo association to coordinate and advance the polo clubs' interests. A committee composed of six members was formed: Henry Herbert as Chairman; Oliver Bird, John Cowdin, Thomas Hitchcock, Edward Potter, and Douglas Robinson, Jr.

At a preliminary planning meeting, Mr. Hitchcock moved that the Westchester Polo Club—the doyen of American polo—be named as the Central Organization of the new entity. This thought was along the precedent that had been set in England when the Hurlingham Club Committee was appointed as the ruling body of the game. However, after careful consideration, the consensus at the meeting was that a new organization, to be called the Polo Association, be formed, with a constitution and rules to govern all polo clubs that should be elected to membership.[1]

The first regular meeting of the Polo Association was held at the Equitable Building in New York City on 6 June 1890. The following clubs were elected to membership and, therefore, can be considered as the founding members: Country Club of Westchester, New York; Essex County, Orange, New Jersey; Meadow Brook, New York; Morris County, Morristown, New Jersey; Philadelphia Polo Club, Pennsylvania; Rockaway, New York; and Westchester Polo Club, Newport, Rhode Island. Henry Lloyd Herbert was elected chairman and Douglas Robinson, Jr., filled the post of secretary.

The Seven Founding Clubs

The story of the Westchester Polo Club is described in Chapter 1. Suffice it to state that the first polo club in America remained as a member of the Polo Association until 1941. A new club with the same name was started in 1993 and promptly claimed to be the original club's successor. Whether or not the practice of claiming instant antiquity for clubs with long hiatuses in their involvement with the game is historically correct remains a matter for much debate.

Rockaway Hunting Club

The origins of the Rockaway Hunting Club go back to September 1877, when seven young blades—John D. Cheever, Edward Dickerson, Jr., Louis Neilson, Edward Nicoll, Edward Spencer, William Voss, and George Work—decided that a paper chase would be a good pastime. The first chase was so successful that they moved on to fox hunting.[2]

The game of polo was started in 1881, Samuel P. Hinckley being the first player. The original field was leased on Central Avenue, near the Lawrence railroad station. The initial players were John D. Cheever, John E. Cowdin, René La Montagne, Sr., Winthrop Rutherfurd, and Joseph S. Stevens. A bit later along came Foxhall Parker Keene and a younger set of players.

Rockaway played Meadow Brook for the first time in 1885, thus starting a long-lasting and bitter rivalry. In that year, the club moved to its new location in Cedarhurst and the polo field was built in front of the clubhouse. Without any doubt, polo's and Rockaway's superstar was Foxhall Keene, the first 10-goal handicap player in the history of the game. No other player was ever rated above Keene while he was active in the game. Foxie Keene excelled in many sports and games: Steeplechasing, foxhunting, sailing, boxing, and tennis, both lawn and court.[3] A racecar driver of good enough skills to be invited by the Mercedes factory to drive one of their cars, Keene carried on his strain of dash bordering on recklessness to the roads and circuits. An English motoring publication, *The Autocar*, judged Keene "the biggest sinner in recklessness," noting the collective sighs of relief that always

John Elliott Cowdin, a 10-goal international player from the Rockaway Hunting Club.

followed his car's passing out of sight.[4] Keene himself was typically nonchalant about his driving. His memoirs recall plenty of instances of near misses and serious accidents. "I very nearly was killed the first time I raced an automobile. This was in the first Paris-Berlin motor race ... when I started out on the long grind to Berlin, I knew absolutely nothing about driving such a race. All I had was my nerve and damn fool confidence in myself."[5]

In the Vanderbilt Cup races held on Long Island, "I took one long chance when I passed Seise (sic), the French driver, in the narrow stretch in front of the grandstand. Both cars were doing close to ninety and there was barely four inches between our wheels. Photographers and officials scrambled over the high board fence in the most ludicrous manner. Later in the race ... I hit a telephone pole at the hairpin turn. It was especially annoying, as I owned the pole, or anyway a third of the company which had put it up."[6]

On a more comical note, Mr. Keene survived being chased on the polo field by an enraged lady, who blamed him for a perceived foul against her husband.[7]

On the polo grounds the Rockaway team, anchored by John Cowdin at Number 2 and Keene at Number 3, respectively, propelled the club's dark blue colors to the very top. Only the best Meadow Brook teams could offer competition at that level. It is thought that this predominance by the two most successful polo clubs was the catalyst for introducing individual handicaps.

The rivalry between the two Long Island clubs was long and deep. This animosity extended to the ladies. That keen observer of the polo scene, James Calvin Coolidge, once wrote:

> Meadow Brook was some twelve miles away but twelve miles in 1895 was a considerable distance. I speak of it as a rivalry between these two clubs but it was more an actual feud. There is a classic incident related of a certain hard-fought match when Rockaway had journeyed over to Meadow Brook, and after a rather serious collision, the Rockaway ladies trouped out on the field and began to whack the prostrate Meadow Brook player with their parasols, holding him responsible for the accident.[8]

Honors were almost equally divided between these two clubs: both took the Polo Association and Added Cups, and the Championship Cup, the most important trophies in the 1890s. Gradually, Meadow Brook began to ascertain its supremacy; however, as late as 1921, Rockaway took the Senior Championship. In 1926, plans were set for a new grounds, to be named Hazard Field in memory of a pioneer polo player, long-time secretary of the Polo Association and its chairman in 1922. The ground was completed in 1929 and inaugurated in 1930 with a match between the English international team and Eastcott, Earle W. Hopping's team. Polo was played until 1932, when difficult financial times bore hard and such luxuries had to go.[9]

Club historian Dr. Benjamin Allison wrote that polo was The Rockaway Hunting Club's laurelled sport. This is a fitting epitaph for the game of polo at this great club.

The Meadow Brook Club

Meadow Brook was incorporated in May 1881 by Francis R. Appleton, Frederick O. Beach, August Belmont, Jr., Wendell Goodwin, and A. Belmont Purdy to support and hunt with a pack of foxhounds and to promote other outdoor sports. However, polo was started earlier than foxhunting, because in 1879 August Belmont, Oliver W. Bird, William C. Eustis,

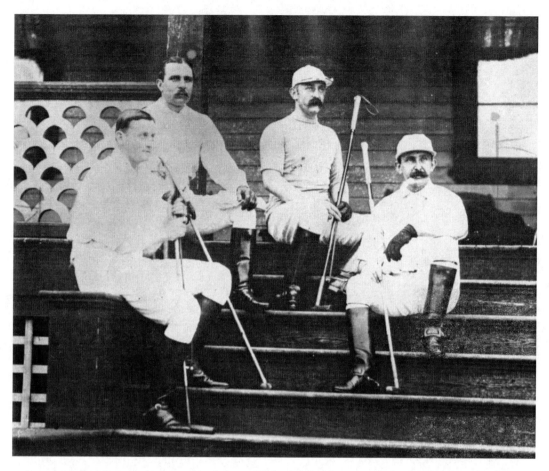

A group of early prominent polo players: Oliver Bird, Thomas Hitchcock the elder, Roger Winthrop and Augustus Belmont.

Thomas Hitchcock the elder, Benjamin Nicoll, and Dudley Winthrop played on a level ground within the Mineola Fair Grounds racetrack. Meadow Brook's polo was founded on the infield of this famous trotting track.[10]

A colonial home owned by A. Belmont Purdy in Westbury was the meeting place for the hunt. Later on, additions were made to construct what became the Meadow Brook clubhouse. The first polo field, later named Number 4 field, was built near the clubhouse; the little brook from which the club took its name had to be diverted.

Meadow Brook thrived, fed by its rivalry with Rockaway, a dozen miles to the south, a significant distance for ponies, players and spectators to travel before the advent of the horseless carriage. A team — Augustus Belmont, Jr., Thomas Hitchcock, Oliver W. Bird, and Roger D. Winthrop — took the first Championship and Added Cups in Newport. This tournament, established in 1890, is the forerunner of the present Open Championship. Another club team won the predecessor of the Senior Championship, before the end of the century. Eventually, the Meadow Brook assumed a place of leadership and authority to be one of the most famous clubs in the world, owner of 263,657 acres.[11] The years of glory extended from the mid–1910s to the early 1950s, when Robert Moses' urbanization plans almost destroyed polo on Long Island.

Essex County Country Club

The Essex County Country Club in Orange, New Jersey, was organized on 23 May 1887 at a meeting at the Mansion House, Orange, and the club was formally organized by the selection of the following: president, Henry A. Page; vice president, A. Pennington Whitehead; secretary, Robert Sedgwick; treasurer, W. Emlen Roosevelt.

William Emlen Roosevelt was a cousin and boyhood companion of Teddy Roosevelt. Born in New York in 1857, he became a financier, developer of railroads and telegraph and cable lines, and a philanthropist. Inventor Thomas Alva Edison was a prominent member.

The new country club held its formal opening ceremonies on Saturday, 4 June 1887, with a polo match on the polo grounds at the corner of South Orange Avenue and Center Street in Orange. Two teams were chosen. The "Blues," headed by T.H. Powers Farr, included Robert Sedgwick, W.W. Tucker, and Charles Pfizer, Jr.; the three-man "Orange" team consisted of Douglas Robinson, Jr., Charles Heckscher, and Samuel Campbell, Jr. The "Blue" team quickly won the first two games, with Farr scoring both goals, before the "Orange" team rallied to win the final three games behind goals by Robinson (twice) and Heckscher. Other early players were John Dallett, Jr., and Peter F. Collier.

Douglas Robinson, Jr., was one of the most prominent real estate operators in New York, the realtor who acquired the land for Penn Station and the Hudson Tubes. A graduate from Oxford University, Robinson married Theodore Roosevelt's sister. He was considered one of the country's outstanding polo players.

Thomas H. Powers Farr was attracted to the Oranges by the variety of sporting activities available there. Born in Philadelphia and raised in New York City, he was educated at Princeton where he played football and was a member of the Glee Club. Farr was captain of Essex County's first polo team, and took up golf only as a less hazardous pursuit after being hit in the eye with a polo ball. He was the club's first Greens Chairman, at the time the Hutton Park Course was built. A banker and railroad financier, Farr eventually left the club in 1923 in protest of the lifestyle of the 1920s, and helped found a "dry club" at Rock Spring.

Polo grew quickly in popularity at Essex County to become the club's banner sport. By June of 1888, a polo field had been built at the northeastern corner of Mt. Pleasant Avenue and Gregory Avenue, in an area called Rolling Green Hills. Polo matches were held there Tuesday, Thursday, and Saturday afternoons throughout the season, and the club team competed against Meadow Brook, Rockaway, Morristown, Philadelphia Country Club, and others. The cost to attend the matches at Essex County was $1 per carriage.

The *New York Herald* carried the following report on one such inter-club match on June 28, 1887:

> The first contests for the Herbert polo trophies—fine silver-handled canes—to be competed for by teams from the Essex County, Meadow Brook, Rockaway, and Pelham clubs, came off yesterday afternoon on the grounds of the Essex County Club on Mount Pleasant Avenue, West Orange, between that club and the Meadow Brook team. The handicap had been arranged so that the Essex County Club received seven goals. The day was faultless—bright, clear, and with cool westerly breezes, and the fashionable society of the Oranges turned out in large numbers, carriages standing three deep around the grounds and in every practicable position.
>
> The Essex County team went in with determination to win or die. Said one of them, "we've all taken out accident policies on our lives and you can bet your life those canes are not going to leave Orange."

Although the Essex County team lost the championship match to Meadow Brook that day, 5 to 3, with their seven-goal handicap allowance, they were able to keep the Herbert trophies in Orange.

Henry L. Herbert, who sponsored the trophies, was a member of Essex County Country Club's first Board of Governors, and also a prominent member of the Rockaway Hunting Club. During the early 1890s, however, polo seemed to be on uncertain footing, at least financially. The Board minutes of 1891 talk of asking the polo members to pay their own rent; in 1893 they were advised to solicit contributions to support their activities; and in 1894 there was talk of enrolling outside members to help pay the bills.

Morris County Country Club

The Morris County Country Club became a Polo Association member on 6 June 1890, with Benjamin Nicoll as delegate. The club was located in Morristown, New Jersey, and the team representing it with Mr. Nicoll, Billy Lord and George Lord Day was one of the most formidable teams in the country. One of the first private fields in the United States was a picturesque and lovely oval ground that Eugene Higgins had at Whippany, near Morristown.

Early players were George L. Day, Rudolph E.F. Flinsch, Norman Henderson, Gustav Kissel, Rudolf Kissel, Benjamin Nicoll, William B. Lord, Robert Stephens, William K. Thorn, Jr., Arthur Whitney and Stephen Whitney.

For some unknown reason the club's polo teams were labeled the Independence team.

Philadelphia Polo Club

The exact date of the formation of the Philadelphia Polo Club is unknown. It was started by Capt. John C. Groome — the man credited with organizing the Pennsylvania State Police and coining the term "trooper" — Harry C. Groome and Harry Pratt McKean, Jr.[12] The Polo Club was absorbed into the Philadelphia Country Club on 23 September 1890, all members being admitted without payment of the initiation fee. The Philadelphia Country Club had been conceived by Mr. William C. Bullitt, a prominent Philadelphian, and some of his friends, who felt a club offering golf and tennis to its members was desirable. Most likely, there were close ties among the membership of both clubs.

The first Polo Challenge Cup was presented by C. Hartman Kuhn on 10 September 1891. The initial matches, including the Kuhn Challenge Cup, were held on The Gentlemen's Driving Park. When completed, the polo ground in Bala was reported to be one of the finest in the country and was the venue for several important tournaments, including Senior and Junior Championships, and the U.S. Open Championship.

Other trophies were donated by James W. Paul, Edward B. Smith and Col. Edward Morrell.[13] His 300-acre estate, Morrell Park, just north of the city, was developed for housing in the 1950s.

Games were played against teams in New Jersey and New York, such as the Independence team of Morristown Country Club, Devon, Rockaway, and the Country Club of Westchester. Philadelphia players included Lemuel C. Altemus, Francis S. Conover, John C. and Harry C. Groome, Albert E. Kennedy, Jay B. Lippincott, Charles E. Mather, Harry

Pratt McKean, Col. Edward Morrell, Philip S.P. Randolph, Mitchell G. Rosengarten, Jr., and Charles N. Welsh.

With the increase in numbers of golfing members some conflict arose between golfers and poloists. A formal complaint was lodged against a golfing member who had been practicing with his iron clubs on the polo field and had cut out many divots while playing there. In retribution for this desecration of polo property, the Executive Committee took drastic action and the Club's secretary was instructed "to call [the member's] attention to his misdoings and to state that a bill for the damages would be sent to him."[14]

Country Club of Westchester

The Country Club of Westchester was started in 1883 by, among others, James Montgomery Waterbury, Sr., who was the first president, Henry A. Coster, William S. Hoyt, Charles Oliver Iselin, De Lancey A. Kane, Pierre Lorillard, Jr., Alfred Seaton, Jr., Lorillard Spencer, Jr., and Francis A. Watson. The location was on Stadium and Rollins Avenues, Pelham.

The Country Club of Westchester developed from a suggestion to organize a tennis club into a determination to found a club where all country sports could be enjoyed by the membership. The newly organized club leased the house and racing grounds of Dr. George L. Morris, at Pelham, and after some alterations, including a large addition, took possession of the property on 4 April 1884, fully equipped with tennis courts, a racetrack, polo field, baseball grounds, traps for pigeon-shooting, a pack of hounds, boats, and bathhouses.

The sale of Dr. George Morris's property made it necessary to find other quarters, and in December 1887, the Country Club Land Association organized and bought Van Antwerp Farm, of about eighty acres, located on East Chester Bay, between Pelham Bridge and Fort Schuyler. Development of the facilities went on, and in the spring of 1888 began to lay out the polo grounds and build a new clubhouse and stables, into which they moved the following year.[15]

Early players included Robert L. Beeckman, James C. Cooley, Sr., Theodore A. Havemeyer, Jr., Edward C. Potter, Marion Story and James M. Waterbury, Sr. For some reason, perhaps the club's location, the teams were sometimes known as the Pelham team. This ground was on Pelham Bay, when Westchester was just a little village in the country, and hounds used to meet at the four corners of the village.

A team — the Waterbury brothers, Harry Payne Whitney and John E. Cowdin — took the Senior Championship in 1903. The final game was played at the Philadelphia C.C. grounds in Bala, against a Bryn Mawr foursome.

The clubhouse burned down on 2 January 1922 and the unabated encroachment northwards of New York City, plus the planned new Lexington subway station near the club, forced the institution to offer the land for housing development.[16]

This Country Club of Westchester is often confused with the Westchester Polo Club of Newport, Rhode Island, and also with the Westchester Country Club in Rye, New York, where polo was played in later years but whose just fame was achieved as a golfing venue of international fame.

Oyster Bay

The Oyster Bay Polo Club was one of the three Long Island polo clubs, the other two being the powerhouses Meadow Brook and Rockaway. Oyster Bay affiliated with the Polo Association on 18 June 1890, just twelve days after the seven founding institutions. The moving force behind the establishment of polo was Francis T. Underhill who built a polo field across from Fleetwood, a house still standing today.[17] Underhill also brought ponies from his ranch in Santa Barbara, which he lent to his friends.

The Oyster Bay players were not a very conspicuous group so far as handicaps were concerned and the melancholy fact has to be recorded that the most illustrious of the names, Theodore Roosevelt, reached a high handicap of one-goal. In addition to the future president and Nobel Prize winner, other recorded names include Francis T. Underhill, who was named delegate to the Polo Association, W.H. Coles, R.H. Munroe Ferguson, Henry von M. Meyer, Alfred Roosevelt, W. Emlen Roosevelt, N. Harry Thorpe, Lucius C. Tuckerman, Walter C. Tuckerman, John B. Van Schaick and John A. Weeks, Jr.

The record shows that Oyster Bay, sometimes with the help of visiting players, played matches against the likes of Meadow Brook second team, Essex County Country Club — where Douglas Robinson, Jr., Teddy's brother-in-law, was a stalwart player — and Morris County.

As to Theodore Roosevelt, he had a tremendous impact upon sports and games in America. When eighteen football players were killed and one hundred badly injured in 1905, President Roosevelt called a meeting of university representatives, Walter Camp of Yale, James Fine of Princeton and Bill Reid of Harvard at the White House and bluntly told them to clean up their act.[18] As a result of this ultimatum the brutality of football was checked by changing the rules, banning mass pushing, preventing freshmen from playing on varsity teams, and opening up the tactics of the game by legalizing the forward pass.

In addition, from his lofty position as president, Roosevelt made athletic endeavors fashionable and encouraged the country's youth to participate in sports. Not least, with the advice of Gifford Pinchot, Teddy Roosevelt promoted outdoor life throughout America. Anyone who has visited our national forests and parks must thank those two men for their farsighted conservation policies.

Polo at Oyster Bay did not resume after the 1894 season and little is known of the subsequent polo endeavors of its members.

Tuxedo Polo Club

The Tuxedo Polo Club was affiliated on 24 February 1891. It had as its delegate Amos Tuck French, from Harvard College, as were several of the 13 players bearing official handicaps. Of those, eleven were rated at zero. Among the players were Winthrop Chanler, Giraud Foster, Wendell Goodwin, Herbert T. King, Richard Mortimer, De Lancy Nicoll, Walker Breese Smith, and Paul Tuckerman.

Other Early Clubs

In 1892 there were 13 clubs affiliated to the Polo Association, every single one of them on the Atlantic coast. To complete the roster of polo clubs in the 19th century, brief mention will be made of those with ties to the Polo Association.

The year 1893 saw the prestigious St. Louis Country Club join the Association's ranks, followed on 6 June by the Monmouth County, in Hollywood, New Jersey. Its players were Peter F. Collier, Robert J. Collier, Dr. Edward Field, Thomas Field, Frederick Hoey, George M. Pullman, Jr., and W.S. Throckmorton. In 1897, this club moved to Long Island and changed its name to Southampton Polo Club.

The Chicago Polo Club was the first club away from the eastern seaboard to join the Polo Association. Its origins are described in Chapter 3. On the same day, 4 March 1895, the Lowell Country Club in Massachusetts also became a member. The initial players were Col. Charles H. Allen, Dr. R.E. Bell, Edmund B. Conant, George C. Dempsey, George C. Motley, Gardner W. Pearson, Thomas Talbot, Edward L. White and William T. White. Just a few months later, on 27 August, the club changed its name to Vesper. Two days after Chicago and Lowell became members, the Devon Polo Club in Pennsylvania gained admission to the Polo Association. This club reached certain renown, with quality players such as Lemuel C. Altemus, George Kendrick, III, Charles Snowden, Jr., and Carlton B. Zeilin.

The Point Judith Country Club in Narragansett Pier, Rhode Island was affiliated on 22 July 1895, although the game had thrived on that location for years. "Polo at the Pier," meaning polo at the Point Judith C.C., meant for more than 30 years national championships, visiting teams from overseas, sometimes club cups and other times matches just for the fun of the game. It also meant polo played on grounds endowed with lush turf considered among the best in the United States. Another welcome feature after five or six chukkers of hard play were the cool, salt-laden breezes that came sweeping from Narragansett Bay, which provided relief to ponies and players alike.

The club came into being thanks to the foresight of Philip S.P. Randolph, a prominent Philadelphian who summered in Rhode Island, was the owner of seaside acreage, and decided to start a place offering polo—and later golf—which sporting people could enjoy in the summer time. And society folks came. Harry Kane, Wally Keith and William Marrow from Baltimore, and Charles Welsh from Philadelphia, were the early ones. They were joined later by the Converses, the Earls, the McFaddens and the Strawbridges from Philadelphia; the Stevensons, the Stoddards and the Webbs from New York; the Burrages, the Clarks, the Dempseys, the Forbes and the Shaws from Boston. They came because polo and horses were uppermost in their minds.

Also joining during the banner year of 1895 was the Genesee Valley Polo Club, in the fox hunting country near Geneseo in upstate New York. Richard Conover, Edward F. Fitzhugh, William L. Littauer, H. Smith, John R. Townsend and Craig and James S. Wadsworth counted themselves among the players.

The nation's capital saw its first polo club become a member on 6 April 1896. Gist Blair, Henry M. Earle, Lewis Earle, Hugh S. Legarè, Capt. Francis Michler, Clarence Moore, David Porter and Dr. Leonard Wood were some of the players. The name Theodore Roosevelt also appears on the club's roster.

The Riding and Driving Club in Brooklyn, later to achieve fame and glory as an indoor polo power, joined in the month of June. Howard Boocock, W.C. Candee, Lewis M. Gibb, G. Herbert Potter, Winthrop M. Tuttle, and Robbins Woodward were the pioneers.

On the same date as the Brooklyn club, Evanston Country Club in Illinois was affiliated. George N. Armsby, Thomas Beard, H. Tracy Kirkman, M. Jay Kirkman, William B. Kirkman, Charles G. Lewis, C.A. McDonald and George F. Slaughter were among the enthusiasts.

Only one club joined in 1897 — the Staten Island Polo Club, in West Brighton. W. Gould Brokaw, Dr. James McKee, C.H. Robbins, George M. Sidenberg, Morton W. Smith,

G.J. Waters and Jack C. Wilmerding, Jr., were the players. Actually, the Polo Association lost ground, because Genesee Valley, Harvard, and Hingham submitted their resignations in that year.

The short-lived Jacksonville, the first polo club in Florida, affiliated on 4 December 1898. W.H. Baker, Montgomery Corse, Albert Huntington, Victor Johnson, D.F. Mitchell — who was the delegate — Lt. William L. Mitchell and Bruce Turton were the initial players. Lt. Billy Mitchell later achieved fame as the father of military aviation in the United States, and is one of the few polo players to be awarded the Congressional Medal of Honor, in his case posthumously, long after his notorious court martial.

The Gould family started their Lakewood Polo Club at Georgian Court in New Jersey, the setting for George Bellows' magnificent trilogy of polo paintings. Also in 1899 the Aiken and the Saratoga polo clubs became formally part of the Polo Association, joined by the Somerset County Polo Club of the pharmaceutical giants Charles Pfizer and Charles Squibb, who were joined by Archibald Alexander, Palmer Campbell, Charles M. Chapin, Percy R. Pyne, Edwin A. and Richard Stevens.

Finally, in 1900, three more clubs joined: Camden, in South Carolina, whose story is related in Chapter 3; Squadron A in New York; and Great Neck, started by the Grace family on Long Island. Joseph Peter, Morgan and William Russell Grace were the founders. Other members included Henry Bell, Walter McClure, Clarence Robbins, Edward Roesler and R. Lawrence Smith.

Rumford Polo Club

A little-known club near Providence, Rhode Island, was the Rumford Polo Club. On 19 March 1903 Rhode Island's secretary of state certified that Abram Barker, Augustus W. Calder, W.R. Callender, Harold Congdon, W.O. Fifield, John R. Gladding, Walter S. Hackney, Walter H. Hanley, Charles L.A. Heiser, John B. Lewis, Stephen O. Metcalf, Thomas B. Owen, Henry W. Sackett and H. Anson Richmond had filed an agreement to form a corporation under the name Rumford Polo Club, for the purpose of encouraging and supporting the game of polo and other sports connected with the use and development of the horse.[19] In addition the above mentioned individuals, some of the polo players were William C. Baker, Harris Bucklin, George H. Eiswald, James C. Gregg, Gerald Hanley, Jesse Metcalf, Charles F. Peckham and Byron S. Watson. The delegate to the Polo Association was Charles Heiser.[20]

Allan Forbes recalled, "The Rumford Polo Club, which did not join the Association until this spring (2 February 1902), played a number of matches at Dedham, Narragansett Pier, Myopia, and on its home grounds, and although beaten in all its games but one, has nevertheless shown a most sportsmanlike quality in entering the Eastern tournaments and doing its share towards making then a success. A friendly rivalry has sprung between this club and the Norfolk Country Club, the latest addition to the Polo Association. The Norfolk County Club played in the Dedham tournament in September and gave a very good account of itself."[21]

Their "friendly" rivals, the polo players at Dedham, could not restrain from poking a little bit of fun at little Rumford. One of the players, Benjamin Nason Hamlin, was quoted in the club's history as follows: "The Rumford polo field in Providence is surrounded by three cemeteries. B. Nason Hamlin says that one is for the players on one side, one for the players on the other side, and the last one for the unfortunate umpires."[22]

The club resigned from the Polo Association on 31 March 1908. Nevertheless, there is a link from the Rumford Polo Club to the present. The trophy for the East Coast Open, now held at Myopia Hunt Club, is the old Perry Cup, donated by Mrs. Marsden Jaseal Perry for competition in 1905.

The 1890 Polo Season

The "Recapitulation of the Season, 1890, June 7th to Sept. 22nd" in the *Polo Association Year Book* makes for interesting reading. "There were 33 match games played, 292 goals made by winners, 49 goals made by losers, 101 goals allowed by handicap, 2½ goals allowed by fouls."[23] It appears that only five fouls were called in the 33 official matches played, at the time when the rules stipulated that half-a-goal was deducted from the offending team's tally.

The unknown writer goes on to list the tournament winners. Rather than current practice, the teams are listed first, followed by their wins. For example, the Meadow Brook players are listed — August Belmont, Jr., Thomas Hitchcock, Jr., Oliver W. Bird, and Robert D. Winthrop — followed by their match wins: Governors Challenge Cup, Clark Cups, Polo Association Cups. While offering the notice of who donated the trophies, in this case the Governors of the Essex County Country Club, and Mr. Farley Clark, it omits the donor of the most important trophy, the Polo Association Cups.

The Rockaway team, with John D. Cheever, Foxhall Keene, John E. Cowdin and Winthrop Rutherfurd, took the Herbert Trophies, and the oldest tournament in competition, the Meadow Brook Autumn Cup, presented by the members in 1885. There is also mention of the Turnure Cups for pairs, donated by Mr. Lawrence Turnure.

CHAPTER 5

Individual Handicaps and the Major Polo Tournaments

On Thursday, 10 July 1890, four gentlemen met at the Café Saravin in the Equitable Building to address the issue of individual handicaps in polo. This was not an ordinary oasis because it carried the reputation as the most aristocratic restaurant in New York City's financial district. The four gentlemen were Oliver Bird, John Cowdin, Henry Herbert and Edward Potter, all members of the Polo Association Executive Committee.

Henry Lloyd Herbert mounted on Louisville Lou. Mr. Herbert, chairman of the Polo Association for thirty-one years, 1890–1921, established the concept of individual handicaps in 1888.

Their brief was to adjudicate individual handicaps to all registered players, a most difficult endeavor. Two years before, Henry Lloyd Herbert had been assigned the task of awarding individual handicaps. Mr. Herbert handicapped 42 players, with Foxhall Keene at the top of the list with a 5-goal handicap. John Elliott Cowdin and William Thorn, Jr., were next with 4-goals; then, at 3-goals, there followed Oliver Bird, Thomas Hitchcock the elder, Winthrop Rutherford, and Robert Winthrop.

This precedent of a maximum rating of five goals was adopted in 1890 for the now official Polo Association handicap list. Foxhall Keene remained at the top, followed by his Rockaway teammate John Cowdin, with a handicap 4. At 3-goals there were August Belmont, Jr., Oliver Bird, Thomas Hitchcock, Edward Potter, T.H. Powers Farr, Douglas Robinson, William Thorn, Jr., and Winthrop Rutherfurd. These ten players represented the best in American polo, their handicaps to take effect from that date until the end of the 1890 season.

The maximum handicap of 10-goals was adopted for the 1891 polo season. Foxhall Parker Keene then became the first player in the history of the game to be recognized as a 10-goaler. [For a list comparing players' handicaps in 1888 and 1891, see Appendix 2.]

Just like most ruling bodies of polo worldwide, another of the first tasks undertaken by the Polo Association was to establish a championship tournament. This resulted in the creation of the Polo Association Cups, a single trophy with four individual cups for each member of the winning team. At the same meeting mentioned above, the following resolution was passed:

> Moved and seconded that the Polo Association shall offer Handicap Cups for teams of four to be won outright.
> To be played for on the grounds of the Westchester Polo Club at Newport, during August of this year.[1]

The first winners—in 1890—were the representatives of the Meadow Brook Club: Augustus Belmont, Jr., Thomas Hitchcock the elder, Oliver Bird and Roger Winthrop. There were four entrants. In the first match, played on 18 August 1890, Harvard Polo Club, with James Burden, Jr., Columbus C. Baldwin, Robert Innes Crocker, and Rodolphe Agassiz, defeated Morristown—George Day, Norman Henderson, Benjamin Nicoll, and William Lord—by 11 goals to 9, giving 5 goals by handicap.

On the following day, Meadow Brook beat Myopia 18 to 10, allowing 10 goals by handicap. The final match was another easy victory for Meadow Brook, which scored 11 goals. The young Harvard team received 9 goals by handicap and was unable to add any tallies to this total.

The event was held in Newport, and thereafter by rotation among different clubs. Rockaway, Myopia, Meadow Brook, Westchester, Brookline in Massachusetts, Buffalo, Bala in Pennsylvania, and Dedham were the venues. As to the players, the best exponents of the game saw their names engraved on the trophy. Legendary names like Rodolphe Agassiz, Columbus Baldwin, John Cowdin, Foxhall Keene, Robert Shaw, Harry Payne Whitney, all 9- or 10-goal players, are on the roll of honor. Frenchmen Charles and Maurice Raoul-Duval were on the winning Meadow Brook 2nd team in 1896, the first foreign-born players to take an important championship in America. Maurice was the best French player up to the start of the World War; in England he took the Warwickshire Cup. Unfortunately, Maurice Raoul-Duval was killed during the battle of Verdun in 1916. Charles, a cavalry officer, survived the conflict.

It should be noted that the Polo Association Cups was an event played on handicap.

After 1898, the Polo Association Cups' results disappear from the pages of the Polo Association Year Book. The Polo Association minutes curtly state that a motion was carried, "To discontinue the Polo Association Cups."[2] Unfortunately, the location of the original trophy is unknown. The complete list of winners appears in Appendix 3.

The Senior Championship

The first championship without handicap took place in 1895 at Prospect Park in Brooklyn, under the name Championship Cup and Added Cups, for a gold vase presented by William Waldorf Astor. For "Added Cups," it was meant individual trophies for the players of the winning team. When the Junior Championship was instituted in 1900, the name of the event was changed to Senior Championship. This competition would last until 1921.

The first game, as all the rest of the matches, took place at Brooklyn's Prospect Park Parade Ground between the team from Myopia, represented by Augustus Peabody Gardner, Bobby Shaw, Rodolphe Agassiz and Frank Blackwood Fay, totaling 28 goals handicap, versus the Country Club of Westchester, which presented the Waterbury brothers, Larry and Monte, Oliver Bird and Edward C. Potter, also a 28-goal team. In a closely contested game, Myopia defeated the favored Westchester by 2¾ goals to 1½ goals. Three days later, on 27 September 1895, the Myopians took the full honors, winning the first national championship for the North Shore club in another tight contest: 4¾ goals to Rockaway's 2¾ goals. John D. Cheever, John Cowdin, Foxhall Keene and Winthrop Rutherford wore the dark blue jerseys of Rockaway, a 29-goal combination.

Bobby Shaw was then raised to 9-goals, and Rodolphe Louis Agassiz reached the 10-goal summit, the first player from Myopia to achieve such distinction. An oil painting depicting Dolph Agassiz by New England artist Howard Smith commemorates the event. It hangs in the Myopia Hunt clubhouse in Hamilton.

The Myopia team was a very fine one and in a great many ways was unique. Their Number 1, Gussie Gardner, stayed farther up field than any other forward in polo and pounced towards goal on the long shots sent up to him by the incredibly brilliant Bobby Shaw and the sound Dolph Agassiz, racing away towards his opponents' goal. And never there was a Back that played deeper than Fay Blackwood, so with Gardner way out in front and Fay hiding coyly in the background, the Myopia team covered a lot of ground. But for a team to engage in the tactics assumed by Myopia meant an enormous amount of work

Myopia Hunt's own Rodolphe Agassiz. Dolph was an international player and achieved a 10-goal handicap.

has to be carried on by the two men in the middle of the game. Agassiz and Shaw, two of the superstars of 19th century American polo, lived up to the task, defeating the top teams in the country. Myopia was in the fortunate position of being able to field such a formidable team.

Next year the table was turned on Myopia. Facing in the first round the Meadow Brook team of William Eustis, his brother-in-law Thomas Hitchcock, Columbus Baldwin and Benjamin Nicoll, they went down to honorable defeat by 6¾ to 3¾ goals. In the second match, Rockaway overwhelmed Buffalo, scoring 20 goals against two of their rivals, which also were penalized ¾ goals. Representing Rockaway were Joseph Stevens, John Cowdin, Foxhall Keene and George Eustis. The final event was quite even, both Meadow Brook and Rockaway scoring eight times each. It came down to penalties: Meadow Brook was penalized a total of 1¾ goals, Rockaway only once, thus winning the championship 7 goals to 6¼.

Meadow Brook took the tournament the next two years, in 1897 with William Eustis, Thomas Hitchcock, Harry Payne Whitney and Benjamin Nicoll. In 1898, Columbus Baldwin played instead of Nicoll. Sadly, it was C.C. Baldwin's swansong. The baby-faced Baldwin, a 9-goal player about to reach polo's summit, died young without reaching his full potential. It was the opinion of many that he would have been the next 10-goal player in America.[3]

The year 1899 was anticlimactic, because the Westchester Polo Club won the tournament by default. Then Dedham, with Allan Forbes, Edward Weld, William Goodwin and Joshua Crane, Jr., took the Senior Championship. Josh Crane was a player who excelled in many games and sports, and with every game had some little gimmick with him; for instance, holding the reins of a double bridle with a wooden bar through which to pass the reins, so instead of holding four reins he gripped one piece of wood; or when putting in golf, Crane would produce a putter stranger than any other known putter in captivity.[4]

The Junior Championship — in our days the Silver Cup, after the years from 1938 to 1973, when it was known under the prosaic name Twenty Goal — was created in 1900 for a trophy presented by Samuel Dennis Warren, the stalwart player and administrator from Dedham Polo Club.[5] There were some conditions applied to teams

A polo team in Newport, 1890s. William Thorn, Harvard's Columbus Baldwin, Moses Taylor and a youthful Harry Payne Whitney.

and players in the Junior Championship. The team handicap was limited to 20-goals; however, the competition was played without handicap. On the other hand, individual handicaps were not restricted; any player could participate. Players who entered the Junior were not eligible to play in the Senior Championship, which followed immediately. There was one exception, because the winning team in the Junior Championship was offered the privilege of a place in the Senior event. A further clause, that eventually signed the demise of the Senior Championship, stipulated that all players in both events had to be members of the club they represented. Furthermore, no player could be handicapped with more than one club.

Lakewood, the Gould family's private club in New Jersey, was the champion team in the following two years. Oddly enough, those conquests came about with borrowed players: Charles Randolph Snowden, the Waterbury brothers, Foxie Keene, Hervey Lyle, and John Cowdin. Actually, the 1902 contest became null and void after the other two teams, Bryn Mawr and Dedham, lodged protests concerning the eligibility of one of Lakewood's players, Lawrence Waterbury. The Polo Association considered the matter and, after hearing Mr. Waterbury's explanation that he had been playing in England representing the Association in the international matches for the Westchester Cup, ruled that the Senior Cup would not be awarded.[6]

The old Country Club of Westchester took the title in 1903, played at the Philadelphia Country Club's grounds in Bala. John Cowdin and Harry P. Whitney teamed up with Monty and Larry Waterbury to win the honors. Myopia followed in 1904 with their second win. Maxwell Norman, erstwhile with the Country Club of Brookline, and a young Devereux Milburn, a graduate student at Harvard Law School, teamed up with previous winners Robert Shaw, II, and Rodolphe Agassiz. Only two teams participated because Dedham withdrew in protest of Bryn Mawr's inclusion of Albert Kennedy, a Philadelphia Country Club player and former captain, on its team. Whether Kennedy should be allowed to play or not caused considerable agitation in the Executive Committee of the Polo Association. Chairman Henry Herbert declined to break a tied vote.[7] The bickering among clubs regarding players' eligibility continued to mar the Senior Championship and eventually contributed to its demise.

No teams participated in the 1905 edition, another blank year.

In the next two years, the top two clubs divided the spoils of victory. The Rockaway Hunting Club, represented by J. Armstrong Rawlins, René La Montagne, Jr., Foxhall Keene and Daniel Chauncey, Jr., was awarded the Championship Cup. It was a hollow conquest because no other clubs submitted an entry for the tournament, which was to have been held at Van Cortlandt Park in the Bronx. Daniel Chauncey, Jr., died two years later, some two weeks after being hit in the head by an opponent's mallet. Young Chauncey had received another serious head injury three years previously.[8]

Then, Meadow Brook's 1st team, with Eugene Reynal, M.F.H., and author of *Thoughts on Hunting Kit*, the celebrated Waterbury brothers, and Robert Beeckman, who later entered politics and was Governor of Rhode Island from 1915 to 1921, took the Championship, defeating the Bryn Mawr 1st team on the historic Westchester Polo Club's ground in Newport.

Once more, 1908 was a blank year for the Senior Championship, because no teams registered to compete.

From 1909 until the entry of America in the European war, the Senior Championship was held at the Point Judith Country Club in Narragansett Pier. It was monopolized by

Meadow Brook teams, with quality players such as Raymond Belmont, Foxie Keene, Devereux Milburn, John S. Phipps, John A. Rawlins, Malcolm Stevenson, James Montgomery Waterbury, Jr., and his older brother Larry. The Long Island club's sky blue-clad players—the robin's egg blue sobriquet was not adopted until 1917—took the prize four times out of seven; only Cooperstown, Bryn Mawr and Great Neck were able to challenge Meadow Brook's hegemony. However, with the Open Championship being reinstated in 1910 and sharing the Narragansett's ground with both the Junior and Senior tournaments, the latter suffered for lack of entries. Sometimes, only two teams entered the Senior Championship.

The chronicle of the Senior Championship, the most important tournament in America until World War I, abounds with stories about great players, of triumphs of this team and that, and the gradual decline in face of the ever-increasing prestige of the Open Championship. After the war, which changed the story of the world, the grip of the Senior Championship became feebler and slowly but surely, in keeping with the trend of the times, the Open Championship became the premier tournament in America.

The rules concerning the Senior Championship had been very sharply designed. The entries represented clubs and all members of a team had to be members of that club. The Open Championship was exactly what it name implies—open to the world—and it is not surprising at all that the restrictions surrounding the Senior Championship were found tedious by both players and administrators of the game. Thus, after 1921, the event was eliminated from the polo calendar, the last winner being Rockaway with Louis Ezekiel Stoddard, Thomas Hitchcock, Jr., Malcolm Stevenson and John Cheever Cowdin.

The Senior Championship had a glorious history. In many ways it is indelibly associated with the carefree days of the game and, indeed, of many good things in this country. Those days, which now seem so infinitely tranquil and easy and comfortable, have gone forever, taking with them so many worthwhile things. Thus, the Senior Championship gave way to the Open, and old names to new.

The Open Championship

The United States Open Championship started in 1904 and since 1922 remains the great event of the polo year. The tournament began not as the most important competition in polo, but as a sideshow to the Senior Championship. The idea of an event open to all, the Open Championship, arose in the fertile mind of Joseph B. Thomas, a sporting gentleman who played polo at the New Haven Country Club in Connecticut. Mr. Thomas was a man of gifted imagination and towering personality.[9]

The event had humble beginnings because only two teams answered the call for the initial tournament. The setting was Van Cortlandt Park in the Bronx borough of New York City; the date Tuesday, 20 September 1904. Four 15-minute periods were played, seven minutes being allowed for rest between each period, and two-minute stoppage time after each goal. Oliver Bird was the referee, and Dr. Harrison Abbott Souther, a veterinarian and polo player from the Hingham Polo Club, served as timekeeper.

Free from the constraints imposed by the Senior Championship regulations, the teams adopted the whimsical names Freebooters and Wanderers. The players were:

Wanderers		*Freebooters*	
Charles R. Snowden (Bryn Mawr)	6	Devereux Milburn (Myopia)	4
John E. Cowdin (Rockaway)	8	R.L. Agassiz (Myopia)	9

James Montgomery Waterbury, Jr., was the younger of the two famous brothers. "Monte" was a ten-goal handicap player and a member of the celebrated Big Four, unbeaten in international play.

Wanderers

J.M. Waterbury, Jr. (C.C. Westchester)	8
Lawrence Waterbury (C.C. Westchester)	9

Freebooters

F.P. Keene (Meadow Brook)	9
Joshua Crane, Jr. (Dedham)	6

The New York Times gave the event ample coverage, referring to the game as "Fast, spirited, well-contested, and brilliant. It resembled the old time matches of which the veterans of Meadow Brook and Rockaway are ever fond of talking over."[10]

Cowdin, Snowden and Larry Waterbury scored for the Wanderers in the first period. Agassiz answered with two tallies of his own in the second, the last one seven seconds after the bell had sounded. The third period was even in goals, Monte Waterbury, Keene, Cowdin, and again Keene scoring in that order. But the Freebooters were penalized ¾ of a goal for a foul committed by Keene and, in addition to that mishap, a ¼ goal for a safety incurred by Crane. No goals were made in the final period; however, the Wanderers were penalized ½ goal for a penalty by Snowden, and the Freebooters ¼ goal for a safety by Keene, the final score being 4½ to 3 in favor of the Wanderers.[11]

In spite of losing the match, it was a creditable performance for the Freebooters; had the contest been played with handicap, the Freebooters would have won the championship. The only handicap change for the next season was Devereux Milburn's, which went up to 5 goals. Although the Milburn name is rightly associated with Meadow Brook, at the time he was playing at Myopia while completing his studies at Harvard Law School.

Of the four individual trophies awarded, only two examples are known to exist. The handsome championship cup presented by Mr. Joseph B. Thomas is modeled after a 17th century tureen, and was sculpted by the talented Sally James Farnham. The trophy is in the custody of the National Museum of Polo in Lake Worth, Florida, having been recovered weeks after a robbery committed on 9 March 2002.[12]

The Open Championship was held in abeyance until 1910, when the event took place at the Point Judith Country Club in Rhode Island. An English team bearing the Ranelagh Club red and white quartered colors won the first round by default from the Rockaway Club, and subsequently defeated Bryn Mawr 12½ to 4¾. Lord Hugh Grosvenor, Riversdale Grenfell, the Earl of Rocksavage and Frederick Gill made up the team in this game. Meanwhile, the Point Judith Perroquets, with Hugh Drury, Frederick Prince, Dolph Agassiz and William Balding, first defeated the New Haven team and then took the measure of the strong Meadow Brook Club, which had John S. Phipps, Monte Water-

The U.S. Open Championship trophy dates back to 1910. Designed by Sally James Farnham after a 17th century tureen, this beautiful trophy was presented by Joseph B. Thomas, polo player and sportsman.

bury, Malcolm Stevenson, and Dev Milburn in its lineup. Englishman Harry Rich replaced Hugh Drury at Number 1 in this game. In the finals, Francis Grenfell, Rivy's twin, replaced Lord Grosvenor. The Ranelagh beat the host club's combination by 7¼ goals to 3½ goals.

It is sad to add that both Grenfell brothers fell during World War I. Francis Grenfell was posthumously awarded the Victoria Cross, Britain's highest decoration for valor. Lord Hugh Grosvenor was also killed during that conflict. As an aside, Francis Octavius—he was the eighth-born child—Grenfell is the only player to have taken the Open Championships in America, England, India and South Africa. This is a remarkable record, and also a reflection of the Edwardians' penchant for worldwide traveling and taking up every opportunity to engage in sports and games.

Following this auspicious beginning, with an overseas team to add to the proceedings, the Open Championship moved on from strength to strength, in spite of interruptions in 1911 and 1915. All the matches were played at the Point Judith Country Club in Narragansett Point, Rhode Island.

The Cooperstown team took the honors in 1912, and successfully defended its title the following year. It consisted of Frank von Stade, Sr., a Harvard product; sculptor Charles Cary Rumsey; financier Chauncey Perry Beadleston; and Malcolm Stevenson. Especially in the latter year they decisively defeated the Meadow Brook team of Watson Webb, Monte Waterbury, Devereux Milburn and Lord Wodehouse, the English 10-goaler. Cooperstown also took the Senior Championship in 1913, a magnificent double.

Without explanation both Meadow Brook and Cooperstown defaulted in the 1914 Open Championship. After two Point Judith teams battled each other in the semifinal round, the Meadow Brook Magpies squad—Norcross L. Tilney, Watson Webb, William Goadby Loew, and Howard Phipps—took the championship. Two days before, this same team had won the Junior Championship from the Aiken Tigers.

While war was raging in Europe, American polo went about its business, but no Open Championship was held. The summer of 1916 saw the debut of 16-year-old Thomas Hitchcock, Jr., in the Open Championship. Playing at Number 1 on the Great Neck team, Tommy showed glimpses of his phenomenal future career and a place among the game's immortals. Great Neck was defeated in the Open competition by 10½ goals to 4. However, not all had been lost for Great Neck because only two days before they faced the identical Meadow Brook team in the finals of the Senior Championship and took the title with a 9¾ to 7¾ victory.

This 1916 Open Championship also saw the first team from California to enter the U.S. Open. Gustave Heckscher, Harry East, Earle W. Hopping and Malcolm Stevenson represented the Coronado Club that beat the Rugby team in the semifinals. The final match pitted Meadow Brook versus Coronado. Oddly enough, this game took place in Westbury, Long Island, far away from Narragansett Pier, and long after the preliminary rounds had been completed on 31 July. The final event for the Open Championship was played on 7 October. Both teams made changes: Elliot Bacon replaced Harry East, and for Meadow Brook, Howard Phipps played instead of Frank von Stade and W. Goadby Loew took Monte Waterbury's place. The final score was 8 goals to 3, favorable to the local team.

When the United States entered the world conflict in April 1917, competitive polo came to an end for the duration. Although many benefit and practice games were played, seventy percent of registered polo players answered their country's call to arms. Out of 1,440 listed players in the Polo Association roster, 1,005 enrolled in the armed services, including twelve that reached general's rank.[13] Two polo players of distinction, Augustus P. Gardner and Charles W. Plummer, lost their lives during the war.

CHAPTER 6

The Westchester Cup:
The Pre-War Years

Following the one-sided British win in Newport there were no official matches for the Westchester Cup until 1902. In his memoirs, Foxhall Keene writes that in 1892 he went to England to try to arrange another visit by an English team. *The New York Herald* published an article stating, "Mr. Foxhall Keene, when he went abroad, was to carry a certain authority granted him by the Polo Association to induce an English team to come over here and try conclusions with our crack teams."[1] According to Keene's version, the mission failed because an agreement regarding the rules of the game could not be reached. The British would allow the hooking of mallets and the offside rule; the Americans would have none of that.[2] A search through the Polo Association's Executive Committee minutes failed to find any mention of a proposed renewal of the international series, or the granting of any kind of authority to Mr. Keene to negotiate on behalf of the Polo Association.

1900 at Hurlingham Club

The persistent Mr. Keene did not falter in his quest to return the International Cup to America. While foxhunting in England, he was instrumental in assembling a team of American players to contest the trophy. They were Walter McCreery, his brother Laurence, and Frank Jay Mackey, a globetrotting Chicagoan who spend much of his time in Europe, and also in Southern California.

Walter Adolph McCreery was born in Zurich to an American father and was educated at Cambridge University. Walter took the silver medal in the 1900 Olympic Games as a member on the Rugby team, and the Hurlingham Champion Cup in 1900 and 1904 with the Old Cantabs team, all former students at Cambridge. His brother Lawrence, who also received his graduate education at Cambridge, took the 1900 Hurlingham Champion Cup.

Jay Mackey was a winner of the gold medal at the Paris games with the Anglo-American Foxhunters team. Mr. Mackey was the donor of trophies bearing his name in Paris, Warwickshire and California. He made his considerable fortune when he started Household International, the forerunner of MasterCard/Visa. Moving to Chicago from Wisconsin, Mackey found that his business' reputation prevented him and his wife, the former Florence May from Minneapolis, being admitted to the circles of prominent society; therefore, they moved first to New York and then overseas. The Mackeys were among the wealthiest Americans living in Europe. They owned a town house in Mayfair and a noted country site,

Beauchamp Hall, in Leamington Spa, Warwickshire. They also became part of the Prince of Wales— later Edward VII — social circle. Meanwhile, at home, the *Chicago Tribune* labeled Jay Mackey — a 5-goal handicap player — "the king of usurers."[3]

Played at Hurlingham, the match was rather one-sided, the British team winning easily by eight goals to only two by the American team. Capt. the Hon. John Beresford, Frederick M. Freake, Walter S. Buckmaster, and the old warrior John Watson represented the Union Jack.

There is some controversy regarding this contest. *The Hurlingham Polo Association Year Book*

A brilliant all-around sportsman, Foxhall Keene before a Westchester Cup match in England under the gaze of fashionable spectators.

lists the event as part and parcel of the history of the Westchester Cup.[4] It is, however, cautiously ignored in the U.S. Polo Association Year Book. Anyway, this 1900 event deserves more recognition than the 1988 competition between the United States and a team from Australasia that was played in contravention of the deed of gift, which clearly specifies that the Westchester Cup is the exclusive domain of America and Britain.

1902 at Hurlingham Club

There is much more documentation regarding the 1902 competition. A formal challenge was sent from the Polo Association to the Hurlingham Polo Committee. A team was selected, comprising the best American players: Rodolphe Agassiz, John Cowdin, Foxhall Keene as captain, and the Waterbury siblings, Lawrence and his younger brother, James Montgomery, Jr., known as Monte.

The pony string left early, accompanied by Foxie Keene, en route to England for the foxhunting season. This proved to be a mixed blessing, because Keene had a bad spill while hunting with the Quorn, injuring his neck and raising doubts as to his availability to anchor the American team.

The American squad played six matches against strong opposition, winning four and being at the wrong end of the score in the other two. Both ponies and players made a favorable impression on their hosts. *The Field* noticed that their hitting was clean, every one used his stick with equal facility on each side, and the ponies ridden by the challengers, although not fast, were handy and responsive to their riders' directions.

On Saturday morning, John Cowdin, the reserve player, was placed at the Number 2 position, previously occupied by Monte Waterbury. Agassiz played forward, and Keene and Larry Waterbury in defense. The English team was Cecil Nickalls, Patteson Nickalls, Walter Buckmaster and Charles Miller. Umpires were William Corcoran Eustis for America and Capt. Gordon Renton for England; Cap. Denis St. G. Daly was the referee.

The start was good for the American team, because Larry Waterbury scored a goal less than three minutes after the throw-in. The second period opened tamely until a breakaway headed by Dolph Agassiz resulted in a goal by Keene. In the third period, Cowdin became a cropper, without suffering bodily injury, only perhaps to his ego. While Cowdin was down, Cecil Nickalls—the Millers' brother-in-law—scored a goal. *The Field* correspondent's commentary is of interest: "While he was down, Mr. C. Nickalls hit a goal, but, of course, the point was disallowed on appeal to the umpire."[5] Therefore, at halftime the Americans led 2–0.

Dryly, *The Field* reports that the second half was by no means interesting, the fourth period being a stumbling one. England kept on pressing, Miller scoring but the goal was nullified for offside. Towards the end of the match, Cecil Nickalls hit a goal for England, the game thus ending 2–1 in favor of the American team, their first win against England.

Why was the second half so uninspiring? The reason is that, being two goals ahead in a tight game, the Americans resorted to a legal tactic allowed by the Hurlingham Rules: If a team hit the ball behind his own backline, play was resumed by a hit-in by the defending team. There is no mention of this tactic in *The Field*'s detailed coverage of the game; however, it was considered an unfair maneuver in England. The American team, under heavy pressure by their opponents, resorted time and time again to hitting behind their own line. As an aside, the Hurlingham Polo Committee quickly changed this rule after the polo season had ended, allowing the attacking team a free-hit from 60 yards, opposite where the ball crossed the back line. This was the modern origin of the safety penalty, called corner in Argentina.[6]

The first game's negative results brought changes to the British team. Frederick Freake replaced Pat Nickalls at Number 2; Charles Miller was dropped from the team, his replacement being his older brother George. The American team was unchanged. The game was a runaway victory for England, the final score being 6–1.

For the third and decisive match, postponed on account of bad weather, England again made changes: Pat Nickalls returned to the team at Number 3, and George Miller moved to the Number 2 position instead of Freake. The American team made one change, Monte Waterbury played at Number 1 because John Cowdin had returned to America to attend to some business commitments.

At the beginning, the match was fairly even, as the first period ended in a one-all tie and the second was a scoreless one. However, in the third period Walter Buckmaster started hitting long shots at goal in an attempt to break the stubborn American defense. In these attempts he was successful and the score started to mount; at halftime it was 4–1.[7] In the second half, the American ponies began to show signs of being tired. As the numbers on the scoreboard deteriorated from the American point of view, Larry Waterbury, Dolph Agassiz and Keene played at times in the Back's position. They were unable to stop the British onslaught. The final score was 7–1, the hosts winning both game and series.

Thus, England retained the cup first won in 1886. It is of interest that the magazine *Baily's* correspondent made the observation that one result of the matches might be the adoption on uniform rules, "so that it will be one of the simplest, as well as the grandest of games."[8]

Regrettably, more than 100 years later, the world leading polo nations seem to be unable to reach an agreement regarding uniformity in the rules of polo.

1909 at Hurlingham Club

No other challenge for the Westchester Cup has matched the degree of advanced planning enjoyed by the American effort to conquer the silver trophy. Once the decision to challenge for the cup was made, the Polo Association placed the organization of the entire project in Harry Payne Whitney's capable hands. Mr. Whitney's first task was to identify and recruit the best American players; then to collect the best polo pony string ever seen on a polo grounds, and thirdly, to assemble the parts into a congenial whole.[9]

Whitney almost always played at Number 3, the most important position on a polo team. A born leader, he felt strongly that the pivot slot was the place for the team captain to be. This was against customary dogma. Since the early days of modern polo, best exemplified by John Watson's towering personality, Back was considered the proper place for the team's leader. The gospel according to Watson also mandated that Back must be basically a defensive player, never venturing near the opponent's goalposts and being content with feeding the half-back and the forwards with booming shots.

In young Devereux Milburn, the Buffalonian now on Long Island by way of Oxford University and Boston's North Shore, Harry Whitney found a player possessed of considerable brawn, complemented with a healthy dose of brains. It was a magnificent amalgam that resulted in a player that exemplified Number 4 play at its best: rock-solid in defense, formidable in attack.

As to the forward contingent, two brothers who had been blooded by their father in the old Country Club of Westchester in Pelham were picked not only for their individual talents, but also for their exquisite combination play. Larry and Monte Waterbury had developed combination play in polo at a time in which individual prowess and effort counted for more that its share on the polo ground. Tried, tested and proven in countless matches, Larry's versatility — he is the only player in the history of international polo to have played in all four positions — nicely complemented his younger brother's keen positional play.

At the time, Foxhall Keene was considered to be the top individual player in America, for no other was ever rated higher than him on the handicap list. Nevertheless, there were two obstacles, one positional, the other, philosophical. Keene, like Whitney, always played Number 3. Harry Payne Whitney, the anointed captain, wanted to assemble a team, each player in the correct slot. Simply put, there was no room for a pair of Number Threes. The second hurdle was the different thoughts about polo exhibited by Keene and Whitney. In his memoirs, Foxhall Keene reminisced,

> He [Dev Milburn] and Harry Whitney made a great combination in the back field. But in a way their style was bad for polo. As Harry could only hit on the offside of his pony, he played everything to pass to Dev and let him go to the side of the field with the ball. Everyone imitated this method of attack, but few could get away with it. It depended on the brilliance of one man.[10]

Two years later, while both were foxhunting in England, Keene asked Whitney about the American team, "Are you going to leave it open to all, or keep it in the family?" When Whitney answered that, as they had taken the Cup, they should have the first chance at defending it, Keene agreed while saying, "I'll come back and give you all the practice you want, but nothing will ever make me go on the team."[11]

Would Foxie Keene have been the ideal alternate player on the American team? Perhaps so; however, Keene never took second place willingly. Therefore, Whitney chose Louis E.

Stoddard, from the New Haven Country Club, who had been playing in Cannes during the winter, as the spare player for the journey to London. Stoddard went on to be a 10-goaler and chairman of the U.S.P.A. for fifteen years during the golden years of polo in America.

Thus the "Big Four," arguably the most influential team in the modern development of the game of polo, was born.

In assembling the polo pony string, Harry Whitney sent his purchasing agents in search of the best horseflesh available. California, England, Ireland and Texas were the primary hunting grounds.

Of that amazing collection of ponies, the star was the California-bred Cottontail, a grand-looking bay gelding ridden by Whitney and purchased from Lawrence McCreery. In the opinion of Col. Edward Miller, the foremost authority on polo ponies, it was the best Whitney ever owned. James C. Cooley thought that Cottontail was the best pony in the history of the game.

Ponies purchased in England included the beautiful chestnut mare Cobnut, who had a perfect conformation. The chestnut gelding Greyling, bred in Cheshire, carried Dev Milburn in the international series.

From Ireland came the bay mare Balada, which was played in Hurlingham's Champion Cup by Walter Buckmaster, and then sold to Harry P. Whitney. Cinders, a grey mare, ridden by Buckmaster, was also purchased by Whitney. La Souris, a grey mare, was bought by Louis Stoddard and loaned to the team. Little Mary, a bay mare, was considered in the American team second only to Cottontail. There was nothing diminutive about Little Mary, because she was a big pony that was loaned to the team by Augustus Belmont. Another Belmont pony was Cinderella, a black mare that had been played by Rivy Grenfell.

Solitaire, a brown mare winner of the prize for best polo pony in Dublin, was bought by Harry Whitney. Summer Lightning was purchased by Robert L. Beeckman and offered to the team. Another Irish-bred mare was Ballin a Hone, purchased by Whitney from Frederick Freake. She was a blazed face chestnut of superb quality and great substance. After Cottontail, Balin a Hone was Whitney's favorite mount. Ralla was the biggest and most powerful of all those celebrated ponies of 1909, a grand-looking chestnut. She had been ridden to hounds and was a temperamental mare; nevertheless, in the hands of a capable horseman she was unsurpassed, yielding in looks only to Cobnut.

Conover, a Texas pony, was owned by Whitney and was ridden by Monte Waterbury. Mohawk Chief was an American black gelding owned by Harold Phipps. When Harry Whitney wired for extra ponies, Mohawk Chief arrived on time to carry Monte Waterbury in the second match.

An Argentine pony that was played by Devereux Milburn was Mallard, a bay gelding. Although not fast enough for American polo, at Hurlingham it was considered a marvel.

Ponies and players on the ready, when the American contingent arrived to London Whitney took upon himself the job of chaperone of his high-living, fun-loving teammates.[12] Since Devereux Milburn arrived in England later than the rest of the team, Louis Stoddard took his slot at Back in the practice games. The American team won all the friendly games with one exception, when a Hurlingham team won a practice game by eight goals to four.

As part of the preparations for the big event, the team, under the name of Meadow Brook, entered the competition for the Ranelagh Open Cup, the second in importance in England after the Hurlingham Champion Cup. They took the tournament with ease, on a slow ground, defeating the Tigers team of the Frenchman Comte Jean de Madré, Ulric Thynne, Col. Chunga Singh and Capt. Brownlow Mathew-Lannowe, by 14 goals to one.

In the semifinals they faced Beauchamp Hall — which had Foxie Keene and Louis Stoddard on its lineup — by seven goals to four. This was the game mentioned by Keene in his *Full Tilt* when he collided with two other players, being knocked out for a while.[13]

The final game was against Roehampton, in which game Meadow Brook gave another sterling performance, taking match and the Ranelagh Open Cup by six goals to one. This impressive victory gave the team some comfort in facing the might of British polo in the forthcoming Westchester Cup matches scheduled to begin only four days later.

Early on, the British realized the supreme qualities of the American team's ponies, and a public appeal was issued for the loan of quality ponies, led by Capt. the Hon. Frederick Guest and Maj. Francis Egerton-Green. Out of the many ponies offered for loan, eleven were selected to play. The remaining eight ponies were the property of the players riding them.

The English selectors had some difficulties in picking their team, which finally presented Capt. Herbert Wilson, Frederick Freake, Pat Nickalls and Lord Wodehouse. The latter was pressed into service just 24 hours before the match because of Charles Miller's illness and Walter Buckmaster's dislocated shoulder in the last practice match for the English squad.

In fact, the series was a no contest, the American winning both matches by scores of 9–5 and 8–2. For the second game, postponed because of inclement weather, the British selection committee made two changes: Harry Rich replaced Capt. Wilson and Capt. John Hardress Lloyd took Lord Wodehouse's position at Back. It made no difference. The disparity between the pony strings and the combination play exhibited by the American foursome was even more overwhelming in the return match.

Out of 28 ponies on their string, the American players saddled a total of 18 mounts. In the second match the ponies played by the American team were as follows:

Larry Waterbury: Little Mary, Cinderella, Summer Lightning and Champion.
Monte Waterbury: Balada, Solitaire, Cobnut, Mohawk Chief and Conover. La Souris was also played in the first game.
Harry P. Whitney: Cottontail, Ballin a Hone, Balada and Greyling.
Devereux Milburn: Mallard, Jack Tar, Ralla and the Roan Mare.[14]

Much praise was heaped upon Lawrence J. Fitzpatrick, who was in charge of fine-tuning the American pony string. The ponies were in perfect trim during the entire period of time the international matches were held. This was no small feat. Fitzpatrick, Mr. Whitney's head groom, was also in charge of the ponies in the 1911 and 1913 challenges. The team players and alternates presented Mr. Fitzpatrick with a beautiful silver cup, suitably engraved, "In appreciation of his care and conditioning of the ponies for the international polo match in 1911." The loving cup is on exhibition at the National Museum and Hall of Fame, following a presentation by the Fitzpatrick family.

After the contest was over, the Westchester Cup was presented to Harry P. Whitney by Lord Frederick Roberts, who when Commander-in-Chief, India, had the foresight to make compulsory the use of polo helmets. The trophy returned to America after an absence of 23 years.

To the English public, as well as the players, the new American style of play was both a revelation and a revolution. In spite of slow grounds and the constraint imposed upon the visitors by the offside rule, the combination of speed, long hitting and smooth interchange of places among the American players left the hosts in a trance. It was an onslaught of constant attack, with even the Back finding himself at times in the Number 1 position.

Action at the 1911 Westchester Cup at Meadow Brook. Umpire Joshua Crane, Larry Waterbury, Noel Edwards, Monte Waterbury, Herbert Wilson, John Lloyd, Leslie Cheape and Harry Payne Whitney.

Pace, accurate hitting, superb ponies at the peak of fitness, and strong leadership were the successful ingredients of the Big Four, the team that changed the course of polo tactics, courtesy of Harry Payne Whitney.

1911 at Meadow Brook Club

On the American side of the pond there was no question of what team would defend the Westchester Cup, following the impressive performance of H.P. Whitney and Company on Hurlingham's Number One ground. The only question facing the selection committee was to name the alternate players. Foxhall Keene, Malcolm Stevenson and Louis Stoddard were to stand on the sidelines. Many supporters offered their mounts to the Defense Committee; among many there was Mr. Walter H. Dupee, of the Coronado Country Club in California, who sent eight of his best ponies at his own expense and risk, but considered himself amply rewarded by having Alverne and Berta, two California-bred ponies, played by Lawrence Waterbury.

Eventually, 36 ponies were selected, of which 17 were used in both games. It is of interest that of the total, eleven ponies were American-bred. The following ponies were used in both games:

Larry Waterbury: Cinderella, Kingfisher, Nellie, Berta, Alverne.
Monte Waterbury: Little Mary, Yaqui, Acushla, Mohawk Chief.
H.P. Whitney: Balada, Hobson, Conover, Cottontail, Ballerina.
Devereux Milburn: Tenby, Ralla, Miss Hobbs, White Rock.

The British team arrived in America towards the end of April, the first match having been scheduled for the end of May. Capt. John Hardress Lloyd was joined by four Army captains, Frederick Barrett, Leslie St. C. Cheape and Eustace "Bill" Palmes, all 10-goalers in India, and Herbert Wilson, a 9-goal handicap player. Lt. Arthur Noel Edwards was the designated spare man.

The team trained intensely, first at Lakewood and then at Cedarhurst. On 22 May, they played a practice game on the International Field at Meadow Brook against a strong local team, Louis Stoddard, René La Montagne, Foxhall Keene and Malcolm Stevenson. The result was a shocker: 11¼ goals were scored by the local team to 1¼ goals for the English team. Several explanations were offered to justify the one-sided result. The ponies were over-trained and got tired towards the end of each period; the team had been practicing on grounds smaller than International Field; the club team was trying very hard, perhaps with an eye on a place on the full international team. In view of the excellent showing by the British team in the international matches, the most logical explanation is two-fold. The visiting team had a limited supply of top ponies and to obtain a further supply would be difficult, if not impossible. It was a question of getting used to their ponies and to the fast American grounds, without tiring the pony string.

Nevertheless, Capt. Hardress Lloyd changed the lineup, inserting Bertie Wilson at Back, himself at Number 3 and Edwards and Cheape at forwards. In the event, the visitors acquitted themselves nobly, scoring three goals — all from Lt. Edwards' mallet — against 4½ for the Big Four. The American ponies performed better than their English counterparts — a scribe noted that Leslie Cheape was certainly the worst mounted man on the field — not surprising since the nucleus of the American string was still the fantastic core of the 1909 ponies.[15]

The second match was described as "the finest game of polo ever seen, being full of accurate hitting, hard riding, and brilliant tactics. Either side would have been unlucky to have lost the day. Every man on the field played up to the top of his form, not a weak link on either side."[16]

To place the second game into perspective, it was the closest result in international play for the unbeaten Big Four. However, grand teams somehow have a knack for winning close matches, just as the Argentine champion team Coronel Suárez would do, time and time again, in its heyday 60 years later.

1913 at Meadow Brook Club

Encouraged by the performance demonstrated by the 1911 team, the Hurlingham Polo Committee issued another challenge for the 1913 season. The Big Four was ready and able to face the challenge; however, it proved to be the occasion for its swansong.

The British felt that the quality of their pony string, compared to the American lot, had let them down. Accordingly, the Duke of Westminster, reputed to be one of the wealthiest men in England, took up the daunting task of assembling their pony string. At the end of the day, 42 ponies were available to the British squad. Walter Buckmaster, the stockbroker who was England's first 10-goal player, was selected as team captain. However, a bad fall, one of many that marred the polo career of this brilliant player, prevented him for taking his place on the team and Capt. Ralph Gerald Ritson was chosen to be the team leader. Lt. Col. Edward D. Miller, the guru of British polo, accompanied the team as manager. The players practiced at Piping Rock, close to Meadow Brook. It was a strong squad, with Leslie Cheape at the top of his form, Noel Edwards, now a captain in the 9th Lancers, playing well, a steady leader in 10-goaler Jerry Ritson, and, at Back, another 10-goaler, Capt. Vivian Lockett.

For all their past glories, the Big Four gave the selection committee some headaches. The team played badly in the practice games, incurring in some criticism that Harry Whitney took to heart, thus, resigning his captaincy of the national team. Foxhall Keene, who had for a long time been waiting in the wings, was appointed captain. With Mr. Whitney gone, so were the Waterbury brothers. The selection committee then announced the anointed team: Louis Stoddard, Devereux Milburn — the best Back in the world at Number 2 — Foxie Keene and Mike Stevenson. It will never be known what this team would have achieved against the fast improving challengers. Fate intervened when four days before the first match, Keene had a fall, breaking his collar bone. The committee beat a hasty retreat; the new team was discarded and the Big Four was Back into the fray.

As it was its wont, the American team started with a tremendous rush, gaining a lead that was held to the end. In the sixth chukker, Monte Waterbury sustained a broken finger, making it impossible for him to hold a mallet. He was ably replaced by Louis Stoddard. The final score was America 5½ goals, England 3 goals.

With Monte Waterbury out of the lineup, Stoddard started at Number 1 and Lawrence Waterbury moved to the Number 2 position. On the British side the old warrior, Sir Frederick Freake, replaced Noel Edwards. The second match was a desperate struggle, both teams scoring five goals each. It came down to penalties; both England and America were penalized ½ a goal for crossing. The difference was ¼ goal for a safety against England, when Capt. Ritson was forced to hit behind his own line to prevent an American goal. Once more, the British team came so very close, only to be bitterly disappointed at the final bell.

Twenty ponies were played by the American team members. Reflecting the improved breeding in the United States, about one-half of the lot were bred in America. Six of the ponies, Berta, Conover, Hobson, Little Mary, Mohawk Chief and Tenby, had played in the 1911 contest. Conover, Little Mary and Mohawk Chief were veterans of the 1909 historic journey to Hurlingham.

The final match was played in a wave of oppressive heat. James Cooley described the situation:

> The second game in 1913 was played on a day when the mercury was trying to break through the top of the glass. Freddie Freake, who played in Capt. Edwards' place, almost succumbed at half-time, and when the game was over neither players nor spectators cared whether school kept or not. All they wanted to do was to rush north or south to the seas and therein dive.[17]

1914 at Meadow Brook Club

The year the First World War started in Europe was a watershed mark in American polo. That great leader, Harry Payne Whitney, retired from international polo and the Big Four was no more. However, the other three members were still there, and the selection committee felt certain that the surging tide of British polo would be, once more, contained. As substitutes, Foxhall Keene, Harold C. Phipps, Charles Cary Rumsey and Malcolm Stevenson were ready.

Lord Wimborne was in charge of the British challenge and with tremendous energy was able to secure an exceptional number of ponies, including the outstanding mare Energy. The selected team included at Number 1 Capt. Henry Tomkinson, a fine horseman who carried the reputation of being able to handle ponies no other player could manage. Captains Cheape and Barrett were at the height of their powers, and at Back it was Johnny Traill, the Irishman from Argentina who was rated at 10-goals. Regrettably, at the last minute Traill was taken ill and was replaced by Vivian Lockett. Maj. Barrett was the field captain.

The American international team in 1914: Lawrence Waterbury, Devereux Milburn, Monte Waterbury and René La Montagne.

The American squad lined up with René La Montagne, Jr., Monte Waterbury, Devereux Milburn and Lawrence Waterbury. This time around it was the British who scored the first goal, and the mistake of taking away Dev Milburn from his accustomed position at the last line of defense was quickly uncovered. Soon after, Milburn and Larry Waterbury exchanged places; however, the damage had been done. At the game's end the scoreboard displayed 8½ goals for the English team against only three for the disappointed Americans.

The second game was closer. The American team started with Devereux Milburn in his usual Back position and played a great game. But so did Capt. Leslie Cheape, one of the top British players in the period before the war. Penalties wrecked the American effort, because the final score was 4 goals for England, a meager 2¾ goals for the United States. And so, the Westchester Cup went across the pond once more.

It could be said the contest up to then was even; three victories for each country, because it is difficult to give full credit to the 1900 competition, which was limited to a single match. Thus ended the first era of international competition between the United States and Great Britain for the Westchester Cup. It was a time during which sportsmanship was at a high point; there were several instances in which both sides refused to take advantage of what appeared to be a situation within the written laws of the game. In his Chairman's Report, Mr. Henry Lloyd Herbert put it as well as it can be expressed:

The ruling spirit of polo the world over is one of absolute fairness no matter how important the match or how bitter the contest — not one infinitesimal unfair advantage of one team or player over another has been known to occur.

Beautiful illustrations of that spirit of honest sport have been shown in all important events and notably in the international matches. In the contest of 1911 the English team was lined up and ready for the ball; the time bell sounded and the ball was thrown in while two of the American team were off the field on account of some small mishap. Captain John Hardress Lloyd of the English team, according to the rule, could have dashed off with his full team of four against only two opponents; instead he gallantly tapped the ball to the side line and awaited the full American team. It was an example of true sportsmanship at a moment when the score was within a fraction of a goal from being a tie, and when the people of England were anxiously awaiting news of an expected victory; also it was in the presence of 30,000 spectators, the larger proportion of who were rooting for the American team. Later in the day the ball was on the end line with the American team all in position for the hit-in; the time bell sounded when the English team was not quite ready but Mr. Milburn withheld his stroke until the Englishmen were in their places. It is this very spirit in all polo and particularly international events which helps to cement the feeling of friendship between neighbors as well as nations.[18]

CHAPTER 7

American Polo Players in the Olympic Games

Polo players from the United States have participated in three out of the five occasions in which polo was an Olympic sport. In Paris 1900, a few American players enlisted on different teams. The polo competition for the Antwerp Games in 1920 was held in Ostende; an American team put together by the Army of the Occupation of the Rhine carried the United States colors. Finally, a representative American team participated in the 1924 games in Paris.

It is hard to explain why there was no polo in the 1932 Olympic Games held in Los Angeles. The host country was at the apex of its world supremacy in polo and there is little doubt that, had the American team competed, they would have carried the gold medal.

For the games held in Berlin in 1936, the U.S. Polo Association declined to send a team, although a full string of ponies was already in Europe for the challenge issued by Britain for possession of the Westchester Cup. Mr. Charles B. Wrightsman, patron of the Texas Rangers team, wished to send a team to participate in Germany. However, the U.S. Polo Association declined to give permission to carry on the enterprise, and so informed the U.S. Olympic Committee. With the Argentines coming over to Long Island to compete for the Cup of the Americas, perhaps it was thought that three international contests between June and September would stretch both ponies and players beyond a reasonable limit.

The minutes of the Executive Committee of the U.S. Polo Association indicate that one of the requirements for American polo to be represented in the Olympics Games was that the Association must be a member of the U.S. Olympic Committee, chaired by Mr. Avery Brundage. There is no record indicating that the U.S. Polo Association leadership ever considered taking such action. The final result is that there was no American representation at Maifeld, in spite of Mr. Wrightsman's sporting offer to finance the team. The absenteeism of the American team was a serious blow to the Olympic polo competition's credibility because the Argentines literally ran away with the gold medal, scoring 26 goals against only five obtained by their two rivals, Mexico and Great Britain.

Paris 1900

The second Olympic Games held in the City of Lights, and more so the polo competition, have been referred as something of a lark.[1] What was and what was not an Olympic event is still a matter of debate among serious students of the Olympic movement. As far

71

as American polo players are concerned, only three participated in the various events: Foxhall Parker Keene, Frank Jay Mackey and Walter Adolph McCreery.

There are two main problems in trying to understand what happened in Paris in 1900. One is the pre-tournament struggle between the International Olympic Committee and the Union des Sociétés Françaises Sports Athlétiques, the latter claiming to be responsible for the organization of all athletic endeavors in 1900. The second is that the Exposition Universelle Internationale, a world fair including sporting events, also took place in Paris that year. And, adding to the confusion, the polo season at the Bagatelle Polo Club extended from May to July.

Several polo tournaments were held in Paris during that summer. Among the most significant events, the first was the Grand Prix Internationale d'Exposition, which is considered by most authorities to be the Olympic competition. It was followed by the Prix de Longchamps, the Grand Prix International de Paris, the Coupe de Bagatelle, the Grand Prix de l'Ouverture, and the Grand Prix de Suresnes.

The competition was held between 28 May and 2 June. Foxhall Keene and Jay Mackey were on the team Foxhunters, a multi-national squad completed with British players John G.H. Beresford, Denis St. G. Daly and Alfred Rawlinson. They took the gold medal, defeating in succession Compiègne (10–0), Bagatelle (6–4), and Rugby (3–1). Capt. John Beresford played in the second game in Keene's position. Walter McCreery, who resided in England, was on the silver medalist Rugby team, with a Frenchman, the Comte Jean de Madré, and two Englishmen, Walter Buckmaster and Frederick Freake. A team from Mexico also entered the competition.[2, 3]

Ostende 1920

Although there was a polo facility near Antwerp — the Antwerp Polo Club founded in Brasschaat by Alfred Grisar in 1905 — in order to avoid congestion the polo competition was moved to Ostende, the trendy seaside resort where polo had first been played in 1903 by the whim of King Leopold II.

The venue itself was the ground inside the Wellington Hippodrome, which assured plenty of stabling facilities for the four competing teams. The Polo Association declined to send a representative team; however, polo in the army was making great strides and the War Department gave permission to the Army Polo Committee to assemble a team. Logistics dictated that the Army of the Occupation of the Rhine, established in compliance of the provisions of the Treaty of Versailles at the end of World War I, should represent the United States.

In preparation for the Olympic competition, a team was selected to travel to England from occupied Germany. After a series of trial matches in Coblenz, Col. John C. Montgomery, Cavalry; Col. Nelson Emery Margetts, a Field Artillery officer; Maj. Henry Terry de la Mesa Allen, Cavalry; Maj. Arthur Ringland Harris, Field Artillery; and Capt. David Sheridan Rumbaugh, Infantry were selected to represent the United States. Col. Montgomery, as Chief of Staff, was unable to make the journey and was replaced by Lt. Joseph Scranton Tate, from the Cavalry branch.[4] The team did well during the London season, when they took the Novices's Cup at Ranelagh.

The team for the Olympic Games was Col. Margetts, Back; Col. Montgomery; and Majors Allen and Harris. Gen. Terry Allen went on to command the First Infantry Division — the "Big Red One" in World War II — and was one of the few polo players to appear on *Time* magazine's cover.[5] It was, nevertheless, a novice team in international competitions, and faced an uphill struggle against the highly rated British and Spanish teams.

Spain was represented by four grandees: the Marqués Alvaro de Villabrágima, considered the best Spanish player ever, at 8-goals; the Duke of Alba and his younger brother the Duke of Peñaranda, and the Conde Leopoldo de la Maza.[6] The Spaniards were beautifully mounted and were considered the favorites to take the tournament.

The British team was composed by three serving officers: Lt. Col. Teignmouth P. Melvill, Maj. Vivian N. Lockett and Maj. Frederick "Rattle" Barrett. Lord John Wodehouse, later Earl of Kimberley, a former 10-goaler, played at Back. Their weakness was on their ponies, because they were mostly mounted on regimental ponies.

The home team was led by Alfred Grisar, the father of Belgian polo and a multi-talented sportsman who had played for Belgium in football and had entered national competitions in cycling and lawn tennis. The team was completed with the Baron Gastón Peers de Niewburgh, who had spent many years in Argentina and was on the team San Carlos, winner of the 1900 Polo Association of the River Plate Polo Championship, ancestor of the Argentine Open. Clément van der Straaten and Maurice Lysen completed the Belgian team. Commandant L. Crockaert was the reserve player.

In a straight elimination contest, Spain defeated the United States squad by the score of 13 to 3. Britain then beat Belgium 8–3. The Americans followed by defeating Belgium by 11 goals to 3 to take the bronze medal, and in the best match of the Games, Britain prevailed over Spain by 13 to 11.[7]

Winning the Olympic bronze medal was a significant achievement for the American Army team. It gave credibility to the Army Polo Committee in its efforts to make polo an important part of the officers' training for war, as it had been from times immemorial.

The military career of the team leader, Col. Margetts, started in the National Guard. His selection by Gen. John J. Pershing as one of his aides de camp to accompany him to France while in command of the American Expeditionary Force gave a boost to his career. Margetts' polo days had started in the Philippines in 1910, where as captain of the 1st Artillery polo team he took the Island Championship three years in a row. Capt. Margetts also won the British Army Championship in Hong Kong. In the 1920s, while being the best Army player in Washington, D.C., he held the delicate post of chief liaison officer between the Army military intelligence section and the military attaches representing the foreign powers in the nation's capital. Col. Margetts died in 1932, shortly after his retirement from active service.

Paris 1924

In the mysterious or at least unrecorded ways of American polo, as described by Nelson Aldrich, Jr., Tommy Hitchcock's biographer, a team was sent to compete in France.[8] It was led by Thomas Hitchcock, Jr., and was formed by Californian Elmer J. Boeseke, Jr., from the Santa Barbara Club; Frederick Roe from Texas; and Philadelphian Rodman Wanamaker, II. This team was far from being a truly representative American team; only Hitchcock would be considered for a place on the best international team. Boeseke was rated at 7 goals, as was Wanamaker. Fred Roe was a 6-goal handicap, and the reserve player, Percy R. Pyne, II, from Meadow Brook Club, was rated at one-goal.

Britain was represented by the Hon. Frederick E. Guest, Lt. Col. John D.Y. Bingham, Maj. Frederick W. Barrett and Wing Commander Percival K. Wise. None of these players made the international team that later that year challenged for the Westchester Cup at Meadow Brook, although "Rattle" Barrett was a former 10-goaler and Wise reached a 9-goal handicap.

On the other hand, Argentina, France and Spain took care to send their best players. Spain presented three players who had been on the silver medal team from 1920: The Duke of Peñaranda, the Marqués de Villabrágima, and the Conde de la Maza, plus the Marqués de San Miguel. Argentina was represented by Arturo J. Kenny, Juan D. Nelson, Capt. Enrique Padilla and Juan B. Miles. The French were Comte Pierre de Jumilhac, Jules F. Macaire, Hubert de Monbrison and the Comte Charles de Polignac.[9] The first match on 28 June at Garches-St. Cloud saw the American team vanquish the host team by 13 goals to one. Three days later, America beat Spain 15–2, and on 3 July, they rather easily took care of the British 10–2. Meanwhile, Argentina was also on a promenade, defeating France 15–2 and Spain 16–1.

What was in essence the final match in this round-robin tournament was played on 6 July, the Americans being considered slight favorites. Played on a muggy, hot afternoon that soon turned into rain, the United States players got off to a quick start when Hitchcock scored a goal less than a minute after the initial throw-in. For the rest of the match the Americans had the lead until the fifth chukker, when the Argentines tied the score. In the seventh and last period, Jack Nelson ran away with the ball and scored the winning tally, making the final score 6–5. It was the first ever gold medal for Argentina, in any sport.

Odds and Ends

The Olympic Games abound with athletes as winners of multiple medals and, in some cases, in different sports. An American polo player from Lakewood, New Jersey, the millionaire Jay Gould, took the gold medal in London 1908 in Jeu de Paume, also known as court tennis.[10]

In 1912 in Stockholm, Jim Thorpe's banner year, John Carter Montgomery, a 2-goal handicap lieutenant in the 7th Cavalry, took eighth place in the Individual Three-day Event mounted on his horse Deceive. As mentioned previously, John Montgomery, by then a major, took the bronze medal at the 1920 polo competition.

Also in Stockholm, Lt. George Smith Patton, Jr., 15th Cavalry, participated in the Pentathlon competition, which consisted of five events: shooting, swimming, fencing, riding, and running. The latter was Patton's best effort, placing third in a field of 32. However, in the shooting competition he placed twenty-first. Patton claimed that he had been penalized for missing the target completely, when in fact the bullet had gone through a previously made hole. If Lt. Patton had been able to prove his point, he would have taken the gold medal. According to Olympic Games historian David Wallechinsky, there is no evidence at all to support George Patton's contention.[11]

In 1920, in Belgium, seven out of eight members on the equestrian team were polo players. Maj. Henry Tureman Allen entered in Show Jumping, as did Maj. John W. Downer, Capt. Vincent Paul Erwin and Capt. Karl Christopher Greenwald. Maj. Sloan Doak and Maj. William Whitehead West participated in Show Jumping and in the Three-day Event.

Finally, Capt. Harry Dwight Chamberlin competed in Dressage, Show Jumping, and in the Three-day Event, in both individual and team categories. None of the officers obtained medals; the best result was a fourth place in the Team Three-day Event, by John Barry on Raven, Harry Chamberlin on Nigra, and William West on Black Boy.[12]

Paris in 1924 saw the return of Maj. Sloan Doak, by now a 3-goal handicap player, who took the silver medal in the Three-day Event, mounted on Pathfinder.

In 1932 at Los Angeles, another veteran, Maj. Harry Chamberlin, took fourth place in the Individual Three-day Event, on his horse Pleasant Smiles. However, the United States took the gold medal in the Team Three-day competition, the first gold medal in equestrian Olympic Games obtained by the United States. Polo player Lt. Earl Foster Thomson on Jenny Champ and Edwin Yancey Argo on Honolulu Tomboy joined Maj. Chamberlin, again riding Pleasant Smiles, on the American team. Harry Chamberlin completed a superior performance by taking the silver medal in the Jumping (Prix de Nations) event, this time around mounted on Show Girl.[13] Polo player Lt. (later Lt. Gen.) Gordon Byrom Rogers was also on the U.S.A. equestrian team.

In Berlin in 1936, the odds were in favor of the German team, which took all the gold medals, some mixed with controversy. Capt. Earl Thomson had a sterling performance in the Individual Three-day Event, taking the silver medal, once more with Jenny Champ.[14]

"Tommy" Thomson, by then a full Colonel, went on to take his third and fourth Olympic medals at the 1948 London Games. In the Team Dressage competition Col. Frank Henry, Lt. Robert Borg and Col. Thomson finished third behind Sweden and France. Then it was found that one of the Swedish riders, Gehnäll Persson, who had been entered as an officer, was a sergeant, promoted to Temporary Lieutenant by royal decree and then demoted to his previous rank.[15] Sweden was disqualified eight months later and the U.S. team was awarded the silver medal. The rules restricting dressage competition to army officers only were soon changed. In 1952 women were also allowed to participate. Sergeant Gehnäll Persson went on to take the Olympic gold medals in 1952 in Helsinki and in 1956 in Stockholm, with his 1948 teammates Maj. Henri Saint Cyr and Gustaf-Adolf Bolstenstern, Jr.

In the Three-day Team event, Col. Earl F. Thomson, mounted on Reno Rhythm, got his fourth medal, a nice addition to the Twelve-Goal Championship obtained with the Fort Bliss polo team 21 years previously, as a young lieutenant. The gold medal United States team was completed with Lt. Col. Charles Anderson, on Reno Palisade, and Col. Frank Henry, on Swing Low, a remount horse, who had been his mount since the 1930s.[16]

Regrettably, after the Olympic successes on 1948, which were followed by outstanding performances in the European horse shows, the Cavalry branch was discontinued by the United States Army and the war horse was confined to the recesses of history.

PART II

Full Blossom:
The Age of Hitchcock,
1922–1939

With due respect accorded to several other practitioners of the game, this time span was dominated by the towering personality of one of the greatest players ever to handle a polo mallet. Thomas Hitchcock, Jr., born into a polo family with deep roots in equestrian endeavors, epitomized the game from his leading role in the 1921 Westchester Cup matches at Hurlingham until his retirement at the end of the 1939 season at Meadow Brook. In the course of his meteoric career Tommy Hitchcock took the Junior Championship at age 16 and made his debut in the U.S. Open Championship. An international player at 21, he became the youngest player to achieve a 10-goal handicap, a record that stood until another phenomenal polo player, Adolfito Cambiaso, made world headlines in 1992.

When Devereux Milburn retired from high-goal and international polo, Tommy Hitchcock became the captain of the American team. As such, Hitchcock took a much more active role than his illustrious predecessors: Thomas Hitchcock the elder, Foxhall Keene, Harry Payne Whitney and Devereux Milburn, a litany of polo greats. They were mostly field captains, which the notable exception of Whitney, whose organizational skills and leadership qualities became legendary. Tommy took upon himself to be a strong voice in the team's selection process, especially in the 1928 and 1930 challenges. His instructions to the American international team on the eve of the 1930 Westchester Cup are still reprinted the world over, some 80 years after they were issued.

His personal life was without reproach. As a teenager, he found his way as a volunteer in the Lafayette Escadrille, a unit of American fighter pilots that saw action in the Western Front. Hitchcock was credited with

77

Tommy Hitchcock on Toughy during the East-West series at Onwentsia.

downing two German aircraft before he was shot down himself. A wounded prisoner of war, he escaped from a train and reached neutral Switzerland. Tommy married Peggy Mellon Loughlin and they had two children. When the United States entered World War II, Tommy Hitchcock joined the Air Force and eventually was posted in England. While testing a Mustang fighter, Lt. Col. Thomas Hitchcock, Jr., crashed near the cathedral city of Salisbury in April 1944. His death was reported on the first page of *The New York Times*.[1]

CHAPTER 8

The Roaring Twenties at Home: West of the Mississippi

The end of the war in Europe ushered an era of prosperity in America that lasted until the financial panic of October 1929. The game of polo also rode on the crest of the wave of unbounded optimism that swept through the country. The Open Championship was resumed in 1919 after a two-year hiatus mandated by the worldwide conflict. Meadow Brook asserted early its supremacy, although their ancient foe Rockaway remained a strong contender for a couple of seasons. Both the Junior and the Senior Championships were competed for in that banner year.[1]

The Westward Expansion

The nation's move west was mimicked in some ways by the game of polo. As early as October 1897, teams from Kansas City and St. Louis participated in a tournament at Fort Riley. The Missouri Hunt and Polo Club in Kansas City replaced the St. Louis Country Club as the most westward polo club affiliated with the Polo Association. A team — Jack Cudahy, Harry Holmes, Paddy Magill and Guernsey — played against the Fort Riley team.[2] The club was formally established in Kansas City in 1904 by John Adams, A. Watson Armour, Harry Holmes, Tom Orr, Dr. St. Claire Street and Tom Velie, among others. Sherman Hall and Bob Thorne joined the team soon after. Stephen Velie, Jr., a 3-goal handicap player, was the delegate.[3] In 1907 this institution merged with the Kansas City Country Club and the latter's name was adopted for both clubs.

In 1912, a Kansas City polo team traveled east to participate in the Junior Championship. Philip Noland, Tom Velie, Stephen Velie and J. Foster Symes were the team members. *The New York Times* wrote:

> There was an upset of the favorites in the first game for the Junior Championship at Point Judith Country Club to-day when the Kansas City Polo Club four after a contest that had many points of interest and in which the Missouri ponies appear to advantage, defeated the Philadelphia Country Club by 7¼ to 6.[4]

However, in the semifinals, the Piping Rock team proved too strong for the Midwestern team, which was defeated 8–3¾. The Kansas City foursome also entered in the competition for the Army and Navy Cup, in which event they were beaten by a different Philadelphia team. This was a most sporting effort for a polo team to travel from Kansas City to Rhode Island, where the best players in the country gathered in the summer.

There was another little known polo club in Kansas City: the Elm Ridge Polo Club, which is mentioned in Hugh FitzPatrick's *American Polo*, the first book on the game by an American journalist.[5] It is possible that Elm Ridge preceded the Missouri Hunt as far as the game of polo is concerned, because FitzPatrick's work was published in 1904. The Elm Ridge Club was an outgrowth of the Kansas City Jockey Club, which was incorporated in 1902. The club possessed what was considered the best horse establishment in the West.[6]

By 1929 play was concentrated on the Nafziger Field at the Kansas City Country Club. A team, Joe Kessinger, Fred Harvey, Frank Baker and Herbert Peet, played in Chicago at the Onwentsia Country Club.

In 1906 the Junction City Polo Club was organized in that town in Kansas, with Dr. T.W. "Fred" O'Donnell serving as delegate. The first team was Dr. O'Donnell, Si Rogers, Louis Loeb and Bruce Grant. Later on, Bill Ebbutt, Jesse Jorgen Langvardt, Sr., Bill and Paul Schmedemann, and Louis and Emil Zumbrunn have been identified as members. There is a record of the club playing frequently against teams from Fort Riley.

The Junction City Polo Club resigned after a few years, in 1910, without ever submitting a list of players to the Polo Association. However, there is a photograph of a Junction City polo team that participated in the 1920 Cavalry School Tournament at Fort Riley. The five players are Hal Pierce, Harold Copeland, Dr. Fred O'Donnell, Harry Thompson and Jack Vickers.[7] The 1921 Year Book lists Harry Thompson as a member of the Kansas City Country Club and John Vickers of the Wichita Polo Club. It seems that in this occasion, four players got together to participate in this tournament. Hal Pierce was a left-handed player who owned a cow-pony named Curly. When Dr. O'Donnell, the team captain of Junction City, instructed Pierce to ride off an opponent, he would ride to the sideboard or to a corner of the field, and hold him there. When Hal was mounted on Curly, it was impossible to get away from him and it was a great source of amusement to see him corner such excellent equestrians as Col. Guy Henry or Maj. John Montgomery, the latter a rider of Olympic caliber.[8]

Nearby, east of Junction City, once named Manhattan, there was a Humboldt Valley Polo team, about which little is known. The young men who met regularly to play on a field on Paul Schmedemann's farm included Carl Best, Bill Ebbutt, Jesse and Pete Langvardt, Bill and Paul Schmedemann, Emil and Louis Zumbrunn, and George Stonebreaker.[9] The cowboys were invited to play at Fort Riley in 1907. In his *History of Fort Riley*, Capt. Woodbury Pride writes:

> The Humboldt Team always brought a crowd of rooters and looked very picturesque coming down the Mormon Trail (roughly the Humboldt Road). They frequently drove ponies hitched to runabouts and buggies, and after arrival, they unhitched them and saddled them up and played them in the polo game. They used stock saddles entirely, and their ponies, as a rule, followed the ball very well. Their teamwork was rather baffling and quite successful for some time. When the player ran over the ball, he turned toward the center of the field and went to the rear of his team. While this left no one ahead of the ball, it produced an absolutely continuous stream of Humboldt players on the ball, and since the field was none too good, the system was far from bad.[10]

The visiting players were royally entertained and a return match was scheduled at the Schmedemann family farm. A team of enlisted men from the 6th Field Artillery was selected to represent Fort Riley. All preparations had been made and refreshments were abundant. The Fort Riley team rode down in wagons and told the Humboldt Valley hosts that the drivers were not to partake of the refreshments. But no one paid attention to the warning. Again, Capt. Woodbury Pride:

The drivers were persuaded to partake of the hospitality of Humboldt. The Fort Riley team won the polo game, but reliable reports are to the effect that some of the players walked part of the way home, and the polo equipment and ponies were scattered. along the road that night.[11]

Concerning this enlisted men's team, Lt. Col. Beverly Browne thought it was the best team in the Army. The players were Sergeant Phillips, 1st Sergeant A.Y. Weir, Sergeant Odle, with Sergeant-Major Basil Conless and Sergeant Flaherty alternating at Back. Sergeant Bloom was a substitute. This team played for about four years, until 1912.[12]

After two or three years the Humboldt boys were getting married and scattered, so the polo games came to an end. Some of the players then moved on the Junction City Polo Club.

St. Louis Polo in the '20s and '30s

At the St. Louis Country Club the old crowd from the late 1890s was gradually replaced by new faces. Traditional names remained, like Davis and Simmons, but others appeared: Charles Bascom, W.H. Cocke, Walter Crunden, Allen Fordyce, Tom Francis, Frederick Gardner, W.B. Goltra, Clarence King, Virgil Lewis, Alexander Primm, Jr., Cupples Scudder, Clifford Scudder the younger, William Stribbling, Festus Wade, Tilton Webster and Clint Whittemore, Jr.

The 1920s and 1930s marked a period of great prosperity for St. Louis polo, when 3,000 spectators "banking the rectangle," according to the *St. Louis Globe-Democrat*.[13] Club teams traveled wide and far to engage other teams in friendly contests and tournament play. A source of comfort was a private railroad car to take players and their wives in those mini-tours.[14]

George Scott, Ira Wright, Mahlon Wallace, J. and Hayward Niedringhaus went to Lake Forest, Illinois, to compete in the 1926 Central Inter-Circuit Tournament. After defeating the North Shore team in the first round, St. Louis lost 14–11 to the eventual winners, Onwentsia, in the semifinal game.

In 1929, matches were played against Chicago, Dayton and Kansas City. A return match was played at Dayton versus the Miami Valley Club. Players included Edward Love, Jr., Hayward Niedringhaus, Edward "Ned" Simmons, II, George Simmons, Mahlon Wallace, Jr., Ira Wright and Eugene Williams.

The Depression affected polo in the Central Circuit most significantly. The 1931 U.S.P.A. Year Book does not mention any national events played in that area. The next notice about St. Louis Country Club teams participating in national championships occurs in 1936, when a St. Louis team — Edward Love, George Forrest, J.B. Gilmore and the redoubtable Hayward Niedringhaus— entered the Twelve Goal Tournament held in Detroit. The St. Louis Country Club foursome reached the finals, where they were defeated by the Grosse Pointe team by 9 goals to six. J.B. Gilmore was a 5-goaler instructor, who went on to the Philippines to manage the Manila Polo Club just before the war.

Prior to World War II, players such as Ned Simmons, Mahlon Wallace, Cliff Scudder, Reni De Rosa, Bucket Hayward, Hayward Niedringhaus, George Doan, Carl Langenberg, Fred Gardner, John, Sam and Dwight Davis, Joe Werner, George Walker and George Simmons were among the most avid enthusiasts.[15]

Another club in St. Louis was the Killdee Polo Club, established in January 1930 with J.K. Van Raalte as delegate. Barney Benson, August Busch, Jr., Willis Engle, Jack Krey,

Arthur Preece, J.C. Roberts, Jr., Roy Sigel, and Adalbert Von Gontard were the other players.

Polo in Colorado after the War

The glory days of the Cheyenne Mountain Country Club came to an end after the First World War when Spencer Penrose saw the game of polo as a way of attracting guests to his new Broadmoor Hotel. Penrose contracted English-born Arthur Perkins, an 8-goal handicap player, as instructor and organizer of polo. The timing was favorable. The Army Remount Service had sent many officers to Colorado Springs, led by Col. Walter Neill. One of the polo-playing officers was Maj. Grove Cullum, who years later would publish a treatise on the selection and training of polo ponies.[16] The Remount staff had barely settled down when retired Maj. Henry Leonard arrived from Washington, D.C., to live there, and became a member of the Cheyenne Mountain Country Club. Maj. Leonard was a soldier and an equestrian of renown. A Marine Corps officer, he had lost his left arm during the Boxer Rebellion in China. The Boxer uprising got its name from the Righteous Fists of Harmony, an anti-imperialism, anti–Christian violent movement supported by the Qing dynasty.

Maj. Leonard was President Theodore Roosevelt's aide-de-camp, who after his retirement became a foxhunter and breeder of thoroughbred horses in Virginia. While in Colorado, he resumed his breeding operation at his Pine Valley Ranch. Maj. Leonard had business ties as well with Bryant Turner, a former polo player who raised ponies at his Trinchera Ranch.

Another polo player was Reginald Sinclaire, who had flown Spad fighters in the Lafayette air squadron — Tommy Hitchcock's unit — during the European war. Learning polo with Sinclaire was William Emslie, an Englishman married to Constance, Joseph Pulitzer's youngest daughter. Others who took the game were Raymond Lewis, a Colorado College tennis player who later became a breeder of champion Hereford cattle, and Lloyd Jones from Detroit. Yet another was Robert Hassler, who made a fortune providing Henry Ford magnetos for his immortal Model T cars. Other visiting teams came from the military garrisons at Randolph

Polo at Cheyenne Mountain Country Club in the 1920s. Colorado's high mountains provide a magnificent background.

Field, Texas, Fort Sill, Oklahoma, and Fort Riley in Kansas. Also from Kansas, Willis Hartman and John A. "Jack" Vickers, president of Vickers Petroleum Co., took teams from Wichita.

Another big spender was Ernest Marland, a Ponca City oil magnate, who used to take entire floors at the Broadmoor Hotel for his players and entourage. Marland, originally from Pittsburgh, made a fortune in West Virginia coal, and later another in Oklahoma, starting an enterprise that eventually became Continental Oil Company, better known as Conoco. Later, Ernest Marland was elected governor of Oklahoma, running on the Democratic ticket, totally opposed to his neighbor Spencer Penrose's staunch Republican ideas.[17]

When the lease of the Cheyenne Mountain's field expired, 23 members subscribed $20,000 to purchase the property; in turn they leased the field to the Broadmoor Polo Association for their games against visiting teams. The club's own team was composed by Reginald Sinclaire, Bob Hassler, Lloyd Jones and Raymond Lewis. Other team members were Jock Hay Whitney, William Emslie and Randall Davey, the Santa Fe artist. One of Davey's paintings, illustrated on the cover of the July 1934 issue of *Polo* magazine, depicts John Edward Madden, Jr., a polo player from Kentucky.

Soon enough it was noticed that a single polo ground could not accommodate all the players who wished to indulge in the game; therefore, Spencer Penrose built another field in 1928, this one with covered stands.

The fast pace of polo slowed down with the onset of the Depression; however the club's youngsters kept on playing. Bill Braid, Jr., Francis "Casey" Jones, Peter Perkins—later an 8-goal international player — and John Puffer were the top of the cream. They played very well, but none better than the girls' polo team that included Josephine Bogue, Peggy Leonard, Hildegarde Neill, Jeanne Sinclaire and Josephine Tutt.

Later on, the Denver Polo Club was organized by Lafayette Hughes and Lawrence Phipps, Jr. Other players were Steven Bull, Oscar Cass, Berrien Hughes, Robert Johnson, J. Foster Symes, Bryant Turner and Bulkely Wells. This club provided plentiful activity during the polo season.

Polo in the Heartland

Far from the main centers of polo, the Northeast and California, the polo clubs in the nation's breadbasket continued to thrive in spite of the tyranny of distance from the higher handicap polo clubs. However, in medium-handicap polo, the country's central teams made their presence felt by taking several national tournaments. Miami Valley Country Club, Chagrin Valley and Fairfield Polo Club are just some examples of the clubs that took national championships at the 12-Goal level during the inter-wars period.

South Dakota

Although the Pierre Polo Club waited until 1946 to seek and obtain affiliation with the U.S.P.A., there had been polo in the area since the 1920s, when officers in the 147th Field Artillery joined forces with local civilian players to start the game. H.I. Lawrence was the main supporter, helped by Emmett C. Lee, maker of well-known saddles, Guy Barnes, Frank Newman and Charles Lee Hyde.

Three teams competed in the 1929 South Dakota State Tournament at Fort Meade: Hot Springs—Mr. Aberg, Mr. Tretsky, Mr. Murphy and alternating at Back, Mr. Martin and Mr. Ickes. The hosts, Fort Meade, presented Lt. A.E. Forsyth; alternating at Number 2 with Lt. Robert Merrick and Capt. H.H. Cameron; Lt. John Murtaugh; and Lt. Charles Feagin, who wrote *Polo: Team and Position Play*, in 1930. The Pierre team aligned Mr. Robinson, A.B. "Pop" Tyler, Barrington Tyler, Frank Newman and Mr. Scurr, alternating in the Back position and Burlington "Bud" Tyler.

Fort Robinson, with Lt. Julius Slack, Lt. R.L. Gervais and Lt. Albert Stubblebine, Jr., alternating at Number 2, Lt. David Erskine and Capt. G.L. Danford; and Minneapolis, with Maurice Krier, Clairborne Hale and I.S. Randall at Number 2, Willis Osborne and Robert Rice, were the other teams that entered the Black Hills Tournament.

The representatives from Fort Meade took the state championship for the second consecutive time, while the Black Hills trophy went to the Pierre Polo Team.

Minnesota

According to Louis Laramie, a saddler with the firm Laramie & Grahn in Minneapolis, polo was introduced by R.F. "Fish" Jones in 1911.[18] The first match, if it can be called a match, took place at the Minnehaha Driving Park. A Mr. Ashbrook, Paddy McGill, his stable manager, and Louis Laramie gave a polo exhibition. Then the Park Board gave permission for the use of the Parade Grounds, where Dr. Elmer Berg, George Kingsley, Will Sexton, Chester Simons and Heit Woodward joined Laramie in some games. In its edition of 23 July 1915, the *Morning Tribune* gives notice of "Minneapolis men at polo on vacant lot," and the announcement that a polo match would take place at the Fair Grounds on Saturday afternoon, 31 July.[19] There is no further news of the game in Minnesota until the autumn of 1921, when Brig. Gen. (then Colonel) Alfred Bjornstad, the commanding officer at Fort Snelling—completed in 1825 in the confluence of the Minnesota and Mississippi Rivers—started the game at this military outpost, known as "the Country Club of the Army."[20]

Civilian and military players then organized the Fort Snelling Polo Association, ponies were purchased, and a short season of basic instruction in polo was carried out before the onset of winter. The following season the Association formed three teams, two made up of Army officers and one of civilians from Minneapolis and St. Paul.

After participating in a local tournament that included teams from the 14th Cavalry and the Wakonda Country Club, both from Des Moines, the teams entered the first annual International Tournament in Winnipeg, Canada, where the Fort Snelling "A" team took the Sifton Trophy, presented by Maj. John Sifton. The St. Charles "B" team won the Junior Trophy competition. The following year the return match was held at Fort Snelling and the local "A" team retained the Sifton Trophy. In 1924 four teams made the journey to Winnipeg: two from the Fort and one each from the Twin Cities. The Fort Snelling Blacks again won the Sifton Trophy.

The fourth International Tournament was held at Fort Snelling in 1925. The Ft. Snelling Blacks—Capt. F.O. Schmidt, Capt. J.A. McCallam, Lt. William Hazelrigg, of the famous Army mount "Whisky," Maj. Charles Lyman, Capt. J.A. Boyers—won the Sifton Trophy once more; the St. Paul Blues (Thomas Engstrom, Charles Finch, L.D. Berry, John Egan, Maurice Krier, Claude Seims) took the Junior Trophy; and the 7th Corps Area squad—

Mr. T. Wilbur Smith, Capt. E. John Brandeis, Capt. M.F. Meador, Capt. C.H. Palmer, Capt. J.C. Rogers—won a newly created tournament, the Open Silver Cup.

The 1929 Northwest Tournament took place at Fort Snelling, where Capt. E.N. Frakes was in charge of polo. Teams representing Fort Des Moines, Freebooters, Pierre, St. Paul, and Snelling Blacks participated. The St. Paul Polo Club was represented by L.D. Berry, Claude Siems, Capt. Arthur Russell and Leo Butler. A strong team from Pierre took the championship honors.

Iowa

The U.S. Army first introduced polo to Des Moines in the 1920s. The soldiers played at the Fort Des Moines parade grounds just south of Army Post Road at SW 9th Street on Sunday afternoons. An article in the *Des Moines Tribune* states:

> The Wakonda club and the Fourteenth cavalry polo teams were the contenders for the championship in the northwest polo tourney at Fort Snelling Monday. The Fort Des Moines team won 6 to 5 although the playing of Captain Wilkinson of the Wakonda team was the brilliant and spectacular event of the contest. The army post team had the utmost difficulty defeating the Wakonda players. The match was the greatest of the tournament.[21]

The Wakonda Country Club, named after the chief god of the Kaw Indians, joined the U.S. Polo Association in 1923, with R.B. Parrott as delegate. Other initial members were C. Carr, V.L. Clark, J. Fleming, Fred and James Hubbell, A. Meadows, Harry Polk, Scott Swisher, Jr., O.P. Thompson and L.W. Wheelock. Regrettably, the Wakonda Polo Club became an early victim of the Depression.

Other short articles from the *Des Moines Tribune* in 1930 and 1931 report that the Fort Des Moines 14th U.S. Cavalry team continued to play polo, with matches against Fort Snelling and the University of Missouri being mentioned. A team — Lt. C.H. Martin, Maj. T.J. Kelly, Capt. P.S. Haydon, and Lt. James Walker — entered the 1929 Northwest Championship at Fort Snelling, Minnesota.

The Pacific Coast: From Washington State to San Diego

The first polo club in Washington State was the Spokane Polo Club, established in 1913 by Robert Cosgrove, Ambrose Cunningham, Dr. J.G. Cunningham, Billy Harris, Fred Miller, John Richards, and Vance Wolverton.

Further south, the Waverly Country Club in Portland, Oregon, affiliated with the U.S. Polo Association in 1912. Some of the pioneer players were E.R., H.F. and Henry Corbett, Sherman Hall, Victor Johnson, Roderick Macleay, B.L. Tone and Lt. Col. Gordon Voorhies, a pioneer in military polo.

By 1928 the Portland Hunt Club joined with the Lake Oswego Club. Team captain was Lee Schlesinger; other players were Tom Barnes, Harvey Dick, William Jenkins and Jake Kamm. The Forrest Hills Polo Club counted Dr. Ralph Matson, Lee Schlesinger, Jacob Kamm and Tom Barnes. Players at Oregon State included a Mr. Hardie, Bill McGinnis, John Henderson and Harvey Dick. The polo club in Seattle had Frank Emerick, Jim Lyon, Dr. Charles Castlen and George Klinefelter.

The year 1907 was a banner year for polo in California. In February, a polo tournament and race meeting were held jointly at the Burlingame and San Mateo clubs organized by the San Francisco–based California Polo and Pony Racing Association, presided by Rudolph Spreckels, of the sugar magnate family. The pony races were held at Mr. Charles Clark's six furlongs private racing track, while the polo matches took place at both El Palomar in San Mateo, and on Francis J. Carolan's Crossways in Burlingame.

The teams from Southern California were hosted by the Associations, which defrayed all the costs, including the entry fees. A month later, the teams met again on the Coronado grounds. The Burlingame and San Mateo teams were made up of the following players: Francis Carolan, the Englishman Capt. Claude Champion de Crespigny, Tom Driscoll, the Frenchman Maurice Raoul-Duval, Walter Hobart, John Lawson, Lawrence McCreery, Cyril Tobin and Richard Tobin. The Riverside team was Robert Bettner, Morgan Flowers, S. Fritz Nave, Gordon Pattee, and W.L. Roberts. The Santa Monica team members included H.G. Bundrem, Frank Hudson, William Pedley and C.W. Redmayne. Santa Barbara was chosen from the three Boeseke brothers, J. Colby and E. Wickenden. The representatives from Los Angeles were chosen from H. Messmore, B.N. Smith, Jr., and Bernie, Harry and Tom Weiss.[22]

The first club from the Pacific Coast to affiliate with the Polo Association was the Coronado Country Club in 1909. It had a beautiful ground close to the Hotel del Coronado and had been host for many years to a summer colony that included several foreign polo players. The first list of players submitted to the Polo Association includes Frank Belcher, Capt. Francis Clark, Lt. Arthur Haldane Doig, Coast Guard Artillery; Walter Hamlin Dupee, a noted breeder; C.G. Hubbard, Victor Johnson, Fritz Nave and Harry Robertson, both from San Francisco, and the Canadians Maj. Colin Ross and G. Noton.

San Mateo Polo Club was affiliated in the same year. El Cerrito, the club's own ground, was complemented by Charles W. Clark's El Palomar ground. William Breese, Thomas Driscoll, E. Howard, John Lawson, and Cyril and Richard Tobin were the highest handicap players, with Thomas Driscoll and Walter S. Hobart showing very respectable 6-goal ratings.

The Santa Barbara County Club followed suit in 1910. Robinson Hill, a marvelous location overlooking the Pacific Ocean and backed by the purple mountains, was secured thanks to funds advanced by Mr. William H. Bartlett. Work to build two polo grounds was started immediately. Initial players included Dr. Bertram Boeseke, a dentist; Edgar Boeseke, Dr. Elmer Boeseke, Sr., his son Elmer Jr., Frederick Leadbetter — a paper mill baron from Oregon who provided the first polo grounds — Edgar Parks, Robert Cameron Rogers and Elliott Rogers. Charles W. Dabney joined the membership later on.

Pasadena Polo Club joined in 1911, with Col. William Hogan as delegate. Players included Dr. William Boucher, a Pasadena veterinarian who was the 1921 Tournament of Roses Marshal; Carleton Burke — who would have such an outstanding career in American polo; John Hobbs, Dr. Zachary Malaby, Edgar G., John B. and John B. Miller, Jr., Robert Neustadt, Dr. Henry Savage, and Harry, Reginald, Bernie and Thomas Weiss, Jr. By 1919, the club had disappeared from the Polo Association's roster. Most of the members moved on to the Midwick Club.

The Midwick Country Club joined the Polo Association in 1913. Located between Los Angeles and Pasadena, the named was adopted from "midwick," meaning between towns. It was a plush club, endowed with a baronial club house and excellent polo grounds. The core of the membership was formed by the members of the Pasadena Polo Club, with the addition of players such as the famous breeder Edward Q. McVitty, Harold Cook, Robert Flint and Tod Ford.

The scene at Midwick in California. Regrettably, this famous club closed in July 1941.

In 1914 the Burlingame Club, in a town where polo had been played as far back as 1876, affiliated with the Polo Association. The Burlingame players were handicapped at other clubs.

Another old-time club, Riverside Polo Club, finally became affiliated in 1914. Robert Bettner, Arthur Holden, Frank Hudson, Dewitt Hutchings, Hillyard Lett, Harry Gordon Pattee, Eric, Lionel, Oswold and William Pedley, Martin Redmayne, G.K. Smith and Alvin Untermyer were the players. Seven-goal player Hugh Drury joined the ranks shortly after.

Del Monte Polo Club joined in 1915. The owner and delegate to the Polo Association was Samuel F.B. Morse, grandnephew of the inventor of the telegraph and the Morse code. Originally from Massachusetts, Morse became enchanted with the Monterey area and acquired large tracts of land. A conservationist and early environmentalist, he developed Pebble Beach. Later players included Harold Cook, Hugh Drury, Capt. Byington Ford, Geo. F. Jones, J.F. Neville and Eric Pedley. The polo season at Del Monte became one of the high points of the polo calendar, attracting top players from the East as well as from European countries.

The Riverside Racing and Polo Club, not to be confused with the Riverside Polo Club, was established in 1921 by Robert Lee Bettner, the breeder Walter Dupee, Col. E.E. Hodgson, Dewitt Hutchings, Thomas Mangan, Gordon Pattee, Thomas Phelan, Frank Winship and J. Harrison Wright. This club failed to thrive and closed after one year.

A year later humorist Will Rogers purchased 345 acres in Rustic Canyon, where he built a horse ranch and polo grounds. Hollywood personalities and fellow polo players included Walt Disney, Robert Montgomery and Spencer Tracy.

Hawaii

According to long-time benefactor of polo in Hawaii, Fred Dailey, the game of polo was brought to the islands by Gordon von Tempski, who had seen the game played in the mainland and decided to start polo in the Big Island. Ranchers and sugar barons started hitting a ball and the game took hold. These were the Baldwins from Maui, the Rices from Hawaii, the Castles and the Dillinghams from Oahu.[23]

The Hawaii Polo Club affiliated with the Polo Association in 1912. Walter Dillingham was the club's delegate and some of the handicapped players were Frank Andrews, George Angus, Robert Atkinson, Frank Baldwin, Harry Baldwin, Samuel Baldwin, William Baldwin, Harold Castle, Arthur Collins, Harold Dillingham, Walter Kendall, Peter Malina, Walter MacFarlane, John Milliken, Arthur, Charles, Harold and Philip Rice, Robert Shingle, and James and Rufus Spalding.

In 1928, the contestants for the Wichman Cup were as follows:

Army: Lt. Ralph C. Bing, Lt. Eugene McKinley, Capt. William H. Craig, Lt. John B. Horton.
Oahu Blues: Wellington Henderson, Harold Castle, Lowell Dillingham, Jay Gould.
Freebooters: Francis Brown, Capt. R.F. Pearson, Curtis Skene, Maj. Carl A. Baehr.
Maui: Asa, Laurence (Chu), Edward and Frank F. Baldwin.

The Wichman Cup was taken by the Freebooters.

The 1929 Inter-Island Championship for the Wichman Cup went to the Maui team made up of Frank Baldwin, his two sons Edward and Laurence, and their cousin Richard Baldwin. Oahu was represented by Jack Walter, Harold Castle, and Lowell and Walter Dillingham.

Idaho

Boise Polo Club was established in 1913 by, among many, Charles Barringer, Albert, Edgar and Harry Chapman, W.H. Estabrook, Harry, Leo J. and Ralph Falk, Herbert Lemp, Edward Ostner, and James Torrence. Mr. Herbert Lemp was Mayor of Boise and polo captain for 17 years, when he was thrown from his pony in a practice match and died a few days later, in 1927.

The 1929 Pacific Northwest Championship was held on Rucker's Field, Vancouver Barracks, in Washington State, with teams from Idaho, Oregon and Washington participating. The Boise team — Art Fletcher, David Whyte, D. Steen Fletcher and Capt. Rogers— took the tournament and confirmed its superiority by defeating an All Stars team made up from the best players of their three opponents, the runners-up, Forrest Hills, Seattle and the 77th Infantry.

Nebraska

An interesting polo club, at least name-wise, was the Ak-Sar-Ben (Nebraska spelled backwards) Riding Club, which was affiliated with the U.S. Polo Association in 1924. Located in Omaha, its delegate was E. John Brandeis, whose family owned the Brandeis Department Store, the largest in Omaha. John Brandeis lived like a young Howard Hughes, playing polo, flying all over the place and doing pretty much anything he wanted to do. Other players were Dr. R. Byrne, Fred Kunce, M. Smith, W. Smith and S. Sommers, barely enough to form one team. Not unexpectedly, the club folded in the following year.

There is, however, a record of an Ak-Sar-Ben team participating in the Rocky Mountain 1925 Intra-Circuit Tournament at Fort Leavenworth: John Brandeis, Capt. C.H. Palmer, Capt. J.A. Boyers and Capt. M.F. Meador. The team lost in the first round to the Kansas City squad.

Texas

San Antonio Polo Club was the first civilian club from the Lone Star state to affiliate with the Polo Association, in 1920, followed by Austin, Dallas and Houston in 1925, Wichita Falls in 1926, and Gillespie and Abilene in 1927. Military polo was very strong in the 1920s in Texas and soldiers mixed with civilians in numerous tournaments at both military bases and private polo clubs.

San Antonio's initial roster had names that became part and parcel of American polo into our days. Charles and Tom Armstrong's descendants are the contemporary links in an uninterrupted family line, one of the longest polo lineages in North America.[24] John Lapham, the Club's delegate, had also roots in New England because the Laphams played at the Ox Ridge Polo Club in Darien and on their private polo grounds in adjacent New Canaan. The Lapham estate, a magnificent Tudor home designed in 1912 by architect W.B. Tubbs, is now the 300-acre Waveny Park, a public recreational facility for New Canaan residents. The park was designed by Frederick Law Olmsted, Jr., the creator of New York City's Central Park. The polo grounds have been left untouched, currently used mainly as a parking area.[25] Other players at San Antonio were Clinton Brown, Holman Cartwright, Robert Maverick, William Meadows, Richard Negley, Sr., Walter Negley, Charles Schreider, Jr., and Frost Woodhall.

Austin Polo Club was started by Sidney Donaldson, George Miller, Charles Cabaniss, Sam Rabints, George Stephens and Hubert "Rube" Williams. A certain Cecil Smith appears on the initial roster of players sporting a 0-goal handicap; a decade later Cecil Calvert Smith would be a 10-goaler on his way to becoming an icon in American polo and one of the game's immortals.

The Dallas Polo Association joined the U.S.P.A. in September 1925. The initial players were A. Cecil Adkins, Eugene De Bogory, W.A. Green, Jr., D. Hughes, H. Hughes and Dudley Mayer. A few years later Dr. George Raworth Williams, a chiropractor who would take the Open Championship in 1958 with a Dallas team that included Bob Skene, started playing at the club.

The Houston Polo and Riding Club affiliated with the U.S.P.A. in December 1925. Stephen and Robert Farish were the main supporters. Other players were George Broun, Earl Cortes, George Dow, G.W. Manford, L.G. Manford, H.V. Neuhaus, George Noble, R.D. Randolph, R. Samuels and Cecil Wilfong.

From San Antonio, John and Charles Armstrong, father and grandfather of current players Charles and Stewart Armstrong, one of the longest polo lineages in North America.

Wichita Falls Polo and Riding Club joined the Association in January 1926. H.D. Cowden, John Fastnow, Dr. J. Fletcher, Jerald Gose, W.M. McGregor, James Minnick, E.R. Palmer, G.E. Prendergast, and David Whyte were the initial members. In 1930, a team — Lt. Albert Barden, Horace Robbins, Capt. C.E. Boyle and C.H. Featherston — took the Texas Mid-Winter Tournament, one of the largest in the country in terms of number of teams competing.

Gillespie County Polo Club, based in Fredericksburg, became a member in January 1927, with W.L. Burke, who brought polo from Houston to the town, as delegate. In the vicinity of town, farmers and ranches raised a peculiar type of large pony that became surprisingly adept for polo. In a short time, the game was in vogue. The players' list reflects the strong German influence in this colony in the Hill Country: Emil Ernst, Herman Fischer, Clinton Harden, Ernst Herfort, Felix, Kurt, Victor and Dr. Werner Keidel, Robert Klett, Silas Kneese, R.L. Kott, Alexander, Elmer and Felix Maier, Eddie Ochs, Harry Priess, York Ratliff and Dr. Otto Witte.[26] Teams including some of the above mentioned players had previously participated in tournaments under the name Fredericksburg without achieving much success. In 1930, the Gillespie County Polo Club became the Hill Country Club.

There was also in Texas a Stonewall Polo Club that participated in several tournaments; however, there is no record of the club seeking affiliation with the U.S.P.A. The players were W. Danze, A. Duecker, E. Duecker, E. Ellenbracht and L. Klein.

The Abilene Polo & Saddle Club joined the U.S. Polo Association in December 1927, with Deane Gill as delegate. Harold Austin, Fred Bayles, Cecil Childers, Willis Cox, Don Davis, George Fry, H.F. Gibson, M.A. Grisham, Bernard Hanks, Earl Hoppe, D.H. Jefferies, Edward Kent, Grady Kinsolving, Caleb Reed, N. Reynolds, Henry Widmer, Talbott Wildman, Herbert Williams and G.W. Yantis were members of a strong polo contingent.

The West Texas Polo Club, in Camp Wood, probably holds the record for most members in a first year of affiliation. No less than 80 players were represented by the club's delegate, J.E. Robbins.

The last polo club from Texas to join the U.S.P.A in the Twenties was Fort Worth. Players included E.A. Compton, Capt. H.G. Conar, J.E. Fitzpatrick, H.F. Gibson, Deane Gill, Fran Kirk Johnson, C.L. Renaud and L.E. Weeks.

Oklahoma and a Bit of Arkansas

In 1924 Ponca City Country Club became the first polo club in Oklahoma to affiliate with the U.S. Polo Association. Ernest Whitworth Marland, already mentioned in the section on polo in Colorado, was the main promoter, with three private grounds on his property. The Marland Oil Co. was considered the most progressive in the oil industry, until a hostile takeover by J.P. Morgan in 1928. The merger with Continental Oil Co. was the forerunner of Conoco.[27]

Mr. Marland, "E.W." as he was called, was all out for polo. If some players could not afford to purchase ponies, he would lend them some. It was also said that some vice-presidents of his company had more to do with polo than with the oil business. Nevertheless, E.W. teamed up with a few of his company employees: players such as John S. Alcorn, a company executive described as "mercurial and convincing," Curtis Allen, S.A. Anthony, Paul Badami, H.B. Copeland, Foy Crawford, S.A. Delleplaine, E. Park "Spoy" Geyer — a geologist who had been a fullback on the University of Oklahoma football team; M.H. Goode, I.G. Harmon, head of the production department; Maj. Don Henderson, an Englishman Master of Fox Hounds; his adopted son George R. Marland, Dr. C.E. Northcutt, Oakley Pappan, A.I. Riley, George Shallemberger and Seward Sheldon — the last two Marland company bright young men. These and others joined the humorist Will Rogers and other celebrities in polo games in Central Oklahoma.[28]

Although there were no polo clubs in Arkansas at the time, a team, Arkansas City, played in the 1928 tournament at Ponca City: C.V. Wilson, M.E. Mollett, R.E. Bates and Curnie Wilson were the players.

Polo in Wyoming

In her *Big Horn Polo*, Bucky King states that in 1907 or 1908 teams from the Big Horn area played against the 12th Cavalry. Photographs showing the Big Horn players—Lee Bullington, John Cover, Malcolm Moncreiffe, Robert Walsh, wearing caps and cowboy hats—contrast with the 12th Cavalry outfit wearing helmets and accompanied by a bugler. Neither the location nor the opponents are identified.[29] However, there is no question that polo had continued in Wyoming, presumably as a training ground for the booming business of selling horseflesh to the eastern establishment and the United Kingdom.

Certainly, teams from Wyoming traveled to Colorado Springs, Glenwood and Denver. In 1913, a Sheridan Polo Ranch team — Robert Walsh, R. Lee Bullington, Malcolm Moncreiffe, and John Cover — made the journey to Denver to participate in the Walsh Senior Cup, an event to be played without handicap for trophies presented by Mr. Thomas F. Walsh. The Polo Ranch lost to a strong Kansas City team. The same team then entered the Walsh Junior Cup, losing to the host 2nd team 8¾ goals to 7. Denver received seven goals by handicap. G.C. Hough, Malcolm Moncreiffe, I. Townsend Burden and John Cover played in the Keene and Phipps Cups. Facing Denver's 1st team the visitors lost again 13½ to 12.

The game in the early 1920s was concentrated at Fort David A. Russell, near Cheyenne, where the persistent efforts of Lt. Col. Henry Meyer brought the game to fruit. Polo started in Cheyenne in 1920, with enthusiasts such as Charles Hirsing, a veteran player, as was Charles Carey. John Elliott and Edward McCarty completed the team. Lacking a polo grounds, the pioneers from Cheyenne were allowed to use the Fort D.A. Russell field.[30]

CHAPTER 9

The Roaring Twenties at Home: East of the Mississippi

Polo in Chicago

World War I played havoc with the clubs in Chicago. At the conflict's end only the Onwentsia Club was able to carry the flag. In 1920 several players met and formed the North Shore Polo Club. Temporary grounds were found in the north end of the city, at Lincoln and Peterson Avenues. The stables and a clubhouse were built by the members. These were Walter Barger, Frank Bering, Eugene Byfield, Sanford Harris, Alfred Hursley, Frank Hayes and Herbert Loberd, among others. In fact, the club was really a reincarnation of the Whip and Spur Club, which had been organized by Eugene Byfield and Maj. Gen. Foreman on the West Side Driving Park in Austin, and later on, at Hinsdale.

The Spur and Saddle Club came into being in 1924. The delegate was Alphon Bahr; other players were J. Droeger, E.B. Emery, Lucius Foster, Edward Hillman, Jr., and F.R. Warren. This club has a brief existence; by 1926 there is no mention of Spur and Saddle in the Year Book.

Oak Brook

Interestingly enough, it was the interest of military polo that started the engine of what would become one of finest polo facilities in the country. The game had started on the property of the Butler estate in 1898.[1] Extra impetus was given in 1914 when some of the private owners stabled their ponies in the premises. In 1921, Paul Butler, president of the Army and Navy Club, in collaboration with Maj. Gen. Harry C. Hale and other leading military officers, started thinking about a large-scale polo operation in the vicinity of Chicago. A suitable tract of land was found at Oak Brook in Hinsdale. Although the original interest in the Oak Brook polo project was largely military, when matters of finance and construction arose the project's management fell upon the capable hands of Mr. Butler.

The Oak Brook Polo Club was chartered on 31 October 1924 by Paul Butler, Gene Gordon Culver and J.W. Butler. Affiliation with the U.S.P.A. was recorded on 19 December 1924. Six fields were planned, including the old grounds on the Butler estate. An interesting feature was that the polo fields were at different elevations, the highest being 40 feet above the lowest. This was done with the thought of preventing cancellations due to inclement weather. Facilities were provided for stabling 160 ponies.

The club received a big help when the organization of the 1929 Junior Championship was awarded by the U.S.P.A. to Oak Brook.

With the demise of polo at the old Meadow Brook Club in 1954, Oak Brook became the best polo facility in the United States and the home of the Open Championship.

Wisconsin

Polo in Milwaukee had started in 1927 in the horse pavilion at the State Park Fair in West Allis. Capt. H. Graham Conan was the catalyst. The outdoor game began on a polo field leased by W.V. Thompson. The Milwaukee Polo Club was named Meadow Brook, and as such could not be affiliated with the U.S. Polo Association. Nevertheless, games were played against teams from Minneapolis, St. Paul, Fort Sheridan, the 124th Field Artillery from Chicago, the 317th Cavalry, the Hunt Club from Evanston, Leona Farms, North Shore, Oak Brook and Onwentsia. The indoor variety was also played at the Fairmount Riding Academy in Milwaukee.

The Game in Ohio

Polo was taken up by the horsemen of Gates Mills, in the Cleveland area, in 1911.[2] The pioneers were Edmond Burke, Jr., and Corliss Sullivan, who had learned the game while wintering in Camden, South Carolina. At a directors' meeting on 6 May of that year a Polo Committee was appointed, with Edmond S. Burke, Jr., as chairman, Arthur "Pop" Baldwin and Frank Newcomer.[3] Eddie Burke, who had some experience in wielding a polo mallet, set the example by shipping three ponies to Cleveland from South Carolina. Arthur Baldwin also had played polo in Hawaii. His sons Henry and Fred were captains of the Yale polo team in different years, and his other two sons, Alexander and Lewis, played polo and hunted in Gates Mills.

The practice field that gave the polo players their start was the parcel of land that had been the site of the Hunt Club horse and pony show. It was located east of Epping Road and south of the Mill Race. Soon it was found to be too small and suitable land was leased from the Gates Mills Improvement Society. A full-size polo ground was then built.

As the sport grew in popularity, more players mounted up, and other private local fields were laid out in the 1910s and 1920s. Eddie Burke built a polo field on his estate in Wickliffe; the Chagrin Valley Hunt club laid out a regulation-size field in 1916; two more grounds were constructed at the Kirtland Country Club; and others at the Circle W Farm of Walter C. White, at the Waite Hill estate of John Sherwin, Jr., and at Halfred Farms of Windsor T. White.

Earle W. Hopping, later to be awarded a 10-goal handicap in England, was selected as coach, and Arthur P. Perkins, another Englishman who reached an 8-goal rating in America — as did his son Peter — was hired as an assistant coach. Arthur Perkins was sent to Texas to purchase ponies; when they arrived in Cleveland the price of the lot was averaged and a purchase price of $300 put on each of the ponies. Interested players then drew lots for the animals.

The first official match was a contest on 7 August 1913 at Edphine Farms between the Chagrin Valley Hunt Club and a squad from Cincinnati. Chagrin Valley came out on top, by the narrow score of 7¾ to 7. A penalty and a safety made the difference. The Chagrin Valley team lined up with Corliss Sullivan, Eddie Burke, Lawrence Hitchcock and Arthur Baldwin. Encouraged by such a successful debut, the green and gold Chagrin Valley polo team traveled to the Thousand Islands Polo Club for a series of matches. Several games were played on the Wellesley Island field. Corliss Sullivan was unable to travel and was replaced by Lewis Williams. The visitors took the series.

In addition to the players mentioned above, other early poloists in the Valley were Laurence Hamill, Parmely Herrick, Livingstone Ireland, Robert Norton, Charles Otis, Samuel E. Strong, George Wade, Japhta Wade, Jr., Thomas White and Windsor T. White.

Polo at Gates Mills became a major pastime because the foxhunters were able to keep their foot in a stirrup during the summer. The competition with Cincinnati became an established event for a cup symbolic of the Ohio Polo Championship, presented in 1913 by Mrs. Carl J. (Frances) Schmidlapp of Cincinnati.

Later on, permanent fixtures were arranged with Buffalo and Dayton. Also, annual journeys were taken to the Thousand Islands for the Mid-Western Polo Championships. After the war, Chicago, Columbus, Detroit, Pittsburgh and Toledo were added to the inter-cities rivalries.

In later years Chagrin Valley benefited from players such as James A. Wigmore, who spent his winters at the Midwick Club in California; Capt. Wesley White, the celebrated polo umpire; Thomas H. White, David S. Ingalls, a newly appointed Secretary of the Navy, and the only Navy ace in World War I; others were Edwin Higbes, II, Tyler Miller, Severance Milliken, Edwin Motch, Jr., and Walter White,

In 1921, the Kirtland Country Club was organized and encouraged several equestrian activities, including polo. Many of the members also played at Chagrin Valley. For example, Pansy Ireland and the Baldwin family were instrumental in getting polo on a firm footing at Kirtland. Quay Findley, Cyrus Ford, Dan Hanna, Woods King, Regan McKinney, Bob Norton, Francis Sherwin, John Sherwin, Jr., captain of the indoors 1st Cleveland Cavalry; Capt. C. Radcliffe and Holden White were other pioneers in Cleveland. Matches between Kirtland and Chagrin Valley became commonplace, the horses first being walked to one or the other club on Fridays for play on Sunday. Vans were then purchased to facilitate the exchange of games between the two neighboring clubs.

The Hunting Valley Polo field was inaugurated in 1931 with a curtain raiser match between the Pioneers, aggregate age 250 years, and the Midgets, aggregate age 50. The youngsters lost 2–1 in the two-chukker game. The main event pitted the Cowboys, James Wigmore, David Ingalls, Cecil Smith — later to be a 10-goaler — and Tom Guy, versus Hunting Valley, with William White, Tom White, Earle Hopping and John Sherwin, Jr. In spite of Cecil Smith's play, the Hunting Valley team won 10–7 in one of the fastest games ever played in the valley, in front of the largest crowd to watch a game in Cleveland.[4]

Club member Courtney Burton played in Mexico in February 1939 as a member of a team of players from Texas. As a result of that trip, Burton initiated the arrangements for a return visit to Gates Mill in August of that year. Severance Millikan and others placed their polo pony strings at the disposal of the visiting Mexican players. In a three-game series, different Hunting Valley players played against the visitors. The Hunting Valley team that won the third and decisive match by 8 goals to seven was Otto Knutsen, Jr., Thomas White, Courtney Burton and Bill Kuykendall from Texas. Gen. Jesús Jaime Quiñones played at Number 3 and was captain of the Mexican team. Lt. Gabriel Gracida, Capt. Alfredo Ramos Sesma and Lt. Jesús Grijalva completed the Mexican squad.

Polo in Dayton started in 1916 when George Mead and Harold Talbott, Jr., purchased polo ponies and the first matches were arranged by Fred Patterson at Community Field, which is now a public golf course. The Miami Valley Hunt and Polo Club was established in November 1919 by Fred Patterson, George Mead, Frank Hill Smith, Edwin Reynolds and Harold Talbott, Jr., for the purpose of promoting polo, hunting, riding and other outdoor sports and for the social entertainment of the members and their guests. The hunting activity never became as popular as polo, largely because it was not a spectator sport. The 1921 Miami Valley team had Colin Gardner, Howell Howard, George Mead, honorary treasurer of the U.S.P.A., and Nelson "Bud" Talbott.

The Carranor Hunt and Polo Club in Perrysburg, near Toledo, was started by two Yale University graduates: James Bell, Sr., its first president, and George Greenhalgh. Mr. Greenhalgh was introduced to polo in Alabama while serving with the Ohio National Guard. After the war, in which he was a colonel of artillery, Greenhalgh returned to Toledo to practice as an attorney. On 16 September 1921 the club was formally organized and two days later a polo game was played against Troop D. The rest of the players were Park Detweiler, Milton Knight and H. Norman Parke. Substitutes were James Bell, Jr., William Knight, Jr., George MacNichol, Jr., Joseph McClure, Jay Secor, Jr., and Duane Stranahan, Sr.[5]

The Carranor Club affiliated with the U.S.P.A. on 19 July 1922. In that same year Earl C. Shawe was hired as polo instructor. Interest in the game continued to increase and a second polo field was leased at Seventh and Walnut streets. This ground was used for practice games while the old field on the Pew property was being reseeded. In the second year of play Malcolm Smith, Sidney Spitzer and Langdon Walbridge joined the ranks. Later players in the Thirties included LaMar Christy, Bower Corwin, George and Hanson Jones, George MacNichol, III, Henry and Rathbun Mather, Frank Stranahan, Jr., and Larry Thompson, Jr.

A Carranor team — James Bell, Jr., George Greenhalgh, Earl Shawe, and Duane Stranahan — took the Central Circuit Tournament at Dayton, defeating the host club, Miami Valley, in the first round, Kirtland in the semifinals, and in the championship match, the Cincinnati squad by 12 goals to 11, after giving five goals by handicap.

Polo at the Carranor Hunt and Polo Club became dormant in 1932; however, it was briefly revived in 1940. Regrettably, the game in Toledo did not survive World War II, but the club continued on, albeit without polo as an attraction.

The Cincinnati Polo Club was established on 18 April 1913 by L.W. Dodd, Julius Fleischman, Col. Max Fleischman, Bruce Graydon, Joseph Graydon, Learner Harrison, William P. Hulbert, P. Lincoln Mitchell, Samuel Pogue, W. Horace Schmidlapp, Dr. Elmore Tauber and Joseph Wilshire.[6]

The club participated in events for the Schmidlapp Cup with other teams in Ohio. This initial attempt to establish polo in Cincinnati came to an early end when the club disbanded in January 1916.

A new Cincinnati Polo Club was organized in 1924. New names were added to the Fleischmanns, Harrison and Mitchell, the old stalwarts from 1913. These were DeWitt Balch, Herman Bayliss, W.J. Fuller, T.S. Goodman, H.B. Smith, Oliver DeGray Vanderbilt and Henry Yeiser, Jr.

Regrettably, this second attempt also failed and the club closed in 1929.

Michigan

The earliest mention of polo in Detroit appeared in a *Detroit News* report of a game in April 1881, in which a Detroit team defeated a Chicago team.[7] No corroboration of this match ever taking place has been found.

Polo at the Grosse Pointe Hunt Club was started in 1911 by Col. Fred M. Alger, Capt. Burns Henry, George Lathrop, Elliott Nichols and Wesson Seyburn.

The Country Club of Grosse Pointe Farms, established on the first day of October 1897 primarily as a golf venue, was affiliated with the Polo Association on 6 July 1920. Polo members were Frank and Herbert Book, Theodore Buhl, J.T. Currie, C.M. Deakin, B.C. Eaton, Capt. Burns Henry, James M. Hibbard, Gordon King, E.E. MacCrone, Neil McMath, William Muir, Frank Nelson and George Stroh. The club's teams later played at the grounds on Nine Mile and Southfield, which opened in 1923.

By 1930 there were several polo clubs around Detroit. The Detroit Riding and Hunt Club (1921), Detroit Polo Club (1923), Michigan Polo Club (1924), and the Grosse Pointe Hunt Club (1927) give some idea of the importance acquired by the game in Michigan.

Polo in the Sunshine State

The first polo club in Florida was the Jacksonville Polo Club, which affiliated with the Polo Association in 1899. Its path was followed by the Orlando Polo Club, in 1906, which ceased operations ten years later. Benjamin Cotton, Walter Cary Elwes, Augustus Emmett, Wyndham Gwynne — the delegate; Augustus Hart, Charles Hiley, Duncan Pell, Hilton Renwick, Edward Sudlow and Seth Woodroff were the founding members. Only three members were rated above a zero handicap: Gwynne himself, Charles Hiley and Louis Nelson, the latter at 3-goals. One of the more curious names was a Victor Starbuck, who is first shown in 1910 and continued to be listed until 1915.[8]

Nevertheless, the game in Florida did not prosper until the early 1920s, when the work of pioneers such as Carl Fisher and Henry Flagler opened the wonderful Floridian beaches to an ever-increasing numbers of sun-followers.

Polo at Miami Beach made news when started in the district known as the Spanish Village. The *Metropolis* newspaper noted that both the bathing beach and the golf course were deserted on the afternoon of the first game of polo.[9]

When the first shipment of horses arrived from Ohio early in the season of 1918 the stables for them had not been completed. A paddock for their temporary housing was hastily put together, feed troughs were improvised from soap boxes obtained from a nearby grocery store, and the mounts of Harold Talbott, Jr., George Mead and other members of the Miami Valley Hunt and Polo Club in Dayton were turned out in the open.

The Flamingo Polo Club in Miami Beach was affiliated in 1920. Within four years the encroachment by developers — sounds familiar — compelled the club to move four miles north to the Nautilus subdivision, at that time a remote section of Miami Beach. Four fields were built on filled-in land on a 12-inch foundation of clay and sand to which was added four inches of topsoil. The new fields were opened on Christmas Day in 1925 in a game where C.G. Fowler, Fred Post, J.C. Andrew and Maj. Louie Beard opposed a team with Carl Fisher, Frederick Prince, Jr., Robert Hassler and Robert Bullock and won.

The polo grounds, known as Nautilus 1, 2, 3 and 4, were located in a plush residential

Polo in Florida in the 1920s. The Chagrin Valley Hunt Club from Ohio and the Flamingo team from Miami at the Nautilus Field.

area. Needless to say, within five years the land had become much too valuable to be kept as polo grounds. Consequently, the polo club had to find grounds for permanent settlement and in April of 1930 a tract of acreage was acquired seven miles north from the center of Miami Beach.

The Gulf Stream Club was started by the Phipps family on a parcel of land near Del Ray. It had a magnificent location, tucked between the Atlantic Ocean and the Intracoastal Waterway. It was essentially a private club for friends and family; however the quality of the game was high. Although play had begun in the mid–1920s, the club did not join the U.S.P.A. until 1935. Its moment of glory occurred in 1941, when John H. Phipps, Michael Phipps, Charles Skiddy von Stade and Alan Corey, Jr., took the U.S. Open Championship at Meadow Brook.

Louisiana

Between 1898 and 1912 polo in New Orleans ranked with some of the best in the South. The New Orleans Polo Club affiliated with the Polo Association in 1903, with players such as Carl Andrews, Clinton Fulton, James Graham, Norvin Harris, William Hero, Frederick Morrill, John Solari, Omer Villere, Marion Weis and Philip Werlein. Teams from this southern stronghold defeated players from New York, Houston, Dallas and Memphis. In 1912 an unfortunate accident put an immediate end to the game in New Orleans. Dr. Logan King, one of the most popular players in New Orleans, was killed in a match and his untimely death was such a shock to his teammates and opponents that interest in the game was allowed to wane. At the outset of the war, polo was no longer played in New Orleans.

However, New Orleans was too sporting a city to permit so magnificent a game to be destroyed. The National Guard units of the city became interested and under the able guidance of Capt. Neal Johnson, the game took a new lease on life, with Government aid in the way of mounts and playing field. Gradually the game revived. The 108th Cavalry and the Washington Artillery had promising teams and a civilian team organized by one of the old timers, Mr. Allen Mehle, was formed to rival them.

The New Orleans Polo Association was formed in 1929 and obtained the use of the old military field at Jackson Barracks. The Cavalry team consisted of John Barkley, Nolte De Russy, Douglas Drennan, Frederick Fox and Fred Wulff, Jr. The Artillery players were James Edmonds, James Edmonds, Jr., Gen. Raymond Fleming, Thurber Richey and Charles Verdier. The civilian team had J.C. Gomila, Joseph Gumble, Lester Gumble, Louis LeFevre and Allen Mehle.

Tennessee

The Memphis Hunt and Polo Club was established in 1925, although there are records of polo teams from Memphis playing in the early 1900s. In September 1925 a team from Memphis traveled to Pinehurst, North Carolina, to play a series of matches against the host club, Sandhills. Allen Wardle, Capt. Fred Egan, Hugh Fontaine and Burr Chapman were twice beaten by Sandhills. It was what is called a learning experience.

Another team from Memphis—Dunbar Abston, Curtis King, Sam Rembert, Jr., and W. Burr Chapman—played in Cincinnati and Dayton. Other players were George Brodnax, Everett Cook, Curtis Dewey, Sid Farnsworth, Robert Galloway, John Gerber, Homer Jones, Ralph Jurden, J.B. McKee, W. Lytle McKee, Hubert Reese, James Stark, Jr., Kenneth Stevenson, McKay Van Vleet and R.E. Lee Wilson, Jr.

The Nashville Polo & Hunt Club affiliated with the U.S. Polo Association in 1923. There is no record of the club participating in U.S. Polo Association events and the club's name disappears from the Year Book after 1924. Identified players were J.M. Bass, Capt. W. Battle, R. Caldwell, M. Davis, Henry Dickinson, R.D. Gleaves, V. Molloy, Frank Murray, Clay Pierce and S.M. Williams.

North Carolina

The Pinehurst golf complex in the Sandhills of North Carolina was created in 1897 by James Walker Tuft, a scion from the American Soda Fountain Company family of Boston. Golf was the first game played at Pinehurst under the guiding hand of Donald Ross, professional player and gifted architect from Dornoch, in Scotland's northern reaches. Pinehurst also hosted equestrian activities from polo to harness racing since the early 1900s. Play was on a ground near the Fair Barn; however, there is no record of the Pinehurst Polo Club being affiliated with the Polo Association. A photograph titled "Polo at Pinehurst, N.C." is in the Durwood Barbour Collection in the Wilson Library at the University of North Carolina in Chapel Hill. The print has been dated between 1905 and 1915.[10] Since the harness racetrack goes back to 1915 and polo was also played on a field inside the track, it can be safely assumed that polo at the Pinehurst resort began at a date circa 1910.

The Sandhills Polo Club in Pinehurst affiliated with the Polo Association in July 1920. William Averell Harriman, from Orange County in New York State, was the prime mover. James and Leonard Tuft, Jackson Boyd, Capt. A. Loftus Bryan and John Tuckerman were the original players. Sandhills had an active winter polo season, hosting teams from Tennessee, the Flamingo Club from Miami Beach, Fort Oglethorpe in Georgia, Aiken in South Carolina, the neighboring Fort Bragg, and teams made up from New York winter vacationers.

The Winston-Salem Polo Club was established in 1923 through the efforts of Thurmond Chatham, who secured the services of Capt. Walter Slocock as coach. Mrs. Richard J. Reynolds gave permission to use her stables and a temporary field on her estate, Reynolda. Games were played against Fort Bragg, Maryland Polo Club and Sandhills. In 1927, Winston-Salem reached the finals of the Southern Circuit Tournament, being defeated by the Fort Oglethorpe squad from Georgia.

A gradual process of disintegration began and only four of the original members remained, Thurmond Chatham, E.A. Dart, E.M. Hanes and J.G. Hanes. Three of those players owned homes in Roaring Gap and had a polo field built; however, they failed to attract other members and polo came to a stop.

The Charlotte Polo Club joined in 1924. The original field also doubled as Charlotte's first airport; presumably play was stopped for landings and take-offs. Players were W.H. Bethea, James Carson, W.M. Cosby, Stuart Cramer, Jr., E.C. Griffith, the delegate; Charles Ivey, Charles and Walter Lambeth, Charles Okey, Jimmy Rust, S.B. Tanner and George Wilson. The Charlotte Polo Club closed in 1927.

Polo in Upstate New York

Following Buffalo Country Club and Saratoga's pioneer ways, the Albany Polo Club was started in 1903. It had a brief existence, because it folded in 1907. In its debut against Saratoga, Charles Sabin, H.N. Kirkland, Harry W. Sage and Charles L.A. Whitney emerged victorious by half-a-goal, 3¾ to 3. The Ballston Cup was their reward. Saratoga took revenge a few days later in the competition for the Hitchcock Cup. Neither team made changes in their lineups; both events were held at Saratoga Springs. The Sanford Cups came next and the novices from Albany drew the strong Buffalo team, John Richmond, Tom Carey, James Averell and George Cary. The final result, 23–1 in favor of Buffalo, tells the story without further words.

The Albany 2nd team entered the Grand Union Hotel Cups in the Saratoga season the next year. Harrison Bird, Henry M. Sage, Frederick Townsend and George Curtis Treadwell, fell to a Saratoga team — Raymond Belmont, Frank von Stade, R.W. Smith, Victor Mather — by another lopsided score: 25¾ to nil. But revenge is sweet, because in the final match for the cups, Albany 1st team, composed by John Manning, Harry W. Sage, James Averell and Charles Whitney, defeated the same Saratoga team that had tormented their club mates by 8¾ goals against none by the locals. On their way to taking the United States Hotel Cups, the two Albany teams met in the first round. Once more, Albany 1st showed no mercy, thrashing their friends by 20 goals to ¾; a safety deprived the Albany 2nd team of at least having at least one goal on the scoreboard.

The final record of the Albany Polo Club in the U.S.P.A.'s Year Book is at Saratoga Springs in August 1906, with Fred K. Pruyn being added to the team.

Polo was started in Rochester in 1903; however, it had been played in the Genesee Valley as early as 1895 by a group of enthusiasts that included Edward Fitzhugh, William Littauer, Craig Wadsworth and James S. "Jim Sam" Wadsworth. When the Genesee Valley Polo Club folded most of its members joined the Buffalo Country Club. Nevertheless, James Wadsworth secured an uneven parcel of land in South Park, Rochester, and play began once more.

The *Democrat and Chronicle* reported that James Averell, Eugene Brown, Luther Gordon, Walter Howard, C.H. Stearns, Norman Van Voorhis, J. Stanley Watson, James Wadsworth and Samuel Wilder were "some of the more expert players."[11] That first season had an international flavor when a team from Calgary crossed the border during their tour of Eastern Canada. Rochester was represented by Norman Van Voorhis, James Wadsworth, Sam Wilder and James Averell. The Calgary team was H.R. Middleton, the Hon. F.A. MacNaughton, Colin Ross and A. Home. Country Club of Rochester teams traveled to Buffalo and Toronto. With Walter Howard in place of Van Voorhis, the team acquitted itself nobly, taking the International tournament in Toronto. However, a return match against a totally different Toronto team that included two British officers resulted in a surprise defeat for Rochester in the two matches, both played without the benefit of an umpire. Matches against Albany also were played, as well as a game against a foursome from Chicago on its way to participate in tournaments in the Eastern seaboard. Matches were played with Kingston, Ontario, Montreal and San Francisco Polo Club. The two matches against San Francisco were described as "colorful."[12]

The game of polo continued to thrive in Rochester until the onset of World War I. It was revived in 1924 under the banner of Rochester Polo Club with the support of Maj. Charles Clifford of the National Guard and it was centered in the Cavalry Armory on Culver Road. Maj. Clifford gathered around him Stalham Baker, Raymond Bantel, Andrew Towson, Col. Kenneth Towson and Allan Steyne

The growth of polo in Rochester was hampered by lack of a proper ground, the old standby field in South Park not being able to provide good footing because of its uneven surface. Nevertheless, games were played against Buffalo, Lake Shore in Derby, Montreal and Toronto, but the club stayed away from major tournaments.

The Game in Buffalo

In the late 1920s there were five fields in activity around Buffalo: Two were at the Buffalo Country Club, two at the Lake Shore Country Club and one at Ess Kay Farm, Seymour Knox's estate. The East Aurora team had the Reginald Taylor–Shorty Knox combination up front, while a pair of veterans, Chandler Wells and Gen. Harold Bickford, handled the defensive strategy.[13] Other players waiting in the wings were Pete Burgard, James Evans, Albert Gurney, Eric Hedstrom, Alfred Schoellkopf and William Schoellkopf. Gen. Bickford, a Canadian, had learned the game in India.[14]

The newly created Lake Shore Hunt Club was responsible for the renewal of polo in Western New York. A polo ground and stables were erected at the Fenton Farm. The individuals responsible for starting the game were Walter Andrews, William Barr, T. Morgan Bowden, John Casa Eguia, Colman Curtiss, Howard Kellogg, Seymour Knox, Stuart Mann, Harry Spaulding and Frank Trubee, Jr. All were experienced horsemen; Colman Curtiss had learned the game while a student at Yale University and the team was built around him. Earl Shaw was contracted as coach and manager. Curtiss was dispatched to William Post & Sons on Long Island, where he selected a carload of ponies that were distributed by lot to the members. Two matches against Grosse Pointe were arranged, and to the surprise of many — some 5,000 spectators witnessed the event — the results were split.

This successful debut encouraged the membership to seek other opponents. Thus, Chagrin Valley, Kirtland, Miami Valley, Toronto, and close-by Buffalo Country Club were met in national tournaments.

In later years the Lake Shore Club benefited from the coaching of Capt. Percy Fleming of the 379th Field Artillery. Their best player was Kellogg Mann, a hard-hitting Back. Other players were Henry Coit, the veteran Howard Kellog, Senior and Junior, Stuart Mann, another veteran, and his sons Kellogg and Nelson, Charles Neale, Walter Schmidt, Frank Trubee, Jr., Gus Watters and Chandler Wells.

Long Island

Polo on Long Island epitomized the golden era of the game in the United States, with the village of Westbury the anointed capital, because the Meadow Brook Club was the most important club in the world and the host of the best polo at both national and international level. In addition to the superb quality of the players, horses, stables and polo grounds, there was the aura of conspicuous consumption by the fabulous wealthy denizens of the North Shore. Those were the years of elegance in dress, of magnificent mansions with perfect lawns, formal gardens and parks designed by top architects. As far as sports and games, talented golf architects developed superior courses, private tennis courts and swimming pools abounded, fox hunting remained the privilege of the few, private yachts were dime-a-dozen and polo reigned supreme.

No one set the scene better than Francis Scott Fitzgerald in his classic novel *The Great Gatsby*. An average day in the season would be a golf game for a healthy wager in the morning, then lunch at a fashionable club, followed by a game of polo at one of the dozens of grounds, either at polo clubs or on private fields. Closing the day would be a cocktail party followed by a dinner and a postprandial reveille that usually would carry on until the small hours of the morning or even sunrise.

As a spectators' game in the 1920s polo surpassed in numbers both tennis and golf during the international matches and the Open Championship events.

Piping Rock Club

Piping Rock in Locust Valley was founded in 1909 and affiliated with the Polo Association in 1912. The Piping Rock name was taken from a large stone located along the ancient trail between Glen Cove and Oyster Bay. Legend has it that Indian tribal leaders conferred and smoked their legendary peace pipes at this site.[15]

In golf architect Charles Macdonald's own words,

In 1911 Roger Winthrop (sic, Henry Rogers Winthrop), Frank Crocker, Clarence Mackay, and other Locust Valley friends wished me to build the Piping Rock Golf Club course. I found they wanted a hunt club as well as a golf-club. Some of the leading promoters thought golf ephemeral and hunting eternal. Consequently, I had my troubles. The first nine holes were sacrificed to a race-track and polo fields.[16]

Charles Blair Macdonald met his match with the Board of Piping Rock. The Board was adamant the golf course must be routed around the two polo fields. It was an argument in which the cantankerous Macdonald did not prevail. In a huff, he left the communications with the club and completion of the course to his talented associate Seth Raynor.

The initial list of players at Piping Rock included J. Leavett Hunt, Ralph Kirlin, Harvey Ladew, John O'Day, Joseph Thomas and Behrens Waters. Most of the later members that played polo were handicapped at other clubs; the reason was that, with the sterling exception of Meadow Brook Club, they played golf at Piping Rock. There is no full history of the club, because it abhorred publicity; Piping Rock was considered the Augusta National of the 1910s and 1920s.[17]

Although the patrician Piping Rock offered several pastimes beside polo, it also was a pioneer in purchasing ponies and offering them for rent to players without or depleted polo pony strings. It proved to be a most successful endeavor, especially for newcomers to the game and low-handicap players. The club also provided lodging and practice facilities for several international polo teams.

The Meadow Brook Club

In the 1920s and 1930s Nassau County was the world center of polo, the village of Westbury its capital and Meadow Brook's clubhouse the seat of power. The huge International Field with its large stands was the site of the best polo in the planet. As one map quaintly describes, the people sat in the East Stands and "The People" in the West Stands, close to the clubhouse. At one time or another, all the best players galloped on the pristine turf of International Field. Hallowed names such as Manuel Andrada, Roberto Cavanagh, Heriberto and Luis Duggan, Lewis Lacey, Charles "Bunny" Land, David and John Miles and Jack Nelson from Argentina; the Ashton brothers and Bob Skene from Australia; England's Gerald Balding, John Dening, Richard George, Eric Tyrrrell-Martin and Lord Wodehouse; Humphrey Guinness, Aidan and Pat Roark from Ireland all contributed to make Meadow Brook the mecca of polo.

They came to do battle with the American heroes, first led in those times by Devereux Milburn and later by Tommy Hitchcock, whose personality was "a riddle wrapped in a mystery inside an enigma," as one scribe put it. Milburn and Hitchcock were blessed with capable lieutenants, a modern band of brothers. The list is long: Winston Guest, born into a noble family in England but an American at heart, Chilean-born Stewart Iglehart, James P. Mills, California's Eric Pedley, Michael Phipps, Billy Post, Malcolm Stevenson, Cecil Smith, Louis Stoddard, Bobby Strawbridge, and James Watson Webb, all 9- or 10-goal players. Perhaps Elmer Boeseke, Jr., could be added to the roster on the strength of one season in which his handicap was boosted from seven to 10-goals for a lone season, only to be then dropped to eight goals.

Just a step below these luminaries were the barely lesser lights: John Cheever Cowdin, scion of a family with polo roots going back to the early days; Raymond Guest, Winston's younger brother; Earle Hopping the younger, whose father was a 10-goaler in England;

Harold Talbott, Jr., and Laddie Sanford, of whom it was said that no boots were more polished, no jersey or breeches more spruced than those of the Hurricanes' patron.

The country roads led to the Meadow Brook Club, not just a polo club but an international port of call, a key fortress in America's strategy of world control. The West stand was the dominant structure which announced that this was an important place. Meadow Brook Club was different: it had style, confidence and urbanity; it belonged to the world of affairs; there was something almost parliamentary and governmental about it. The word "establishment" would not have been in vogue at that time, but it was the most important place in the world of polo, a defining institution.

Mrs. Frederick Prince, whose Princemere estate in Pride's Crossing was one of the main social and polo centers in Boston's North Shore, wrote about Meadow Brook:

> There never was a more glamorous sight than the Number 1 Polo Field at Meadow Brook on the day of an International Game—the emerald green grass, the blue-painted stands, the length of the field on each side, topped by the national flags, and, prior to the game, the parade of the world's finest polo ponies.[18]

Within a few miles radius of Meadow Brook Club there were plenty of private polo grounds. Old Westbury was the site of two Whitney's fields: J.H. Jock's Greentree and H.P.'s Straight Field. The Heckscher's ground later became the Bostwick Field, where Pete Bostwick popularized the game by offering inexpensive tickets to watch high goal polo. The John S. Phipps grounds, now the Old Westbury Gardens, the William Grace Field, the Elliott C. Bacon grounds, the Frank von Stade's polo field, Watson Webb's private grounds, and the Sparrow Hawks, where Mrs. David Iglehart taught children the game's basics on her estate, were also located in Old Westbury. All this was part of what F. Scott Fitzgerald quaintly referred to as the consoling proximity of multi-millionaires.

Harold Talbott's field was the home of his own team, Roslyn. Also in Roslyn was the Childs Frick field. The Post family had a ground in East Williston, site of many polo pony auctions. And finally, in Westbury proper there were the Hitchcock Field, home ground of the celebrated Meadow Larks, and the Preece Field.

There were many other polo grounds in Nassau County in an area extending from the Sands Point Polo Club on the Sound to the Atlantic Ocean shore in the south, where Fort Neck, Merokee Polo Club, the Corroon Field in Massapequa, and the waning Rockaway Hunting Club in Cedarhurst kept polo going.[19]

Polo in New Jersey

Polo at Peapack Valley Polo Club in Gladstone was carried out at W. Thorn Kissell's property, October House, where a field was laid out. The club affiliated with the Polo Association in 1907 and resigned in 1912. Players included William Camman, Seymour Cromwell, Arthur Fowler, Fred Jones, Jr., Charles and Emile Pfizer, Kenneth Schley, Charles Squibb, Richard Stevens and John Wilmerding.

After the war, the game of polo in New Jersey reflected the boom years of the 1920s, but not for everyone. The Whippany River Polo Club, successor to the Morris County, one of the Polo Association's founding fathers, once a club of wide fame frequented by players of international repute, went through lean times. It possessed a wonderful polo ground that boasted a turf imported sod by sod from Ireland. Douglas Fonda, H. Beddell Albright, Jr., and Jesse and Manton Metcalf, Jr., took the Monmouth County Cup in 1922.

Then in 1928, Dr. John Richards, a player of great repute in arena polo, took renewed interest and assembled a team with promising players such as Cyril Harrison and Gerard Smith. The team, completed with Texan Hubert "Rube" Williams at Back defeated a Meadow Brook squad of Cornelius Whitney, Harold Talbott, Jr., J. Watson Webb and Gerald Dempsey, to the surprise of every one, not least the Meadow Brook players, considered heavy favorites. The club also played games against Princeton; however, it became an early victim of the Depression. A link to the earliest organized polo in the United States was then lost.

The Rumson Country Club, dating back to 1901, had its own cup, presented by Mr. Bertram and Gen. Howard Borden in 1912. It hosted the 1922 U.S. Open Championship and the Herbert Memorial Trophy. Among their winning teams were W. Strother Jones, Jr., General Borden, Manton Metcalf and J. Ford Johnson, Jr., a foursome that took their own Rumson Country Club Cup and the Monmouth County Cup in 1923.

The Monmouth Polo Club, successor of the Deal Polo Club in West End, started operations in 1919. Robert Lehman, Cyril Carr, Milton Erlanger and Walter Sleigman won the J.E. Stern Cup at Suneagles in 1923.

Old Oaks Polo Club was started by the Borden family in 1927. Arthur Borden, his father Gen. Howard Borden, Cyril Carr and Rube Williams won the Southeastern Circuit Championship. However, its moment of glory occurred when the veteran James Calvin Cooley, an accomplished polo writer, Arthur Borden, Gerald Balding and Hubert "Rube" Williams took the 1928 Junior Championship. They defeated an U.S. Army team, putting an end to a string of three consecutive wins by a military team.

It is noticed that in 1929 there were five polo clubs within a short distance of Newark: Essex Troop, Norwood, the magnificent Suneagles in West End; Eatontown, Deal's successor, and Spring Lake.

Polo at Norwood Country Club was started in December 1919 by Louis Gimbel and his brother Adam, Herbert Glass, Verner Reed, Allison Stern and Herbert Winn, with grounds in West End. Cyril Carr, Paul Ladin, Milton Erlanger and Monroe Eisner won the Suneagles Tournament in 1927.

Suneagles, also in West End, was the club of Ferdinand Fleischman, Max Phillips, C. Powell, Fred Wettach and Herbert Winn. It began in 1923, when Max Phillips, H. Bedell Albright, Jr., Terence Preece and Paul Ladin took the Eatontown Cups, and did not survive the shock of the Depression.

Eatontown, also started in 1923, which had indoor polo star Archie Kinney, Robert Lehman, Cyril Lee and Herbert Winn as core players, eventually became another casualty of the lean years in America.

The Spring Lake Polo Association purchased 22 acres of land for building two fields. Harry Maxwell was president; E.A. Kertscher, Jr., Frederick Duggan and James Eben were some of the members. A team — Lt. Eric Molitor, Harry Maxwell, Alex Bullock and David Drage — took the Sandhills Fall Tournament at Pinehurst.

The romantically named Beau Geste Polo Club in Shrewsbury began in May 1928. The Allenhurst Polo and Riding Club started in 1928 and promptly won the Suneagles Polo Tournament with a squad composed by Walter Hardy, Jack Henley, Sanders Wertheim, Jr., and Warren Sackman, the later another prominent indoor polo player.

Other clubs in New Jersey affiliated toward the end of the decade were Oraworth in 1929; Elkwood Polo Club optimistically began activities in June 1930, at the same time as Fairlawn, and the Saddle River Club in January 1931, as well as Burnt Mills.

Pennsylvania

The Philadelphia Country Club, one of the founders of the Polo Association in 1890, broke new ground in 1919 when it purchased two ponies for use by the members. The notice also stated, somewhat uncertainly, "It is believed that these ponies are suitable for Ladies' use."[20] Both the Senior Championship and the Open Championship were held at the club's grounds at Bala in 1919 and 1921. A team representing the Philadelphia Country Club entered the Open Championship in 1921: Thomas Stokes, W. Standley Stokes, A. Lowber Stokes and Barclay McFadden were defeated by the U.S. Army 1st Team in the first round.

In January 1920, the club's Board sent out to the members the gloomy announcement that no wines or liquors could be stored or served in the Club House. It appears that scant attention was paid to the notice, because three years later another prohibition notice was mailed to the membership advising that that the U.S. Government intended to strictly enforce the law.

Returning to polo, the club in conjunction with the Bryn Mawr Polo Club sponsored an International Tournament that included the Frenchman Comte Jean de Madré famous Tigers team with Jaswant Singh and Jagindar Singh, both to be 10-goalers, and a British Army team. Tickets were quite expensive: $125 for a box plus $100 for a parking space. Nevertheless, it was a financial success for the club, bringing in six thousand much needed dollars to the coffers.

However, it proved to be the twilight of high-goal polo at the Philadelphia Country Club. Interest in polo was flagging, as more and more members took up golf as a pastime. In 1928, a Philadelphia team — Henry Coxe, Carroll Coyle, Wister Randolph and Barclay McFadden — took the Alexander Memorial Trophy and the Wooton Challenge Cup at Bryn Mawr.

The Devon Country Club, which dated back to 1895, was quite active until the onset of war. Players included Thomas Doughtery, Jr., J.S. Knight, John McFadden, Edward McVitty, the noted breeder; E.M. Leache, Lowber Stokes and Thomas Stokes. The club resigned in 1919.

The green shirts of Bryn Mawr remained the most powerful force in Pennsylvania polo. The list of successes is impressive: The Senior Championship in 1914; finalist in the 1912 U.S. Open, and six Junior Championships between 1905 and 1920. The name Strawbridge, father and son, both winners of the Open Championship, is indelibly associated with Bryn Mawr Polo Club in that trendy Philadelphia suburb. Bobby Strawbridge, besides being an international player, served as chairman of the U.S. Polo Association from 1936 until 1940, and again from 1946 to 1950. Players of note at Bryn Mawr included Alexander Brown, who would drown in the Delaware River when his airplane crashed into the waters; John Converse, Albert Kennedy, Henry Harrison, George Kendrick, III, C. Randolph Snowden and Charles Wheeler.

The Penllyn Polo Club was established in 1906 by Alfred Biddle, Francis Bond, William Hart, Edward and Harry Ingersoll, Harry Markoe, Jr., and Henry and Richard Vaux. It had a checkered history, because it resigned in 1910, was reelected in 1923, and again in 1932. In 1923, a Penllyn team — George Earle, III, Albert Smith, Barclay McFadden and M.H. Dixon — took the recently established U.S.P.A. National Twelve Goal Tournament, defeating the Army team in the final match.

The Pittsburgh Polo Club was established in 1907 by A.W. Bell, Dallas Byer, H.L. Collins, Percy Donner, A.R. Hamilton, Julian Huff, George Laughlin, Jr., Grant McKinney,

John Ricketson, Jr., and Harvey Van Voorhis. It had a brief existence because it resigned in 1911.

Another club in Western Pennsylvania was the Westmoreland County Polo Club established in October 1913, in Greensburg. Several players from the defunct Pittsburg Polo Club joined the new entity: A.R. Hamilton, Burrell and Julian Huff, and George Laughlin. They were joined by J.D. Callery, Jr., Alexander Coulter, William Frew, Leslie Johnson, George McNary and Samuel Upham. This club resigned in December 1919.

New England Polo in the 1920s

Massachusetts

The Danvers Riding and Polo Club was formed about 1937 by Lester Crossman, Cyrus Newbegin, John and Buddy Pickering, Joseph Poor and John Semons. They were joined later by Everett Crossman, Kenney Fossa, Judge Daniel Manning, Arthur Mason, the Pennell brothers, Gardner and Linden, and Bobby and Ted Poor. Although there was much polo played, as amply recorded in the contemporary press, the club did not affiliate with the U.S. Polo Association. Perhaps the close relationship with the Myopia Hunt Club made the affiliation with the U.S.P.A. redundant in the Danvers club membership. The Crossman family albums, kindly loaned to the author by Chris Crossman Vining, Les Crossman's daughter, contain no information on this matter.

Myopia Hunt Club retained its status as the patrician polo venue of Boston's North Shore. Although not any longer the powerhouse in national polo that it was at the turn of the century, the game continued to thrive on Gibney's Field, although at the mid and low handicap level. Myopia's second team was organized by Dudley Rogers. They created a new mystique and even had different team colors—blue with a horizontal white stripe—from Myopia's traditional scarlet and yellow. With players such as the Burrage brothers, Albert and Russell, Thomas Mandell, Bayard Tuckerman and Jock Whitney, they took more than their share of tournaments.

It was also a time of fathers and sons playing together. Robert Gould "Bobby" Shaw, II, the 9-goal player of the early 1900s, played with his four sons, Gould, Alexander, Louis and Paul; Dudley Clark with Forrester and George; and Frederick Prince, Sr., with Fred the younger. A six-goaler, Forrester "Tim" Clark was an outstanding athlete at Harvard: captain of polo, a member of the varsity rowing eight and a football player. During the war, he rose to the rank of lieutenant colonel in the Armored Corps. When he returned to civilian life, eventually he ran H.C. Wainwright & Co., the family's investment bank.

There was also sadness, a reminder of how a dangerous a game polo can be. On a hot summer day in 1929, George Clark and James Mandell had a head-on collision during a game between old rivals Dedham and Myopia at Westwood. For Jimmy Mandell, recently graduated from Harvard, the collision was fatal; for George Clark it meant years of recuperation and recovery.[21]

Myopia organized an invitational tournament that usually gathered eight or nine teams, including the Myopia first team and the Seagulls; a Princemere squad that had the habit of bringing along a superstar such as Tommy Hitchcock or Lewis Lacey; and teams from Montreal, Norfolk, Dedham, Pittsfield and Narragansett.

Rhode Island

Point Judith Country Club was the only active polo club in Rhode Island during the 1920s. However, it remained as a citadel of good taste and excellent polo throughout the 1920s. A team — Pete Bostwick, Billy Post, Gerald Dempsey and Joseph "Cocie" Rathborne — took national honors when they won the Inter-Circuit Championship, defeating the Cavalry School team in the final match. This was, needless to say, a team made up of vacationers at the Pier in the late summer of 1928.

The club hosted the Twelve Goal National Tournament on several occasions and the Eastern Division Inter-Circuit Championship. The onset of the Depression was a huge blow to polo in Rhode Island. The polo section of the club changed its name to Narragansett Polo Club in March 1936.

Connecticut

The Taconic Polo Club in Hartford was the first one in the Nutmeg State. The date of affiliation was 25 February 1904 and play was carried on at a field in the Hartford Golf Club. This was far from an ideal location because it was on a low ground and it was flooded for days when it rained. An agreement was then reached with the Charter Oak Park to lay out a regulation polo ground on the park's infield.

Walter Lippincott Goodwin was elected delegate and the initial players included Douglas Dodge, R.F. Ely, R.L. Jones, R.G. Keeney, Hugh Legarè, P.S. Ney, Joseph Thomas, Jr., and S. Russell, Jr. Another founding member and a colorful character was John James "Jack" Nairn, who years later would start polo in Cimarron, New Mexico, together with Waite Phillips and Ed Springer, of the CS Ranch.

Most of the games played by the Taconic team were in New Haven, Narragansett and Pennsylvania. The Taconic Polo Club resigned in 1910, only to be reelected a year later. The final bell for the club was sounded in February 1913.

The New Haven Country Club joined the Polo Association on 19 April 1904 and resigned in December 1912. Among the players, who included several undergraduates at Yale University, were L. Hastings Arnold, Jr., Frank Baldwin, Chauncey Perry Beadleston, Frank Butterworth — once a great fullback, later a dashing polo player — Colman Curtiss, Edward Hoyt, Henry Parmelee, Howard Phipps, Louis Stoddard, H.Q. Towbridge, R. Pierpoint Tyler and Seward Webb. The club leased the old Hamden Driving Park, where the stables were put in working order. Two moments of glory marked the short trajectory of the New Haven Club in polo's firmament: the victories in the Junior Championship in 1908 and 1909. Frank Seiler Butterworth, Hugh Drury, Louis Stoddard, Joseph Thomas, Jr., and James Watson Webb were the men that brought back-to-back championships to New Haven.

Polo at the Ox Ridge Hunt Club, established in Darien in 1914, began two years later. The starting polo players, all rated at 0-goals, were Paul Colbron, John Farrell, Philip Gossler, Frederick Howard, Bruce Jenkins, John Lapham, W.D. Macdonald, Dr. Howard Stout Neilson and E.P. Sharrett. The club participated mostly in local tournaments and developed a healthy rivalry with their Westport neighbors, the Fairfield County Hunt Club.

In the late 1920s one of the players was Martin Quigley, the publisher of the magazine *Polo*. Other players were Arthur Buckley, Anson Hurd, Jr., and William Ziegler, Jr.

The Fairfield Polo Club was started in Greenwich in 1923; it promptly changed its name to Greenwich. The first players were Lt. Frederic Bontecou, Thomas Cawthra, G.F.

Cronkhite, Henry Flower, Jr., Stafford Hendrix, C.D. Huyler, C.D. Mallory and William Ruxton.

This club's activity was limited to local and Circuit tournaments with the exception of a team that entered the 1926 Junior Championship at the Westchester Biltmore Country Club in Rye, New York. Lt. Frederic Bontecou, H.L. Platt, C. Reddington Barrett — a member of the Yale University championship team — and Richard Allison were defeated in the first preliminary by Bryn Mawr.

The Greenwich No. 1 team took the New England Circuit Championship in 1928, defeating their brethren Greenwich Larks in the final game. Watson Pomeroy, Reddington Barrett, Richard Allison and George Sherman, Sr., were the team members.

The Fairfield County Hunt in Westport had its beginning when William Averell Harriman commissioned the noted sculptress Mrs. Laura Gardin Fraser to design a polo medal. To study her subject she borrowed mallets, mounted a horse and started knocking a ball around at Stuart Benson's property. Another lady, Mrs. Lila Howard, joined her. The sight of two women trying polo attracted local attraction, even in a horsy community such as Westport.

Soon men joined the fray and local games were organized. Charlie Clapp, Clark and Nancy Fay, Oscar Howard, Lila's husband, and Donald Perkins played on a field by the Saugatuck River, bounded by Clinton Avenue and Redcoat Lane, on what was the Arthur Dolge property. Polo was played first in Westport, then on a field opposite Charles Stillman's house on Hulls Farm Road, with two stone gate posts serving as goals. That field and the stone gate posts are still extant, although polo has not been played on that parcel of land since the late 1920s.

The club was founded in 1923 and affiliated with the U.S.P.A on 11 October 1926. The current property on Hulls Farm Road was purchased in 1924 and Rudkin Field, donated in perpetuity by Henry Rudkin, Sr., still hosts charity polo games.

Samuel Hopkins, Jr., came from Yale in 1927 to assume the positions of coach and general manager. By then polo had prospered and the ranks had swelled. Alfred Allen, Joseph Bulkley, Lawrence Cornwall, Willard Emerson, Sr., Irving Fearn, John Fitzgerald, Allen McKay and Nathaniel Wheeler were the new addicts. An early member was Thomas Glynn, who as an undergraduate at Harvard College had taken the Intercollegiate Championship. Throughout his long life Tommy Glynn became an iconic figure in the polo scene in the northeast, reaching a respectable 4-goal handicap. But it was his coaching and mentoring of young and old players and his uncanny eye for a horse that endeared "Mr. Polo" to every one who knew him.

The onset of World War II ended polo at the Fairfield County Hunt Club for the duration. The game was resumed as soon as possible after the end of the hostilities, in the spring of 1946.[22]

Maine, New Hampshire and Vermont

Civilian polo was first played in Vermont when a number of polo players who were Mr. Winston Churchill's[23] guests at his home in Cornish, New Hampshire, crossed the Connecticut River and played two exhibition games at the Vermont State Fair in White River Junction, on 23 and 25 September 1908. Playing as the Myopia Freebooters, Dudley Rogers, Harrison Tweed, James Watson Webb and Frank von Stade defeated a Squadron A team from New York, composed of Alexander Pratt, Leavitt Hunt, Joseph Hunt and R.C. Lawrence.[24] Robert C. Lawrence was a 3-goal handicap player from the Rumsom Country Club. Near Burlington, polo was much in vogue at Fort Ethan Allen; the Parade Ground, where the matches took place, is still an open space. The only other institution where the game was played in Vermont in the 1920s was at the Norwich Military Academy in Northfield, and also at Mr. Webb's private field in Shelburne.

In New Hampshire the Cornish Polo Club was established by Griswold Hayward, Charles Platt and A.E. Wade in 1926.[25] There was a very good polo grounds on Mr. Hayward's estate. Like many other small clubs in New England, the Yankees showed its individuality and most of the clubs did not join the U.S.P.A.

A polo tournament was held in August 1929 in Dixville Notch, New Hampshire, at the Balsams Hotel, owned by the owner, Capt. Frank Doudera of the New York police force. There was a very fine polo field, surrounded on three sides by steep wooded hills and looking down on the fourth side into a magnificent valley.[26] Four teams competed: Fort Ethan Allen from Burlington, Vermont; Governor's Island from New York; the Boston Pilgrims and the U.S. Army Freebooters. The Boston Pilgrims—Cyrus Newbegin, Carl Adams, Dudley Milliken and Samuel Hopkins, Jr.—took the trophy.

In the state of Maine during the late 1920s the South Portland Polo Club was started by Colonel Byers and Mr. Charles Sims with about a dozen players. At about the same time, the Falmouth Foreside Polo Club was formed by Alexander Gordon and Payne Payson, with about the same number of players. Polo was also played at Bar Harbor and Lewiston.[27]

Virginia

The first polo club in the Old Dominion was the Fauquier County in Warrenton, which affiliated with the Polo Association on 9 February 1909. William Skinker was the main promoter, assisted by Fletcher Harper, Harry Groome, the club's delegate; E.H. Leache, who had played at the Devon Country Club, Fred Okie and John Butler Swann. Other initial players were R.C. Barclay, Clinton and Warren Davis, D.F. De Butts, W.W. Drake, T.L. Evans, M.W. Faile, John Gaines, J.D. Hall, H. and R. Hordern, H.M. Lutrell, J.K. Maddux and Joseph Warren.

The first recorded match played by Fauquier County was held in Washington on 2 October 1909 against an Army team. W.F. Wilbur, C.H. Smith, William Skinker and C.P. Wiley alternating at Number 3, and J. Butler Swann. The Fauquier foursome took the game by 4 goals to 3½.

In July 1910 another team traveled to Narragansett Pier in Rhode Island to participate in the Freshmen Cups. New Haven defeated Fred Okie, C.P. Wiley, John Butler Swann and E.H. Leache by the conclusive score of 6¼ to 2 goals. In the Rhode Island Cups, Fauquier County defeated the Myopia 3rd Team by 7½ to 1½ goals. In this game, a Mr. Mallett replaced C.P. Wiley. Regrettably, English-born Butler Swann, Harvard Class of 1898, died from a head injury sustained during a practice game. This fatality engendered a pall upon the game in Virginia. Nevertheless, there was enough enthusiasm for the game left for Henry Halff,[28] Courtlandt Dixon, II, Lawrence Rumsey and Conn Gano to take the Southern Circuit Cup and reach the finals of the Partridge Cup. Both events were held in Aiken.[29] The Fauquier County Polo Club submitted its resignation in May 1914.

After the war was over, the club, now renamed Fauquier County Country Club, was reelected to the Polo Association. The new polo grounds were in The Plains, a few miles south of Middleburg. Some of the prewar old gang remained: Raymond Belmont, John

Gaines, Walter Goodwin, Fletcher Harper and William Skinker. They were joined by Thomas Atkinson, Maj. Louis Beard, Barrington Elliott, E. Carter Foster, H. Sage Goodwin, Walter Goodwin, Jr., Barry Hall, William Hulbert, Charles Oliver Iselin, Jr., John Walker, Arthur White and Rodney Woodward.

In 1927, the club became the Fauquier-Loudon Polo Association. D. Bachelder, R. Bishop, William Emory, H. Frost, H. Frost, Jr., W. Frost, Richard Kirkpatrick, John Skinner, Baldwin Spilman, Jr., Albert Stagg and Turner Wiltshire were the new additions.

The second polo club in Virginia was Melrose, in Casanova, which affiliated with the Polo Association in 1916. The ten initial members included William Weightman, the delegate; R.B. Barrett, a Mr. Drake, H.L. Edmonds, F.J. Grace, Orson Hoyt, William Wilbur, J. Williams and Samuel Wortham. It also had among its members a man of the cloth, the Rev. William Marshall. The club closed in 1921.

CHAPTER 10

The Open Championship
After World War I

The return of polo to normalcy after the war did not take place until 1919. Only three teams competed for the Open Championship held at the Philadelphia Country Club ground in Bala, in late September. Cooperstown — Louis Stoddard, Tommy Hitchcock, Pad Rumsey, Robert Strawbridge, Jr. — took the measure of Rockaway — Perry Beadleston, Earle W. Hopping, Malcolm Stevenson, Robert Strawbridge, Sr. — by six goals to 3¾. In the final match, Meadow Brook — Frederick Prince, Jr., J. Watson Webb, Frank von Stade, Sr., Devereux Milburn — took the championship by 5 goals to 4.

There was much more year-round polo activity in 1920, starting in Camden, South Carolina, on January 3 and extending to September 26 in Dayton, Ohio. The Open Championship was played at Meadow Brook during the already traditional month of September. Four teams competed: Bryn Mawr, Cooperstown, Meadow Brook and Rockaway. The final game matched Cooperstown versus the host team. It was not much of a contest, Meadow Brook taking both match and championship, scoring 12 goals against three by the occasional adversary. Meadow Brook's foursome was Frank Skiddy von Stade, Sr., J. Watson Webb, Robert Strawbridge, Sr., and Devereux Milburn.[1]

The tournament returned to Bala, Pennsylvania for the 1921 competition. It marked the debut of an Army team in the Open and it was an auspicious one, because that Army

James Watson Webb is the only left-hander to achieve a 10-goal rating. The photograph shows Webb wearing the green and white quartered Shelburne jersey.

team — Maj. Arthur "Jingle" Wilson, Maj. Harry Chamberlin, Lt. Col. Lewis Brown, Jr., and Maj. William Erwin — defeated the host team, Philadelphia Country Club, 10–5. The vagaries of the draw picked the best two teams in the first round. Great Neck — Louis Stoddard, Rodman Wanamaker, II, J. Watson Webb and Robert Strawbridge, Jr. — beat Meadow Brook — Frank von Stade, Capt. Frederick Guest, Elliot Bacon and Devereux Milburn — scoring 9 goals against 8 by the defending champions. This was the first year in which the new rule allowing free hits after a penalty was enacted, doing away with the cumbersome practice of deducting fractions of a goal for fouls and safeties.

Rockaway then postponed the Army team's dream of reaching the finals, only to be defeated by Great Neck in the championship game.

For the first and only time the U.S. Open Championship was held at Rumson Country Club, in New Jersey, following the inaugural Herbert Memorial Tournament.

The inclement weather — the U.S.P.A. Year Book called it "miserable" — that plagued the careful arrangements by the host club continued into the U.S. Open Championship. The expected results carried through the preliminary matches. Shelburne took the measure of Flamingo; Orange County defeated All Ireland and Meadow Brook beat Eastcott, all with great facility. The Argentine Federation team was the beneficiary of a bye into the first semifinal, in which they defeated Shelburne 12–8. In the second semi-final, Meadow Brook beat Orange County by 7 goals to 4.

The final match showed the best two teams in the tournament. The score at halftime was close, 6–4 in favor of the visitors. Early in the fourth period, David Miles collided with Milburn and was almost forced out of the game. Miles remounted, his leg wrapped in polo bandages and adhesive, his foot in a tennis shoe. In an incredible performance David Miles ended as the high scorer in the game, which was taken by the Argentine Polo Federation team 14–7. Dev Milburn, no mean judge of men, said of David Miles, "If there is a better 10-goal player better than David Miles, show me, because I don't see anyone."

Thus, for the second time in its short history, the U.S. Open Championship went to a foreign team, the first one being Ranelagh in 1910.

In 1923 a Meadow Brook foursome took the honors by defeating a British Army team in the final match. The original team — Averell Harriman, Tommy Hitchcock, Robert Strawbridge, Jr., Devereux Milburn — underwent changes when Harriman was injured in the opening match versus the English team wearing the Hurlingham Club's colors. R. Penn Smith took his place, only to be replaced in turn by Morgan Belmont, a higher handicapped player, for the final match. Mr. Penn Smith got the consolation of being on the Meadow Brook team that took the Monty Waterbury Cup, with J. Watson Webb, Frank von Stade and Devereux Milburn.

Just like any year in which there is international polo, the 1924 U.S. Open paled when compared to the Westchester Cup. More than 35,000 spectators watched each match versus England, while the Open Championship and the Monty Waterbury Cup matches were witnessed by about 20,000 people. Ten thousand spectators watched Princeton take away the intercollegiate title from perennial powerhouse Yale. Polo was a hot ticket in those days.

History was written in Westbury because for the first time in the history of the event, the Open Championship was taken by a team from California. The Midwick foursome had traveled east with the purpose of entering in the Junior Championship, played at Rumson Country Club in August, which event they proceeded to win with relative ease. This success encouraged the team to participate in the Open Championship.

The healthy pattern of distributing the 10-goal superstars among different teams was

The picturesque polo grounds at Rumson Country Club on New Jersey's south shore, site of the 1922 U.S. Open Championship.

continued. Thus, Tommy Hitchcock was a member of the Wanderers, Watson Webb played on his own Shelburne, Devereux Milburn with the Freebooters. In the first round, Midwick, with Edgar "Teddy" Miller, Eric Pedley, Arthur Perkins and Carleton Burke, defeated Laddie Sanford's Hurricanes, a team based on the British team that had competed in the Westchester Cup. In spite of Lewis Lacey's efforts, Midwick prevailed 14–11. The eight teams were reduced to four after the preliminary round. In the semifinal, Wanderers defeated Orange County and Midwick did the same with Shelburne. The final match brought victory to the Californians, in spite of Hitchcock's superhuman performance. The final score was 6–5 in favor of Midwick, after trailing in the last period. Henry Lacey, Lewis' younger brother, played at Number 1, with Hitchcock at Number 2, Elmer Boeseke, Jr., another Californian, at Number 3 and Louis Stoddard at Back. It was a struggle of team play against individual brilliancy. As usual, sound combination play prevailed over personal endeavor.

Only four teams entered the 1925 competition. Meadow Brook had C.V. "Sonny" Whitney, Tommy Hitchcock, Elmer Boeseke and Dev Milburn — the clear favorites. They beat the Hurricanes, with Stephen Sanford, Pat Roark, Lord Wodehouse and Maj. Louis Beard by a surprisingly narrow score, 6 goals to 5. Orange County beat Princemere by a substantial margin. The final game, played in late September in front of a large, colorful audience, was another surprise; with Orange County coming from behind three times to finally win 11–9. William Averell Harriman, James Watson Webb, Malcolm Stevenson and John Cheever Cowdin carried the spoils of victory.

An Argentine team of international caliber participated in the 1926 Open Championship. Carlos Land, Jack Nelson, Luis Lacey and Manuel Andrada wore the light blue and white national colors. They defeated Harold Talbott's Roslyn by 10 goals to three and in the semifinals overwhelmed Averell Harriman's Orange County 13–3, after scoring six unanswered goals in the first period. This high-standard performance made them slight favorites in the championship match versus Laddie Sanford's Hurricanes, a team that had found its way by beating Boston's North Shore Princemere by a single tally, 10–9. The final was an epic encounter, one of the best final games in the history of the championship. With the score tied at 6-goals apiece, Sanford picked up a loose ball and, taking advantage of the phenomenal speed of his mare Fairy Story, ran unchallenged towards goal and scored, putting the final touch to a great contest.

The Westchester Cup was played for again in 1927. That story is narrated elsewhere in this book. The Army-in-India team made it to the final game, after taking the best of Eastcott, Earle W. Hopping's team, and then defeating the holders, Hurricanes, by 8 goals to 7 in a most creditable performance. The team was Capt. Richard George, Capt. John Dening, Maj. Eric Atkinson and Lt. Humphrey Guinness. They met Sands Point, a new team made up of Averell Harriman, Thomas Hitchcok, Jr., Louis Stoddard and J. Cheever Cowdin, that had successfully defeated the Magpies and subsequently the U.S. Army team. It was a close contest until early in the third chukker, when in an ill-conceived attempt to score a goal Capt. George crossed behind Cheever Cowdin's pony. Capt. George became a frightful cropper, surviving the accident with only a fractured collar bone, which put him out of action. Lt. Col. George de la Poer Beresford took his place; however, the momentum was lost and Sands Point went on to take the championship by 11 goals to 7.

Once more, 1928 was an international year, that of the first series for the Cup of the Americas between Argentina and the United States. The Argentine team, its pony string depleted by an equine influenza epidemic, did not enter the Open Championship. Nevertheless, three of the team joined local clubs. The burly Back Manuel Andrada played on the Eastcott team, Lewis Lacey was on the Sands Point squad, and Juan Miles wore the robin's egg blue of Meadow Brook. Only four teams competed in this championship, which was played in two consecutive days in October because of the repeated postponements of the Cup of the Americas matches. This situation added fuel to the fire started by those who argued that frequent international games detracted and disrupted the smooth running of the Open and other important tournaments. This isolationist viewpoint is still present in the twenty-first century, as evidenced by the postponement of an international match against Argentina at 30-goal level, scheduled for 2010 in Palm Beach, following the path created by the successful restart of the Westchester Cup in 2009.

Nevertheless, the United States Army team — Capt. Candler Wilkinson, replaced during the first game by Lt. Morton McDonald Jones, Capt. Charles Gerhardt, Capt. Peter Rodes and Capt. George Huthsteiner — beat the Eastcott team by 9 goals to 8 to reach the final game. Meadow Brook then defeated Sands Point, also by only one tally, 10–9, on a goal scored in the ninth period by John Miles.

In the final match, Meadow Brook, with Cornelius V. Whitney, Winston Guest, John Miles and Malcolm Stevenson, ran out the victors by a score of 8 to 5. As an aside, it must be wondered what the reaction would be in 2010 if teams were asked to play the semifinals and the finals of the U.S. Open Championship, back to back, on a Friday and Saturday.

Learning from the lessons of the previous year, the 1929 Open Championship had an earlier start than usual, because the first preliminary match took place in August. Six teams entered and the early games were rather one-sided: Sands Point won over Eastcott and Greentree defeated Old Aiken, a team made up of youngsters that had taken the Junior

Championship and was trying to emulate Midwick's double of 1924. The first semifinal set a record, probably unbroken: Hurricanes beat Roslyn in 12 chukkers. In the last chukker of regulation time, with the scoreboard showing seven goals for each team, Harold Talbott pulled a riding muscle and was unable to continue. Aidan Roark, Pat's younger brother, came in to do battle against his celebrated sibling. The elder Roark ended the stirring contest with what was described as "an inspiring shot."[2] What was remarkable is that Roslyn, trailing 7–2 at halftime, managed to shut down the Hurricanes for all but one minute of eight periods. The period by period scoring is interesting:

Hurricanes	2	1	1	3	0	0	0	0	0	0	0	1
Roslyn	1	0	0	1	3	1	1	0	0	0	0	0

The second semifinal was an amusing game, won by Sands Point 14–10 over Greentree. Sands Point had Averell Harriman, Earle Hopping the younger, Tommy Hitchcock and Charles Schwartz, while Greentree presented Jock Whitney, Elmer Boeseke, Jr., Eric Pedley and Winston Guest. Most people thought Greentree would be easy victors. They probably forgot that it was not wise to count Tommy Hitchcock out. However, Winston Guest, who had played a powerful game at Back against the Argentines in the previous year, decided to concentrate on the offense and let the defense take care of itself, or rather, have Eric Pedley, a natural superb offensive player, take care of the defense. Peter Vischer, editor of the respected *Polo* magazine, wrote:

> As an exhibition of individual prowess, Mr. Guest's performance against Sands Point was quite fascinating. He stormed up and down, hit tremendous shots, achieved some extraordinary results. He even introduced an entirely new idea into the game: given a free shot at the enemy goal, following a foul, he jumped off his horse and started digging up the ground with his heel to make a tee for the ball![3]

The championship game lived up to everyone's expectations, including the 12,000 people who witnessed a beautiful game. Only one foul was whistled by the umpires, Capt. Charles Tremayne and Capt. Wesley White, for an obvious cross. This is a record that surely will never be beaten.[4] The score was tied at 4-all at halftime, very much of a close fight. Capt. Pat Roark played superbly and the left-hander Watson Webb succeeded in keeping Hitchcock at bay. In the seventh period, the game was still

Earle W. Hopping, Sr., and Harold Talbott. Earle senior was a 10-goaler in England, while Talbott played at Dayton, Long Island, Florida and England with a 7-goal handicap.

tied, at seven. Webb scored a huge goal in the seventh, and Hurricanes dominated the final chukker, scoring three more goals.

The decade then closed with Hurricanes repeating its victory of 1929, this time against Templeton, the Guest's family team. Templeton got to the finals by defeating Eastcott 18–4 and Sands Point in the semifinals 16–8. Raymond and Winston Guest, Lewis Lacey and Lt. Humphrey Patrick Guinness, Royal Scots Greys, formed the Templeton squad.

Seven teams entered, including, once more, a youthful Old Aiken team of Elbridge Gerry, James Mills, Stewart Iglehart and Joseph "Cocie" Rathborne, a portent of things to come. Hurricanes made only one change from the 1929 team: Eric Pedley replaced James Watson Webb. They survived a monumental scare in the first round when Roslyn — Harold Talbott, Jr., Cecil Smith, Rube Williams and Gerald Balding — took the heavily favored Hurricanes to a hair-raising 10–9 win in the ninth chukker. The semifinal game between the title holder and Greentree — Pete Bostwick, Elmer Boeseke, Tommy Hitchcock, Jock Whitney — was a dandy, Hurricanes coming out the winners 15–13. It was also, in the opinion of the unnamed *Polo* reporter, one of the roughest that Meadow Brook saw that summer.[5] The umpire, Capt. Wesley White, blew the whistle no less than 13 times, a high figure for those days. Ten of the penalties were converted into goals, five by each side. The championship game was also touch and go, Hurricanes finally prevailing by 6 goals to 5 in a good match. Hurricanes started the final chukker leading 6–4. With less than a minute to go, Lewis Lacey hit an under-the-neck shot for a goal. Templeton won the ensuing throw-in, and, once more, Lacey set sail towards the Hurricanes' goals. His last shot hit a divot and the ball went wide. Lady luck prevented the game from going into overtime.

CHAPTER 11

The Golden Era
of the International Matches

The 1921 Westchester Cup at Hurlingham

In the aftermath of the unexpected defeat suffered by the American team in 1914 at Meadow Brook, the Polo Association was keen to recover the Westchester trophy as soon as feasible. However, the carnage inflicted upon British young men during the Great War, as the first worldwide conflict was then known in Europe, forced a delay to allow England to recover and be able to mount a meaningful contest.

Many British polo players paid the ultimate price during the war. Among the international players who had defeated the United States team in Westbury, Long Island, was one of the greatest ever, Capt. Leslie St. Clair Cheape, killed on Easter Sunday in Palestine. Another player from that team, Capt. Herbert Wilson, and Lt. A. Noel Edwards, from the 1911 and 1913 international teams, also died. Promising and accomplished players that surely would have been candidates for international honor after the war, such as the twins Francis and Rivy Grenfell, Lt. Edward Leatham and Lt. Brian Osborne, also lost their lives in the war to end all wars.

American polo players also were killed in the conflict, most notably Maj. Augustus Peabody Gardner, a polo player from Myopia Hunt Club and a member of Congress who resigned his seat to join the army, and 2nd Lieut. Charles W. Plummer, 88th Aero Squadron, a Harvard graduate shot down in his plane over the Vesle River in August 1918.

When the Polo Association made overtures to challenge for the cup in 1920, the Hurlingham Polo Committee, the ruling body of the game in the United Kingdom, requested that the contest be postponed for one year. This was agreed to by the Americans. Nevertheless, preparations began in earnest. The players were selected and a formidable string of polo ponies was assembled and sent to England under the care of H.V. Colt in December of 1920, well ahead of the scheduled matches for the month of June.

Devereux Milburn was appointed team captain and the rest of the squad consisted of Tommy Hitchcock, at the time an undergraduate at Brasenose College in Oxford, J. Watson Webb, Louis Stoddard, and Charles "Pad" Rumsey. Upon arrival in England, the American team was lavishly entertained by their hosts, most notably by Buck's Club members.[1] The visitors were also invited to a luncheon with King George V. Regrettably, Devereux Milburn was unable to attend because of an attack of lumbago. Most sportingly, the English players conveyed to the Hurlingham Polo Committee their wish that the first match be postponed. The good sportsmanship reflected in the English players' request was not supported by the

Committee, which citing the lateness of the request and the fact that no postponement was asked by the Americans, reluctantly decided that the match should take place. At any rate, Milburn recovered and took his place on the team.

In front of an audience that included King George V, Queen Alexandra, Princess Victoria, the Prince of Wales and Alfonso XIII, King of Spain, the match started under a bright sun. England lined up with Lt. Col. Henry Tomkinson, Maj. Frederick Barrett, Lord Wodehouse and Maj. Vivian Lockett. The United States, wearing white shirts, were represented by Louis Stoddard, Thomas Hitchcock, Jr., Watson Webb and Devereux Milburn.

The American team took off in the first chukker on goals by Webb and Hitchcock and was never headed during the match. The score's progression tells the story: 2–0, 3–1, 5–3, 5–4, 7–4, 9–4 and 11–4 at the end of the seventh and final period. J. Watson Webb was high scorer with five tallies; Hitchcock scored four goals and Milburn and Stoddard, one each. For England, Tomkinson scored three goals and Barrett one.

The teams remained the same for the second match. Once more, the American team pressed hard from the first throw-in and finished the period three-nil on two goals by Webb and one by Stoddard. This three-goal cushion obtained by the Americans proved fatal for the British team, because the final tally was 10–6 in favor of the challengers. Essentially, the British played even with the Americans for the game's last six chukkers. Louis Stoddard scored four goals, Watson Webb three, Hitchcock two and Dev Milburn closed the proceedings with a penalty shot. On the British team, Barrett, Tomkinson and Lord Wodehouse scored two goals each.

Thus the Westchester Cup returned to America, in whose hands it would remain until 1997. The large American contingent that had traveled to England to witness the series celebrated the victory with unabashed joy. The staid British supporters watched with a mixture of surprise and bewilderment when a long conga line was formed by American men and women in an impromptu celebration of their team's success.

The Argentine Polo Federation Tour

In 1922 a team representing the Argentine Polo Federation, an organization recently created in an attempt to change the archaic ways of the Polo Association of the River Plate, traveled to England with their own pony string.[2] The team — Juan Miles, Jack Nelson, David Miles and Lewis Lacey — was unbeaten during the London season, taking the Hurlingham Champion Cup and the Roehampton Open Cup. The second string team also took several tournaments. The team's success resulted in an invitation from the U.S. Polo Association for the team to cross the North Atlantic to participate in the U.S. Open Championship and other tournaments.

The Argentine team made its debut at the Rumson Country Club in New Jersey, competing in the Herbert Memorial Trophy. Giving five goals by handicap to the Orange County team — Averell Harriman, Charles Rumsey, Malcolm Stevenson and Morgan Belmont — the visitors were defeated 13–10. The game was played on a ground that was soaked from an all-day rain that continued to fall during most of the match, making heavy demands on the players.

The two other foreign teams, Eastcott and All Ireland, failed to get past the first round, being defeated by Flamingo (James Cooley, Harry East, Benjamin Gatkins, Frederick Prince, Jr.) and Shelburne (Louis Stoddard, Raymond Belmont, Watson Webb, Robert Strawbridge,

Jr.). The Herbert Memorial Trophy, established in memory of the longest serving U.S.P.A. chairman, was taken by Meadow Brook, with Frank von Stade, Sr., Tommy Hitchcock, Elliot Bacon and Devereux Milburn.

The 1922 U.S. Open Championship has been described in Chapter 10, The Open Championship after World War I.

The quality of play shown by the Argentines was such that there was really a popular demand for a series between the American international team that had recovered the Westchester Cup the previous year, and the Argentine team. Louis Stoddard, who had played so well at Number 1 at Hurlingham, was unable to take part because of an injury; his place was then taken by James Calvin Cooley. For some unknown reason, the team played under the name Meadow Brook.

The matches were held at the Meadow Brook Club on October 4 and 7. In two close matches the Meadow Brook foursome, Cooley, Hitchcock, Webb and Milburn, restored the American superiority in the realm of polo, winning both games by scores of 7–4 and 5–4.

The Argentines had unequivocally demonstrated at Hurlingham and Rumson that there was a new power in world polo. However, the results of the series at Meadow Brook showed that the United States was still on top of the heap.

Two days before the start of the matches against the Argentine Polo Federation team, an interesting game took place at Meadow Brook. Louis Stoddard, Tommy Hitchcock, Watson Webb and Devereux Milburn, a 40-goal team, faced Flamingo: James Cooley, Harry East, Malcolm Stevenson and Frederick Prince, Jr. Giving eight goals by handicap, Meadow Brook was defeated 16–11. This was the first instance of a 40-goal team taking the field.

Polo historian Dennis Amato would argue with some validity that the "Big Four" was the first 40-goal team in the history of the game. The Waterbury brothers, Whitney and Milburn, were raised to 10-goals by the Hurlingham Polo Committee following their victory in the 1909 Westchester Cup. However, the Polo Association in America did not award the 10-goal rating to Milburn and Whitney until 1917, when Whitney had already retired from international polo. With the exception of Milburn, it was essentially an honorary rating, because the Waterbury brothers were also given a 10-goal handicap in 1917. They had previously been rated at 10-goals; Larry in 1900 and Monte in 1902. The bottom line is that the Big Four were a 40-goal team, but they never played competitively together with the magic 10 after their names.

1924 The Westchester Cup at Meadow Brook

The 1924 challenge by the Hurlingham Club's Polo Committee resulted in what was the weakest series for the Westchester Cup. The main reason was the disparity in quality of play between the two teams. America's colors were, once more, worn by four men who were eventually tagged with the sobriquet "the second Big Four." James Watson Webb, the left-hander now playing at Number 1; the incomparable Tommy Hitchcock, Malcolm Stevenson and Devereux Milburn, mounted on the best ponies money could buy, constituted an unbeatable combination.

Britain was represented in the main by serving army officers. Maj. Thomas "Billy" Kirkwood and Lt. Col. Teighnmouth Melvill alternated at Number 1, while Maj. Frank Hurndall and Maj. Geoffrey Phipps-Hornby did the same in the Number 2 slot. Maj. Eric Atkinson played in the pivot position. Canada-born Lewis Lacey, one of the world's top players, was at Back. However, it was an ailing Lewis Lacey. During a practice match he sustained a shoulder injury that required a mechanical contraption in order to protect the shoulder's socket. To this injury, an acute attack of shingles was added, a benign but painful viral condition on his chest that presented itself just before the start of the series.

The presence of the Prince of Wales on the stands did much to assure substantial gate receipts and was a source of great moral support for the embattled British team. Nevertheless, no amount of royal encouragement could alter the imbalance on the field of play. In spite of Lacey's superhuman efforts, ably supported by Eric Atkinson, the disparity between the two teams was enormous. The final scores, 16–5 and 14–5, are indicative of what transpired on the polo grounds.

1927 The Westchester Cup

Three years later, once more at Meadow Brook, it was a different story, although when all was said and done the final result was identical: America wins!

The United States presented, for the last time, the Second Big Four. It would be the swansong for team captain Devereux Milburn, one of polo's immortals, who had come into the limelight with his magnificent performance at Hurlingham's Number 1 polo ground in the unforgettable year of 1909. It would also be the last international appearance of J. Watson Webb, a player who no other than Lewis Lacey thought the most difficult to contain. The redoubtable and stern Mike Stevenson was at Number 3, almost in the twilight of a most distinguished polo trajectory. And, at Number 2, it was Tommy Hitchcock, near the crest of an outstanding polo career.

To face the daunting task of recovering the Westchester Cup, the Hurlingham Polo Committee, the ruling body of the game in England, took a gamble. Amidst much opposition, the H.P.C. asked the Indian Polo Association to select, provide appropriate funding, and represent Britain in this challenge.

The selected players were Capts. John Dening, Richard George, Claude Pert and Charles "Pat" Roark, and Majors Eric Atkinson and Austin Williams. Lt. Col. George de la Poer Beresford was in charge of the polo pony string. Pert, Williams, Roark and Atkinson played in the first match. Following an unsatisfactory performance from the British point of view, Capts. George and Dening replaced Capts. Pert and Williams. This new lineup played very well; the three unanswered goals scored by the Big Four in the first chukker was the difference at match's end.

The matches were ably described by Frank S. Butterworth in *The Sportsman*:

The long trail, the high hopes, the tremendous preparations for lifting the highly prized international sport trophy, The Westchester Cup, ended for the British in defeat in two straight games on September 10 and 14, after magnificent polo. No more inspiring or more perfectly played game has been seen in any match between England and America that the first one played by the American four, each of whom equaled or surpassed the best game he had ever shown.

Four men that day played unbeatable polo, and England was overwhelmed, scoring only three goals, while America scored from one to three goals in every period excepting the second. And because England was outpaced and outplayed by super polo, the game was not a great contest; the joy came in seeing such fine individual and team play, at a speed that few of us will see again on any field.

From the first throw-in America seized the ball, assumed the mastery, and began scoring, piling up 13 goals. Team captain Milburn played his best game. It was quickly evident that Stevenson

Trophy presentation following the 1927 Westchester Cup. Mrs. Thomas Hitchcock, Sr., her son Tommy, Malcolm Stevenson, Watson Webb and Devereux Milburn.

was in rare form, and that Milburn could play with confidence that his Number 3 was not only in harmony but effective, and the great Back proceeded to open up all his longest and best shots in defending his goal and turning to offense.

It was Hitchcock, the incomparable, who set the standard of play. His influence on the team is almost as remarkable as his individual skill — so remarkable, indeed, that it can almost be said that as Hitchcock plays, so will the team play. His own scoring ability, out of 13 goals he scored six, his feeding to others, his talent for coming back on occasions and getting the ball and sending or carrying it to the antagonist's goal, his booming drives, and his ability to hit all sorts of shots and score from difficult angles. His knowledge of polo and team play were all shown from the start.

At Number 1, the most difficult position in polo, Webb played his elevated game. Well mounted, true and at times uncanny in his hitting, always in his place for scoring or riding-off, and showing skill in handling Atkinson, he, too, played at top speed and form. The two British defensive players, Atkinson and Roark, played better than the forwards, and there were flashes of team play. The hitting of the British four was not accurate, and it was not improved by the hurrying that they were subjected.

The second game, however, was not a runaway. In fact, barring the first period, in which Hitchcock scored three times, it was a hard fought game. Those three tallies were the difference at day's end, the score being 8–5. For this second game, captains Dening and George replaced Williams and Pert. Dening particularly, made a difference in the match. On the other hand, the American team could not possibly duplicate their form of the first day.[3]

1928 The Cup of the Americas at Meadow Brook

The wishes of the Argentine Polo Association for a more prominent role in international polo could not be met by their entry into the challenges for the Westchester Cup. Lord Cowdray, representing the Hurlingham Polo Committee, and Louis Stoddard, on behalf of the U.S. Polo Association, made it quite clear to Juan Nelson during his visit to America in 1927 that competition for the Westchester Cup was entirely restricted to teams representing England and the United States. Therefore, Mr. Nelson proposed a series for the Championship of the Americas. This challenge was readily taken by the U.S.P.A., to the chagrin and indignation of the Federación de Polo de Mexico, which objected strongly to their national team being left by the wayside. For all their good intentions and justified annoyance, the level of polo in Mexico in the late 1920s did not came close to the high level achieved over the years by the Americans and lately reached by Argentina.

There was unnecessary turmoil in the selection process for the American team. With the retirement of Devereux Milburn from international polo the American captaincy passed unto the hands of Thomas Hitchcock, Jr., and the laborious series of selection matches began. James Watson Web announced that he would not be a candidate; this left the middle of the team rock-solid with Hitchcock and Mike Stevenson. The question was: Who would be Number 1 and who would be Back?

Early form indicated that Capt. Candler Wilkinson would be the best in the forward position; however, he played himself, as well as his mounts, into the ground and lost his sharp edge. This left Averell Harriman and Laddie Sanford as the most likely candidates. Stephen Sanford was selected. Newly appointed captain Tommy Hitchcock would have none of that; he wanted Harriman to play. In the last practice match, the Argentine reserve, strongman Manuel Andrada played opposite Laddie Sanford. Although beautifully mounted, Laddie was averse to heavy bumping. Andrada took Sanford out of the picture during the entire game. Sanford was out and Harriman in, even though the program had already been printed with Stephen Sanford's photograph and his position listed at Number 1.[4]

At Back, the issue came down to John Cheever Cowdin and Winston Guest. Cowdin was selected. Once more, Hitchcock threw his considerable weight around and Guest was inserted into the lineup at the eleventh hour. These two instances resulted in an unseemly public humiliation of two popular American players, as Richard Ely Danielson put it in the magazine *The Sportsman*.[5] J. Cheever Cowdin took his demotion very hard; his dream of representing his country, as his father John Elliott Cowdin had done before him, was shattered. Cowdin quit polo and moved to California.

For their part, the Argentines selected Arturo Kenny, a gentleman-rider of great repute on the flat, at Number 1; team captain Juan Diego "Jack" Nelson at Number 2, Juan B. Miles in the pivot position and Lewis Lacey at Back. The pony string, one of the strongest to leave the River Plate shore, became the Achilles' heel of the South American enterprise. An equine influenza laid the entire contingent low; it would be a considerable amount of time before they would be able to regain their true form. A sporting offer by the U.S.P.A. to lend available mounts was politely — and perhaps foolishly — rejected with thanks by the Argentine delegation. Thomas Nelson, Jack's cousin, was in charge of the ponies. Tommy moved in the stables at Mitchel Field, adjacent to the Meadow Brook Club, and worked tirelessly to restore the ponies' health. The start of the series was postponed. When it started, it became the most competitive international polo series up to that time.

The first match, played in a light drizzle, proved to be anybody's game; many keen observers felt that the American team was lucky to win by one goal, 7 to 6. The rain made Arturo Kenny's glasses foggy, with the result that with impaired vision he had difficulty with his shots at goal and positional play.

The second match saw the Argentine team in top form, winning by 10 goals to 7. This defeat, the first on home ground since 1914, made changes necessary. Banking his team chances on a totally offensive mode, Tommy Hitchcock moved to Stevenson's slot at Number 3, and Earle Hopping, the younger, made his international debut at Number 2.

Soon after the start of the third and decisive game, it became obvious that the Argentine ponies were not in the game. Three hard matches in the space of eight days were too much for the hard-pressed, convalescent ponies. The United States ended up comfortable winners, scoring 13 goals against seven by the Argentines.

In the chronicle of international matches in the twentieth century, there can be no possible doubt that the contests between Argentine and America were the most interesting and very assuredly the most closely contested. It was a wonderful beginning to a series that, most regrettably, has not been resumed since 1980.

The Argentine Ponies

Several of the Argentines ponies bought for high prices at auction did not perform according to expectations. Two prime examples were the mare Judy and the gelding Jupiter, both purchased by John Sanford for his son Laddie. The hammer prices at Post's auctions in Westbury were $13,000 and $22,000, both top prices at the 1926 and 1928 sales, respectively. Judy, champion polo pony in Argentina, was awarded the Best in Show prize at the Meadow Brook meet. Jupiter was a big, magnificent horse in the right hands. Difficult to ride, only Lacey's masterful equitation got the best out of Jupiter. Both failed in high-goal polo; Judy just faded away and Jupiter had his jaw broken while being ridden by Dev Milburn. The poor chestnut ended his life pulling a cart at the Sanfords' farm in Amsterdam, New York.

The Irishman Capt. Charles T.I. Roark, a 10-goal player, was in charge of Sanford's polo pony string and thought that both horses were duds. This had Mr. John Nelson by the ears because he felt that Jupiter and Judy were two of the best polo ponies ever to leave the shores of Argentina. Jack Nelson, who had successfully trained and played Judy, went to see the horses and found them looking like stuffed owls. Mr. Nelson was of the opinion that both ponies had been over-fed and under-exercised by Sanford's handlers, a remark that Capt. Pat Roark did not appreciate. Jack Nelson, one of Argentina's most respected breeders, who knew a thing or two about horses, was of the opinion that some polo ponies, such as Judy, had to be worked into the ground to get them appropriately conditioned for high-goal polo.[6]

1930 The Westchester Cup

England tried, once more, to recover the Westchester Cup in 1930. Their selection committee went through a large number of practice matches, some said far too many, trying to figure out what would be the best combination to face the formidable American team. Capt. Charles Tremayne, a veteran 7-goal player, was appointed to be team captain as well as being in charge of selection of the team's other three members. The rationale given by Lord Cowdray, chairman of the Hurlingham Polo Committee, was that that was the most likely way to ensure that those selected would be a team, rather than four individual players. Capt. Maurice Kingscote, from the Cirencester Club, was in charge of the ponies.[7]

The English side as originally selected was Maj. Geoffrey Phipps-Hornby, Capt. Pat Roark, Capt. Tremaine and Lt. Humphrey Guinness. The initial trial matches did not bode well for the team. It became clear to observers that both Maj. Phipps-Hornby, a member of the 1924 team, and Captain Tremayne were not up to the international standards required to offer battle to the Americans. Several changes were made during the ensuing trial matches at Beaufort, Hurlingham and Roehampton. Lewis Lacey, the world's best Back at the time, was inserted at Number 1; although his opponent was his friend Johnny Traill, another 10-goaler, Lacey played remarkably well. The rest of the team was Gerald Balding, Pat Roark, and his brother Aidan at Back. Eventually, that was the selected team.

For its part, the U.S.P.A. announced the names of 16 players invited to participate in the official test matches. Thomas Hitchcock, Jr., was appointed captain and chairman of the Defense Committee, and was also given the power to select its members. In other words, Tommy Hitchcock was allowed to have absolute control. For his committee, Hitchcock chose the savvy Carleton Burke, his father Thomas Hitchcock, who had played in the 1886 contest, David Iglehart, George Mead, Charles Schwartz and John Hay Whitney. The trial matches began in July, at a rate of two a week on the grounds of Piping Rock and Sands Point. The final selection fell upon Eric Pedley, whom Tommy Hitchcock thought was the best American Number 1 ever, the young Earle A.S. Hopping, proven as an asset in the 1928 final match against Argentina, and, at Back, Winston Guest.

The English team had to make a last-minute change because Aidan Roark developed an infection in his throat. He was replaced by Lt. Humphrey Guinness. Gerald Balding played Number 1, Lacey at Number 2, and Pat Roark at Number 3. The problem was that the team, both in practices and during the series, did not possess a true Number 1.

The Americans ran victors with relative ease, although the general opinion was that this was the most serious threat to the United States supremacy since the series were resumed after the war.[8] The games were far closer than the five-goal differential in both games. The first match was quite even, 7–5, until the seventh chukker, when the American team went into high-gear on its way to a 10–5 win. In the second game the English team started ahead; however, in a critical sixth chukker the British ponies appeared to be "cooked" and the Unites States team pulled away for a 14–9 victory.[9] Horse power, as usual, made the difference. Eric Pedley made the most of his many chances at goal, while Gerald Balding had

The 1930 Westchester Cup at Meadow Brook. Pat Roark breaks away, followed by Tommy Hitchcock (3), Lewis Lacey (2), Winston Guest (52 on saddle-cloth) and Gerald Balding. Earle Hopping the younger is in the foreground.

fewer shots at goal during the entire series than Pedley had in a few periods. The offensive spirit advocated by Tommy Hitchcock in his pre-game instructions (still being quoted in print) paid handsome dividends.

1932 The Cup of the Americas at Palermo

In the spring of 1932, arrangements were made to send a squad of players to Argentina under the leadership and direction of Carleton Burke. The six players were Elmer Boeseke, Jr., Winston Guest, Stewart Iglehart, Seymour Knox, Michael Phipps and Joseph Cornelius "Cocie" Rathborne. Later, James Mills and William Post, II, were added to the team. Surprisingly, young Earle Hopping, who had played so well in the international contests of 1928 and 1930, was left aside. As to Tommy Hitchcock, it was mentioned that pressures of work prevented him from traveling to South America.

Twenty mounts were shipped to Buenos Aires. They left New York on 16 June aboard the *Clan Grande* in charge of Paul Amos, and two more were forwarded from Australia by the Ashton brothers. Some other 20-odd horses were to be placed at the disposal of the players in Argentina by the Argentine Polo Association. Of the twenty ponies going forward, five were owned by the U.S.P.A., four by Seymour Knox, three each by Guest, Iglehart and Phipps, and two by Rathborne. Of the two traveling from Australia, one was consigned for

Californian Carleton Burke took the 1924 U.S. Open and was a successful manager, leading U.S. teams to victory in the Cup of the Americas, the Argentine Open and the West team in the East-West series.

Guest and one for Phipps. It is interesting to note that of the twenty mounts that went to Argentina from the United States, ten were geldings, nine mares, and one a stallion. As to breeding, thirteen were Argentineans going back home, three were bred in the United States, two from Chile, one Australian, and one English.

It was a young team; certainly not the strongest side the United States could have assembled, because it lacked Tommy Hitchcock. This not only meant that it lacked the greatest player in the land but it missed a playing captain tested by the fire of competition, an active leader known to have an unsurpassed will to win.

On the other hand, the team had in Carleton Burke an experienced leader who could direct his young charges from the sidelines. Carty Burke played a significant role in American polo in 1924, when he took a team of youngsters from California to New York ostensibly to win the Junior Championship, and ended up by taking not only the Junior but the Open Championship as well.

The team had international experience, because Boeseke had played on the United

States team captained by Tommy Hitchcock in the Olympic tournament on 1924 at Paris, and Winston Guest had appeared twice at Meadow Brook, against Argentina in 1928 and against England in 1930.

A strange official communiqué was then issued by the U.S.P.A., stating in part: "If the team picked is successful in the Open Championship of the Argentine it will represent the United States in an International series with a team representing Argentina on the dates named."[10]

Whether "successful" in the Argentine Open meant winning the championship, it was not indicated. There are several other references to this imposition by the U.S. Polo Association upon their Argentine counterpart. It is hard to imagine that the international series would not have been held, under some banner or other. The expense of hosting a visiting team was an enormous financial task for the Argentine Polo Association in the lean years of the 1930s; therefore, gate receipts were absolutely essential to cover the expenditures.

Nevertheless, the U.S.P.A. has demonstrated an ambivalent attitude in regard to international contests. There are some examples of such attitude. The first Championship of the Americas in 1928, as the Cup of the Americas was then known, had no permanent trophy of its own. Robert Kelley stated that an appropriate cup was to be presented to the winning team and the announcement was very nearly made when the conservative faction within the U.S. Polo Association won the day, holding that the Westchester Cup must remain the feature of international polo.[11] Therefore, only individual trophies were awarded. A photograph of the American team receiving a large cup from Mrs. Louise Hitchcock is shown in the 1929 U.S.P.A. Year Book. This particular trophy has not been traced. In the 1936 contest, the American team, instead of the customary national team's white colors, wore a red jersey in the first match and Jock Whitney's Greentree pink colors in the second, a reminder that perhaps the U.S. Polo Association did not really consider the Cup of the Americas a true international event. In 1949, in Buenos Aires, the American team displayed Meadow Brook's colors in both the International 30-goal series and in the World Championship. The same situation occurred in the 1953 Coronation Cup in England, when the American team appeared in Meadow Brook's blue colors.

Another request made by the U.S. Polo Association was that Tommy Nelson, who had earned his laurels in the 1928 series, be placed in charge of the American polo string. This request was honored by the Argentine Polo Association. Mr. Nelson, once more, won kudos for his superb work in preparing the American team's mounts.

After several practice games and participation of a few American players in local teams competing in the Hurlingham Club's Open Championship, a Meadow Brook team was selected to enter in the Argentine Open. Mike Phipps, Winston Guest, Elmer Boeseke, Jr., and William Post defeated Venado Tuerto, a 16-goal team, by 19 goals to 6. In the semifinals, the Meadow Brook team beat Hurlingham, a 25-goal side, in a disappointing performance, with both Guest and Boeseke, the latter having difficulties with his mounts, showing poor form. The final score, 11–5, did not reflect the flow of the game. Only a superior performance by Billy Post at Back saved the day for Meadow Brook. In a drastic move, by the time the final match came about, Boeseke and Phipps changed positions.[12] Their opponent in the final match was Santa Paula, the holders of the U.S. Open Championship. However, it was not the full Santa Paula team. Juan Reynal had his leg just out of a cast and it was thought unwise for him to risk playing. Bad luck continued to pursue Alfredo Harrington, Santa Paula's Number 1. Just before the finals at Meadow Brook, Harrington had his leg shattered when entering the ring during the Polo Pony Show. This time around, his leg was again broken during the Hurlingham Open. Luis Nelson, Jack's brother, replaced him in the Open Championship.

Nevertheless, in a stirring match, in which Santa Paula led most of the way, Meadow Brook eked out a narrow victory, 8 goals to 7.

The American team selected to play in the international series was Mike Phipps, Elmer Boeseke, Winston Guest and Billy Post. They wore white shirts with two horizontal red and blue bands. Argentina lined up with Arturo Kenny, Jack Nelson, both veterans of the 1928 series; and José Reynal and Manuel Andrada, Santa Paula's bulk wards. It turned

Mike Phipps, Winston Guest, Elmer Boeseke and Billy Post achieved a magnificent double in 1932: the Argentine Open Championship and the Cup of the Americas. This foursome created history as the only foreign team that took the Abierto at Palermo.

out to be a wonderful contest. The first match ended with a 9 to 6 goals win for the American team; the second game went to Argentina, 8–7 in a sudden death extra chukker, and the decisive match a 12–10 score in favor of the United States.

The Cup of the Americas series received ample coverage, James Mills writing for *Polo* and Cocie Rathborne for *The Sportsman*. Here we have Cocie Rathborne's report:

> I went in with Tommy Nelson with the ponies the day of the first match, and how those horses traveled six times from Hurlingham to Palermo and back, without ever injuring one another or themselves, is incredible. They are ridden into freight cars, lined up twelve and at times fourteen in a car alongside each other, closely packed in, and have to ride for an hour on a very bumpy train. Each petisero (groom) squats down in front of the horse's front legs, and why none of them were not trampled upon is another mystery. Then on arriving at Palermo the horses are ridden and led through heavy traffic for about five or six blocks before they reach the field.
>
> As far as the ponies go, I believe we had a slight edge. I was talking to Fred Post on the boat going home, and his idea was that our ponies stood up better, and were in better condition. He felt that Tommy Nelson had used more "horse sense" in training our ponies and that they showed it on the field. Our ponies were not as fast, perhaps, as some of the Argentines but they were under control much better.
>
> The Argentines were better horsemen than we, with the exception of Billy Post. They seemed able to get to the ball quicker, and get around quicker. The hitting was in our favor, especially with our forward shots, which proved to be much longer than theirs and showed the result of practicing at speed on good grounds.
>
> If I were asked for any special reason why we won, I should say it was because we were able to break the teamwork between Andrada and José Reynal, and thus "upset their apple cart," as Carty Burke put it. When we were beaten in the second game it was because our players played a defensive game and did not break up their opponents' offense.[13]

This time there was a handsome trophy to be presented to the winners. The Cup of the Americas was manufactured by Mappin & Webb, based upon an ornate design known as the Warwick Vase, now part of the Burrell Collection in Glasgow, Scotland.[14]

Thus, the young American team returned to New York bearing two of the most important trophies in the world of polo: The Argentine Open Championship Cup and the Cup of the Americas.

1935 Presidente Abelardo Rodríguez Luján Cup

In April of 1934, an American Army polo team traveled to Mexico City to compete for a cup presented by Mexico's president Abelardo Rodríguez Luján. The following players were selected: Maj. Charles Smith, Maj. Joseph Swing, Capt. Chester "Stub" Davis, Capt. Lucien Truscott, Lt. Charles McFarland and Lt. Gordon Rogers, all experienced players.

The first match was held on April 8, resulting in a victory for the U.S. Army team of Capt. Davis, Maj. Smith, Capt. Truscott and Lt. McFarland alternating at Number 3, and Maj. Swing. The Mexican Army team lined up with Capt. Jesús Gracia, Capt. Antonio Nava, Capt. Antonio Pérez and General Quiñones. The final score was 12–4.

The next game, played on April 15 between the same two teams, with the exception of Capt. Truscott who was injured, resulted in a close win for the Americans, 9–8. With the series defined, an exhibition game was played on April 22. Lt. Rogers alternated with Capt. Smith and Capt. Truscott returned to the lineup replacing Maj. Swing at Back. The Mexican Army team, Captains Gracia, Nava, Quintín Reyes and Pérez, won by 7 goals to 5. All the games took place at Campo de Marte, the site of the 2008 F.I.P. World Championship.

This same team represented Mexico in a return series played at Potomac Park in Washington, D.C., in September. The U.S. Army team was Capt. Chester Davis, Lt. Edwin Walker, Lt. George Read, Jr., and Major Charles Smith. Both games were taken by the American Army team, by scores of 11–6 and 12–8. Following the precedent set in Mexico City, an exhibition game was held at the conclusion of the series. In this match, Lt. John Stadler replaced Maj. Smith. The American team was again victorious, 14–4.

1936 The Westchester Cup at Hurlingham

The Westchester Cup was intended to be played for every three years in the holder's home grounds. The economic situation did not allow the Hurlingham Polo Committee to launch a challenge in 1933; therefore the next challenge was scheduled for the year of the Olympic Games, in the month of June. The Hurlingham Club in Fulham, a London suburb, was the venue.

The United States Polo Association planned the overseas journey with care. A drawback was Tommy Hitchcock's absence from the team. Winston Guest, by now a seasoned international player, was trusted with the team's captaincy, playing the Back position. Stewart Iglehart, about to reach a 10-goal handicap, played at Number 3. The forwards slot presented a bit of a problem, because both Michael Phipps and Eric Pedley excelled in that critical position. The decision was made to place there Eric Pedley, while Mike Phipps, a much better Number 1 than a Number 2, went to the second forward position. In the event, Phipps was far from his best, particularly in the first game. The reserves were Elbridge Gerry and Robert Strawbridge, Jr. Of note is that Cecil Smith, already having achieved a 10-goal handicap, who was playing the London season on Charles Wrightsman's Texas Rangers team, was not invited to be part of the American squad. No reason was given for this notorious omission.

Eric Pedley was thought by Tommy Hitchcock to be the best American player at Number 1.

The British had some problems with their selection. A year before the Westchester Cup was held, a Hurlingham team was sent to Long Island to compete in the U.S. Open Championship. The team—Capt. Hugh Walford, Capt. Percival "Tony" Sanger, Eric Tyrrell-Martin and Capt. Humphrey Guinness—was defeated in the first round. Capt. Michael Ansell replaced Capt. "Chicken" Walford in the Monty Waterbury Cup. Things did not go well either in this handicap tournament. A scratch team, Long Island, beat Hurlingham 16–10, after receiving one-goal by handicap from Hurlingham. After wholesale changes, the British team that took the field had the benefit of only one practice game playing together. Hesketh Hughes, Gerald Balding, Eric Tyrrell-Martin and Humphrey Guinness made up a 31-goal side that matched the American team as to total handicap. Capt. Bryan Fowler and Capt. George Prior-Palmer were selected as alternates. Rao Rajah Hanut Singh, the brilliant 9-goaler from India, was unable to play because of a shoulder injury sustained during one of the practice matches.

The team selected did not enjoy the confidence of the London press corps. Peter Vischer, *Horse & Horseman*'s editor who had traveled to England to report on the series, wrote that the announcement was greeted with catcalls and boos of the London newspapers, which were particularly cruel to Hesketh Hughes, being told in no uncertain terms that he was no polo player.[15]

The United States took the first match 10–9, with a little bit of luck on their side. It was such a close match that either side could easily have been the winner. The American weakness at Number 2 was not of major importance on Hurlingham's Number 1 ground, because it was considerably shorter than Meadow Brook's International Field. Therefore, Iglehart and Guest, both long-hitters, were able to reach Pedley who had 24 shots at goal in the series, scoring a total of 11 goals, the highest of any player on the field. Mike Phipps had a total of four shots in both games, scoring only once.

Stewart Iglehart was the outstanding player on the American side. He had to do plenty of work because of the sag at Number 2, and also had to protect his own goal to cover Winston Guest's frequent forays up-field. In his international debut, Iglehart rose to the challenge in rare form and showed admirable style.

Winston Guest was an important factor in America's victory. His hitting was excellent, long and accurate. However, he paid little attention to the British attacks and was frequently out of position, adding considerably to Iglehart's worries.

The second game was played ten days after the first because of intermittent rains, which made the luscious turf at Hurlingham virtually unplayable. It was another grand match, won by the Americans 8–6 after a terrific battle.

As to the British, they surprised their supporters and confounded their critics. They proved beyond any doubt how wrong they had been in their pre-games dire predictions. Hesketh Hughes, the hardy Welshman who had received his polo education in Argentina, amply justified his selection, scoring a total of nine goals, by far the highest of his team. In the first game, Hughes accomplished perfect accuracy in his strikes at the American goal: six shots, six goals. It is sad to record that Hugh Hesketh Hughes, a 2nd Lieutenant in the Welsh Guards, was killed near Dunkirk in the early stages of World War II.

Both Gerald Balding and Eric Tyrrell-Martin played high-class polo in the middle of the field, where most games are won and lost. Humphrey Guinness was once more the star of the British team, showing his development as a great Back since the 1930 contest. His knock-ins were of great length, as good as Winston Guest's, and he also made a great number of saves near his goal. His weakness, if any, was that he permitted himself to ride inferior mounts, in comparison to the rest of the players.

Thus, a Westchester Cup series that most observers though would end in a comfortable success for the American team turned out to be one of the best ever, and certainly the most competitive during the inter-wars period.

1936 The Cup of the Americas at Meadow Brook

After asserting its supremacy in the world of polo in June 1936, the United States relinquished that lofty position without a meaningful fight with the up-and-coming Argentines. The failure of the U.S. Polo Association to send a representative team to Berlin has been described in Chapter 7 on the Olympic Games. Much more puzzling is the decision by the American ruling body of the game to entrust the defense of the Cup of the Americas to the winner of the U.S. Open Championship.

Some months after the event, Peter Vischer shed some light on the issue:

> There you have the reason for last year's curious arrangement with the Argentines. The leaders of polo wanted the Argentines to play in our Open Championship tournament, win it if they could, and then go on and play the best available United States side. And what a battle it would have been!
>
> But, with the memory of the British experience still fresh in their minds, the American leaders didn't dare to take a chance on the Argentines. Suppose they too would be beaten in the first round, as the British had been? Where would the tournament be then? And how would the very considerable expenses of the Argentine invasion be met? How could they possibly have guessed what a whirlwind this Argentine side would have turned out to be?
>
> So, because the Argentines might have been licked, they were not invited to play in the Open. And because the American leaders still wanted to give proper emphasis to the Open, they devised the rather clever scheme of letting the winning Open team meet the Argentines for the Cup of the Americas. With results long known to all.[16]

The available U.S.P.A. minutes are silent as to why the time-honored, well-proven selection process of an international team was set aside. It is possible that an assumption was made that Templeton — a team made up of three members of the international team at Hurlingham, Winston Guest, Stewart Iglehart and Mike Phipps, together with Jimmy Mills, an alternate in the American squad — would surely win the Open Championship. As it was, Tommy Hitchcock had other plans. After all, his Greentree team sponsored by Jock Whitney was the holder of the U.S. Open. In the event, Greentree defeated Templeton in an extra period.

However, the real problem was the selection process. Whichever team took the Open Championship, top players would be off the international team. If Templeton had won, how could Tommy Hitchcock's absence from a representative team is justified? Was it proper not to take Cecil Smith or Eric Pedley into consideration? Quite obviously, it is not possible to guess what the thoughts were of the U.S.P.A.'s Executive Committee. In selecting a team that was not the very best America could assemble, and which also included a foreigner, three possibilities must be considered.

The first was the scheme related by Mr. Vischer: the glittering prize of representing the United States would add significant interest to the U.S. Open Championship. Did it occur to the authorities that out of the seven teams that had entered the tournament, three had foreign players in their lineups?

The next possibility is that with the U.S. Polo Association's recurrent policy of allowing non-official teams to carry the national colors— such as in the 1924 Olympic Games, the 1932 Argentine Open, the 1949 World Championship, and the 1953 Coronation Cup — the same should be in this international series. It was a face-saving method. Proof is in the fact that in the second game of the 1936 series, facing almost certain defeat after the initial game's 21–9 thrashing, the American international team wore Greentree's jerseys.

The third possibility is that by claiming that the team was not truly representative of America's polo prowess, it could provide some explanation in case of a loss. It also has been raised the issue of overconfidence, which, if true, amounts to neglect.

Whatever the reasoning, the U.S.P.A. authorities bear a heavy responsibility for the debacle of the 1936 Cup of the Americas. It marked the ascent to the top by Argentine polo, a position still untouched 75 years later.

While defending the decision to allow the winners of the U.S. Open to defend American interests in the competition, Peter Vischer felt that it was absurd to let Gerald Balding play for the United States three months after he had played for England against America in the Westchester Cup.[17]

The matches can be quickly recounted. The American team was Pete Bostwick, the Englishman Gerald Balding, Tommy Hitchcock and John Hay Whitney. They faced the newly anointed Olympic gold medalist, Luis Duggan, Roberto Cavanagh, Andrés Gazzotti and Manuel Andrada. In their two matches at Maifeld, this same quartet had beaten Mexico 15–5 and Great Britain 11-nil. Superbly mounted, this team was felt to be the best — up to that time — that had ever left the River Plate.

The first match was even, eight-all at halftime. Then the Argentines unleashed an unrelenting attack that overwhelmed the American team for a final result of 21 goals to 9. It was the worst defeat for an American international team since the initial Westchester series in 1886.

In a most sporting gesture, Jock Whitney, the American Back rated at 5-goals, offered to stand-down in the second match. His offer was rejected by the U.S.P.A. and the second game resulted in a dull 8–4 win for Argentina.

In the final analysis, a poor decision by the U.S. Polo Association negated the chance of a most wonderful international series between America and Argentina. A team made up of Pete Bostwick or Mike Phipps, Tommy Hitchcock, Stewart Iglehart and Winston Guest would certainly have shown the best polo in the world. Sadly, the opportunity was missed and the mighty clash was not to be.

The Westchester Cup at Meadow Brook, 1939

Encouraged by the good showing of British players against the American team at Hurlingham, when they were beaten by only very narrow margins, England once more challenged the United States for the Westchester Cup, a trophy that Peter Vischer described as "the most hideous old trophy offered in any sport."[18]

Britain mounted the best possible organization ever. The Hurlingham Polo Committee budgeted 35,000 sterling to cover the costs, and successfully raised that amount, making it a patriotic duty for British sportsmen to subscribe to the recovery fund. Lord Cowdray was appointed non-playing captain of the team. The players were sent to California early in the year, with plenty of time to weld themselves together as a unit on the fast American polo grounds at the traditionally fast American pace.

Maj. Noel Leaf was sent to Argentina to buy a string of horses, with Hesketh Hughes as an advisor, because of his experience living and playing polo in Argentina. Gerald Balding went to India to borrow all the good ones he could from the stables of the Indian princes. They asked Bob Skene to bring the best he could find in Australia. They combed England's best pony stables.

It did not worked out as expected. At the end of the series, out of all ponies played, the Hurlingham Polo Committee had provided eight, Indian princes seven, the Viscount Cowdray had sent out four from his own string, the Duke of Roxburghe three, Gerald Balding, Bob Skene and Major Leaf had furnished two each, and Ricardo Santamarina, Eric Tyrrell-Martin, and a sporting English lady, Mrs. Marjorie Whitefoord, one pony each.[19] When the critical time came, the British team, short of good mounts, had to buy ponies from the well-known Long Island dealer, Godfrey Preece.

For some unexplained reasons, some of their best players were left out of the final team. The great Irishman Pat Roark, widely thought of as the best British player in the inter-wars era, and a former 10-goal handicap, was left out. A lack of form was offered as the reason, but his play during the California season was reminiscent of his former glory and raised questions among the polo community. Those questions were never answered because Pat Roark sustained a fatal head injury during a practice match at Del Monte. Capt. Roark had recently married an American socialite, Patsy Hostetter Smith; their son was born a month before Pat Roark died two days after his accident.

Eric Tyrrell-Martin, a 9-goal player, had won high praise for both his leadership and individual play on the 1936 British team; however, he was relieved of his captaincy and acted as an alternate. The accomplished Indian player Hanut Singh, another 9-goaler, was not considered. Fully considered by the Americans to be Britain's best, Capt. Charles Roark, was not even invited to try out. Nor were any of the great Indian stars persuaded to join the British squad, even though the spectacular Rao Rajah Hanut Singh would have played in 1936 had he not, a few days before the opening match, been injured. Capt. Humphrey Guinness, who had played so well at Back in 1936, was on military duty in Palestine and could not be spared.

Additionally, the ponies were in two railroad accidents going from California to the East, and two of them died, one being killed outright, the other succumbing to pneumonia. Maj. Noel Leaf, in charge of the pony string, developed a serious infection, was taken to hospital, and died there.Truly, it seemed a doomed expedition for the British.

For the United States, it was an embarrassment of riches. If the team originally selected, Michael Phipps, Cecil Smith, Stewart Iglehart and Tommy Hitchcock, could not beat any team in the world, there was something very wrong in the handicap ratings. These four superstars were thought to be a perfect team; moreover, there were plenty of players almost as good to take their places. Pete Bostwick, Ebby Gerry, Winston Guest, James Mills, Eric Pedley, Billy Post: the list is interminable They had reserves of top ponies, all experienced in international contests. They were playing at home, in front of supporting crowds, under conditions they liked. And they had a tradition of winning, broken but once in the last thirty five years.

The American team was well-mounted, under a formula that required each player to mount himself and have his string ready for action. It is of interest that Tommy Hitchcock had no mounts of his own; Sonny Whitney lent him four ponies, Jock Whitney three, and Raymond Guest and Seymour Knox, one pony each.

When the time came to put the American team on the field, it was found that Iglehart, not fully recovered from a gastric malaise, was playing below his best form. It was personally unfortunate for him, but not really serious for the United States' chances, because his announced replacement, Winston Guest, was performing so well in the trial matches that the side was still considered unbeatable. Nevertheless, in the last practice game, Cecil Smith suffered a nasty spill. The great Texan was concussed and it was felt that he could not play without danger to himself. At the fifty-ninth minute of the eleventh hour the American team had to be revamped. Michael Phipps stayed at Number 1; Tommy Hitchcock, who had not played the demanding and traditionally strong Number 2 position in an American team for ten years, moved up to fill the breach. Stewart Iglehart, whose form was improving rapidly, was called back into the lineup and Winston Guest was inserted at Back, a position that he had successfully filled against Argentina in 1928, and in the Westchester matches of 1930 and 1936. It was a formidable combination.

After much debate and argument, the British side was Bob Skene at Number 1, Aidan Roark at Number 2, team captain Gerald Balding at Number 3, and at Back, Eric Tyrrell-Martin, again into the good graces of the selection committee.

The day of the scheduled first game, June 4, dawned with rain and bad weather forecast. Members from both teams met and debated for some time before deciding to go ahead with the game. With the heavy ground, it was the polo that failed to live up to international standards. The field's condition did not favor fast play and long hitting. The Americans got out in front, but by the fourth chukker the British came within one goal. In the second half the American team scored five goals against only two by the visitors, both in the last chukker when the issue was already decided. Hitchcock and Phipps were the high scorers, with four goals each; Guest had two and Iglehart one tally. For Great Britain, Balding and Skene had three goals each, and Roark one.

Neither team made changes for the second match, which was held one week after the initial contest. It was more of the same story as in the first game. Britain stayed close during the first five periods; however, they were able to score only one goal, again in the last chukker. The final score, 9–4, reflected the American superiority. Tommy Hitchcock closed his outstanding international polo career being the high scorer, with four goals. Mike Phipps scored three goals; Iglehart and Guest, one each. For Britain, Bob Skene had two goals, and Roark and Tyrrell-Martin, one each. Many years later, Bob Skene made the observation that before the start of the series, he was hitting all the penalty shots with great accuracy. When the day of the matches came, Gerald Balding took the penalties, scoring three in the first game and none in the second. Bob Skene commented that had he been allowed to hit the penalties, the matches might have had a different outcome.[20]

Nevertheless, the young Australian's play caught the eyes of spectators and critics alike, who discerned in his performance the sterling qualities that would take him to the top of the game and a place among polo's immortals.

Since the outcome of the Westchester Cup was decided in only two games, an interesting special match was arranged. The visiting officials put up some prizes for a game on handicap against the highest team the United States could assemble. Therefore, Mike Phipps, Cecil Smith, Tommy Hitchcock and Stewart Iglehart, a 40-goal combination, faced Bob Skene, John Lakin, Gerald Balding and Eric Tyrell-Martin. The American team gave 10 goals on handicap, and was defeated by 16 goals to 14 goals. At the end of the fifth chukker the score was 14–13 in favor of the British team, and the crowd expected an American victory. In the last three chukkers the visitors outscored the U.S. team 2–1, displaying the best polo they showed in this country, in what the Year Book vividly described, "[t]he last three periods of this match were as great as polo has seen anywhere."[21]

This historic game was the first one to show a 40-goal team in competitive action since the special match between Meadow Brook — Stoddard, Hitchcock, Webb and Milburn — and Flamingo, held in October 1922.

The Avila Camacho Cup

In 1941 the president of Mexico, Gen. Manuel Avila Camacho, an enthusiastic polo player, presented a trophy bearing his name to be played in a series of matches between the United States and the Republic of Mexico. Two series were held in that year, in late February and early March, and later in the month of November, both in Mexico City.

The American players who journeyed to Mexico City in February were Roy Barry, Sr., Harry Evinger, Michael Phipps, Cecil Smith and Robert Strawbridge, Jr. Four matches were played; in the first one, Strawbridge took Cecil Smith's place because of a fall suffered by the superstar from Texas. Among those playing for Mexico were Maj. Antonio Nava Castillo, Capt. Guillermo Gracida, Capt. Alberto Ramos Sesma, and Lts. Guillermo Cisneros and José Villalobos.

Four matches were played: The American team took the first and third games by scores of 6–5 and 9–1, while the Mexicans won the other two games 7–4 and 8–5.

The Anahuac Field in Mexico City was formally dedicated in November and another American team participated in the ceremonies and in a three-game series. In the first game, Henry Lewis, Cecil Smith, Winston Guest and Harry "Dutch" Evinger defeated the Mexican team of Lt. Gabriel Gracida, Lt. Jesús Grijalva, Capt. Alberto Ramos Sesma and Guillermo Cisneros by 6 goals to 5. The U.S. team clinched the series in the second game, which was won by 6 to 4 goals. Mexico presented the same lineup as in the first game, while Michael Phipps replaced Henry Lewis on the American squad.

With the Avila Camacho Cup safely in American hands, a third match was played. The Americans made no changes, while the Mexican team was Maj. Eduardo Gallardo, Maj. Antonio Nava Castillo, Maj. Juan Gracia Zazueta and Capt. Alberto Ramos Sesma. The United States players defeated the local team by the score of 12–4.[22]

It is of some interest that in the next Year Book published by the U.S. Polo Association, in 1949, and in subsequent editions, there is no mention of the series played in February and March of 1941— only the one held in November.[23] The first Mexico–United States international series of 1941, having ended in a tied contest, has been relegated to oblivion.

CHAPTER 12

Polo During the Depression

The worldwide economic turndown had a significant impact on the game of polo in America. Although the Open Championship continued its merry ride, it had fewer players and fewer teams. International tours came to an almost total stop. An exception was Seymour Knox's Aurora team journey to England, where they took the Hurlingham Champion Cup and Roehampton's Open Cup. The team was made up of Seymour "Shorty" Knox, Harold Talbott, Elmer Boeseke, Jr., and Billy Post.

Aurora also undertook another journey in 1937, in this case southwards to Buenos Aires, in order to participate in the Argentine Open Championship. Seymour Knox, Frank Skiddy von Stade, Jr., Capt. Pat Roark and Lindsay Howard beat Los Pingüinos in the first round. However, they fell to Santa Inés in the semifinals. In the handicap tournament for the Copa Provincia de Buenos Aires, Aurora, with Col. Howard Fair, of the Canadian Army, and Lewis Smith in place of Pat Roark and Skiddy von Stade, the latter just out of Harvard, lost in an extra chukker to Los Indios.[1]

The Junior Championship

The oldest American polo trophy is the Silver Cup, which was the prize given to the winner of the Junior Championship, dating back to 1900. In 1938, the competition was renamed the Twenty-Goal Championship, reflecting the highest handicap allowed to enter the tournament. It is known as the Silver Cup since 1974.

The Army polo teams continued to exercise their supremacy in medium-goal polo in the early 1930s, taking the tournament in 1930 and 1932, being runner-up in 1934. The winning players' names are mentioned in the Notes to Chapter 15 on Military Polo. Successful civilian clubs included Roslyn (Raymond Firestone, Seymour Knox, Harold Talbott and Billy Post), Aknusti (Averell Harriman, Jimmy Mills, Ebby Gerry and Robert Gerry), Burnt Mills (Stephen Farish, Harry East, Arthur Border and John Mather), Aiken Knights (Pete Bostwick, James Curtis, Winston Guest and Dunbar Bostwick), Hurricanes (Laddie Sanford, William Reynolds, Terence Preece and Aubrey Floyd), Santa Barbara (Harry East, Alex Bullock, Eric Tyrrell-Martin and Charles Jackson, Jr.) and Bostwick Field (Edward Gerry, Pete Bostwick, Robert Gerry and Charles von Stade).

Following the tournament's name change to Twenty Goal Championship, the League of Nations—a team formed by Jay Secor, Australian Bob Skene, George Oliver and Belgian Robert Loewenstein—were the winners. The remaining victors before the onset of World War II were Great Neck (Gerald Dempsey, Joseph P. Grace, Jr., Stewart Iglehart and Edward

137

Carpenter) and, once more, Bostwick Field, with Sidney Culver, Pete Bostwick, Charles von Stade and Alan Corey.

The Twelve Goal Tournament

The need for a U.S.P.A. national competition at a lower handicap level was recognized when in 1923 a Twelve Goal championship became part of the regular polo tournament schedule. It was played without handicap, with no player with a handicap higher than four-goals allowed to participate. The initial event was held in Narragansett Pier and was taken by the Penllyn Club from Pennsylvania over the U.S. Army team.

Despite this early hiccup, Army teams dominated the Twelve Goal Championship throughout the 1920s and 1930s (teams are listed in the Notes to Chapter 15). Only Midwick and Santa Barbara from California, Miami Valley and Gates Mills from Ohio, Oak Brook in Illinois and Pegasus from New Jersey were able to occasionally break the Army teams' grip in this important competition.

The Twelve Goal Inter-Circuit

Another 12-Goal tournament was added in 1925 with the institution of the Inter-Circuit Championship, to be decided among the eight winners of the Intra-Circuit elimination tournaments. The trophy for this handicap competition was donated by the heirs of Mr. Julius Fleischman and was presented by his son-in-law, Henry Yeiser, Jr., from the Cincinnati Polo Club.

The Intra-Circuit winners were Bryn Mawr, Chagrin Valley, Fort Bliss, Fort Leavenworth, Fort Oglethorpe, Midwick and Rockaway. The U.S. Army team from Fort Bliss took both tournaments in 1925, played at the Philadelphia Country Club in Bala. The runner-ups were Rockaway in the Twelve Goal and Midwick in the Inter-Circuit.

Just as the military teams dominated the Twelve Goal Championship in the inter-wars period, they achieved prominence in the Twelve Goal Inter-Circuit. The civilian teams that took the championship during that time span were the Farish's Houston Huisache on three occasions, Chagrin Valley twice, Point Judith, Fairfield, and the Blue Hills Farms team from Philadelphia.

California

An Argentine team, named El Pampero, visited California in 1931. The players were Juan Benitz, Santiago Cavanagh, Luis Duggan, Daniel Kearney and Juan Reynal. Their first match was in the Teddy Miller Memorial at Midwick Country Club, in which event they drew the Hurricanes, with Stephen Sanford, Pat Roark, James Colt and Lindsay Howard. Hurricanes, the eventual tournament winner, defeated the Argentines 15–11.

Opposite, top: **Aurora in England: Harold Talbott, Elmer Boeseke on the famous Red Ace, team captain "Shorty" Knox and William Post, II. This team took the Hurlingham Champion Cup and the Roehampton Open Cup.** *Bottom:* **The Roslyn team members receiving the 1931 Junior Championship trophy from Mrs. Howard Borden. The happy winners are Raymond Firestone, Seymour Knox, Harold Talbott and Billy Post.**

Lindsay Howard from San Mateo Polo Club taking a drink at the pony lines.

El Pampero then tried its luck in the Pacific Coast Open Championship, taken the previous year by their compatriots from Santa Paula. In the first round they avenged their loss in the Miller Memorial, defeating the same Hurricanes team by 9 goals to 8. The final match was between the host team, Midwick, and El Pampero. Midwick took the championship by virtue of an 8 to 6 goals win. Neil McCarthy, Elmer Boeseke, Jr., Eric Pedley and Howland Paddock represented Midwick.

In a special match at Fleischman Field in Santa Barbara, El Pampero met the Hurricanes and won the game 17–8, receiving 4 goals by handicap.

In December 1931, for the first time a Mexican team made its appearance on the Pacific Coast.[2] It was a good side, rated at 18-goals and quite worth it, mounted on twenty-five of the best mounts available in the republic to the south. The players included team captain Julio Muller, a magnificent horseman and an accomplished striker, playing at Number 3; José Conian, Capt. Juan García, Capt. Antonio Nava Castillo and Lt. Antonio Pérez. Both Muller and Nava Castillo played on the Bronze medalist team in the 1936 Olympic Games.

The Mexicans made a favorable impression in their matches on California soil, particularly because of the unselfish team play they exhibited. Their first game was against a California foursome: Hal Roach, Snowy Baker, Eric Pedley and Clair Brunson. It was an event that was part of the official opening of the new Riviera Country Club grounds on 6 December. Those were the grounds where it was hoped that the Los Angeles Olympic polo matches would be played; however, there was no polo at the Games. Although the Mexican team was defeated in extra chukker, their good reputation was upheld.

In the second match, played on 13 December 1931, the Mexican team scored a 9–6 victory over the California four led by Eric Pedley at Number 3, with Reginald "Snowy" Baker[3] playing the Number 1 position, Neil McCarthy at Number 2, and Carl Beal at Back. The third and deciding game went to the Mexico in a dramatic struggle, 13–12. The Mexican team was Capt. Juan García, José Cobian, Capt. Nava Castillo and Julio Muller. California was represented by Hal Roach, Eric Pedley, Dr. H. Wilson and Clair Brunson.

There was another visit by Mexican players in 1937. Maj. Juan Gracia Zazueta, Maj. Antonio Nava Castillo, Capt. Alberto Ramos Sesma and Lt. José Villalobos played at Midwick for the Eric L. Pedley Cup. In a three-game series, the local team took two of the three games. James Rogers, Howland Paddock, Eric Pedley, William Tevis, Arthur Perkins, Eric Tyrrell-Martin and Aidan Roark played for Midwick.

A Mexico-California All Stars series was then held at the Golden Gate Polo Club in San Francisco. Four matches were played; California took the last three encounters. In the last game, Maj. Francisco Medina replaced Lt. Villalobos on the Mexican team. Just as at Midwick, several players played on the California teams: George Pope, Jr., Eric Tyrrell-Martin, Tom Guy, Charles Howard, Jr., and Alex Bullock.

Midwick remained the premier club in California in the 1930s and hosted important tournaments such as the Pacific Coast Open and the Teddy Miller Memorial. Santa Barbara, with its stunning grounds overlooking the ocean, hosted the James Wood Colt, Jr., Memorial and the Pacific Coast Intra-Circuit Championship. Del Monte was the scene of the Pacific High Goal Tournament and its own Del Monte Open. Other renowned clubs were Will Rogers' Uplifters Ranch in Santa Monica, now bulldozed into a street, movie producer Darryl Zanuck's Los Indios, the Riviera Country Club and the Army team at Presidio in San Francisco. San Mateo and Burlingame joined to better face the financial constraints imposed by the economic situation; fortunately, the club still survives.

The California winter was the most crowded in the polo calendar, after the Eastern Circuit's summer season. There was no competition between the two largest polo centers in America because the Pacific Coast season extended from February to late April,

Eric Pedley at Del Monte; Jimmy Mills and Hal Roach in the background. The 1935 Pacific Coast Open Championship.

when polo in the East Coast began in earnest, to last until late September with the jewel in the crown, the U.S. Open Championship at Meadow Brook.

Polo came to an end for Midwick in July 1941 when the 210-acre property that included clubhouse, golf course, swimming pool and tennis courts was sold at public auction for $178,000—five hundred dollars more than a bid offered by a group of club members.[4] The property was then sold to the Midwick Development Company, which subdivided it for residences. Streets were named for the polo players and golfers who frequented the club.

Michigan

The hard times of the early 1930s affected Michigan, and Detroit in particular, because of the drop in demand for new automobiles. Somehow, polo kept on going. Teams from the Detroit area included the Triple Cs, the All-Stars, Ivory Rangers, Freebooters, Majors, the Birmingham Rockets and Ramblers, the Brookwood Blues, the Blue Eagles, Cavaliers, Lancers, Broncos, the Pontiac Chiefs, Rangers and the Franklin Hills. The Detroit Polo Club's Gold Hats were named by a bowler, L.A. Young, who promised the name to his teammates if they won.

The main polo grounds were the Ivory field at Lahser and Eight Mile; Roy's Ranch on Walnut Lake Road in Walled Lake, and fields in Union Lake, Milford, Grosse Pointe at Cook Road Field, Seven Mile and Mack, White Lake and other cities such as Flint and Mt. Clemens.

Wealthy families often sponsored their own teams, such as the Hammond family team. Edward P. Hammond, Jr., related to the Chicago Hammond-Standish meat packer family, belonged to several clubs including the Bloomfield Open Hunt, where his sons played the game. Known as the Hillwoods or The Hammond Brothers, George, Fred, John and Ted became famous players.

Vivian M. Baluch wrote,

> High-goal polo developed here because of the indulgence of three men—L.A. Young, who owned the fields, built the clubhouse, sponsored the early Gold Hats, and in later days made several brave efforts to revive the game; Phil Grennan, a nonpareil among sportsmen, an able though fragile competitor and a national influence; and Marvin Harrison, who went so all-out in his devotion to the game that his high-goal polo expenditures eventually bankrupted him.[5]

The game of polo was supported in the Detroit area by several such sponsors, including John Ivory, Sr.[6] John F. Ivory, Jr., played at Number 1 on the winning team in the 1947 East-West series. A 5-goal handicap player—seven indoors—he started the Ivory Polo Club in 1946, which remained active until 1976.

New England

The W. Cameron Forbes Trophy was started in 1938 as emblematic of the New England Polo Championship. The Grand Old Man of American polo, William Cameron Forbes, age 68, played at Number 1 for Dedham in the initial match of the trophy named after him. R. Bennett Foster, Dudley Milliken and Robert Almy were his teammates. They defeated Danvers Polo Club, only to be beaten in the semifinals by the eventual winners, Myopia, with Charles Rice, Paul Fox, Forrester "Tim" Clark and Frederick Ayer, Jr. In the second semifinal, Pittsfield won over Connecticut's Farmington Valley Polo Club.

In 1939, this competition was divided into two divisions, Eastern and Western, the respective winners meeting in the finals. In a close match, Pittsfield, with William Rand, Jr., Zenas Colt, Arthur Mason, Jr., and Frank Butterworth, Jr., defeated Myopia, Charles Rice, Paul Fox, Tim Clark and Fred Ayer, 5–4. These same two teams met again in the final match the following year, Paul Fox replacing Rand on the Pittsfield team, and Bennett Forbes taking Fox's slot on the Myopia team. Pittsfield won once more time.

This trophy was again played for from the early 1960s into the 1980s, mostly between Fairfield County Hunt Club and Myopia Hunt, which generated some terrific battles on the polo ground and great parties after the final bell.

The original trophy was lost while in custody of the Myopia captain, Forrester "Tim" Clark, who at the time dryly made the remark that it almost broke him to replace the silver cup.[7]

The Northeastern Circuit

The main competition remained the Monty Waterbury Cup, established in 1922 by Meadow Brook Club members, to be played on handicap by the teams participating in the Open Championship. Regrettably, the Monty Waterbury Cup, which honors the memory of one of the greatest American players, is now relegated to a secondary role, displaced from its former position as a top tournament by the C.V. Whitney Cup.

Some controversies in the finals of the Monty Waterbury Cup between Templeton and Roslyn are worth mention. There were arguments concerning goals. Three times shots whistled over the posts from difficult angles, so that neither the goal judges nor the umpires could really tell if goals had been scored or not. *Horse and Horseman* commented:

> Polo was once described as a game played by millionaires but decided by Italian day-laborers standing behind the goal-posts with red flags in their hands. Wouldn't it be a good idea to have two competent judges placed at a wide angle behind the judges [sic, posts] in matches of national significance?[8]

It is interesting that the same questions are being asked regarding flag persons in the current Florida season. Some things never change in the world of polo.

After Meadow Brook, Rumson Country Club in New Jersey remained the main polo center, with its showcase Herbert Memorial Tournament still going strong. But also Aknusti, Blind Brook, Bostwick Field, Cortland, Loudonville, Piping Rock and Ramapo Valley in New York, and Burnt Mills, Monmouth Country Club and Pegasus in New Jersey had thriving local polo seasons as well as active participation in inter-circuit tournaments, as well as the occasional national competition.

Maryland

The Maryland Polo Club had a beautiful field set in a natural amphitheater that allowed the occupants of many rows of automobiles to view the action on the entire field from a vantage point. The location was in Stevenson, near Baltimore. An old farmhouse was tastefully renovated and became the essence of taste combined with comfort and friendly informality.

The club was affiliated in 1926; the main tournaments were the T. Dudley Riggs, Jr.,

Memorial and an Invitational Tournament. Matches were held with the 6th Field Artillery at Fort Hoyle, the Maryland National Guard 110th Field Artillery, and military teams from Washington. One of the players on the Sixth Field Artillery was Lt. A.C. McAuliffe, who as Gen. Anthony McAuliffe, in temporary command of the 101st Airborne Division, would become the hero of Bastogne during the Battle of the Bulge in World War II. Players of note at Maryland Polo Club included Bonsal Brookes, Henry Dentry, Wallace Lanahan, Styles Tuttle, Edwin Warfield, and the Foster brothers, John and Arthur Jr.

Polo in the Northwest

During the 1930s there was polo in Portland, Seattle, Spokane, Wiley City and Yakima. The Toppenish Polo Club in Yakima was re-started in 1933 by Fred Jensen and G.A. Gibson. Play was at Mr. Gibson's property. The officers were W.S. Doran, W.R. Winn and Dr. Frank Shearer. Dr. Shearer was still stick and balling in 2009, at age 104.[9] Players included Billy Coleman, Bill Drake, the Jensen boys, George and Stanley, Carroll Lawrence and Fred Wilson.

In order to provide competition, Mr. Gibson got a group interested in polo to start the game in Wiley City, not far away, while Seattle had the Olympic Polo Association.

Polo in Spokane had Phil Alexander, Paul Graves, Ken Hauser, Dr. Kalez, Bob Mills and Wally Rothschild as the main supporters. It also had a woman player, Mrs. David Oglesbee, whose husband organized the Evergreen Polo Club in Spokane.

The Northwestern Polo Championship for the Cunningham Trophy was contested in Spokane. It also included teams from Calgary and Kamloops from Canada.[10]

Southwest Polo

The polo season in the Southwest was centered in San Antonio, around the strong Army contingent and the civilian game at the San Antonio Polo Club, the base for the Farish family's polo enterprise. The Houston Riding and Polo Club maintained the flame bright and Albert "Buster" Wharton's El Ranchito from Fort Worth added interest to the regional tournaments. There was polo in Dallas, supported by Dr. Raworth Williams, which offered stiff competition to Houston's powerhouse Huisache.

The Shreveport Riding and Polo Club in Louisiana faced several teams from Texas, and its team of James Harris, Rudolph Humberson, William Kuykendall, Hersdhell Scivally, Clarence Starks and Dr. A.V. Young was successful in the late thirties.

It is of interest that in the 1930s and 1940s the Luchesse Cup was played at the San Antonio Polo Club and players such as Cecil Smith, Roy Barry and George Oliver have their names engraved on the trophy. At the time of writing, 2010, a Luchesse team is making its mark in Florida's high-goal polo, as the winners of the 20-goal Ylvisaker Cup.

Polo in the Southeast Circuit

The game in this circuit, which extended from Pennsylvania to Florida, hit an all-time low. When polo in Miami disappeared, Gulf Stream, the Phipps' family club in Delray

Beach, was the only active club in Florida. The only other clubs were Aiken and Camden in South Carolina and the Augusta Polo and Riding Club in Georgia.

By 1939 the Philadelphia area, once a booming center, had only the 1st Troop Philadelphia Cavalry as an active club. Virginia counted the Fauquier-Loundon Polo Association as its lonely club and neighbor West Virginia the Greenbrier Polo Club.

This club in White Sulphur Springs affiliated with the U.S.P.A. in 1932, at the height of the Depression. Brownell and Leslie Combs, II, Lawrence McClung, C. Kendall McDowell, Gould Shaw and A.R. Winters were the enthusiasts who started the game at this fashionable spa. A highlight of the 1934 season was the Mexico-Greenbrier series. Two matches were played late in the season, in the month of October. The Greenbrier players were Leslie Combs, William Fergus, Charles Neale and Gould Shaw, reinforced by Warner Atkins from Camargo, and Stanley Taylor, from Miami Valley. The Mexican Army team won both matches, 9–6 and 9–4. The team was made up of Captains Chaves, Juan Gracia Zazueta, Antonio Nava Castillo and Quintín Reyes.

The Fauquier-Loudon amalgam had Robert Clark, Charley Cushman, H. Frost, Sr., and Jr., Walter Goodwin, William Hulbert, Richard Kirkpatrick, John Rawlings, Charles Sabin, D.C. Sands, Henry and John Skinker, Baldwin Spilman, Jr., J.F. Walker, Arthur White and Turner Wiltshire. Matches were played at Maryland Polo Club, White Sulphur Springs and Washington, D.C.

The 1933 East-West Series

In the absence of meaningful international competition, the U.S.P.A. organized in 1933 a two-out-of-three-match series between the best teams each section of the country could muster. This East-West clash aroused enormous attention, fueled by a press corps that characterized a polo competition as a test between a complacent and confident Eastern seaboard upper class which had ruled American society as well as polo ever since the onset of polo in the United States, against what was popularly known as cowboy polo. The East-West series then became a symbolic event. Will Rogers, America's favorite humorist, with his knack for an appropriate *bon mot*, referred to the games as a challenge between the bunkhouse and the drawing room.

Thus, the stage was set for a contentious encounter at Onwentsia Polo Club, just north of Chicago. There were careful and thoughtful preparations by both sides and the host club. Temporary stands were erected; the teams had Carlton Burke as non-playing captain, assisted by Neil McCarthy in charge of the West team and Tommy Hitchcock, the world's best player, as leader of the East contingent, as playing captain.

The East team in the first game was Mike Phipps, Tommy Hitchcock, Winston Guest and his younger brother Raymond. The West team had Aidan Roark, Elmer Boeseke, Jr., Cecil Smith and his pal Rube Williams. Under ideal weather conditions and in front of a crowd estimated at 15,000 that overflowed the stands, the West squad took off from the very beginning and run away for a 15–11 win. Rough play, a feature that became the hallmark of the series, was evident. Fearless Rube Williams was stunned when he collided with a goalpost. In the fifth period Cecil Smith crossed Raymond Guest too close to his pony's hind legs and fell, unconscious. The game was delayed for approximately 40 minutes; after waving off the ambulance, Smith kept on playing, finishing the top scorer, with six goals to his credit.

For the second game, Hitchcock made changes in the East's lineup. Winston Guest was moved to the Number 1 position, young Earle Hopping, who had a reputation for not shying away when the going got rough, was at Number 2, then Hitchcock at Number 3 and Raymond Guest at Back. The changes proved beneficial to the Eastern squad, which won by a four-goal differential, the same as in the first game. The scoreboard showed a 12 to 8 margin. Regrettably, in the first period Tommy Hitchcock went down, courtesy of Boeseke, and then the tall Californian himself hit the turf, courtesy of Hopping. Elmer Boeseke injured his foot, and Tommy Hitchcock's fate was more severe, because he suffered a concussion that most likely was the eventual cause of his losing his 10-goal rating.

There was more havoc in the seventh period when Rube Williams challenged both Hitchcock and Hopping, and badly fractured his leg. When Ray Harrington asked Rube why he did not give way, the cowboy's laconic answer was: "They could've given way just as easily as I could."[11] Alternate Neil McCarthy came in as a replacement, but the die was cast.

Hard play characterized the East-West series. Here Rube Williams scores for the West in spite of Winston Guest's close marking.

Carleton Burke, the West's manager, came to the conclusion that his team could not possibly win the third game with a 4-goaler in the lineup. Therefore, an urgent telephone call to Eric Pedley had the California star on a flight from the Pacific Coast, arriving with plenty of time for Sunday's defining match.

Then a situation extraneous to the contest raised its ugly face. While having dinner at a restaurant with Maj. Frederick McLaughlin, one of the event's main organizers, bachelor Cecil Smith was served with a warrant charging him with criminal assault. A nurse, Eugenie Rose, who had been tending to Hubert Williams in hospital, reported to police that Cecil Smith had offered her a ride home after work and attacked her. An understandably distraught Smith admitted that he had offered the woman a ride, but adamantly asserted that they had not stopped. The charges were dropped soon after without explanation. Rumors abounded. Apparently, there had been heavy betting on the series outcome, with the serious money behind the East squad. It was thought that the charges would affect Smith's play, which had been superb.

The polo community stood unequivocally behind Cecil Smith. The committee representing the U.S. Polo Association issued a document stating that the charges were groundless. For their part, the East team players published a notice saying that "We are convinced there is no word of truth in this foul accusation against his good name."[12]

Played in front of a crowd numbering 25,000, the final match showed Cecil Smith at the top of his game. The West team placed Eric Pedley at Number1 and Aidan Roark at Back. The score was 6–4 at half time, in favor of the West, and 8 to 6 at the end of the sixth chukker. Then the West team scored four unanswered goals to ice game and series. Unfortunately, the roughness continued. Elmer Boeseke was knocked out near the goalpost, and his celebrated mount, Red Ace — recently enshrined in the Hall of Fame's Horses to Remember category — captivated the crowd when he trotted back to his rider and nuzzled him.

By all accounts, it was a rough series, which prompted changes in the rules of the game, most notably to prevent the situation that involved Hitchcock, Hopping and Williams. From then on, when two players were together, the third one had to give the right of way. Robert Kelley wrote,

> Riding at terrific pace, and fighting for every break of the game, the West, which had entered the series the underdogs, won a smashing victory over the East by taking the first game, one of the most sensational and roughest in years, 15–11; losing the second 12–8; and coming through with a revamped line-up to a notable triumph in the third and final match, 12–6.[13]

The 1933 East–West series changed the game of polo. The record shows that more fouls were committed and more serious injuries occurred in this competition that in any important contests, before or since. There was too much desperate chance-taking and bumping at an angle. The new generation of players was impatient of the old technique brought to perfection by Watson Webb, by riding alongside his opponent and by superior horsemanship, riding him off the line of the ball, to either make a stroke himself or leave the ball for a teammate. The exponents of the new school started using the horses as weapons, bumping-off instead of riding-off, some times at outrageous angles.

Many years later, Heriberto Duggan, one of the finest riders in Argentine polo, mentioned that during the 1937 U.S. Open Championship, he carefully rode-off Tommy Hitchcock away from the ball. Minutes later, Tommy bumped him with such force that his teeth rattled.[14] But then, that was the American style of riding-off in the 1930s.

The Western polo commentators ran wild with excitement, feeling that a new era had began. According to the gospel in the West, the game no longer belonged to Long Island; it belonged to the entire country.

Eastern observers took a more cautious view. Robert Kelly, again in *The Sportsman*, wrote "As the Open and Monte Waterbury [tournaments] gallop merrily along to the close of the summer season, there is a feeling in the air that the game is going to change. Something is to be done about the dangerous increasing roughness of American polo."[15]

Writing for *Country Life*, Arthur Little also voiced his concerns:

> One of the most unpleasant repercussions from the East-West rivalry, from the official viewpoint, was the publicity given to the lusty mayhem committed on the field at Onwentsia Country Club, Chicago, where the bold Westerners spared neither themselves, their mounts, nor the opposition in proving that polo is a game not always distantly removed from the rodeo.[16]

Nevertheless, the myth popularized by Will Rogers remains fixed in people's minds: The hillbillies beat the dudes and took the polo championship of the world right out of the drawing room and into the bunkhouse.

Hillbillies? Elmer Boeseke was the son of a prosperous doctor and polo player, who was one of the founders of the game in Santa Barbara. Neil McCarthy was a wealthy lawyer in Los Angeles who counted many movie stars as his clients in legal matters. Eric Pedley, son of a British engineer, had a significant personal fortune. Aidan Roark, a scion from the famous Irish polo-playing family, a prominent figure in the Hollywood set as an executive with 20th Century–Fox, married tennis champion Helen Wills, arguably the best woman player ever. Carleton Burke was a wealthy and important figure in California polo and turf circles.

The two Texans merit a separate paragraph. Cecil Calvert Smith not only became one of the game's immortals, but also was a gentleman with innate dignity and manners that enabled him to fit comfortably at the finest social occasions. The ebullient Hubert Winfield Williams had a fine sense of humor. When an inquisitive journalist asked him about his middle initial, Rube facetiously told him, "Windshield." So it was for years. Rube played hard, but always within the limits of the game's rules.

But perhaps the East-West series conclusion was a reflection of the western indifference towards the northeasterners, if not in financial riches, at least in status and prestige.

The West-East Series of 1934

The incredible success of the series at Onwentsia convinced the U.S. Polo Association's hierarchy that a second edition would be another bonanza for the game of polo. The East's injured pride needed a quick redress, while the Western champions were willing to prove that the performance rendered at Lake Forest was no one-time wonder.

Instead of a more neutral site, such as Texas, the eastern citadel of the Meadow Brook Club was selected as the venue for the resumption of the series. Although fairly well attended, the spectators seemed to be lost in the immense robin's egg blue stands. Prices for the West Stand, the best side to watch the games, were high, and postponements due to inclement weather cut down attendance to the event.

With Tommy Hitchcock out of commission because of the concussion suffered on the Onwentsia grounds, an injury that was aggravated by another fall on the Piping Rock's ground towards the end of the selection process, the East selectors opted for a young team, Mike Phipps, Jimmy Mills, Winston Guest and William Post. As to the West, Carleton Burke was again appointed to be in charge. Burke selected the same side that had done so well in the third match at Onwentsia: Pedley, Boeseke, Smith and Roark.

In the first match, the West went ahead 8–4 on the strength of three goals in the sixth period, and seemed to have the game in control. However, in a burst of scoring seldom seen in high-goal polo, the East marked six tallies in the seventh chukker, to take the match by 10 goals to 8.

There was more discouraging weather after the opening game, which forced yet another postponement. Carleton Burke decided to shuffle his squad, placing Smith at Number 2, Roark at Number 3 and Boeseke at Back. The East team stayed put, showing quiet confidence.

The second game started with a burst by the East side, that reached the interval ahead by three goals, 9 to 3. They hung on for a close 14–13 win. Frank von Stade, Sr., who was placed in charge of the team in early summer, received the strong support of his committee, James Cooley, Dev Milburn and the veteran Larry Waterbury.

Attendance at the two matches was not as expected considering the quality of the selected teams. This gave some support to those who suggested that international events were beneficial from the financial and sporting points of view, a contrary view of those who were of the opinion that international visits disrupted the domestic polo schedule. The public responded with their feet. At Meadow Brook, they wanted to see royalty, Indian princes and their turbaned grooms, talented Argentine players, their gaucho attendants and their fantastic string of polo ponies. For some reason, the home talent, which was as good any foreign team had exhibited, was not enough of a draw in the middle of the depression, when a dime was almost as big as a house. The 15,000 spectators in the first game and the less than 10,000 in the second match would have been a sizable crowd at Onwentsia. At Meadow Brook, they seemed to be lost in the ample stands. The bottom line is that the East-West series was not renewed until 1947.

The Reorganization of the United States Polo Association

In 1936, polo in the United States had a new leader in Robert E. Strawbridge, Jr. This brilliant young player, a veteran of international play and a member of six victorious Open Championship teams despite his youth — he was only 39 years old — was unanimously elected chairman of the U.S. Polo Association at the annual meeting in New York on 21 January 1936. He succeeded Louis Ezekiel Stoddard, head of the association since 1922, who had announced at the annual meeting a year before that he would retire at this time. Following a time-honored tradition since the inception of the old Polo Association, an active player returned to the leadership of American polo, just as an active player, Stoddard, had replaced the late William Hazard 14 years previously.

Not everything was wine and roses at the annual meeting because a bitter factional fight marked the gathering. Incoming chairman Bobby Strawbridge called the situation "a grave constitutional question."[17] The administration in power, led by Louis Stoddard with the strong support of Devereux Milburn, was strenuously opposed by a group led by Thomas Hitchcock, Jr., Charles Wrightsman and Winston Guest. There was little the two factions could agree upon, with the exception that Robert Strawbridge the younger should be the new chairman of the U.S. Polo Association, and also, that the annual dues of each club be reduced from $150 to $25, plus an additional $5 for each player registered.

Both sides asked for sweeping changes in the constitution of the Polo Association, and the Hitchcock group demanded as well revisions in policy on such matters as the selection and management of international teams. The two sides could not agree, however, on either the proposed changes or on the time and methods of making them.

Two rival plans, the Milburn Plan and the Hitchcock Plan, were submitted. In brief, the Milburn Plan called for the subdivision of the U.S.P.A. into six circuits: Northeastern, Southeastern, Central, Rocky Mountain, Southwestern and Pacific Coast. The delegates of the clubs of each circuit were to elect their own committee and the chairman of that committee. The association would have officers as at present, and an executive committee of 17 members, consisting of the officers, the chairman of each circuit committee, a representative of the Army Polo Association appointed by the Army, and seven members at large.

The Hitchcock Plan was simpler, calling for similar circuits, with the delegates of the various clubs in each circuit electing their own presiding officer, to be known as "circuit governor." These governors, together with five others of their own choosing, would constitute an executive committee that would have complete control and management of the

Elbridge Gerry, a 9-goal handicap player and a winner of the U.S. Open Championship, was chairman of the U.S.P.A. during the dark years of World War II.

U.S. Polo Association, including the election of a chairman, vice-chairman, secretary and treasurer.

The election showed that the incumbent forces could not be defeated, as is often the case in reform matters. Every vote taken was won by the administration, the votes on two rival slates of officers being 32 to 21, which showed just about what the division of power was.

Robert Strawbridge, Jr., was the candidate for chairman on both tickets presented. The administration slate called for the return to office of every incumbent, making the election of officers a vote of confidence rather than anything else. F. Skiddy von Stade, Thomas White, and Carleton Burke were reelected vice-chairmen. Seymour Knox, Nelson Talbott, James Mills and John Lapham were reelected to the executive committee. J. Ford Johnson, Jr., was renamed secretary and Elbridge Gerry treasurer, replacing long-time serving Frank Sheridan O'Reilly.

The defeated slate was as follows: Thomas White, Stephen Farish and Charles Jackson, for the offices of vice-chairmen. Winston Guest, John Hay Whitney, Stewart Iglehart, for places on the executive committee. Gerard Smith ran for secretary and John H.H. "Ben" Phipps for treasurer.[18]

The End of an Era

In summary, the 1930s were a matter of survival by polo clubs awaiting the return of prosperous times. There were, of course, several bright spots: the continuing success in the Westchester Cup against British teams, the wonderful double at Palermo in the Argentine Open and the Cup of the Americas, the terrific struggles for the U.S. Open Championship, and the East-West series. It was also characterized by the fortitude of all polo institutions, large and small, in maintaining the spirit of the game in the face of adverse circumstances far beyond their control. In spite of heavy odds against them, the men in charge of polo in America showed their mettle in doing their best to preserve polo going on and securing its continuing success. It would be a long and arduous process, interrupted by the Second World War, but eventually it would bear fruit in a remarkable recovery following the lean years.

CHAPTER 13

The Open Championship
Until the War

The 1931 Open Championship, played at its usual venue, the Meadow Brook Club, provided a surprise because the Argentine team Santa Paula walked away with the trophy. It was the third foreign team to take the crown since the Ranelagh team had done so in 1910. The Santa Paula had planned the event with great care and much anticipation. The previous year they had sent the pony string to California, where they won all their matches, including the Pacific Coast Championship. They left their ponies in America; therefore, they were well acclimatized when the Eastern season began.

There was another team from Argentina participating in the tournament, the Hurlingham squad. John Miles, John Benitz, David Miles and Lewis Lacey appeared to be a team with great possibilities; however, they were defeated in the semifinal round by the Hurricanes. In the Monty Waterbury Cup, Hurlingham beat Sands Point, only to be defeated in the semifinals, again by the eventual winners of the tournament, in this particular instance Templeton. This tournament marked the final appearance of a glorious veteran, because a 7-goal, white-haired Devereux Milburn made his presence felt on the champion Templeton team, playing at Number 3 with the young lions, Mike Phipps, and the Guest brothers, Winston and Raymond.

The road to the championship was not an easy one for Santa Paula. Although their mounts were in superb form thanks to the ministrations of the celebrated Tommy Nelson, bad luck dogged the players. First, on the eve of their first game against Roslyn, Manuel Andrada injured his right thumb in the course of a practice game at Mitchel Field. A strong man, he played and had a bad spill, which rendered him unfit to play the semifinals against Greentree. Therefore, Andrés Gazzotti replaced him at Back, a position that was not customary for him. With a patched-up team, Santa Paula beat Greentree and they were in the finals, against the holders, Hurricanes. Further trouble awaited Santa Paula. The day before the final match it was the Polo Pony Show at Meadow Brook. Santa Paula's Number 1, Alfredo Harrington was riding into the ring to show one of his ponies, when something startled his mount, which shied away and in so doing, smashed Harrington's leg against a post. With one player in the hospital and another with his arm in a sling, the future loomed dark. Two physicians advised Andrada not to play. With a shrug of his shoulders, Andrada leaned over to Tommy Nelson and asked him, "What pony shall I play in the first chukker?"

The next afternoon, Andrada was at Back, as well as Gazzotti, once more out of position at Number 1. In spite of his swollen thumb, "Old man Andrada simply picked up his team and hurled it at the Hurricanes goal."[1] In a big upset, Santa Paula defeated Hurricanes by 11 goals to 8.

In a prescient commentary prior to the Open Championship, Robert Kelley described the changes in tactics developed by Thomas Hitchcock, Jr., and Santa Paula's counterpoint:

> Hitchcock has been credited with the change to hard, long-hitting and galloping, and probably justly so. The present trend of polo became the official, or standard, type of polo immediately after the third game between this country and Argentina in 1928. From that point on, pace, pace, and more pace has been the thing. Speed, long hitting, and practically nothing else. And there is no time to think. You have to make quick guesses. So far, in international play, which sets the style, the plan has been successful. This country has so far been able to put on the pressure and to keep it on until the other side cracked. This country has never had to try to stem any cracks in its defense, because there have not been any cracks. I would not be too sure about the invincibility of the United States until an American side has had to chase another.
>
> There are reasons for the success of the Santa Paula team. Over and above everything else was its spirit; but, mechanically, it was its superbly worked-out, short-passing game that gave it the victory. Certainly here at last was a perfect demonstration that you need not be a slugger to win in polo. It was the theory of team play put into action, and most theories never reach action.[2]

In marked contrast to previous years, the 1932 Open Championship had no foreign teams entered. In the preliminary matches Aurora won over Hurricanes and Eastcott, in one of the competition's best matches, defeated Sands Point, Tommy Hitchcock's team, in a close encounter, 6–5. Templeton, named for Raymond and Winston Guest's father's estate in England, easily took the measure of Aurora, 13–6. In the second semifinal, Greentree got by Eastcott 11–10 on a goal by Gerald Balding in the ninth chukker; however, an injury to Cecil Smith marred the contest. Close to the end of the sixth chukker, Cecil Smith's Texas pony, Glider, tripped while going at full speed, and went down. After a prolonged wait, Smith continued to play; later it was found he had a broken bone in his elbow.

The final match was a walk-away for Templeton. With Cecil Smith out of the lineup, Eric Tyrrell-Martin was called to duty. Templeton was a well-oiled machine: Mike Phipps, Winston Guest, Stewart Iglehart and Raymond Guest liked to play together and had a sound knowledge of each other's abilities. What had promised to be a quality final ended up as a one-sided, uninteresting match, which Templeton won 16–3. Rather sarcastically, Peter Vischer wrote:

> The last game was hardly a polo match, let alone the final contest of an Open Championship; it was more like an early June morning at Grace Field, with one side having a grand time doing as it pleased and the other trying desperately, even to the point of unexpected switches in position, to do something right.[3]

This Open Championship also served as the selection ground for the American team due to travel to Argentina. Three of the players on the champion team, Winston Guest, Iglehart and Phipps, were selected among those traveling to Buenos Aires and the glory of Palermo.

The first match of the 1933 Open Championship proved to be sweet revenge for Greentree, because the luck of the draw decreed that they play Templeton. Popular opinion held that this match would settle the championship there and then. There were some changes in both teams. In the defending champion team, Cocie Rathborne replaced Raymond Guest at Back, while in Greentree Ivor Balding took Hubert Williams' place. "Rube" was still nursing a broken leg, an injury sustained during the East-West series at Onwentsia Polo Club. Cecil Smith's uncanny accuracy in scoring from penalty shots—he tallied five—sealed the game for Greentree, 14–13.

Templeton, the 1932 and 1934 U.S. Open Champions. Raymond Guest, Stewart Iglehart, Winston Guest and Michael Phipps.

Aurora again drew Hurricanes in the first round, and once more took their measure in another close match, 8–7. Westbury, with Sonny Whitney, Barney Balding, Harold Talbott and John Fell, defeated Sands Point 11–7. With Tommy Hitchcock out of the polo season because of the concussion suffered in the same East-West series that claimed Rube Williams' leg, Robert Lehman, the Hoppings, father and son, and Raymond Guest wore Sands Point orange colors. In a battle of the Balding brothers and the Whitney cousins, Greentree ended up on top, 14–9.

The final game then was between Aurora and Greentree, with little to choose between the two sides. Aurora had a balanced team, beautifully mounted. But Greentree had Cecil Smith, to say nothing of Jock Whitney's string of ponies. Aurora led at halftime 6–5, but had a superb fifth chukker, when four goals crossed Greentree's posts. Aurora never looked back and ended deserved winners, 14–11.

Because of the mayhem and resultant publicity given regarding the number of fouls during the East-West series, Peter Vischer, *Polo* magazine's editor, counted every single foul committed — or whistled, if you prefer — during the Open Championship. Mr. Vischer's findings make interesting reading in view of the large number of fouls called by today's umpires. In the Open Championship's six matches, 55 fouls were called, an average of 9.2 fouls per game, or slightly more than one a chukker. Let us remember that eight chukkers was the norm in those days. Mr. Peter Vischer's assessment was that there were far too many. The champion team, Aurora, had an average of only two fouls per game called against them. The runners-up, Greentree, averaged 4.3 fouls per game. The Hurricanes, which came to within one goal of beating Aurora, committed seven fouls in their only game. Westbury averaged 5.5 fouls called against them. Sands Point and Templeton, which did not win a single game, were charged with ten fouls each. Fouls, then as now, are expensive.[4]

The same four players that had won for Templeton the 1932 Open did the trick in 1934. Mike Phipps, Winston Guest, Stewart Iglehart and Raymond Guest beat the defending champions, Aurora, 10–7, in the best match of the tournament. Six teams entered; first-round matches resulted in the elimination of Aknusti, the Gerry brothers' combination, and the Aiken Knights, by Eastcott and Greentree, respectively. Both winners fell in the semifinals. Therefore Aurora, with Billy Post replacing Ebby

Top of the swing at speed for Cecil Smith, who is wearing Greentree's shirt. For a long number of years the gentlemanly, soft-spoken Cecil Smith was at the summit of polo in America.

Gerry, faced Templeton. Although the team from East Aurora played well in its 11–7 win over Greentree, Elmer Boeseke was below form. He was playing Number 2, which forced James Mills to the unaccustomed Number 3 position.

In the final game, Boeseke played Back, which allowed Mills to return to his usual place; however, Billy Post, perhaps the best Back in America at the time, had to play Number 3. By the time Aurora settled down, Templeton had a 5–1 lead. Aurora was able to tie the score at seven-all in the seventh chukker, but the ponies were spent. Winston Guest led a furious attack that netted three goals for Templeton before the final bell sounded.

The 1935 Open Championship had a bit of foreign flavor rendered by the presence of a team representing the Hurlingham Club. With a challenge for the Westchester Cup looming within the next few months, the English selection committee dispatched a representative team to test the waters. Under the watching gaze of Col. R. Gerald Ritson, a former 10-goaler and a member of the 1913 international team, the team played a few practice games before the Open Championship inaugural game against the Hurricanes. The selected Number 1, Capt. Michael Ansell, injured a hand and was unable to play. His place on the team was taken by Capt. Hugh Walford. Capt. Percival "Tony" Sanger, Eric Tyrrell-Martin and

Left: **Princeton product William Post's classical swing. The 1933 U.S. Open, Aurora vs. Greentree.**
Right: **Thomas Hitchcock, Jr. Like Dev Milburn in his day, Tommy lent an air of adventure and enterprise to the game. The U.S. Open, Greentree vs. Hurricanes at Meadow Brook.**

Capt. Humphrey Guinness formed the rest of the team. After leading 7–5 at halftime, Hurlingham had a bad fifth chukker and never recovered. They were able to score only one goal in the second half of the game, losing 9–8. The Hurricanes had Laddie Sanford, Robert Gerry, Bobby Strawbridge and Cocie Rathborne. On the same day, Aurora—Shorty Knox, James Mills, Elbridge Gerry and Billy Post—defeated Westbury, with C.V. Whitney, Earle Hopping the younger, Cecil Smith and Rube Williams.

The tournament's third match was the only easy one for the winners, Greentree. They defeated John Fell's Long Island team at no more than a gallop. Then came the match between Aurora and Westbury, which was a battle all the way. Hurricanes were ahead in the last chukker, 10 goals to nine, but Aurora would not give up. Shorty Knox tied the score and Ebby Gerry iced the game shortly before the final bell.

The semifinal game between Greentree and Templeton was thought by many to be the decisive match for the championship. It was a choppy game, in which Templeton failed to finish scoring opportunities, including a 40-yard penalty with only seconds to go before game's end. Greentree, however, made most of the chances that came its way. With the scored tied at halftime, Greentree took 13 shots at goal, converting six into goals. In the same time span, Templeton had 14 shots, and made only five of them good. The scoreboard showed 10–9 at the final gong.

This left Aurora and Greentree to fight it out for the championship. It was a close-run thing, a pretty a polo game as you could ask for.[5] Greentree led 6 to 5 in the eighth chukker, but Aurora would not give in. Ebby Gerry tied the game with seconds to go, and into a ninth period they went. The play went on for a full period; when the bell sounded, Tommy Hitchcock got possession of the ball far away from the Aurora goal posts; passed it to Balding, who passed to Pete Bostwick, who set sail for goal, scoring a dramatic tally to take both game and championship. It was a match to remember.

The 1936 Championship had to share the spotlight with the Westchester Cup and the Cup of the Americas, while polo at the Olympics was ignored by the U.S. Polo Association. Nevertheless, Jock Whitney's Greentree successfully defended its title, this time beating Templeton in the final stanza, with the same four players on the team. Only Cooperstown in 1912 and 1913 had achieved that feat. The Hurricanes came close when they won in 1929 and 1930; however, the players were different.

The preliminary rounds were just an appetizer for the expected struggle between the titans: Greentree and Templeton. Greentree was the defending champion. Templeton, with Bobby Strawbridge replacing Stewart Iglehart, had a magnificent season in England, taking the Roehampton Open Cup, the Hurlingham Champion Cup and the Coronation Cup.

Three games were played on the first day. At Meadow Brook's International Field, Greentree met and won over Aurora, who was missing team captain Seymour Knox because of a family bereavement. Sands Point was the venue for Texas defeating Roslyn in a close match. And at Bostwick Field, Hurricanes beat Old Westbury. Templeton drew the first round bye and proceeded to crush Texas 16–5 in the semifinals. In the other semifinal match, Greentree ran away from the Hurricanes, 13–9.

Thus, the stage was set for the final game, with great expectations for an exhibition of good polo. The spectators were not disappointed because Templeton and Greentree delivered a superb, close and exciting game that went into sudden-death overtime.

The usual tactic of a whirlwind offensive from the start, employed countless times by

Another successful American team in England was Templeton. Mike Phipps, Jimmy Mills, Winston Guest and Robert Strawbridge, Jr., with the Roehampton Open Cup.

Cecil Smith and William Post clash at Meadow Brook. Despite the heavy bump, both players are in control of their mounts as befits those two excellent horsemen.

Tommy Hitchcock, did not materialize. On the contrary, Templeton jumped to a 2-nil start. It took some time for Hitchcock to reorganize his team; at halftime it was 6–5 in favor of Templeton. The fifth chukker showed Templeton at its best, obtaining an 8–5 lead. Somehow, by sheer effort Hitchcock slowed down Templeton, but with less than two minutes to go, Templeton was still ahead by one goal, 10–9. In his own, inimitable way, James Calvin Cooley described the scene:

> Greentree swept towards the south end of the field, which goal Templeton was defending. That south end is where the ponies stand, twenty-five or thirty on each side, Greentree on one side, Templeton on the other. And as Greentree attacked in that last desperate effort to tie the score, the yells and whoops of the Greentree grooms and helpers and sympathizers made a bedlam, and tired ponies being led around to cool out pricked their ears and wondered what it was all about. They had done their share and while thousands of people were getting as big a thrill as they ever had at polo, the ponies were thinking that they'd like to call it a day and go home and stand relaxed and comfortable on clean straw, digging into some sweet, fragrant hay. But for eight ponies there was more to come.[6]

A Templeton player crossed the line of a Greentree man and the whistle went. It was sad that the player penalized was Stewart Iglehart, who more than the others had kept Tem-

Stewart Iglehart hitting a near-side forehand shot. Winston Guest and Tommy Hitchcock follow the play.

pleton where it was. Tommy Hitchcock rode to take the 40-yard penalty. Of course, he did not miss.

Yes, there was an extra chukker. Both Iglehart and Hitchcok tried their luck at goal, but Whitney and Guest denied them the score. Winston Guest just managed to send the ball towards the corner. Wild scrimmage ensued, the ball popped towards Bostwick, who send it to Hitchcock, who passed to Balding, who scored.

Another final Open Championship game for the ages.

In 1937, a new team rose to the top of American polo: Old Westbury. It was a fine team, combining the best traditions of the east with the new spirit of the west. It was well-organized, wonderfully mounted, seasoned, and got to the top by a combined effort. It was assembled by Cornelius Vanderbilt Whitney, who had inherited a winning tradition from his father, the legendary leader of the first "Big Four," Harry Payne Whitney.[7]

The Old Westbury win brought Cecil Smith his first Open Championship. Playing at Number 2, between Mike Phipps and Stewart Iglehart, the tall Texan went about his business in his usual quiet, crisp and efficient way. Iglehart played as he had performed at Hurlingham the previous year: a brilliant and resourceful player, at his best when the going gets harder. With an efficient Phipps up front, and a solid Sonny Whitney at Back, Old Westbury's victory was no surprise. What was surprising was the ease with which it came about. They reached the final round by overwhelming Aknusti 16–3 and Templeton 19–5.

In the other bracket, Shorty Knox's Aurora was defeated 15–8 by the visiting Argentine team San José. In the semifinal round it was sweet revenge for Greentree, champion for the last two years but badly beaten in the Cup of the Americas. The San José team — named after the Duggans' estancia in Argentina — had in its lineup three members of the Cup of the Americas team: Manuel Andrada, Luis Duggan and Andrés Gazzotti. The fourth wheel was Heriberto Duggan, Luis' younger brother who at a 5-goal rating made an excellent impression as a surprisingly clever player endowed with wonderful equitation. The Argentine pony string was not up to the previous year's standard, the reason being that many of the latter were now carrying Greentree players.

Greentree got off to a lightning start, achieving a 5-goal advantage. San José got within one goal in the seventh chukker and scored what would have been the tying goal. However, a 40-yard penalty was called against the visitors and Tommy Hitchcock rammed the penalty shot to ice the game. It was, by far, the best match of the 1937 U.S. Open Championship.

The final game was anticlimactic. Old Westbury took 28 shots at goal, scoring 11 goals. For its part, Greentree had 20 shots at goals, making good on only 6 occasions. Balding and Hitchcock had eight shots at goal each, converting only four times: Hitchcock thrice and Balding a lonely tally.

In 1938, Old Westbury retained its championship with ease. The team was just too powerful for the opposition. Mike Phipps was on his way to achieve a 10-goal rating in spite of a shoulder injury that grounded him for the second match, Cecil Smith was all the way a 10-goal player, dominating in offense, scoring an average of one goal per chukker throughout the tournament. Stewart Iglehart, another 10-goaler, completely overwhelmed Tommy Hitchcock in the final match. And Cornelius Whitney at Back played above his handicap.

With such a talented, well-mounted team, the path to victory was easy. Old Westbury defeated Aknusti — the Gerry brothers, Elbridge and Robert, the talented Pat Roark, and Raymond Guest — by a categorical score of 13 to 7. In the semifinals that took care of Aurora, a good side with Seymour Knox, Frank von Stade, Lewis Smith and Ricardo Santamarina scored 14 goals against 8. In the finals, they overwhelmed Greentree 16 to 7.

This powerful Old Westbury was broken up and only four teams contested the 1939 Open Championship. Bostwick Field, with Pete Bostwick, Robert Gerry, Jr., Ebby Gerry and Eric Tyrrell-Martin, had a hard-earned win over Westbury, which had Gerard Smith, Earle A.S. Hopping, Stewart Iglehart and Robert Strawbridge, Jr., in its lineup. No matter how well Iglehart played, the more homogenous Bostwick Field had the upper hand, 9–8. A new Greentree, Peter Grace, Jr., Bob Skene, Tommy Hitchcock and Jock Whitney, then defeated the Texas Rangers by 14 goals to 11. Charles Wrightsman, Cecil Smith, Eric Pedley and Winston Guest played on the losing side.

The final match was touch and go throughout the game. Only once a team enjoyed a two-goal advantage, which did not last long. Ebby Gerry had an outstanding game and pushed Bostwick Field to the first of its two Open Championship titles.

In 1940, the Open Championship was played in matches of six chukkers, for the first time since eight chukkers became the norm. It was felt that with international play out of the question because of the war in Europe, it would be an appropriate manner to induce younger and lower handicap players to enter the most coveted trophy in North America.

Six teams answered the call. A notable absence was that of Tommy Hitchcock, for the first time since 1933. The title holders, Bostwick Field, presented a new team: Stephen

Four Gerry brothers from Aknusti: Edward, Elbridge, Henry and Robert junior. One of the few all-brother top polo teams.

Sanford, Pete Bostwick, Charles von Stade and Billy Post. They defeated a Westbury team composed of Jay Secor, Cornell University's star Clarence Combs, Earle Hopping the younger and Henry Gerry. In the second match, Aknusti, with Gerard Smith, Robert and Ebby Gerry, and Alan Corey, Jr., won from Texas: Charles Wrightsman, James P. Mills, Cecil Smith and George Oliver, Jr. Great Neck, with Yale's George Mead, Jr., J. Peter Grace, Jr., Stewart Iglehart and Bobby Strawbridge, drew a bye in the semifinals. They beat Bostwick Field 4–3. In the second semifinal Aknusti defeated another bye team, Gulf Stream, which had the brothers Ben and Mike Phipps, Winston Guest and Cocie Rathborne, rather comfortably 11 to 6.

In the final game, after a big tussle, Aknusti won the championship with a 5 to 4 win over Great Neck. The Long Island team took some measure of revenge when they turned the tables on Aknusti in the Monty Waterbury Cup, the most important tournament played on handicap.

The last Open Championship before Pearl Harbor was held in September 1941, with an entry of five teams. Two scratch sides, Pelicans and Texas, played the initial match. The Pelicans, Laddie Sanford, Winston Guest, George Oliver and Cocie Rathbone, beat Texas 9 to 7. The Texas team had Walter Hayden, Jr., Cecil Smith, Jay Secor and Harry "Dutch"

Evinger. The second game presented Gulf Stream, representing the family club in Florida, with John "Ben" Phipps, Michael Phipps, Charles von Stade and Alan Corey, another Yale product.[8] They rather easily beat Westbury, a team that had been re-arranged on the eve of the tournament. Gerald Dempsey, Earle A.S. Hopping, Stewart Iglehart and Holden White played for Westbury.

Aknusti then defeated the Pelicans, and faced Gulf Stream in the championship game. The twins Edward and Henry Gerry, older brother Elbridge, and Pete Bostwick made up the team, named after the Gerry family estate in New York State's Delaware County. Ebby Gerry played brilliantly; however, Gulf Stream proved to be too strong and took the title away from Aknusti.

CHAPTER 14

The Game at the Universities

The game of polo had been practiced at a few colleges in a more or less haphazard fashion ever since Harvard College started the trend in 1883. Maj. Gen. Robert Lee Bullard, the commander of the Second Corps Area with headquarters on Governors Island, presented in 1923 a bronze of two polo players to be emblematic of the Intercollegiate Championship.[1] Two successful tournaments were held on the parade grounds of Fort Hamilton in Brooklyn. Then Gen. Bullard retired and the Intercollegiate was left without a home. The need for an organization to support and direct polo at the universities became paramount. To that end, the Intercollegiate Polo Association was formed on 2 March 1925 at a meeting held in the offices of the U.S. Polo Association in New York City. The organization's charter members were Cornell University, Norwich University, Pennsylvania Military College, Princeton University, U.S. Military Academy, Virginia Military Institute, and Yale University. Mr. Alvin Devereux of Princeton was elected president; Governeur Morris Carnochan of Harvard, secretary and treasurer, and Frank O'Reilly, of the U.S.P.A., assistant treasurer and secretary. The rest of the members of the Executive Committee were Maj. Richard Anderson, Cornell; Maj. Archibald Arnold, Yale; Col. Frank Edwards, Norwich; Maj. Arthur Holderness, U.S. Military Academy; Lt. Col. Frank Hyatt, Pennsylvania Military Institute; and Maj. Harding Polk, Virginia Military Institute.[2]

In 1924, the University of Arizona polo team was crowned king of the west. "Then came east the Arizona team to give battle to the Princetonians. Princeton, however, speedily decided the issue by scoring two clean-cut victories in succession, and the Westerners returned mournfully westwards."[3]

Princeton University

The game of polo started at Princeton University in 1903. William G. Devereux of Glenwood Springs, Colorado, was elected captain, and Charles H. Dugro of New York City, treasurer and manager. A field west of the infirmary was secured. The following undergraduates joined the Princeton Polo Association: Lynn M. Adsit, Pierce Archer, Jr., David Baird, Jr., Walter Devereux, Jr., Charles Nicholl, Jr., Alexander Pratt, Percy Pyne, II, Leland Ross and Harry Yarrow.[4]

A later article in *The New York Times* reads: "The Polo Association received another lot of ponies last week, and the sport is on in earnest. Several games are scheduled for this month. The game which was to have been played here with the Freebooters of Philadelphia has been changed to that city for May 16."[5]

This seminal event finds confirmation in the 1904 Year Book. The record is that of a "Special Match by permission of the Committee," played at Devon, Pennsylvania on 15 May 1903. Harry Yarrow and Charles Dugro alternated at Number 1 for Princeton; the other team members were Leland Ross, Walter Devereux, and William Devereux at Back. Devon's team was composed by William Carter, Horace Hare, George Harrison, Jr., and Craig Biddle. Devon won the match by 11¼ to 5 goals.[6]

When the Reserve Officer Training Corps (R.O.T.C.) was established at Princeton with Maj. McMahon as commanding officer it became feasible for the undergraduates to obtain horses provided by the government. At the same time a number of graduates that had played polo in their younger days met at the Nassau Club. The result was the organization of the Princeton Polo Association. It was a large and distinguished group. Charles Munn, Class of 1881, represented the senior brigade. Albert Kennedy, Class of 1890, was an 8-goal handicap player with the Goulds' Lakewood Polo Club and a winner of the Association Cup and the Junior Championship. Other relative old-timers were Knox Taylor, Richard McGrann, James Barnes, John Converse, winner of the Senior Championship with Byrn Mawr; William Green, Percy Pyne, II, who would be a reserve on the American team in the 1924 Olympic Games; Courtland Nicoll, Leland Ross from the original Princeton team; future coach and author of a manual of polo Walter Devereux, Jr.; Alexander Pratt and Henry Yarrow, both from the first Princeton team; Alexander Perry Osborn, Alfred Ely and Charles Frick. More recent graduates were Fitz Eugene Dixon, Alvin Devereux, and James Devereux. Maj. McMahon and Lt. Robert Horr were also present.[7]

The Princeton Polo Association joined the ranks of the Polo Association on 17 January 1922. Thomas Bancroft, Charles Barkhorn, Charles Boynton, Jr., William Colket, Richard Ellis, Stuart Harrison, Richard Keith, Lewis Norris, Frank Richardson, Jr., Edward Shober, Charles Taylor, II, Augustine Weishaar, Clarence Wheelwright and Robert Williams, Jr., were the initial recruits.

Princeton took the Intercollegiate Arena tournament for the John R. Townsend Trophy in 1922.[8] Elgar Stabler, Alton Hall and William Fleming defeated Yale University at New York's Armory. Then Princeton took the measure of Yale 11–5 on an outdoors match. The Tigers were Elgar Stabler, William Fleming, Alton Hall and James Bathgate, III.

In 1923 the Princeton polo team was runner-up to Yale for the Intercollegiate Championship Trophy presented by Maj. Gen. Robert Bullard. The following year, the Princeton team — Charles Newbold, David Holbrook, William Jackson, Thomas Bancroft — now coached by Capt. J.W. Andrews, won the trophy. Every member of the team went the way of graduation into the real world and Maj. Fay Brink Prickett, who undertook as coach, was presented with the problem of shaping out a competitive team out of inexperienced players. Naturally, Princeton did not fare well for a few years, but in 1927 the team captained by Harold Erdman was runner-up to Yale. In 1928, Arthur Borden was captain; John Shaw and Redmond Stewart, Jr., with Frank Hitchcock, of Westbury, New York, younger brother of the international player, completed the team.

In that same year the Walter B. Devereux, Jr., Memorial Field was dedicated and in 1933 a Princeton team — John Kemmerer, Jr., Raymond Firestone, William Sullivan, and Mahlon Kemmerer — took the Intercollegiate Tournament held at the Westchester Country Club in Rye, New York. The Harvard College team was runner-up.

Yale University

According to Myopia polo player and writer Crocker Snow, Jr., the first intercollegiate polo game took place between Harvard and Yale in 1907 at Myopia Hunt Club's Gibney Field in Hamilton, Massachusetts.[9] Gibney Field, one of the oldest polo grounds in the world, was the site for the Harvard squad practice matches. Neither the teams nor the result is known.

What is known is that a Yale team played Squadron A at Cortlandt Park on 10 June 1903. This was the first appearance of the recently organized Yale team in a formal game. A. Moore, Louis Stoddard, Lydig Hoyt and Chauncey Hamlin played for Yale. The Squadron A team was Herbert Barry, Leavitt Hunt, R.G.D. Douglas and Joseph Hunt; they took the match by 8 to 5½ goals.[10]

On 21 June 1922 Yale played a game against Princeton, the first one since 1904. Henry Baldwin, Jonathan Bulkeley, Samuel Hopkins and Alan Cairns played for Yale.

In 1926 Yale University started a magnificent run that yielded ten championships. Fred Baldwin, Frederick W. Guest, C. Reddington Barrett and William Muir were that team's members.[11]

The varsity team — Fred Baldwin, Winston Guest, Reddington Barrett, Richard Simmons— retained the championship trophy in 1927, when the Phipps Field was opened for play. Oliver Wallop, John H.H. "Ben" Phipps and H.C. Adams also played during the event, which on this occasion was played as a round robin. The year 1928 yielded another championship for Yale. Oliver Wallop, Peter Folger, John H.H. Phipps, Fred Baldwin and Hardie Scott played in the final round, which had reverted to a single elimination format. Pennsylvania Military College was the runner-up. Ben Phipps became notorious when he brought a skunk to church while a student at Groton. Not unexpectedly, in the aftermath, he enrolled at Exeter.

In 1929 Harvard placed a parenthesis in Yale's winning streak, by defeating the Bulldogs by six goals to three. But in 1930 Yale recovered the crown with a most powerful team: Hardie Scott, James Mills, Stewart Iglehart and Joseph C. "Cocie" Rathborne. Michael Phipps also played on this team, which included two future 10-goalers, Phipps and Iglehart, plus Mills and Rathborne who would reach a lofty 8-goal handicap — something of an anomaly in a college game. Hardie Scott went on to be elected to the U.S. House of Representatives for three terms. The Princeton four was runner-up in that year.

In 1932, Yale University, having gained permanent possession of the Bullard Trophy, added for the second time its name to the Gouverneur Morris Carnochan Cup, being once more represented by a

The 1937 Inter-Collegiate Championship was held at Governors Island in New York Harbor. Mott Woolley of Yale is leading Oliver DeGray Vanderbilt in a first round match won by the gentlemen from Princeton.

team of Open Championship caliber. The handicap principle was applied for the second time in the tournament and added much to the interest in the tournament. The Yale team was Michael Phipps, James Mills, Stewart Iglehart and Dunbar Bostwick. In their prime that would have been a 34-goal team. Later that year, Mike Phipps accomplished a magnificent double when he took the Argentine Open Championship and the Cup of the Americas at Palermo. Stewart Iglehart was a reserve for the American international team in the Argentine tour. In the intercollegiate tournament, played at Rye Turf and Polo Club, old rival Harvard was runner-up. The final score was 13–9, Harvard receiving 7 goals by handicap.

Yale took four additional championships before Pearl Harbor. In 1935 Robert E.L. Wilson, III, Peter Dominick, Joseph Peter Grace, Jr., and Jay Secor, Jr., again defeated Harvard. This competition was held on Governors Island. In 1939 at the Burnt Mills Polo Club in New Jersey, William Chisholm, Alan Corey, Jr., C. Mott Woolley, Jr., and Collister Johnson once more took the best of Harvard College. While the war was raging in Europe, William Chisholm, George Mead, Jr., Alan Corey, Jr., and Frank Goodyear, Jr., beat Princeton, a good team that replaced Harvard as the bridesmaid. This tournament took place at the Hon. W. Cameron Forbes' field, in Westwood, Massachusetts. A team from the University of Arizona played, and was defeated by Princeton in the semifinals.

In the last Intercollegiate Championship played four-a-side, in the spring of 1941, the Yale squad, John Daniels, David Wilhem, George Mead, Jr., and Robert Johnson, again defeated Princeton University in the final match, which took place at the Blind Brook Turf & Polo Club, in Port Chester, New York.

Pennsylvania Military Institute

Polo was tried at the Pennsylvania Military Institution (now Widener University) in 1915.[12] It was felt by the university that a polo program added significantly to the school's reputation.

The 1928 team indoor team took the Townsend Trophy: Daniel Jones, James Whitehurst and Charles Bower. Herman Neuwieller, John Pickering and Jack Smith were other players.

Cadets played polo as an intercollegiate sport between 1923 and 1948. There were very few opportunities to play polo in the immediate postwar years.

The institution became a casualty of the antimilitary feelings in vogue during the Vietnam war and elected to change its name to Widener University.

Cornell University

The spread of polo at American colleges and universities lends particular interest to the growing pains of the sport at a great institution like Cornell, in Ithaca, New York.

Although a few students showed a keen interest in the game, it took time to become a working organization.

Polo was started at Cornell in 1919, when Maj. Thomas Christian, a Virginia Military Institute graduate, and Maj. Ralph Hospital organized the Field Artillery Unit of the Cornell Reserve Officers' Training Corps.[13] The first official Cornell polo team was composed by the following undergraduates: Richard Burke, Caesar Grasselli, David Morse, John Pflueger and Walter Schmidt.[14]

There was a Cornell Officers' Polo Club, composed of two officers in the Field Artillery unit, Capt. Hugh Gaffney and Lt. Arthur Hammond, and two students. This team played polo as it could, at Madison Barracks in the summer, at the Tompkins County Fair in Ithaca in August, at Governors Island in September, and at nearby Cortland.

In 1929, Cornell had the Cayuga Heights Polo Club, an organization of exactly four students: Paul Deming, Myron Fuerst, John Hertz, Jr., and George Olditch. Since there was no official polo at Cornell University, the Cayuga name was adopted. This team "occasionally has the temerity to challenge some organization," but it had neither mounts, nor field, nor coach, nothing but a desire to play polo for the sheer joy of it. One of the reasons polo was not on a firmer footing at Cornell is because there were no facilities whatever for winter practice. Ithaca has a long winter and a cold one and it is impossible to play polo most of the college year without a riding hall.

In spite of all the difficulties, games were played against Cortland Polo Club, Ohio State University, Norwich Military Academy, West Point, Yale University, the 104th Field Artillery at their armory in Syracuse, and other National Guard Units in the early 1930s.

As an aside, an interesting situation occurred when All-American Bartholomew Viviano, Class of 1933, played polo and was also captain and fullback on the Cornell football team. Bart Viviano led Cornell football to an 18-5-1 record in three years

That Cornell was alive to the possibilities of polo may be judged from the results of a meeting among Col. Joseph Beacham, Jr., Commandant of the Cornell R.O.T.C., Maj. Ralph Hospital and Cornell's President Livingston Farrand, regarding the feasibility of securing a riding hall similar to the one built at Princeton. President Farrand expressed himself in full sympathy with the idea, which bore fruit in the fall of 1934, when the Riding Hall with a gallery for 300 spectators was inaugurated. Paul Schoellkopf, an influential alumnus from Western New York, was instrumental in securing appropriate funds. The Riding Hall and the stables were located between the Cascadilla Creek and Dryden Road, now Route 366.

In the early 1970s the wooden stables and the R.O.T.C. Riding Hall had developed major maintenance problems, becoming unsafe and in urgent need of a solution. The old Warren Farm site across the heating plant east of Schoellkopf Stadium was selected. Following an intensive fund-raising campaign, in which John T. Oxley and Dolph Orthwein were major contributors, a practically new stables and arena with a gallery capable of accommodating 800 spectators were erected. The new stables were donated by Adolphus Orthwein, Sr., and his family, all closely connected with polo in St. Louis. Peter Orthwein, Class of 1968, was an outstanding collegiate player and captain of the championship polo team.

With an adequate arena fully operational, Cornell University quickly became a strong contender in collegiate polo. In 1937, Stephen Roberts, Clarence Combs, Jr., and Thomas Lawrence took the Indoor Polo Championship. Dr. Roberts became a much beloved polo coach at Cornell from 1942 until 1972. Clarence "Buddy" Combs is one of only three players who achieved a 10-goal goal rating in the indoors game, the others being Winston Guest and South African Joe Henderson.

Women's polo took off at Cornell when the R.O.T.C. under the coaching of Maj. Charles Ferrin started a team of Alice Nathalie Colvocoresses, Ruth Sharp, Anne Simpson and Virginia Yoder. The team played about three games a year against the Wilkes Barres Whipettes at the 109th Field Artillery facilities. Women's polo stopped in 1938 when Maj. Ferrin was transferred and the Dean of Women decided that polo was not a game for females after one player had a few teeth knocked out by an errant mallet.

However, intercollegiate women's polo came back with a vengeance in 1972. The Cornell team took the Championship a dozen times between 1979 and 2009, besides being finalist in 14 occasions: an enviable record, which included five titles in a row in 1984–1988. Pam Wood, Janet Burgess and Cindy Preston took the first title for Cornell. In the following years, players such as Elizabeth and Harriet Antczac, Marisa Bianchi, Anne Broeder, Mary Buck, Kelly Chambers, Caroline Hahn, Karen Lowe, Taylor McLean, Renee Ravesloot, Mary Ricciuti, Melissa Riggs and Rachel Smith were the outstanding players for Cornell, who also achieved three championships in a row in 2000–2002.

Cornell men's polo was revived in 1946 after World War II, under the captaincy of Cecil D. Cooper, but the intercollegiate crown, now played indoors and three-a-side, proved to be elusive until 1955 when Albert Mitchell, Camilo Saenz and Alberto Santamaría trounced Yale 19–5 in the finals. Cornell University went on to win the Indoor Intercollegiate Championship a total of eleven times. The Colombian connection of Saenz, the Santamarías—Alberto and Guillermo—and Pablo Toro was beneficial to the Big Red in the 1950s. Patrick Baker, Bennett and Peter Baldwin, Frank "Butch" Butterworth, Patrick Dix, James Greenwell, James Morse, Paul Mountain, Peter Orthwein, James Reynolds, John Walworth

The Cornell University polo squad in 1961. Mounted: E. "Pat" Baker, Frank "Butch" Butterworth, John Walworth and Ben Baldwin. Standing: Coach Dr. Stephen Roberts, J. Allan Leslie, Thomas Henderson, James Morse and Kevin Freeman. In front: Allen Schwartz and Nathaniel Grew.

and Stanley Woolaway all contributed to the titles in the 1960s. Patrick Dix in Spokane, Butch Butterworth and Peter Orthwein at Fairfield Hunt Club in Connecticut, and all three players in the Florida season reached respectable handicaps and became part and parcel of high-goal polo.

The Cornell University men's polo team then suffered a drought as far as championship titles is concerned, until 2005, when Brian Fairclough, Senter Johnson, Jeffrey Markle and Nicholas Grew took the Intercollegiate crown by defeating the University of Virginia in a thrilling match, 21–19.

Harvard College

Harvard, the first university to take up the game of polo, revived old glories when Frank Stranahan, Jr., Alexander Shaw, William White and Robert Pinkerton took the intercollegiate championship in 1925. In 1929 Harvard defeated Yale in the finals. James Cotton, Elbridge Gerry, Forrester "Tim" Clark and James Mandell did the honors. Tim Clark missed a few polo games because of his duties as No. 6 in Harvard's Varsity eight while training for the annual contest versus Yale in New London. It is quite unusual to hold a mallet and grab an oar during the same season; however, the giant from Myopia managed to achieve such a feat.

During the 1930s Harvard took three Intercollegiate Championships. In 1934, Edward Gerry, Lowell Dillingham, Thomas Davis and Henry Gerry defeated the Pennsylvania Military Academy in the final match at Blind Brook Turf & Polo Club in Rye, New York. A team from the University of Missouri participated in the tournament.

Edward Gerry, twin brother Henry Gerry, A. Townsend Winmill and Frank S. von Stade, Jr., took the trophy in 1936. The U.S. Military Academy at West Point was runner-up. The Robert L. Gerry Trophy became the trophy emblematic of the Intercollegiate Championship. The competition took place on Morris Memorial Field, Governors Island, in New York's Bay.

The difficulties encountered by the colleges located in the western states convinced the authorities at the U.S.P.A. in 1937 to establish two championships, Eastern and Western. Harvard took the 1938 Eastern competition, which was held at Burnt Mills Polo Club. It was a sweet victory for the Crimsom, because they defeated Yale in the finals. R. Bennett Forbes, H. Gaylor Dillingham, Frank von Stade, Jr., and Bronson Rumsey took the honors.

Virginia Military Institute

There is notice that Virginia Military Institute, the second oldest military school in America, had a polo team in 1921. A photograph in that institute's archives bearing the caption V.M.I. Polo Team shows four mounted players in polo gear. Only one individual is identified: Cadet Walter Ames, Jr. (Class of 1922) is on left. There is also another photograph of the 1922 Virginia Military Institute polo team: Leon Daube '23, Wilson Cary Marshall '22, Ruxton Ridgely '23, and Morton Winchester '23.

Another photograph of the 1923 team getting ready for a match is also in the archives. The players are identified as James Girand, Graham Penniman, Leon Daube, and [Henry or James] Barrow, all Class of 1923.[15]

After World War II, polo was resumed on the Parade Ground in 1955.

Collegiate Polo in the West

Polo at the University of Oklahoma at Norman was started in 1919 by Maj. Charles Bahr. Both private and government horses were procured. Norman being only 50 miles from Reno, the Army's largest remount depot, it was relatively easy to obtain horses. The 1928 team was made up from Ralph Garretson, Thomas McHenry, Meredith Miles, Edgar Mills, Charles Stanley and Clyde Watts.[16]

The University of Oklahoma participated in the 1931 Intercollegiate Tournament in 1931. The team from Norman — Clyde Watts, J. Brac McKinley, Joe Chastain and Joe Barnhill — was unlucky because the draw placed them against the U.S. Military Academy in the first match. The West Point squad went on to take the championship.

Oregon State University begun its polo program in 1921, on mounts issued by the R.O.T.C. In the 1920s the team played Stanford and Utah universities, Portland Polo Club, Seattle Polo & Hunt Club, an Army team from Vancouver Barracks in Washington and a Canadian team from Lake Douglas in British Columbia, losing only one contest. Varsity players included Twain Bodmer, Boeseke, Cornutt and Bill McGinnis.

Polo at the University of Arizona in Tucson began in 1922 when ten undergraduates answered Lt. Col. Ralph Parker's call for volunteers. After some six weeks of training on government mounts the property of the R.O.T.C. a team played a match against the Douglas Country Club.[17] Later on, Arizona played against Fort Huachuca at Douglas and Fort Bliss in Texas.

The following year a Southwestern Intercollegiate Championship was organized. Teams from Arizona, New Mexico Military Institute, University of Oklahoma and Texas A & M participated, with the University of Arizona emerging as the champions. In 1924, a team traveled East and met Princeton University, being defeated but not disgraced.

There is a photograph of the University of Arizona polo team in Newell Bent's *American Polo*. The caption indicates that the players, wearing checkered shirts, chaps and cowboy hats, were the 1924 Western college champions. The stern-looking undergraduates are identified as Harry Saunders, Paul Sawyers, James Heron and Montgomery Goody.[18]

By 1929 there were several teams in Tucson: the Jaycees, sponsored by the Junior Chamber of Commerce, composed by former University of Arizona players and the Old Pueblo Mustangs, comprised of officers who were instructors at the college and Army reserve officers in Tucson. The grass polo grounds in Tucson carried the reputation of being the best between Los Angeles and San Antonio.

Stanford University in Palo Alto was twice runner-up in the Western Intercollegiate Championship. Matches were played against other universities and teams such as Burlingame, Oakland and the Presidio of Monterey.

New Mexico Military Institute had a good run between 1924 and 1928 by winning all but four of the matches. Varsity players were William Dritt, John Kizer, J. Braxton McKinley, Leonard Smith, Thomas Thompson, Richard Wittenburg, Lewis Brown, III, and Arthur Wilson, Jr. Both Brown and Wilson were sons of two outstanding Army polo players: "Vief" Brown and "Jingle" Wilson.

When the U.S.P.A. decided to split the championship into Western and Eastern divisions, the Western competition was held at the Uplifters Polo Club in Santa Monica, California. The University of Arizona team, Charles Mosse, George Evans, Boyd Branson and George Judson, Jr., took the championship. The runner-up was Stanford University from Palo Alto.

The University of Missouri had a good team in 1930, with W.E. Cheatham, E.B. Reaves, L.A. Scott, A.E. Terwilliger and John Kizer.

In 1938, the University of Southern California's Jack Anderson, Robert Stack, Robert Rogers and Charles Wheeler took the trophy, after defeating Stanford in the finals. The tournament was played again at Uplifters Polo Club. Robert Stack, U.S.C.'s Number 3, went on to a career as a movie star, besides being an excellent shot. He became a familiar figure on the sidelines of polo clubs around the country long after his polo-playing days were over.

By 1941, although there was no official intercollegiate tournament, there was active play in the West, with Stamford playing a full schedule of eight games. Other colleges with teams on the field included the University of Arizona, California Agricultural College, New Mexico Military Institute and University of Utah.

International Polo in England

An invitation from Cambridge University in 1958 resulted in a tour by the U.S. Intercollegiate Polo Team, under the guidance of the U.S. Polo Association. George "Frolic" Weymouth, from Brandywine, Peter Baldwin from Hawaii, Richard Riemenschneider from Milwaukee, and Stanley Woolaway, also from Hawaii, were the selected players. All were experienced: Weymouth, Riemenschneider and Woolaway were team captains at Yale, Virginia and Cornell, respectively. Peter Baldwin was the star player at Cornell University.

The team gathered at Brandywine under the guidance of Ray Harrington and Jimmy Mills for training and practice games. Upon arrival in England, the team had a practice game at Cowdray Park on ponies lent by their gracious host, Lord Cowdray. The American undergraduates then played the Maharaja of Cooch Behar's team in the Pimm's Cup, being defeated by one goal in the match's waning seconds. The following Sunday the Americans played against Cambridge University at Woolmers Park, Arthur Lucas' estate. The American undergraduates defeated their Cambridge counterparts 11–4, and started a string of victories which continued at Cirencester and at Windsor Park.

The official tour being over, the team was invited to play in two low-goal tournaments, the Gloucestershire Cup at Cirencester and the Holden White Cup at Cowdray Park. The collegiate team took the Gloucestershire Cup, after beating three opponents. Nineteen teams entered the Holden White Cup, where the U.S. team lost 7–3 to Cheshire, the eventual champions. Windsor Holden White was a scion of the White family in Ohio; he took up residence in England, where he became patron of the Polo Cottage team.

As a token of appreciation towards their several hosts who loaned their ponies and provided housing, the Americans presented the Gerald Balding Cup, which is still played for at Cirencester Park.

Women's Intercollegiate Polo

To give the ladies due credit, collegiate polo started in 1915 in an arena in New York City. An article in *The New York Times* so states:

> Probably the first polo game ever played by teams of college women was watched by a large crowd last night at the Central Park Riding Academy. It was the opening match of the season, held under the auspices of the Alumni committee on Athletics of Barnard College.

The players on the teams represented a number of colleges, including Vassar, Bryn Mawr, and Wellesley. The sides lined up as the Blue and the Red. The former won by 4 goals to 0.

The women played a splendid game, and many of the spectators who went there expecting to see a burlesque on outdoor polo were pleasantly surprised and applauded the numerous good plays that were made.

Both sides mixed it up, and apparently enjoyed a scrimmage as much as Devereux Milburn, or any of the international four. Miss Jean Moehle of the Blues was particularly aggressive, and was on the ball every minute. She sat deep in her saddle and had a fine, free swing on either side of her pony. There were one or two bad "crosses," but there was also a lenient referee, and they were overlooked.

The Blues, consisting of Miss Jean Moehle, Emma L. George, and Lillian Schoedler, started to rush matters immediately the ball was thrown in, and with the aid of surprisingly good work soon had the sphere in front of the Reds' goal. But Miss Kate Chambersand cleared and then the Reds started pressing, and Miss Lillian Schoedler was called upon to save, which she did in fine style. However, the Blues would not be denied, and Miss Emma L. George fastened on the ball in midfield and dribbled up to within ten feet of the goal, and scored the opening point for the winners. Two more were added before the period close. The Reds played with a little more ginger in the second half, and the Blues were only able to add a single tally to their total.

With practice, the college women would give the famous Meadow Larks of Long Island a good tussle. On the side of the Reds were Miss Kate Chambersand, the Misses Elmina and Alva Wilson.[19]

Chapter 15

Polo in the Military

Robert Lee Bullard, a lieutenant general in the U.S. Army, tells how military polo started in America. In the early 1880s a cavalry regiment marching to a new station in the Western states' prairie country stopped at a small city for the night. Among the residents there were some men who had played polo in England and they suggested a match be played against a regimental team. This was accepted. The struggle that followed was the first polo match played by an Army outfit. A croquet ball and hockey sticks were produced for the five-a-side encounter, which was played for three periods, each lasting 20 minutes. The civilian hosts took the match by a score of 5 goals to 2.[1]

With due respect to Maj. Gen. Bullard,[2] a strong supporter of polo in the United States, this is an interesting narrative; however, the lack of details makes it hard to accept it as fact. There is no mention of which regiment was involved, and the town's name remains a mystery. Nothing is known about the players.

The first written mention of polo in the military appears in *Outing* magazine: "The officers of the U.S. 4th Cavalry, stationed at Fort Walla-Walla in Washington State, will be honored in future histories of polo as the founders of the first regular regimental club."[3]

It was Lt. Edward B. Cassatt, from a Pennsylvania horsy family, who had the idea of starting polo.[4] A regimental polo club was formed on or about 1 March 1892, establishing a committee chaired by Capt. James Lockett,[5] and composed of Lt. Robert A. Brown,[6] Lt. Cassatt and Lt. Gordon Voorhies.[7] None of the officers had played the game of polo before. As to ponies, there was ample supply of the local breed, known as Cayuses, at $15 each, which proved to be easily trained and quite suitable for the game. The problem was that there were no other opponents nearby. It is quite likely that polo at remote Fort Walla-Walla[8] failed to thrive after Maj. Lockett was transferred to the Presidio in San Francisco.

The game received a full start in 1896 at Fort Riley,[9] in Kansas, by lieutenants Sterling Price Adams, Terry Allen, Brook Payne, and Samuel Sturges, and Maj. Charles Treat. The practice games were held on what was known as the "Hogback," a flat ridge between Godfrey Court and the streetcar track. Later the parade grounds of the Cavalry and Artillery Posts were used as polo fields.

In October 1897, the Junction City *Republican* stated in its Fort Riley column: "The polo teams from Kansas City and St. Louis will be here to play. The officers of the Post are practicing hard."[10]

Around that time, polo was also carried on at nearby Fort Leavenworth.[11]

Polo at West Point was started in 1900 when Col. Albert Mills was Superintendent of the Academy and the Commandant of Cadets was Col. Charles Treat, who for many years would represent the Army Polo Committee in the U.S. Polo Association. A few ponies were obtained and Capt. Cassatt — who had started the ball rolling in Walla-Walla — and Lt. Col. Robert Howze, who succeed Col. Treat as Commandant, became polo instructors for both officers and cadets.

In 1902 the Army Polo Association was affiliated with the Polo Association. Play was carried on by cavalry regiments at many army stations in the continental United States: Assinniboine in Montana; Grant in Arizona; Riley in Kansas; Robinson in Nebraska; and Walla Walla in Washington.[12] The 25th Infantry Polo club was in Fort Niobrara, Nebraska,[13] and two cavalry regiments stationed in the Philippines played polo near Manila. The U.S. Military Academy at West Point, New York, also boasted a polo club.[14]

The first list of polo-playing Army officers appears in the 1908 Polo Association *Year Book*. Twenty-five officers are listed, all with a rating of 0 goals, with the exception of Maj. Treat at 2-goals, and Capt. Sterling Adam, Capt. Henry T. Allen, Lt. Carl Muller and Lt. Samuel Sturgis, all rated at one-goal.[15] In 1928, 1,152 officers were listed on the Polo Association handicap list.

The best Army team in the 1910s was the 10th Cavalry: Lieutenants Henry R. "Hank" Adair, Ephraim Graham, Carl Muller and Bruce Palmer.[16] The 10th was stationed in Fort Robinson and was one of the visiting teams at Colorado Springs. They were nicknamed the "Buffalo Soldiers" because it was a segregated unit, officered by West Point graduates. When transferred to Fort Ethan Allen in Vermont, after long service in the West, the polo team acquitted itself well in their matches against Eastern teams.[17]

In March 1912, an 11th Cavalry team from Fort Oglethorpe in Georgia traveled to Camden, South Carolina, in order to participate in the Camden Championship Cup. They took the initial game against the Camden 2nd team; this is the first recorded win for a military team in the Polo Association Year Book.[18] The team was Capt. George Vidmer, replaced during the game by Lt. E.R. Harris; Lt. Clark Chandler, Lt. Richard Kimball and Capt. George Langhorne. The 11th Cavalry then lost the next two matches against Camden 1st and Aiken. Nevertheless, they took the Camden-Aiken Cups defeating the Camden Freebooters team. The expedition was composed of "five captains and lieutenant, five privates to take charge of the ponies, and probably five army wives."[19] Subsequently to this event, Army teams from Fort Oglethorpe were frequent visitors to Camden.[20]

The Army Championship was played in Washington, D.C., in July 1912. Teams from the 11th Cavalry, Fort Myer, 5th Field Artillery, Washington, West Point, and the 6th Field Artillery participated in the week-long event.[21] The two Field Artillery teams met in the finals, the 6th being the winner. This team — Lieutenants Alfred Sands, Cortlandt Parker, René R. Hoyle, and Louis Beard — went on to Narragansett Pier, the summer place for the gathering of the best American polo players. It was considered a learning experience; however, the Army team, with Lt. Joseph Rumbough in place of Lt. Sands, reached the finals of the Overture Cup, losing to a Bryn Mawr squad.

In the Army and Navy Cups, also played at the Pier, the Army team, now with Lt. Sands back on the lineup, beat teams from Meadow Brook and Camden before falling against a different Bryn Mawr team in the semifinals. It was an auspicious debut for the young Army team. This 6th Field Artillery team which also included lieutenants Harvey Highley and Ralph Pennell became the best in the American Army in the 1910s.

The participation of an American Army team in the 1920 London season and in the Olympic Games in Belgium has been described in Chapter 7.

The 1920s was the golden age of military polo in the United States. For the first time, an Army team entered the U.S. Open Championship in 1921. The event, held at Bala in

Pennsylvania, saw the Army team — Maj. Arthur H. Wilson, Maj. Harry Chamberlin, Lt. Col. Lewis Brown, Jr., Maj. Walter Erwin — face the Philadelphia Country Club. It was an auspicious start, because the military squad came out the winners by 10 goals to 5. In the semifinals the Rockaway team of Morgan Belmont, Tommy Hitchcock, Benjamin Gatins and John Cheever Cowdin defeated the Army representatives 14–9.

The soldiers served notice when the U.S. Army team took the Junior Championship in 1922. Maj. Arthur H. Wilson, Maj. Louis Beard, Lt. Col. Lewis Brown, Jr., and Maj. William Erwin were on the winning team. They defeated a strong Meadow Brook team — Averell Harriman, Elliot Bacon, Morgan Belmont, Robert Strawbridge, Jr. — in the final game, held at the Point Judith Club in Narragansett Pier. The Army polo team made a habit of taking the Junior Championship because they won the cup a total of seven times between 1922 and 1932.[22]

In 1927 an Army polo team entered the U.S. Open Championship. Candler Wilkinson, Charles Gerhardt, Peter Rodes and George Huthsteiner, all captains, prevailed over the Ramblers team in the first round, only to be defeated in the semifinal game by the eventual Open Champions, the Sands Point team of Averell Harriman, Thomas Hitchcock, Jr., J. Cheever Cowdin and Louis Stoddard.

The following year the U.S. Open Championship was played at Meadow Brook following the completion of the series for the Cup of the Americas versus Argentina. The Army presented another team to compete in the Open Championship. The start of the international series was delayed due to the sickness of the Argentine pony string. Accordingly, the Open was played late in the season, over two days in October. Only four teams participated in the tournament. In the first game, the U.S. Army team defeated Eastcott by a single tally, 9–8. The same four players that had represented the Army in 1927 made up the team. In the course of the match, Capt. Candler Wilkinson was hit in the face by a hard-driven ball and was replaced by Lt. Morton McD. Jones. The injury prevented Capt. Wilkinson from playing in the final game against Meadow Brook, which had beaten Sands Point by a single goal, 10–9. The Meadow Brook foursome — Cornelius V. "Sonny" Whitney, the Argentine ace Juan Miles, Mike Stevenson and Winston Guest — proved too much for the Army squad, winning match and tournament by 8 goals to 5. Nevertheless, it was a creditable performance rendered by the U.S. Army team.

The final game for the U.S. Open Championship was also the semifinal game for the Monty Waterbury Cup, in those times played for on handicap by the teams entered in the U.S. Open Championship. Meadow Brook gave the Army team five goals by handicap; therefore, the Army team won 10–8. The final game for the Monty Waterbury Cup was between the Army team and Sands Point, which had Elbridge Gerry, Averell Harriman, Tommy Hitchcock and Stewart Iglehart. The Sands Point team won the match, 13–11, after giving 2 goals by handicap. It should be noted that the Army team had to play three hard matches in five days, while Sands Point, loser in the opening round of the Open Championship, had a four-day rest. This must have told on the stamina of the Army's ponies.

Military Polo Successes in the Twenties and Thirties

Army polo teams had their share of success in the medium-handicap tournaments held in the inter-wars period. These competitions were the National Twelve Goal Cham-

The U.S. Army polo teams were quite successful in the 1920s and 1930s. This is the team that took the Junior Championship in 1930: Lt. Morton Jones, Capt. Candler Wilkinson, Capt. Peter Rodes and Lt. Homer Keefe. The silver cup is presented by U.S.P.A. Chairman Louis Stoddard.

pionship and the Twelve Goal Inter-Circuit Championship, the latter held among the winners of each circuit.

From 1925 until 1938, different military teams, starting with Fort Bliss[23] and ending with the Field Artillery School, took these two championships a total of fourteen times.[24]

Mention must be made of the two Intercollegiate Championships taken by the West Point Military Academy. In 1931, cadets George Grunert (replaced in the final game by Gordon Cusack), Laurence Rodgers, Royden Beebe, Jr., and Bruce Von G. Scott won the championship at the Rockaway Hunting Club on Long Island, defeating Harvard in the final game.

The 1937 Eastern Intercollegiate Championship was held at Morris Field on Governors Island, New York. The polo ground was named as a memorial to Col. Wyllis Virlan Morris, head of the American Army delegation in its successful trip to Argentina in 1930. Col. Morris was killed in a polo accident while playing at Meadow Brook in 1931. Fittingly, the winning team was the representation from West Point. The team was Henry Wilson, William West, III, Arthur Harrison Wilson, Jr., and William Brett. Cornell University was runner-up, with Stephen Roberts, Clarence Combs, Jr., Thomas Lawrence and Walter Naquin, Jr.

International Matches with the British Army Team

The most significant events in the history of United States Army polo were the 1923 and 1925 series against the British Army. The idea originated with the U.S. Polo Association, and on its behalf Gen. John J. Pershing, Commander-in-Chief of the U.S. Army, wrote to the Earl of Cavan inviting a British team to play in America. In his letter of acceptance Lord Cavan strongly suggested that the teams be made up only by officers on the active list of each army, and that the ponies be the property of the officers, or of the War Department. This would preclude the borrowing or leasing of ponies for this series by either side.

In replying to the Earl of Cavan's letter, General Pershing wrote:

> Your letter rings with just the sort of sportsmanship that deeply appeals to me. The conditions you strongly advocate are exactly along the line our team is training; an example to all the world for clean sportsmanship.[25]

The U.S.P.A. arranged that the matches be held on Meadow Brook's International Field on Long Island at the height of the polo season. Named the International Military Title, the trophy was presented by the Meadow Brook Club and took place from 12 September to 18 September, as three matches were needed to decide the contest. The U.S. Army team was Maj. Arthur Wilson, Maj. John Kerr, Lt. Col. Lewis Brown, Jr., and Maj. Louis Beard. England was represented by Lt. Col. Teignmouth Melvill, Lt. Walter McCreery, Maj. Frank Hurndall and Maj. Eric Atkinson. The U.S. Army team came out winners, by scores of 10–7, 10–12 and 10–3.

Great credit was given to Lt. Thomas McCreery, who was in charge of the American pony string. The ponies had been under his care for three months prior to the event and were in top form for the series. Lieutenant McCreery had been in charge of the ponies for the Army team that had taken the Junior Championship against strong and well-mounted civilian teams.

A return series was played in England in 1925. Once more, there were painstaking preparations for the American Army team. Maj. Louis Beard was put in charge and ordered to make an inspection of Army posts in search of men and ponies. As a result, six players, together with grooms and ponies, were assembled at Mitchel Field,[26] right next to the Meadow Brook Club, for a summer of polo experience in 1924. The matches were to be played in June 1925, so men and ponies were sent to Florida for practice during the winter. Their host was Mr. Carl Fisher — of Indianapolis Speedway fame — who most generously provided training facilities. The team left in March, the horses being fed English hay on board to get them accustomed in time for the change in feeding. Once in England, the ponies were conditioned slowly, in a sensible way.

When the first match took place at the hallowed Hurlingham ground the American team was ready and won by a score of 8 goals to 4. The second game was also won by the United States, 6–4. The American team was Maj. Arthur Wilson, Capt. Charles Gerhardt, Capt. Peter Rodes and Maj. Beard. The British Army team was Capt. Richard McCreery, his younger brother Walter, Capt. John Dening and Maj. Dennis Boles. In the second game there was a collision between two English players in the fifth chukker; Capt. Dening had to be replaced by Maj. Vivian Lockett. King George V and his consort Queen Mary attended the game, adding a royal touch to the proceedings.

On the English side the McCreery brothers, Richard and Walter Selby, had American blood in their veins, because their father Walter Adolph McCreery was an American living in Europe and had participated in the 1900 Olympic Games.[27]

The international military series were scheduled to be resumed in 1929; however, the onset of the worldwide financial crisis resulted in the cancellation of the event.

Matches with Mexico

In the spring of 1924, the Mexico Polo Club invited a military team from Fort Sam Houston in order to improve the standard of the local game. Maj. Clifford King, Lt. G.C. Benson, Lt. Morton McD. Jones and Lt. Edward McGinley, together with Mr. John Lapham, made up the team. The team played under the name Whips, and won all four games by scores of 9–1, 10–2, 12–1 and 16–3. The American ponies outpaced the local mounts, with the exception of Manuel Campero's fine string. Henry Lacey, Jorge Parada and Maj. E.L.N. Glass, Military Attaché in the American Embassy, were the best local players.

Following play for the Southwestern Circuit Cups in February 1926, a team of Maj. Clifford King, Maj. Frank Andrews, John Lapham and Lt. J.M. Clark, representing Fort Sam Houston, met the Polo Club of Mexico in a two-game series. The Fort Sam Houston team won both games by only one goal in each, the last one in an extra period. The Mexican team was Manuel de Campero, Archibald Burns, Lt. Col. Jaime Quiñones and Julio Muller.

The 1st Cavalry Division was garrisoned at Fort Bliss, Camp Marfa and Fort Clark in Texas. In December 1926, under the command of Brig. Gen. Edwin Winans, a team played in Torreon as guests of the Mexican president, Gen. Plutarco Elías Calles. The tournament also had two military teams and one civilian team from Mexico.[28] Only Lts. Eugene McGinley and Morton McDonald Jones have been identified as members on the American Army team.

The United States Army Team in Argentina

In 1930, the Argentine Polo Association sent an invitation to America for a U.S. Army team to participate in the Open Championship and in a special series against an Argentine Army team. This was accepted and the following squad was selected to travel to South America: Col. Wyllis Morris, as head of the delegation, and Capt. Wesley White, as official umpire. They were joined by Maj. Candler Wilkinson, Quartermaster Corps (Cavalry); Capt. Peter Rodes, 16th Field Artillery; Lt. Morton McD. Jones, Cavalry; 1st Lt. Homer Kiefer, Field Artillery. Later on, Maj. Charles C. Smith, 14th Cavalry, was added to reinforce the team.[29]

The announcement of this visit produced great excitement in Argentine polo circles because it was the first official team from overseas to play in Buenos Aires. The year 1930 was a black year in the history of Argentina because on 6 September a military coup ousted the legitimate civilian government, thus ending 80 years of uninterrupted elected presidents, the longest in the country's annals. It is sad to record that just as in the occasion of the 1978 soccer World Cup held in Argentina, the military government used the tools of an international sporting tournament to mask unsavory political events.

Nevertheless, the tour of the American Army team was a great success. The team selected to play in the Open Championship was formed by Lt. Jones, Capt. Wilkinson, Capt. Rodes and Maj. Smith. They defeated in the first round Los Pinguinos, a team formed by four Braun Menéndez brothers, and in the semifinals, Las Rosas, a strong team that counted the brothers David and John Miles, both international players. The final match was against Santa Paula, the best team in Argentina, which would go on to take the U.S. Open Championship at Meadow Brook in 1931. The U.S. team was ahead for most of the game; however, Santa Paula began chipping at the Army's lead and in the last chukker the redoubtable Back Manuel Andrada ran the length of the field to score the winning goal.

When the final bell sounded the noise was such that neither the umpires nor the players heard the toll. When the public realized the game was over, the Palermo Number One ground was invaded by the joyful crowd. Capt. Wesley White wrote "During the nineteen years that I have played and watched polo I have never seen such an enthusiastic crowd. They seemed to lose all control of themselves and there was so much noise it was impossible for the umpires to hear the final bell. When it became evident that the final bell had rung, a crowd of about five thousand swarmed onto the field, lifted the Santa Paula players from their ponies, and carried them to the center of the grandstand for the presentation of the trophies."[30]

Postscript

The United States Cavalry, the heart and soul of military polo in America, is no more. The death knoll sounded in June 1943, when the dismounted First Cavalry Division left Fort Bliss in Texas en route to Strathpine, Queensland, in far away Australia. They did their duty well. Gen. Douglas MacArthur wrote, "No better record had emerged from the war than that of the First Cavalry division."[31] The only American cavalry to serve in World War II was an improvised provisional troop organized by the Third Infantry Division in the Sicilian and Southern Italy campaigns.[32]

Gen. John Knoles Herr, a 5-goal polo player winner of the Junior Championship in the glory days, whose destiny was to be the last Chief of the U.S. Cavalry, fought a hopeless battle to the end of his days in an attempt to maintain a semblance of a mounted unit. It was not to be.

As part of the State Department Exchange Program a military team traveled to Pakistan and India in 1962 to participate in the Annual Pakistani National Tournament. Colonels Ted deSaussure, Jackson Shirley (Ret.), James Spurrier, William West and Lt. Col. Jack Burton embarked on a five-week journey. The U.S. Military team won the first match, 7–4, against the Mixtures Polo Team. In the semifinals they defeated the Darvishes by 4 goals to 2½. The final match was against the Kahrian Polo Team; giving one goal on handicap, the U.S. team was beaten 4–2. The Pakistani players were Maj. Gen. Sahibzada Yakub Khan, Brig. Hesky Baig, Brig. H.M. El-Effendi, Col. M.S.A. Baig and Lt. Col. Jehanzeb Khan.[33]

After this tournament, the American delegation was joined by George Oliver and Peter Perkins for a series of exhibition matches, which continued when the squad crossed the border into India, playing two games in New Delhi, one of them being against the 61st Cavalry, the last Indian cavalry unit.

There was a revival, sort of, in 1992, when a team from Fort Knox hosted a team from the Louisville Polo Club at Brooks Field, the military post's parade ground. Fort Knox was represented by Maj. John Rogers, Maj. Evan Miller, Capt. Eric Besch, Capt. Alan Huffines—who shared the Number 1 position with Maj. Miller—and Sergeant (ret.) Paul Vollmer. The Louisville team was Cissy Maloney, John Barker, William Fires and Nana Lampton. The Fort Knox team won 5–1; however, the Louisville foursome was victorious in a return match.

Two weeks later, at Potomac Polo Club near Washington, D.C., Lt. Col. Robert Shoemaker, Maj. Mark Gillespie, Captain John Chick and Lt. Michael Mason, U.S. Navy, defeated a multinational team of Brig. Gen. T.J. Shergill from India, Maj. Rich Miles and Sophie Stoner from England, Imad Badran from Jordania and Jost Spielvogel of Germany.[34]

Top: The inaugural Westchester Cup was played in Newport. Raymond Belmont mounted on Domino is wearing the yellow Westchester Polo Club jersey. The other ponies are Red Skin, Flirt and Cody. Oil on canvas by Gustav Muss-Arnoldt. *Above:* Polo on the prairies as depicted by A.W. Springstein in the late 19th century.

Left: California-bred Cottontail, Harry Payne Whitney's grand-looking bay gelding. In the opinion of Col. Edward Miller, an authority on polo, it was the best Whitney ever owned. James C. Cooley thought that Cottontail was the best pony in the history of the game. Oil on canvas by Melinda Brewer. *Right:* Devereux Milburn on Jacob, oil on canvas by Franklin Voss. Jacob, an international pony in the Westchester Cup, was bred in Texas by John C. Jacobs.

A Back for the ages. Devereux Milburn depicted by Richard Adam. Milburn established a standard of play at the Back position that has never been surpassed.

"The Polo Set — Palm Beach," an oil on canvas by Edward Cucuel, captures the glamour of the 1920s (private collection, Alex Pacheco photograph).

Left: Miss Hobbs. A superb example of a polo pony mare, played by Devereux Milburn in the Westchester Cup. Oil on canvas by Franklin Voss (private collection). *Right:* Paul Brown depicted the game of polo like no other American artist. This is just one of his many watercolors (private collection, Alex Pacheco photograph).

Top: Four mares from Harold Talbott's string, painted by Franklin Voss: Abdication, Delysia, The Vamp and Broken Crown. *Above:* "Mallet Work" by Sam Savitt. The scene is the Fairfield County Hunt Club in Westport, Connecticut, where Savitt was a frequent visitor sketching his polo art (private collection, Alex Pacheco photograph).

BTA ladies team: Karlene Beal Garber, Caroline Anier from France, Kristy Waters and Susan Stovall.

Left: Marcos Heguy for Jedi and Adam Snow for Coca-Cola battling it out in the U.S. Open Championship at Royal Palm Polo (Museum of Polo, Alex Pacheco photograph). *Right:* Dawn Jones, Tommy Lee Jones and Tommy Wayman share a laugh. The Joneses' San Saba team from Texas has achieved its share of successes.

Left: Guillermo "Memo" Gracida dominated the U.S. Open with sixteen wins to his credit, most likely an unreachable record (Museum of Polo, Alex Pacheco photograph). *Right:* Jeff Hall playing for Zacara during the Florida high-goal season (Museum of Polo, Alex Pacheco photograph).

Adolfito Cambiaso has defied John Donne's ancient admonition: "No man is an island, entire of itself." Like he often does, Cambiaso carried the Crab Orchard squad to three U.S. Open Championships in a four-year span. This is the winning 2010 team: George Rawlings, Adolfo Cambiaso, Beverly Rawlings, Julio Arellano and Hilario Ulloa (courtesy Frederic Roy).

Above: Lengthening shadows in Aiken provide the background for Maureen Brennan's Goose Creek team, three-time winner of America's oldest trophy, the Silver Cup. José "Cote" Zegers, Adam Snow, Maureen Brennan and Martín Zegers (courtesy Maureen Brennan). *Left:* S.K. "Skeeter" Johnston, III, was the patron of the Everglades and Skeeterville teams and the prime mover behind the North American Polo League. His demise following an accident on the polo field was a terrible blow to his family and his countless friends. The polo community worldwide grieved his passing. Here he is at the top of the swing, wearing the Skeeterville shirt, competing in the U.S. Open Championship at International Polo Club, Wellington (courtesy Mrs. Leslie Johnston).

Above: Ambassador Glen Holden is a towering figure in polo. Prime mover at the prestigious Santa Barbara Polo Club in California, president of the Federation of International Polo, member of the Polo Hall of Fame, Mr. Holden has made an enormous contribution to the game as player, organizer of a World Championship, administrator, counselor and patron. Glen with his charming wife Gloria on the occasion of the tournament celebrating his 80th birthday (courtesy Amb. Glen Holden, Sr. Kim Kumpart

photograph). *Right:* Tommy Wayman hitting a neck shot while playing for Southern Hills at Palm Beach Polo. The pony is La Fortuna, one of the celebrated Santamarina's greys, bred by Dicky Samtamarina and his wife Frances, née Post (courtesy Mr. and Mrs. Thomas Wayman).

Top: Thomas Biddle, Jr. (right), occupies center stage in a match at I.P.C. Palm Beach. Tommy, one of the longest hitters in polo, took the U.S. Open Championship in 2002. Julian Daniels, playing for Faraway, stretches long for a hook (Museum of Polo, Alex Pacheco photograph). *Above:* This oil by the hand of Thomas Worth depicts a match circa 1890 between Rockaway and Essex County, two of the Polo Association's founding clubs (courtesy Mr. F. Turner Reuter, Jr., and Red Fox Fine Art).

PART III

The Road to Recovery, 1946–1975

CHAPTER 16

The Home Front, 1946–1960

The Second World War took its deadly toll on the ancient game of polo. One of the best-ever polo players, Thomas Hitchcock, Jr., was killed in England when his fighter plane crashed towards the end of a test flight. A few of the more promising young players also paid the ultimate price. Among them, Charles von Stade, winner of the 1941 U.S. Open Championship and a scion of a family with deep roots in American polo—for his father Frank had taken three U.S. Open crowns in the 1910s—was killed when his Jeep hit a mine in Germany, just a few weeks before the war's end in 1945. George Meade, from Dayton, Ohio, a 5-goaler who also played at Meadow Brook, and Jack Milburn, a Meadow Brook Club member, also lost their lives during the conflict.

Organized polo in the United States got going again in 1946. A team from Argentina, Miraflores, now a defunct club, played several matches at the Fairfield County Hunt Club's Rudkin Field in Westport, Connecticut. During their tour of the Northeast, Eduardo Brown, Carlos Torres Zavaleta, Oscar Tricerri and Federico Vogelius entered the U.S. Open at Meadow Brook. Their quest for the Open crown was unsuccessful; however, Miraflores took the Monty Waterbury Cup, in those days still played on handicap by the teams participating in the Open Championship.

The finals of the 1946 Open Championship saw six Mexican players take the field. Under the name Mexico, Gabriel, Guillermo, Alejandro and José Gracida won from Los Amigos, in which Stewart Iglehart and Michael Phipps joined Antonio Nava Castillo and Alberto Ramos Sesma. For the fourth time a foreign team took the U.S. Open—the only occasion in which four brothers were on the winning team.

While the Gracidas' Mexican team was ready to defend its championship crown, three American teams announced their lineups for the 1947 competition. Stephen Sanford's Hurricanes had Joseph P. Grace, Cecil Smith and Alan L. Corey, Jr., a powerful combination. When 10-goalers Stewart Iglehart and Mike Phipps arranged a team together, Laddie Sanford threw a tantrum at the U.S. Open Committee meeting. When the Committee overruled his objection at having two top players on the same team, Sanford said "I won't play and neither will Cecil Smith."[1]

Faced with such a childish threat and the prospect of only three teams participating in the Open Championship, the authorities relented. Pete Bostwick and Michael Phipps then signed up Peter Perkins and Tom Mather to play under the Bostwick Field banner. Stewart Iglehart, left to scramble on his own, secured Clarence Combs, Pedro Silvero and George Oliver onto a team named Old Westbury, no relation to Sonny Whitney's team of the 1930s. The team worked well. In the semifinals, they defeated the Hurricanes 11–10, with Combs and Argentine professional player Silvero scoring five goals each.

World War II took its toll. Among the dead was Capt. Charles von Stade, a winner of the U.S. Open and a most promising young player.

In the other semifinal game, Mexico beat Bostwick Field, only to lose the championship game to Old Westbury by 10 goals to seven.

The years 1948 and 1949 belonged to Laddie Sanford's Hurricanes. With Cecil Smith in the pivot position, another Texan, Larry Sheerin, and Peter Perkins, son of the Englishman Arthur Perkins who had won the Open in 1924, the Hurricanes easily won all their matches.

In 1948, Hurricanes faced Great Neck in the final game. Great Neck had Eddie O'Brien, Peter Grace's stable manager, J.P. Grace, Jr., George Oliver and Alan Corey, Jr. Alan Corey was hit by a ball in the semifinal game and was concussed. Carlos Menditeguy took his place for the rest of the match. Corey returned to the lineup for the finals, where a goal by Cecil Smith in the game's waning minutes gave the title to Hurricanes, 7–6.

In 1949, the Argentine player Roberto Cavanagh replaced Perkins at Number 2. The final match pitted the Hurricanes and El Trébol, an Argentine team that had had a successful campaign in the Northeast, and also at Oak Brook in Illinois. In his biography of the Sanford family, Alex Robb wrote:

> The presence of Roberto Cavanagh in the Hurricane lineup was a story in itself. Juan Perón was in power in Argentina at the time, and the Hurricanes, with whom the Argentine Cavanagh was playing, were expected to meet the Argentine team in the finals. Before the finals, Roberto attended a cocktail party at the Argentine embassy, where he was advised that his compatriots must not be beaten in the decisive match. Rumors floated about that Cavanagh would throw the game. But Roberto Cavanagh never played better than he did in the match against El Trébol, and when he returned to Argentina he was not allowed to play polo for two years.[2]

This is absolute nonsense. There was no sanction in Argentina against Roberto Cavanagh. Furthermore, it was Cecil Smith who became the Hurricanes' star of the game. The score, 9–2 at halftime, 10 goals to 4 at the final bell, reflects the absolute superiority of the Hurricanes. The gigantic Roberto returned to Argentina to play in his usual slot on the Venado Tuerto team, with his cousin Juan, and the Alberdi brothers, Enrique and Juan Carlos. This team, wearing the sky-blue and white of the international Argentine team, was unbeaten in the following two years, winning the Argentine and Hurlingham Open Championships, the World Championship, and the Cup of the Americas. Only a broken fibula prevented Roberto Cavanagh from participating in the 1949 Argentine Open at Palermo.

The United States Open Championship in the 1950s

The Meadow Brook Club in Westbury continued to be the venue for the U.S. Open Championship until 1953, when Robert Moses' plans cut a swath through the polo grounds. The only exception was in 1952, when the tournament was awarded to the Beverly Hills Polo Club in California.

The 1950 Open Championship featured the participation of a team from California, its expenses being taken care of by the U.S.P.A. Robert Fletcher, Clarence Combs, Bob Skene and Carlton Beal put an end to the Hurricanes domination of the event when they defeated Stephen Sanford's team 10–9. The final game pitted Bostwick Field—winners over Brookfield—against California. This match produced the best polo of the tournament, the score being tied at halftime. Then gradually Bostwick Field pulled ahead to take match and championship by seven goals to five. Pete Bostwick, George Oliver, Alan Corey and Devereux Milburn, Jr., formed the winning foursome.

The team from California was successful in the Monty Waterbury Cup, defeating Bostwick Field 9–5 in this important handicap competition. The last main national tournament, the 20-Goal Championship played at Bostwick Field, was taken by Milwaukee, with Pedro Silvero, Juan Rodríguez, George Oliver and Robert Uihlein, Jr., capping a most gratifying season.

Milwaukee did even better in the following year, because they took the Open Championship, with Peter Perkins replacing Juan Rodríguez at Number 2. They defeated Meadow Brook 6–2, in a game marred by whistling numerous fouls, many of which were disallowed by the referee, Robert Strawbridge, Jr. The Meadow Brook Club was represented by Charlie Leonard, Buddy Combs, Alan Corey and Albert Parsells.

For the first time in its history, the 1952 U.S. Open Championship took place in California, on the Beverly Hills polo grounds. Unfortunately, soon after the fields were sold for development; the astronomical rising prices in real estate in Santa Monica made the sale a necessity.

Only three teams entered the competition: Beverly Hills, San Francisco and Los Pingüinos, the holders of the Argentine Open Championship. Jaime Rincón Gallardo, Iván Mihanovich, Cecil Smith and Mariano Gutiérrez Achával formed the team. Cecil Smith replaced Heriberto Duggan in the match against Beverly Hills; however, he also injured a knee and was not able to play up to his usual top form. The heavily favored Argentines lost to the host team 7–5. The final game was against San Francisco, a team that had Victor Graber, Eric Pedley, William Linfoot and Robert Smith on its lineup. Bob Skene led Beverly Hills to a 9–6 victory, confirming his outstanding level of play. His teammates were Robert Fletcher, Tony Veen and Carleton Beal.

The end of a tradition going back to 1916 occurred when the last United States Open Championship was held at Meadow Brook Club. Only four teams answered the call. Meadow Brook had Henry Lewis, III, Philip Iglehart, Alan Corey and Pete Bostwick. This strong team ran over Milwaukee in the first game; Pedro Silvero, Ray Harrington, Al Parsells and Robert Uihlein played for Milwaukee. In the second game, Chicago, with Paul Butler, Lewis Smith, Cecil Smith and Thomas Healey, overwhelmed the Hurricanes 14–4. Laddie Sanford, Clarence Combs, George Oliver and Devereux Milburn, Jr., a good team, did not have a good outing.

The final game between Meadow Brook and Chicago ended with a 7–4 win for the host club. A glorious chapter in the history of American polo then came to an end. The contributions of the Meadow Brook Club to polo in the United States can only be characterized as monumental.

The 1954 Open was then held at the Oak Brook polo complex near Chicago, with four entrants. CCC–Meadow Brook[3] enlisted Don Beveridge, Pete Bostwick, Alan Corey and Harold Barry. They defeated the strong Milwaukee team in the first game, and Brandywine in the finals. Brandywine had beaten Oak Brook in a preliminary game. Thus, a combination of East and Midwest players took the Open at its new home. This same team took the Monty Waterbury Trophy and the Butler National Handicap, a wonderful triple.

The entries increased to six teams for the 1955 Open Championship. Oak Brook defeated Meadow Brook in the first game, and Milwaukee did the same with Detroit Rangers. In the latter team, Northrup Knox, later to be captain of the American international team in the Cup of the Americas and U.S.P.A. chairman in the 1960s, made his debut in the Open Championship. The results of the semifinal games, Brandywine defeating Oak Brook and CCC beating Milwaukee, placed two evenly matched teams in the championship match. CCC, with Don Beveridge, Dr. William Linfoot, Paul (Bill) Barry and Harold Barry, took the U.S. Open crown 9–8 after being behind 7–3 at the interval and 8–7 at the start of the final chukker. Brandywine had the veteran Dr. Raworth Williams, Ray Harrington, Clarence Combs and William Mayer.

The path to recovery continued in 1957, when the Open Championship attracted seven teams, including one from Mexico. In the preliminary rounds Brandywine took the first game from Detroit CCC, Aurora beat Boca Raton, and California won over Oak Brook. The semifinals matched Mexico: Rubén Gracida, Capt. Jesús Sonora, Julio Muller and Gabriel Gracida; the second semifinal was between Brandywine and California, which had Vic Graber, Peter Perkins, Bob Skene and Carlton Beal. In a very close game, Brandywine won 11–10, while Aurora defeated the Mexican combination 10–8. Thus, the final match was between Aurora and Brandywine. It turned out to be one of the best finals in

The winners of the 1954 U.S. Open Championship at Oak Brook: Harold Barry, Alan Corey, Pete Bostwick, Mrs. Maryland McCorming doing the honors, and Don Beveridge.

the long history of the U.S. Open Championship. Norty Knox had a spectacular game, scoring six goals, while Ray Harrington played just as brilliantly, netting five goals for Brandywine. The rest of the Aurora team nicely complemented its captain's performance, with Bill Ylvisaker playing a sound game at Back, and Seymour Knox, III, and Lewis Smith playing an aggressive game as forwards. For Brandywine, Bill Mayer was a solid Back and Buddy Combs was an effective Number 3. It was a hard match, with seven falls recorded. Two extra periods were needed, until Clarence Combs scored the winning tally for Brandywine, for an 11–10 win.

In his *Aurora at Oak Brook*, Seymour Knox, Jr., wrote: "Before closing, I should like to add, as coach, father, substitute and interested spectator, that I have never seen, in all my 35 years as a polo player and spectator, a more exciting or thrilling polo game."[4]

The Beveridges added another victory in the U.S. Open in 1957, with Don Beveridge, nephew Robert Beveridge, George Oliver and Harold Barry as members of the Detroit CCC squad. This team defeated in succession Russell Firestone's Circle F, John Oxley's Tulsa, which included Bob Skene, and in the final match, Aiken, which had Vincent Rizzo, Pete Bostwick, Alan Corey and Devereux Milburn, Jr., in its lineup.

Dr. Raworth Williams, who had been playing polo in Dallas since the 1920s, finally realized his dream of taking the U.S. Open Championship. The team was assembled around two players from California, Dr. Billy Linfoot and Bob Skene. The fourth wheel was Luis Ramos, handicapped at 5-goals. On its way to the title, Dallas defeated Oak Brook 7–5, Boca Raton in the semifinals 14–7, and a team unimaginatively named Solo Cup 7 to 6 in the championship game. Del Carroll, Ray Harrington, Bill Mayer and patron Russell Firestone were their opponents.

The 1959 U.S. Open Championship proved to be another heartbreaking loss for Aurora, once more in double overtime. Things started well for the Knoxes' team, when they beat a Meadow Brook that included Enrique Alberdi, in the opening match of the championship. In the semifinal round, Aurora defeated Oak Brook, with Cecil Smith, 9–5.

The other finalist was Circle F, with Delmar Carroll, Ray Harrington, William Mayer and Russell Firestone. Circle F found its way to the finals by first beating Detroit CCC 10–8, and then taking the measure of Solo-Cup Tulsa 7–6. The Aurora team was Seymour Knox, III, Northup Knox, Lewis Smith and Horacio Castilla, an Argentine 4-goal player. At halftime the score was Circle F five, Aurora two.

Aurora slowly fought its way back and tied the game in the sixth period via a Lewis Smith goal from the field. By this time, the excitement was tense and Aurora fouled. Ray Harrington's shot from 40 yards was blocked by Norty Knox and the goal was saved when the ball hit Knox's arm. Then, Circle F fouled and a 60-yard penalty was awarded. Lewis Smith missed and regulation time ended in a tie, 7–7.

In the sudden death period both teams missed chances at goal until another penalty was called against Circle F. Lewis Smith offered the chance to Norty Knox; however, he could barely hold the mallet and declined to take the shot. Smith missed again and the seventh chukker ended. Midway through the eighth period Delmar Carroll found the ball near the boards, and dribbled towards goal; his last shot hit the goalpost and went in. The 1959 U.S. Open was history.

Only five teams entered the last Open Championship of the decade. The defending champions, Circle F, defeated Solocup Tulsa, John Oxley's team, which included Bob Skene, and Oak Brook CCC, with Don Beveridge, Wayne Brown, Cecil Smith and Harold Barry, won over Milwaukee. In the semifinal game, Royal Palm decisively beat Circle F 13–6, to face Oak Brook CCC in the final match. In a game that saw the Beveridge brothers on opposing teams, Oak Brook CCC was the winner by a score of 8 goals to 5.

The Renewal of the East-West Series

The East-West series was held at the Meadow Brook International Field in 1947. As a reflection of the times, it was a single match affair. The West team, Jack Ivory from Detroit, Peter Perkins, George Oliver and Thomas Guy, defeated the East squad by a score of 9 goals to seven. George H. Bostwick, Jr., Peter Grace, Jr., Stewart Iglehart and Alan Corey represented the Eastern interests.

In 1951, two contests were held, in Arlington Farms, Illinois in the month of August, and at Meadow Brook in September. In Illinois, William Ylvisaker, Bob Skene, Cecil Smith and Harry Evinger defeated Pete Bostwick, Albert Parsells, Alan Corey and Devereux Milburn, Jr., taking two of three encounters played. Stanley Taylor replaced Cecil Smith in the final game.

At Meadow Brook, only two games were needed by the West squad to take the honors. William Ylvisaker, Bob Skene, Harry Evinger and Tom Cross won over Pete Bostwick, Albert Parsells, Alan Corey and Devereux Milburn. Both teams made changes before the second game: Peter Perkins and Cecil Smith replaced Skene and Cross, while in the East team Clarence Combs took Milburn's place.

This event was the swan song of the once immensely popular contest between the Western and Eastern schools of polo. In the 1970s and the 1890s a Junior East-West series competition took place at Oak Brook and in Florida between promising young players.

Each side won twice. Lyle Graham, Willie Hartnett, Heath Manning, Jr., Joe Muldoon, Jr., Paul Rizzo, Nicolás Roldán, Robert Sieber, Jr., and Adie von Gontard, III, starred for the East. Stewart Armstrong, Kris Kampsen, Corky Linfoot, Alan Martinez, Jamie Uihlein, Robin Uihlein and Billy Ylvisaker did the same for the West team.

Michelle Gracida, Memo's daughter, was the only woman to participate, being on the 1996 winning East team, while Jake Sieber from Cincinnati played for both East and West.

Meet Me in St. Louis

After the war, a number of players at the St. Louis Country Club continued to enjoy the game as they brought it to younger men. It was a mixture of the old and the new: Taylor Bryan, Wills Engle, Roland Hoerr, John Krey, Frederick Luyties, Dolph Orthwein, John Otto, Clifton Scudder — a surname dating back to the very origins of the club — and Adalbert and Paul von Gontard. Following a match, players frequently gathered to enjoy a shandi-gaff, a thirst-quenching drink of half beer and half ginger ale. To further encourage polo, in 1946 the club purchased ten ponies for the use of members.[5]

The so-called brewer's series took place at the Club during Memorial Day weekend in 1954. Milwaukee, the polo club owned by Robert A. Uihlein, Jr., whose family owned the Schlitz brewery, played against a team lead by Adolph B. Orthwein, from the Anhauser-Busch family. The series ended in a draw, each team winning one game. Robert Walker, Pedro Silvero, Robert Uihlein and George Sherman played for Milwaukee, while the host team was Robert Human, John Otto, Dolph Orthwein and Theodore Martin. In the second game, Louis Werner, II, and Wills Engle replaced Human and Otto on the St. Louis team.

A special match was held that year against a team from Topeka. Theodore Martin, Dolph Orthwein, Taylor Bryan, III, and Wills Engle defeated Topeka 8–2. The visitors were Jack and Jarrett Vincent, Mark Mollett and William George. Games versus Mission Brook, from Kansas City, were also held, the St. Louis Country Club team winning on both occasions.

The St. Louis Country Club hosted in 1959 a special series of matches against the Mexican team El Roble and visitors from Memphis, Milwaukee and Louisville. In the final game, Robert Human, Thruston Petton, Paul von Gontard and Adolphus Orthwein were defeated 6–4 by Louisville's Byron Hilliard, Robert Wilson, III, Warner Jones and C. Virgil Christian. It must have been a bitter pill to swallow for Dolph and his teammates, because Virgil Christian was the St. Louis Country Club's resident professional.

Illinois

While Oak Brook rose to prominence as the most important club in America from the mid–1950s to the 1970s, there were several other polo clubs of significance in Illinois. Arlington Farms was affiliated in June 1946, one of the first five clubs to join or rejoin the U.S.P.A. after the war, the others being Broadmoor in Colorado, Pierre in South Dakota, San Francisco in California and Squadron A in New York.

Arlington Farms, located in Libertyville, was started by Leonard and Edward Bernard, Jr.; other members included William Fergus, William Grant, Leo Hulseman, Charles Jelke, Jr., John Mather and Dan Peacock. A team, William Ylvisaker, Tom Cross, Cecil Smith and John Hulseman, took the Twenty Goal Championship in 1951, Arlington Farms' high watermark. In 1953, the club moved to Omaha, Nebraska.

Other clubs in Illinois were North Shore, which re-affiliated in 1947, the short-lived Mill Creek in Wadsworth that joined in 1950, and Healy Farms, established in McCook by

Michael, Thomas and James Healy, Jr. This family club took the Inter-Circuit Championship in 1951, with Jerome Fordon as the team's fourth member.

Pennsylvania Polo

There were no clubs in the Keystone state affiliated with the U.S.P.A. until the short-lived Bishop Hollow Polo Club in Newtown Square joined in September 1950. Alvin Busch, Robert Dilworth, Edward James, the Charles Maloneys Senior and Junior, Charles Martyn, Patrick Tarone, Norman Taylor and Edward Yetter were the enthusiasts that started this little-known club.

Then the Brandywine Polo Association, destined to become an important polo center, was created in 1951 by James McHugh, Col. Howard Fair, Charles Maloney, Jr., and Albert G.S. Stewart. The club leased from the Philadelphia Country Club the historic Bala ground, before moving to permanent quarters at Toughkenamon, on Route 1, south of Kennett Square. The old farmhouse on the 150-acre site was renovated and refurbished into a club-house. Professional player Ray Harrington was hired as playing-coach and manager.

Brandywine organized several popular tournaments during the month of August. The Polo Ponies Memorial 12-Goal Tournament, the 8-Goal Gerald Balding Cup, and the Tar Baby Plate attracted a large number of entries from many clubs from Massachusetts to Virginia.

Longtime member Fred Fortugno, who has played polo longer than most, joined Brandywine in 1958 and went on to achieve many successes with his own Mallet Hill Polo Club.

Polo in the Northwestern Circuit

The game had some rough going when several clubs lost their polo grounds because of the suburban growth of many cities. Fort Hays, Old Ironsides in Topeka, Kansas, and Mission Brook in Missouri all suffered that predicament. Polo at Broadmoor in Colorado cancelled the season due to lack of water to keep the fields safe for polo.

On the other side of the ledger, two new clubs were inaugurated. Clark Hetherington started the Broad Acres club in Norman, Oklahoma, and John T. Oxley in Tulsa sponsored the Tulsa Polo and Riding Club, which joined the Hartmans' Fairfield Polo Club in Wichita, Kansas, to create the Northwestern Circuit Invitational Four-Goal Tournament with the aim of encouraging newcomers to the game and low-handicap players to enter a big tournament without the need to possess enough ponies and lots of experience. As part of the conditions to enter this handicap tournament, no player could use more that three ponies and no player could be handicapped at more than one-goal.

Seven teams participated in the initial tournament, by far the largest number in the circuit. The Fairfield team, John Knightley, Eugene Ralston, William Ralston and Ralph Hartman, won over Tulsa, John and Jack Oxley, Duke Merrill and Mancel Fore.

Oklahoma, a team that had John T. Oxley, Leslie "Bud" Linfoot, Clark Hetherington and C. Robert "Kay" Colee, took both the National Inter-Circuit Championship and the National Twelve Goal Championship at Santa Barbara, California. It was a very nice double for the Okies.

Polo in the Northwest Circuit. The Fairfield Polo Club team with the spoils of the 1962 Invitational Tournament at Tulsa Polo and Hunt Club: William Wayman, Bill, Julian, Peggy and Gene Ralston, and John Burnell.

Polo in Detroit

During the 1950s, Detroit industrialist Andrew D. (Don) Beveridge sponsored the Triple Cs and also served as a playing captain. He had his nephew, Bobby Beveridge, Harold Barry from Texas, and George Oliver from Florida on his team, which was formed in 1951. As related in the section on the U.S. Open Championship in Chapter 16, CCC had more than its share of tournament wins. Among those, mention must be made of the Twenty-Goal Championship, the Butler National Handicap in no less than three times, and the Monty Waterbury Trophy.

The sport was supported in the Detroit area by many such sponsors, including John Ivory. Mr. Ivory, who died in 1971 at the age of 83, had made his fortune with the John F. Ivory Moving and Storage Co. His father, a saddler in Queenstown, Ireland, moved to Norwich, New York, where he taught his son how to ride horses. The Ivory Polo Club, where Jack Ivory starred, was a power in arena polo ever since its affiliation to the U.S.P.A. in November 1946.

Also in Michigan, the game was played at Grand Rapids, which joined in 1950, and later at the Kentree Polo Club.

Connecticut and Massachusetts

The 1951 New England Championship for the W. Cameron Forbes Trophy was taken by the Fairfield County Hunt over Farmington Valley, near Hartford, and the Pittsfield Riding & Polo Association. William Crawford, Jr., John T. Mather, William McMath and William Crawford, III, were on the winning team. Fairfield Hunt retained the Forbes Trophy the following year.

Pittsfield had a successful 1952 season, when Charles Wheeler, Herbie Pennell, Zenas Colt and Joseph Poor took the National Inter-Circuit Championship, after defeating Fairfield County Hunt in the final game of the Northeastern Intra-Circuit tournament. Pittsfield took the measure of the Milwaukee Shamrocks, at Blind Brook, in Purchase, New York.

It was a good year for the Northeast, because Blind Brook took the National 12-Goal Championship as well. Thomas Glynn, Adalbert von Gontard, Jr., Cyril Harrison and Jack Crawford were on the championship team.

Fairfield Hunt continued its winning streak when they took the National Inter-Circuit Championship, defeating Dallas 10–3 at Meadow Brook. Bill Crawford, his son Randy, Zenas Colt and Tommy Glynn played on the Fairfield team.

However, Fairfield lost in the finals of the National Twelve-Goal Championship to Farmington Valley's Barclay Robinson, Zenas Colt, Frank Butterworth and Albert Marenholtz, 9–6. In this game, Henry Lewis and George Sherman played instead of Zenas Colt and Thomas Glynn.

The Forbes Cup was resumed in 1956; Farmington-Blind Brook took a close match from perennial contenders Fairfield County Hunt, once more led by Tommy Glynn, 7–6. Frank Fox, Adalbert von Gontard, Frank Butterworth and Albert Marenholtz played for the winners.

Farmington Valley retained the Forbes Cup in 1957, with Frank "Butch" Butterworth, III, in place of Adie von Gontard. After a hiatus, Fairfield County Hunt won again in 1960, with the William Crawfords, father and son, Stuart Feick and George Haas, Jr.

A most welcome event was the return to the fold of the Myopia Hunt Club, resurgent after the parenthesis imposed by World War II. Gibney Field had gone to grass, while the practice ground was utilized by the golfing community as a handy driving range. Former Harvard collegiate star Forrester Clark and Crocker Snow, Sr., were the two enthusiasts that brought polo back to Myopia. Both men were veterans from World War II. Clark had been in the Armored Corps in Europe, while Snow was leading B-29 Super Fortresses over Japan. Upon receiving news that Army horses were available at Fort Sill, Tim Clark purchased a box car and had them shipped to South Hamilton. The first practice game was on Crocker Snow farm's landing strip, located in Ipswich, the players mounted on Army horses, hunters and pre-war polo ponies.

The next step happened in the mid–1950s, when Donald V. Little, a B-47 pilot and Snow's stepson, took to arena polo while stationed at Tucson. When Charlie Barnes, Crocker Snow, Jr., and Adam Winthrop visited him in Arizona, they took to the game like ducks to water. When they returned to the North Shore, the first game was played in May 1958 by five men: Neil Ayer, Lester Crossman, Charles Rice and the Snows, father and son. In his fascinating account of polo at Myopia, Crocker Snow, Jr., makes the interesting observation that only five players also participated in the first game ever at Myopia, some seventy years earlier.[6]

Ohio

In 1948, the only club left in Ohio was Harbor Hills Polo and Riding Club, on the shores of Buckeye Lake, north of Columbus. It had originally been started in 1935 by Otis Harris and Walter Shapter, Jr. Large crowds numbering 5,000 attended polo every Sunday, and the after games parties would go on until sunset. Ralph Barnett, Frank Harris and Edward Kennedy were some of the players.

In April 1952, Otis Harris started the Columbus Farms Polo Club in Galloway, together with Hal and James Everett, Alan Holman, Dick and Trent Smith. The Salem Saddle and Polo Club joined in 1953, organized by James Pidgeon, Jr., Anthony Sheen and Wilford Smith.

The Mahoning Valley, in Poland, came into being in 1955. Curtis Crum, Edward Roberts, Albert and Stanley Strouss, and Philip Thompson were the initial players.

Disrupted by World War II, the outdoor game in Cleveland was revived on a much smaller scale when William Herbert Greene, Jr., organized a polo team in 1952; by 1953 the team was playing an eight-game schedule in the Penn-Ohio league supported by the Cleveland Polo Association, made up of about 200 enthusiastic non-playing members. Players included Jack Arnold, James Bahr, Harrison Hartman and Richard Knepper.

Polo in Toledo was resumed at the Springbrook Polo Club, at Harpst Farm Field on Corey Road, organized by Dan McCollough, with Nelson "Dan" Abbey, Jr., Jack Hankison and Henry Weiss. Players from the Carranor Hunt and Toledo polo clubs, both in abeyances, also joined the new entity.

The Cincinnati Polo Club was revived in 1958 by Edward Kennedy, James Anderson, Frank Longevin, Otto Salsbery, Robert Sieber — whose sons Jake, John and Robert Jr. would later have outstanding intercollegiate careers— John Stark and Milton Stulbarg.

The Dayton Polo Club, where polo had for the first time been played in 1916 by George Mead, was formed in 1959 by Nelson Mead. The highlight of the season was the match against Cincinnati for the Howell Howard Trophy, first played since 1932. Other games were played against Columbus, Louisville and Toledo.

Finally, Walter Shapter, Jr., one of the players who restarted the Harbor Hills club, founded El Rancho Polo Club in Columbus. Alva and W.J. Durrett, Frank Harris and Albert "Bud" Strauss were members of El Rancho team.

Florida

The game in the Sunshine State was kept alive at the Phipps' Gulf Stream club in Delray Beach. The polo season included an East-West contest, sponsored by the Delray Beach Chamber of Commerce. Eight of the country's best players participated in the contest, which attracted some 6,000 spectators. The West team, Ray Harrington, Cecil Smith, George Oliver and Harold Barry, an aggregate of 35-goals, won 11–6, over Michael Phipps, Philip Iglehart, Stewart Iglehart and Pete Bostwick, a 33-goal handicap team. It was the highest handicap polo game played in the United States since 1939. Regrettably, the sale of the club's property was announced in April 1956.

A new club was formed by Maj. Frederic Collin, the owner of Blind Brook in Purchase, New York; it was named Palm Beach Polo Club, with three regulation grounds on Military Trail, Congress Avenue and Dillman Road, in West Palm Beach. The club had a busy

George Bostwick, Jr., played polo longer than most. Pete Bostwick took the Monty Waterbury Cup in 1932 on a team that included Tommy Hitchcock and Eric Pedley, and then again in 1981 with his sons Charlie and Ricky. The end came in 1982 during a game at Gulfstream Polo Club in Florida.

inaugural season, with many players from the northern regions of the country and also from the Dominican Republic, France and Cuba.

The Beveridges also started polo at Boca Raton. Those were the initial steps in the game's boom that would eventually make Florida the most active polo area in the world during the winter season.

The Tennessee Polo Waltz

The Dogwood Hunt and Polo Club of Chattanooga, Tennessee, began its operations in 1956. S.K. Johnston, Jr., whose father, a Dogwood founding member, had started polo in the Chattanooga area in 1937, was one of the players.[7] "Skey" Johnston would go on to be Chairman of the U.S. Polo Association from 1984 to 1988 and was one of the last left-handed polo players in America. Other players were Howard Bickerstaff, Jr., Glen and Kenneth Dalton, Robert Easterly, James Franklin, James Irvine, Jr., John McGauley, Jack Miller, Alex Wells and Bert West.

The Dogwood polo team got off to a good start when they defeated state rival Memphis Polo Association in a very close game, which was decided in an overtime period. Matches were also played against teams from Fort Oglethorpe in Georgia, the Governor's Horse Guard and Camden.

The temporary loss of the polo grounds forced the Dogwood team to play their annual tournament in 1959 on a smaller than regulation field. Playing three-a-side, Sam Lowe, Jack Miller and Skey Johnston on the Bendabout team took the championship after defeating Chattanooga and Mariwood.

The Bendabout team in polo—named after the Johnston's ranch in McDonald—was revived after the turn of the century, when Gillian Johnston, Skey's daughter, fielded her own Bendabout team in the high-goal seasons in Florida, Wyoming and Aiken, South Carolina.

Polo in Memphis was also restarted in 1956. Oddly enough, the Memphis Polo Association was assigned to the Northwestern Circuit. Old-timers Dunbar Abston, Everett Cook, Homer Jones and Lee Wilson, who had played in the 1920s, joined newcomers Percy Aden, Winston Cheairs, Jr., Edward Cook, Arthur Herman, who was the delegate and prime mover, Frank King, Arnold Klyce, Eli Long, Jr., James Maddox, Barclay McFadden, Jr., and Frank Norfleet in the revived club. Its location allowed the Memphis squad team to play against teams in Oklahoma, Arkansas and Missouri, as well as in its home state of Tennessee.

Other Clubs in the Southeastern Circuit

Camden was the first club to resume operations after the war. In February 1946, John Daniels, David Williams, Jr., Cyril Harrison and Carl Lightfoot played a one-sided home game against Augusta, the result in favor of Camden 8–1.[8] Daniels and Williams, both undergraduates at Yale University when the war started, joined the armed forces, Dave Williams as a P-51 fighter pilot and his brother-in-law Jack Daniels as an artillery officer in former polo player George Patton's Third Army.

The Western Carolina Polo Club, located in Asheville, was affiliated in 1950. Dr. Arthur Christian, Bruce Benedict, Ray Ferguson, Gerald Graham, Thomas Matlack and Edward Tejan were the first players. The club closed in 1953.

The venerable Aiken Polo Club celebrated in 1957 the seventy-fifth anniversary of polo in town. The Diamond Anniversary Cup was taken by Aiken, Charles Leonard, Pete Bostwick, Alan Corey and Devereux Milburn, over Aurora, Jack Ivory, Shorty Knox and his two sons, Norty and Sey. It was the largest crowd of locals and members of the winter colony to witness a game at Whitney Field since the war.

Four clubs in the Commonwealth of Virginia affiliated with the U.S. Polo Association. In October 1957, the Warrenton Polo Club was started by Arthur W. Arundel, C. Venable Barclay, William Chewning, William Clark, Jr., Wesley Dennis, Kenneth Edwards, John and William Gulick, John Hopewell, Curtis Lee and Dr. E. Douglas Vere Nicoll.

The Belvoir Polo Club then joined in 1959: Donald Beggs, Col. Frank Bower, Capt. Robert Ehrlich, Col. Jackson Shirley, Col. James Spurrier and Stuart Updike were the original members.

The Farmington Hunt Club in Charlottesville joined in 1960. Members were Carlton Barrett, Jr., Dr. Herbert Jones, Jr., Thomas Farrell, Henry Koch, Dr. Douglas Vere Nicoll and Rodger Rinehart, Jr.

In the same year, Winchester Polo Club was affiliated with the U.S. Polo Association; the initial playing members were Beverly Byrd, Joseph Claffy, John Cussen and John Day.

Maryland added the Dollbaby, in Germantown, and Stoney Creek in Rockville, in 1960. There were dual memberships. However, the initial members in each club were Mark and Halter Cunningham, Albert Puelicher, Jr., Leo Racca, Jr., and Col. William West, in Dollbaby; while Stoney Creek had David Ferguson, Allison and Edward Miller, and Robert Rawlins.

As an appendix, the St. Croix Polo Club, in the Virgin Islands, was granted affiliation with the U.S. Polo Association in 1956 and was assigned to the Southeastern Circuit.

CHAPTER 17

International Contests After the War

The Avila Camacho Cup

Soon after the stoppage of hostilities the U.S. Polo Association scheduled two international series with their counterparts in Mexico City, the Federación Mexicana de Polo. The first contest was held at the Meadow Brook Club on Long Island in September 1946. The United States selected a powerful team: Michael Phipps, Cecil Smith and Stewart Iglehart, all three experienced practitioners of international high-goal polo. They were joined at Back by Peter Perkins, who was making his debut as an international player. As to the Mexicans, they relied upon the skills of the four Gracida brothers, Gabriel "Chino," Guillermo "Memote," Alejandro "Cano" and José "Pepe." The American squad took both games, by 10 to 4 and 11 to 4 goals.

The second series took place at the Austin Polo Club in Texas, in November. The Gracida brothers again represented Mexico, while on the United States team Stephen Sanford replaced Mike Phipps and Peter Perkins' slot at Back was taken by John T. Mather, a safe and redoubtable 7-goal handicap player.

Following a lopsided first encounter, won by the American team by 7 goals to nil, the second game was a close one, finally taken by the U.S. squad 11–9. With the three-game series already decided, William Barry entered the team at Number 2 and Cecil Smith took Iglehart's place at Number 3. This final match was won by the United States by 11 goals to 4.

There was a long hiatus until 1974, when through the efforts of Claude H. Barry, U.S.P.A.'s Border Circuit governor, the Avila Camacho Cup was contested at Las Anitas Polo Club, in Ciudad Juárez. Russell Corey, Allan Scherer, Lester "Red" Armour and Robert Beveridge represented the United States, while Francisco "Paco" Camarena, Julio Muller, Alberto Muller and Pablo Rincón Gallardo played on the Mexican team.

Three matches were played. The American team won all three, 9–4, 9–6 and 9–4. The second match was the best of the series because the Mexicans, after being down 4 goals to 2 at halftime, equalized the game at 5-all in the fifth chukker. Beto Muller electrified the Mexican partisans when he scored to put his team ahead. However, Red Armour tied the game as the period ended, with the scoreboard showing two sixes. The last period was all the way America, which scored three unanswered goals to clinch the series.

Once more, Las Anitas was the venue for the 1975 contest. William Sinclaire from Colorado, Thomas Wayman, Red Armour and Bob Beveridge played for America. Mexico had Paco Camarena, Javier Rodríguez Luna, Antonio Herrera and Pablo Rincón Gallardo.

The United States team won the first match by 8 goals to seven. Then a serious problem for the American team arose when both Armour and Beveridge fell ill on Monday and were confined to bed. Neither of the two should have played in the second match, scheduled for Wednesday, but they did, although they were unfit. Mexico played well and took the match with ease, scoring 12 goals against only four made by the Americans.

The defining game on Sunday produced an outstanding polo match, the American team in front 5–4 at the break. The Mexican team repeated its Wednesday form and went ahead 7 to 6 in the fifth chukker. It was nine-all in the sixth period, with the real possibility of sudden death overtime looming on the horizon. The Mexican umpires, Julio Muller and Manuel Nava then whistled a 60-yard penalty against the home team and Tommy Wayman hit a high, unstoppable strike through the goalposts. Match and series were over.

The International Series at Beverly Hills

In the spring of 1949, Russell Havenstrite, a strong supporter of polo in California, made the arrangements for a visit by the Venado Tuerto team from Argentina, at the time the best in the world at a 36-goal aggregate rating. Only three of the starters made the journey: Juan Cavanagh and the Alberdi brothers, Enrique and Juan Carlos. The visitors also brought along as reserves Eduardo Brown, Nicolás Ruiz Guiñazú and Jorge Tanoira, the father of the 10-goaler Gonzalo Tanoira.

Venado Tuerto made its debut in the Pacific Coast Open Championship at the Beverly Hills Club in Pacific Palisades. Juan Cavanagh, Nicolás Ruiz Guiñazú and the Alberdi brothers defeated El Ranchito, with Albert "Buster" Wharton, Robert Fletcher, Tom Guy and Harold Barry. In the final game the Hurricanes, Laddie Sanford, Cecil Smith, George Oliver and Harry Evinger, beat Venado Tuerto by 6 goals to 5.

This unexpected setback shook the Argentine contingent and a telephone call was made to Roberto Cavanagh to join the team. Roberto flew his own Cessna airplane all the way from Argentina on time to play in the three-game international series. Played in April, this international series was the best staged in the United States since the halcyon days of the Westchester Cup in the 1910s.

In the first game, the full Venado Tuerto team defeated the United States 15–10. Eric Pedley, George Oliver, Cecil Smith and Aidan Roark played for America. One week later Aidan Roark now at Number 1 and Harry "Dutch" Evinger at Back turned the tables on Venado Tuerto 14–12, in a thrilling match. The third and decisive match was awaited with great anticipation. Regrettably, George Oliver was unable to play. The U.S. team underwent realignment. Roark, who had played brilliantly in the second match, remained in the Number 1 position; Eric Pedley was recalled to the lineup, Cecil Smith played at Number 3, and Dutch Evinger was the last line of defense. Without Oliver on the team, the American squad was unable to repeat the outstanding form they had shown in the previous game and went on to defeat by 11 goals to seven.

To place the American team's achievement into perspective, their win over Venado Tuerto on 17 April was one of the few defeats inflicted upon that team in a period of ten years, from 1946 to 1955. One can only wonder what would have happened had George Oliver played in the last game.

The visitors from Argentina played in several tournaments, occasionally mixing with local players in different teams. In the finals of the Pat Roark Perpetual Tournament, Tortugas, with Nicolás Ruiz Guiñazú, Roberto Cavanagh, Enrique Alberdi and Eduardo Brown,

International polo at Riviera Country Club in Pacific Palisades. Hurricanes defeated Venado Tuerto in the finals of the 1949 Pacific Coast Open. Nicolás Ruiz Guiñazú, George Oliver, Enrique and Juan Carlos Alberdi.

a 30-goal combination, defeated the 26-goal Freebooters, R.B. "Monk" Jowell, Juan Carlos Alberdi, George Oliver and Charles Huthsing, 7–6.

El Trébol Tours the Midwest and Long Island

The late summer and early spring of 1949 saw another top polo team from Argentina, El Trébol, play high-goal games in Chicago, as well as in New York State. The visiting team was built around Carlos and Julio Menditeguy, two former 10-goalers, supported by Juan Reynal and Horacio Castilla at 5-goals each, and Carlos Alonso and Iván Mihanovich as alternates.

The tour began in mid–July at the Oak Brook Polo Club in Hinsdale, with a three-game series, all easily taken by El Trébol. The scores were 10–8, 9–5 and 13–3. The U.S.A. team was William Barry, William Skidmore, Peter Perkins and Harry Evinger.

The so-called Argentine series was held at Blind Brook, Bostwick Field and at the Hamilton Club in Brooklyn. El Trébol defeated Blind Brook 7–4, lost their first game in America to Bostwick Field 8–7 and beat Fort Hamilton 8–7. Bostwick Field had Pete

El Trébol, another team from Argentina, visited the United States in 1949. Bostwick Field, with Pete Bostwick, George Oliver, Alan Corey, Jr., and Devereux Milburn, Jr., cut El Trébol's string of victories. Mrs. Dolly Bostwick presented the trophies.

Bostwick, George Oliver, Alan Corey and Devereux Milburn, Jr. Winston Guest had one of his last appearances playing Back on both the Blind Brook and Fort Hamilton squads.

The tour then moved on to the Meadow Brook Club grounds for the U.S. Open Championship, described in Chapter 16. Briefly, El Trébol beat Chicago and Mexico, before staging a disappointing performance in the finals, losing 10–4 to the Hurricanes. In the Monty Waterbury Cup, played on handicap by the teams entering the U.S. Open, El Trébol avenged the loss to Bostwick Field by 6 goals to three. In this match, Iván Mihanovich played instead of Julio Menditeguy and Clarence Combs took Peter Perkins' place. The final game was scheduled for the following day and, with the Argentine team packing their bags to return to Buenos Aires, it was played between Bostwick Field and Hurricanes, the latter emerging as the winners.

The 1949 International Season in Argentina

This 1949 high-handicap polo season in Buenos Aires had no parallel in the game's history. Representative teams from the United States, Chile, England and Mexico competed in several tournaments from early October to mid–December. It began in October with a 24-Goal tournament featuring Chile, England and two Argentine teams, Civilians and Military. The United States declined to participate. However, an American squad wearing Meadow Brook's colors, Pete Bostwick, Peter Perkins, Alan Corey, Jr., and Devereux Milburn, Jr., entered the Open Championship, taking the measure of the Military team in the first round, 14–8, in a demonstration of excellent polo. However, in the second round an inspired La Concepción team produced the biggest surprise of the tournament by defeating Meadow Brook 14–12, in what turned out to be the best game of the Open Championship. So, the expected clash of titans, Meadow Brook facing Venado Tuerto, did not take place to the great chagrin of the fans, and, not the least, of the Argentine Polo Association's treasurer.

In the Open Championship's subsidiary tournament, the Copa Provincia de Buenos Aires, played on handicap by the teams defeated in the Open, Meadow Brook beat La Herradura, the team of the four Gracida brothers, Rubén, Gabriel, Guillermo and Alejandro, by a score of 10 goals to 9. Devereux Milburn had returned to the States; therefore Clarence Combs, Jr., played in the Number 2 position and Peter Perkins moved to Back. It was a stronger team than the one that had entered the Open Championship. However, Militares, the same team that had been defeated by Meadow Brook in the Open, won the semifinal game 19–12, after receiving eight goals by handicap. In this match, Enrique Alberdi played instead of Buddy Combs. El Trébol went on to take the tournament.

An Inter-American series between 30-goal teams from Argentina and the United States then squared off for the Ministry of Agriculture Cup. These two games provided the best games of the season. The American team was the same: Pete Bostwick, Buddy Combs, Alan Corey and Peter Perkins. The Argentine Polo Association selected Ernesto "Tito" Lalor, Juan Cavanagh, Heriberto Duggan and Juan Carlos Alberdi. Two hard-fought matches ensued, the Argentine combination winning the first game 11–9 and the second 10–9 in sudden death overtime. Heriberto "Pepe" Duggan scored the golden goal.

The last tournament of the season was the World Championship, played on the flat with no handicap limit. Argentina presented the full Venado Tuerto squad: Juan Cavanagh, Roberto Cavanagh, now recovered from a broken fibula that prevented him from entering the Open Championship; Enrique Alberdi, the team's captain and president of the Argentine Polo Association; and his younger brother Juan Carlos Alberdi. Mexico presented Rubén, Gabriel, Guillermo and Alejandro Gracida. The United States team, still wearing the Meadow Brook Club's robin's egg blue jerseys, aligned Pete Bostwick, Peter Perkins, Bob Skene — there in Buenos Aires as a member of the Cowdray Park and English teams, but on his way to California and U.S. citizenship — and Alan Corey, Jr., at Back. In the opening game the United States defeated Mexico with relative ease, 12–7. Argentina followed with a conclusive victory over the Mexican squad, to go on and meet the United States in the final game. The Argentine team came out on top, 11–5. In this series, Alan Corey, the American Back, played the best polo of his career.[1]

This is, so far, the only world championship of polo played without handicap restrictions. Although sanctioned by the U.S. Polo Association, that ruling body had not considered the team an official international team. To the Argentine public, it really did not matter. Thus ended an exciting — as well as exhausting — international polo season at Palermo.

The 1950 Cup of the Americas at Palermo

Buoyed by the experience of the 1949 journey to Buenos Aires, the U.S. Polo Association decided to send an official representative team to challenge for the Cup of the Americas, with former Chairman Robert E. Strawbridge, Jr., as non-playing captain. The American squad was initially based on the Bostwick Field team — Pete Bostwick, George Oliver, Alan Corey and Devereux Milburn, Jr.— that had taken the Open Championship at Meadow Brook in the autumn of 1950. However, Alan Corey sustained an injury that left him unfit to play. The rest of the players were Delmar Carroll, Peter Perkins, Jules Romfh and Lewis Smith. As to mounts, ten ponies were shipped to Argentina, to be complemented by 16 local mounts provided by the hosts.

Bostwick Field entered the Argentine Open, which was played before the series for the Cup of the Americas. George "Pete" Bostwick, Peter Perkins, George Oliver and Lewis Smith, in that order, formed the team. In the first round, Bostwick Field found a tough nut to crack in La Espadaña — Carlos Debaisieux, Tommy Garrahan, Héctor Zavalía and Louie Garrahan — a 22-goal combination that had qualified for the Open by virtue of their victory in the Cámara de Diputados Cup. It was a close-fought match, the result being in doubt until the final chukker, when the visitors went ahead by two goals, 11–9.

Four days later, Bostwick Field easily defeated the military team San Jorge, scoring 11 goals against only six for San Jorge. George Oliver established himself in the eyes of the Argentine aficionados as a great player, showing with advantage his well-earned 9-goal handicap rating. Oliver was ably supported by Peter Perkins, who repeated the good form he had demonstrated in the previous year's high-goal season.

The final match took place one week after the semifinal round. The holders, Venado Tuerto, had defeated their archrival El Trébol in the first semifinal, by a score of 11–9, in what was called at the time "the match of the century." So, Juan Cavanagh, Roberto Cavanagh, Enrique Alberdi and Juan Carlos Alberdi faced the American invasion. Venado Tuerto won the contest after a good match, the final score being 14–8 in their favor. Down 2–7, in the fourth period Bostwick Field scored three consecutive goals to cut the margin to two tallies. But the American squad ran out of steam after that. The result reflected the difference in handicaps, 31-goals for Bostwick Field and 37-goals total for Venado Tuerto, at the time the best team in the world.

The series for the Cup of the Americas created great expectations for a gigantic clash: the best of Argentine polo versus the best of American polo. The American squad made one change from the Bostwick Field team: Del Carroll replaced Pete Bostwick at Number 1. Argentina was, once more, represented by the Venado Tuerto foursome.

In the first match the American team started very well, at times outplaying their fearsome opponents. Ahead in the first and third chukkers, the U.S. team played above their handicap, taking control of the game. At this stage, the American ponies seemed faster and stronger than the Argentine string. Only after the mid-break did the Argentine team assert its supremacy. The final score was 14–11; however, the level of play was much closer than that.

The second match was postponed because of rains, the bane of the Argentine Open in spring. It was held on a heavy field, which slowed down the tempo of play. Interestingly enough, only three fouls were whistled by the umpires during the entire game. Argentina scored two goals from the two initial throw-ins, and never looked back. The final score had the same differential as in the first game: 11–7. George Oliver played a great game. The prestigious magazine *El Gráfico* called his play "sensational" and referred to his multiple plays as "Oliver, always Oliver."[2]

In the final analysis, the United States team acquitted itself nobly. Once more both teams' aggregate handicap differential tells the story: had the matches been played on handicap, the Americans would have been the winners by two goals in each event. The local press again marked George Oliver as the best figure for the Americans, followed by Peter Perkins. If there was a weakness in the team, it was at Back, because Del Carroll did well against the hard defensive tactics of the Alberdi brothers. The consensus was that the best combination would have been Bostwick, Carroll, Oliver, and Perkins, in that sequence. This was the team initially selected to represent Bostwick Field in the Argentine Open Championship. The superb performance delivered by Peter Perkins during the 1949 polo season was still fresh in the public's mind.

The Coronation Cup in 1953

In the British Isles of the early 1950s an age of austerity was gradually giving way to an era of consumerism and comparative affluence. The Tories were sanctioning enterprise and the accession of a new, young queen had prompted thoughts of a new Elizabethan age. In time, something called youth was to create its own culture, but for the moment full employment and Royal participation breathed life into English polo. In what was dubbed the Royal Year of 1953 everybody knew about Edmund Hillary and Tensing climbing to the summit on Mount Everest, and Sir Winston Churchill's Nobel Prize for literature.

To celebrate Queen Elizabeth II's coronation at Westminster Abbey the Hurlingham Polo Association took out the Coronation Cup from safekeeping and brought it into competition for the first time since 1939. The Coronation Cup had been presented by the Ranelagh Club in 1911 to commemorate the accession to the throne by George V. It was to be played for by the winners of the four major London tournaments: The Hurlingham Champion Cup, the Ranelagh Open Cup, the Roehampton Open Cup and the Inter-Regimental Tournament. If a foreign team was invited to the London season, usually it was allowed to enter the competition. And so it proved to be the case in the inaugural event when a team representing the Indian Polo Association took the cup.

Invitations for the 24-goal tournament were sent to the major polo-playing nations; Argentina, Chile, Spain and the United States participated, in addition to England, and local clubs Cowdray Park and Woolmers Park. The U.S. Polo Association, following the policy applied in the 1949 season in Argentina, was represented by a Meadow Brook Club team, George Bostwick, Jr., Philip Iglehart, Ricardo Santamarina and Devereux Milburn, Jr., at the time Chairman of the U.S. Polo Association. Dicky Santamarina, breeder of the famous "Santamarina Greys," was married to Frances Post. Actually, every team except England and Chile had at least one Argentine player in the lineup.

In the first match of the competition the American team faced Cowdray Park, which had Lt. Col. Peter Dollar, Enrique Alberdi, Rao Rajah Hanut Singh and Teófilo Bordeu. In a close, hard-fought game, Cowdray Park prevailed by 10 goals to 7. In this straight-elimination format, Meadow Brook was relegated to the handicap competition for the Duke of Sutherland Cup.

The final of the Coronation Cup, played at Cowdray Park in the rain, was between Argentina and England, the visitors winning the tournament in another close encounter; the final tally was 7–6.

The American team drew a bye in the first round of the Duke of Sutherland Cup, getting a free pass to the semifinals, where they defeated Woolmers Park 6½ to 6. John Lucas, older brother of the celebrated Claire Lucas Tomlinson, Z. Singh, Prem Singh and Carlos de la Serna played for Arthur Lucas' Woolmers Park, his estate in Hertfordshire. In the final match they faced Cowdray Park, the team that had beaten them in the first round of the Coronation Cup. Cowdray Park had John Lakin replacing Hanut Singh. This time the American team prevailed by the minimum difference, 6 goals to five, after trailing in the last period by one goal.

The Meadow Brook team was now clicking and in a special match held at Cirencester Park they defeated England 9½ to 9, with a spectacular goal by Pete Bostwick with less than 60 seconds to go before the final bell.

Other International Matches

During the 1950s there were a few visits to foreign countries undertaken by club teams. A notable one was the visit to Biarritz and Deauville by Frederic Collin and Stephen Sanford's Blind Brook Hurricanes. Maj. Collin, Juan Rodríguez, George Oliver and Sanford took the 1952 Gold Cup at Deauville, defeating the Hurlingham team 7–6 in the finals, after trailing 3–0.

In February 1953, George Sherman, Jr., John Ivory, Jr., Clarence Combs, Jr., and William Nicholls, a team that played as New York, traveled to Bogotá, Colombia, in order to participate in various tournaments, including the Colombian Open Championship. The New York team played five games, winning all but one. They also participated in two games in mixed teams with Colombian players, at Mondonedo and Potrero Grande. This was the first visit ever of an American team to Colombia.[3]

Oak Brook–CCC ventured to Mexico City in 1954, led by their respective patrons, Don Beveridge and Paul Butler. To add extra punch, Cecil Smith and Roy L. Barry joined the team. Four matches were played, the locals winning the first two encounters and the Americans the last two. The opposition was very strong, which reflected the increased maturity of Mexican polo. Playing on different teams, four Gracida brothers, Alejandro, Gabriel, Guillermo and Rubén, played with Erwin Anisz, Roberto Borunda, Jaime Rincón Gallardo, Alberto and Julio Muller, Memo Ruiz and Luis Vinals.

In November 1957, a Milwaukee team played in Lima, Perú. Robert A. Uihlein, Jr., was captain, playing in his usual position at Back. The rest of the team members were David Ellis, George Sherman and Mexican ace Gabriel Gracida, a frequent sight on Milwaukee's polo grounds.

The team played six games on handicap, winning two and losing four. The Milwaukee wins were against the Calipsos, which counted Argentine 9-goaler Enrique Alberdi on its ranks, and San Isidro, the Mulanovich's family team, reinforced by Antonio Grana.

The Cup of the Americas in 1966

After a 14-year hiatus, the Cup of the Americas was resumed at Palermo as part of a crowded international polo season. The Argentine Polo Association contributed to the celebrations associated with the 150th anniversary of independence from Spanish rule, with a 30-goal tournament that included teams from the United States, the British Commonwealth and Argentina's Junior Team.

The American team was carefully selected and given extra time for practice. The U.S. Open Championship was moved to Santa Barbara in the spring of 1996, a change from the traditional September dates. Test matches were held at Oak Brook, coincidentally with the playing of the Butler National Handicap. A selection committee comprised of Alan Corey, Jr., George Sherman, Bob Skene and Cecil Smith elected Northrup Knox as playing captain, with Harold "Chico" Barry, Roy Barry, Robert Beveridge, Dr. William Linfoot, Jack Murphy, Allan Scherer and Lewis Smith completing the rest of the American squad.

Once settled in Argentina, the U.S. team elected not to enter in the Argentine Open Championship because it was felt that the ponies were not yet ready. The 30-goal team — Norty Knox, Bob Beveridge, Chico Barry and Jack Murphy — drew the British Commonwealth team in the first match for the Copa Sesquicentenario. Patrick Kemple from Rhodesia, Sinclair Hill from Australia, and Ronald Ferguson and Paul Withers from England defeated the American team 13–8 on the Number One ground at Palermo.

Several postponements due to rain, a common occurrence in springtime in Buenos Aires, meant that the 30-goal match against Argentina was held between the games for the Cup of the Americas. The Argentine Junior 30-goal team — Alfredo Harriott, Gastón Dorignac, Juan Carlos Harriott, Jr., and Gonzalo Tanoira — having previously beat the Commonwealth 24–2, then took the measure of the U.S. Team 13–6. In this match, Roy Barry took his cousin's place at Number 3. The Argentine team was a most powerful one; some observers felt that it was a stronger team than the one selected for the Cup of the Americas. This team took the Hurlingham Open as well, and when handicaps were modified at season's end, the aggregate was 34-goals.

The first match for the Cup of the Americas saw the American team, with Norty Knox, Billy Linfoot, Roy and Harold Barry, meet the Argentines, Gastón Dorignac, Horacio Heguy, Juan Carlos Harriott, Jr., and Francisco Dorignac. It was a close contest at the beginning, with the Americans trailing 6–5 after three chukkers. Gradually, the Argentines pulled away to win 10–6.

One week later, the same teams met, once more. Argentina made a positional change, Heguy and Gastón Dorignac trading places. The U.S. team gave as good as they took, the score being 11–10 towards the end of the sixth chukker. However, a weak knock-in allowed Horacio Heguy to jump on the ball and score a crucial goal. In the seventh and last chukker, Argentina scored two more goals to win the match 14–10. It was a great game, one that could have gone either way. The American team played an excellent game, closely marking their opponents throughout the match, thanks to the superb performance by their ponies, which had reached their peak at the right time. Count Reigh, Paul Butler's pony, was awarded the series' Best Playing Pony Prize.

Years later, Frankie Dorignac, who played on two winning teams in the Cup of the Americas, felt that the American team in the 1966 series was by far their toughest opponent, compared to the 1969 squad.[4]

Once More, the 1969 Cup of the Americas

When Northrup Knox left Argentina following the 1966 Cup of the Americas series, the question was not whether the series would be renewed, but when.[5]

Norty Knox was again designated captain and the rest of the players were Harold "Chico" Barry, Bennie Gutierrez, Ray Harrington and Billy Linfoot. Harold "Joe" Barry later joined the team as an alternate. A suitable string of ponies was secured with some difficulty, because polo ponies of international caliber were hard to procure; many of the better mounts were just not for sale. Nevertheless, a commitment was made to the Argentine Polo Association to enter an American team in the Open Championship, following the completion of the matches for the Cup of the Americas.

Gutierrez and Dr. Linfoot played in the Hurlingham Open on borrowed ponies; the Cup of the Americas' horses were much too precious to risk before the matches.

Argentina was represented by the same foursome that had been so impressive in the 1966 series: the Dorignac brothers, Juan Carlitos Harriott and Horacio Heguy. The U.S. team was Bennie Gutierrez, Norty Knox, Doc Linfoot and Harold Barry. As in 1966, the matches were played over seven periods, a compromise reached between both associations. High-goal polo in Argentina lasts eight chukkers, and only six in the United States.

The Cup of the Americas at Palermo's Number 1 Field, 1969. Norty Knox, Benny Gutierrez, Doc Linfoot making a goal-saving backhander, and the ever-present Juan Carlos Harriott, Jr.

The first game started with the Argentines off and running hard: 2–0, 3–0, 5–1 and 6–1 was the progression in first four chukkers. Then Bennie Gutierrez took the Back position and things improved noticeably for the American team. The goals scored in the last three periods were six for Argentina and five for the United States. It was, however, too late to make a meaningful challenge.

The second game was more of the same medicine. Argentina got off to a 7–0 start and never looked back. In the middle of the third period, the front legs of the pony mounted by Chico Barry tangled with Horacio Heguy's pony's hind legs, with the result that Barry landed on his hand, spraining his thumb. Chico was unable to continue; in came Ray Harrington at Number 1 and Gutierrez moved to Back. The final score was 18–6.

At the year's end handicap changes, the Argentine team became a 40-goal team, when Horacio Heguy and the Dorignac brothers were raised to 10-goals.

A disheartened U.S. team played in the Argentine Open Championship, in a round robin format.

The team, now with Knox at Number 1, Ray Harrington at Number 2, Linfoot at Number 3 and Barry at Back, drew Coronel Suárez, the defending champion since 1961, in the first game. The final score, 21–9, tells the story. Northrup Knox was of the opinion that this Coronel Suárez team was even better than the Cup of the Americas squad.[6]

The second match, against the Dorignac's Santa Ana, was interrupted after four chukkers because of rain, the score being Santa Ana 4 goals, U.S.A. 2 goals. The match was resumed four days later, with Santa Ana winning 8–6 in an encounter that the U.S. team should have won. The Americans went ahead 5–4, only to miss several penalty shots.

The last game was against Mar del Plata, Juan José Alberdi, Jorge Tanoira, Gonzalo Tanoira and Alfredo Goti. Both teams had lost their two previous matches; Mar del Plata, with Gonzalo Tanoira on his way to a 10-goal rating, took the game by 20 goals to 10.

When the American polo squad returned home, the U.S.P.A. took a jaundiced look at the series of events and lowered all handicaps. The highest U.S. rated players were at 8-goals. This massive reduction affected the entire rankings and it took a few years to stabilize all the players' ratings, including low-handicapped players.

Team Journeys to England

In the summer of 1960 a Meadow Brook team led by Alan Corey, Jr., and completed by William Hudson from Dallas, the professional Juan Rodríguez from Florida, and George C. Sherman, Jr., the new U.S. Polo Association chairman, traveled to participate in the English polo season and also some tournaments in France. Alan Corey, III, also played in some of the matches.

Meadow Brook was defeated by Centaurs, Baron Evelyn de Rothschild's team, in the first round of the Cowdray Park Gold Cup. In the subsidiary tournament for the Midhurst Town Cup, Meadow Brook first defeated a team from Argentina, La Espadaña, and then Cowdray Park, only to lose the final to Silver Leys, a club whose origins dated back to 1890, and was now sponsored by Alfie Boyd Gibbins. In the Cowdray Park Challenge Cup, the oldest club's tournament first played in 1911, the local team with Rao Rajah Hanut Singh on its lineup beat Meadow Brook by a single tally, 5–4.

Meadow Brook finally achieved success when they took the Westbury Cup at the Household Brigade Polo Club in Windsor, now named Guards Polo Club. They defeated the home team and Queen Elizabeth II presented the trophy to team captain Alan Corey, Jr. Following a loss in the Horse and Hound Trophy, the team moved on across the English Channel to the resort town of Deauville.

Meadow Brook lost to Laversine in the first match of the Silver Cup. This team was sponsored by Baron Elie de Rothschild, from the family's French branch. However, with Argentine Carlos Miguens in place of Juan Rodríguez, Meadow Brook took the Jean de Madré Cup, established to honor the good Comte Jean, who in 1923 had brought his Tigers team all the way to the United States eastern seaboard to play the summer season.

The Plainsmen, a team formed by John Armstrong, his son Charles, and the Orthwein brothers, Steve and Peter, participated in the 1969 English polo season. The team reached the finals of the Royal Windsor Cup, played on the Guards Polo Club grounds in Windsor Park. The competition posted 20 entries. In the semifinal round, the Plainsmen defeated Friar Park 5–4½. In the final game they faced Lushill — Capt. Frederick Barker, Howard Hipwood, Peter Perkins, Peter Gifford — and were leading 3–1 in the last chukker; then

Lushill made it 3-all after. The Plainsmen missed a 30-yard penalty. They were unlucky to lose in sudden-death overtime, in a chukker that, following local rules, had widened goals.

The Plainsmen also reached the semifinal round of Cowdray Park's Gold Cup, the tournament emblematic of the British Open Championship, in which ten teams were entered. They met Windsor Park — Lord Patrick Beresford, his brother the Marquis of Waterford, the Duke of Edinburgh, Paul Withers — which had a comfortable lead until halftime, when the Americans fought to get on top and eventually the game was tied at 7-all. Just as time was expiring, Windsor Park managed to score, thus winning 8–7. Windsor Park went on to defeat Pimms in the championship game.

Brig. Jack Gannon, the Hurlingham Polo Association's Joint Honorary Secretary, wrote

> A most welcome American side, the Plainsmen, comprising J. Armstrong, his son C. Armstrong and the twin brothers S. and P. Orthwein came with well trained ponies for the season. The run of the ball was unkind to them in close finishes, causing them to lose by a goal or half a goal against eventual winners throughout.[7]

Two teams from America, Boca Raton and Greenhill, participated adding international flavor to the 1970 English season. Joe Casey, Jack Oxley, Roy Barry and John Oxley defeated 13 goals to 10 Windsor Park, the holders, in the finals of the Gold Cup, the only open highgoal tournament in Britain at the time. The Cowdray Park Gold Cup was established in 1956 as emblematic successor of the Hurlingham Champion Cup. The winning team was considered as the season's champion. It was the first championship gained by an American team since 1938, when Charles Wrightsman's Texas Rangers took the Hurlingham trophy.

The Americans went back to England in force the next year. Oak Brook had Heath Manning, Sr., New Zealander Anthony Devcich, Dr. William Linfoot and Ronnie Tongg. James "Hap" Sharp entered his own Greenfield Farm, with Cristián Zimmermann, later replaced by Rube Evans, Harold and Joe Barry. Both teams reached the semifinals in the Queen's Cup, being defeated by Jersey Lilies and Stowell Park.

For the Cowdray Park Gold Cup, the Oak Brook team was entered as Columbia, Heath Manning's club in South Carolina. In the first round, Columbia defeated Cowdray Park 11–10 in an extra chukker, and Greenhill Farm beat Stowell Park, 8 goals to seven. In the semifinals, Columbia met Windsor Park to win 8–7, and Pimms had a close call with Greenhill Farm, winning 9–8. So to the final game, where Pimms scored four unanswered goals in the first chukker before Billy Linfoot answered with a goal. By halftime, the scoreboard showed five goals for each team. Columbia entered the last chukker 8–6 ahead. Brigadier Jack Gannon described the last period,

> But quite a historical last chukker followed, Gonzalez at his best broke through twice to make it 8 all, next moment Gonzalez was off again for Zorrilla to make it 9–8 only for Linfoot to make it 9 all. Pimms attacked again and again Zorrilla put through for 10 to 9. But as spectators excitedly looked at the clock closing on time the gallant Linfoot made it 10 all. There was still time to start again and almost immediately Roland Ferguson galloped clean through the game at top speed to shoot from an awkward angle, and the ball sailed high over the goalposts and between them for Pimm's victory by 11 to 10. Time came following his shot.[8]

James R. Sharp's Greenfield Farm, which spent much of the summer season playing on European grounds, took the Cowdray Park Gold Cup in 1975, defeating the much fancied Jersey Lilies by 9 goals to five in the championship match. Hap Sharp, Tommy Wayman, Lester "Red" Armour, III, and England's Maj. Ronald Ferguson were on the winning team.

The Coronation Cup Is Resumed in 1971

England's Coronation Cup, which dates back to 1911, had last been played in the coronation year of 1953, as related above. There being several American players in England, it was arranged to have a single match to define the outcome of this prestigious trophy.

Ronnie Tongg, Dr. William Linfoot, Harold L. "Chico" Barry and his son Harold A. "Joe" Barry faced Mark Vestey, Howard Hipwood, Julian Hipwood and Paul Withers at Cowdray Park. The American team totaled 28-goals and the English side only 22-goals. Played on the flat, the U.S. team won the match 9–6. Had

This team took the 1974 King's Cup at Puerta de Hierro, Spain. James "Hap" Sharp, Tommy Wayman, Lester "Red" Armour and Robert Graham. Hap Sharp left a successful career as a driver with the famous Chaparral racers to become an international player and patron of the game. His Greenhill Farm team was successful in both the U.S. Open Championship and England's Cowdray Park Gold Cup, emblematic of the British Polo Championship, among a string of victories in American and European grounds (courtesy Mr. and Mrs. Thomas Wayman).

the contest been played on handicap, the English team would have been the winners.

For the 1972 contest, the venue changed to the Guards Polo Club at Windsor Great Park. As a second match on International Day following the Coronation Cup, a contest between Young England and Young America was held. Played on a rainy day, Young America won the game in the last chukker via a penalty by Lester "Red" Armour.

The main event saw the English team handicapped by a fractured thumb in Paul Withers' left hand. The soaking conditions made his cast soft, and by the middle of the first period, Withers had to be replaced by Lord Patrick Beresford. William Cort Linfoot, his father Dr. Billy Linfoot, Roy Barry and Chico Barry played for America. Under conditions not suitable to the American running style of play, they did well to retain the Coronation Cup by a score of six goals to three.

The following year a patched-up American team of Bill Ylvisaker, Tommy Wayman, Dr. William Linfoot and Chico Barry made a remarkable comeback in the last chukker, edging the host team 7–6, after trailing 6–4 in the fifth period. Dr. Linfoot scored the winning goal with a 40-yard penalty with only 20 seconds remaining on the clock. The Hipwood brothers, Paul Withers and Maj. Ronald Ferguson, played for England.

In the Young England versus Young America match, Benjy Toda, Corky Linfoot, Red Armour and Billy Ylvisaker defeated their opponents 10–3, in the Wills Trophy.

For the fourth year in succession, the American team took the Coronation Cup in 1974, again on the Guards Club polo grounds, before a crowd estimated at 30,000, with Queen Elizabeth II in attendance. Once more the winning goal was scored in the final seconds, on a crisp shot by Tommy Wayman. Bill Ylvisaker, Roy Barry and Red Armour completed the United States team. It was a low-scoring game, tied at three goals apiece in the third chukker, the issue being decided by Wayman's score. England had Maj. Ferguson, playing out of his normal position at Number 1, Howard and Julian Hipwood, and Paul Withers.

Harold "Chico" Barry playing on Hap Sharp's Greenhill Farm team in England facing Ronnie Driver's Jersey Lilies. The Queen's Cup at Windsor Park.

Following this contest, the matches against the United States were interrupted. International Day became the scene of matches for the Coronation Cup between England and other countries, and also mixed teams, such as Rest of the World, North America, South America and Rest of the Commonwealth. The United States versus England international matches were not resumed until the Westchester Cup of 1992, which resulted in another American victory.

CHAPTER 18

Women's Polo in America

The development of women's polo in the United States was delayed, as in all polo playing countries, by unspoken restrictions imposed by codes of propriety, unsuitable female attire and male polo players' skepticism as to the ladies' ability to play. There was no doubt whatsoever as to their ability to ride, astride or sidesaddle; women's prowess on the hunting field had long-time ago proved their skill and courage in the pursuit of deer and fox. The concerns were about their capacity to withstand the physical toughness prevalent in early polo, when close encounters in the melees, hard bumping on the open field, and relative disregard in crossing the ponies' paths were common occurrences in the course of play. In the 1890s, the game of polo was in fact a very rough one.

One of the earliest and perhaps the first notice of women's polo in the United States appeared in *The New York Times* in March 1901. Under the heading "Women Play Polo" the brief report stated:

> There was great interest among the Winter colony in the polo game between teams of women that was scheduled for today. The weather had moderated and was delightful and a large number witnessed the contest. The women have practiced for some time. Those who rode "man fashion" seemed quite at home. Mrs. Hitchcock, Jr., was Captain of the "Reds," with Mrs. George Eustis, Mrs. N.K. Hayes, and John Sanford. The "Blues" were captained by Miss Langhorne, the other members being Mrs. Shaw, Mrs. R.L. Stevens., and Mr. Stevens. The game resulted 2 to 3 in favor of the Blues. Reginald Brooks acted as referee.[1]

A description of all the participants in this game and the stories of their lives could fill many pages. Mrs. Hitchcock, Jr., was the formidable equestrienne Louise Eustis Hitchcock, Tommy's mother. As an aside, Thomas Hitchcock the elder was Thomas Hitchcock, Jr.; when Tommy was born, his father dropped the Junior, but never used the Senior after his name. John Sanford was Stephen "Laddie" Sanford's progenitor, who bankrolled Laddie's tremendous buying sprees on horseflesh.

Mrs. George Eustis was the former Miss Marie Eustis, the daughter of U.S. senator and Minister to France, and a cousin of her husband. Marie divorced George in May of 1901. George Peabody Eustis, a noted architect who designed several homes in Aiken including the palatial Milburn home, the Pink House and the Knox residence in 1908, married Rosamond Street, who was also his cousin.

Richard Stevens was a player at the Somerset County Polo Club, in Bernardsville, New Jersey. The umpire, Reginald Brooks, was the Langhorne sisters' brother-in-law. Miss Nora Langhorne was the youngest of Chiswell Langhorne's five daughters from Albemarle County, Virginia. By far, the most colorful personality was Mrs. Shaw. Nancy Witcher "Nannie" Langhorne married Myopia's 9-goaler Robert Gould Shaw, II, in 1897. She was described as "[a] magnificent horsewoman, as a child won the admiration of the Deep Run here by her abandon and daring. Later she attracted attention by her incomparable seat in the Myopia, Norfolk and Meadow Brook hunts."[2]

The marriage did not last long after the birth of their only son, also named Robert Gould Shaw. During a transatlantic voyage, Nannie met, and soon married, Waldorf Astor, eldest son of William Waldorf Astor. Waldorf Astor had been captain of the Oxford University polo team, and heir to a huge fortune. As a wedding present, the father of the groom gave the couple Cliveden, one of England's great country houses. Lady Astor became involved in politics and was the first woman to sit in the House of Commons, where she became known for her wit and powers of repartee.

To return to our story, it is very likely that women played polo at Aiken most of the time, probably under the leadership of Mrs. Louise Hitchcock. However, there are no records in print of such events.

The next mention of women's polo is also an article in *The New York Times*, whose headline read: "Women Play Polo: Miss Eleanor Sears and Sister Players Cause Sensation at Narragansett Pier." The article went on to describe some aspects of the game:

> In this resort of sensational happenings, as far as the late season is concerned, at least another event in which women participated took place to-day on the polo field.
> A polo team comprised of Miss Eleanor Sears, Miss Handy and two other girls opposed a team of men made up of C.P. Beadlestone, C.C. Rumsey, Devereux Milburn and a member of the victorious international field.
> About four periods were played, and the young women acquitted themselves very creditably. Two of them rode astride, and because the other two rode sidesaddle they were considerably handicapped, but nevertheless played a surprising strong game against their male opponents.[3]

The two ladies who wore riding habits were Mrs. Antelo Devereaux and Mrs. Charles Rumsey. The men's team was top notch, with Devereux Milburn, Pad Rumsey, Perry Beadlestone, all winners of the Open Championship. The fourth, unnamed member was either Harry Payne Whitney or one of the Waterbury brothers.

Another press clipping, also related to polo at the Pier, is dated 3 August 1912 and titled "Women Polo Players Put up Fast Game."

> The women followers of sport on the polo field who made up the Meadow Larks team at last have a rival, and these young women must now look to their laurels.
> On Tuesday, the Black Birds, a new polo team here, under the leadership of the Misses Jeanette and Dasha Allen, daughters of Major Henry T. Allen of Washington, defeated the Meadow Larks in a spirited match at the Point Judith Country Club.
> The Misses Allen, who are newcomers here, play polo with considerable dash and in their initial match at Narragansett defeated the Long Island "Larks" by a score of 5 to 1. Miss Jeanette Allen was the heroine of the game. She gave a fine exhibition of fast riding, and scored four goals for the Black Bird team.
> There are several other events scheduled in the Ladies Polo Tourney here. Among other young women who play polo at the Pier are Miss Emily Randolph, Miss Hannah Randolph, Miss Helen Hitchcock of Newport, and Miss Kate Penn-Smith of Philadelphia.[4]

Two ladies, Mrs. Thomas Hastings, who had been fundamental in establishing the Ladies' Four-in-Hand Driving Club, and Mrs. Thomas Hitchcock started women's polo on Long Island. Mrs. Hasting called for a meeting of expert horsewomen at her home on the North Shore, where it was decided to organize matches for women. They started with practice games on private polo grounds such as the Bacon and Phipps fields in Westbury, and at the Grace field in Great Neck. Under Mrs. Hitchcock's tutelage, progress was such that they moved on to the back fields at the Meadow Brook Club.

The Meadow Larks were the youngsters, boys and girls, coached by Mrs. Thomas Hitchcock at both Aiken and Long Island. Among them were her four children, Celestine, Tommy, Helen and Frank, and Marion Hollins, the gifted all-round athlete who was the prime exponent of the polo-playing girls. Other students of Mrs. Louise Hitchcock included Kitty Penn-Smith, Mrs. John S. Phipps, Emily Randolph, later Mrs. Philip Stevenson, and Flora Whitney. Flora was Harry Payne Whitney's daughter and married G. Maccullough Miller. She became president of the Whitney Museum and its savior after the death of Gertrude Vanderbilt Whitney.[5]

The indefatigable Louise Hitchcock continued her coaching in the 1920s. Among her female students were Elizabeth Chase, Eve and Mollie Crawford, Rita Dolan, Marjorie Le Boutellier and Paula Murray. Some of the boys she taught became famous and covered themselves, their team, Old Aiken, and American polo with a mantle of glory. They are hallowed names in the history of the game: George "Pete" Bostwick, Gerald Dempsey, the Gerry brothers, Raymond and Winston Guest, her own son Frank Center Hitchcock, Philip and Stewart Iglehart, Jimmy Mills, Billy Post and Cocie Rathborne. All had their primary polo education courtesy of Louise Eustis Hitchcock.

Women's polo moved along slowly. Later on, in 1913, the *New York Evening Post* wrote,

Miss Helen [sic] Hollins played on the Aiken team and Miss Helen Hitchcock on the Meadow Larks in a polo match yesterday at Piping Rock, and Aiken won by 7½ to 1½ goals. Miss Hollins gave a fine exhibition of polo, and Miss Hitchcock was not far behind in both offense and defense, and both rode as hard as men. Miss Hollins scored three goals, and Master Thomas Hitchcock made four, the latter showing great promise. Mrs. Thomas Hitchcock gave the cups to the winners.[6]

It seems that Helen Hitchcock and Marion Hollins were the stars of distaff polo. Once more, *The New York Times*:

A polo game in which women starred and were the recipients of much praise was that played on field No. 1 of the Piping Rock Club this afternoon, between Aiken and the Meadow Larks. The reward consisted of four individual cups presented by Mrs. Thomas Hitchcock. Aiken beat the Larks, 7½ to 1½.

The line up:

Aiken — Allen Devereux, G. [George] Gilder (alternate), Master Thomas Hitchcock, Miss Hollins, F.S. [Frank Skiddy] Von Stade.

Meadow Larks — Mr. [William Walter] Phelps, Helen Hitchcock, George Hecksher, F. [Frederick] Prince.

Miss Hollins played a remarkable game. Her maneuvering over the field and the perfect handling of her mounts was a noticeable feature. Mr. Hitchcock and Godfrey Preece furnished her with mounts. Both Miss Hollins and Miss Hitchcock exhibited the daring of men. In their defensive tactics they were not only hard riders but skillful horsewomen and players. Master Thomas Hitchcock showed promise of a future great player. He captured four of the goals scored and Miss Hollins tallied three. Mr. Von Stade put the eighth through the posts for Aiken. The latter lost one-half goal for crossing, and the Larks also forfeited a half goal as a penalty.[7]

Regarding the players, A.J.A. Devereux was a member of the Bryn Mawr Polo Club, George Gilder was a member of the Smithtown Polo Club on Long Island and Frank von Stade was a three-time winner of the U.S. Open Championship. For the Meadow Larks, William Phelps played at the host club, Piping Rock Club, Gustave Maurice Heckscher was a Meadow Brook member who took the Junior Championship, and Frederick Prince, Jr., was from Boston's North Shore — a 6-goal handicap player who won two Open Championships on Meadow Brook teams. The ladies most certainly played in very good company.

The same can be said of the season in Narragansett. If the Misses Hollins and Hitchcock were the stars of women's polo on Long Island, Mrs. Philip Stevenson, née Randolph, and Miss Eleonora Sears carried the same weight on Rhode Island:

> Zest was given to outdoors sports on Monday by the advent of Miss Eleanor S. Sears of Beverly Farms, Mass., who arrived here to visit Mr. and Mrs. G. Maurice Heskscher of New York. Miss Sears was entertained at luncheon on Monday by Mr. and Mrs. Heckscher, and soon after was whirled away in a motor car to the Point Judith Polo Club. A match was arranged there to follow a special game between the Wanderers and Point Judith. Miss Sears was chosen Captain of one polo team, the Reds, and Mrs. Philip Stevenson was chosen Captain of the Whites. It recalled old times at Narragansett, when the present Mrs. Stevenson was Miss Emily Randolph.
>
> The line-up of the two teams was as follows: The Reds—Captain, Miss Eleanor Sears, S. Harold Freemen of New Jersey, Thomas Hitchcock, Jr., of Westbury, L.I., and Maurice Heckscher.
>
> The Whites—Captain, Mrs. Philip Stevenson of Westbury, L.I., Rodman Wanamaker, M.C. [Max] Fleischman, and Philip S.P. Randolph.
>
> The match followed the contest between the Point Judith poloists and the Wanderers after 5 o'clock. Both Captains, Miss Sears and Mrs. Stevenson, gave an exhibition of clever riding and dashing play.[8]

The early start of women's polo at college level has been described in Chapter 14, "The Game at the Universities." Collegiate polo started in 1915 at the Central Park Riding Academy in New York City, under the patronage of the Alumni Committee on Athletics of Barnard College. The players on the teams represented a number of colleges, including Bryn Mawr, Vassar and Wellesley.

Women's polo was played mostly on Long Island, Aiken and Narragansett Bay. Nevertheless, staid Boston finally came on line, perhaps ushered on by Eleonora Sears, whose determination to compete in many sports and games usually reserved for men opened the gates for women's entrance in sports. The notice read:

> Polo played by women's fours, a distinct novelty in this country, though an established competition in England, is contemplated as a special feature of the interclub polo contests at the meeting of the Boston Fair Association at Readville, Sept. 30, Oct. 1 and 2. It is planned to form two or more teams of young women, who will play for special trophies.[9]

Eleonora "Eleo" Sears was an all-round sportswoman. Born into a wealthy Boston family, her uncle Richard Sears was the first U.S. tennis champion. Eleonora participated in all kind of sports: tennis, polo, squash, sailing, riding and shooting. She excelled in tennis, being four times national champion in doubles, twice each with her friend Hazel Hotchkiss, later Mrs. Wightman, and also with Molla Bjurstedt. She took the mixed doubles title, partnering with Willis Davies, and was finalist in singles in 1912, losing to Mary Browne. However, horses were her most enduring passion.[10]

The Game in the Midwest

Audrey Scott was the pioneer of polo in Chicago when she organized the Chicago Women's Polo Club in 1924, and the game in Ohio got its start in Cincinnati in 1922, when Mrs. Harrison B. Smith organized two teams to play indoors.[11] Regrettably, there is no further information about the subsequent existence of these two initial efforts.

Years later, again in Cincinnati, Earle W. Hopping, a 10-goaler in England, coached several women led by Louise Fleischman, later Mrs. Henry Yeiser, Jr. The group included Mrs. James Benedict, Mrs. Harold Lion, Dorothy Rawson, a Miss Resor, Mrs. Lawrence

Smith and Mrs. Samuel Stephenson. In Cleveland, the team of Miss M. Allen, Mrs. Gregory (Isabel) McIntosh and Pansy Ireland also played indoors.

In Omaha, Nebraska, Daphne Peters organized a women's team.

Elisabeth Ireland, the First Woman to Obtain an Official Handicap

In 1914 a woman appeared in the horse shows polo classes whose activities in all forms of Chagrin Valley sports made her into a legend. Elisabeth "Pansy" Ireland, later Mrs. Parker B. Poe, was a rare, accomplished and unique character. Her equestrian career started in the usual way: horse shows, hunting, point-to-points and polo. She also was an avid reader of sporting literature. An excellent horsewoman, Pansy won a national championship at Madison Square Garden on a horse named Sun Rise.

She owned a farm in Kentucky, where she bred hunters and thoroughbreds, and a plantation in Thomasville, Georgia, where she had a herd of Jersey cattle and also bred American foxhounds. Elisabeth organized the first women's polo team in Chagrin Valley, keeping the game alive during World War I. Among those girls who played polo were Katharine Haskell, Florence Hale, Katharine Holden, Eloise McLaughlin, Caroline Pickands, Delia White and Kathleen York. The later was the main protagonist of an amusing incident. The week before her scheduled wedding to Thomas White, in the course of a game, a ball made contact with one of her eyes; the resultant shiner caused much concern in the bride's family. Tom White, being a polo player, would have none of that family nonsense, and the best make-up available carried Kathleen through the critical walk down the aisle.

In due time, Pansy Ireland became the first woman to be listed in the U.S.P.A. handicap list, her gender unbeknown to that august body. The name E. Ireland, Kirtland Country, followed by her handicap, 0, appears in the 1925 and 1926 Year Books.[12] When the ruse was discovered, her name was promptly deleted from the official handicap list. However, her name again appeared in the Year Book until 1935.

The Game in California

It is said that in America, all trends begin in California and then progress eastwards. This was not the case with the game of polo, where Mrs. Andrew Chaffey earned the sobriquet "mother of California polo" in recognition of her pioneer efforts on behalf of the game. Nevertheless, Dorothy Wheeler started polo in Santa Cruz in 1922 with her husband Deming on a dirt, or "skinned," field on the Wilder ranch north of the town. In addition to Melvin and Deloss Wilder, the owners, participants included Sam Leak, Jr., Frank Wilson and Dr. Golden Falconer. Dorothy was the only woman player.[13]

In July 1923, a new field was constructed on Bay and California Avenues. Matches were played against teams from Berkeley, Del Monte, Stanford and the U.S. Army. A better ground within the racetrack in Aptos was found and the Aptos–Santa Cruz Polo Club was founded. Then Marion Hollins came to town and women began to join the game, which attracted many spectators. Her grand design was Pasatiempo, a 750-acre property that would offer a top golf course, and a polo ground within a housing development. Now there were two women's teams in Santa Cruz: Pasatiempo and Pogonip.

Reginald "Snowy" Baker, a transplanted Australian, initiated polo at the Uplifters Polo Club in 1925.[14] That same year, women's polo was an established game in Santa Barbara, promoted by Mrs. Deming (Dorothy) Wheeler. The ladies moved on from stick and ball sessions to occasional participation in men's practice chukkers and then progressing into full-fledged games. From the dirt field allotted to the women, they moved to the turf polo grounds, including players like the promising Medora Stedman, Canada-born Doreen Ashburnham, Mary Chapin, later Mrs. Allen Beemis, Alice Hanchett, Mrs. Charles Jackson, Jr., and Mrs. Grace Terry.

A tournament was then organized at Will Rogers' Uplifters Polo Club in Santa Monica between teams representing the host club, Santa Barbara and Santa Clara. During this competition, Mary Rogers showed promise as a future star player.

However, the best woman polo player in America was the remarkable Marion Hollins, United States' amateur golf champion and responsible for the design and construction of two world-class courses, Cypress Point and Pasatiempo. When the celebrated golf architects Dr. Alister MacKenzie and Seth Raynor advised her that a hole was far too long for a water-carrying par-3, Marion took a brassie and hit the ball across the ocean.[15] Where it landed, it is now the sixteen green at Cypress Point, the world's most photographed golf hole.

Marion Hollis was perhaps the first American multitalented sportswoman. Besides golf and polo, she was an accomplished driver, fond of fast cars and steering a four-in-hand through some narrow streets in Paris with a confidence born out of assiduous practice. Miss Hollins was instrumental in the founding of the Pacific Coast Steeplechase and Racing Association, with circuit racing in northern California. Marion was also an excellent tennis player, as were her friends Eleonora Sears and Helen Wills, both national champions. Helen Wills, later married Aidan Roark, the Irish polo player who made California his home. In preparations for many of her tournaments, Wills practiced at the Pasatiempo tennis courts, built by Marion Hollins, and also played many exhibition matches at her friend's club.

The 1930s were the heydays of California's polo. The Girls' Championship of Santa Barbara was played for on the Fleischman Field on 27 March 1931. The team named Palomas (Doves), Alice Erving, Violet Tuckerman, Frances Tuckerman and Mrs. Deming Wheeler, defeated the Golondrinas (Swallows), Patricia Collins, Margot Flick, Mary Collins and Elizabeth Sherk, by 5 goals to 3. It is significant that this particular game was included in the U.S.P.A. Year Book.[16] This mention is perhaps the first acknowledgement by the U.S. Polo Association that, yes indeed, women played polo somewhere in the United States.

The Pacific Coast Women's Polo Association organized a tournament that gathered nine teams at the Pasatiempo grounds. In the finals, Pasatiempo, Rose Donnelly, Mrs. Floyd (Leone) Hart, Marion Hollins, Dorothy Wheeler, defeated Riviera, Mrs. Orville Caldwell, Audrey Scott, Mrs. Carl Beal, Mrs. Gilbert Proctor, by the score of 5–3. The winning and runner-up teams were invited to go on an exhibition tour of Texas and Arizona.[17]

Therefore, in November 1934, nine California players led by Mrs. Spencer (Louise) Tracy headed for Texas on a barnstorming journey in two aircrafts and two cars. The women played games in Abilene, an event that generated a large amount of publicity. The next two games, at Fort Worth and Austin, had to be cancelled because of heavy rains that turned the polo grounds into thick mud. Nevertheless, the girls from the University of Texas, the only female team in the state, traveled to San Antonio for a match against the Californians.

The team then moved on to Tucson, where the University of Arizona men's team defeated the visitors, on a soft sand field, a surface unfamiliar to the ladies. Next stop was

Yuma, where the match was held at night on the High School's football stadium, with the purpose of attracting a large crowd. On a hard, fast field, the woman played the best game of the tour. The finale took place in Los Angeles; much to the relief of the player's relatives, none had sustained an injury. There is a photograph in *Polo* magazine showing some of the players: Mrs. Deming Wheeler, Mrs. Gilbert Proctor, Mrs. Carl Beal, Miss Audrey Scott and Mrs. Spencer Tracy.[18]

In 1934, seven clubs got together and formed the Pacific Coast Women's Polo Association and started to organize tournaments.[19] The founding clubs were Berkeley, Douglas School for Girls in Pebble Beach, Fullerton, Pasatiempo, Riviera, Sacramento and Santa Barbara. The main tournaments were the Governor's Cup, the Lady Chaytor Trophy, the Pacific Coast Handicap, the U.S. Open, and the Senior and Junior Handicap tournaments.

Other clubs that became affiliated with the P.C.W.P.A. included the Capitol Chukkerettes, Las Amigas, Salinas, San Francisco and San Jose. The Association also published a handicap list, with Mrs. Floyd (Leone) Hart at the top.

The summit was reached in 1937 when the newly renamed U.S. Women's Polo Association organized the initial Women's Open Championship, which was played for until 1940. Riviera, Santa Barbara, Las Amigas and Pogonip are the recorded champion teams. The complete rosters are in Appendix 7.

Women's polo in California. The final game of the 1938 Open Championship between Pogonip (light shirts) and Santa Barbara (dark shirts). Wilma Kann, Elaine McInerney, Ann Jackson hitting the ball, and Willamette Keck. Santa Barbara took the match, 4–3.

The Game in the Rockies and the Northwest

Polo in Colorado started in 1920s, when Josephine Bogue, Peggy Leonard, Hildegarde Neill, Jeanne Sinclaire and Josephine Tutt began practice chukkers and then matches against the boys' team at Cheyenne Mountain Country Club in Colorado Springs.[20]

In Boise, Idaho, Julia Davis, Bessie Falk, Suzanne Dabney Taylor and Mrs. Cora Irigh formed a team that played exhibition matches at equestrian gymkhanas, sometimes in mixed teams.[21]

Seattle offered a welcome change because the male members of the Olympic Riding and Driving Club encouraged the formation and active participation of a ladies' polo team.

Polo in the Philadelphia — Washington Corridor

On a cold and rainy day in November of 1925 a group of 18 young women met in Col. Ola Bell's office, headquarters of the Third Corps Area in Baltimore at the request of Mrs. Thomas Jefferson Randolph Nicholas. Something new in the way of sports for women in Maryland was to be attempted: polo.

Col. Bell introduced Capt. W.R. Hamby, who would act as a coach. He mentioned that the Washington, D.C., women's team had sent out a nationwide challenge to other women's teams, and he hoped to coach a team from Baltimore that could meet this challenge. Practices started at the Armory, using the Third Corps Area ponies.

The first match took place at the 103rd Regiment Armory in Philadelphia against a team captained by Miss Elizabeth Altemus, Miss Lydia Clothier and Miss Good. Mrs. Nicholas, Miss Catherine Bosley and Miss Mary Fussellbaugh represented Baltimore. A gallery of 500 spectators watched the Philadelphia ladies crush their opposition by the unlady-like score of 15-nil.

One month after the Baltimore women players were organized, a team was formed at Chestertown on the Eastern Shore of Maryland by Alverta Brice, Mrs. Richard Carvel, Edith Humphries, Elizabeth Wickes and Rowena Woods. Eventually, three matches were played, the Baltimore women winning all three. Then the challenge from Washington was accepted and in May 1926 on the Atamasco Field in Baltimore, Washington taking the honors. This result was repeated a week later on the Potomac Field.[22]

In February 1927, the Baltimore team, Catherine Bosley, Alverta Brice and Miss Burch, traveled to Cincinnati where they played on ponies borrowed from their hostesses' team, Mrs. Joseph Viner, Mrs. Henry C. Yeiser, Jr., and Mrs. Laurence R. Smith. Cincinnati defeated their orange-clad rivals by 8 goals to 4½.

A repeat 3-game series was played against Washington: Maude Preece, Lydia Archbold, Elizabeth Jackson and Mrs. William Thomas. The Baltimore players were Katherine Schmidt, Catherine Bosley, Alverta Brice and Mrs. Amos Koontz. Baltimore took revenge, winning the series two games to one.

Similar teams were started in Philadelphia thanks to the enthusiasm and support of Mrs. John Hay Whitney, née Altemus, and in Washington by Miss Lydia Archbold, a wealthy socialite who later became Mrs. Elliott Strauss.

Polo in the Southeast

As expected, polo at all levels thrived in Aiken, the cradle of women's polo, during the winter season. The towering presence of Louise Hitchcock made sure that the game remained part and parcel of the northern colony amusements and pastimes.

Just south of the border in Georgia, some women players started polo in Augusta; they received support from Army wives in nearby Fort Oglethorpe.

Further northwest, in Asheville, North Carolina, Mrs. Cornelia Vanderbilt Cecil organized a polo group from her palatial Biltmore mansion. Eliza Cox, Elizabeth Martin and Mrs. V. Oldsmith are the names associated with women's polo in Asheville.

The U.S. Polo Association and Women's Polo

Besides Elisabeth Ireland, two other women managed to evade the gaze of the U.S.P.A. censors, according to a brief note in the magazine *Polo*. Miss Pansy Ireland of Cleveland, Miss Mary Henry Broderick of Austin and Mrs. Gilbert Proctor of Los Angeles were mentioned as being officially rated by the Association.[23] A review of the pertinent Year Books reveals that M.A. Broderick appears in the 1932 edition; then as Mary Henry Broderick in 1933 and 1934. Being so brazen probably cost her the erasure of her name from the 1935 version.

Mrs. Gilbert Proctor does not appear in any of the U.S.P.A. Year Books. However, she entered in the Annual Eight Goal Tournament as a player on the Riviera Country Club team and became the first woman to enter in a U.S.P.A. sanctioned tournament.[24]

The removal of the players' names from the U.S.P.A. Handicap List provoked consternation in some circles. Peter Vischer, the respected editor of *Polo*, the only specialized magazine devoted to the game, wrote a letter to the U.S. Polo Association:

August 15, 1935

Dear Mr. Kelley,

I think it was a dirty trick to take the ladies out of the handicap list, and just to show you the charm of one of the people to whom you did such an injustice, so that it may be forever on your conscience, I send you the enclosed picture.

Very truly yours,

(signed) Peter Vischer

Attached to the letter is a photograph of Elisabeth Ireland in polo garb.[25] There is no recorded response from the U.S. Polo Association's authorities.

The enterprising Dorothy Wheeler, chairperson of the Women's Polo Association in California, wished to obtain recognition and support from the U.S.P.A. in her endeavors to promote the game. Mrs. Deming Wheeler wrote a letter to Frank S. O'Reilly, at the time holding the office of secretary-treasurer of the U.S. Polo Association, requesting recognition of the entity.

Mr. O'Reilly answered to the effect that he thought that the general feeling among the polo players was the game was not a woman's game. Undaunted, Dorothy Wheeler then wrote to the newly elected chairman of the Association, Robert E. Strawbridge, Jr. His response was more measured; it was still negative, however, stating that the U.S.P.A.

could not take any official part in the governance of women's polo. The pertinent minutes read:

> The question of the recognition of formal women's polo was discussed at great length. Mr. Strawbridge read the formal request of the Pacific Coast Women's Polo Association, for recognition and affiliation with the United States Polo Association. It was finally decided by the meeting to leave to Mr. Strawbridge and Mr. Kelley the writing of a letter informing the Women's Polo Association that, while the United States Polo Association desired to encourage polo in every possible way, it was not the policy of this Association to make any attempt to identify itself with women's polo.[26]

Thus, Mr. Robert Strawbridge, a stern Quaker from Philadelphia's Main Line, slammed the door in the face of women, and the California polo players in particular.

The women polo players in the Golden State responded by starting a new club in Santa Cruz, Marion Hollins' base at the Pasatiempo Golf Club. They named the club Pogonip, after the Native American word for the formation of frost on trees. Although male polo players were accepted, the primacy was entitled to the women. The California ladies persevered on their own, establishing the already mentioned Women's Open Championship and publishing a Year Book and their own handicap list.

One of the stars of women's polo in California was Mrs. Floyd (Leone) Hart from Sacramento. Born in San Antonio, she moved to California and organized polo teams and played until 1937. Leone Hart became the top ranked female player in the U.S.W.P.A., with a rating of 9-goals, probably the equivalent of a four-goal handicap today.

The start of World War II essentially put an end to organized polo in America for the duration. Nevertheless, a women's benefit match for the Navy Relief charity attracted 8,000 paying spectators to Golden Gate Park in San Francisco.

During the war, with many polo players away in the armed forces, the majority of sports were halted. However, at the St. Louis Country Club an enterprising group of equestrian ladies thought of polo as a way of passing the time. Three ladies, Mamie von Gontard, Ann Bates and Zoe Lippmann, decided to practice polo and formed their own team. While their primary objective was to exercise the horses, they did play practice matches among themselves, making their effort most unique.[27]

In England after the war, women were welcomed to the polo grounds; two polo players, Mrs. Philip (Celia) Fleming and Mrs. John (Daphne) Lakin, Lord Cowdray's younger sister, were on teams that took the Cowdray Park Challenge Cup in the late 1940s, when the game in Britain was struggling to recover from the war.

The gains painfully obtained by women players before the world conflict were lost when peace was declared. There is no notice of women players participating in U.S.P.A. events until 1973. There are only anecdotal stories of women playing here and there; however, there was place in organized polo for the ladies.

A funny happening occurred in 1962 at the St. Louis Country Club, where several girls who had excellent riding skills took up polo. Soon enough, a game was arranged between teenagers, boys versus girls at the club. Joe Carpenter, a boy who played polo on his school team, had returned home for a vacation. In a moment of inspiration, the enterprising girls dressed Joe in female clothes and a wig, introducing him as "Josephine," a new friend keen to try polo. The boys could not cope with the polo skills demonstrated by the guest player. To make things worse, one of the boys asked "Josephine" out during the match. Smiling under the helmet, wig, and padding, "Josephine" courteously declined. It was only later that the trick was revealed, with much hilarity on both sides.[28]

Women's Polo After the War

Sue Sally Hale from California was the most prominent figure in women's polo in the United States. However, her struggle to gain recognition and eventual admiration was long and difficult. She had to face the hostility and veiled disdain of players and officials who displayed the outraged rigidity of those threatened by changing times. However, encouraged by the support of a few, Hale soldiered on. There are reports that she had to hide her hair under the helmet and sometimes she had a fake moustache. *The New York Times* wrote that she also entered tournaments as A. Jones, her maiden surname.[29] Most likely, she utilized this ruse in local tournaments because a search of Year Books from 1955 to 1972 failed to identify such a name.

Nevertheless, it was much more than her abilities as a player that endeared "Sue Sal" to her admirers in the polo community. She performed an outstanding effort in mentoring, coaching and encouragement of many polo players on the West Coast. Perhaps her most satisfying personal achievement was winning the first U.S. Women's Championship with her two daughters, Stormie and Sunset, the latter better known as "Sunny." The National Museum of Polo and Hall of Fame awarded Sue Sally Hale the 2004 Philip Iglehart Award for lifetime contributions to the game of polo. Regrettably, she unexpectedly died a few months before the award's presentation.

Her daughter Sunny continued the family legacy of excellence when she took the 2000 U.S. Open Championship on Tim Gannon's Outback team. Sunny Hale became the women's top handicap in the world at 5-goals, an accolade that she shared with England's Claire Lucas Tomlinson. Sunny is the founder and president of the American Polo Horse Association, an organization deeply involved in the collection, recording and preservation of polo horses' pedigrees.

As an example of how far the clock has moved, in 2010 Sunny Hale was elected governor-at-large of the U.S. Polo Association. This represents a sort of belated vindication of her mother Sue Sally's efforts on behalf of the game.

In a long-overdue move, the 1973 Year Book listed four women in its roster of players: Elizabeth Dailey from Mokuleia in Hawaii, Sue Sally Hale from Carmel Valley, Virginia Merchant, from National Capitol Park, and Jorie Butler Richardson from Oak Brook. University players included Kathy Barrett, Sandra Datschovsky, Gail Flynn, JoAnn Kavanaugh, Dorothy and Mary Prowell, Janet Schwartz and Sallie Wilhite, all from Texas A&M, and Amoret Cardeiro, Janet Fates and Louise Lippincott, from Yale University. However, when at the start of the 1971-1972

Sue Sally Hale, who paved the way for women's polo in America.

season Yale University sent to the U.S. Polo Association the list of men and women players, the members of the first Yale women's team, Amoret Cardeiro, Cricket Fates, Jennie Freeman and Deborah Lee were erased, with the exception of Amoret Cardeiro.[30] Obviously, the U.S.P.A. censors tried to be gender-specific; however, the fact remains that Amoret Cardeiro was the first woman to be listed in the U.S.P.A. Year Book after World War II.

Daniel Wallace, coach of the Yale University polo team, deserves a mention in this chapter on women's polo because it was his support and coaching that allowed undergraduate Deborah Lee to become the first woman to compete — against Harvard in a 14–9 winning effort — on the men's squad. The year was 1972 and the event caused national and international news. *The New York Times* and the magazines *Parade* and *Sports Illustrated* sent reporters to the game and the Associated Press wired the story overseas. That is how Debbie's mother, in Japan at the time, heard about her daughter's achievement.[31]

Soon after, the University of Virginia and Cornell University started to organize teams. The only games Yale played in their inaugural season were against those colleges. The Yale varsity squad went on to take the first Women's Intercollegiate Championship in 1976, the centenary of polo in America. Captained by Molly Baldridge, the Yale team included Jaquelynn Chazey, Anna Hewitt and Liz Hetch. They took the trophy donated by Katrina Hickox Matheson of Katydid Farms, mother of Yale varsity player William Matheson.

In November 1975, the Carmel Valley Riding and Polo Center organized the first all-girl polo tournament in more than 30 years. Four teams competed for the SSH Perpetual Trophy. In the first game, the Central Valley team, Cathy Whaley, Mary Alizon Walton, Mimi Bommersbach and Mary Lambert, defeated UC–Davis, Cathy Mills, Betsi Sumida, Sue Fredericks and Noel Madigan. The second game pitted Carmel Valley's Brenda Lambert, Judy Ale, Teresa Beiger and Barbara Atkinson versus Santa Barbara, which had Carol Borucki, Becky Rainsford, Sue Reeves and Betsy Walton on their lineup. The host club won the match, placing them in the finals against Central Valley.

In the match for third place, Davis, with Vicki Hauman in Sumida's place, ran away with the victory. The final game was very close, Central Valley winning by three goals to two.[32]

The Women's U.S. Handicap tournament was created in 1979 as the showcase for women's polo. Carmel Valley took the first edition, with Sunset Hale, Susan Welker, Sue Sally Hale and Stormie Hale. Many of the top players in the country have their names engraved on the trophy, such as Yvette Biddle, Leigh Eckstrom Butterworth, Alina Carta, Kim Kelly, Jolie Liston, Lesley-Ann Masterton from Jamaica, Maggie Mitchell, Nancy Romfh, Susan Stovall, Oatsy von Gontard, Susan and Mary Alizon Walton. Regrettably, this important tournament has been in abeyance since 2003.

Many other women have contributed to the growth of the game. In her time, Vicky Armour was perhaps one of the best female players in Florida; however, she abandoned playing to dedicate herself to purchasing and training polo ponies.

Out in California, Susan Stovall for many years was a player-manager of Eldorado, one of the largest polo clubs in the United States. Mary Alizon Walton, the youngest of the sisters, made headlines when she was on the Robert Louis Stevenson School Interscholastic championship winning team with Peter Young, Sean Cooley and Matthew Upchurch. Her sister Susan Walton took the U.S. Women's Handicap a total of six times, twice with Mary Alizon on her team.

In Texas, Dawn Jones is a regular feature on the San Saba team, while Leigh Ann Hall had her moment on top of the world when she took the Silver Cup, the oldest polo tournament in America, with her Pueblo Viejo team.

Melisa Ganzi in Florida is one of the high profile patrons of the game, as well as in the winter season in Colorado and at Santa Barbara during the summer months. As a supporter of the game, Melisa's offer to put her polo pony string at the disposition of the British team was crucial to the success of the 2009 Westchester Cup.[33]

There are several sponsors who play in the Florida season. Maureen Brennan's family purchased the gorgeous Llangollen property in Virginia — Jock Whitney's wedding present to his bride Mary Elizabeth Altemus — where Maureen's successful Goose Creek team is based. Goose Creek achieved back-to-back wins in the Silver Cup at Aiken with the same four players, an unusual occurrence.

Cathy Stewart Brown's summer play is in Nashville, Tennessee; in winter, she brings her Wildwood team to Gulfstream in Lake Worth. Barbara Uskup, together with her husband Tom, is one of several players that have taken part in the development of Aiken as a major polo center, with strong polo season in the fall and in the spring.

Women in the U.S. Open Championship

Gillian Johnston, Skee Johnston's daughter and a third generation polo player, was the first patron to take the U.S. Open Championship on her own Coca-Cola team in 2003 at the Royal Palm grounds in Boca Raton, Florida. Adam Snow, Miguel Novillo Astrada and Tommy Biddle were her teammates.

Canadian-born Julie Roenisch was the first woman to participate in the Open in 1992 on Frederick Mannix's Fish Creek team, with her husband Rob, Hector Galindo and Alejandro "Piki" Díaz Alberdi. Although beaten by Hanalei Bay in the finals of the U.S. Open Championship, that same Fish Creek team took the handicap tournament for the C.V. Whitney Cup.

Deborah Couples won the 1992 East Coast Open at Myopia in 1992; that success moved her to enter the U.S. Open two years later with her own All-America Polo team, which included Rob Walton, Dale Smicklas and Tommy Biddle. She was the first female patron to play on her own team. Good luck evaded the squad, which lost all four qualifying matches.

In 1999, both Sunny Hale and Gillian Johnston made their debut in the U.S. Open at Palm Beach Polo Club; Sunny on the Lechuza Caracas team and Gillian on Skee Johnston's Coca-Cola. Both teams failed to qualify for the final match. Nevertheless, Hale went on to take the championship the following year with Outback, and Johnston did the same with Coca-Cola in 2003.

Julie Nicholson Boyle, a winner of the Bronze Trophy, and Kristy Waters Outhier, a former star player on the Texas A & M squad, were alternates in the 2001 runner-up team, Steve Van Andel's Orchard Hill.

Alina Carta and Dawn Jones were on Tommy Lee Jones' 2006 San Saba team that did not qualify for the semifinals, and KC Beal on the BTA squad, which had a similar fate. Elizabeth Shannon Iorio, a hunter and jumper rider, was the sponsor and player on the pink-clad Laurence Wallace team, which had Luis Escobar, Mike Azzaro and Agustín Merlos in its lineup.

Finally, Melissa Ganzi played on the Audi team in the 2008 U.S. Open Championship. The team won one game and lost two in its bracket and failed to advance further in the tournament. Juan Bollini, Santiago Chavanne, Francisco de Narváez and Gonzalito Pieres were also on the squad.

International Polo

Two games between American and Canadian teams were played on the Westchester Biltmore polo grounds in Rye, New York, in 1928. The United States was represented by Mary Leary, Mrs. James Hewlett, Sally and Becky Lanier. The Canadians were Dorothy Hogan, Bunny Dewdney, May Atkins and Violet May. The American team won both matches, by scores of 7–1 and 12–3.[34]

CHAPTER 19

Indoor Polo

Polo in America as an indoor game started at Dickel's Academy in the winter of 1876. Most likely, James Gordon Bennett and his friends did not realize that they were starting a new game, but in fact it was the first time that the indoor version had been played anywhere.[1]

Although these initial and haphazard attempts at polo were of the indoor variety, the game promptly established itself as an outdoor pastime. Almost nothing is known about arena or indoor polo for several years after the experience in New York City. For several years a variant of the games was played in a desultory sort of way by using a soccer ball and hitting it with broomsticks with sawed-off bristles. The broomsticks were not very successful at shooting goals, and it became apparent that the outdoor mallet would have to be used. This meant a smaller ball, and experiments along those lines were started almost immediately. As a result, the current ball is a miniature of the original soccer ball.

Around 1901, Earle W. Hopping, Harry R. Guthrie, John C. "Jack" Wilmerding, Jack de Saules and a number of other enthusiasts started playing in the arena at the top of Tchchor Grands' Sale & Riding Academy, at 61st Street and Central Park West in New York City.

The game began to arouse interest and men at Brooklyn Riding and Driving Club soon took it up, and so did the Central Park Riding Academy and Durland's Riding Academy. In 1904, *The New York Times* reported on the first match at Durland's:

> Polo as an indoor game, with the mallet and regulation willow ball, was introduced as a novelty last night at the Durland Riding Academy on West Sixty-sixth Street. The game followed the regular music ride, in which nearly fifty riders took part. The polo game was characterized more by all-around amusement than by any exhibition of science, for the latter was out of the question in the limited space that the players had in which to hit the ball. The goals were placed at the extreme end of the riding ring, and after the first throw-in, the mêlée of horses was generally the most prominent feature of the game, while the mallets of the contestants flew wildly up and down in the air.
>
> Three periods of ten minutes each were played and the men were glad when the final period closed. The team captained by H. Branchley won by 5 goals to 4. J.C. Wilmerding was Captain of the defeated team. He was the only player who has ever appeared prominently on the polo field, but during the last year or two he has done little tournament play. He only made one goal. Sidney Holloway gave good assistance to Wilmerding's team, while Marshall Clapp and William Montgomery did effective work for the winning team, Montgomery making two goals. The winning team consisted of H. Branchley, William Montgomery, Marshall Clapp, and H. Schoen. The defeated four were J.C. Wilmerding, J.C. Punderford, Sidney Holloway, and George Mills.[2]

It is interesting that the wooden ball was used indoors, when the smaller than regulation soccer ball had been already successfully tried. However, traditions die hard in the game of polo.

When Dickel's Academy moved north to West 56th Street, many of the players were well aware that the indoor game had been played there first of all, in the old place at Fifth Avenue and 39th Street. They had tried it a bit at the beginning of this century, but it wasn't until about 1906 or 1907 that it really obtained any foothold.

The National Indoor Polo Association

A short article from *Outing* magazine informs that approximately 60 enthusiasts formed the National Indoor Polo Association in 1910, in New York City. The officers of the novel institution were Harry Gugenheimer, president; Jack Wilmerding, vice-president, Dr. F.T. Robeson, secretary, and Harry Guthrie, treasurer. The article mentions that it was planned to make the association national in scope and that clubs in various parts of the country have been invited to join the new association.[3]

No other notice has been obtained regarding the eventual development and ultimate fate of the National Association.

The Indoor Polo Association

Soon after that came the organization of a team at Durlands which included Archie Kinny, Earle W. Hopping and Jack Breen. Archer W. Kinny, later treasurer of the Indoor Polo Association and one of indoor polo's best players, began about that time, as well as T.K. Alford, E. Maher, Charles Lang and George Sherman. The group formulated some rules and regulations and went along until 1915, when the Indoor Polo Association was organized with George C. Sherman as president, T.K. Alford as vice-president, Charles Lang as secretary and E. Maher as treasurer.[4]

The clubs in 1921 were Brooklyn Riding and Driving Club, Durland's Polo Club, New York Riding Club, 101st Cavalry, Squadron A and The Riding Club, all in New York City; the U.S. Military Academy at West Point also had a club. In Pennsylvania there were the First and Second Troop Polo Associations and the University of Pennsylvania. Virginia Military Institute had a polo club in Lexington, and in New England, Yale University in New Haven and Norwich University in Northfield boasted about their strong teams. Finally, Princeton University in New Jersey was the home of the first intercollegiate champions.[5]

Following the cessation of hostilities in Europe in 1918, there was a good deal of interest shown in the game. The celebrated Squadron A joined the I.P.A., and in 1920, the Riding Club, which was then located at 7 East 57th Street, took up the game actively. Play started at the big arenas, such as the Squadron A Armory, the 101st ring in Brooklyn, and the 105th Field Artillery in the Bronx.

With the formal organization of the Indoor Polo Association, the game started the steady forward progress that reached its summit in the 1930s. A problem that faced the Association was the difficulty to standardize the playing surface. The game was held at riding arenas, in the rings of military armories and in polo clubs, which varied in size, footing, lighting and other details; therefore, the visiting teams were often at a significant disadvantage.

The Indoor Polo Association Championships

The initial competitions offered by the I.P.A. were the Senior Trophy, presented by John R. Townsend, the Junior Trophy, donated by Thomas Leeming, the Rookie Trophy, presented by Walter Bliss, and the Intercollegiate Trophy, also presented by Mr. Townsend.

The initial championship for the Senior Trophy in 1921 was taken by the New York Riding Club, with George Sherman, Archie Kinny and H.S. Crossman.

The first championships in all four classes were held at the Squadron A Armory on 94th Street and Park Avenue, in New York City, from 4 March to 18 March 1922. The Riding Club, Dr. John Richards, Henry Blackwell and Robert Granniss, a 16-Goal combination, defeated the New York Riding Club 9–6, and in the finals, the Squadron A team by 12 goals to 7½. Squadron A had previously beaten Durland's Polo Club 11–8½. All Indoor Polo Association's tournaments were played on handicap.[6]

Brooklyn Riding and Driving Club took the Junior Trophy, The Riding Club won the Rookie Trophy, and Princeton University the Intercollegiate Trophy.

Then the tournaments underwent title changes. The Senior was renamed Class A Championship, the Junior became the Class C, and the Rookie Trophy became Class D. A new cup, donated by Wilson Powell, Jr., was added to the schedule as Class B Championship. Both the I.P.A. and the U.S.P.A. in their respective annuals have reversed the donors' names in both Class B and C results.

A new tournament was added to the schedule in 1926, the Open Championship, for a trophy donated by Charles Danforth. The Yale University team, Reddington Barrett, Winston Guest and William Muir, took the honors. Then the Brooklyn Riding & Driving Club took the prize three years running. Carl Pflug, Gerard Smith and Warren Sackman accomplished this feat. Then in 1930, The Optimists, Michael Phipps, Winston Guest and Lt. Morton Jones, stopped Brooklyn's streak.

A new team, Los Nanduces, named after a South American rhea by Lt. Jones, who had been to Argentina with the Army team, took the Open trophy. Gerard Smith and Cyril Harrison completed the squad. Winston Guest's Optimists regained the indoor crown, with Stewart Iglehart and Warren Sackman. The following year they held on to the trophy, this time with Mike Phipps instead of Sackman.

The indoor Open Championship then fell into abeyance until 1940, when it was revived for one year only. Winmont Farms, with Walter Hayden, John Pflugh and Robert Eisner, were the champions.

The Indoor Polo Association and the U.S. Polo Association

The Indoor Polo Association wanted nothing to do with the U.S. Polo Association. Although a few players practiced both outdoor and indoor polo in the 1920s, notably Winston Guest, Averell Harriman, Earle A.S. Hopping the younger, Stewart Iglehart and Mike Phipps, there was very little crossover. In the late 1920s A.G. Blaisdell, executive secretary of the Indoor Polo Association, stated that "We do not take outdoor prowess into account, because we have found the many fine players outdoors are quite helpless in the defter, quicker, more kaleidoscopic indoor game."[7]

The feeling of the indoor players was that their favorite version had suffered because of the wide impression that it was a makeshift substitute for the real game of polo, a sort of winter-weather retreat. The indoor polo aficionados felt that the two games were separate and distinct, even though indoor polo belonged to the same ancient family roots.

The I.P.A. touted its advantages over the traditional outdoor polo. Among those perceived benefits—some of which had validity, like the question of expense—significantly smaller number of ponies needed, year-round availability, large number of arenas (in the 1920s), less danger to horse and rider because of the soft ball, a sure-footing on a tanbark surface and more appeal for the public in general because of the smaller playing surface which allowed the spectators to sit very close to the action.[8]

Nevertheless, both ruling bodies went their separate ways until 1954, when the diminishing number of players made economic sense to merge both organizations. Both chairmen, Devereux Milburn, Jr., and George Sherman, Jr., reached an agreement and both entities united under the banner of the U.S. Polo Association.

George Carter Sherman, Jr., son of the first president of the Indoor Polo Association, was elected vice-chairman of the U.S.P.A. and eventually became chairman from 1960 until 1966.

International Competitions

In 1923 the Indoor P.A. decided that the game had made such progress that an international competition was in order. An invitation was sent to England to come to this country, which was readily accepted. The English team, Capt. L.W. Walford, Capt. W.F. Holman and Frederick Egan, with Capt. Kenneth McMullen as an alternate, were given practice games in New York, then in Philadelphia, Cincinnati and Chicago, cities where indoor polo had been taken up with enthusiasm.[9]

The British players brought with them seven ponies with them, all but one belonging to Capt. Walford. After the international series was over, the Cincinnati Polo Club purchased all the ponies.

Back in New York, the first game of the best three of five series for the John R. Townsend Challenge Cup was held at the Squadron A Armory on 6 March 1923. The American team, composed of Archer Kinny, Dr. Hugh Blackwell and Robert Granniss, the team's captain, won the 4-period match by 4½ goals to one. The U.S. team scored six goals, but committed three fouls, so 1½ goals were taken off the scoreboard. The English team was McMullen, Holman and Egan.

The second match was played two days later at the same venue; both teams kept their lineups intact. Again, the U.S. team ran away with the ball, scoring 12 goals against a single tally by Capt. Egan. One point was deducted from the U.S. score because of fouls by Blackwell and Granniss.

The third match, played on March 10, ended, once more, in another victory for the Americans, 10–4. Not a single foul was whistled by the referee, Maj. Willis Crittenberger. The British team made one change, Capt. Walford replacing Kenneth McMullen.

The outcome having been decided in three matches, the last two games were exhibition matches, which attracted capacity crowds to the Armory.

No less than eighty-three years passed before the competition for the Townsend Trophy[10] was resumed at the Shallowbrook Polo Club in Somers, Connecticut. Anthony Vita from Shallowbrook, Peter Daly from Meadowbrook on Long Island, and Michael Zeliger retained the trophy. The English team was James Lucas, John Horswell and William Crisp.

The issue was decided by the total aggregate goals in two matches. England won the first match 16–15 and the United States the second by a score of 17 to 14 goals, including a few 2-pointers by Tony Vita. In arena polo, a goal scored from behind the center line counts for two goals.

In 2008, John Gobin, from Aiken and Wellington, Dr. Adair Seager from Virginia, and Californian Billy Sheldon won the Townsend Trophy once more at Chetwood Polo Park in The Plains, Virginia. The final score in the single match was 16–14. Dominic State—from Great Plains—Maurice Ormerod and his father, Giles Ormerod played for England.

Other Indoor Tournaments

The U.S. Arena Championship, successor to the I.P.A. Open Championship, was re-established in 1980. Joy Farm, from Illinois, took the championship in a final match against Chicago. William Stevens, Richard Warren and James Stevens played on the winning team. Joy Farm retained the title, with Charles Stevens replacing Richard Warren.

The tournament then moved east. Chris Knowles' Fox Lea, Guy Gengras' Essex Leasing twice, and Guy Gengras again, this time around on the Conco team, were the winners.

The West Coast was the next stop. Comancheros, Empire Polo Club, Indian Palms and Westin were the winning team during this sojourn west.

In 1993, the Arena Championship moved back east. Los Gallos, Tack Room's Bond-street, and Shallowbrook on four occasions were the winning teams, punctuated by a solitary victory for San Diego.

Yale had an impressive win in 2001, when Robert Arnold, David Eldredge and Jim DeAngelis scored 32 goals in their championship final, against ten tallies by Shallowbrook. That translates into eight goals per chukker, more than one a minute, for the winners, and a total of 42 goals in the match. Pity the scorekeeper!

For the next three years, the tournament moved to Virginia, where Tullyroan and the Seagers' Chetwood won the tournament. In 2005, Westport's Tack Room won the Championship, which was held at West Hills on Long Island. CCSA won in California, and Nash Tigers and La Union at the Great Meadow Polo Club in the Commonwealth of Virginia, the last one in 2008.

Women's Indoor Polo

In February 1934, a match took place at the Armory in New York City between teams representing Saxon Woods in White Plains and Ramapo Valley from New Jersey. Although not officially sanctioned by the Indoor Polo Association, the game took place with the implicit support of the I.P.A. The match was played interjected between matches played by men; nevertheless, it was the first indoor game played by the distaff side in the city.

Mrs. Arthur Faubel, Jane Gardner and Jane Dunn, the latter as captain, represented the Saxon Woods Hunt Club. Mrs. Frank (Martha) Clarke was the Ramapo Valley's team captain, with Dora Bruce and Jean Pitcher.[11]

Professional Indoor Polo

An attempt was made to bring the professional game to Los Angeles by J. Albert Garcia. Al Garcia met Dr. Robert G. Walton, a transplanted English physician, later president of the U.S. Polo Association, and the National Polo League was established in 1983 as a joint venture between Walton's Polo Inc. and Equestrian Centers of America, the corporate owners of the Los Angeles Center.[12] The venue was the Los Angeles Equestrian Center Equidome, at Griffith Park, near Burbank. The L.A. Lancers were the home team, which played every week against teams labeled as Chicago, Hawaii, New England, San Antonio, San Francisco, Washington D.C., and the like. The team of Bill Walton, F.D. Walton and polo manager Dan Healy compiled an impressive winning record, drawing crowds of up to 4.000.

However, the partnership between Dr. Walton and Al Garcia came to an end after two seasons. In 1984, financial problems forced the Los Angeles Club to file for reorganization under Chapter 11 provisions.[13] Later on, the Los Angeles Colts achieved the same domination that the Lancers had obtained in their prime. Thomas Goodspeed, a University of Connecticut product with two Intercollegiate Championships in his C.V., took over the reins as general manager and was instrumental in launching a highly successful instructional program. Tom Goodspeed went on to reach a 9-goal handicap in arena polo. Dr. Walton started on his own the National Polo League, which did quite well in Texas. Joseph Henderson, a South African player on the Colts team, became the third arena polo to achieve a 10-goal handicap, following Winston Guest and Dr. Clarence "Buddy" Combs' footsteps.

It proved to be a temporary respite for the Los Angeles Equestrian Center. Gibraltar Savings, the savings and loan bank holding the $10 million note, found itself in trouble with the federal authorities and went into receivership itself. Management of the L.A.E.C. was transferred to a Burbank development firm, Del Ray, which had no interest in polo.[14]

CHAPTER 20

Polo at Home, 1961–1975

The decade of the 1960s was a period of slow growth for polo in America. The main events were the two challenges for the Cup of the Americas by United States international teams led by Northrup Knox. The Open Championship remained the high point of the polo year; however, the entries remained rather consistently at a low level.

The U.S. Open Championship

Paul Butler's Oak Brook remained the venue with only two exceptions: Santa Barbara in 1966 and Memphis in 1968. The first change, which brought the Open to California for the second time in its history, was the need to test the top American players for the squad that later in the year would travel to Buenos Aires to compete for the Cup of the Americas.

The decade opened with Milwaukee's second championship crown. Two Mexican players, Guillermo Gracida, Sr., and Julio Muller, joined George Oliver on Robert Uihlein's redshirted team. Throughout the tournament Milwaukee was the team to beat and they defeated Beaver Ridge Farm in the finals by a score of 13 goals to 9. Don Beveridge, Bill Ylvisaker, Harold Barry and John Armstrong played on the Beaver Ridge Farm team.

Persistent rains—according to the Chicago Weather Bureau it was the heaviest rainfall in history—forced the transfer of some games to Uihlein Field in Milwaukee; furthermore, the final match was played on a Wednesday to accommodate CBS-TV to film the match for the program Summer Sports Spectacular. Bud Palmer provided the narrative, and Col. Maharaja Prem Singh was the "color man." The ratings are unknown.

In October, the Milwaukee team traveled to Long Island to compete in the Monty Waterbury Cup, an event in which they were successful.

The big news of the 1962 event was the presence of Juan Carlos Harriott, Jr., on the Tulsa-Aiken team, with John Oxley, Pete Bostwick and Vincent Rizzo. They defeated Oak Brook with ease, but then ran into the Linfoot-Skene Santa Barbara combine, losing 12–5. Santa Barbara, with Ronnie Tongg and Roy Barry completing the team, met in the finals Royal Palm — Bert Beveridge, Robert Beveridge, Harold Barry and Ray Harrington — a team that had defeated the holders, Milwaukee, in the semifinals.

In one of the better U.S. Open finals ever, Santa Barbara eked out an 8–7 win. When the final bell sounded, two Royal Palm players were heading alone towards the Santa Barbara goalposts. The rule mandating that a match ends with the second bell was and is an unjust one; it should be repealed. If an NFL game would end with a player running unimpeded towards the end zone, the tumult would be enormous.

Nevertheless, it was the greatest final match since the 1959 final between Aurora and Circle F. This same Santa Barbara team went off to take the Butler National Handicap.

The following year the U.S. Open returned to California, to be played at the beautiful Santa Barbara grounds. Therefore, the traditional September dates were changed to earlier in the year, the month of June. Only four teams participated, Crescents, Santa Rosa, Tulsa and the host club.

The visitors from Oklahoma, John Oxley, Ray Harrington, Harold Barry and Robert Beveridge, defeated Santa Barbara by only one goal, while the Crescents had an easy win over Santa Rosa. In the final game, Tulsa defeated Crescents, William Atkinson, Leslie "Bud" Linfoot, Roy Barry and Erwin Anisz, by 7 goals to 6. Both games won by Tulsa went into overtime.

In the National Twenty Goal Tournament, contested at the Milwaukee Polo Club, Tulsa, with Raul Salinas in Bob Beveridge's place, was defeated by Oak Brook, James Kraml, Jr., Charles Smith, Cecil Smith and Jack Murphy, 10–7. These two teams were the only entrants.

Concar-Oak Brook won three matches to take the 1964 U.S. Open. Bud Linfoot, Charles Smith, Julio Muller and Jack Murphy defeated the defending champions, Tulsa, then Santa Barbara, and in the finals, the Solo Cup Crescents, a good team with Vic Graber, James Kraml, Jr., Bob Skene and Roy Barry. The final score was 10 goals to 9 and the match was televised nationally.

Charles Smith and Jack Murphy continued their successful Open Championship partnership when they took the tournament in 1965. Ronald Tongg and Dr. William Linfoot completed the squad, which defeated Tulsa in the first match and Bunntyco in the finals. John Armstrong, Ray Harrington and Roy Barry and Richard Bunn were the losers to Oak Brook–Santa Barbara. The latter team kept their winning days in the National Twenty Goal Tournament, with Hugo Dalmar in Dr. Linfoot's slot.

This was the year in which the Willis L. Hartman Award was given to the best playing pony in the U.S. Open. Donated by Mr. Hartman from Wichita, Kansas, the trophy is a solid silver polo pony, manufactured by the royal jewelers in London, Garrard & Co.[1] The trophy itself resides in the Museum of Polo in Florida. Lovely Sage, owned by Ruddy Tongg, was given the first Hartman Trophy.

Because of the time constraints imposed by the selection of the American team that would travel to Argentina to enter the 1966 edition of the Cup of the Americas and the 30-Goal international tournament, the U.S. Open was played in May at Santa Barbara.

Five teams entered the competition. Tulsa, with John Oxley, Ray Harrington, Harold Barry and Jack Murphy, defeated Santa Barbara–Milwaukee in the first match and the Mexican team Hermosillo in the semifinals. Fountain Grove, from Santa Rosa, with Robert Walter, Bud Linfoot, Roy Barry and Allan Scherer, beat Aurora in a close match, 6 goals to 5. In the final game, Tulsa handed Fountain Grove a 10–5 defeat.

The celebrated Rotallen, Norty Knox's pony, was awarded the Willis Hartman Trophy.

The 1967 U.S. Open Championship drew a record low of two entrants, the lowest number since the tournament's inauguration in 1904. The championship match was not much of a contest, Bunntyco–Oak Brook running away with an 8–2 win over Milwaukee. Del Carroll, Ray Harrington, Jack Murphy and Richard Bunn made the winning team. This was the fourth consecutive championship win for seven-goaler Jack Murphy, a record that stood until Memo Gracida's six victories in a row from 1992 to 1997.

This year Penrage Dandy, Delmar Carroll's pony, took the Hartman Trophy.

The first Willis Hartman Trophy for the best playing pony in the U.S. Open Championship went to Lovely Sage, owned by Ruddy Tongg and played by Dr. William Linfoot. Mrs. Carol Oxley presented the trophy.

For the first time in its history the U.S. Open Championship moved south to Memphis, Tennessee. Five evenly matched teams competed. In the opening game, the pre-tournament favorite Milwaukee defeated Aurora. The semifinals matched Midland versus Oak Brook and Milwaukee against the defending champions, Richard Bunn's Bunntyco. Midland and Milwaukee won their matches, both by a two-goal differential. In the final game, played in mid–October, Midland, trailing in the last period by one goal, finally won 9–8. George Landreth, Ray Harrington, Roy Barry and his cousin Harold Andrew "Joe" Barry formed the winning foursome.

George Landreth and Joe Barry had previously taken the National 12-Goal Tournament held at the Fairfield Polo Club in Wichita, Kansas, and then the National Inter-Circuit Tournament at Oak Brook. Orlando de Hoyos and Bob Beveridge completed the Midland squad in both occasions.

Ragamuffin, one of the famous three "R" ponies owned by Northrup Knox, joined her stable mate Rotallen as a winner of the Hartman Award.

Six teams gathered at Oak Brook for the 1969 U.S. Open Championship. The first match featured the always powerful Milwaukee team against William Farish's Houston. As expected, Milwaukee came out on top, 9–8. In the second game, Tulsa-Greenhill defeated

Oak Brook rather easily. James Sharp, taking leave of his Chaparral racing sport cars, Tommy Wayman, Argentine Gastón Dorignac and Bill Atkinson went on to the semifinal match versus Tulsa-Fairfield. Four minutes into the first period, Gastón Dorignac had a bad fall and was taken to the hospital. Ray Harrington, sitting on the sidelines, was called onto the field. Ray buckled on a pair of chaps, and off he went, helping Greenhill to a 7–3 victory. Harrington also had cause for satisfaction, because his pony Ever Ready was awarded the Willis Hartman Trophy.

The final game was touch and go, with Milwaukee — Hugo Dalmar, Benny Gutierrez, Harold Barry and Bob Uihlein — ahead by one goal at halftime. Tulsa-Greenhill went ahead 8–6, only for Milwaukee to even things at 9-all at the start of the final chukker. With about two minutes left in regulation time and the score tied at 10 goals, Tommy Wayman scored. Just seconds before the bell, Milwaukee's desperation final shot went wide of the goalpost and Tulsa-Greenhill took the Open crown.

James "Hap" Sharp came back to win his second consecutive Open Championship with his Tulsa team. Only three teams answered the call and Tulsa defeated both with ease, Bunntyco 15–5 and Oak Brook 9–3. Reuben Evans, Chico Barry and Joe Barry completed the team. Bonnie, Harold Barry's pony, was given the Hartman Trophy.

In the Twenty Goal Championship played at Milwaukee, Oak Brook, with Corky Linfoot replacing Hugo Dalmar, surprised the Open Champions Tulsa by 9 goals to 7.

Tulsa-Greenhill started well on the quest for a third consecutive U.S. Open championship when they defeated Milwaukee 7–6 and Jack Oxley's Tulsa 8–3. In the second semifinal, Oak Brook, with Hugo Dalmar, Charles Smith, Allan Scherer and Robert Beveridge, took Houston by 11 goals to six. Tulsa-Greenhill had basically the same team; the only change was Corky Linfoot for Rube Evans. Things kept on going well for the green shirts; they led by three goals at halftime, a differential that persisted through the fourth period. Then Oak Brook exploded for five goals, and regulation time ended knotted at 7-goals each. Charles Smith scored the winner after some three minutes of play in overtime.

Harold "Joe" Barry followed in his father's footsteps when Moonshine was awarded the Willis L. Hartman Trophy.

Greenhill-Tulsa, with the same lineup that competed in the Open Championship, took the Twenty Goal Tournament by defeating the host team, Milwaukee.

Only four teams contested the 1972 Open Championship. Defending titleholder Oak Brook was uncertain regarding its lineup, which started with Hugo Dalmar, Charles Smith, Bart Evans and Bill Atkinson. Several changes were made along the game's progression; it ended with Dalmar, Atkinson, Smith and Evans. After a poor start, Oak Brook recovered and lost to Milwaukee by only one tally, 9–8. In the other semifinal game, Tulsa, with Del Carroll, Jack Oxley, Allan Scherer and Patrick Dix, defeated San Antonio 7–5. Therefore, Bill Ylvisaker, Tommy Wayman, Benny Gutierrez and Robert Uihlein, III, wearing the red shirts of Milwaukee, faced Tulsa. It was 4–3 at the half, Milwaukee in the lead. Then Tommy Wayman showed the form that would take him to a 10-goal handicap and Milwaukee danced its way to a 9–5 win.

Delmar Carroll got his second Hartman award when Magazin was selected as the best playing pony in the tournament.

Six teams participated in the 1973 Open Championship. A new team, Norman Brinker's Willow Bend from Dallas, beat Tulsa, led by John Oxley, back into the fray. In the second match, the defending champions from Milwaukee were defeated by Houston, with Will Farish, Delmar Carroll, Red Armour and Chuck Wright. In the semifinals, Willow Bend

This Oak Brook team took the 1971 U.S. Open Championship: Hugo Dalmar, Charles Smith, Jorie Butler, who presented the trophies, Allan Scherer and Robert Beveridge.

continued its winning ways, winning 8–2 over the Mexican team of Jaime Bermúdez, Alberto "Beto" Muller, Julio Muller and Pablo Rincón Gallardo. Oak Brook then took care of Houston with a 10–6 victory.

The championship game was a win for Oak Brook, with Hugo Dalmar, Bill Atkinson, Charles Smith and Robert Beveridge. The final score was 9 goals to four. Bob Beveridge's Chips Royal took the Hartman Trophy.

The 1974 U.S. Open Championship had only three competitors: Houston, Milwaukee and a last minute assembled Oak Brook squad. The later proved no match for Houston, which galloped to a 9–6 win. The final game was between Milwaukee, with Del Carroll, Tommy Wayman, Joe Barry and Robert Uihlein, Jr., and Houston, William Farish, Red Armour, Roy Barry and Charles Wright. It was a close and exciting match, which was tied at 6-all at the end of the fifth period. The last chukker was a full blast affair, neither side sparing horses nor effort. An overtime period seemed to be a certain bet; however, a foul by Houston with the clock showing 15 seconds remaining, sealed the Texans' fate. Tommy Wayman took the penalty from eight yards and the game was over.

Top: International 8-goaler Benny Gutierrez marking Ray Harrington, another eight-goal handicap player. *Above:* The 1974 U.S. Open Championship was taken by this Milwaukee team: Delmar Carroll, Tommy Wayman, Joe Barry and Robin Uihlein.

The grey pony Delta Dawn, owned by Norman Brinker and ridden by Roy Barry, was awarded the Hartman Trophy.

Four teams lined up for the 1975 U.S. Open Championship. Tulsa-Dallas defeated Oak Brook and Milwaukee beat Good Hope Farms in the semifinals. The final match was marred by a heavy field that contributed to a sloppy game. In addition, 33 fouls were called by the umpires, bringing the game to almost a standstill.[2] Milwaukee played with Robert A. "Robin" Uihlein, III, Thomas Wayman, Harold A. "Joe" Barry and James Uihlein. Little Lou Dee, played by Tommy Wayman, won the Willis Hartman Trophy.

The Gold Cup

A new tournament was created by the U.S.P.A. in 1974, the Gold Cup, to be played by teams up to 24-goal handicap, at the time the highest level in America. The first edition was held at Oak Brook, with four teams entered. Milwaukee defeated Tulsa and Houston did the same against Oak Brook, in overtime, when Houston won the throw-in and Delmar Carroll ran untouched to the goal.

The final was tied at 5-all into the final period, that ended in another tie, 8–8. In overtime, Tommy Wayman scored three minutes into the period, giving Milwaukee the first Gold Cup. Robert Uihlein, III, Tom Hughes and Joe Barry completed the Milwaukee team.

In 1975, Tulsa-Dallas got its revenge when they defeated Milwaukee in the final game of the Gold Cup, played at Uihlein Field, Milwaukee's home ground.

International Visits

In 1961, a team from Chile, Lo Castillo, played a three-game series at Santa Barbara. Jorge Undurraga, Alberto Correa, Francisco Echenique and Jorge Lyon won two games and lost one against different combination of Californian players. In two of the games, Ronnie Tongg from Hawaii and local superstar Bob Skene played on the Chilean team.

The international presence continued at Santa Barbara the following year, when a Hurlingham team, Lord Patrick Beresford, his brother the Marquis of Waterford, Maj. Ronald Ferguson and Charles Smith-Ryland defeated the host team in a close match, by 8 goals to 7.

Uihlein Field in Milwaukee and the Oak Brook complex were the sites of a visit from a team representing Cowdray Park in 1963. Lord Patrick Beresford, Paul Withers, Australian Sinclair Hill and Maj. Ronald Ferguson, with the Marquis of Waterford as spare, played two matches for the Robert A. Uihlein International Cup. The two games were split, Cowdray Park winning 11–3 and losing 8–7, then being declared the winners on aggregate goals.

The visit was marred by an equine viral illness that affected all 14 ponies brought over from England and more than 100 among the local mounts. Some games were conducted playing only five periods in order to save mounts for the Butler National Handicap. In this tournament, the Oak Brook team, in a most sporting mode, defaulted to Cowdray Park in what was to have been the semifinal game so they could loan their ponies to the visitors. In the other semifinal, Tulsa beat Milwaukee, earning the right to face Cowdray in the finals. Tulsa, a 25-goal team, with Jules Romfh. Ray Harrington, Harold Barry and John Oxley gave two goals on handicap to Cowdray Park, a 22-goal team. Those two goals made the difference, Cowdray Park winning the Butler National Handicap 12–10.

Cowdray Park from England took the 1963 Butler National Handicap at Oak Brook, Illinois. Paul Withers, Australian 10-goaler Sinclair Hill, John Oxley and Jules Romfh.

In California, the Hermosillo team of Guillermo Gracida Hoffmann, Alberto Muller, Gabriel "Chino" Gracida Hoffman and Javier Garza took the 1963 Pacific Coast Open Championship, first beating the host team, Santa Barbara, and then the Crescents in the finals. Victor Graber, Allan Scherer, Roy Barry and Erwin Anisz played well in a losing effort.

A team from Pakistan led by Brig. Gen. Hesky Baig visited the U.S. in 1973. The other members were Podger and Wicky El-Effendi, Tariq Afridi and Shahid Ali. For two weekends, the visitors played against Santa Barbara. Playing against Pakistan were Harry Hicks, Bill Mayberry, Chuck Rogers and Wendy Kerley. Santa Barbara won the first game 6–5 and Pakistan took the second 8–6.

The Pakistanis played many games in the United States, including those at Central Valley, Brandywine, Fairfield Hunt and Myopia.

Also in 1973, a team from Kenya, Antone Allen, Geoffrey Kent, Mark Milligan and Don Rooken-Smith played in Houston. Almost every member of the local club loaned ponies for the three matches played. Houston played Glen Holden from Santa Barbara, Juan Rodriguez, Chuck Wright and Frank Yturria. A severe gash in his left elbow disabled Glen Holden; his place was taken by Bill Guest. The Kenyans then left for Dallas and another week of polo.

Las Garzas, a team from Argentina, visited the Northeast for a few weeks in the summer of 1974. The squad, named Las Garzas (The Herons) after the Podestá family's estancia, was Roberto Fernández Llanos, Tomás Garrahan, Ernesto Pinto, Alfredo and Oscar Podestá, a 16-goal combination. Three days after disembarking at JFK Airport, the visitors played at Brandywine without the possibility of becoming familiar with their mounts because the Friday practice game was rained out.[3] Dixon Stroud, Fred Fortugno, Benny Gutierrez and Harlan Williams played for Brandywine, Gutierrez scoring five goals and Fred Fortugno three tallies. Oscar Podestá was the high scorer for Las Garzas, with three goals, in a match dominated by the play of eight-goaler Benny Gutierrez. Final score was Brandywine 10, Las Garzas 6.

The visitors then moved on to Connecticut, where they played two games at Fairfield County Hunt Club, which had organized the tour. A courtesy exchange of ponies between Fairfield and Meadowbrook allowed both teams to be fully mounted. Fred Braunstein, Frank Mortimer, Dave Rizzo and his son Paul shipped their strings for two games at Fairfield. In mid-week, a combined team, Ernesto Pinto, Butch Butterworth, Peter Orthwein and Oscar Podestá, took the silver. The Sunday game was close until halftime, when Fairfield pulled away to win 8–4. Adie von Gontard, Jr., Adie von Gontard, III, Peter Orthwein and George Haas played for Fairfield.

Bethpage on Long Island was the next stop. In reciprocity, Fairfield players Frank Butterworth, George Haas, Horace Laffaye, Peter Orthwein and Adie von Gontard brought their best ponies for the big event at Bethpage State Park, the first visit by an Argentine team since El Trébol toured in 1949. Good publicity meant that Bethpage Park was mobbed and a huge crowd cheered the Argentines to victory over the Hurricanes, five goals to three, all scored by Dave Rizzo on penalty shots.[4]

Tom Dowd at Potomac was the host for the match against Las Garzas. The team was completed by Robert Beer, Benny Gutierrez and Vinnie Rizzo. Leading 5–0 in the fifth period, Las Garzas eased-on and took a 7–4 win.

The tour ended at Myopia in Hamilton, where the Argentines were introduced to arena polo, which they thoroughly enjoyed. Roberto Fernández Llanos had to return to his home country; therefore, Ernesto Pinto played at Number 1 and Alfredo Podestá and Tommy Garrahan moved to the Number 2 and 3 positions, respectively. Bill Mulcahy, Crocker Snow, Jr., Adam Winthrop and Darnall Boyd represented Myopia. The score was tied at five goals with two minutes to go, when Oscar Podestá took a penalty from the center of the field and Tommy Garrahan followed with a neck shot through a maze of mallets and legs to score the winner.[5]

This almost forgotten tour was most significant for American polo because it marked the start of the invasion by Argentine players to the United States. As a result of this tour, George Haas was invited to play in Argentina, where he was introduced to Gonzalo Tanoira. The following year, Tanoira played on the Fairfield team that entered to U.S. Open Championship at Oak Brook, together with Peter and Steve Orthwein. This event started the large-scale practice of patrons inviting players from Argentina to play in America, which has remained a feature of the polo landscape to this day.

The Butler National Handicap again had an international component when a local squad competed in a single match against a Mexican team. Roberto Borunda, Alberto Muller, Julio Muller and Pablo Rincón Gallardo were defeated by Oak Brook's William Ylvisaker, Allan Scherer, New Zealander Stuart Mackenzie and Thomas Hughes, by 11 goals to 4.

Santa Barbara continued its international commitment when the club received a visit from the Pergamino Polo Club from Argentina. Captained by Marcos Uranga, the visitors were Camilo Aldao, Eduardo Huergo, now president of the Federation of International Polo, Miguel Lagos Mármol and Angel Paz. In the first match, Aldao, Paz, Huergo and Uranga were defeated 7–6 by Harry Hicks, Glen Holden, Sr., Miguel Lagos Mármol and Chuck Rogers.

For the second match Santa Barbara sent Ken Berry, Billy Linfoot, Bud Linfoot and Chuck Rogers, a team that defeated Pergamino by 9 goals to 6. The final game was for the Ambassador's Cup. Aldao, Uranga, Lagos Mármol and Huergo played on the winning Pergamino team. Glen Holden, Ken Walker, Dr. William Powell and Harry Hicks represented Santa Barbara. The final score was 9–6.[6]

American Teams Abroad

American teams followed the 1962 Army Polo Team visit to Pakistan in 1964 and 1968. Victor Graber, Richard Riemenschneider, Bob Skene, Roy Barry and Albert Puelicher, Jr., played three matches versus the Pakistan Polo Association team. The results favored the American team 11–5, 14–3 and 6–12. Brig. Hesky Baig, Brig. Gul Mawaz Khan, Col. M.S.A. Baig, Maj. Sahibzada Azmat Ali Khan and Podger El-Effendi represented their country.[7]

The 1968 series ended in a draw, Pakistan taking the first match 11–3 and the United States the second game, 7–5. Robert Beer, Stephen Orthwein, Col. William West and Col. Harry Wilson were the American representatives. The Pakistan Polo Association team was Syed Shahid Ali, Maj. Jaffar Kahn, Podger El-Effendi and Tariq Afridi. However, the United States team took the National Open Polo Tournament at Lahore. Raymond Guest, Jr., Steve Orthwein, Col. Wilson and Col. West formed the winning team.[8]

Iran celebrated its 25,000th anniversary in 1968. As part of the festivities an American team was invited to play in Teheran and the U.S.P.A. chose Myopia to represent America. Michael Andrew, Don Little, Crocker Snow, Jr., and Adam Winthrop, with Standish Bradford, Jr., as alternate and Norman Vaughn as coach and referee, undertook the long journey to the Middle East. Over a period of one week, the Myopia team got used to their allotted mounts, all Arab stallions, split two practice matches played on a skin field dotted with pebbles, and managed to take the first of two games. The second and final match was played with Queen Farah Diva in attendance. Both teams played with vigor, with some players wearing goggles as protection against flying pebbles. The local team won the game by the minimum score, one goal to nil.[9] The author has witnessed only one other game with the same score, at Ox Ridge between Fairfield and Myopia for the Governors Cup on 11 September 1979.[10]

In April 1973, the Langham Stables team, bankrolled by John Coates from the Blairstown Polo Club in New Jersey, played the season at the polo grounds at Mandelieu, near Cannes in southern France, taking two of the five tournaments they entered. William "Corky" Linfoot, Lester "Red" Armour and Dr. William Linfoot completed the American team

The Pan American Equestrian Games were held at the Aurora Jockey Club and the Elgin Polo Club in Guatemala City in November 1973, with polo as one of the featured events. Glen Holden, Sr., took Jeff Davis, Dr. William Linfoot and his son Corky in representation of the United States. Guatemala, El Salvador and two teams from the Elgin Club, the Blues and the Whites, completed the entry. The American team proved to be the strongest, winning all five matches they played.

Trophies New and Old

In addition to the already mentioned Gold Cup, and the change of name for the Twenty Goal Tournament, renamed the Silver Cup in 1974, the U.S.P.A. created some new tournaments during the time span related in this chapter. A new competition, the Sixteen Goal Tournament, was started in 1964. During its ten years of existence, the Sixteen Goal produced some worthy winners. The initial one was Palm Desert, which had Heath Manning, Bud Linfoot, Allan Scherer and Tony Veen in its lineup. Tim Leonard's Sunny Climes and Cloudy Clime took the tournament when it was moved to the Midwest. St. Louis Country Club won the Sixteen Goal with a family team, Dolph Orthwein, his sons Steve and Peter, plus the classy 8-goal player Bennie Gutierrez. Milwaukee, the Uihlein's team, would not be denied on two occasions, with Tommy Wayman and his father Bill, Harold Barry and, again, Benny Gutierrez. The new Meadowbrook, with a changed spelling, won the tournament in 1972, with Fred Fortugno, Allan Scherer and the brothers Alan and Russell Corey.

The Fourteen Goal Tournament was established in 1972. Seven teams gathered at Oak Brook. Milwaukee — Edward Lutz, Robin Uihlein, Tommy Wayman and Robert Uihlein — took the initial edition, defeating Fairfield-Myopia by 9 goals to seven. The two bitter New England rivals joined forces in a team that had George Haas, Don Little, Jim MacGinley and Adam Winthrop.

Two years later, the Fourteen Goal Tournament became the Continental Cup.

In 1974, the Sixteen Goal was changed to the America Cup. By then based in Florida, John Oxley's Boca Raton team took this tournament a record seven times between 1973 and 1981, six of those being consecutive wins.

The Monty Waterbury Cup, played for on handicap since 1922 by the teams entering the U.S. Open Championship, became part of the Northeastern Circuit schedule when the Open was moved to Illinois. In 1956, it was played at Piping Rock on Long Island, one of the last polo tournaments played at that magnificent club. By 1961, the third oldest polo competition in the United States was in abeyance. Circuit Governor George Haas, Jr., was instrumental in reviving the historic trophy in 1975. Most appropriately, his Fairfield County Hunt Club team won the tournament, played at Hickox Field, with the final match being held at Bethpage

Steve Orthwein (6-goals) and Bill Ylvisaker (7-goals) in action at Oak Brook, 1960s. Both men eventually were elected chairman of the U.S. Polo Association.

State Park. George played inspired polo in this tournament, with plenty of help from Delmar Carroll, Peter Orthwein and Myopia's Adam Winthrop.

The North American Cup was also instituted in 1974, alongside the Gold Cup and the Sixteen Goal tournament. The Tulsa squad, with Corky Linfoot, Dr. William Linfoot, Jason "Jim" MacGinley and John T. Oxley, were the first winners.

The Monty Waterbury Cup, first played for in 1922, was revived in 1976. This is the winning Fairfield County Hunt team at Bethpage State Park on Long Island. Adam Winthrop, Peter Orthwein, Del Carroll and George Haas.

The Growth of Polo Across America

In 1950, there were 55 clubs affiliated with the U.S. Polo Association. This total rose to 88 in 1960, 112 clubs in 1970 and 127 in 1975, excluding 20 colleges and one affiliate member, the Manila Polo Club. At a time, the U.S.P.A. jurisdiction extended from the West Indies— the St. Croix Polo Club in the Virgin Islands— to the Philippines.

Comparisons among the different circuits are not valid because the geographical limits changed along the years. For instance, the Pacific Coast Circuit, which counted 15 clubs in 1950 and 20 in 1960, went down to 18 in 1970, when the northern regions became part of the new Pacific Northwest Circuit, which had ten affiliated clubs.

The largest circuit in 1960 was the Central, with 21 entities. When the new Midstates Circuit was created, it had 12 clubs, while the Central went down to 15 clubs. Nevertheless, the overall pattern was one of undiminished growth.

The Central Circuit

This circuit extended from East Aurora in New York to St. Louis in Missouri, and from Shakopee, Minnesota, home of the High Path Polo Club, down to Louisville in Kentucky. The main center was the Oak Brook Polo Club in Hinsdale, Illinois, home of the U.S. Open Championship, the Gold Cup and the Butler National Handicap. North of Chicago was the Milwaukee Polo Club, which also hosted the Gold Cup and the Twenty Goal Tournament.

Cincinnati, Cleveland, Columbus Farms and El Rancho in Columbus, Dayton and the Springbrook in Toledo were centers of polo in Ohio, while the Kentree in Grand Rapids, the Detroit in Milford, and the Ivory in Detroit maintained the flame going in Michigan. Milwaukee and Joy Farms were in Wisconsin, while the St. Louis Country Club in Clayton, Missouri, had been a hotbed of the game since 1893, mainly supported by the Orthwein family. Also in Missouri was the Mission Brook, successor of the Missouri Hunt and Polo Club, then Kansas City Polo Club, the former having been founded in 1904.

In 1965, Iowa City had the only polo club in the state.[11] Other clubs included Duluth and Twin Cities in Minnesota, Green Bay in Wisconsin, Northern Illinois, in Elburn, Onwentsia in Lake Forest and Springfield Polo Club in Dugald, Manitoba.

The Northeastern Circuit

The cradle of American polo remained strong after the lamented departure of the original Meadow Brook Club. Myopia regained its position as the major polo club in New England and the contests for the Cameron Forbes Trophy with the Fairfield County Hunt of Westport, Connecticut, became the stuff of legends. Ox Ridge Hunt, in Darien, was reformed and provided a worthy adversary to neighboring Fairfield, the two clubs at times pooling resources. The riding arena at Ox Ridge allowed polo players from Greenwich to Fairfield who were unable to travel and play in Florida, to keep their ponies in reasonable condition during the long winter months.

Farmington Valley, near Hartford, had a checkered existence, but was a welcome source of polo for the northern part of Connecticut. The Northeastern Circuit even extended to the Province of Ontario, where the Chukker Hill Farms in Gormley and the Toronto Polo Club conducted their activities.

The Northwestern Circuit

At one period during its existence the Northwestern Circuit comprised polo clubs from Pass Christian in Mississippi to Pierre, South Dakota and as far west as Colorado. Even the state of Tennessee was split in half, with Memphis Polo Club being part of the Northwestern and Dogwood in Chattanooga allotted to the Southeastern Circuit.

Oklahoma was the main center of polo in that Circuit, with clubs such as Broad Acres in Norman, the Tulsa Polo and Hunt Club and Greenhill Farms in Tulsa. Kansas had the Fairfield Polo in Wichita, while the game in Colorado was played at the Plum Creek Polo Club in Sedalia, and the Red Rock Rangers Polo Club in Monument. Colorado Springs, where polo had been played in 1886, had a revival when the Colorado Springs Polo Club returned to the fold.

The Pacific Coast Circuit

This large circuit has always been a powerful player in American polo. The big cities in California, Los Angeles, San Diego and San Francisco have always had polo clubs in their suburbs. However, polo in California has a history of a myriad of polo clubs, small and big, where the game thrived. Central Valley in Oakdale and later in Stockton, Fountain Grove in Santa Rosa, Headlands in Point Lobos, La Jolla Farms, Menlo Park, Red Diamond in Pomona, Santa Rosa, Sleepy Hollow in Carmel, Valencia in Pasadena and later in Garden Grove, and White Horse Valley in Napa were some of the clubs that kept California as a shining example of polo at all levels.

When the expansion moved eastwards towards the desert, Eldorado and Palm Springs became two of the largest polo clubs in the nation, while old timers Santa Barbara and San Mateo–Burlingame maintained their long traditions in the game.

Polo in Hawaii never stopped after the war. Walter Dillingham's Hawaii Polo & Racing Club in Honolulu was the only affiliated club in the islands in 1950. Ten years later there were two: the Tongg family's Pupukea and Fred Dailey's Waikiki Polo Club, which later moved to a scenic location in Mokuleia on the north coast beaches. In the 1970s, Waikoloa became the first polo club on the Big Island.

The Pacific Coast Circuit also encompassed Arizona, which had the Pima County in Tucson, and the Scottsdale Polo Club, just north of Phoenix. Other clubs within the circuit were the Portland Polo Club in Oregon, the Flying Y in Yakima and the Spokane Polo Club in Washington State.

The Canadian Calgary Polo Club, in Alberta, was also part and parcel of the U.S. Polo Association. This club hosts the oldest polo competition in the Americas, the Calgary Challenge Cup, which was first played for in 1892. When the Pacific Northwest Circuit was established, the polo clubs in Alberta, Oregon and Washington were transferred to the new circuit.

The Southeastern Circuit

Polo in the Southeastern Circuit experienced a tremendous growth, from five clubs in 1950 to twenty-seven in 1970. The game in Florida was most prominent in Boca Raton with the Royal Palm, started by the Beveridges, and then taken over by John Oxley. Gulfstream in Lake Worth was in a certain way the spiritual successor of the old Gulf Stream, which had been founded by the Phipps family in the 1920s. There was also a polo club in Ocala, where polo began in 1971. Later on, Oxford Downs in Brandon and Tampa Polo Club joined the Association.

In the 1960s, Georgia had the Atlanta Polo Club and the Northeast Georgia Polo Club in Hollywood. In addition to Aiken, polo in South Carolina was played in Camden, Columbia and Hilton Head.

The Commonwealth of Virginia boasted several clubs: Belvoir, Casanova, Farmington Hunt in Charlottesville, Winchester in Berryville, Blue Ridge in Front Royal, Deep Run in Richmond, Keswick, Middleburg, and Reston in Oakton.

Alabama had one club, Point Mobil Clear, in Mobile, while Mississippi counted the Gulfport Polo Club. The game was played in Louisiana in Baton Rouge, and at Sugar Oaks in New Iberia.

In Tennessee, the Nashville Polo Association was affiliated in 1969; meanwhile, the old Dogwood Polo Club, where S.K. Johnston, Sr., had started the game in the late 1930s, changed its name to Chattanooga Polo Association. The polo players, led by S.K. Johnston, Jr., remained the same.

Pennsylvania added several clubs to the established Brandywine. Lancaster in Rothsville, Chukker Valley Farms in Gilbertsville, Mallet Hill in Cochranville, and West Shore in Mechanicsburg. Mallet Hill specified its colors as green and mushroom white, after Alfred Fortugno's mushroom farm in Oxford.

The game in Maryland thrived at several clubs. Dollbaby in Germantown, Potomac, Stoney Creek and Washington Polo Club all clustered in Rockville. The District of Columbia had one club, the National Capitol Park, site of many games near the Washington Monument.

When the Eastern Circuit was created in 1971, the polo clubs located in the District of

Columbia, Pennsylvania, Maryland and Virginia were made part of the new Circuit. They joined Joe Muldoon's Gone Away Farm in Poolesville, Maryland, and new arrivals Woodland in Belvoir, and Rappahannock in Castleton, Virginia.

The Southwestern Circuit

Every club in the Southwestern Circuit in 1960 was situated in Texas: Polo Association of Dallas, El Ranchito in Vernon, San Antonio, and Paso del Norte in El Paso. Up to 1975, Houston rejoined the Association and Lone Oak, Midland, Wichita Falls, John Armstrong's Rio Grande in Kingsville, San Patricio in New Mexico and Sugar Oaks in Louisiana were added to the roster.

The Pacific Northwest Circuit

The map of polo clubs in North America changed with the reorganization of several circuits. The new Pacific Northwest Circuit incorporated the polo clubs in Oregon, Washington and Alberta previously attached to the Pacific Coast Circuit. The clubs in the new administrative division were Big Horn, Cheyenne and Jackson Hole in Wyoming, Tacoma in Washington, and Dead Horse Polo Club in Bend, Oregon.

PART IV

American Contemporary Polo

CHAPTER 21

The International Panorama

The age of the jet aircraft made the world smaller and long-range travel much easier than ever. However, in spite of this comfort in traveling, the quantity of international polo did not increase, at least at the top level. The rate of players traveling around the world, either as professionals or just for enjoyment, increased exponentially. American players went far and wide, from Australia and South Africa, to China and Singapore. The polo seasons at Deauville, Paris and Sotogrande were filled to the brim with foreign players, with a good number coming from the United States.

At the highest levels of the game, the Cup of the Americas was played for only twice, an away and home affair in Buenos Aires and San Antonio. The Avila Camacho Cup was played again in 1976 at Houston, Texas; the Westchester was revived, sort of, at Lexington, Kentucky, and then formally at Windsor Park in England. The creation of the Federation of International Polo in turn spawned the 14-Goal World Championship, first held at Palermo in Buenos Aires in 1987.

The Avila Camacho Cup

The international competition against Mexico was continued in 1976 at Houston Polo Club. Three matches were played; all saw the Mexican team as winners, 7–4, 14–6 and 12–5. The Mexican team was Guillermo "Memote" Gracida, Sr., Guillermo "Memito" — as he was then known — Gracida, Jr., Javier Rodríguez Luna and Pablo Rincón Gallardo. The United States was represented by William Farish, Charles Smith, Roy Barry and Richard Latham. With the exception of Norman Brinker at Back — he was unable to play because of injury — this foursome had taken the U.S Open and the Gold Cup early in the year. In reporting the series, *Polo*'s editor Ami Shinitzky commented that the American team was suffering from battle fatigue after a long campaign that also included the 20-Goal tournament just prior to the Avila Camacho competition. Young Guillermo Gracida at 5-goals was the attraction of the matches, while his father played a very wise Number 1, overpowering Dick Latham, the American Back, eluding him again and again.[1]

The Avila Camacho Cup was played for again in Texas in May 1981, on this occasion at Retama Polo Center. Mexico took the first game 11–6, with Rubén, Carlos and Guillermo Gracida, and Pablo Rincón Gallardo. The United States had William "Corky" Linfoot, Joe Barry, Charles Smith and Robin Uihlein. In the second game, Owen Rinehart replaced an ailing Robin Uihlein and the American team came out on top, 9 goals to eight.

Then the rains came down in earnest and the third and decisive game had to be postponed until September. The U.S. was unable to field the same team. Charles Smith pulled a riding muscle in a previous game and Rinehart and Uihlein had commitments to play in Chicago. Attempts were made to reinforce the team with Bart Evans and Tommy Wayman; however, both were unable to bring their ponies into fitness on short notice. Linfoot remained at Number 1; Robert Walton, Joe Barry and Seth Herndon, in that order, completed the team. Mexico won 13–9, and the Avila Camacho Cup remained south of the border.

In 1988 at Palm Beach Polo and Country Club, the issue was decided in a single game. Mexico kept the trophy, after defeating the American squad by 9 goals to six. Roberto González Gracida and his cousins Carlos, Guillermo and Rubén defeated Rob Walton, Tommy Wayman, Owen Rinehart and Dale Smicklas. The American team was seldom in the game in a closely contested match. The score at halftime was 5–3 in favor of the Mexican team. The scoreboard read 9–5 with little time left before Owen Rinehart scored the match's last goal.

While the Gracidas had been playing and assiduously practicing together, the American team had only two practice games before the big event. In his post-game comments, Rinehart mentioned horses and organization as the main reason for the American poor show, added to lack of team practice.[2]

The Cup of the Americas

Following a lapse of ten years, the Cup of the Americas was once more placed into competition. The United States had high hopes for a competitive series, based upon the

Team USA in the 1988 Avila Camacho Cup: Dale Smicklas, Owen Rinehart, Tommy Wayman and Rob Walton.

increased number of high-handicap players in the 1970s and the pleasant surprise of the victory by a Texas-USA team over Coronel Suárez in the finals of the World Cup at Palm Beach Polo. Granted, this was not the full Coronel Suárez team; nevertheless, it was a powerful team: Horacio Araya, Ernesto Trotz, Juan Carlos Harriott and Celestino Garrós. Bart Evans, Tommy Wayman, Red Armour and Joe Barry's achievement in overtime bode well for the American international team's chances at Palermo.

With Steve Gose's financial support, careful preparations were carried out to ensure that the selected team would enjoy ample support. Fifty horses, a veterinarian, grooms, a farrier, families and helpers left Florida in September, with enough time to acclimatize for the matches scheduled for November.

Harold "Joe" Barry exemplified American polo in the 1970s and 1980s.

The task at hand was daunting. Barring injuries, the Argentines surely would nominate Alberto Pedro Heguy, Horacio Heguy, Juan Carlos Harriott and Alfredo Harriott to represent the home country. That was the case, with Cacho Merlos and Gonzalo Tanoira as alternates, if needed. This team, nicknamed the "Forty-goal machine," is considered the best club team ever in the history of the game, based upon its record number of victories in the Argentine Open Championship, 13 in fifteen years of competition. Only the equally powerful Santa Ana, with Gastón Dorignac, Héctor "Cacho" Merlos, Daniel González and Francisco Dorignac, was able to break Coronel Suárez's hegemony in the Abierto.

The American squad was composed by Lester "Red" Armour, Joel Baker, Harold "Joe" Barry, Roy Barry, William "Corky" Linfoot, Charles Smith and Tommy Wayman. Harold "Chico" Barry was appointed as the team's coach. Rather than select the starting team at an early stage, coach Barry decided to try many different lineups during the weeks of preparation. After many changes and spirited discussion, the American team in the initial match at Palermo was Charles Smith, Tommy Wayman, Red Armour and Joe Barry. A large contingent of American supporters undertook the long journey to Buenos Aires, hoping to witness a good showing by the United States team. Regrettably, it was not to be. The 40-goal machine was working at full speed, ahead 12 goals to two after four periods and 18–6 at the match's end.

The usual spring showers in Buenos Aires forced the postponement of the second match for two weeks. A few extra mounts were secured and the team was revamped, again after much argument and further discussion. Red Armour was moved forward to Number 1, a position he was not used to play. Tommy Wayman remained at Number 2; Joe Barry was switched to Number 3, and his cousin Roy played Back. Although the team as a whole played better than in the first game, it was not enough. Pressed at times, but not consistently, the U.S. team was defeated again, this time by 16 goals to six.

Press coverage of the Cup of the Americas made the front page of the Buenos Aires' dailies. Attendance was more than 20,000 for each of the games, which was transmitted live on television, with millions watching—such is the impact of high-goal polo in Argentina.

In the United States, recriminations began the morning after, as expected. Ami Shinitzky, writing in *Polo*, felt that one of the reasons for the defeat was that no one was in charge within the American organization.[3] According to Shinitzky, the U.S. Polo Association assumed a supporting role only because Steve Gose had provided the financial support and made the arrangements. However, the U.S.P.A. was the organization that sent the team to Buenos Aires in representation of the national colors.

It seems the lessons learned in 1966 and 1969, when Northrup Knox's shoulders tried to uphold the dual responsibilities of player and captain, were not applied. Chico Barry was overwhelmed, because he had gone to coach, not to manage the countless problems that always arise during a foreign tour.

The Cup of the Americas was played with the understanding that it would be a home and away competition. Therefore, in 1980 the matches were held at the Retama Polo Center, Steve Gose's concoction near San Antonio.

Argentina sent the same team that was so successful at Palermo, with Alfredo "Negro" Goti and Gonzalo Tanoira as reserve players. In a scenario reminiscent of the 1928 Cup of The Americas, the pony string developed a viral infection and a persistent cough that forced a one-week postponement. Dr. Alvaro Pieres, older brother of Alfonso, Gonzalo and Paul, was in charge of the ponies, spending countless hours tending to the ponies. One of their best, La Purita, was bitten by a snake. Alberto Pedro Heguy stated that La Purita was the best polo pony he ever played.[4]

Regardless of the difficulties endured by the Argentines, the United States team performed nobly. There were several factors involved in this change of fortune only months after the debacle at Palermo. In the first place, the Americans were playing at home. Some four years prior to this series, Gonzalo Tanoira, who was at Oak Brook competing for the U.S. Open Championship, expressed the opinion that if a 35-goal team series between the Unites States and Argentina were to be held in America, the host team would take the series.[5] The inclusion of Guillermo "Memo" Gracida at Number 1 became a great asset to the American team. That allowed Wayman, Armour and Barry, the core of the United States international team, to play in their accustomed positions.

In the first game, Argentina was leading 6–5 after four of the seven chukkers to be played. The crucial period was the fifth period, when the Argentines scored three goals, without reply from the Amer-

Alfredo Harriott, Argentina's Back, and Red Armour playing Number 3 in the first match for the Cup of the Americas at Palermo in 1979.

icans. The final score was 11–8. It was the best result for America in all matches since 1932. At the game's end there was a huge sensation of relief in the Argentine camp, because the feeling was that they had passed a severe test with unhealthy ponies. Reminiscing about the game, Juan Carlos Harriott, Jr., remembers the players' shirts and pants stained with blood from the horses coughing in the course of the game.[6]

The concern about the ponies' health was such among the Argentine contingent that the possibility of giving the Americans a walkover for second match was discussed. However, the ponies recovered well enough and the second game went on as scheduled, without any changes on both teams.

The second game was even for six chukkers but four consecutive goals were scored by the visitors at the beginning before Memo Gracida found the goalposts. That four-goal differential stood until the final bell, with Argentina the victors by ten goals to six. Players and observers were of the opinion that the second game was better than the first. Juan Carlos Harriott, who finished his high-goal and international career at Retama, thought that this particular match was the best of all eight he had played for the Cup of the Americas.

The Young Cup of the Americas

An interesting competition was held in 1984 at Palermo in Buenos Aires as a Cup of the Americas' version for young players. Bobby Barry, Gene Fortugno, Calixto García Vélez, Owen Rinehart and Dale Smicklas, coached by Tommy Wayman, played two consecutive games against Chapaleufú and Los Cóndores.

The preparation of the American team was rather haphazard. Tommy Wayman was called in at the last minute to coach the team and the players had to pay for their own transportation.[7] Although Gene Fortugno and Cali García had arrived early to take part in some tournaments, the other players, particularly Owen Rinehart who had a commitment to play in the Boehm International Challenge Cup, arrived much later and had to struggle with their mounts.

In the first game Chapaleufú, with cousins Alberto, Gonzalo, Horacio and Eduardo Heguy, just overwhelmed the Americans 19–5. Los Cóndores, the González's family team, with Mariano González, Santiago Gaztambide, Martín Zubía and Santiago Trotz, defeated a much improved American team by 8 goals to six.

George Haas, a member of the U.S.P.A. International Committee who went along with the team, felt that the challenge proved to be a good experience for the young players. Tommy Wyman agreed with that observation, adding the players had acted as gentlemen on and off the field. Gene Fortugno commented on the speed of the Argentine players, "We didn't have time to think — you just have to react. In the States you have more time to see the play develop. If you wait, they have someone on you."[8]

The Coronation Cup

The Coronation Cup had evolved into a one-game match between England and an invited team. In 1987, an American team labeled by the Hurlingham Polo Association as North America played against the English team of William Lucas, Alan Kent, Julian Hipwood and Howard Hipwood.

The North American team rode primarily British ponies. Team captain Owen Rinehart had previously taken the Coronation Cup on a multi-national team, Rest of The World. On this occasion, John Yeoman lent him Piqui, who was named Best Playing Pony. Yeoman also facilitated the mounts for Mike Azzaro. Rob Walton's horses were loaned by Muktar Mohammed from Nigeria, and Norman Lobel and Bryan Morrison loaned Dale Smicklas' mounts. At 6-goals, Mike Azzaro was thought by the British to be the cheapest handicapped player around.[9] Nevertheless, the Pegasus Triumphant M.V.P. trophy was awarded to Rob Walton.[10] The American team was ahead by one point midway through the match; however, they gradually pulled away to win by 8 goals to five.

The following year, the United States team of Mark Egloff, Michael Azzaro, Rob Walton and Dale Smicklas was defeated 8–7 by Andrew Seavill, John Horswell and Lord Charles Beresford. Queen Elizabeth II and some 20,000 spectators gathered on Smith's Lawn to watch a come-from-behind English team win on a late goal by team captain Julian Hipwood. With several Americans playing the British season, Owen Rinehart could have picked a 33-goal team to face the locals. When Hipwood picked a 22-goal team, the Americans had to scale down their aggregate handicap. Then Owen Rinehart stood down in favor of Mark Egloff. It was a close game throughout, played under threatening, cloudy skies. With the score tied at seven all and about one minute from time, Julian Hipwood met a knock-in and found the flags to give England the victory.

The Westchester Cup with an Asterisk

The negotiations for the renewal of the Westchester Cup began in earnest in March 1986, when the Hurlingham Polo Association proposed that it be held at Guards Polo Club as part of England's largest polo event, Cartier International Day.

The interests of the U.S.P.A. were represented by S.K. Johnston, Jr., the Association's chairman, and Allan Scherer, the executive director. The Hurlingham P.A. was represented by its chairman, Brig. Peter Thwaites, and Maj. Ronald Ferguson. The British proposal for a single match to decide the winner was rejected by the U.S.P.A., which preferred the two-out-of-three games format as a better way to decide the issue, a practice that had been followed in the Westchester Cup ever since the beginning in 1886. The American position was that it should be held in the United States, as the trophy's holders. The question of sponsorship became a thorny one, because of the English request of 120,000 pounds—approximately 200,000 American dollars—to cover the costs of the expedition.[11] In addition, the British officials felt that the marketing arrangements limited the participation of their sponsors.

The bottom line was that the Hurlingham Polo Association and the U.S. Polo Association could not reach an agreement regarding location, number of matches and sponsorship. The negotiations were then discontinued. This situation persuaded the U.S. Polo Association to look for other options in order to stage the competition.

Arrangements were then made for an Australasian team, with two New Zealanders, Graham Bray and Graham Thomas, and two Australians, Stuart Gilmore and Jaime MacKay, with Jim MacGinley as alternate, to compete for the Westchester trophy. Joey Casey, Jake Sieber, Bart Evans and Jeff Atkinson were selected to play on the United States team.

It is of interest that after all the arguments about one singles match against the best two out of three, it was agreed to hold two matches, the event being decided on aggregate goals. So much for tradition.

Played in early October in Lexington, Kentucky, the American team had an almost insurmountable lead with a 10–3 win in the opening match. The Australasian team took the second match by nine goals to six; however, it was not enough to turn the tide. Some of the members on the hastily formed Commonwealth team were more familiar with the American players than with their own teammates. Lack of familiarity with each other's patterns of play bedeviled the visiting squad.

A nostalgic note was sounded with the presence on the sidelines of Bob Skene, the great Australian-born player who had participated in the 1939 contest at Meadow Brook. His nephew, Jaime MacKay, was the captain of the Australasian team.

The original Westchester Cup was prominently displayed at the awards ceremony; however, a different trophy — one of the individual cups given to each member of the winning American team in 1927 — was awarded to the United States team.

This competition is listed in the U.S.P.A. year books under the heading "Australasia vs. United States (Westchester Cup)," along with a photograph of the second trophy.[12] There is no mention of the event in the Hurlingham Polo Association yearbooks.

The Westchester Cup Proper

The first postwar renewal of the competition with England for the Westchester Cup took place at Guards Polo Club in 1992, when the U.S. Polo Association waived its right to hold the challenge on home grounds, as stipulated in the trophy's deed of gift.[13]

With both Adam Snow and Owen Rinehart playing in the British season, the middle of the U.S. team was sent. Rob Walton was selected for the Back position and young John Gobin was flown in a few days before the event to play at Number 1.

The British team was William Lucas, Cody Forsyth from New Zealand at Number 2, Alan Kent at Number 3, and team captain Howard Hipwood at Back. Interestingly enough, there was brotherly competition on the sidelines, because Carlos Gracida coached the American team and Memo Gracida did the same for the British squad. Brook Johnson, an American playing in England, selected 14 of his ponies for the American team, while the ecumenical Kerry Packer loaned two ponies to both England and the United States.

The game itself was reckoned to be one of the best ever in the long history of the Westchester Cup and the only one to extend into double overtime. Howard Hipwood was the dominant player in the first half, hitting powerful backhanders and well placed knock-ins. The score was 5–4 England midway through the contest. In the last chukker of regulation play the American team was holding a one-goal advantage when a foul was whistled in favor of England, some 90 yards out and near the boards. John Gobin went off the field to change ponies, followed by Cody Forsyth. Thinking that Hipwood would take a long circle before hitting the penalty, Adam Snow also went to change ponies. Seeing the opportunity of three-on-two, Howard Hipwood tapped the ball, and passed it to Kent, who scored the tying goal with less than three minutes to play.

The first overtime was all nerves. Two penalty shots were awarded, both from the center of the field, to each team. Will Lucas had the best chance to score, but his under-the-neck shot went wide. Finally, in the eighth chukker of a fantastic match, Adam Snow picked a loose ball 60 yards from the American goal, ran along the boards, and when marked by Forsyth left the ball to Rinehart, who sent it towards the English goal. John Gobin, the lowest handicapped player on the field at 4-goals, then made a difficult, backhand cut shot towards goal that eluded Alan Kent's desperate attempt to stop the winning tally.[14]

With the British so tantalizing close to winning in 1992, it was no wonder that a challenge for a rematch was forthcoming in 1997. The second of the postwar revivals was held, once more, on Cartier International Polo Day at the Guards Polo Club in Great Windsor Park. Since John Goodman's Isla Carroll team was playing in the English season, it was relatively easy to assemble a team to answer the challenge from the Hurlingham Polo Association. Both teams were rated at 28-goals. Julio Arellano, Michael Azzaro, Guillermo Gracida and John Goodman were picked to represent the United States. The H.P.A. selected a well-balanced team: William Lucas, the New Zealander Cody Forsyth, Howard Hipwood and Andrew Hine.[15]

Joe Barry, the United States coach, had some reservations before the match about the pony string: "As great as our ponies are, there is a limit to how long they can remain in peak condition. Being in the finals of two tournaments, both with a large number of entries, winning all those games took a lot out of the horses."[16] Barry's words proved to be prophetic. As the game progressed, the American mounts appeared sluggish in comparison to the English pony string. At halftime, the scoreboard indicated 9 goals for England, 3 for America. Joe Barry made a move, placing Goodman at Number 1, Arellano at Number 2 and Mike Azzaro at Back. The changes worked, because in the second half the U.S. team outscored their rivals by six goals to three. However, it was a bit late. The final tally, 12–9, was a reflection of what happened on the field of play. After 83 years of drought, the Westchester Cup returned to England's possession.

The America's Polo Championship

Not to be confused with the Cup of the Americas, this high-goal event was organized in September 1987 by Peter Brant's Greenwich Polo Club in Connecticut. Because of its high rating, it was the most important international match in the 1980s. Nevertheless, both the Argentine Polo Association and the U.S. Polo Association distanced themselves from any recognition of the event as an international contest between the two nations. The 39-goal Argentine team was billed as "Best of Argentina" and the United States team as "North America," a 38-goal team. The trophy itself is a George III gilded sterling silver cup made in London in 1784 by silversmiths John Wakelin and William Taylor.[17]

Tommy Wayman, Carlos Gracida, Memo Gracida and Owen Rinehart played six chukkers of the best polo seen in this country for some time, against Benjamín Araya, Alfonso Pieres, Gonzalo Pieres and Ernesto Trotz. The last chukker began with the Argentines leading 11 goals to 7. Tommy Wayman scored three goals in the final period, and the game ended 11–10.

The event had all the trappings of a big occasion. CBS filmed the match for national television, and the usual number of celebrities were on hand as well as corporate sponsors that footed the advertisement for television time. As a polo event, it was an unqualified success.

Heavy rains almost disrupted the 1988 event; however, a determined Peter Brant hired helicopters to hover over the field and effect a semblance of dryness. The heavy field was not the cause of a slower match compared to the previous year's edition; it was the umpire's whistle. Gonzalo Pieres had an outstanding performance, scoring eight of Argentina's 11 goals. At the match's end, the scoreboard read 11–8. The South American squad was the same as on the previous year; in the American team, Mike Azzaro played instead of Tommy Wayman.

The third and last of the America's Polo Championship took place in 1989. The Argentine team remained the same; the Americans were Mike Azzaro, Tommy Wayman, Owen Rinehart and Dale Smicklas, a 32-goal combination. The match lived up to the public's expectations. The American team played well but faltered in the last chukker and the South Americans took the trophy again, this time by an 11 goals to seven score.

The Federation of International Polo and the World Championship

The Federation of International Polo came into being thanks to the Herculean efforts by Marcos Uranga, at the time president of the Argentine Polo Association. In December 1982, the inaugural meeting took place in Buenos Aires. George Haas, Jr., was the United States representative. Marcos Uranga was elected president, a post he held until 1995, when Glen Holden, Sr., from Santa Barbara, succeeded Uranga as F.I.P. president. In turn, Patrick Guerrand-Hermès from France took over the Federation's reins after Holden's mandate came to an end. Differences of opinion between M. Guerrand-Hermès and the three major polo organizations, Asociación Argentina de Polo, Hurlingham Polo Association and United States Polo Association, led to the president's resignation in November 2009.

James Ashton from Australia was appointed interim president, pending confirmation by the General Assembly to be held in 2010. Mr. Ashton, scion of a prominent family with deep roots in Australian and international polo, regrettably met his fate during a polo match in Thailand. James Ashton, a man of great integrity, keen organizational ability and extraordinary personal charm, had started his mandate with a clear vision of the F.I.P.'s worldwide mission. His untimely passing was a terrible blow to his family and to his many friends.

U.S. Polo Association chairman Thomas Biddle, Sr., was appointed interim chairman by the F.I.P. Council of Administration. At the General Assembly held in Lake Worth, Florida, in April 2010, Eduardo Huergo of Argentina was elected as the new president. At the same meeting, Argentina was selected to be the venue for the next World Championship, to be held in September 2011.

The United States Record in the F.I.P. World Championships

Among several initiatives brought forth by the Federation was the establishment of a World Championship. The competition was limited to national teams of no more than 14-goals aggregate handicap. The rationale for such a low handicap limit was to allow many countries to enter the competition, according to geographical areas. Zone 1 was allotted to Central and North America. In the zonal preliminaries, held in San Antonio, the United States lost to Canada and Mexico and failed to qualify for the first World Championship, which took place in Buenos Aires in 1987.

The American team was formed by Billy Maybery from Santa Barbara, Mike Azzaro, team captain Tom Gose, and Tommy Biddle, Jr., from Aiken. Mexico had Javier José Celis, Armando González Gracida, Pablo Rincón Gallardo and Manuel Nava. Canada, with Rob Roenisch, Rene Vlahovic, Dave Offen and Cliff Sifton, was the surprise of the tournament, which had a double round-robin format. When the first round was finished Canada had a 2-0-1 record, Mexico 2-1-1, and the United States a dismal 0–3. In the decisive game, Mexico defeated Canada by 8 goals to six. The United States final match against Canada did not take place.

In 1989, the United States won the Zone preliminary by defeating Canada and Mexico in Florida, with Darin "Bunky" Martin, John Wigdahl, Charlie Bostwick and Horton Schwartz, and qualified to play in the second World Championship, held in Berlin on the same polo ground where the 1936 Olympic Games were contested. Julio Arellano, Charles Bostwick, Horton Schwartz and John Wigdahl made up the team, with George Haas and Allan Scherer as alternates. The United States drew the easier of the two brackets, defeating West Germany 12–8 in the first game and France 16–4 in game two. They had to face Chile, a team that had also beaten France and Germany, in the final qualifier. The match ended in a 6-all tie; the F.I.P. Rules do not allow overtime play. Nevertheless, the U.S. team got into the final by virtue of a better goal average.

They were to face England, which was allowed to compete although they had not joined the F.I.P. as yet. England had surprised Argentina 9–6 to enter the finals, and was considered the favorite. Coach Allan Scherer was dissatisfied with the team's performance in the virtual semifinal game and made some changes. Schwartz was moved from Back to Number 3, Bostwick went to Number 2, and Wigdahl to Back; Julio Arellano remained at Number 1. In order to deceive the British about the changes, the American players wore the original numbers on their shirts. The final match was a close run thing, with the Americans down 6–5 at the end of the fifth chukker. A wonderful play by Charlie Bostwick, who picked the ball near the American goalposts and ran the length of the field for the equalizer, was the spark that got the team going again. John Wigdahl scored the winning tally with some two minutes left on the clock.

The next World Championship was held at the beautiful San Cristóbal Polo Club in Santiago, Chile's capital city. The United States received an automatic entry in the final round as the championship holders. Coach Red Armour enlisted eight players: Ken Cresswell, Peter Cumming, Jake Devane, John Gobin, Matthew Gonzales, Charles Muldoon, George Olivas and Dale Schwetz. All saw action during the tournament.

On opening day, the United States met Chile in front of a vociferous partisan home crowd. Cresswell, Muldoon, Olivas and Cumming, in that order, fell behind 4-nil in the first chukker and never caught up, losing the match by 15 goals to three. For the second match against Mexico, Gobin and Schwetz joined Olivas and Cumming, earning a well-deserved win over Mexico, 13–8. The American team then faced Argentina in the semifinals. Francisco Bensadón, Delfín Uranga, Marcos Di Paola and Patricio Garrahan defeated the United States 16–8. Many observers thought the Argentine team was under handicapped, although Bensadón's handicap was raised to four goals midway through the tournament. One American supporter made the comment that the experience was like "taking a knife to a gunfight."[18]

The United States and England battled for the bronze medal. Coach Red Armour allowed Jake Devane and Matthew Gonzales to see some action in this match. The Americans were ahead by two goals by the middle of the last chukker, but two penalties tied the game and within seconds of the bell, England scored the winner, for a final score of 10–9.

The United States did not qualify for the 1995 contest in Switzerland. The preliminary round against Canada was played on home ground at the Palm Beach Polo Club in April. Brian Middleton, Charlie Bostwick, Ricky Bostwick and Brad Scherer represented the United

Jeff Hall, who played for America in the 2009 Westchester Cup, is one of the young lions in American polo.

States, while Jeff Begg and Don Pennycock alternated at Number 1 for Canada, with Rob Roenisch, Dave Offen and Mike Jordan completing the squad.

The American team took the first game by 9 goals to 5. Canada won the second game 8–5 and the third and final game by 9 goals to 8.

As the host country, America was present in 1998 in Santa Barbara. The selected players were Carlos Arellano, Andrew Busch, Anthony Garcia, Jeff Hall, Stevie Orthwein, Billy Sheldon and Tony Vita. Jeff Blake was also chosen, but a facial injury prevented him from playing in the tournament. The squad was coached by Rege Ludwig.

The festivities prior to the tournament had some controversy because all the Brazilian players had had their handicaps lowered within six months of the World Championship. The issue was solved by arbitrarily having Brazil compete as a 17-handicap team.[19]

In the first match on Sunday, England defeated the United States by 10 goals to 5, after giving two goals on handicap. Wednesday was a better day for the American team, which beat Guatemala 12–7, after giving Guatemala two goals by handicap. In the first semifinal, the U.S.A. team, Billy Sheldon, Tony Vita, Jeff Hall and Andy Busch, faced Argentina's Lucas Labat, Pablo Spinacci, Gerardo Collardín and Ramiro Guiñazú. Argentina led by one goal at halftime. Coach Daniel González had a serious talk with his players during the interval, with the result that they scored six unanswered goals while shutting off the American team. The final score was Argentina 10, U.S.A. 3.

The game for third place between America and England was held in San Diego. The starters for the American team played the first three periods and the second team the last three. England won by two goals.

The sixth World Cup Championship was held at Werribee Park in Melbourne, Australia, and is still considered the best organized of all the F.I.P. championships. Credit is due to James Ashton for his leadership in securing more than 280 horses from all over Australia. Each pony was photographed and hoof-branded to facilitate inspection and prevent time overplay.

The issue of handicaps continued to plague the competition; both Brazil and England played at 16-goals.

The American team, Carlos Arellano, Jason Crowder, Matthew Ladin, Chris Nevins and Dale Schwetz, participated in an 18-goal league at Eldorado Polo Club in California. Although they won only one match, coach Steve Crowder pronounced himself satisfied with the team's performance, taking into consideration that most other teams counted a professional player among their ranks.

The United States team drew Argentina in the first game. Carlucho Arellano suffered a knee injury but continued to play; Mariano Uranga had a head trauma that took him out of the game and the tournament, a heavy blow for the Argentine team. Argentina won a tough match. The U.S. team then beat India 10–8 and England 11–10, which was enough to put them in the semifinals when the English squad surprised Argentina 12–8.

The semifinal match against Brazil could have gone either way, but Brazil prevailed 9–8, after giving two goals by handicap and trailing at halftime 5–2. In the match for the bronze medal, the American team failed again, as it had done in Chile and in San Diego. The pattern of allowing all the American players to participate in the match for third place continued, with negative results for the team at large.

The 2004 World Cup was held at the majestic Chantilly, north of Paris. The French authorities led by Patrick Guerrand-Hermès spared no effort in making the venue a spectacular one. At times, it appeared that the festivities overwhelmed the polo.

The United States squad was Joe Wayne Barry, Jason Crowder, Chris Gannon, Alan Martinez, Stevie Orthwein, Joseph Stuart and Dan Walker, again coached by Steve Crowder. The first game was against Chile; Gannon, Martinez, Crowther and Barry lost 9–8. In the second game, versus Australia, Orthwein replaced Barry, who had sustained an injury to his hand. The United States team played well, defeating Australia 12–7. The last preliminary game was against France, which surprised the Americans, scoring seven goals against only 4 by the U.S. team. This defeat marked the exit for the American squad.

The Zone A elimination competition was held at Costa Careyes in Mexico, in May 2007. Team USA included Nick Cifuni from Memphis, Chris Nevins from Houston, Stevie Orthwein, Jr., from St. Louis and Florida, Joseph Stuart from Nashville and the brothers Miguel Angel and Santiago Torres. The American team that played against the Dominican Republic in the opening match was Santiago Torres, Miguelito Torres, Chris Nevins and Stevie Orthwein. Team USA won 11–9. Later that day, Canada defeated Guatemala by 12 goals to 5½. Canada then proceeded to eliminate the Dominican Republic from the tournament with a 14–3 victory. The United States team made changes for the match against Guatemala: the Torres brothers were replaced by Joseph Stuart and Nick Cifuni. The U.S. barely defeated Guatemala by half-a-goal, six to 5½ goals.

The final game to decide which team would go on to the World Championship to be held in Mexico City. The honor belonged to Canada by defeating Team USA 7–4.

Therefore, it is now of a period of reflection and waiting for the ninth F.I.P. World Championship to be held in Argentina in 2011.[20]

The F.I.P. Centennial Cup

There is a trophy displayed at the Museum of Polo and Hall of Fame in Florida engraved with the names Yvette Moore, Tom Biddle, Jr., Rick Sears and George Haas. A photograph of the cup appears prominently in every U.S.P.A. year book with the notation that it was not played from 1991 to 1992 and from 1994 to 2008.

This single event took place at the Gulfstream Polo Club in Lake Worth in 1993, by teams representing USA-Canada, Argentina, Caribbean and Australia. The tournament was designed to foster ties between polo-playing nations. Looking at the team's rosters, it appears to be more a junket than a meaningful tournament.

The Argentine team was David Wayne, from the Mobile-Point Clear in Alabama, Ricardo Mihanovich, Agustín "Negro" Aguero and Peter Winkelman, from Skaneateles, New York. Caribbean was represented by Mike Bucci, sometime Myopia's polo captain, Raúl Brea, Julio Arellano and Norberto Azqueta. Finally, Australia's colors were defended by Allan Scherer, the well-known American international and U.S.P.A.'s Executive Director, Dr. Ted Brinkman from Meadowbrook and Gulfstream, Scott Campbell from Long Island, and Peter Yunghans, an F.I.P. official from Australia.

In the first game, USA-Canada defeated Caribbean 7–4; then Argentina beat Australia by 8 goals to four. In the finals, USA-Canada overwhelmed Argentina 8–1. The game for third place was taken by the Caribbean team over Australia by a score of 7–1.

American Tours Abroad

In May 1974, a 25-goal team from the United States visited South Africa. Allan Scherer, Red Armour, Dr. Linfoot and Bob Beveridge played a test match on the Shongweni grounds against the South African team of Raymond D. "Jim" Watson, Michael Miller, Pieter Potgieter and Terence Craig. At the end of six chukkers the game was tied at 8-all; Armour scored in the seventh and the teams exchanged goals in the final 8th period, with the U.S. on top at the end 10–8.

The second test was cancelled because of rain, and in the third game at Inanda, the American team came from behind, 8–11, in the eighth chukker to tie the game and take the Benson & Hedges international series. Roy Barry, who flew in to replace an injured Billy Linfoot, played at Number 3.

The United States team also played matches against the South African Polo Association President's team at Lions River, a 12–1 victory. Then they played against Natal at Shongweni, were they again won 12–10. Jack Oxley replaced Bob Beveridge in the last period.

Playing against East Griqualand on the Meadowbrook field at Matatiele, the American team suffered their first defeat, 9 goals to three. The team was Jack Oxley, Allan Scherer, Red Armour and Robert Beveridge. Against the Orange Free State at Roderick Park in Bloemfontein, the Americans were again beaten, 7–6, even though Roy Barry was on the team. The last match was against Transvaal on the Inanda ground. Scherer, Armour, Barry and Beveridge came out easy winners by 12 goals to six.

In April 1976, an American team traveled to Australia for a three-game series. Robin Uihlein, Dr. William Linfoot, Joe Barry and Bill Ylvisaker played test matches against an Australian combine rated at 26-goals. The Australians provided the visitors with 27 fine ponies and large crowds, ranging from 12,000 at Warwick Farms to 47,000 at the Royal Agricultural Fairgrounds, were treated to a major polo event. The Americans took all three games, 14–7, 8–7, on a pony-goal in extra chukker, and 14–8. In the last game, John Walker from New Zealand played instead of Dr. Linfoot, who had suffered a concussion.

In 1980, Caltex Zambia, through Bryan and Carol Foye, presented the Cal Tex Polo Trophy to be competed for by any visiting team from the United States. Gene Gilmore from Kentree, Leslie Johnson from Fairlane Farms, Richard Warren from Joy Farm and George Alexander from Greene Valley traveled to Zambia, where they played five games against various local teams at Lusaka and Mazabuka, invited by Mike Newham, the chairman of the Zambia Polo Association. The opponents were Lusaka and Zambia B, which defeated the visitors, Zambia on two occasions, and Mazabuka. The American team took the last three matches. The Zambian team was Guy Robinson, Keith Coventry, Mike Newham and Paul Taylor.[21] In a nice gesture, George Alexander donated to the Mazabuka Polo Club a very much needed time clock.

A second American team consisting of James Gilstrap from Willow Bend, Bill Lesley, Fredrick Walton from Modesto and H.L. "Buzz" Welker from Willow Bend and Tulsa toured Zambia in April 1981. They beat the Zambian team of Paul Taylor, Gordon Kirby, Guy Robinson and Keith Coventry by 8 goals to three.

A third American visit took place in 1985, with Buzz Welker, Corky Linfoot, Harley Stimmel and Jim Vaughn.

Steve Gose took his Retama team to Sydney, with his son Thomas, Joe Barry and Memo Gracida. They won the Easter International for the Morton Cup and the Easter International, both in 1981.

Four players, two wives and one supporter arrived in New Zealand for a two-week tour of the North Island. Steve Flores, Joel Baker, Mike Conant and Peter Baldwin lined up in that order. The first game was at the celebrated Kay family's KihiKihi. Missing Mike Conant, the game ended in a 9-all draw.

The next game was at Waimai, where the visiting team, now with Conant at Number 3, obtained their first win. Auckland was their next adversary at a game played in Clevedon; Maui won 6–5. After a four-day break, Maui entered the New Zealand Open. They were defeated 5–4 by Jim Watson, Cody Forsyth and the brothers Paul and Stephen Kay.

Then Maui defeated Cambridge and on the next day faced Taupiri on a ground that resembled more like a dustbowl than a polo field because of a severe drought. Maui ran out the winners and received their trophies looking as if they had just come out the local coal mine.

During a break, some of the team visited Ken Browne's Lanherne, where they had a friendly game; Oatsy Von Gontard Baker took part. Although most grooms are females, women polo players were unknown in New Zealand and several aspiring players stood on the sidelines to cheer Oatsy on.

The next day Maui played against the Auckland provincial team of Chris Jones, Cody Forsyth, Tony Devcich and Graham Thomas, winning 6–5 in an exciting game. The tour's last game was played at Clevedon against another Provincial team, with Nick Jones, John Walker, Jim Watson and Stephen Kay. The Provincial side combined well and defeated Maui 8–4 in a game most will remember for the appearance of a mounted streaker, who caused umpire Graham Thomas to be deposited in a ditch while giving chase.[22]

An American team labeled Texas played two test matches in South Africa in June 1982. Charles Armstrong, Bobby Barry, Geoffrey Kent, Steve Orthwein and Tommy Wayman were the members of the touring party. Kent, Orthwein, Wayman and Armstrong opened the tour with a 7–7 draw against a combined Orange Free State–Transvaal team at Inanda Polo Club in Johannesburg. During the game, Steve Orthwein came off his pony and injured his back. As a result of this injury, Orthwein was replaced by Bobby Barry in the test against South Africa, also played on the Inanda grounds. South Africa had Stephen Erskine, Mike Miller, Dale Osborne and Richard Kimber. One of the largest crowds ever at Inanda watched the South Africans win 7 goals to five.

The Texas team then moved on to Lions River in Natal, where the visitors played on different South African teams: Wayman on Lidgetton, Armstrong on Caversham, Orthwein on Nottingham Road and Barry on Dargle. From Lions River, the players left for Durban, where they played at Bridgemead against a combined Natal–East Griqualand side. After switching Steve Orthwein to Back from Number 2, the Texas team overcame a deficit and won by 13 goals to eleven.

The second test match and last game of the tour was held on the Shongweni grounds. The South Africans left their international team unchanged, while Orthwein returned to the Texas team at Back. The Springboks took the game 10–6.

In 1988, a team from Hawaii, Anthony Mullins, J. Campbell from Zimbabwe, Tommy Harris and Michael Dailey, went to Australia and took the March International Tournament in Sydney.[23]

An American team led by South African–born Joe Henderson traveled for a three-match international series in 1991 in his home country. Joel Baker, Rick Bostwick, Greg Linehan and Fred Walton were the rest of the players. The first test at Shongweni had the Springboks— Murray Rattray, Harry Mandy, Russell Watson and Will Rogers— wearing the green and yellow jerseys. The U.S. team, Bostwick, Baker, Henderson and Walton, earned a hard-won victory by 11 goals to nine.

The second test was also held at Shongweni between the same teams. The Americans took the game 13–7. The last test match took place on the Inanda grounds. Both teams made changes; Linehan played at Number 1 for America and the Springboks replaced the forwards with Andrew Erskine and Clark Rattray. The U.S. team also won this game.

Another American team reinforced by Adolfo Cambiaso played in South Africa in the 1996 BMW Internationals. James Armstrong, Orrin Ingram, Tod Rackley and Guerry "Boone" Stribling, Jr., completed the team. The first test was played on the Bridgemead ground. *Polo Post* reported:

> Never before has the South African public been so enthralled with the play of a single man. There were shouts of horror as he swept the ball away from his South African opponents, refusing to be hooked and whoops of sheer amazement as he galloped down the sidelines tapping the ball in the air five or six times, before dropping it to the ground and racing off to score another goal.[24]

In this match the United States team was Ingram, Armstrong, Cambiaso and Rackley. The final score was 11–9, favorable to the American squad.

The second test was played at Inanda on a chilly day. Those who braved the icy wind were treated to another exhibition like never before. After the first chukker, the U.S. team was ahead 6–0, on four goals by Cambiaso and two by Stribling, who replaced Armstrong on the American side. The final score was U.S. 19, South Africa 9. Clive Hill, Buster MacKenzie, Clive Mandy, Russell Watson and Selby Williamson were the South African representatives.

Isla Carroll had a successful campaign in Britain in 1997. John Goodman's team was built around Memo Gracida in his customary position at Number 3. With young Englishman Matt Pennell at Number 1 and Argentine Juan Ignacio "Pite" Merlos at Number 2, it was the team to beat. They defeated the Black Bears 13–10 in the finals of the Queen's Cup at Guards Polo Club in Windsor Park. Then they lost in the finals of the Cowdray Park Gold Park to Hubert Perrodo's Labegorce, anchored by Memo's younger brother, Carlos Gracida.

CHAPTER 22

Polo in America in the Late Twentieth Century

The last quarter of the twentieth century witnessed a tremendous growth burst in American polo. The number of players increased from approximately 1,230 in 1975 to 2,856 in 1990 and 3,037 in 2000. There were 147 affiliated clubs in 1975, 212 in 1990 and 223 in 2009.[1]

The international scene highlights were the encouraging performance offered in the Cup of the Americas by the United States team at Retama Polo Center, the gold medal obtained by the 14-goal American team in the Federation of International Polo's World Championship at Maifeld in Berlin, and the successful defense of the Westchester Cup at Guards Polo Club in England.

The United States Open Championship 1976–2000

Paul Butler's Oak Brook Polo Club remained the site of the U.S. Open until 1978, when it moved to Steve Gose's Retama Polo Center in Texas. In 1976, six teams entered to competition; Fairfield Hunt and Tulsa drew byes into the semifinals. In the preliminary matches Oak Brook, with Geoffrey Kent, Martín Braun Lasala from Argentina, Red Armour and Bill Ylvisaker, defeated Wilson Ranch, with William B. Wilson, Pat Dix, Juan José Alberdi, another Argentine, and Allan Scherer, by 9 goals to seven. Defending champion Milwaukee, with Robin Uihlein, New Zealander John Walker, Joe Barry and Steve Gose, faced Gold Cup winners Willow Bend, with Will Farish, Charles Smith, Roy Barry and Norman Brinker. This match went into overtime, Willow Bend escaping with a 10–9 win.

In the first semifinal Tulsa, with Bill Sinclaire, Tommy Wayman, Bart Evans and Jack Oxley, pulled away to take the game away from Oak Brook, 11–6. The second semifinal was marred by controversy. Fairfield Hunt had 10-goaler Gonzalo Tanoira, George Haas, and the Orthwein brothers, Peter and Steve. At halftime Willow Bend was ahead 5–3, with the crowd delighted with Tanoira's magnificent display and at the same time, quite displeased with the officiating.[2] In the fourth chukker, Willow Bend widened its lead as the unfortunate result of an accident. While Steve Orthwein was carrying the ball, his mount's girth broke and he fell, head first. Sensing the danger of the situation, the Fairfield players and two of Willow Bend's players stopped to aid the fallen player. However, the umpires did not blow the whistle; play went around Orthwein toward the Fairfield goalposts and Willow Bend scored a goal. Then the whistle went.

Most people though that play should have been stopped. The umpires neglected to apply Field Rule 22, which addresses accidents. The wording is very clear. "If any part of a pony's gear becomes broken or unfastened and there is a possibility it could cause an accident the Umpire shall stop play immediately and allow the player to make the necessary repairs or replacements before restarting the play."[3]

Polo's magazine editor Ami Shinitzky, never one to mince words when he noticed injustice, wrote an editorial reaffirming the need for the highest standards of professionalism in umpiring. In Shinitzky's own words, "Not only should the umpire in all tournaments be extremely knowledgeable and able on the field, but all possible implications of partiality, by virtue of involvement or vested interests (no matter how far removed), must be avoided."[4]

Perhaps the explanation for the reference to vested interests was the fact that the grey mare Sweet Be, winner of the Hartman Trophy, played by Charles Smith of the Willow Bend team, was the property of Richard Latham, who was one of the officials in the Fairfield versus Willow Bend match.

It has been written that the Willow Bend players were correct in keeping the

One of a mighty Texas contingent: Bart Evans on Chica Boom.

ball in play.[5] Perhaps it was so, but a comparison with another incident in the same U.S. Open Championship is worth mentioning. During the Tulsa versus Oak Brook game, Red Armour lost his mallet; his opponent Tommy Wayman stopped, picked Red's mallet with his own and handed it to Armour, in a nice gesture of sportsmanship.[6]

The score at the end of the controversial fourth chukker was 8–3 in favor of Willow Bend. Led by Gonzalo Tanoira, Fairfield tied the game at 9-all, with less than 30 seconds to go. From the ensuing thrown-in, play went towards Fairfield's goalposts, Will Farish picked the ball and, eluding Steve Orthwein's hook, scored the winner.

Compared to the semifinal game, the final match was a disappointment for the spectators because Willow Bend achieved an easy win, 10 goals to Tulsa's five tallies.

The format for the 1977 U.S. Open and the Butler National Handicap was changed, adopting a formula popular in Argentina. Each first round match would have two winners, on the flat and by handicap. It proved to be quite successful. So was the number of entries, thirteen. When it was announced that Paul Butler was selling most of his property to the village of Oak Brook, it became evident that the organization of U.S. Open had to take steps towards making the event self-sufficient. The drive for corporate sponsorship was evident.

Even the most casual observer could tell which way the wind was blowing when a red flag with golden arches was fluttering at International Field. McDonald's was behind the United States Open Championship with something more than cheeseburgers.

Twelve teams entered the dual competition. After the 23 games need to complete the preliminary rounds, Retama, with Corky Linfoot, Memo Gracida, Joe Barry and Steve Gose, and Wilson Ranch, with "Willie B" Wilson, Fortunato Gómez Romero, Antonio Herrera and Ernesto Trotz, faced each other in the finals. Retama won by 11 goals to seven.

In the Butler National handicap, San Antonio, with Stewart Armstrong, Bob Beveridge, Daniel González and Charles Armstrong, defeated Lone Oak, 8–6. Thus, four teams from the heart of Texas filled the slots in the finals.

The same format continued in the 1978, with the addition of another handicap tournament, the A & K Trophy. Therefore, no less than 36 matches, including the President's Cup, were played to decide the three semifinalists, one from each bracket. The titleholders and favorites, Retama, were derailed by a determined Tulsa team, Michael Carney, Ronald Tongg, Red Armour and Seth Herndon. Abercrombie & Kent, with Geoffrey Kent, David Wigdahl, Antonio Herrera and Stuart MacKenzie, drew a bye and defeated Tulsa in the finals 7–6.

In the Butler Handicap, Smallwood, with Heath Manning, Jr., Paul Rizzo, Tom Harris and Russell Corey, first defeated Fairfield Hunt 8–7, with George Haas, Steve Orthwein, Gonzalo Tanoira and Peter Orthwein; then scored an easy victory, 9 goals to 5, over Jet Mix.

This was the last Open Championship held at Oak Brook. In 1979, Retama became the new home of the most prestigious American polo tournament, held in the southwest for the first time in its history. Eight teams entered the tournament, which had a 24-goal top handicap limit and 18-goals as a minimum. The practice of simultaneous games on handicap and on the flat had proved to be successful, and was kept at Retama. Two 18-goal teams, Palm Beach and Blanco, were entered with realistic hope of doing well in the handicap tournament.

There were no surprises; the two favorites, Huisache, with Joel Baker, Alejandro Soldati, Charles Smith and Will Farish, at times spelled by Ken Fransen, met Retama, with Corky Linfoot, Memo Gracida, Joe Barry and Steve Gose. Regrettably, Alejandro Soldati broke his shoulder in the game against Blanco and was unable to play in the finals, won by Retama 6–5. Alabama, Steve Gose's wonderful grey horse, was judged the best playing pony in the U.S. Open for the second time.

Only six teams participated in the 1980 U.S. Open: Redwood, Retama, Southern Hills, Tulsa, Valdina Farms and Willow Bend. The lateness of the polo season — the championship game was held on 26 October — kept the numbers down, in addition to heavy rains that forced a one-week postponement of both the Open and the U.S. Handicap finals. Local favorite Retama, with Carlos Gracida, Memo Gracida, Joe Barry and Steve Gose, and Southern Hills, with Rubén Gracida, Tommy Wayman, Julian Hipwood and Seth Herndon, were the strongest teams on handicap. However, Willow Bend, with Joel Baker, Charles Smith Roy Barry and Norman Brinker, made it to the finals, to meet Southern Hills.

Due to an injury suffered by Julian Hipwood, Southern Hills was obliged to make changes in its lineup. Patron Seth Herndon moved up to Number 1, Jake Sieber came in at Number 2, and Tommy Wayman and Rubén Gracida moved to Number 3 and Back, respectively. By all accounts, it was a rough game.[7] At halftime, Southern Hills was up by three goals, a differential that they maintained to the game's end; the final score was 9 goals to six.

Eight teams answered the call for the 1981 U.S. Open. The teams were divided into two brackets, the winners to play one game for the championship. The situation was complicated by the sudden onset of an equine flu manifested by running noses and cough. Some teams were more affected than others. Boca Raton withdrew after one game, and Rolex A&K was minus nine horses. After the third round in Bracket A, Rolex and defending champion Southern Hill were tied with a 2–0 record. Rolex took the crucial match by 10 goals to six. In Bracket B, Retama defeated Fort Lauderdale 13–6.

Before the championship game, to everyone's surprise, Rolex A&K, due to the depleted state of their string, requested that the match be played at a later day during the Florida season. Furthermore, with the usual end-of-season fatigue, the team felt that its remaining ponies would suffer undue stress.[8] The request was promptly denied on the grounds that all other teams had been affected by the virus.

With no other alternative to play or forfeit the match, Rolex A&K changed its strategy. Since Stuart MacKenzie had lost his entire pony string and had to play on borrowed horses, he would play a deep Back to cut off the speedy Carlos Gracida, Retama's Number 1. Secondly, Geoff Kent at Number 1 would play farther back to support Joel Baker in marking Joe Barry, although it meant leaving Norman Brinker unguarded.

In spite of their pony shortage, Rolex A&K started the game at full-blast speed, scoring four goals in the first chukker. At halftime the score was 7–3. The fifth chukker was critical for Rolex because it was their weakest period pony-wise. They hung on to enter the final period leading by two goals. Early in the last chukker, a penalty was whistled against Rolex some six yards from the goal, but at an acute angle. Rather than take the hit from the 30-yard line, Retama chose to take the penalty from the spot where the infraction had taken place. Memo Gracida made an easy tap to bring the ball closer to the center of the goalposts and out of nowhere MacKenzie met the ball and cleared the danger. With four minutes to go, Memo Gracida hit wide of the goal, missing another opportunity to close the gap. Then Joe Barry scored, but time ran out. Final score: Rolex A&K 10, Retama 9.

The 1982 U.S. Open at Retama had the usual sponsors from the southwest with the welcome addition of Peter Baldwin's Maui team from Hawaii. The first match produced the unlikely score 3–2, Maui over Tulsa. In spite of this hiccup, Tulsa, with Dick Albert, Julian Hipwood, Howard Hipwood and Podger El-Effendi, made it to the finals, with a little help of San Antonio, which won the only game of the tournament against Maui. In the other bracket, Retama, with Rubén, Carlos and Memo Gracida, and sponsor Steve Gose at Back, came out on top. In the championship match Retama's horsepower was the deciding factor in their 11–6 victory.

Five entries battled for the 1983 U.S. Open: defending champion Retama with Tom Gose, Carlos Gracida, Memo Gracida and Steve Gose; Fort Lauderdale, Jack Oxley, Fortunato Gómez Romero, Rubén Gracida and Bart Evans; San Antonio, at 21-goals the weakest entry, with Charlie Bostwick, Charles Armstrong, Rick Bostwick and Calixto García Vélez; and two 26-goal teams, Southern Hills and Valdina. Southern Hills had Seth Herndon, Charles Smith, Tommy Wayman and Dale Smicklas, while Valdina counted on Matt Gose, Owen Rinehart, Red Armour and Joe Barry. Each team had to face the other four; the best two teams were to meet in the finals.

As it often happens in this situation, there was much speculation and uncertainty as to which teams would meet in the championship game. Retama finish its matches with a 3–1 record and seemed to be certain of a place in the finals. Three other teams remained in the running: Fort Lauderdale, Valdina and Southern Hills. Fort Lauderdale would have to defeat Southern Hills, but more importantly, they needed San Antonio to beat Valdina. Southern Hills beat Fort Lauderdale 6–4 and long faces abounded in the Fort Lauderdale camp because San Antonio was expected to be an easy prey for the powerful Valdina. But the unexpected happened and the beautifully mounted San Antonio won the game by 11 goals to nine. The three pretenders were tied at 2–2. With a better goal average, Fort Lauderdale was in the finals. San Antonio went on the take the handicap tournament, played on the Saturday before the final of the Open Championship.

Memo Gracida was unable to play because of a broken collarbone and was replaced by Howard Hipwood. Fort Lauderdale then altered its lineup, placing Rubén Gracida at Back and Bart Evans at Number 3, to be closer to Howard Hipwood who had a reputation of not backing off when the going was getting rough. Retama and Fort Lauderdale stayed within two goals of each other throughout the match, with Evans and Hipwood battling in the middle, where polo games are lost and won. In the final chukker, Fort Lauderdale took the lead and the epic match ended 8–5 in their favor. Jack Oxley realized his dream of winning the U.S. Open, seventeen years after his father John had accomplished that feat with his own Boca Raton team.

The 1984 U.S. Open continued to draw half-a-dozen teams while the Gold Cup, the only other 26-goal tournament in America, routinely attracted many more teams. For instance, in 1978, the last time the U.S. Open was held at Oak Brook, 12 teams participated. When it was moved to Retama, the number of teams varied between six and eight. At the same time, the Gold Cup was transferred from Milwaukee to Florida. In 1982, the Gold Cup had 21 teams, compared to seven in the U.S. Open; the figures in 1893 were 19 and five, and in 1984, 19 in the Gold Cup and six in the Open. These numbers raised increased concerns within the polo community. Even though Steve Gose had raised a magnificent establishment at Retama, the issue of "location, location," so beloved by real estate brokers, was raised time and time again by sponsors. Most felt that it was too far away and it took to long to play the three featured tournaments: the U.S. Open, the U.S. Handicap and the President's Cup.

Nevertheless, eight teams planned to start the tournament in September; however, Tom Wigdahl's team from Chicago pulled out and Jimmy Newman's Cibolo had to scratch at the last minute when Roberto González Gracida ran out of horses. One bracket had the perennial host team, Retama, Alan Connell's Las Cachinas and Old Pueblo, sponsored by John Hall. The titleholders, Jack Oxley's Fort Lauderdale, joined San Antonio and Tom Mudd's Santa Clara. Then, after a prolonged drought, the rains came in two waves, firstly pushing the entire schedule back one full week and then forcing a pause after only four of the six preliminary games had been played. As a result of the weather delays, Santa Clara had to pull out of the tournament because of Howard Hipwood's commitments in England.

Fort Lauderdale was the winner of the first bracket. It took 14 days to find out which team would face the defending champions. Retama took one bracket with a sudden death overtime 11–10 win over Old Pueblo and a 9–6 victory over Las Cachinas. In a sort of replay of the previous year's finals, Fort Lauderdale and Retama battled for the trophy. It came down to a Gracida show, Carlos and Memo dominating center stage, while Steve Gose played a sound Back, and son Tom kept Dale Smicklas quite busy. The final score was 9–6, Retama.

Bad weather was a factor, once more, in the 1985 U.S. Open at Retama, delaying several games for the six entrants. Bracket A consisted of newcomer Carter Ranch, with 2-goal patron Preston Carter, Carlos Gracida, Memo Gracida and Mexican Pablo Rincón Gallardo;

Hall of Famer Owen Rinehart, a 10-goaler from Charlottesville, Virginia. A winner of the U.S. Open Championship and the Westchester Cup.

Old Pueblo, with John Hall, Joe Barry, Corky Linfoot and Joel Baker; and Santa Fe, with H. Ben Taub, Oscar Bermúdez, Bobby Barry and Roy Barry. It came to Old Pueblo versus Carter Ranch. Both came out winners: Carter Ranch 14–13 in the Open and Old Pueblo 16–14 in the Handicap. It was the best game of the entire tournament.

In Bracket B, Fort Lauderdale, with Jack Oxley, Rob Walton, Owen Rinehart and Bart Evans, defeated Lone Star; however, the latter beat Retama, Tom Gose, Tommy Wayman, Rubén Gracida and Steve Gose, in overtime. This left the Floridians to fight it out with Retama for the final slot. In this encounter, Retama, with Bil Walton replacing an injured Tom Gose, both won and lost. They won the game 8–7, but lost the bracket to the best goal differential accumulated by Fort Lauderdale.

On to the final match, that was played one week later. It was a choppy match, marred by many penalties. Tied at 8-goals in the fifth chukker, Pablo Rincón Gallardo scored what turned out to be the winning goal with a perfect neck-shot. Memo Gracida then converted

Carlos Gracida, one of polo superstars, wearing Ellerston White's shirt.

a 60-yard penalty to make the final score 10–8. Carlos Gracida was then raised to the magical 10-goal handicap and a place among the game's immortals. Lone Star took the United States Handicap, with Jimmy Newman, Charles Smith, Paul Rizzo and Fayyaz Uddin.

The last U.S. Open Championship played at Retama took place in 1986 because of the financial hardship incurred by the club. Seven teams answered the call, divided into two brackets. Bracket A had had one of the pre-tournament's favorites, Fort Lauderdale, with Jack Oxley, Carlos Gracida, Bart Evans and Joey Casey. Completing the bracket were Retama

I, with Roberto González Gracida, Rubén Gracida, Memo Gracida and Steve Gose; this team was thought to be somewhat weak horse-wise. Texas Lone Star, with Jimmy Newman, Bobby Barry, Wicky El-Effendi and Chuy Báez, and defending champion Carter Ranch, with Preston Carter, Stewart Armstrong, Charles Smith and Fayyaz Uddin, completed the roster.

Bracket B had the other favorite, Retama II, with Mike Azzaro, Tommy Wayman, Owen Rinehart and Tom Gose. The other two teams were San Antonio, with Charlie and Rick Bostwick, Alejandro "Piki" Díaz Alberdi and Charlie Armstrong, and Miller Draft, who had sports car racer Alan Connell, Julian Hipwood, Fortunato Gómez Romero and Dale Smicklas in its lineup.

The three initial matches saw Retama I take an 11–10 win in the Open Championship against a tough Carter Ranch squad that took the handicap 16–11. The next day Miller Draft met Retama II in one of the tournament's best matches that went into overtime. Owen Rinehart converted a long 5B penalty from the spot of the foul to win the day for Retama II. The day's second game saw Fort Lauderdale defeat Lone Star 11–7 in the Open and lost 12–11 in the U.S. Handicap.

Then, as feared, the rains came and all action was suspended for eight days, wrecking the schedule, especially for the U.S. Handicap as well as the 8-goal President's Cup. When resumed, the tournament results were a 12–5 win by Retama I over Lone Star, a 13–12 victory for San Antonio over Miller Draft, and an 18–7 romp by Fort Lauderdale over Carter Ranch. Eventually, Retama II and Fort Lauderdale reached the finals. Retama II started well and obtained a lead that was challenged by Fort Lauderdale only in the last period for a final 8–7 score. And so the era of Retama came to an end.

The U.S. Open returned to California after 21 years. Eldorado club in Indio was the venue for this tournament that attracted eight teams. Bracket 1 had Aloha, BTA/Barron Thomas Aviation and Old Pueblo from Texas, and Fort Lauderdale. Bracket 2 had Fish Creek — a name in Canadian polo going back to 1903 — from Alberta, Peter Baldwin's Maui and California's own Gehache and Los Potros.

In the first bracket all three teams ended with a 2–1 record; net goals decided that Aloha, with Dartmouth's product Robert Fell, Carlos Gracida, Memo Gracida and Warren Scherer, went to the finals. In the other bracket Los Potros, with Mike Azzaro, Hector Galindo, Owen Rinehart and patron Jim Gilstrap, was undefeated. In a fine game, Aloha won game and championship, giving Bob Fell the U.S. Open trophy in his first try.

The championship's location was then moved to the Kentucky Horse Park in Lexington. U.S.P.A. chairman S.K. Johnston, Jr., pointed out that Lexington's central location made it within a one-day drive for clubs east of the Mississippi and even for some west.[9] The U.S. Open attracted five teams; every one had at least a foreigner in the lineup. This invasion of imported players and their role in both low and high-goal competitions was a topic of conversation among spectators and a matter of serious discussion at the U.S.P.A. semiannual meeting. Not surprisingly, a decision was not reached on the issues of limiting the number of foreign players on a team, or on the touchy subject of limiting an individual player's handicap to no more than three-quarters of the maximum tournament handicap.

The teams' composition reflected the fact that the Westchester Cup was to be played following the Open Championship. Therefore, players from Australia and New Zealand were available to play. Each team played four matches to decide the finalist for the Open and the handicap tournament for the C.V. Whitney Cup. Johnnie Walker/Boca Raton was rated at 25-goals; all the rest at 26-goal handicap. Cellular Farms had Adam Lindemann,

Benjamin Araya from Argentina and Stuart Gilmore and Jaime Mackay from Australia. Coca-Cola, Skeeter Johnston's team, had Argentines Marcos Heguy and Eduardo Novillo Astrada and Jeff Atkinson. Fort Lauderdale, with Jack Oxley, Joey Casey, Argentine Ernesto Trotz and Bart Evans, was one of two Oxley entries from Florida. John Oxley had Argentines Santiago Araya and Juan Badiola, plus Stuart Mackenzie from New Zealand. Frenchman art dealer Guy Wildenstein presented Carlos and Memo Gracida on his Diables Bleus squad, with Okie Ted Moore at Number 1. When the qualifying round was completed, the two Oxley entries were to decide the handicap tournament that was taken by Fort Lauderdale 15–10.

There were no unbeaten left; both finalists had taken a tumble in the preliminary round: Coca-Cola lost to Fort Lauderdale 11–10 and Les Diables Bleus was defeated by Coca-Cola 10–6. The match was even at even at 5-goals in the third chukker when Eduardo Novillo Astrada went down and injured his shoulder. Although Taio finished the match, his sore shoulder prevented him from scoring any more goals and Les Diables Bleus went on to an 11–8 win.

Only four teams competed in the 1989 U.S. Open: defending champions Les Diables Bleus, Fort Lauderdale, Michelob and Black Bears. The later team was Swiss patron Urs Schwarzenbach's team based in England, who was perhaps trying to emulate Anthony Embiricos' win in the World Cup in Palm Beach. It became obvious that the sponsors voted with their feet; the participation in the most important polo tournament in the United States was the lowest since 1975.

All four teams played each other; Black Bears won all their matches, including a 9–7 victory over Les Diables Bleus, their opponents in the finals. Both teams were rated at 26-goals. Black Bears, with Urs Schwarzenbach, Mike Azzaro, Owen Rinehart and Memo Gracida, faced Guy Wildenstein team, who had Alejandro Agote, Juan Ignacio "Pite" Merlos and Dale Smicklas.

Guillermo "Memo" Gracida's penchant for meticulous preparation paid handsome dividends on game day. When the rains started on Thursday and continued steadily on Friday, the Diables Bleus horses underwent a change of shoes in anticipation of having to play on a soggy field on Sunday. In Memo's own words, "When the rain started on Thursday, we talked to the blacksmith and began to change the shoes. We used larger caulks on the back and in the front we used nails with the biggest heads possible."[10]

The Black Bears ponies slipped, slid and three fell during the game, including those ridden by Azzaro, Rinehart and Smicklas. None of Les Diables Bleus became a cropper. By the last chukker the ground's condition had deteriorated to such an extent that all players had to slow down. Les Diables Bleus took the second of their three consecutive victories at Lexington. Memo Gracida took his eighth Open Championship, breaking the record held by W. Ray Harrington.

Michelob took the C.V. Whitney Handicap on Monday in front of a sparse crowd with a goal by Bart Evans with 12 seconds remaining in the clock. The many-times postponed President's Cup was taken by Toronto 10–9 over Richland with David Offen scoring five goals.

Les Diables Bleus retained the U.S. Open Trophy in 1990, making it three-in-a-row. Memo Gracida and patron Guy Wildenstein remained on the team; they were joined by the brothers Pite and Sebastián Merlos, the latter handicapped at 4-goals, although his rating in Argentina was 6-goals. The question must be asked: Where was the U.S.P.A. Handicap Committee?

The other teams were Fred Mannix's Fish Creek, Adolphus Busch's Michelob, the perennial Fort Lauderdale and Ron Bonaguidi's Hanalei Bay. The latter team, directed by Carlos Gracida and completed with Alejandro Agote and Mike Azzaro, met Les Diables Bleus in the final match. Young Julio Arellano stepped in before the final game because of Wildenstein's sudden illness. Les Diables Bleus controlled the game in achieving a 9–5 victory.

Most regrettably, controversies marred the 1991 U.S. Open, the last one to be held at Kentucky's Horse Park. Five teams entered, with three of them, Grant's Farm Manor, Michelob and Michelob Dry, linked to the Anheuser-Busch brewery in St. Louis. The other two teams were Jack Oxley's Fort Lauderdale and Gone Away Farms from Maryland. Michelob Dry, with Philip Lake, Adam Snow, Owen Rinehart and Bobby Barry, ran away in the preliminary round with an unbeaten record. Michelob and Grant's Farm Manor had identical 2–2 records, and the latter qualified by virtue of better net goals.

Allegations flew when Fort Lauderdale lost 11–6 to Gone Away Farms. Had Fort Lauderdale beaten their opponents, its record also would have been 2–2; however, the goal differential among the three 2–2 teams would have been in Michelob's favor because Fort Lauderdale had previously defeated Grant's Farm Manor, 11–6. Adolphus Busch, IV, filed a protest with the U.S.P.A. with the allegation that Fort Lauderdale intentionally lost the game with Gone Away Farms, also asking the Association to review its play-offs procedures. Perhaps there was bad blood between the Michelob and Fort Lauderdale camps as a result of an incident during their contest. In the fifth chukker, Adolfo Cambiaso collided with Martín Zubía who was knocked unconscious. Cambiaso dismounted and handed his reins to Gracida. Adolphus Busch also dismounted and shoved Cambiaso to the ground; the action was not noticed by the umpires but was caught in a video camera. No action was taken against Busch; however, a penalty 1 was awarded against Fort Lauderdale. When Michelob was unable to produce a substitute for Zubía, a rare penalty 10 was assessed against Fort Lauderdale and Memo Gracida — at 10-goals the player closest to Zubía's 9-goal rating — was sent off the field and the teams finished the match three-a-side. Fort Lauderdale was unable to regroup. At the time, they were leading 5–3; however, they failed to score a single goal following the incident and lost the match 9–5. In reality, sportsmanship was the big loser.

Michelob Dry and Grant Farm's Manor met in a meaningless last game of the preliminary play-offs, Michelob Dry winning 13–9. The final game for the C.V. Whitney Handicap was next, between feuding Michelob and Fort Lauderdale. Umpires Red Armour and Bart Evans called 24 penalties during the match, which was taken by Fort Lauderdale 9–8 via a winning score by Adolfito Cambiaso.

The U.S. Open final match between friendly rivals Grant's Farm Manor and Michelob Dry was tied at 4-all at halftime and 8–8 at the end of regulation time. Within minutes of the overtime throw-in, Billy Busch found a loose ball and passed it to Carlos Gracida, who scored the championship goal for Grant's Farm Manor.

At the end of the season, Owen Rinehart became the first American-born player to achieve a 10-goal rating since the legendary Tommy Wayman.

The Open returned to California in 1992. It was sweet revenge for Ron Bonaguidi's Hanalei Bay, runner-up in 1990. With Julio Arellano, Carlos and Guillermo Gracida, the team was considered the odds-on favorite after the tournaments leading to the U.S. Open at Eldorado. Fred Mannix's Fish Creek was one of the two entries by the Calgary patron, the other being Millarville. Fish Creek had two Argentines, Francisco "Pancho" Bensadón and Julio Zavaleta, plus 10-goaler Owen Rinehart. Millarville, at 24-goals two points lighter than Fish Creek, had Rob Roenisch, Hector Galindo, Piki Díaz Alberdi and Julie Roenisch, Rob's wife and the first woman to participate in the U.S. Open Championship. She played well up to her 2-goal rating. The other two teams, BTA from Texas and a mixed Lodesworth/Sidelines, compiled a losing record in the preliminary round. Fish Creek qualified for the finals; however its 5 net goals compared unfavorably with Hanalei Bay's 31 net goals. And so it was. The Gracida duo was too much power for Fish Creek and they took the championship with a convincing 13–6 victory. The second Mannix team, Millarville, won the U.S. Handicap over Lodesworth/Sidelines.

Eldorado was again the host club in the 1993 U.S. Open which had only four entrants: Fish Creek, BTA, and Gehache, all rated at 26-goals, and Revo, a 22-goal team with C.V. Whitney Handicap's aspirations. Revo lost all their four matches, including the finals of the C.V. Whitney against BTA. The final match between Fish Creek, with Fred Mannix, Piki Díaz Alberdi, Julio Zavaleta and Joe Henderson, versus Gehache, with Rubén Gracida, Mike Azzaro, Memo Gracida and Glen Holden, was a tight match in that the underdogs from Canada were ahead into the fifth chukker, and again with three minutes to go in the game. Gehache tied the game and with 48 seconds remaining, a safety was called against Fish Creek. While Diaz Alberdi was being attended to for his injured shoulder, cagy Memo Gracida practiced shots at goal from the 60-yard line. While not explicitly prohibited by the rules of the game, it was nevertheless a questionable show of sportsmanship. Memo converted the penalty, Gehache won the ensuing throw-in and the game was over. For this match, Fish Creek moved Joe Henderson up, and lining-up at the throw-ins backwards, which disoriented Gehache. The sponsor's initials in Spanish, GH, gave the name to the team. Glen Holden became the oldest player to take the U.S. Open Championship.

The U.S. Open Championship returned to New York in 1994. Reflecting the Big Apple's prices, the entry fee was set at $25,000. In spite of the five-fold increase over other 26-goal tournaments, eleven teams, from Peter Orthwein's Airstream to Raúl Villalobos', Villagers, registered to play. Bethpage State Park on Long Island and Greenwich Polo Club in Connecticut were the main venues. Division I was taken by Aspen, a team that posted a 5–0 record. The other favorite, White Birch, won Division B with a 4–0 record, following a much-discussed game against divisional runner-up Calumet Farm. In a clash of Heguy cousins, Bautista on White Birch and Eduardo and Alberto "Pepe" on Calumet Farms, in the fifth period Pepe crashed into Bautista, who was unable to continue. There was no available 10-goal player to take Bautista Heguy's place; therefore the umpires apply a Penalty 7, giving White Birch the choice to sit out either of the Heguy brothers on the Calumet Farm team. Although Alberto Heguy was judged to have committed the foul, Eduardo "Ruso" Heguy was sent to the pony lines. The remaining six players continued a game plagued by fouls, invectives and intimidation. It was a sorry situation for the spectators which had every right to watch a fine match played by talented players. Mariano Aguerre converted two penalties to give White Birch a 10–8 win and a place in the finals.

These two teams, Aspen and White Birch, met in the final game at Bethpage on a field rendered unsuitable for an U.S. Open final because of heavy usage. There had been matches played on that field in five of the previous eight days, including the final of the Handicap tournament the day before the finals and several periods of a celebrity exhibition match. Aspen was ahead 3–1 at halftime, but Mariano Aguerre scored three goals in the fourth chukker to put White Birch ahead. Then it was Carlos Gracida's turn, for he scored three times in the fifth, while Aguerre scored once towards the end to make it a one-goal difference entering the last chukker. In the last chukker, Bautista Heguy scored three goals; however, one was disallowed by the umpires. After Heguy's last goal, with White Birch ahead by one goal and only 43 seconds remaining, Bauti took his time returning to the lineup. Rather than throw-in the ball, as mandated by the rules, umpire Gene Fortugno blew the whistle, stopping the clock. Carlos Gracida gained the ball at the throw-in and raced towards the goalposts closely followed by Mariano Aguerre. Gracida scored to send the match into overtime. White Birch was penalized during the throw-in, and again in the ensuing play. Carlos Gracida converted the 30-yard shot to win the match by 8 goals to seven.

White Birch's bad luck in the U.S. Open continued in 1995. For the first time, the C.V. Whitney Handicap was a separate tournament played just before the Open. White Birch took the C.V. Whitney by defeating Revlon 12–10. Four teams reached the semifinals. One was Airstream/Cellular, a team that changed its name to Sotheby's just before the tournament started, with two good amateurs in Adam Lindemann and Peter Orthwein and two talented Argentines, Nachi and Bautista Heguy. They faced Outback Steakhouse, with Julio Arellano, Sebastián Merlos replacing an injured Carlos Gracida, Memo Gracida and Tim Gannon. The other semifinal had White Birch, with Brandon Phillips, Adolfo Cambiaso, Mariano Aguerre and Peter Brant, versus Revlon, with David Offen, Tomás Fernández Llorente, Cristián Laprida and Michael Tarnopol. Both winners had an easy time: White Birch defeated Revlon 9–4 and Outback beat Sotheby's 15–4.

Compared to the previous year's dramatic finals, this one was anticlimactic. Mariano Aguerre suffered a ribcage injury while blocking an open goal penalty and was eventually unable to continue, being replaced by Todd Offen. Outback Steakhouse galloped to a 15–6 victory. The consolation final for the Tommy Hitchcock Memorial was taken by Sotheby's with 14 goals against Revlon's 13 tallies.

The U.S.P.A. awarded its 1996 Open Championship to Palm Beach Polo & Country Club in Wellington, Florida. The major polo competition has remained within the confines of the Sunshine State ever since. Eleven teams participated in the event, with Outback and White Birch competing in one semifinal and Casa Manila and Pony Express/Grant's Farm Manor in the other. Outback, with Valerio Aguilar, Mike Azzaro, Memo Gracida and Tim Gannon, defeated White Birch, with John Hensley, Adolfo Cambiaso, Mariano Aguerre and Steve Dalton replacing injured Peter Brant, 10–7. For their part, Casa Manila, with patron Wesley Pitcock, Marcelo Caset, Marcos Heguy and Luis Escobar, beat Pony Express/Grant's Farm Manor, which had Bob Daniels, Bautista Heguy, Gonzalo Heguy and Andy Busch, 15–12. The final match was dominated by Outback, defeating their rivals by 16 goals to nine.

The White Birch team took the handicap tournament for the C.V. Whitney Cup when they defeated Pony Express/Grant's Farm Manor 13–10.

Nine hopeful teams gathered for the 1997 U.S. Open. Following three weeks of preliminary matches, the semifinals were Coca-Cola, with S.K. Johnston, III, Adam Snow, Owen Rinehart and Miguel Novillo Astrada, versus Isla Carroll, with Martín Estrada, Mike Azzaro, Memo Gracida and John Goodman; the other semifinal game was White Birch versus Revlon, with Eugene "Tiger" Kneece, Tomás Fernández Llorente, Cristián Laprida and Michael Tarnopol. All were 26-goal teams. Both were decided by identical scores, 9 to 7, with Isla Carroll and White Birch to meet in the final game.

As usual, White Birch made several substitutions along the course of the U.S. Open, but Hensley, Cambiaso, Aguerre and Brant played in the finals. For once, White Birch was out-horsed by Isla Carroll, the winner by 10 goals to six. Regrettably, several cases of

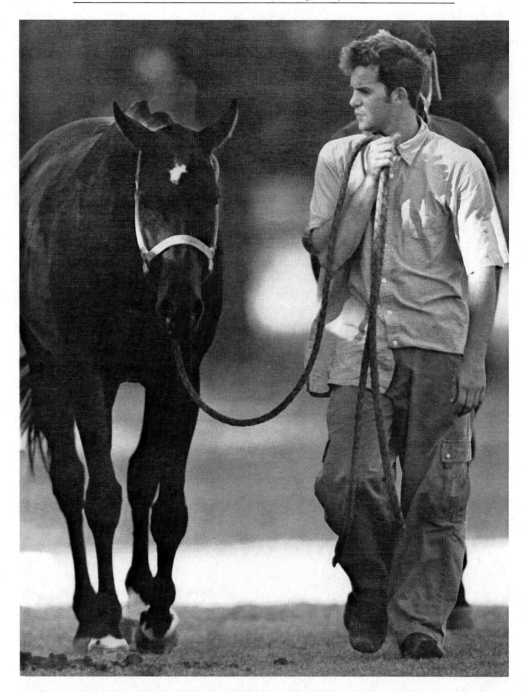

The unsung workers. A groom leads a tired horse after a hard-fought game in Palm Beach.

unsportsmanlike conduct occurred during the game that culminated in an ugly confrontation between Aguerre and Azzaro at match's end.

Ten teams started the 1998 U.S. Open but only eight finished their scheduled games. Division 1 had heavy favorites Isla Carroll, the Busch family's Bud Light/Grant's Farm, Escue, sponsored by Sheik Adus "Shimmy" Qureshi and named after his initials, Pony

Express and Templeton. Division 2 counted Tommy Boyle's C-Spear, Skeeter Johnston's Coca-Cola, former champion Outback, Revlon and White Birch. It was a magnificent field.

The road to the semifinals was complicated. In the Division 1, Pony Express appeared to be safe in one of the two spots with a 3–1 record; the only blemish was a 12–8 loss to Isla Carroll. Escue defeated Bud Light/Grant's Farm, lost 12–11 to Pony Express, and surprised Isla Carroll, defeating the favorite 13 goals to 11. Isla Carroll beat Bud Light/Grant's Farm, Pony Express and Templeton. Then Templeton withdrew from the tournament prior to their engagement against Escue. By their action all the games involving Templeton were removed from consideration into the final standings and Escue was placed into the semifinal round. All three teams in contention ended with a 2–1 won-lost record. Isla Carroll had +2 goals, Escue +2 and Pony Express -3. The two top teams went on to the semifinals and hard-luck Pony Express, innocent victim of a bad rule, went on to win the C.V. Whitney Handicap, with Bob Daniels, Javier Novillo Astrada, Pancho Bensadón and Miguel Novillo Astrada.

Division 2 also had a withdrawal, when White Birch's superstar player Mariano Aguerre was injured in a preliminary match. His withdrawal did not affect the standings as much as the one by Templeton in Division 1 because it occurred early in the round. Both Coca-Cola and Outback had 2–1 records, with the former in first place because of better goals differential.

Isla Carroll faced Outback in what was perceived as a critical semifinal match, because most pundits felt that Tim Gannon's team with Adolfo Cambiaso, Lolo Castagnola and Santiago Chavanne had the best chance to unseat the defending champions. However, it was not to be. In a thrilling match, Isla Carroll defeated Outback 12–11 with only 30 seconds left to play in regulation time.

Later that same day, Escue defeated Coca-Cola, with Skeeter Johnston, Adam Snow, Owen Rinehart and Roberto González Gracida, by 8 goals to 7 in a hard defensive battle.

If the road to the finals was difficult, the day before the last game was even worse. In his *Polo Players' Edition* report on the U.S. Open story Peter Rizzo tactfully made reference to certain "distractions" affecting the Escue team.[11] Federal marshals threatened to impound most of Escue's polo ponies as a result of a financial dispute. The final match almost did not take place. Things quieted down thanks to the timely intervention of Héctor Merlos, father of the two Escue 10-goalers, team captain Juan Ignacio and Sebastián. The rest of the squad was 15-year-old Nicolás Roldán, who went from taking the Avendaño Junior tournament in January to the U.S. Open in April, and South African Stuart "Sugar" Erskine, a former member of the Isla Carroll team who was looking forward to prove that his 6-goal handicap was better than the one sported by his replacement. In the final game, Erskine and Roldán exchanged places, Erskine going to Back and Roldán to Number 1.

Sebastián Merlos did a superb job in keeping Memo Gracida at bay, while older brother Pite converted critical penalty shots. The score at halftime was Escue 7, Isla Carroll 5. At the end of the fifth chukker, with Escue clinging to an 11–10 lead and being out-horsed by Isla Carroll, Pite Merlos scored a most important goal, to put Escue ahead by two. In the last chukker only one goal was made, appropriately enough by Sebastián Merlos. Pite Merlos was MPV and his pony Torcaza (ring-dove) was awarded the Willis Hartman trophy as the Best Playing Pony.

In 1999, ten entrants made a most satisfactory U.S. Open that started in mid–March. A newcomer, Lechuza Caracas from Venezuela, served notice when they defeated White Birch 10–9 in the tournament's first game. Other powerhouses, such as Coca-Cola and Isla

Outback's one of five U.S. Open victories. This is the 1999 team: Tim Gannon, Jeff Blake, Adolfo Cambiaso and Bartolomé "Lolo" Castagnola.

Carroll, fell by the wayside during the preliminary rounds. The semifinals saw Pony Express defeat Everglades Polo, with S.K. Johnston, III, Tomás Fernández Llorente, Owen Rinehart and Eugene Kneece, by 12 goals to nine. Casa Manila, with Wesley Pitcock, Roberto González Gracida, Luis Escobar and Matías Magrini, went down to Outback in a heartbreaking 12–11 overtime loss.

The final match between Pony Express, with Bob Daniels, Nicolás Roldán, Gonzalo Heguy and Bautista Heguy, and Outback, with Tim Gannon, Jeff Blake, Adolfo Cambiaso and Lolo Castagnola, proved to be an entertaining game, in which lady luck turned against the team from Massachusetts. The Cambiaso-Castagnola horsepower was a little too much for the Heguy brothers. The final score was 13–9 in favor of Outback, a team that took its third Open Championship.

The World Cup: Gould, Michelob, Piaget, Cadillac and Regina

William Ylvisaker, an individual always ready to implement ideas to benefit the game, was the prime mover in establishing an all-professional high-goal competition offering a

$25,000 purse. As chairman of Gould, Inc., a billion-dollar electronics corporation, Ylvisaker was in a position to spearhead the project under the banner of the Polo Corporation of the Americas, with the enthusiastic support of Paul Butler, who provided the venue for the competition at his Oak Brook Polo Club. The other sponsors were John Coleman, from Fremont Hotel, and Donald Little, from Kidder Peabody.

Two teams were selected to do battle for the first Gould World Cup. The White team, Corky Linfoot, Tommy Wayman, Red Armour and Bart Evans, added up to 30-goals. The Blues, Dr. William Linfoot, Charles Smith, Roy Barry and Joe Barry, had a total of 31-goals. Nothing like that had been seen in the United States since the trial matches for the Cup of the Americas.

It was a fast game, characterized by short intervals between chukkers, quick knock-ins and throw-ins, and best of all, only seven fouls called on each team. In the sixth chukker, Corky Linfoot tied the game at 7-all, only to have his father score to give the Blues the lead, once more. A 40-yard penalty with less than 30 seconds left on the clock allowed Tommy Wayman to send the match into overtime.

In the sudden death period, Bart Evans, White's Back, saved a certain goal with a neat backhander inches from the goal line. In the subsequent play, Red Armour scored the winning goal for the Whites. It was a marvelous exhibition of polo, in front of a crowd of 8,000. It was a huge success.

Next year the total purse went up to $150,000 with two-thirds of the total amount donated by oilman and polo player Carlton Beal.[12] The lure of greenbacks attracted six teams: Chapaleufú (38-goals) and Nueva Escocia (33-goals) from Argentina, Rancho Portales (30) from Mexico, and three American teams, California (28), San Antonio (25) and Texas (33 goals). The draw was conducted to ensure that an American team and a foreign team would meet in the finals. The two highest rated teams, Chapaleufú and Texas, drew byes into the semifinals.

Nueva Escocia, with Ezequiel Fernández Guerrico, Eduardo Moore, Eduardo Novillo Astrada and Jorge Tanoira, defeated Rancho Portales, with the sponsor Francisco Olazábal, Gastón Dorignac, Juan "Pierrou" Gassiebayle and Francisco Dorignac, by 8 goals to six. In the second preliminary California, with Corky Linfoot, Memo Gracida, Antonio Herrera and Bart Evans, bested San Antonio 12–8. Stewart Armstrong,

Tommy Wayman was the first American 10-goaler since the days of Bob Skene and Cecil Smith. His play reminded old men of the golden days.

Héctor "Cacho" Merlos, Daniel González and Charlie Armstrong played for San Antonio.

On to the semifinals, where Texas beat California 9–4 to meet Chapaleufú, a 14–7 winner over Nueva Escocia, in the final game, scheduled for a week later. The rains came in earnest in mid-week, raising serious doubts as to whether it would be possible to hold the match. A postponement was not viable because the Argentines had commitments in the high-goal Argentine season. Three helicopters were contracted to hover over the polo ground and the show was on. In spite of a heavy field, the game moved along, helped immensely by the two umpires, Maj. Ronald Ferguson and Allan Scherer, who kept fouls to the minimum being slightly more permissive than usual, without losing control of the game. At no time there was any question about the umpiring.

Texas jumped to a two-goal led in the first chukker, only the see the scoreboard at two-all in the second. The game was a tie, 4-all, in the third period, and then Chapaleufú began to pull away for a 10–7 victory. It was the best polo seen in the United States in a long time; however, only half as many spectators watched the game, compared to the previous year. Gonzalo Tanoira was the player of the match and Tommy Wayman's Orphan got the best pony award.

After a one-year hiatus due to lack of sponsorship the World Cup was resumed in 1979 at the new Palm Beach Polo Club in Wellington, Florida. The brewery Anheuser-Busch was the new sponsor, so the title was changed to Michelob World Cup.

Five teams with a minimum 26-goal handicap competed for the $150,000 purse: Anadariya from Nigeria had Usman Dantata with Argentines Ezequiel Fernández Guerrico, Eduardo Moore and Gonzalo Pieres. Coronel Suárez, the perennial champion from Argentina, featured Horacio Araya, Ernesto Trotz, Juan Carlos Harriott, Jr., and Celestino Garrós. Retama had Julian Hipwood, Memo Gracida, Antonio Herrera and Steve Gose, while San Antonio sent Stewart Armstrong, Cacho Merlos, Daniel González and Charlie Armstrong. The big American hope was USA-Texas, with Bart Evans, Tommy Wayman, Red Armour and Joe Barry, a 34-goal combination that matched Coronel Suárez' aggregate.

San Antonio was out of contention early in the round robin, losing to both Anadariya and Retama. Both winning teams substituted freely introducing higher-rated substitutes. Although a legal practice because the games were played on the flat, it nonetheless created some ill will.[13] Anadariya continued to substitute to such an extent that that by the time they were out of the competition no fewer than seven players had been on the field.

The two strongest teams, USA-Texas and Coronel Suárez, met the winners of each round robin in the semifinals. USA-Texas beat Retama 11–4 and Coronel Suárez won over Anadariya 10–5. On to the final, where Coronel Suárez squandered leads of 4–0, 6–2 and missed a 40-yard penalty in overtime. Bart Evans scored the winning goal; Celestino Garrós was MVP and George Haas' Oscuro was chosen best playing pony.

There was much jubilation among the American fans with this result, since the four winning players were on the anointed team to do battle for the Cup of the Americas later that year. Sage Harold "Chico" Barry was more cautious: "It had to give them a boost, but when they get there it'll be a different story."[14]

The entries for the 1980 Michelob World Cup numbered four. Horacio Araya, Daniel González, Juan Carlos Harriott and Celestino Garrós returned with a team named El Malón (The Indian Raid), while Usman Dantata sponsored a Nigerian team, Hallal, with Julian Hipwood, Gonzalo Pieres, Gonzalo Tanoira and Antonio Herrera. The other teams were

Macondo, from Colombia, with Jaime Serrano, Horacio Heguy, Héctor Merlos and Francisco de Narváez, and the previous year's winners, now under the Retama banner. Three of the world's 10-goalers were in action at Palm Beach Polo.

This time the format was a straight elimination one, with the losers playing for the third spot. Hallal showed its mettle in the first round, when they defeated Macondo 12–5. In the second game, Retama, the probable team for the Cup of the Americas to be played on home ground within a month, Armour, Wayman, Barry and Evans, defeated El Malón by 8 goals to five. It was not a good tournament for Harriott's team, because in the match for third place Macondo came up on top.

The final game was a grand spectacle. Prince Charles was there; ABC television was there, *Time* magazine was there, as well as a capacity crowd. As to the game, with the Cup of the Americas looming near, the American partisans were the recipients of an electric shock. Not that Hallal was expected to win; it was the way they achieved the feat. After a quick goal by Armour from a throw-in, Hallal scored nine consecutive goals before Retama got their next one on a penalty conversion. Joe Barry kept Retama's hopes alive with six penalty conversions, not missing a single one. The final score was Hallal 13, Retama 8.

Four teams contested the 1981 World Cup. At 35-goals, Macondo was the highest handicapped team with the brothers Horacio and Alberto Heguy, Alfredo Harriott and patron Jaime Serrano. Boehm-Palm Beach had Alfonso Pieres, Julian Hipwood, Gonzalo Tanoira and Howard Hipwood, a 34-goal combine. White Birch, with Carlos Gracida, Gonzalo Pieres, Eduardo Moore and Héctor "Juni" Crotto, added up to 32-goals, and finally, Rolex Abercrombie & Kent were rated at 30-goals, with Geoffrey Kent, Antonio Herrera, Alfredo Harriott and Stuart MacKenzie.

Rolex A&K surprised Macondo with a 9–6 win and Boehm-Palm Beach dispatched White Birch 8–7 in a closely fought game. The final match was won by Boehm-Palm Beach by 14 goals to 8. For the third year in a row, Gonzalo Tanoira was voted MVP and Negrita, played by Alfonso Pieres, got the Best Playing Pony award.

Boehm successfully defended its title in 1982 and Gonzalo Tanoira was again the MVP. Peter Brant's White Birch, with Cacho Merlos, Gonzalo Pieres, Eduardo Moore and Juni Crotto, won its bracket with victories over Rolex A&K (13–8) and Piaget (11–6). Piaget overwhelmed Rolex A&K by 17 goals to three in the battles of the watches. In the other bracket Boehm, with Alfonso Pieres, Julian Hipwood, Gonzalo Tanoira and Howard Hipwood, defeated Macondo 10–2 and Retama 11–6; Macondo qualified for the third place match with a 9–8 win over Retama. In an excellent final game, marred by charges of biased umpiring, Boehm defeated White Birch 13–11.

Piaget became the World's Cup new sponsor in 1983, an event that attracted four teams. Anadariya, once more sponsored by Usman Dantata, had Carlos Gracida, Julian Hipwood, Memo Gracida and Howard Hipwood. Boehm–Palm Beach presented Juan Martín Zavaleta, Gonzalo Tanoira and Celestino Garrós. Prudential-Bache Securities had Jake Sieber, Alan Kent, Wicky and Podger El-Effendi. White Birch–A&K, jointly sponsored by Peter Brant and Geoffrey Kent, fielded Benjamín Araya, Antonio Herrera, Gonzalo Pieres and Bart Evans.

Anadariya edged out Boehm-Palm Beach 10–9 and White Birch defeated Prudential-Bache Securities. In the finals, Anadariya beat White Birch by 10 goals to eight. Julian Hipwood was chosen MVP, and Phyllis, owned by Peter Brant and ridden by Benjamín Araya, was Best Playing Pony.

The usual number of teams, four, entered the 1984 contest. The Concord, a 33-goal team bearing the name of one of Piaget's watch brands, with Benjamín Araya, Tommy Wayman, Owen Rinehart and Joe Barry, found the Broilers a pesky rival in the first game. A 32-goal combination, Alan Kent from England, Alfonso Pieres, Cristián Laprida, and Juan Martín Zavaleta, took the game away from Concord with a 10–8 victory. Boehm, the team of the two Gracida and the two Hipwood brothers, defeated Four Flags in an interesting match 14–10. Four Flags, with Charles Armstrong from the United States, Rubén Gracida from Mexico, Fortunato Gómez Romero from Argentina, and Pakistani Podger El-Effendi, trailed 5–1 at the end of the first chukker, a differential they were unable to discount for the rest of the game. Julian Hipwood broke his thumb in the fourth chukker, courtesy of Fortunato's mallet; he was replaced by Jesús "Chuy" Báez.

The heavily favored Boehm team flew in Antonio Herrera to replace Julian Hipwood in the finals. With the game tied at four-all at halftime, the rains and Boehm's surge appeared simultaneously. The final score was 11–7 for the porcelain makers.

The year 1985 was the first of four successive wins by White Birch Farms, from Greenwich in Connecticut. Only the visiting Tramontana from England stopped White Birch's string of victories, which were continued with yet another championship in 1989. Three Pieres brothers, Paul, Alfonso and Gonzalo, with Peter Brant at Back, took the first title. The same team won in 1986, defeating Retama 8–7 in the finals.

In 1987, it was with 5-goaler Juan José Boote, whose ancestors the Gibson brothers had started playing polo in Argentina at estancia Los Yngleses about 1887, in the Number 1 position replacing Paul Pieres. They defeated Cadillac, with Bill Ylvisaker, Memo Gracida, Carlos Gracida and Dale Smicklas, by 8 goals to six.

A year later, future superstar Mariano Aguerre was in the Number 1 slot, helping White Birch in gathering its fourth consecutive World Cup title. Rated at 4-goals, Aguerre was named the finals MVP.

A new sponsor, Cadillac, became the marquee name for the 1989 World Cup. Only three teams entered the 30-goal tournament. Greek shipping magnate Anthony Embiricos crossed the Atlantic Ocean from England to play with Carlos and Memo Gracida and 7-goaler Hector Galindo. His team Tramontana had been quite successful in Britain, winning Cowdray Park's Gold Cup four years in a row. The other entrant was the Palm Beach All-Stars, with Charlie Bostwick, Bil Walton, Red Armour and Alex Garrahan. They drew White Birch in the first game, and lost 15–7. Stewart Armstrong from Texas was added to the White Birch team. Most of the match was played in heavy rain, with Tramontana defeating White Birch 10–8. The streak was broken.

Only three teams, Michelob, Tramontana and White Birch, entered the 1990 World Cup. Michelob, with Charlie Bostwick, Mike Azzaro, Owen Rinehart and Dale Smicklas, defeated Tramontana, with Roberto González Gracida, Carlos Gracida, Memo Gracida and Anthony Embiricos, in the first match. The final result was not totally unexpected, but the goal differential certainly was; Michelob doubled-up Tramontana 14–7. Therefore, White Birch, with 19-year-old Bautista Heguy at 7-goals, Mariano Aguerre, Gonzalo Pieres and Peter Brant, was a 31-goal combination, one goal above the limit. In his column "Personally Speaking," Ami Shinitzky took a strong exception to the change:

> It had been announced, as in prior years, as a 30-goal event. In order to accommodate something for someone, however, the level was raised (allegedly by consent) to 32-goals just weeks before. What transpired next was a nasty turmoil among the teams and the host club, with accusations and threats of boycott that weren't resolved until the eve of the draw.
> On the day of the final, the club was again abuzz with fresh rumors, later confirmed; one

team Michelob, agreed in exchange for a guaranteed share of the prize money ($5,000 per player) to allow the other, White Birch, to come to the field as a 31-goal team. The club, peculiarly, chose to look the other way.[15]

This note provoked a letter to the editor from Charlie Bostwick, stating that he had not received any money.[16]

Nevertheless, White Birch went on to take the match 13–9 and with it, their fifth World Cup in six years. The magnificent Levicu, a bay mare owned by Peter Brant and ridden by Gonzalo Pieres, was given the Best Playing Pony Award, while Bautista Heguy was MVP.

The 1991 World Cup was notable for several occurrences. The first was the American debut of 15-year-old Adolfito Cambiaso, a 6T (for temporary) goal handicap player on Adam Lindemann's Cellular One team. For the first time since 1984, White Birch was not in the final game; furthermore, they did not win any of the other high-goal tournaments in Palm Beach. Neither did the vaunted Diables Bleus, winners of the last three U.S. Open championships, nor the Gracida brothers, although Carlos took the 22-Goal Prince of Wales Cup at Windsor Polo Club in Vero Beach.

It was a season of transition, with perennial bridesmaid Michelob winning the World Cup, at last. Philip Lake, Martín Zubía, Owen Rinehart and Dale Smicklas outlasted Les Diables Bleus in the finals by 11 goals to seven.

Regina became the fifth sponsor of the World Cup. Rolex A&K, after suffering the embarrassment of losing in the first round of their own Rolex Gold Cup — "very bad timing," conceded team captain Geoffrey Kent — took the World Cup by defeating White Birch 10–9 in the finals. Geoffrey Kent, Adolfo Cambiaso, Carlos Gracida and Juni Crotto were on the team.

In 1993, Budweiser bested White Birch in a boring, defensive game. There were six teams, Cellular One, Michelob/CS Brooks, Rolex A&K and Les Diables Bleus.

The 1994 season in Florida was highlighted by a controversy regarding temporary handicaps, especially Ignacio "Nachi" Heguy's 7T. Marty LeGrand, who succeeded Ami Shinitzky as editor of the magazine *Polo*, wrote an editorial pointing out that Nachi Heguy, who had been temporarily rated at 7-goals during the previous Palm Beach season, had been raised to 8-goals in Argentina; his team in America had won 12 of the first 13 games played.[17] Patron Adolphus Busch, IV, and the U.S.P.A. National Handicap Committee chairman Lester Armour, III, took opposite points of view in the same issue of *Polo*. Busch pointed out the absurdity of waiting four months before the U.S.P.A. raised Heguy's handicap to 9-goals, He also voiced his concern that such practice could contribute to the loss of new and established patrons committed to polo.

In reply, Red Armour pointed out that no request for review reached him until April. Furthermore, Armour felt that his position as umpire at most high-goal games during the Palm Beach polo season might look inappropriate if he took action single-handedly.[18]

From a neutral point of view, it is apparent that a hard-to-explain absolute lack of communication among club managers, team sponsors and U.S.P.A. officials led to the controversy, fueled by a culture of "I thought somebody else was taking care of the matter."

Nevertheless, with Nachi still at 7-goals, Les Diables Bleus beat White Birch 17–11, and defending champions Budweiser 13–9, to face Cellular One in the finals. Nachi Heguy, Carlos Gracida, Memo Gracida and Guy Wildenstein took the World Cup by 12 goals to seven.

Only five teams, Henryk de Kwiatkowski's Calumet, Les Diables Bleus, Redlegs, Villagers and White Birch, participated in the 1995 World Cup. The finals pitted Calumet, with Henryk and his son Stephan alternating at number, and the three brothers Pepe, Ignacio and Eduardo Heguy, versus White Birch. The team from Greenwich had Australian Nick Manifold, Adolfito Cambiaso, Mariano Aguerre and Peter Brant and Todd Offen alternating at Back. Cambiaso's 11 goals powered White Birch to a 16–12 win, its sixth World Cup conquest.

The World Cup was contested only two more times; Isla Carroll took the trophy in both opportunities. Two teams entered in 1996, Isla Carroll and White Birch. Isla Carroll, with Mike Azzaro, the Gracida brothers and John Goodman, won the cup from White Birch's Neil Hirsch, Bautista Heguy, Mariano Aguerre and Adolfo Cambiaso by a single tally, 12–11.

The same two powerhouses met in 1997 to decide the winner. The game went into overtime, Isla Carroll winning 15–14. Hector Galindo, Mike Azzaro, Memo Gracida and John Goodman played for Isla Carroll, while sponsor Neil Hirsch, Mariano Aguerre, Adolfo Cambiaso and Bartolomé "Lolo" Castagnola represented White Birch.

The World Cup then faded away from sight after 21 uninterrupted years as Americas' highest polo competition.

The Rest of the High-Goal Tournaments

The U.S.P.A. Gold Cup was created in 1974 as a second tournament to be played next to the U.S. Open Championship. Initially held at Milwaukee to complement the U.S. Open at Oak Brook, it was moved to Florida as the crown jewel of the winter season. Both Royal Palm in Boca Raton and Palm Beach Polo in Wellington were the venues. In 2002, the Greenwich Polo Club in Connecticut became literally the home of the Gold Cup, when local team White Birch took the trophy all three years.

The Gold Cup site was then awarded to New Bridge Polo Club in Aiken for a couple of years before returning to Florida as one of the unofficial Triple Crowns of polo at International Polo Club. In its heyday the Gold Cup attracted many more entries than the U.S. Open at Retama, Lexington and the California desert. It was "the" tournament to win, in spite of its single elimination format. The lure of gold attracted other high-goal handicap tournaments, such as Royal Palm's International Gold Cup, Palm Beach Polo's International Open, Gold Cup of the Americas and Cartier's Polo Challenge.

Through the years, White Birch is the team with most wins in the Gold Cup, a total of an even dozen to this date. Retama, Cellular One, Boca Raton and Crab Orchard have taken the trophy twice.

The Silver Cup, the Oldest U.S.P.A. Tournament

Originally known as the Junior Championship, the Silver Cup was presented in 1900 by Samuel Warren, the captain of the Dedham Polo Club. It has been played for without interruptions, with the exception of the years of the two world wars. The venue for the Silver Cup changed through the passage of time; by 1976 it was held in Texas.

The most successful teams during this period of time were those fielded by the Busch family under the banners of Grant's Farms Manor and Bud Light, with a total of six wins along an eight-year span. John and Leigh-Anne Hall achieved three victories with their own

Old Pueblo and Pueblo Viejo, a number matched by Steve Gose's Retama. Norman Brinker's teams, Willow Bend and Chili's, took the Silver Cup thrice; Wilson Ranch, sponsored by Willie B. Wilson, had wins in 1976 and 1978; while Fort Worth, with Jay and Matthew Upchurch, had back-to-back victories in 1988–89. Another two-time winner was John Goodman's Isla Carroll.

In 2006, the U.S.P.A. awarded the Silver Cup to Royal Palm Polo Club in Florida. BTA, from Midland, Texas, took the tournament. The next year it was moved to Aiken, where Maureen Brennan's Goose Creek based at the old Llangollen grounds near Middleburg in Virginia took the Silver Cup three years in a row, with Adam Snow and the Zeger brothers from Chile, José "Cote" and Martín. Llangollen was Jock Whitney's present to his wife, Mary Elizabeth Altemus. It has now been restored to its former glory by the Brennan family.

The U.S. Handicap — C.V. Whitney Cup

When the U.S. Open Championship was held at Oak Brook the Butler National Handicap occasionally served as a sort of handicap tournament for the team entering the U.S. Open. Retama Polo Center then became the host for the Open and a new tournament, named the U.S. handicap, was formally instated for the teams entering the U.S. Open Championship. A small cup was presented to the captain of the winning team as well as individual prizes to the team's players. This changed when the site was moved to Lexington. A large trophy, engraved with the name C.V. Whitney Cup, was presented to the winning team. The U.S.P.A. Year Book enumerates the winners of the C.V. Whitney Cup retroactively to 1979, when Tulsa took the Handicap Tournament at Retama. White Birch with five wins and Jack Oxley's Fort Lauderdale with four are the most successful teams in the U.S. Handicap.

The big loser in all this is the Monty Waterbury Cup, the third oldest official U.S.P.A. trophy in active competition, which dates back to 1922 and was the tournament played on handicap by the teams participating in the U.S. Open until 1953. When the site of the U.S. Open Championship was transferred to Oak Brook, the Monty Waterbury Cup, always played under the aegis of the Meadow Brook Club, having been presented by James Waterbury's friends at the club, fell into relative obscurity until its revival in 1975.

Polo in the Northeast

The game of polo remained strong in the Northeastern regions of the country.

In Rhode Island, where polo in Newport dates back to 1876, Dan Keating revived the game at a ground on Glen Farm, in Portsmouth. The club hosts a popular international series against visiting foreign teams every summer. The club affiliated with the U.S.P.A. under the hallowed name of Westchester Polo Club — the first polo club in America. After its days of glory, the original institution lingered on until World War II. If there is any link between both clubs, it is a very tenuous one indeed.

Myopia Hunt Club in Massachusetts is the oldest club affiliated with the U.S.P.A., an occurrence that happened in 1890. For several years Myopia hosted the East Coast Open and the Cameron Forbes Cup as the main tournaments, along a busy season that extended from late May to mid–September. Nick Roldán, whose father Raúl is from an Argentine polo family that started playing in the 1920s, showed early promise on the Gibney Field. Nick realized such auspicious beginnings by being the youngest player to take the U.S. Open Championship with the Escue team, a 9-goal rating and a place on the Team U.S.A. in the 2009 Westchester Cup. The auld rivalry with Fairfield County Hunt remained active as ever until the late 1990s, when polo at Rudkin Field in Westport faded into the sunset.

In Connecticut, the mantle was taken over by the Greenwich Polo Club in Conyers Farms. Peter Brant's concoction hosted a few of the matches in the U.S. Open Championship and the full schedule for the Gold Cup. The America's Championship, for three years at 36-goals plus level — the highest handicap event in the world of polo outside of Argentina — drew national television coverage, but regrettably ended its course early because of lack of meaningful sponsorship after a sterling start.

Polo at Greenwich, White Birch's home ground, featured the top handicap tournaments during the summer season. The Tommy Glynn Cup, first started at Fairfield in 1975, moved to Greenwich and is still one of the main events at Greenwich Polo Club. Its great players included the Pieres brothers, Alfonso, Gonzalo and Paul, Benjamin Araya, Ernesto Trotz, Milo Fernández Araujo, Bautista, Gonzalo and Horacio Heguy. It witnessed the development of Mariano Aguerre from a 3-goaler into a perennial 10-goal handicap player under the tutelage of Héctor Barrantes and Gonzalo Pieres, who would became his father-in-law. A youthful Adolfito Cambiaso wore White Birch's white and green colors, reaching the finals of the U.S. Open.

Polo in the northern reaches was played at Quechee, Sugarbush in Waitsfield, Vermont, and at several clubs in the Quebec Province, such as Montreal, and Ganaraska in Ontario. Maine had the Down East Polo Club in Falmouth, organized in 1984, but now unfortunately inactive.

Upstate New York had the resurgent Saratoga Polo Club in Saratoga Springs, which developed a crowded calendar in August with the venerable Monty Waterbury Cup as the season's highlight.

The Skaneateles Polo Club had been started on the shores of Cayuga Lake by the Winkelman family: father Dwight, son Peter and son-in-law David Chase. It is now continued by Martin Cregg, David Chase's son-in-law. Nearby was the Cortland Appleknockers, which had veteran Pedro Silvero— winner of the U.S. Open in 1947 and 1951— as resident professional. Other New York polo clubs included Chuck Elmes' Blue Sky, Buckleigh, Gardnertown, Central New York, Mashomack, Pawling and Western New York.

Villages Polo Club was established by Pete Bostwick and his sons Charlie and Ricky in Gilbertsville. It had its moments of glory, hosting the Monty Waterbury Cup and other tournaments. When the Bostwick siblings gave up polo, the club disappeared from the U.S.P.A. roster.

Long Island had Bridgehampton, Southampton and West Hills, as well as the renamed Meadowbrook Polo Club in Westbury, now run by Luis Rinaldini.

The Eastern Circuit

The long tradition of the game from New Jersey to Virginia remained vibrant during the final quarter of the twentieth century. Virginia by far counted the largest number of clubs, more than a dozen, while the oldest was Brandywine in Pennsylvania, dating back to 1951.

In Virginia, the Middleburg Polo Club was started in 1961. The polo grounds are in Amissville. Also in Amissville is the Kievit Polo Club. Near Middleburg, the Foxlease Polo Club, at the Steiner family property in Upperville, has been in operation since 2000. Roseland was started by David King at the family vineyard in Crozet. Chester B. Fannon's Rappahannock in Laurel Mills was another polo club in Virginia.

In Charlottesville, home of the successful University of Virginia male and female polo teams, Robert Rinehart with help from UVA's coach Louis Lopez started the Charlottesville Polo Club in 1982. Tayloe Dameron founded the Shirley Plantation Polo Club in Charles City. Finally, the Virginia Beach Polo Club was started in 1987 at Alpha Omega Farm in the rural Pungo area of Virginia Beach.

The main polo clubs in Maryland were the Potomac, first started by Thomas Dowd and later taken over by Joe Muldoon, home ground of his successful Gone Away Farm team, and Dan Colhoun's Maryland Polo Club in Monkon.

There were several clubs in New Jersey, among them Amwell Valley, started by W. Bryce Thompson, Brookview in Freehold, Colts Neck, Cowtown in Woodstown, Far Hills in Lebanon, Shannon Hill in Liberty Corner and Tinicum Park in Bucks County. Most of these clubs played each other as well against Bucks County and Lancaster in Pennsylvania at a 12-goal level.[19]

Polo in Pennsylvania was maintained by veteran clubs such as Brandywine, Lancaster, Mallet Hill and West Shore. A new club, Burnt Chimney in Coatesville, was added to the ranks in 1999. It is of note that Alfred E. "Fred" Fortugno served as Circuit Governor without interruption from 1972 to 2009, a most unusual record of commitment to the game of polo.

Polo in the Southland

With the exception of Florida, Aiken was the main venue for polo in the Southern states. The winter season was extended to the month of May and later from mid–September to early November. The 302 Polo Club was started in 1999. Jack and Martha Daniels' old Camden was joined by Midfield Polo Club, helping to maintain polo alive in that town. In Charleston, Palmetto and Quinby both joined the U.S.P.A. in the 1990s.

Tennessee had plenty of polo. The Johnston family kept the flag flying at Bendabout Farm, while Memphis, Nashville — including Sassafras Polo Club — and Franklin boasted busy polo clubs.

Most of the polo in Georgia was centered on Atlanta. The Atlanta Polo Club, established in 1969 by Adolph Northern, Jr., and Ben Smith, Jr., changed its name to Atlanta Columns Drive in 1985. Play was near the Chattahoochee River; then the club was served notice that the site would become a National Park. Dolph Orthwein resorted to moving the club to his private ground in Vinings, and the club underwent another name change, to Atlanta Vinings.

The Columbus Polo Club, located in that town, joined the U.S.P.A. in 1979, with the Upatoi Cup as the main tournament.

The polo boom that started in the 1980s gave rise to several new clubs in Georgia. Evans Polo Club started in 1982; in 1986, Pat Domeniconi formed the Atlanta Southeastern some 40 miles from Atlanta on Route 400. Harbor Polo Club, in Alpharetta, was active from 1989 to 1992, while Scuppernong, also in Alpharetta, was formed by Jack Cashin in

The Father/Son Tournament. Skeeter Johnston, Skey Johnston, Jules Romfh and Jay Romfh.

1988 and remains in activity. Foxhall, in Carrolltown, was active from 1984 until 1989, when it resigned, only to seek re-affiliation in 1995, now with grounds in Douglasville. Rose Hill Plantation in Savannah, and Golden Isles on St. Simon Island were two other clubs in activity in the 1980s.

The next decade showed a slowdown in new clubs; only Mount Vernon in Monroe and Red Hills in Thomasville joined the U.S. Polo Association.

The game of polo in Alabama was restricted to the Birmingham Polo Club in Shelby County and the Blue Water Creek Polo Club in Muscle Shoals.

In North Carolina, the Charlotte Polo Club was reformed in 1985 by Charlie Carson, a grandson of James H. Carson who had founded the original club in 1924. North Carolina Polo Club in Louisburg, a revived Pinehurst in that golfing resort, and Chukker Downs in Rougemont were the other polo clubs in North Carolina.

Mississippi had the Gulfport Polo Club since 1972. It was joined by the Jackson Polo Club in 1984.

In Louisiana one found the Central Louisiana Polo Club in Opelousas, Innisfree in Folsom, Louisiana Polo Club, also located in Folsom, the short-lived North Shore in LaComb, Palmetto in Benton, and a revived Sugar Oaks in New Iberia which joined the Baton Rouge Polo Club.

The Centenary of Polo in the United States

Among the celebrations commemorating the beginning of polo in America, a Centennial Polo Game took place on the Morris Memorial Field in New York Harbor's Governors Island in July 1976.[20] Taking advantage of free entrance a large crowd took the ferry from Manhattan and overflowed the safety zone along the sidelines, making play difficult. Admiral William F. Rea, III, in 1812 naval uniform regalia, presented the trophies to the winning Fairfield Hunt team of Lyle Graham, Horace Laffaye, William Whitehead and George Haas, Jr.

The National Museum of Polo and Hall of Fame

Tucked in the corner of Lake Worth Road and Lyons Road, in the western fringes of the town of Lake Worth in Florida, stands the National Museum of Polo and Hall of Fame, a unique institution in the world of polo. The concept of a polo museum was started by Philip Iglehart, a 6-goal player and a winner of the U.S. Open Championship. Mr. Iglehart was joined in his endeavor by H. Jeremy Chisholm, a polo player and sporting art dealer; Leverett Miller, also a polo player at nearby Gulfstream Club; and George Sherman, a former chairman of the U.S. Polo Association.

The first site of the Museum of Polo was in Lexington, Kentucky, where it opened its doors in 1988 hosting a temporary exhibition. Construction of the present site in Florida began in 1996 and was completed one year later. Benefactor Philip Iglehart donated one-third of the land, while the Beal family, S.K. Johnston, Jr., the Orthwein family and John T. Oxley subscribed for the balance.

The institution is a self-sustaining, not-for-profit educational organization, totally independent from the U.S. Polo Association. Its mission statement commits the Board of Directors to ensure that the Museum of Polo remain dedicated to fostering an appreciation of the development of the game by collecting, preserving, exhibiting and interpreting its collections, as well as honoring those who have made outstanding contributions to the sport.

The permanent collections

Philip Iglehart leading Clavel. In later years, Mr. Iglehart was the leading light in establishing the National Museum of Polo and Hall of Fame.

are most impressive. Place of pride corresponds to the U.S. Open Championship trophy, crafted by artist Sally Farnham and presented by sportsman Joseph B. Thomas. Also on exhibit are the main U.S. Polo Association trophies, such as the Gold Cup, the C.V. Whitney Cup for the U.S. Handicap Championship, the Monty Waterbury Cup, the Hall of Fame Cup, and the oldest U.S.P.A trophy offered for competition, the Silver Cup, originally the Junior Championship trophy that dates back to 1900. There are also hundreds of polo trophies, from a 1884 cup awarded for a pairs tournament, donated by Mrs. Charles Cary Rumsey, Jr., to contemporary prizes.

Among the international trophies, the exhibits contain a gilded replica of the Westchester Cup that was the trophy for the International Challenge tournament at John Oxley's Royal Palm Polo Club, as well as a smaller version in silver manufactured by Tiffany & Co., the designers of the original Westchester Cup in 1886. The Federation of International Polo's Centennial Cup, presented to the U.S.P.A. in 1990 to commemorate its one-hundredth birthday, is also displayed. The Lawrence J. Fitzpatrick Bowl was presented to Larry Fitzpatrick by the players and alternates of the 1911 American international team in appreciation of his care and conditioning of their ponies for the Westchester Cup.

The polo works of art in the collection are impressive, starting with a Chinese scroll from the T'ang dynasty presented by Leverett Miller, Harry Payne Whitney's grandson. There are many paintings by such notable artists as Larrence McKenna, Alejandro Moy, Gustav Muss-Arnoldt, Thomas Pearl, Sam Savitt and Franklin Voss. Melinda Brewer has painted all the polo ponies honored with the Horses to Remember Award; they are displayed in two separate walls. The Hall of Fame Wall is covered with plaques identifying the inductees and their achievements.

Polo bronzes include works by Herbert Haseltine, Georges Malissard, Rob Roenisch and Charles Rumsey. Finally, the Philip L.B. Iglehart Library contains hundreds of books, videos, old films, magazines, programs and posters. The library is open to researchers in quest of information about the game of polo.

The Museum's Director, George DuPont, Jr., and Brenda Lynn, the Director of Development, are always available to conduct guided tours, an incredible experience that include temporary exhibitions, mallets from the 19th century, Tommy Hitchcock's wooden horse and innumerable polo artifacts covering the entire span of the world of polo.[21]

CHAPTER 23

The Literature of Polo in the United States

History and Development

The most important work about the game in the United States is *American Polo* by Newell Bent, a 2-goal handicap player from Boston. This work was published in 1929 and set the standard for future writers on the subject. With topics ranging from the game's origins to famous polo players, passing through breeding the polo pony, international matches, the handicap system and the penalties after fouling, this book became the bible of the game in America.

The next significant effort was *The Endless Chukker*, published in 1978 to coincide with the centenary of polo in America. It offers a large number of illustrations, many unrelated to polo but illustrating significant moments in the history of these United States. A specially bound edition was also offered and it has become a collector's item. Ami Shinitzky, the creator and long-time editor of *Polo Magazine*, and Don Follmer produced an entertaining volume.

Chronologically, *The Book of Sport*, edited by William Patten, another player from the Boston area, is the first publication to address polo in this country. The chapters on polo are written by luminaries such as John E. Cowdin, Henry L. Herbert and Foxhall Keene. This work gives useful and first-hand information about the early development of polo in America.

Books addressing regional polo include Addison Geary Smith's *Mallet and Hounds*, published under the pseudonym "Addison Geary." It covers polo and hunting in the Buffalo and Rochester areas in upstate New York.

Sports in Norfolk County, by Allan Forbes, describes in exquisite detail equestrian sports in Boston's neighboring Norfolk County, with plenty of historical illustrations and fascinating vignettes from a participant in those early matches in New England. Just as *Not a History of the Dedham Polo Club*, this book is a must read for those interested in polo in New England.

The well-known haberdashers Brooks Brothers published in 1927 the booklet *Polo*, which at four and one-half by three inches is the smallest book on the game.

Frank Milburn, Devereux' grandson, wrote an interesting book, *The Emperor of Games*, from the vantage point of a member of a family with deep roots of polo in this country.

The latest addition to the history of the game in America is Horace Laffaye's *The Evolution of Polo*, a sociological study that includes much material about the development of the game in the United States.

Club Histories

There are a few works dedicated to put on the record the activities of several clubs that offered the game of polo as a choice pastime. The standard was set early on, when an unknown writer — probably Allan Forbes— hiding behind the curious pseudonym "Author Escaped," published *Not a History of the Dedham Polo Club*. It is, however, a detailed description of the polo activities in that ancient club, related with a fine sense of humor and a touch of irony. Nevertheless, it provides entertaining and accurate reading material. *Not a History of the Dedham Polo Club* is a rare book in the realm of polo and commands a high price when it appears for sale.

Club polo in New England has been well served by Allan Forbes in *Early Myopia*, a nice chronicle of the North Shore's golfing, polo and hunting institution. The story of this traditional club and its members was updated in 1975 by Edward Weeks' *Myopia*.

The game at Harvard College is related by Amos Tuck French, Class of 1885, in *Harvard Polo Club*, which provide much information on its origins and early years. Since French was one of the players, that has a strong flavor of personal knowledge of people, ponies and events. The book was dedicated to the memory of Raymond Rodgers Belmont, "one of the best." Only 50 copies were printed. A valuable reference work is *Harvard Polo Club 1883–1905*, which contains a list of every undergraduate that played at that university.

Cornell University is well served in Dr. Stephen Roberts' *Wearers of the C* and in *An Autobiographical History of Collegiate Polo and Its Players at Cornell University, 1919–1972 and Beyond*, an indispensable source for those interested in the development of collegiate polo.

The History of the Philadelphia Country Club, by Jane P. Alles, carefully relates polo events that occurred in Bala, until the game disappeared from the club. Polo merits a great deal of attention in *The History of the Rockaway Hunting Club*, a beautiful encased book by long-time and honorary member Dr. Benjamin Allison.

Polo in the Midwest receives special attention in J. Bland Van Urk's *The Horse, the Valley and the Chagrin Valley Hunt* and *The Story of Rolling Rock*. There are extensive references to several polo clubs in the region.

Recently published in 2009, *St. Louis Country Club— A Legacy of Sports* is a comprehensive history of the club that now stands as the second oldest polo club in America. The author is James F. Healey and the book itself is a gem in contents, including illustrations, paper quality and binding.

A wonderful book is *Nothing Could Be Finer*, a detailed chronicle of the game in Camden, South Carolina. The special, leather-bound edition is quite scarce. The author is John H. Daniels, author, benefactor, bibliophile and strong supporter of the game throughout his life, who represented Yale University in polo and played in Camden all his life. Mr. Daniels donated his extensive collection of sporting books to the National Sporting Library in Middleburg, Virginia, which in his honor created the John H. Daniels Fellowship, a coveted honor for researchers in the field of sports and games.

Polo in Colorado is well detailed in *The Grizzlies— A History: The Cheyenne Mountain Country Club*, by Marshall Sprague. The early days of the game in eastern Colorado and its further development in the Pike's Peak region are charmingly described.

Bucky King is a life-long resident in Wyoming. Her small book, *Big Horn Polo*, is the main resource about the game, from its introduction by British pioneers to the late twentieth century.

Another regional history is *55 Years of Polo in Minnesota 1922–1977*, by Orville Volkmann. Primarily, it is a book of clippings and letters, which are a good primary source of information. Only 200 copies were printed.

Geoff Shackleford, better known as a distinguished golf writer, produced the well-illustrated *The Riviera Country Club*, in Pacific Palisades, California. Although most of the work is about the royal and ancient game, there is abundant coverage of the vicissitudes of polo at Riviera.

Polo in the military is partially covered by C.R. Farmer in *Polo — The King of Games*, which includes notice of the game in the Philippine Islands and some garrisons in the United States.

Biographies and Autobiographies

This genre is surprisingly lean, considering the significant numbers of American polo players that achieved world-wide fame and glory. There are just four autobiographical tomes, perhaps a reflection of most polo players' reluctance to write about themselves and share their life's experiences.

The multi-talented Foxhall Parker Keene recorded his sporting memoirs in collaboration with Alden Hatch in *Full Tilt*, a Derrydale Press imprint. It is a personal view of Keene's spectacular trajectory, a series of events that Foxie himself described as "a life of pure delight." However, like many reminiscences written towards the last stages of human lifespan, facts are at times blurred. Nevertheless, it is an important record of sporting life in both the gilded age and the roaring twenties.

Carl Beal's *Into Polo* is a candid recount of the oilman and polo player who made such enormous contribution to the game.

An entertaining and informative set of books, written by Seymour H. Knox, Jr., *Polo Tales and Other Tales*, in two volumes, and *Other Tales in Other Years*, recount the Knox family's involvement in polo, since the early beginnings in Buffalo in the 1920s to the spectacular challenges for the Cup of the Americas in the 1970s. Other books on polo written by Shorty Knox and his son Norty are described in the Competitions section.

Clark Hetherington, a life-long supporter of polo in Oklahoma and active participant as well during the Florida season, recounted his experience as player, coach, club owner, university team mentor, administrator and much respected referee and Chief Umpire. The book's title is *Six Chukkers of Love*, honoring his unremitting love for his sweetheart at the University of Oklahoma and then wife. It is a well-written autobiography which depicts college life and sports at the outbreak of World War II, the struggles of the game in the immediate post-conflict period, and its eventual bloom across the United States.

Fred Daily, hotelier and a bastion of polo in Hawaii, tells about in the game on the islands as seen through the eyes of Moki, his beloved polo pony. *Polo Is a Four Letter Word* is an entertaining book, full of first-hand information and certainly a little treasure about polo in Hawaii.

Moving on to biographies, but still in Hawaii, Elizabeth Layton produced a detailed account on Ronnie Tongg's polo life. Describing in *The Golden Mallet* Tongg's career year by year, the author takes us in a whirlwind world tour, from California to Great Britain to Argentina.

One of the best biographical works is Nelson W. Aldrich, Jr.'s *Tommy Hitchcock — An*

American Hero. Drawing upon family archives and extensive research, this book is a careful and well-written account of Hitchcock's fascinating life and times.

Another short biographical study of Hitchcock is Nigel à Brassard's *Tommy Hitchcock — A Tribute,* which was privately published in England as a limited edition.

Blair Calvert wrote *Cecil Smith: Mr. Polo,* a biography that compares with Nelson Aldrich's superb work on Hitchcock. It is a literary feast that both American polo superstars are the subjects of outstanding biographies.

David E. Outerbridge, amateur golfer and writer, composed*Champion in a Man's World: The Biography of Marion Hollins.* This superior American athlete, who excelled at polo, golf and tennis, receives a high quality study of her fascinating life, from the glitter of a comfortable Long Island upbringing, to transatlantic voyages, polo at Aiken, Long Island and the Pacific Coast, her involvement in the creation of two superb golf courses, Cypress Point and Pasatiempo, to her sad end in California, almost destitute and totally forgotten. In this carefully researched biography, Marion Hollins, the best American sportswoman of the 1920s, finally receives that recognition she fully deserves.

The Whitney family, so prominent in polo circles from the late 1890s until the onset of World War II, has been the subject of several books. *The Whitneys,* by Edwin Hoyt, is a good reference source. Jeffrey L. Rodengen's *The Legend of Cornelius Vanderbilt Whitney,* commissioned by John Hendrickson and with a foreword by Marylou Whitney, paints a rosy picture of C.V.'s privileged life. The game of polo receives scant coverage.

Alex M. Robb wrote *The Sanfords of Amsterdam,* which contains much material about John Sanford and his son Stephen. Like many biographies commissioned by relatives, it must be read with an open but cautious mind regarding facts and opinions.

The latest addition is *Alan Corey — 9 Goals,* a compilation of photographs, clippings and other memorabilia performed by his youngest son, W. Russell Corey, a 6-goal international player. This work has been privately published; however, there is great demand that it be made available to the general public.

Profiles in Polo, edited by Horace Laffaye, consists of thirty-four biographical essays of individuals who had a significant impact on the game of polo. The American players Foxhall Keene, Harry Payne Whitney, Devereux Milburn, Tommy Hitchcock, Cecil Smith, Stewart Iglehart and Joe Barry are covered by different authors.[1] Bob Skene and Memo Gracida, a pair of 10-goalers that obtained American citizenship, are also included.

The latest biographical endeavor is *Prides Crossing,* a full-scale biography of Eleonora Randolph Sears, the pioneer sportswoman who excelled in several sports and games, including polo. The author is Peggy Miller Franck, who had access to primary sources so far untapped.

Finally, Alphons Stock's *Polo: International Sport* is a coffee-table size book with one or two-page biographical information and a full-page image of the player in question. It was produced in a small quantity, all volumes signed and numbered.

Competitions

Frank Gray Griswold, one of the pioneers of polo in America, wrote *The International Polo Cup* in 1928. This small book covers the story of the Westchester Cup from its inception in 1886 to the 1927 contest. The coverage is irregular. While the 1914 contest at Meadow Brook, the 1921 matches at Hurlingham and the 1927 series in America receive extensive coverage, the rest of the matches are only briefly mentioned and the 1902 series is totally ignored. Gray Griswold also recounted some of the Westchester Cup contests in his 8-volume *Sports on Land and Water*.

The English author Arthur W. Coaten, editor of *The Polo Magazine* from its beginnings in 1909 until its demise in 1939, covered the same subject in three volumes of *International Polo*, published between 1912 and 1922.

Works describing individual series include Nigel à Brassard's delightful *A Glorious Victory, a Glorious Defeat*, which meticulously describes the first challenge played after the Great War, on the Hurlingham grounds in 1921. It also describes the involvement of Buck's Club in English and international polo. This book was published privately in a limited edition of 500 copies to benefit charities.

The Knox family from East Aurora, New York is responsible for several books on polo. Patriarch Seymour Knox's first literary effort was *To B.A. and Back*, a fine book about the visit of a representative American squad to Buenos Aires, where they took both the Argentine Open Championship and the Cup of the Americas. Shorty Knox followed with *Aurora in England*, in which his own team had a successful London season, and then with *Aurora at Oak Brook*, in which he describes the preparation and competition for the 1957 U.S. Open Championship at Oak Brook, which ended with a heart-breaking loss in overtime.

His son Northrop R. Knox, the leader of two American challenges for the Cup of the Americas in 1966 and 1969, recorded in his diary the day-to-day activities of the American team in Argentina. These two volumes, *To B.A. and Back, Again* and *To B.A. and Back, Once More*, are a fascinating record of two gallant attempts to recover "La Copa" from the grasp of the powerful Argentine teams led by Juan Carlos Harriott, Jr.

Theory and Practice

The first book on the game was a slim volume by Hugh L. FitzPatrick titled *Equestrian Polo*. It saw the light of day in 1904, and contains advice on the game and equipment, how to play the game, and points about the ponies. Also included are the results of the Polo Association Championships and the ranking of players. Half the book is devoted to advertisements extolling the virtues of Spalding Athletic Goods, which is not at all surprising since the book was one of the Spalding Athletic Library, with offerings from Archery to Wrestling, at ten cents per volume.

Then came William Cameron Forbes' *As to Polo*, one of the most profound polo books ever written, which remains a classic of polo's literature a century after being first published. Cameron Forbes' penetrating discussion of the game — lines of running, angles of hitting-in, individual tasks, different phases of play — brought a startlingly new technical discussion to polo literature, raising it to a level of sophistication previously unheard of and rarely exceeded since. Yet for all his modern thinking, Cameron Forbes had little to say about individual players that excelled in his time. This classic went into six editions between 1911 and 1929, with minimal changes to the text, and it is now being reprinted by on-demand presses. *As to Polo* was translated into Spanish by Dr. Carlos Rodríguez Egaña, sometime president of the Argentine Polo Association, with the title *Manual de Polo*, bearing identical covers. There are also versions in Japanese and Thai.

As to Polo was an outgrowth of *A Manual of Polo*, a booklet written in 1910 by Forbes while governor-general of the Philippines. It was designed for the use of the Civil Government team; however, the U.S. Army 14th Cavalry, then stationed in Fort Stotsenburg,[2] requested and was granted permission to print this manual. *A Manual of Polo* offers many pearls: "Drive fiercely at the ball as though the whole game depended upon it" is a favorite one.[3] "Any two men riding parallel down the field side by side can be certain that they are playing very bad polo, probably inexcusable."[4] And finally, "...no stroke can possibly be successful unless the eye is glued to the ball at the time the mallet hits it."[5]

Walter B. Devereux, Jr., from the polo pioneering Colorado family, Princeton graduate and polo coach, wrote *Position and Team Play in Polo*, a well-known and frequently used book with several well-designed and clearly printed diagrams. The Spanish Marqués de Viana translated the book with the long-winded title *De la posición y forma de jugar un team y equipo en el polo*. The Spanish version is limited to 200 numbered copies.

Following the publication of Walter Devereux's opus in 1924, no other instructional books appeared in America until 1973, when Col. Harry Disston published *Beginning Polo*, a short but highly readable manual aimed at neophytes, but containing sound advice for more experienced players.

Frederic Roy, the Wellington-based journalist who performs a yeoman's work with his celebrated *The Morning Line*, wrote in 1993 *Your Polo Game*, a thoughtful and forward-looking treatise on arena, or stadium polo as the author prefers that variant of the game to be named. The work is nicely illustrated by Rollin McGrail, whose charming and whimsical drawings are a regular feature in *The New Yorker*.

An important treatise on the game and its ponies is Robert D. Lubash's *Polo Wisdom*, subtitled "You can talk, but can you play?" It was published for the Polo Training Foundation in 2003. It is an up-to-date and comprehensive book by an experienced polo player, covering all aspects of the game and its off-the-field organization, including sound advice of transporting polo ponies.

Also worthy of mention are William G. Langdon's trilogy: *Polo — A Way of Life, Team Play* and *Fouler*; James J. Nero and Ami Shinitzky's compilation of the thoughts on the game of Dr. William R. Linfoot — a 9-goal international player — titled *Linfoot on Polo*; and Steven Price and Charles Kauffman's *The Polo Primer*.

Finally, there are two tracts written by superior polo players. The first one is "The Science of Hitting in Polo," initially published in *The Spur*. In this short work, Devereux Milburn managed to write about the game of polo with something of the style and generosity of spirit with which he played it.

The second is the famous set of instructions given to the members of the 1930 international team selected to play in the Westchester Cup by team captain Tommy Hitchcock.

Polo Ponies

There are two superb books on polo ponies. One is Lt. Paul G. Kendall's *Polo Ponies — Their Training and Schooling*, published by the famous Derrydale Press in 1933. The other is also by an Army officer, E. Grove Cullum. The title is *Selection and Training of the Polo Pony*, published in 1934.

Worth of mention are the two volumes of the *Polo Pony Stud Book*, published under the auspices of The National Polo Pony Society, an organization now defunct, but that had great influence in the 1920 and 1930s as organizer and sponsor of many polo pony shows and competitions that attracted large entries and a sizeable number of interested spectators.

The U.S. Polo Association has published a much needed manual, *Polo Pony Welfare Guide and Guidelines*, which is distributed free of charge to polo clubs and polo players.

Polo and Society

Almost every individual club programs contain an article explaining the game of polo and its history, directed mostly to spectators lured to watch a polo game for the first times in their lives. They are informative and well-illustrated, and serve an incalculable force in keeping their interest and perhaps attracting even more people to the traditional Sunday afternoon polo events.

More serious efforts are two books. Don Carberry, a player from the Bishop Hollow Polo Club in Pennsylvania, wrote in 1965 *Pedestrian's Guide to Polo*, a short, basic polo guide for novice spectators. More comprehensive is Richard McMaster's *Polo for Beginners and Spectators*, published in 1954, in hard cover. The cover depicts a match between American and Argentine team at the Riviera Country Club in California, with Eric Pedley leading six others players after the ball. Maj. McMaster was a U.S. Army cavalry officer. The foreword is by U.S. Army polo legend Maj. Gen. Terry de la Mesa Allen.

Reference

The Polo Encyclopedia, published by McFarland in 2004, contains more than 10,000 entries arranged alphabetically, from "Abbott, Keneth Oswald," a South African player, to "Zwartberg," a South African polo club. Stephen A. Orthwein, Past Chairman of the U.S.P.A. and of the Museum of Polo and Hall of Fame, contributes a thoughtful introduction to the work. The book was written by Horace A. Laffaye.

Umpiring

The art of umpiring a polo game, a most difficult task at best, has Capt. Wesley J. White, the outstanding umpire of his time, as a powerful spokesman in his *Guide for Polo Umpires*, published by the U.S. Polo Association in 1929. This invaluable work went through several editions, the last one in 1963. Capt. White's basic philosophy in umpiring is clearly and succinctly expressed: If there are rules of the game, it is essential that they be obeyed by the players and enforced by the umpire.

R. Quinton Marshall wrote *The Polo Umpire's Primer*, in 1989. In this book the umpire's task is described in a friendly way, with very little discussion of the nuances in the rule book. It gives good advice on how to conduct a polo game; however it pales in comparison with the master's work. The book is based on R. Dan Thompson's theories on how a polo game should be conducted, and on Harry "Dutch" Evinger's on the field examples. Carlton Beal wrote a brief preface to the book.

Art

Books by Paul D. Brown depicting polo scenes include *Hits and Misses* and the instructional manual *Polo — A Non-technical Explanation of the Galloping Game*, commissioned by the U.S. Polo Association in 1949. Robert Strawbridge, Jr., the U.S.P.A. chairman at the time, contributed a short Foreword. The book was designed to answer basic questions regarding the game, the mounts, their tack, and the players in simple language. The illustrations showing the rules are the best ever seen in print. Paul Brown recreates outstanding plays and goals through the rich history of American polo from the mid–1920s on. It is a book that should be in every polo aficionado's library.

Other works by Paul Brown that include scenes depicting polo are *Ups and Downs* (1933), *Spills and Thrills* (1936) and *Good Luck and Bad* (1940). All describe equestrian incidents, mostly polo and steeplechasing.

Another important art book is Warren Halpin's *Hoofbeats*, published in 1938. The work is divided into four sections: Polo, Hunting, Steeple-chasing and Miscellaneous. Stewart Iglehart, a 10-goaler, wrote the section on polo. In addition to the trade edition of 1550 copies there is a deluxe edition of 160 copies, with a hand-colored frontispiece.

Photography

Polo in America received extensive coverage in *Chakkar — Polo around the World*, edited by the dean of polo writers, Herbert Spencer. It is a magnificent opus, in large format and superb photography. The book includes several essays on different facets of the game, written by luminaries like the Duke of Edinburgh, Hanut Singh, Juan Carlos Harriott, Jr., Lord Louis Mountbatten, Baron Elie de Rothschild, Ricardo Santamarina, Bob Skene and Cecil Smith. Published in 1971, *Chakkar* set a bar that has not yet been surpassed.

In 1992 Penina Meisels, a San Francisco–based photographer, published *Polo*, a book dedicated exclusively to photos of the sport. Her father is a veterinarian that played polo on the Cornell University team. Meisels' photography adds a new dimension to the illustration of the game because of her unique style.

Annuals

Among the many yearly publications dedicated to polo, the oldest and most complete is the set of year books published by the Polo Association from 1890 to 1923. In 1924, the polo ruling body changed its name to United States Polo Association. A small format was initially used; however, starting with the 1923 edition, the larger blue cover year book has been published until now. The only gap is between 1943 and 1948. Regrettably, the 1949 edition does not include information about the 1946–1948 seasons. This is a black hole in the history of polo in the United States. For information on the game on those lean years, interested readers and researchers must consult contemporary newspapers.

The Indoor Polo Association also published year books from 1923 until its merge with the U.S.P.A. in 1954. As expected, there was a gap in publication during the war years. The data pertinent to indoor polo were then included in the Blue Book, as the U.S. Polo Association year books are popularly known.

The United States Women's Polo Association published a year book from 1937 to 1941. These volumes are extremely rare. The U.S. Women's Polo Association was a bit of a misnomer as it was basically an association of women's polo clubs only in California.

The *Spalding Polo Guide* was published by that sporting goods manufacturer. Copies of this work have been found between 1911 and 1923. It contains a wealth of information on the game, including polo in English-speaking countries, a description of the game, nervousness and the horse, results of national and international tournaments, notices of polo in different states, officers and members of the Polo Association and its circuits, and the rules of the game.

There are also regional publications such as the *California Polo Annual*, published by the American Polo Association. When the Pacific Coast clubs in that organization joined the Polo Association in New York City, it ceased publication.

A few individual clubs also published annuals. Most include the club's directive bodies, list of members, and results of both club competitions and away tournaments and matches. The Meadow Brook Club and Rockaway Hunting Club annuals are the most complete in this particular genre. Also worth of mention is the rare *Peninsula Polo Annual*, an illustrated record of the season of 1912–13 in San Mateo, Hillsborough and Burlingame in California.

Magazines

Many publishers have navigated through the dangerous shoals of polo magazines, from national publications to individual club publications. The first sporting publication to include polo in its pages was *Outing*, that was started in 1882 as *Wheelman* and ceased publication in 1923. It is an important source for the game in its early stages.

The Spur, long considered a publication aimed at the idle rich, also contained occasional articles on the game; however, polo was a secondary interest for the magazine's editor and perhaps to its readership as well.

The breakthrough came about in 1927 when the first issue of *Polo* hit the news stands. For more than a decade, under the able editorial guidance of Peter Vischer, *Polo* and its successor *Horse and Horseman* reported the game comprehensibly and with admirable objectivity. Many years later, in 1967, Peter Vischer edited an anthology of articles and illustrations that had appeared in both publications.

A high quality magazine was *The Sportsman*, edited by Richard E. Danielson. Started in 1927, a decade later it merged with *Country Life*. Although its polo coverage did not reach the proportions of *Horse and Horseman* because *The Sportsman* devoted its pages at all games and sports, it was always on the side of the ideals of the amateur code but at the same time recognizing the skills and achievements of the professional athletes.

Polo News was the monthly official publication of the U.S. Polo Association. In 1974, Ami Shinitzki took over the editorial reins and the title was changed to *Polo*. As time went by, the magazine significantly improved its coverage, becoming the illustrious successor of its namesake of the 1920s and 1930s. Sometimes contentious, always informative, the magazine had no competition in the American scene. When it was purchased by Westchester Media, the Ralph Lauren enterprises brought suit seeking to force the magazine to change its name, during the course of the clothier's ill-advised attempts to obtain exclusive copyrights for the word "polo." As part of the legal settlement, the publication's name underwent a change to *Polo Players' Edition*. It still thrives under the editorship of Gwen Rizzo, now based in Lake Worth, Florida.

CHAPTER 24

American Polo in Art

The scope and quality of the artistic production relevant to the game of polo in the United States are so vast that it merits a book of its own. This chapter is an attempt to familiarize the reader with some of the extraordinary paintings and sculptures that depict polo in America. Rather than describe the works by event or subject, an alphabetical approach has been selected.

Richard Benno Adam (1873–1937), a German artist who visited America, drew pictures of four American 10-goalers, Foxhall Keene, Devereux Milburn, Thomas Hitchcock the elder and James Watson Webb, in *The Sportsman*. This series of illustrations also included a portrait of Mrs. Thomas Hitchcock in hunting kit. Foxhall Keene's picture appeared in the frontispiece of *Full Tilt*, Keene's autobiography, and Milburn's drawing was illustrated in the 2009 Westchester Cup program.[1] Milburn is depicted in polo garb, while Hitchcock is shown training horses and Webb is in ratcatcher attire.

Cecil Charles Windsor Aldin (1870–1935) was a distinguished English artist best known for his dog subjects, who included polo scenes among his works. Only two of his paintings have a link to polo in America. The first is a pastel and watercolor of Velocity, a grey pony ridden by Capt. Vivian Lockett in the Westchester Cup. Prints were published by Welbeck under the title *Activity — A Polo Pony* as one of a series of four, The others were *Brains*, showing a bay hunter and foxhounds, *Strength*, Squire Benyon's Shire Horse, and *Quality*, a show jumper.[2]

The second painting is *Dull Polo!* impressions of a match between British and American Army teams in 1925.[3]

George Denholm Armour (1864–1949) was a Scot sporting artist whose horse portraiture could seldom be faulted. Armour was one of the outstanding British artists of his time, together with Lionel Edwards, Gilbert Holiday and Sir Alfred Munnings. In 1913, Armour came to America with the Westchester Cup team and was made an honorary member of the Meadow Brook Club. George Armour painted several scenes with the Westchester Cup as the main subject, including *D. Milburn (U.S. Back)*, *A Practice Match at Piping Rock*, *Larry Waterbury Scoring*, *Capt. Ritson Making a Run*, *Saving a Goal*, *A Polo Match* and *Mounted Polo Player*, thought to be the Duke of Westminster, who was the team's sponsor.[4]

Carroll Kinney Bassett (1906–1972) was a fine steeplechase jockey who rode for Marion DuPont Scott. His bronzes were cast for himself and his friends. There is a fine bronze of a polo player in the National Sporting Library in Middleburg, Virginia.

Kathleen Beer, wife of polo player Robert Beer, was the proprietor of the Beresford Gallery, in Maryland and Saratoga. She was an accomplished artist on her own. Some of her watercolors are *Tommy Wayman on Orphan*, best playing pony at the Gould Gold Cup, a watercolor of the Chilean polo player Gabriel Donoso, *Dribbling on the Boards* and *Fighting It Out on the Boards*.[5] Mrs. Beer also painted her husband, the founder of Potomac Polo Club, in polo garb.

Elizabeth Bell, a contemporary artist, painted Delmar Carroll and some of his favorite ponies. She also depicted Frivolity, one of Robin Uihlein's ponies, and John T. Oxley on Cat-A-Joy.[6] The latter work of art hangs in the Museum of Polo and Hall of Fame. Both mount and rider are enshrined in the Polo Hall of Fame.

George Wesley Bellows (1882–1925) painted only three works depicting the game of polo, all masterpieces by this great American artist. In April 1910, Bellows' patron, Joseph B. Thomas—who commissioned the U.S. Open Championship trophy—arranged for him to visit the Gould estate in Lakewood, New Jersey, where polo matches were a great enthusiasm of the well-to-do. Bellows was swept away by the visual spectacle of the environment, the game and the audience. In his own recollections, "I've been making studies of the wealthy game of polo as played by the ultra rich. And let me say that these ultra rich have nerve tucked under their vest pocket. It is a great subject to draw, fortunately respectable."[7] Upon his return to New York City, Bellows immediately painted two versions of a polo match, *Polo Game* and *Polo at Lakewood*, followed by a third version in November, *Crowd, Polo Game*. The artist considered *Polo Game*, the simplest and smallest of the trio, his best to date. Nevertheless, all three paintings brilliantly capture in bold, fluid strokes the near collision of riders on the field that signals the thrill of the sport, as well as the determination of the players, tempered by touches of elegance in the spectators' attire and reinforced by the silk hat of a coach driver.

Only *Polo at Lakewood* is available for public viewing, in Bellows' birthplace, Ohio, in the Columbus Museum of Art. The other two paintings are in private collections.

Crowd, Polo Game was in the collection of Mrs. John Hay Whitney and was sold at Sotheby's in New York in December 1999. The hammer price was 27.5 million dollars, the highest price paid up to that time for an American painting, surpassing the previous record of 11.1 million set by *Cashmere*, a work by the hand of John Singer Sargent.

Cuthbert Bradley (1861–1943) was an English painter of numerous polo subjects, among them a watercolor of Stephen Sanford on My Girl, displayed at the Cartier Polo Retrospective Exhibition in Palm Beach. Other paintings by Bradley are *Ranelagh — Mr. Milburn on Teddy Roosevelt, Mr. J. Watson Webb, the left-handed American No. 3 going thirty miles an hour, Lewis Lacey on Marie Sol*, a mare played in the 1930 Westchester Cup, and the famous *Jupiter*, also owned by Lacey.

Franklin Bennett (1908–2005) painted an oil depicting Bob Skene on a grey pony, signed and dated 1960. A copy of this painting was presented to the Museum of Polo by Mrs. Elizabeth Skene.

Melinda Brewer is a contemporary artist recognized as one of Canada's foremost wildlife artists. She discovered polo at the Montreal Polo Club, and was smitten. Among many polo subjects, she has painted every winner of the Willis Hartman Trophy for the best playing pony in the U.S. Open Championship. The paintings hang in the Museum of Polo and are a significant historical record of some of the top polo horses in America.

Paul Desmond Brown (1893–1858) and American polo art go together hand-in-hand. His production of polo drawings and watercolors is immense. His style emphasizes hard edge lines, with color a secondary adjunct. Paul Brown worked primarily on paper in pencil, pen or ink, crayon, and gouache, although he produced some work in oil. After some tentative beginnings in the late 1920s, mostly in pen and ink, Brown's work reached full maturity with his watercolors in the 1930s. His opus covers most of the main polo events on the east coast, prominently showing the international competitions and the U.S. Open Championship.[8]

Paul Cadmus (1904–1999), when commissioned by the Relief Art Project to paint a game of polo, went to Governors Island and watched a polo game for the only time in his long life. The result was an oil titled *Aspects of Suburban Life— The Spill.* Like his better-known *Golf,* it is a satirical view of games played by wealthy individuals during the Depression. The melodramatic fall of horse and rider, the exaggerated facial expressions of concern by the well-dressed spectators, the photographer rushing to snap a photo of the accident, all contribute a comment to the social scene during those difficult times. Seventy-five etchings of the same scene were also made.

The colorful Tobiano, presented by Lewis Lacey to Tommy Hitchcock, became a favorite of the crowds at Meadow Brook. Eduardo Rojas Lanusse said of Tobiano: "A cat made into a horse," such was his agility. This watercolor by Melinda Brewer hangs in the Museum of Polo in Lake Worth.

Bunny Connell is a contemporary American artist based near Big Horn, in Wyoming. Although she does not identify her subjects, her sculptures are the result of first-hand, daily experience. The first of her polo series was *To the Boards,* which was followed by *Turning the Play,* shown on the cover of Bucky King's *Big Horn Polo, Gotcha* and *Head to Head.* Bunny Connell is one of the most important American sculptors.

Alice Carr de Creef (1899–1996) produced a bronze of Bob Skene on the famous horse Stormy, commissioned by the Skene family. Only two examples were cast; one is in the Skene home and the other in a private collection.

Ron Crooks (b. 1925) painted *The Backshot,* a large polo scene in California said to be a portrait of Cecil Smith. It is a fine painting, with all the trappings of a sunny California afternoon, the beautiful mountains providing a stunning background.

Edward Cucuel (1875–1951) painted the magnificent *The Polo Set— Palm Beach.* A dapper polo player is shown engaged in conversation with two elegant ladies on a lawn. The background is the Atlantic Ocean, with a large yacht near the shore. The brilliancy of this work makes it one of the best American polo paintings. This work was sold at Sotheby's in 1989.

Kenneth MacIntosh Daly was born in California where he watched Cecil Smith, Bob Skene and other star players at the Riviera Club. Among his numerous works on polo are *Groom Shadows,* a scene at Eldorado Polo Club, *On the Ball, Maui,* and *Peter Baldwin et al.* commissioned by the Hawaiian player. In this work, Daly portrays "Team Peter." Baldwin is the central figure on his favorite pony, surrounded by wife Gini, his groom Herman Louis DeCoite, and three of his ponies.[9] Daly also painted portraits of Héctor Barrantes and Gonzalo Pieres.

Randall Vernon Davey (1887–1964) was one of the few artists who also played polo, in his case at Broadmoor in Colorado when the artist was based in Santa Fe. One of his polo paintings is *Portrait of a Polo Player,* which appeared on the cover of the July 1934 issue of the magazine *Polo.* The sitter was Ed Madden, Jr., who played at the Iroquois Hunt and Polo Club in Lexington, Kentucky.

Lionel Dalhousie Robertson Edwards (1878–1966) was a sporting English artist of the first rank. Watercolor was his favorite medium, although later in life he used oils frequently. His work was very sensitive, showing a superb understanding of horses and a great ability to paint fine landscapes and skies. Edwards painted *The Westchester Cup America v. England, Hurlingham 1909*, a depiction of the Big Four in England. Other works include *Polo — An Ounce of Blood Is Worth a Pound of Bone*, *A Run Down the Boards*, *The Winning Goal* and *Riding-Off*.

Sally James Farnham (1876–1943) is best known for her magnificent silver trophy emblematic of the U.S. Polo Open Championship. She also produced a polo-related bronze, *Will Rogers on His Pony*.

Laura Gardin Fraser (1889–1966) designed the Horse Association of America Medal presented to the winner of the best playing polo pony in each U.S.P.A. club. She also sculpted a polo pony commissioned by

Bronze by Laura Gardin Fraser presented by the U.S.P.A. to those individuals that loaned ponies to the 1927 International Series.

the U.S. Polo Association for presentation to those who loaned mounts for the 1928 Cup of the Americas series. Another of her works is *Miss Buck*, a polo pony that was owned by Averell Harriman. There is an example of this bronze in the Museum of Polo. *Long, Long Trail*, a bronze bas-relief depicting polo player Theodore Roosevelt, is at the Theodore Roosevelt High School in Des Moines, Iowa.[10]

Joseph Webster Golinkin (1896–1977) best polo works are a series of watercolors depicting scenes from the 1930 Westchester Cup series at Meadow Brook.[11]

June Harrah, a contemporary American sculptor, modeled a bronze, *Two Players, One Intention*, in 1982. She was a founder, together with other artists including Henry Koehler, Marilyn Newmark and Sam Savitt, of the American Academy of Equine Art.

Herbert Haseltine (1877–1962) is considered the best animalier of the twentieth century. Born in Rome of American parents — his father was the talented painter William Haseltine — he went to Harvard where he graduated with the class of 1899. Herbert Haseltine was one of the first polo players in Italy. Then he moved to Paris, where his mentor Aimé Morot encouraged him to send one of his works to the Paris Salon. The result was that his first attempt at sculpture, *Riding-Off*, received an honorable mention. Seven casts were made; there are examples in the Cleveland Museum of Art, the Virginia Museum of Fine Art in Richmond, the National Museum of Racing in Saratoga, the Racquet Club in New York and the Hurlingham Club in London. Another example was destroyed in a fire in the Bagatelle Club in Paris; the remnants are still at the club. Another example is *Polo*, of which examples were cast in 1907 and 1908. There is a one-third life size at the Knickerbocker Club in New York, dated 1907.

The Meadow Brook Team was commissioned by Harry Payne Whitney and cast in 1911.

This, the most important bronze in polo, shows Devereux Milburn on the Roan Mare, followed by Harry Payne Whitney on Cottontail, Monte Waterbury on Little Mary and Larry Waterbury on Cobnut. An example was presented to the Hurlingham Club, and it is in the entrance hall. A second cast is at the Whitney Museum of Modern Art in New York. There are also individual bronzes of each player.

The Whitney Museum also has an example of *Ralla*, one of Harry Whitney's ponies. In conformation, she was perfect, yielding in beauty only to the incomparable Cobnut. A single cast of *Polo Pony Yearlings* was commissioned by W. Averell Harriman, dated 1924.

In 1921, the Royal Agricultural Show inspired a series of British Champion Animals. The polo pony selected by Haseltine as a model was Perfection, a heavyweight pony bred in Ireland that carried Capt. Henry Tomkinson in the Westchester Cup.

Haseltine also sculpted *Chilly and Sunbeam* for Jock Whitney. Chilly was a favorite dog and Sunbeam a polo pony, purchased in 1927 from the British international team. The plaster model was completed in May 1940 and was sent to the foundry, just days before the German army invaded France. The foundry sustained severe damage during one of the rare air raids; however, the founder had taken the model to his own village outside of Paris, where he hid it from the Germans. Seven years later, Haseltine returned to Paris, to find the caster working on his bronze.

Charles Gilbert Joseph Holiday (1879–1937) was one of the outstanding sporting artists of the twentieth century. His contemporary Lionel Edwards said of him, "no one can, or ever could, paint a horse in action better than Gilbert could."[12]

His polo masterpiece is *The 1936 Westchester Cup* which hangs at the Hurlingham Club. The draftsmanship is perfect, the ponies are magnificent. A goal has just been scored, emphatically signaled by the flag-person, wearing a silk long-coat. It is likely the Americans have scored the goal: the British players are near the goalposts and an American player is raising his mallet in jubilation. The old Hurlingham grandstand appears in the background, with three flags on top of the roof. Six of the eight players can be identified with certainty. The British Back, Lt. Col. Humphrey Guinness, is to the right, wearing his blue pith helmet. Gerald Balding, the Number 2, is returning to the center of the field, while Eric Tyrrell-Martin is next to Guinness; both can be identified by their respective helmets, a blue polo cap and a number 2 on Balding's shirt and a white pith helmet worn by Tyrrell-Martin. Further back, Hesketh Hughes is side-by-side with Winston Guest; the latter wears his trademark blue polo cap. Stewart Iglehart is between Humphrey Guinness and the American player who has scored a goal. Iglehart was the only American to wear long sleeves. The two other American players, Eric Pedley and Mike Phipps, cannot be identified with certainty.[13]

Gilbert Holiday painted other works related to American polo. One is *The Shot from the Grey Pony*,[14] depicting J. Watson Webb, the American left-handed player, and an interesting cartoon, *Polo at Eltham*, showing a practice match at the Royal Artillery ground in Avery Hill, Eltham.[15]

Thomas Holland (1918–2004), a California-born artist, produced a large number of polo bronzes with great accuracy and feeling for the game and the ponies. Among his works are *Go for Goal*, which is a representation of Bob Skene, *The Neck Shot*, *Ride-Off*, *Turn the Play*, which made the cover of *Polo* in its October 1986 edition, *On the Near Side*, *Follow Through*, and *The Tommy Hitchcock*, which was presented annually by *Polo* magazine for excellence in the game of polo.

Carroll Nathaniel Jones, Jr. (1917–2009) graduated from Yale University with a B.A. in Fine Arts, and lived in Stowe, Vermont, most of his life. Jones painted his subjects with a first-hand experience developed when he played polo as a young man. *Myopia*, a work in oil, was featured in the cover of *Polo* magazine, in January 1981. This painting is at the Myopia Hunt Club. Most of his works, which were done on commission, are in private homes.

John Gregory King (b. 1929), an English painter who studied with Lionel Edwards, was one of the founders of the Society of Equestrian Artists. John King is on the forefront of British sporting artists. He painted *Smith's Lawn* depicting the match Young England versus Young America at Guards Polo Club in Windsor on 5 August 1972. The central figure is Prince Charles, followed closely by Benjy Toda. As an aside, the game was won 5–4 by the Young America team, on a goal by Red Armour in overtime.

Henry W. Koehler (b. 1927) went to Yale University and developed an interest in fox-hunting and later in polo. He has produced many polo paintings, almost always without identifying his subjects. His work is highly thought of and is in many museums and private collections.

Edmund Larch Lewis (1835–1910) was known as a painter of marine and coastal pictures. During his stay in Rhode Island he went to watch polo games at the Point Judith Country Club at Narragansett Pier. Two similar works came out of the impromptu visit. The first one is *Polo: Myopia and Dedham*, a game played on 6 August 1898. The players are Charles Rice, Bobby Shaw, Harry Holmes and Frank Fay for Myopia, and Allan Forbes, Cameron Forbes, Charles Foster and Samuel Warren for Dedham. The background is a nice view of Narragansett Bay with several boats sailing. This painting is in the Dedham Country and Polo Club. The second painting, dated two days later, is *Westchester vs. Point Judith*; in this case the background is woods and a tower in the Thomas Hazard's estate, now the religious center Our Lady of Peace.

Henry Frederick Lucas-Lucas (1848–1943) was a prolific English painter based in Rugby. Many ponies that played in the Westchester Cup matches were painted by Lucas-Lucas. Among them are Charmer, a bay mare the property of Walter Jones, My Girl, a brown mare played by Charles Miller, Luna, a bay mare played by George Miller, and Blue Sleeve, a grey mare owned and played by Pat Nickalls in the 1909 contest. Lucas-Lucas was one of the artists who tried his hand in the Westchester Cup; his painting *England versus America at Hurlingham* is dated 1921 and was offered for sale by Sotheby's.

Kenneth Stevens MacIntire (1891–1979) moved from Wiscasset, Maine, to California, eventually in Sonoma County. His production of polo paintings, totaling 38 in all, was purchased by a California collector who in turn sold the works to two brothers in Rhode Island.[16] The collection was then dispersed; the Museum of Polo has a painting of Laddie Sanford on Gartara. The famous Irishman Pat Roark was one of his sitters. Another interesting oil painting is *The Bell*, a rather prosaic theme that comes alive in MacIntire's deft hand.

J. Edward B. Martin is a contemporary American artist of equestrian scenes. His *Potomac Park, Washington, D.C.* was offered at auction by Sotheby's in 1988.

Rollin McGrail is a contemporary American artist famous for her contribution to the *New Yorker*. Her whimsical cartoons of polo related subjects are much sought after. An outstanding work is her painting *The British Are Coming!* in commemoration of the English invasion of Palm Beach on the occasion of 2009 Westchester Cup in 2009. The original work was sold for a hefty sum at an auction benefit for the Museum of Polo and Hall of Fame.

George Ford Morris (1873–1960) painted many and varied equestrian subjects. Two of his polo paintings are *A Gentleman Up on a Polo Pony*, a large oil on canvas signed and dated '23, and a portrait of William Post, II, the international 8-goal player, signed and dated 1930.

Sir Alfred Munnings (1878–1959) is one of the great masters of equestrian art. He worked mostly in oils, but also produced watercolors. Munnings was a controversial president of the Royal Academy because of his strong dislike of modern art. His polo paintings include *Brigade-Major Geoffrey Brooke*, a polo player well known for his *Horse-Sense and Horsemanship of To-Day*. *Making a Polo Ground* shows Frederick Prince's polo grounds at Prides Crossing in Massachusetts under construction. The celebrated *Devereux Milburn, the American polo player, changing ponies* is one of the outstanding paintings in the world of polo. Several prints were made of this painting, which originally was in the Milburn home and now is in a private collection. Two U.S.P.A. chairmen sat for Munnings: Louis Stoddard and Robert Strawbridge, Jr.

Another polo player from the Meadow Brook Club, William Goadby Loew, was painted wearing his Magpies jersey. In his autobiography, Sir Alfred described a rather poor impression of his client,

> There was another sitter who, although as rich as Croesus, beat me down and haggled for hours over what he was to pay. For some stranger reason or other, when painting him in his dining room — keeping the butler from setting the lunch-table — the picture insisted on being better than others which I had worked on much harder. His polo shirt was black and white, his team — the Magpies. I can see him yet: a tall fellow, on the rather low saddle-horse, his mallet over his shoulder, the large dining room table pushed aside; the butler coming in....[17]

LeRoy Neiman is an American artist with a large following. Two of his works on polo, *Prince Charles* and *Polo*, were illustrated in the magazine *Polo*.[18]

Marilyn Meiselman Newmark, a fellow of the National Sculptors Society, was a student of Paul Brown on Long Island. She sculpted *Game's End* in an edition of 30 casts to benefit the Polo Training Foundation.[19]

Gustav Muss-Arnoldt (1858–1927) made his reputation as a painter of sporting and gun dogs. Two polo players appear in one of his foxhunting pictures: Augustus Belmont, Jr., commissioned *The Meadow Brook Hounds Meet at the Old Westbury Pond on Long Island*. This painting also includes Theodore Roosevelt. In the Museum of Polo's collection there is a painting of Raymond Belmont on Domino, at the Westchester Polo Club in Newport, dated 1887. A similar painting hangs in the Meadowbrook Polo Club on Long Island. The other three ponies are Red Skin, Flirt and Cody.[20]

James Lynwood Palmer (1868–1941) was born in England and at age 17 he ran away to Western Canada to avoid being forced into law or the diplomatic service, neither of which appealed to him. After eleven years working in cattle ranches but always keen on sketching, he took a batch of horses to New York. Gen. Field of the U.S. Army saw his sketches and started him on his artistic career. One of his polo works is *The Old Polo Grounds*, oil on panel, en grisaille, dated May 1892. It is signed Lynwood Palmer / Claude Prescott so it is a collaborative work.[21]

Raymond Pease (1908–1990) was born in Vermont. While living in Weston, Connecticut, Pease frequented the polo games at the Fairfield Hunt Club in Westport. Pease painted several watercolors of the matches with Las Garzas from Argentina. *Near the Boards* shows Roberto Fernández Llanos, wearing a red helmet and blue shirt, George Haas and Adie von Gontard, of the Fairfield club, and umpire William Whitehead following the play in the background. There are at least two versions of this painting.

Another painting is *Tail Shot*, with the Fairfield Hunt clubhouse in the background. The players are, from left to right, Peter Orthwein, Butch Butterworth, Nick Biafore, Horace Laffaye, Kent Logan and umpire Frank Butterworth, Jr.[22]

Henry Rankin Poore (1859–1940), born in New Jersey, returned to the United States after a period of time studying in Europe and began teaching in Philadelphia. A polo painting, *The Opening Charge, Hutton Park*, was painted about this time. Another work on polo, *Return from the Game*, commissioned by the Essex County Country Club, appeared as an illustration in the magazine *Outing*.[23]

Alexander Pope (1849–1924) is considered by many to be the major Boston trompe l'oeil painter of the late nineteenth century. He started his artistic career as a sculptor. From this period dates his *Standing Polo Pony*, cast by the Gorham Company Founders. There is another version of this bronze with a mounted player, said to be James Gordon Bennett.[24]

Frederick Sackrider Remington (1861–1909) went West as a young man to seek his fortune and became a popular illustrator of cowboy and Native American life. Among his numerous polo drawings is the illustration for Rudyard Kipling's *The Maltese Cat*, the charming story of a polo match in India from the perspective of a veteran and aged polo pony.

The Frederick Remington Art Museum in Ogdensburg, New York is dedicated to his work. His major representation of the game is *Polo*, a dramatic bronze showing a spill, cast in 1904. In his own words, "Group of three horses and riders in a game of polo. One horse has fallen and rider is caught under him. The second horse and rider are leaping directly over the fallen man. Third horse standing with two hind legs upon the belly of the fallen horse."[25]

John Rogers (1829–1904) created *Polo*, a plaster and metal cast of two players going for the ball, next to a flag, which could indicate a goalpost or a corner flag. Consistent with the polo attire of the period, the players wear forage or pillbox caps. John Roger's designs were patented and were for sale at very reasonable prices to appeal to the average buyer. Only five examples of *Polo* are known to exist.[26]

Charles Cary Rumsey (1879–1922) was an 8-goal player from the Buffalo polo family as well as a talented sculptor. After schooling in Paris, Rumsey returned to America where he was commissioned to model equestrian bronzes for August Belmont, Thomas Hitchcock and Harry Payne Whitney. Good and Plenty, Hitchcock's celebrated horse, is in the Metropolitan Museum of Art. His polo bronzes include *Frank Skiddy von Stade, Sr.* and *John R. Fell*. However, his best is *Polo Player on Pony: Harrison Tweed*. Harrison Tweed was on the Harvard polo team and later played at Meadow Brook.[27]

Pad Rumsey's career included three U.S. Open Championships, the Senior and Junior Championships, and the Ranelagh Open Cup in England, when he was a member of the American squad for the 1921 Westchester Cup. Rumsey was killed in an automobile accident the day after his Orange County team had defeated the visiting Argentines.

John Singer Sargent (1856–1925) drew a magnificent portrait of Eleonora Randolph Sears in charcoal on paperboard, signed and dated 1921. The portrait captures Sears' inner fire, best reflected in her steely eyes and shining hairdo. Eleo was delighted with the portrait; she rushed to have it framed at the Copley Gallery and ordered photographic copies to give to friends.[28]

Sam Savitt (1917–2000) was the spiritual successor to Paul Brown in American polo. Savitt wrote and illustrated more than 120 books, including the *Glenlivet Guide to Polo*. Sam Savitt lived for many years in equestrian North Salem, in New York State just west of

Connecticut, in his home "One Horse Farm." His was a familiar figure at the Fairfield County Hunt Club and at the Greenwich Polo Club, where he spent afternoons sketching polo games. Among his numerous polo paintings is *George Haas and Feather*, which for many years adorned George and Babs Haas' home in Weston. The painting is now in the library room of the Museum of Polo and Hall of Fame. Another important painting is *Mallet Work*, painted at the Fairfield County Hunt Club, signed and dated 1990. This painting was the cover for the November 1991 issue of *Polo* and was also featured as a full double spread in the center of the same publication.

Sam Savitt also produced several posters illustrating the rules and many other features of the game of polo.

John Rattenbury Skeaping (1901–1980) was an English painter and sculptor with a very individualist style. He spent most of his life in Southern France near the Camargue, breaking horses and rounding up cattle. An important twentieth-century artist, Skeaping felt that individuality and self-expression were an artist's strengths. He also

The versatile and controversial Eleonora Sears, who pioneered the role of women in American sports and pastimes. Charcoal on paper by John Singer Sargent, 1921.

produced wood and bronze sculptures. His works on the game include *Polo Group* exhibited at Ackerman's in 1978, *Polo Player*, also at Ackerman's, and a watercolor, *Polo at Gulfstream*, offered for sale in 2001.

Rodney Skidmore is an American contemporary artist based in Maine who started playing polo at age 54 at the Down East Polo Club. Most of his paintings are done on commission. Many of his paintings depict the Florida winter season, the Rolex Gold Cup being one of his favorite subjects. One of his best paintings is *Rolex Gold 91*, a watercolor showing a scene from a match between the Rolex A&K team and White Birch. Peter Brant and Geoffrey Kent are in the foreground, simultaneously turning to catch up with the play. Juan Badiola, Carlos Gracida and Adrian Wade are also in the picture. Skidmore chose to depict this match because he was intrigued by the long-standing sporting rivalry between Kent and Brant.

Another interesting composition by Rodney Skidmore is a watercolor *The Orthweins*, signed and dated 2006, which depicts six members of the famous St. Louis polo family charging after a polo ball.[29]

Howard Everett Smith (1885–1970) in his time was considered one of the top American equestrian artists. It is possible that his professional training as a veterinarian gave him an insight into the intricate muscular anatomy of the horse. His sketches of polo at Myopia Hunt Club led to his being commissioned to paint some of the leading thoroughbreds, such as Battleship, Man-O-War and Troublemaker. Smith moved west, settling in Carmel, California, were he did fine etchings of cowboys and horses reminiscent of Frederick Remington's images.

Howard Smith produced several fine etchings based upon his experiences at watching games at Myopia; among those is *Along the Boards* with his signature on one of the field's boards. An oil of Myopia's own 10-goaler Rodolphe Agassiz hangs at the club.

Joseph H. Sulkowski is a contemporary American painter based in Franklin, Tennessee. He studied at the Academy of Fine Arts in Philadelphia and at the Art Students League in New York City. Sulkowski depicts dogs, thoroughbred horses, landscapes and still life. His polo paintings include *Rolex Gold Cup Action at Wellington*, set in Florida, *Polo Pony*, a nice study of a grey pony, with a polo mallet and ball on the ground, *Still Life with Polo Tack* and *A Master Stroke*, showing U.S.P.A. chairman Skey Johnston playing in the July Invitational at Edwin Warner Park, in Nashville.[30]

Diana Thorne (1895–1965) was born in Winnipeg, Canada. She illustrated several books on the game, including *Polo, Pepito the Polo Pony* and *Roughy*. Her action sketches show good movement, are direct and strong. Her etching *Exciting Moment* is a good example of her work. Diana Thorne also painted watercolors, including a depiction of the 1939 Westchester Cup, a painting of Tommy Hitchcock and a 1930s match between Templeton and Greentree.

Bror Thure de Thulstrup (1848–1930) was born in Stockholm, Sweden and studied at the Art Students League in New York City. He was an illustrator for the magazines *Daily Graphic, Leslie's* and *Harper's Weekly*. His claim to polo fame resides in the fact that he was the illustrator for the first Westchester Cup match in Newport, Rhode Island, in 1886. His work was published in *Harper's Weekly* and has been reproduced many times. He also exhibited his *Polo Girl* at the Art Institute of Chicago in 1914.

Franklin Brooke Voss (1880–1953) was born in New York into a sporting and artistic family. A fine horseman and polo player, Voss hunted with the Rockaway and Meadow Book hunts, and later with the Elkridge-Harford Hounds, of which his brother Edward, also a talented sporting artist, was the M.F.H.

The works of Franklin Voss related to polo include *Devereux Milburn on Jacob*, a recently rediscovered painting which now hangs at the Museum of Polo. Devereux Milburn is shown wearing Meadow Brook's blue shirt, mounted on Jacobs, a famous polo pony bred in Texas. Other celebrated polo ponies painted by Voss are Glimmer, Lapwing and Miss Hobbs. Miss Hobbs was featured in the U.S.P.A. Year Book as an example of a superb polo pony mare.[31]

Polo at Meadow Brook, a watercolor painted in 1927, shows Devereux Milburn and James Watson Webb riding-off. The work is quite unusual because Voss seldom painted action scenes and rarely utilized watercolor as a medium.

Other significant polo paintings by Franklin Voss are *Mike White's Polo Ponies*,[32] and *A Quartette of Mares in the Fine String of Mr. Harold Talbott, Jr.* showing Abdication and Delysia, both English-bred, The Vamp, from Texas, and Broken Crown, born in England.[33] Finally, there is the brilliant *Grooms Bringing the Polo Ponies onto the Field*, dated 1941. The horses are Formula, Ask Me, Isabelle, Luxury, Royal Coquette, Full-Tilt and Trilby, accompanied by two terriers, Peanut III and Badger II.

Andy Warhol (1928–1987) was born Andrew Warhola in Pittsburgh and became a famous pop artist and filmmaker. A silk-screen and mixed media portrait of Memo Gracida was on the cover of *Polo*'s tenth anniversary issue, May 1985.

Larry Dodd Wheeler (b. 1942), a member of the American Academy of Equine Art, has painted many equestrian subjects from the sporting landscapes of Maryland and Virginia. His polo paintings include *Between Chukkers, Sidelines* and *Portrait of Robert Beer*. Wheeler also painted in oil Kaliman, a pony owned by Guy Wildenstein and ridden by Memo Gracida, a winner of the Willis Hartman Trophy for the best horse in the 1987 and 1989 U.S. Open Championship. Kaliman was named after a Mexican comic's character.

CHAPTER 25

American Polo in the Twenty-First Century

The Growth of the Game in America

The unabated expansion of polo in the United States is reflected in the statistics compiled by the U.S. Polo Association. In 1950, there were 56 clubs affiliated with the U.S. Polo Association.[1] The 2009 Year Book lists 261 member clubs; in addition there are 40 school and college members. There are polo clubs in 42 states, and affiliates in Argentina, Canada, the Dominican Republic and Jamaica.[2]

Currently, California is the state with the second largest number of affiliated polo clubs, 25. Polo in California is centered in the venerable Santa Barbara, a polo club that will celebrate its centenary in 2011. The club is the venue for the most important summer polo season, starting with the Bob Skene Trophy and culminating with the Pacific Coast Open, a competition for the massive Spreckels Cup.[3]

Further south, another Spreckels Cup is competed for at the San Diego Polo Club in Rancho Santa Fe. This is a 16-Goal tournament which draws a significant number of entries. The U.S.P.A.'s 16-Goal Rossmore Cup is also played at San Diego. The Eldorado Polo Club, site of two U.S. Open Championships, still is the main polo club in the desert. The main tournament is the Pacific Coast Governor's Cup.

The Hawaiian Islands Circuit comprises five affiliated clubs: Hawaii, Honolulu, Kauai, Maui and Mauna Kea. The major competition is the 12-Goal Master's Cup; the other three U.S.P.A. tournaments are the Congressional, Constitution and Sportsmanship Cups.

Geographically, the Pacific Northwest is the largest U.S.P.A. circuit. Its nineteen clubs are located in Wyoming, Oregon, Idaho, Washington, Utah and Alberta, Canada.

Polo in Wyoming, dating back to 1882, remains alive and well. In Big Horn, near Sheridan, the Flying H Ranch is the site for a busy 20-goal polo season during the month of August. The Skeeter Johnston Memorial Cup was started as a North American Polo League event for a silver trophy commissioned by the Johnston family and designed by Mariano Draghi.

Teams from Calgary have participated actively in the California and Florida seasons, notably Fish Creek, Millarville and The Hawks, all sponsored by that great patron of polo, Fredrick Mannix, Sr. The Calgary Polo Club is also the venue for the North America Cup, an official U.S.P.A. tournament

The game has experienced a revival in Colorado. High Prairie Polo Club in Lone Tree hosts the Congressional Cup and the Governor's Cup; Roaring Fork in New Castle, the

Rocky Mountain Circuit Player's Cup; Willow Creek in Elizabeth, the Amateur Cup; and Denver Polo Club in Littleton, the Centennial Cup.

Aiken has become a hotbed of polo with several new clubs near town, where the ancient Aiken Polo Club still reigns. New Bridge, Russell McCall's creation, hosted the Gold Cup and the historic Monty Waterbury Cup; 302 Polo Club was the venue for the Silver Cup and Maureen Brennan's Goose Creek team string of victories in this tournament, which is the oldest in the United States, predating the U.S. Open by four years. The Continental Cup and the Northrup Knox Cup are also played in Aiken, the Knox family from Buffalo being winter residents starting in the early 1930s. The game of polo has been played in this tranquil South Carolina town since 1882.

The Northeastern Circuit is the largest in the country, with 43 affiliated clubs. The Greenwich Polo Club in Connecticut is the main center for high-goal polo, having been the venue for the Gold Cup and enjoying a busy season from Memorial Day to Labor Day, punctuated by a spell at the Hamptons on Long Island in midsummer. Fairfield County Hunt Club is but a shadow of itself, compared to the halcyon days of the 1970s and 1980s.

In the New Haven area, the Butterworth's Giant Valley Farm, where polo has been played for a century, still witnesses low and mid–goal polo. The Yale University male and female polo teams are considered a significant power in intercollegiate polo, as is the University of Connecticut in Storrs. The UConn women's team took the championship from 2005 to 2008, matching the University of California at Davis' 1980–1983 record string of four consecutive championships. The streak came to an end at Charlottesville when the host team, University of Virginia, the eventual champions, beat Connecticut in a shoot-out in the semifinals.

The East Coast Open at Myopia was for many years the centerpiece of the summer season and remains so, although the last time it was played at Greenwich. Frequent winner White Birch is the current holder of the Perry Trophy. This trophy, emblematic of the East Coast Open, dates back to the old Rumford Polo Club in Rhode Island.[4] The Cameron Forbes Cup, for so many years the coveted prize for the New England Championship, has been relegated to a lesser place in the scheme of polo things in the northeast. So much for tradition.

The polo season at the Hamptons is an important part of polo in the Northeastern Circuit. The Bridgehampton Polo Club hosts the Mercedes-Benz Challenge and nearby Southampton Polo & Hunt Club the Independence and Southampton Cups and the 12-goal Club Championship.

Saratoga Polo Club, first revived by Peter Brant, Will Farish and Richie Jones, later on under the aegis of Bill Ylvisaker and currently run by Jim Rossi, offers a wonderful opportunity to enjoy polo during the August racing season at that old spa. The original polo ground has been carefully restored and attracts quality teams from as far as Kentucky.

In little Rhode Island, Dan Keating has revived the game at a ground on Glen Farm, in Portsmouth. The club hosts a popular medium-goal international series against visiting foreign teams every summer.

Polo in the Commonwealth of Virginia has remained a low-key pastime, reminiscent of country polo in England. Friends and relatives enjoy the game on numerous private polo grounds scattered around the land, without having to endure the pressure of serious competition. Both the thrill of victory and the agony of defeat are brought into constructive perspective on the hunting fields of the Piedmont country.

Winter polo in Florida attracts the largest number of players in the United States. With the concomitant equestrian events at Wellington, this village can certainly be called the equestrian capital of America and perhaps the world. It has been estimated that more than 12,000 horses winter around Wellington.

The 2010 U.S.P.A. Year Book lists no less than 28 clubs in Florida, part of the Florida-Caribbean Circuit.[5] Just in Wellington's vicinity there are many clubs and private grounds. Gonzalo Avendaño's Patagones, Jan Pamela Farms, Joe DiMenna's Equuleus, El Sur, the Johnston's Everglades, Mark and Melissa Ganzi's Grand Champions, Isla Carroll, Mario González de Mendoza's La Posta, Far Niente, Tommy Lee Jones' San Saba, Luis Escobar's Santa Clara, Frank MacNamara's Southampton South, and South Forty are some which enjoy private polo grounds. The big guns, Camilo Bautista's Las Monjitas and Víctor Vargas' Lechuza Caracas, have large establishments, and in the case of Lechuza, a beautifully appointed pavilion overlooking one of the best polo grounds in the Wellington area.

Unfortunately, the Royal Palm Polo Club in Boca Raton closed its doors after 49 years of uninterrupted high-goal polo. Royal Palm was the venue for the U.S. Open Championship, the Gold Cup and just about every major championship in the United States. The stadium on Glades Road was the best from the spectators' viewpoint because of the unlimited 180-degree vision. It was a sad day for polo when the Oxley family decided to discontinue operating this great facility.

Another great club that bit the dust, literally, was the Palm Beach Polo and Country Club. Bill Ylvisaker's concoction, in his times P.B.P. & C.C. was arguably the top polo club in the world. With more than a dozen polo grounds, a grand stadium, a wonderful player's club, the winter season attracted the best players in the world, from the European shores to the South American beaches, passing through Australasia, the polo-playing countries in Africa, and teams from the Philippines. Greed and financial mismanagement brought the club to its knees. A hurricane severely damaged the stadium, which was razed to the ground shortly after.

Nearby, the International Polo Club Palm Beach took up the challenge of becoming the top club in Florida. With the purchase of the old Outback grounds, I.P.C. now has six polo fields plus access to the adjacent Isla Carroll's polo grounds. The club hosted the 2009 Westchester Cup, an unforgettable occasion. The true and real Triple Crown of Polo, that is the U.S. Open Championship, the Gold Cup and the U.S. Handicap for the C.V. Whitney Cup, is also held at this club. Add to that galaxy of trophies other 20-goal plus tournaments, such as the Joe Barry Memorial Trophy, The Hall of Fame Cup, the Ylvisaker Cup, and the Lester Armour Trophy, International Polo Club is currently the Mecca of American polo.

Polo on Florida's East Coast also has active clubs in Vero Beach and in Hobe Sound, as well as in Palm City. The old Gulfstream Polo Club on Lake Worth Road still goes on, having temporarily dodged a bullet in the form of a developer's bid to convert the old polo grounds into a shopping center. The future remains uncertain for this wonderful polo club.

Further inland, Stephen Orthwein started the Port Mayaca Polo Club, near Lake Okeechobee. The club has five polo fields and stabling for 120 ponies. The principal tournaments are the 16-goal Live Oak Challenge, the Women's Tabebuia Annual Tournament and the Port Mayaca Lakes 12-goal Tournament. A new polo club, just established in 2009, Port Mayaca has thousands of acres ready for development within a first class polo facility.

Sarasota has a vibrant polo season, thanks to the initiative of Robin Uihlein, a member of the Milwaukee U.S. Open championship team in the 1970s. The Robert A. Uihlein, Jr., Memorial Cup, the Wayne Brown Tournament, both winners of the U.S. Open, and the Ringling Cup are some of the tournaments organized by the Sarasota Polo Club.

The Villages Polo Club has a wonderful stadium, which was the site of the 2009 Avila Camacho Cup against Mexico. It also hosts international matches with visiting foreign teams. Florida's gulf coast polo is centered in the Tampa Bay Polo Club in Plant City, started by Edward Kampsen and Riviere Thomas.

There are also polo clubs in Hobe Sound, Ocala, Palm City and Vero Beach, a powerful testimony of the attraction that polo has in the southern reaches for players, sponsors and spectators alike.

The United States Open Championship

The 2000 U.S. Open was significant because for the first in its history a woman was on the champion team. Sunset "Sunny" Hale, Sue Sally's daughter, played at Number 1 on Tim Gannon's Outback squad. The eleven entrants were placed in three divisions; the top two teams in Divisions 1 and 2 to meet in a quarterfinals round. The two winners were then to meet in the semifinals with the top two teams in the five-entry Division 3. Such are the vagaries of an uneven schedule.

In the quarterfinal round Isla Carroll defeated Mike Price's Templeton in overtime, and Crab Orchard did the same in its match against Mega. The semifinals matched Outback, with Sunny Hale, Adolfo Cambiaso, Lolo Castagnola and Phil Heatley, against Crab Orchard, with George Rawlings, Matías Magrini, Memo Gracida and Silvestre Donovan. Outback eked out a 12–11 win. In the second semifinal game, Skeeter Johnston's Everglades, a team completed with Tomás Fernández Llorente, Owen Rinehart and Tommy Biddle, defeated a dispirited Isla Carroll team. In the morning of the match, news reached the Palm Beach polo community that Gonzalo Heguy had been killed in a motor vehicle accident. Gonzalo Heguy's cousins Eduardo and Nachi were on the Isla Carroll team.

Therefore, the final match featured two teams from the tough Division 3. Outback had defeated Everglades 13–7 in their divisional match and was considered the heavy favorites. However, the score at the end of the fourth chukker was 7 to 5, Outback in front. The expected mismatch had turned into a game well worthy of a final championship game. However, in the critical fifth period, Cambiaso took charge, as he often does when the going gets tough. Mounted on best playing pony Garantía, Adolfito led Outback to a 10–7 advantage and an eventual final score of 11 goals to 8. Everglades played well, but Outback played even better.

Outback made it three-in-a-row U.S. Open championships in 2001. Again, eleven teams made it a complicated draw; this time there were only two brackets, the two top teams to advance to the semifinals. Division 2 winners Pony Express, with Bob Daniels, Nicolás Roldán, Bautista Heguy and Alejandro Agote, went into overtime with Division 1 second-place Orchard Hill, with Stuart Erskine, Julio Arellano, Eduardo Heguy and Steve Van Andel. A 30-yard penalty by Julio Arellano defined the match. The other semifinal game was between Outback, with Santiago Chavanne, Brazilian Fabio Diniz, Adolfo Cambiaso and Chris Gannon, against Venezuela's Lechuza Caracas, with Víctor Vargas, Sebastián Merlos, Pite Merlos and Kris Kampsen. The score was tied 13-all at the end of the fifth chukker. Once more, Cambiaso elevated his level of play when most needed, scoring four times in the last chukker of an 18–14 festival of goals.

In both the semifinal and final matches Kristy Waters, a Texas A&M product, substituted for team sponsor Steve Van Andel. The score at halftime was 8–6 in favor of Outback;

however, Outback's horsepower began to rise in the second half and allowed the favorite to post a 14–12 win.

The 2002 U.S. Open stayed in Florida's east coast but the venue moved 20 miles south to Royal Palm Polo Club in Boca Raton. Fifteen teams made it a populous tournament; again an odd number of entrants made the draw rather complex. During the draw, players and sponsors made it known their concern about the lack of a quarterfinals round. A week later, officialdom changed its mind, and a quarterfinals round was added. In the first semi-final game Orchard Hill, with Jeff Hall, Julio Arellano, Eduardo Heguy and Steve Van Andel, defeated Lechuza Caracas, the team of Víctor Vargas, Sebastián Merlos, Pite Merlos and Pascual "Lito" Salatino. The score was 13–11.

In the second semifinal, Coca-Cola, with Gillian Johnston, Adam Snow, Miguel Novillo Astrada and Tommy Biddle, upset favorites Los Banditos, with Brandon Phillips, Mike Azzaro, Memo Gracida and Dave Dollinger, by 10 goals to 9. Gillian Johnston, the team's sponsor, scored the winning goal in overtime. The championship match was a good running game, with the playing surface in perfect condition. Orchard Hill led 8–6 at the half; however, Coca-Cola tied the game at 10-all in the fifth. In the decisive sixth chukker all the players were mounted on their best playing pony nominees; it was all Coca-Cola, Adam Snow and his grey mare Pumbaa. The final score was 13–10. Snow was MVP and Pumbaa best playing pony.

Adam Snow completed an unforgettable year when the U.S. Polo Association raised his handicap to 10-goals at season's end.

The tournament remained at Royal Palm for the 2003 edition, which had eleven entrants. The format was changed once more, with the two top teams in each division meeting in the semifinals. C-Spear, with Tommy Boyle, Matías Magrini, Carlos Gracida and Jeffrey Hall, won its division with a 5–0 record. Lechuza Caracas, with Víctor Vargas, Sebastián and Pite Merlos and Jorge Rodríguez, took second place on net goals from Las Monjitas and Texas Polo.

In the other division Isla Carroll posted a 4–0 record despite several lineup changes. The team started with John Goodman, Mike Azzaro, Memo Gracida and Brandon Phillips. An injury to Gracida brought Hector Galindo in and Phillips out, so the higher handicapped Tommy Biddle could play. Then Galindo was injured and Sugar Erskine was his replacement. The last playoff game saw Memo Gracida and Brandon Phillips back; but John Goodman was out, his place taken by Galen Weston. Second place went to Millarville, on net goals over White Birch and Pony Express.

Adam Snow, a third generation polo player from Myopia, was captain of Team USA in the 2009 Westchester Cup (Museum of Polo, Alex Pacheco photograph).

In the semifinal round, C-

Miguel Novillo Astrada playing on the Johnston's Coca-Cola team. The final match for the 2002 U.S. Open Championship at the Oxley's Royal Palm Polo Club in Boca Raton, won by Coca-Cola over Orchard Hill (Museum of Polo, Alex Pacheco photograph).

Spear defeated Millarville 13–8 and Lechuza Caracas beat Isla Carroll 14–13 in overtime. The final match provided a comfortable victory for C-Spear by 14 goals to seven.

On the occasion of the Open Championship's centenary the tournament was held at the new International Polo Club Palm Beach, located in Wellington. Thirteen teams were divided into three brackets. Division 1 included five teams playing against each other, with the top three advancing to the quarterfinals. Divisions 2 and 3 had four teams each that played across brackets, with the top five teams advancing to the quarterfinals. Therefore, all 13 teams would play four qualifying games. The first semifinal between Isla Carroll and Lechuza Caracas must be one of the longest matches on record because of an accident in the first chukker. Memo Gracida and Sebastián Merlos came together; Merlos fell, injured his shoulder and was unable to continue. A foul was called on Gracida and Lechuza Caracas invoked a Penalty 7, which removed Memo Gracida from the game, as the nearest higher handicapped player to Merlos. The officials discussed the ruling for almost one hour before deciding to play out the remaining 27 seconds of the chukker prior to allowing another substitute on the Lechuza team. Then the issue came that, since Isla Carroll had a 17-goal aggregate and Lechuza only 16, another player should substitute to make the handicaps even. Gastón Ururi was then replaced by Jorge Rodríguez in a three-a-side game. Nevertheless, Isla Carroll took a boring game by 12 goals to 11.

Memo Gracida was astonished. After the game was over, he said, "We are playing the U.S. Open.... You cannot play three-against-three polo. It is cruel for the horses, it is unfair to the players, unfair to the patrons and unfair for the crowd that stays to watch a polo game, not a rule game."[6] All of this is very interesting in the light of what came after that same day, in the course of the second semifinal game between Catamount and White Birch.

The crowd moved over to the main field to watch two very good and evenly matched teams decide which one would face Isla Carroll in the finals. At halftime, the teams were locked-up at 5-all. In the fourth chukker, Pelón Escapite knocked down Del Walton against the boards. Rendered temporarily unconscious, Walton was not allowed to continue playing, quite rightly. A Penalty 7 was invoked, and Escapite was ordered off the field. At least, there was no squabble about Pelón Escapite being 4-goals and Del Walton 3-goals. However, for the second time and on the same day, a U.S. Open semifinal game was finished with three players on each team. Catamount led 11–10 after five chukkers, and Peter Brant took out himself and Julio Arellano came on the field. The move paid off, because at the end of regulation time the scoreboard read 12–12. Mariano Aguerre broke away early in the overtime period to score the winning goal.

The final was anticlimactic. Although White Birch had beaten Isla Carroll 14–9 in bracket play, this time around Isla Carroll came on to obtain a 10–6 victory. Califa, ridden by Mariano Aguerre, was judged Best Playing Pony and Francisco Bensadón was Most Valuable Player. For Memo Gracida, it was his sixteenth U.S. Open title, a record unlikely to be surpassed.

In the spring of the year 2005, there was a simple, rather large asterisk in White Birch's record: They had not taken the U.S. Open, even at the peak of their brilliancy. Finalists in four instances, the Greenwich-based team had been defeated by Aspen in their first attempt at the Open crown in 1994, as the result of a controversial call. The other three finals were runaways for Outback and Isla Carroll, However, 2005 proved to be the year of White Birch, on the strength of their victories in the Hall of Fame Cup over Skeeterville, the C.V. Whitney Cup over Black Watch, both 26-goal tournaments, and the U.S. Open Championship over Skeeterville.

Even before the U.S. Open started, there was controversy involving White Birch. The Hall of Fame Cup started the high-goal season in February; White Birch won the first game with Julio Gracida, Memo's son, Lucas Criado, Mariano Aguerre and Peter Brant. Then 4-goaler Martín Ravina took Brant's place for the next two games and Brant returned to play the final against Skeeterville. White Birch came from behind a 7–3 score, to win 11–10. Then in the C.V. Whitney Cup, Peter Brant missed three of the four opening games.

The White Birch team was doing very well, beating their opponents by an average of six goals. Before the finals, there were claims of cheating and ringers, and the Handicap Committee met twice to address Ravina's handicap. The Committee's decision was that his handicap would remain at 4-goals.[7] With Peter Brant on the team, White Birch defeated Black Watch in overtime. In their first match in the U.S. Open, White Birch defeated Isla Carroll 12–4. The U.S.P.A. Handicap Committee met again, changed their tune, and raised Martín Ravina's handicap to 6-goals, effective immediately. This handicap change placed White Birch at 28-goals; however, the team was allowed to play as long as they gave their opponents the handicap differential. White Birch then beat Catamount 18–10, allowing them two goals on handicap. Black Watch was the next victim, by 14 goals to 11. Then Peter Brant returned to the team and they lost to Old Pueblo 12–11. The return of Brant meant that Ravina could not play any longer; therefore, when Brant was unable to play in the quarterfinal match against Loro Piana, Del Walton took his place in a 12–9 win.

In the semifinals, White Birch again met Catamount, taking a close game 11–10. The second semifinal was a contest between the two Johnston entries: Bendabout, with Gillian Johnston, Alejandro and Miguel Novillo Astrada and Tommy Biddle, versus Skeeterville, with Skeeter Johnston, Owen Rinehart, Julio Arellano and Lucas Monteverde. When asked which team he would root for, Skey Johnston replied, "I think I'll go fishing."[8]

The final match was an excellent polo exhibition, which result could have gone either way; it was one of those games in which it is sad that one team has to lose. Peter Brant was expected to play; however, he stood aside to let young Del Carroll Walton play. The halftime break saw White Birch ahead, six goals to four, but Julio Arellano tied the game in the fifth. Lucas Criado tied again 9-all in the sixth chukker. Arellano and Criado converted penalty shots in the chukker and regulation time ended with the scoreboard reading 10–10. The large crowd was on their feet, mostly cheering for Skeeterville.

The overtime was not long. Skeeterville had a couple of shots at goal that went wide of the mark. Then the umpires called a 30-yard penalty against Skeeterville, and after a few tense moments, Lucas Criado split the goalposts with a high, unreachable shot. White Birch's curse in the U.S. Open was broken.

The 26-goal tournament season in 2006 was an interesting one. Russ McCall probably made the best investment, money-wise, when he contracted Adolfo Cambiaso to enter New Bridge/La Dolfina, completed with Nick Roldán and Matías Magrini. With Sunny Hale in the lineup instead of Nicolás Roldán, New Bridge/La Dolfina took the 22-goal Ylvisaker Cup. The full team then took the 26-goal Hall of Fame Cup, trouncing Isla Carroll in the final by 13 goals to 5. Later in October, New Bridge ended a successful season when Russ McCall, Magrini, Cambiaso and Gonzalo García del Río took the Gold Cup over Maureen Brennan's Goose Creek team.

New Bridge/La Dolfina did not enter the remaining 26-goal tournaments, to the great relief of their opponents. A new team, Jedi, with Torsten Koch, Pablo MacDonough, Juan Martín Nero and Alejandro Agote, entered the C.V. Whitney Cup and won all their matches, defeating Lechuza Caracas in the final match 8–6. Sponsor Erich Koch then took his squad behind closed doors on South Shores Boulevard, as is his wont.

With both winning teams of the previous 26-goal tournaments out of the way, the U.S. Open Championship seemed to be up for grabs. However, Las Monjitas' pony string managed by Guillermo Fernández Llanos peaked at the right time. Camilo Bautista, Adam Snow, Eduardo and Ignacio Novillo Astrada ran over Skeeterville 15–9, squeezed by Lechuza Caracas 11–10, and thrashed ERG 12–5 to reach the semifinals unbeaten. Orchard Hill's

Steve Van Andel, Jeff Hall, Héctor Galindo and Francisco de Narváez beat Pony Express in their semifinal match 14–12.

The semifinal game between Mokarow Farms and Las Monjitas was a great disappointment. In the third chukker, Kevin Mokarow collided with Guillermo Willington in one of the worst wrecks in a long time. Both ponies suffered serious injuries and Kevin Mokarow was unable to continue; Carlitos Gracida came in to the game as a replacement. A rare Penalty 1 was called against Mokarow Farms. In the fifth period, Guillermo Gracida was asked to leave the field after an incident with Eduardo Novillo Astrada. Mokarow continued the game with only three players until the chukker ended. Then Julio Gracida entered, but the die was cast. Las Monjitas won 8–4 in a match that most were glad when it was over.[9]

Steve Van Andel's Orchard Hill was in their third U.S. Open finals; it was the first one for the Colombian team. Las Monjitas jumped to a 4–1 lead in the first chukker and was never caught. The final tally was 12–6. Eduardo Novillo Astrada was MVP and Adam Snow's bay mare Amy was awarded the best playing pony Hartman Trophy.

More controversy marred the 2007 U.S. Open Championship before it had even started. During a Gold Cup semifinal match that would decide the seeding for the U.S. Open, members of La Herradura team incurred the displeasure of the International Polo Club Organizing Committee for not trying too hard in their contest versus Lechuza Caracas.[10] The game was a sham. Within a few seconds of the start, Fred Mannix left the field after telling the umpires he was unwell. J.J. Celis replaced Mannix. Lechuza Caracas won the game 18–7, with most of the spectators gone before halftime. The 11-goal differential put La Herradura safely in the Open Championship's Bracket 1, considered the weakest of the four.

To their credit, the I.P.C. Committee took a drastic action. At a meeting held after the Lechuza-Herradura game, four players, Kris Kampsen, Javier J. Celis, Memo and Julio Gracida, were banned from competition for the rest of the year in events organized by the club. Guillermo Gracida filed an appeal with the U.S.P.A. The parent body of polo in America revealed itself to have the spine of a jellyfish. Under the lame excuse that it had no jurisdiction over the event, the guardian body of the game's integrity washed its hands off the affair, ignoring its own rules.[11] Furthermore, the Chairman, Jack L. Shelton, sent a letter to Gracida stating that all four suspended players were in good standing with the U.S. Polo Association and could participate in its events.[12]

Frederick Mannix, Jr., was spared the rod and proceeded to assemble a team, Millarville, to participate in the U.S. Open. Started under such inauspicious conditions, the 2007 Open proceeded according to form. In the semifinals, Jedi bested White Birch and Crab Orchard ran like an express train over Orchard Hill, last year's finalist.

The finals game promised to be a battle of the titans, because Jedi had defeated Crab Orchard 10–8 in bracket play. A battle it was, indeed. Jedi, with Torsten Koch, Pablo MacDonough, Juan Martín Nero and Cristián "Magoo" Laprida, led 3–1 early in the game. Crab Orchard, with David Stirling, III, Matías Magrini, Adolfo Cambiaso and George Rawlings, equalized matters at the half. Then Crab Orchard surged ahead, only to allow the game to be tied in the fifth chukker. Going into the last period Jedi came within one goal and Magoo Laprida tied the game at 14-all with less than a minute to go. From the ensuing throw-in Matías Magrini won the ball and passed it to an unmarked Adolfo Cambiaso, who ran the half length of the field to score the championship-winning goal.

The game of polo suffered a terrible loss during the season when the much respected Skeeter Johnston, patron of the Everglades and Skeeterville teams, died after an accident during a practice game. Skeeter was one of the founding members and principal sponsor of the recently formed North American Polo League, an entity dedicated to improve the organization and scope of the professional game in the United States.

Crab Orchard retained the U.S. Open Championship in 2008. Jeff Blake and Ignacio "Nachi" Heguy replaced David Stirling and Matías Magrini in the pink team.

The ugly face of match fixing made its appearance again during the playoff matches following the preliminary bracket play. Crab Orchard, Las Monjitas and Skeeterville, all three sporting 2–0 records, advanced to the quarterfinals. That situation left five slots open for the six teams with 1–1 records. The three games were played in a single day, one after the other. A careful examination of the possibilities determined that in the first match, that pitted Audi against Zacara, both teams would advance if the final result was a one-goal differential. As the final bell sounded, Zacara was ahead 9–8. Pony Express was facing elimination if they lost their encounter with Black Watch by more than two goals. The finals tally was Pony Express 10, Black Watch 9. Both teams qualified for the quarterfinals, leaving Isla Carroll and White Birch in a win or die situation to qualify for the last available slot in the competition. It was perhaps the best game of the entire tournament, with White Birch winning via a Mariano Aguerre goal with 35 seconds left on the clock.

Crab Orchard, White Birch, Pony Express and Las Monjitas moved on to the semifinals. Both games ended with identical scores, 12–11; Crab Orchard over Pony Express and Las Monjitas eliminated White Birch.

The final game, held in front of a crowd estimated to be 8,000, was fast-moving and interesting. Crab Orchard had a three-goal lead at halftime. Both teams traded goals during the second half; the final score was Crab Orchard 15, Las Monjitas 12. Jeff Blake was MVP, playing well-above his 6-goal handicap, and Adolfito Cambiaso's Silvia was best playing pony.

George Rawlings' Crab Orchard team passed up the opportunity to take three consecutive U.S. Open championships when he made the decision to take the year off from high-goal polo. Nevertheless, the 2009 U.S. Open Championship will be remembered forever because of the tragedy that befell the Lechuza Caracas' pony string. The nineteenth day of April, 2009, is the darkest day in the history of the game of polo.

There were eight teams entered, a number that simplified International Polo Club's polo manager Jimmy Newman's perennial problems in dealing with unbalanced entries. James A. Newman, a winner of the C.V. Whitney Cup in his polo-playing days and manager of several polo clubs from Retama to Palm Beach, deserves a word of recognition for his dedication to the game, his diplomacy in dealing with polo superstars and at times overbearing sponsors, and his intestinal fortitude in tackling thorny situations. Jimmy Newman is one of a band of unsung heroes in polo.

Early favorites were Audi and Lechuza Caracas, after Audi's 8–7 win over Lechuza in the finals of the C.V. Whitney Cup and Lechuza Caracas' one-goal victory over Audi in the Gold Cup. The U.S. Open would define which one of those powerhouses be the top team in America.

In Division I, Lechuza Caracas, Las Monjitas and White Birch were 1–1, and Black Watch was out of the picture with a 0–2 record. The last game would decide which two teams would advance to the semifinals. The game never took place because of the incident that resulted in the death of more than 20 horses of Lechuza Caracas' pony string. White Birch, with Jeff Blake, Pancho Bensadón, Mariano Aguerre and Peter Brant, and Las Monjitas, Camilo Bautista, Adam Snow, Eduardo and Ignacio Novillo Astrada, moved on following Lechuza Caracas decision to forfeit the game.

After the preliminary rounds in Division II, Audi, with Marc Ganzi, Nicolás, Gonzalito and Facundo Pieres, qualified for the semifinals together with Orchard Hill's Steve Van Andel, Hector Galindo, Lucas Criado and Pablo MacDonough.

In the first semifinal game Orchard Hill was leading by a single tally in the last chukker; however, Audi came out strong and scored four goals to Orchard Hill's single point, for a 12–10 win. The second semifinal was a good game, Las Monjitas winning the contest by 11 goals to nine over White Birch.

The final was rather disappointing from the spectators' point of view. It was the acme of contemporary polo: a slow, dribbling-controlled match with both teams unable or unwilling to open up the game and take chances. Las Monjitas had a 7 to 5 goal lead at halftime. Gonzalo Pieres, Sr., was in Audi's tent and changed the team's lineup, placing Ganzi at Back. The game's tempo remained the same: a defensive struggle marked by few field goals. It was no surprise when it went in to overtime. An errant backhander was picked by Facundo Pieres some 50 yards from Las Monjitas' goalposts and Facundo scored an easy goal for a 9–8 win.

Eduardo Novillo Astrada and Adam Snow were jointly awarded the MVP prize, while Eduardo's grey Flecha took the Willis Hartman Trophy for best playing pony.

The 2010 U.S. Open Championship gathered nine teams, rated from 24 to 26-goals. Bracket 1 had Lechuza Caracas, newcomers Valiente, and Las Monjitas all at 26-goals, and Bendabout/The Wanderers at 24-goals. The five-team Bracket 2 had defending champion Audi, Crab Orchard, Pony Express, Orchard Hill, and 25-goal team Piaget, Melissa Ganzi's team that had started the season as Grand Champions. Missing from the high-goal season was perennial power White Birch.

The semifinals found Audi meeting Lechuza and Valiente facing Crab Orchard. The defending champions had in its lineup three members of the 2009 squad: Marc Ganzi, Facundo and Gonzalito Pieres, plus Ignacio "Iñaki" Laprida. Lechuza Caracas, with Victor Vargas, Guillermo Caset, Juan Martín Nero and Santiago Toccalino, was given a good chance of defeating the championship holders. It was not to be. Audi ran up a 5-nil score at the half. However, Lechuza, led by an impressive performance by 10-goaler Juan Martín Nero, came within one goal of making the score board even. With less than 15 seconds left in the game, a shot at goal by Nero found a pony's leg and the ball deflected sideways, from where Audi hit it to the boards, ending the game. The final score was Audi 7, Lechuza Caracas 6.

The other semifinal had previous champion Crab Orchard, with Hilario Ulloa, Julio Arellano, Adolfo Cambiaso and George Rawlings, versus Valiente, with Bobby Jornayvaz, Cristián "Magoo" Laprida, Miguel and Ignacio "Nacho" Novillo Astrada. In this match, Crab Orchard was a comfortable winner, scoring ten goals against seven by Valiente.

The subsidiary tournament for the U.S. Open is the Hall of Fame Cup. The final match was played on the Saturday before the U.S. Open championship match on Sunday. Orchard Hill, with Steve Van Andel, Lucas Criado, Pablo MacDonough, and Hector Galindo, prevailed over Pony Express, with Bob Daniels, Matías Magrini, Carlos Gracida and Bautista Heguy. In this final match, Tomás Goti played instead of Bautista Heguy, who had returned to Argentina.

The final game of the Open Championship was expected to be a great game between two teams that were considered the top in the tournament. In bracket play, Audi had defeated Crab Orchard in a thriller, 13–12 in sudden-death overtime. In spite of this early result, opinion shifted towards Crab Orchard as the favorite because of Cambiaso's reputation as a big match player and the extraordinary form of young Hilario Ulloa, rated at 9-goals in Argentina and at 8-goals by the U.S.P.A.

Rain throughout the match made things difficult for both teams. Marc Ganzi became a cropper following the initial throw-in, five seconds into the game. Amazingly, there were no other falls during the rest of the game, the grounds holding well. Although Audi scored the first goal, Adolfo Cambiaso began to dominate the game, as he often does. Crab Orchard led 7–3 at the halftime break, cut short by heavy rain that sent the divot-stumpers and champagne-seekers running for cover.

In the second half, led by Facundo and Gonzalito Pieres' superb play, twice Audi cut the deficit to only two goals; however, Crab Orchard always seemed to regain control when things became tight. The final tally was Crab Orchard 13, Audi 8. Hilario Ulloa was voted MVP and Julio Arellano's magnificent True was best playing pony. Thus, Crab Orchard took the Triple Crown, having previously taken the C.V. Whitney Handicap and the Gold Cup.

There was no question as to which was the best team in the United States 2010 high-goal polo season.

The 2009 Westchester Cup

The impetus for the revival of the Westchester Cup arose at a meeting of the Museum of Polo chaired by Steve Orthwein in February 2008. It was pointed out that the following year would mark the centenary of the first American victory in the Westchester Cup, a landmark event in the annals of polo because the winning "Big Four" team revolutionized the game's tactics and team preparation. A small committee was established, and Col. David Woodd, the Hurlingham Polo Association chief executive, was contacted regarding the possibility of a challenge by a top American team. The British authorities were enthusiastic about the renewal of the oldest international competition at the highest possible level.

In England, Nicholas Colquhoun–Denvers, the H.P.A. chairman, and John Tinsley, chair of the international committee, were rock-solid in their determination to make the Westchester Cup revival a reality. On this side of the pond, Thomas Biddle, Sr., chairman of the U.S.P.A. and Stephen Orthwein for the Museum of Polo were instrumental in making the innumerable arrangements. Arduous negotiations followed, which were satisfactorily solved thanks to the spirit of cooperation on both sides of the Atlantic Ocean.

A single match took place, following the pattern of the last two competitions, held at the Guards Polo Club in 1992 and 1997. The International Polo Club Palm Beach was the venue; 21 February 2009 was the date. The most pressing problem was how to mount the visitors in an equitable way. Melissa Ganzi was the first to offer her pony string to the British team. Many others followed,

Thomas Biddle, Sr., is the current chairman of the U.S. Polo Association. Based in Aiken, South Carolina, Mr. Biddle continues a long line of polo players who were elected to guide the destinies of the game of polo in the United States. The international matches for the Westchester Cup and the Avila Camacho Cup were revived during his tenure (courtesy Mr. Thomas J. Biddle, Sr.).

allowing the first English international team since 1939 to play polo on a United States ground. It was a formidable achievement taking into consideration the less than favorable economic situation in 2008.

The selected American team was Mike Azzaro, Julio Arellano and Nick Roldán, under Adam Snow's captaincy. Bad luck pursued Team USA. Julio Arellano broke a bone in his hand during one of the first practice games at Hobe Sound, and was out. Mike Azzaro had a spill and fractured his collarbone just days before the event. The team that took the field was Jeff Blake, Adam Snow, Nicolás Roldán and Jeff Hall. England presented James Beim, Mark Tomlinson, London-born Eduardo Novillo Astrada and team captain Luke Tomlinson. Roberto González Gracida and Carlos Gracida were the umpires. By mutual accord between the team captains, a provision was made to stop play around the middle of each chukker to allow for a change of ponies.

Following the usual pomp and circumstance associated with international events, the match started with the English team pressing the issue and obtaining a two-goal advantage at halftime, with one received by handicap. American coach Owen Rinehart made lineup changes: Snow to Number 3 and Roldán to Back, with Jeff Hall moved up front at Number 2.

The changes gave quick results with three quick scores by Roldán, Hall and Blake to put Team USA on even terms. The fourth period ended tied at 7-all. In the fifth chukker, the Americans took the lead for the first time, by 8 goals to 7. The fifth chukker ended 9–9. Only one goal was scored in the last period, which proved to be the winner with two minutes and 42 seconds left to play.

The Westchester Cup returned to England. However, as Polo Museum's chairman Steve Orthwein stated in the official program, "Regardless of which team wins, this renewal of the Westchester Cup will have delivered to our historic sport a great victory. This is the most significant polo competition to take place in the United States in over a quarter of a century."[13]

The 2009 Avila Camacho Cup

After eleven years of rest on Memo Gracida's mantelpiece, the Avila Camacho was taken to the Villages Polo Club in Lady Lake, Florida, for its tenth edition. As previously mentioned in Chapter 11, the U.S.P.A. *Year Book*, for some unexplained reason, does not record the first series played in Mexico City in February 1941; only the November contest is mentioned.

The United States team was John Gobin, Carlos Arellano, Kris Kampsen and Tommy Biddle. Mexico lined up with Pelón Escapite, Julio, Carlos and Memo Gracida. The American team received two goals by handicap, and jumped to a 5–1 lead in the first period, increased to 7–2 in the second. By the fourth chukker the Mexicans had tied the match at 8-all, but two more scores by Mexico matched goals by Gobin and Biddle. The end of the fourth period made it Mexico 10, USA 9. The match was 13-all in the fifth chukker and 15–15 with some two minutes remaining in regulation time. With 48 seconds left on the clock, Memo Gracida intercepted a pass from Gobin to Biddle and scored the wining tally.

It was an entertaining, open match, which pleased the 4,000 spectators enormously. Tommy Biddle was high scorer for America with six goals, while Carlos Gracida made 10 goals, six as the result of penalty shots.[14]

The Avila Camacho Cup returned to the Gracida household, once more.

CHAPTER 26

Current Polo Issues
in the United States

As the ancient pastime of polo slid into the twenty-first century many issues of vital importance to the well-being of the game in America remained unsolved or confined to the backburner. Among those are the difficult question of drug usage, the thorny problem of umpiring, the constant changes of the rules, the increased number of professional players at all levels, the decline in the standards of sportsmanship, the difficulties in applying a fair individual handicap, the quest for participation in the Olympic Games, the issue of safety on the polo grounds and its attendant medical response to accidents, and finally, the role of the U.S. Polo Association vis-à-vis the game's sponsors and the individual clubs.

Certainly, it is a long list; however, unless problems are recognized and openly discussed, they will never be solved.

The State of the Game in 2010

The most welcome news is that the "tapping" game, a nightmare for the umpires and an annoying sight for the spectators, is gradually disappearing from the polo grounds. The credit for this positive development must be given to the three leading national polo associations, American, Argentine and English, that with a minimum of fuss introduced changes to the laws of the game that favored the need for a more open game. Javier Tanoira, a seven-goal Argentine player, produced a manuscript, "Reflections on Argentine Polo," translated into English by Sharon Chavanne, that had a significant impact upon the game.[1]

The Florida winter of 2010 presented the best polo played in years because the new rules as adopted by the U.S. Polo Association have been successful in opening up the game, coupled with the return of the backhander stroke as a play-making and offensive weapon. The players enjoy the game, the spectators take pleasure in watching the action, and the stress on the ponies is considerably less than the "stop, go, stop, turn and go," so prevalent only a season ago. This change in the pattern of polo started in Britain, followed in the Argentine high-goal season, and, happily, moved on to the polo grounds in Palm Beach County.

The Game's Administration

More than fifteen years ago, Marty LeGrand wrote a provocative editorial in *Polo* magazine. Among her comments there was a sentence that merits serious consideration in regard

Santiago Chavanne, a winner of the U.S. Open with Outback, playing on the Mount Brilliant team during the 2010 high-goal season. Jeff Hall and Gonzalo Deltour rush into coverage for Zacara, followed by Francisco Irastorza (Museum of Polo, Alex Pacheco photograph).

to the future of polo in America: "A good sport has gone astray in the last 10 to 15 years thanks to the insidious influence of big money, big mouths, big egos and too little backbone among those whose job is to enforce polo's code of conduct."[2] Many keen observers of the game agreed with her comments, then and now. There is no question that without the enormous amount of dollars spent by the patrons of the game, polo in the United States could not possibly be played at a 26-goal level. However, at times the influence exerted by the sponsors of polo has had deleterious influence upon the conduct of the game.

An egregious example was the issue of Gonzalo Pieres, Jr.'s handicap. At the end of the winter 2008 season, Gonzalito, one of the world's top players, a 10-goaler in Argentina and England, had his handicap raised to 10-goals by the U.S.P.A. Handicap Committee. His sponsor became upset because with that change, Pieres would not be able to be part of his team in the 20-goal California summer season and in the 26-goal U.S. Open in Florida. Within a short period of time, Gonzalito Pieres' handicap was back to nine-goals. There were very few people that would disagree with the notion that Gonzalo Pieres, Jr., was a true 10-goaler. The implied threat to remove a team from competition was akin to blackmail, and the lack of backbone shown by the U.S.P.A. authorities confirms Ms. LeGrand's observations.

Another player on Audi's team was Gonzalo Deltour, an Argentine who many observers thought was under-handicapped at three-goals. U.S.P.A. officials observed his performance and determined that "although he was playing well, he was fairly handicapped."[3] Audi, with Sugar Erskine and Marc Ganzi completing the team, were unbeaten in the California season, winning every tournament, with an overall 10–0 record.

The ripples extended into the 2009 U.S. Open Championship. In the final match between Audi and Las Monjitas, with only seconds to go, Las Monjitas was ahead by one goal — Gonzalito's handicap — when brother Facundo scored to take the game into overtime. Facundo scored again in extra time to seal the championship for Audi.

The issue of proper individual handicapping is crucial to the well-being of polo. We are all in agreement that handicaps are arbitrary values; nevertheless, a great measure of fairness must be applied by the Handicap Committee. The question of a "prestige" handicap for a prominent individual still comes up quite often and it will remain current as long as the era of patron polo remains the standard in high-goal polo.

Another issue related to proper handicapping is that of the "ringer," usually a young foreign player sporting a much lower handicap than his apparent ability as a polo player. This raises loud cries of cheating and bad feelings among players. It is not an easy situation to solve. The fact is that a young player on a well-endowed team will be given mounts much superior to the ones he has been riding up to then. Taking into account that horses account for roughly 75 percent of the game — some say more than that — it should be no surprise that suddenly the tyro is playing three or four goals better than his official handicap. This is borne out by the fact that after the tournament is won with a concomitant handicap raise, when the young player is left to his own resources, more often than not he is unable to maintain his new handicap. Another fact to be considered is that the "ringer" may be playing on a team with Mariano Aguerre or Adolfo Cambiaso, both well-known by their ability to nurse promising youngsters to higher levels of play.

For the great majority of polo players, membership in the U.S.P.A. is a matter of fact, especially in medium and high-goal polo. At low-handicap level, there are probably many players that do not bother to seek membership with the ruling body; they play polo for the sheer fun if it. At the club level, the feeling among the players seems to be that the U.S. Polo Association is a far-away entity, removed from the problems and struggles of the smaller clubs, quite different from those faced by the big institutions hosting the main national tournaments. In these quarters the question often asked is, "What do we get from the polo association?"[4] The perception is that the U.S.P.A. is asleep; its coffers are full but its energy is dissipated and its heart is empty. Sometimes it seems that everyone in polo is preoccupied with making money and no one is bothering about running the game properly.

There are one or two grave constitutional defects in the administrative body that controls American polo, one being the continuing re–election of delegates and officers, in one position or another. There seems to be a rotating-door culture, which makes it extremely difficult for dissenting voices to gain admission to the Association's higher councils. The reform in allowing the membership to elect the delegates-at-large has been a big step forward; however, in the first election all the candidates selected by the Nominating Committee gained election; none of the other candidates were successful.

Nevertheless, the game of polo has survived and prospered as a gracious pastime played and administered by decent, affable people. It prides itself on a code of conduct that makes it virtually unique among its peers and rivals. The challenge for the future is to ensure that the game can withstand the corrosive effect which money has had on other sports and to maintain that special ethos which, we would like to think, sets polo apart.

Money in Polo

Teddy Roosevelt, polo player, Nobel Prize winner and American president, believed in sports as a means of developing strength of body which led to vigor of mind and character. T.R. was against professionalism and the commercialization of sport. He was quoted as saying: "When money comes in at the gate, the game goes out at the window."[5]

The game of polo is following the path of many professional sports. It was a game in the 1890s. Then it became a cult in the roaring twenties and a small business in the late 1970s. Today, it is big business, and in common with other sports and games, polo is at risk of becoming a victim of its own professional success. The more our talented athletes sell themselves to the entertainment business, the more they lose the sense of fun and joy in competing.[6] The biggest problem in the world of sports today is that it is now becoming not only less fun but also increasingly subject to corruption. Adding to the problem is the inadequate disciplinary control by governing bodies, many of which lack the moral courage to impose adequate sanctions and penalties on offenders.

The current fact in polo is the ever-increasing dominance of the profit motive. That is, a shift from what was an amateur approach to games to the spirit of what is in it for me. The U.S. Polo Association must guard against the well-endowed sector of the entertainment industry masquerading as sport. The game has been organized with great devotion, integrity and caution, not always with imagination.

Probably today, most professional polo players would laugh when told the story of Alberto Pedro Heguy, the Argentine 10-goaler, telling the umpires during a final match for the Open Championship that he had hit the ball for a safety.[7] Compare that attitude with recent incidents during soccer's World Cup: Diego Maradona scoring against England with the notorious "hand of God" score, and, just recently, Thierry Henry's obvious hand goal for France in the match that eliminated Ireland from going on to compete in the final round in South Africa.

The Question of Drugs

This is a most complicated issue that besets all sports and games. The question of human usage cannot be answered until the U.S.P.A. implements a randomized drug-testing program conducted within strict scientific parameters by independent, federally approved laboratories. The sooner this is done, the better for the game of polo and the welfare of the players. The consequences of an accident on the polo grounds incurred by a player under the influence of drugs are too horrifying to contemplate.

The U.S. Polo Association's Code of Conduct states: "The United States Polo Association requests that all USPA member clubs and individuals honor and adhere to the following Code of Conduct:" Under Provision 6, it reads, "Always compete without the use of drugs and/or alcohol."[8]

Compare this bland directive with the Hurlingham Polo Association's stand on the same issue: "Doping is the use by an associate member (player or official)—hereafter collectively referred to as 'player,'—of any Banned Substance and is strictly forbidden according to the terms of this Regulation."[9] There is neither ambiguity nor hopefulness in the H.P.A.'s wording.

In regard to the use of drugs in horses, the H.P.A. has paved the way in a sustained effort to stamp out the use of stimulants, and there is no one who is honestly interested in the game's welfare that will not applaud its efforts. However, it is a delicate subject and has to be handled with care because certain medications have the potential to be utilized as "tonics," a euphemism for performance-enhancing drugs, or plainly stated, doping.

The question has been raised about administering medications that may contain stimulants to sick animals. The answer was given a long time ago by James Calvin Coolidge: "It stands to reason as a perfectly sensible attitude that horses that developed a cough and therefore are in need of cough medicine, or fail to clear up their feed, and so in need of therapy, are really in no condition to play, and should not be sent to a match."[10] The practice of doping must be eliminated if the U.S. Polo Association is going to substantiate its claim about caring for the ponies' well-being, as mentioned in Provision 4 of its own Code of Conduct.

The use of noxious medications was brought into the limelight in April 2009, when more than twenty ponies of the Lechuza Caracas team perished just before a quarterfinal U.S. Open match at International Polo Club Palm Beach. Everybody got into the act and seemed to have an opinion in the matter, from the Humane Society of the United States to the ever-present media.[11]

The State of Florida Agriculture and Consumer Services Commissioner Charles H. Bronson ordered an investigation. At the time of writing, one year after the event, no report has been made public regarding the results of the investigation.

This incident raises issues regarding the use of medications supposed to decrease the recuperation time after exercise. Biodyl, a substance used in France but prohibited in the United States, contains selenium, an element essential in normal metabolism but deadly in toxic doses. An overdose of selenium was identified as the cause of death of the ponies. The fact is that selenium does not either improve performance or decrease recuperation time to normal after exertion. A review of the pharmacological literature failed to find a single scientific article regarding a beneficial effect of selenium supplements.[12] The question must be asked: Why was selenium prescribed and administered?

Although at the time of the Lechuza Caracas incident there was a 34-member Equine Welfare Committee chaired by Clint Nangle, U.S.P.A. Chairman Thomas Biddle, Sr., appointed an ad-hoc Polo Pony Welfare Committee to look into ways to prevent such an occurrence from ever happening again.[13]

A pilot program was started in 2010, with full implementation in 2011. The U.S. Polo Association has engaged the services of the U.S. Equestrian Federation, which is the national governing body for equestrian sport in America for the Equine Drugs and Medications Program, to administer the testing. At their annual meeting in October 2009, the U.S.P.A. Board of Governors unanimously approved a by-law change that requires individual members of the U.S.P.A. to submit their horses for random blood and/or urine testing. The Association has also amended the by-laws to include disciplinary action against any member convicted of a civil animal-abuse violation.

The International Scene

As the year 2010 unfolds, the world's polo hierarchy is well defined: England and the United States as likeable underdogs and Argentina as a ruthless imperial power.

One of the problems in international polo is the low index of competitive balance among the polo-playing nations. Competitive balance is in important part of professional sports. In any other business a company would be pleased to watch its competitors to file for bankruptcy; however, sports franchise owners are bound together by an inherent common interest in maintaining a viable league because their business is selling to the public a competition on a field, court or rink. Uncertainty of outcome is a powerful magnet for attracting the fans to stadiums or TV sets.

This lack of competitive balance at the top is the long-term result of differences in the evolution of the game in each individual country. The adoption of polo in the differing communities, societies, and nations was soon followed by adaptation. The rules of the game were basically the same, but the way polo was played by policemen in Burma, shepherds in New Zealand, cattlemen in Australia and settlers in Argentina differed from each other as they differed in the game played by cowboys in Texas, British settlers in Iowa or Wyoming, and Harvard undergraduates in Watertown.

Each social group approached polo with its own attitudes, preferences and priorities, tempered by available resources. They wished to play polo in their own way and the players went about their pastime according to local conditions and customs. Perhaps uniformity was sought, but it was rarely attained.

Argentina was blessed with ready-made polo grounds on the flat pampas and an abundance of horseflesh, which was improved by British thoroughbreds. Two world wars depleted the resources in both the United States and Britain. This differential at the high level of the game has remained untouched since the end of World War II.

Competition with Argentina has not occurred since the 1980 Cup of the Americas at San Antonio. The reluctance of the Argentine Polo Association to compete for the Cup on handicap basis, although quite understandable, prevents the issue of a meaningful challenge by the U.S.P.A.

On the other hand, the Westchester Cup may have a bright future. When the British team traveled to Florida for the 2009 contest, the understanding was that a return match would take place in England within the next three years. Initial negotiations have taken place between the two associations.

Polo and the Olympic Games

The return of polo as an Olympic sport remains a dream. The tremendous popularity of the Olympic five-ring circus with its attendant enormous infrastructure needed to accommodate the multitudes that congregate every four years has made the possibility of polo, an elite game played by less than 20,000 people world-wide, a remote proposition. So far, the efforts of the U.S.P.A. International Committee have failed to bear fruit, while an entry in the Pan American Games is still a remote possibility.

If and when the game of polo becomes part of a truly comprehensive international event it must be played without handicap limitations. International competitions at the top level are restricted to the very best individuals and the top teams. The issue of fair and equitable handicaps has been a thorn in the side for the officials charged with running the Federation of International Polo World Polo Championships at the 14-goal level.

Umpiring

The call for better umpiring has been heard for a long time, but in recent years has reached a crescendo. The long-awaited introduction of a professional program was supposed to dramatically improve the quality of umpiring on the field. Regrettably, that lofty goal has not been achieved. In the eyes of impartial observers, the quality of high-goal polo officiating has significantly decreased since the balmy days of Benny Gutierrez and Red Armour, the best two-men crew since the war's end. Perhaps that quality of umpiring was made possible because both Red Armour and Benny Gutierrez were once two very good polo players.

The current crop of umpires has failed to reach high expectations. When Steve Lane, chief umpire instructor, went to England at the invitation of the Hurlingham Polo Association to assess the quality of umpiring in the British Isles, his main criticism was poor positioning on the field. Other deficiencies noted by Lane were inconsistency in making calls and weak field discipline. He felt that during the Gold Cup, the umpires got right 80 to 84 percent of the calls. He stated that in America the percentage was 94 percent and was of the opinion that since only six umpires officiated at high-goal in the United States, while in England the number was 13 umpires, it was easier to achieve uniformity.

An informal survey of high-goal players in Florida indicated that the most significant fault on the part of the umpires was the lack of uniformity in making calls. An infraction would be let go by and a similar play seconds later would be whistled. The second most common complaint was a perception of arrogance on the part of the umpires. The third observation was that the umpires called relatively minor infractions while instances of dangerous riding were allowed to go unpunished. This latter criticism was echoed by polo legend Gonzalo Pieres, Sr., while watching games in the course of the 2009 U.S. Open Championship.

One of the problems in contemporary polo is that, by and large, the umpires lack presence, that undefined qualification, on the polo grounds. Instead of exuding an air of confidence and quiet authority, many umpires depend on the red flag to maintain professional respect and field discipline. Such an attitude invariably leads to further anger and loss of control.

The peer review system in umpiring must be upgraded. It is difficult to criticize one of your own peers, who may be your partner in the next polo game. The umpires and referee's performance on the field must be recorded and also observed by an independent body of experienced players and retired officials, persons of substance and influence, who are in a much better position to be objective in their evaluation of umpires' skills.

Until an impartial, away from the fray method is adopted, the complaints about poor umpiring will continue to plague the polo scene.

George Oliver, a 9-goal international player, expressed some thoughts on umpiring and players' behavior. "A player's early training sets the tone for his conduct on the field," Oliver stated in an interview. That was where he believed the polo players of his day enjoyed the best of times. Recollecting his memories of the Meadow Brook Club, George Oliver said,

> There you were taught respect for the rules and sportsmanship, and it was made possible by the interest of gentlemen such as Mr. Devereux Milburn, Sr., Mr. von Stade, Mr. Iglehart, and Mr. J.S. Phipps. These gentlemen were not only helpful in all phases of polo—horsemanship, sportsmanship, teamwork and teaching the right way to play the game—but they did not hesitate in

setting you right; they let you know what you had done wrong, and made it clear that you were not to do it again. Players now are put on the field before they are ready, and on horses they can't ride. Then they are put on practice games, often with no umpiring, hardly the formula for instilling respect for the rules.[14]

The governing bodies, both at the national and club level, must support the umpires without hesitation. An integral part of this support includes strict application of decisions rendered by disciplinary committees; otherwise the system will crumble. Years ago in 1994, a high-handicap player, Cristián Laprida, was fined $2,000 and suspended for one game by the club's disciplinary committee. The player showed up the following day, ready to play. An arrangement had been made between the club and the sponsor to exchange the suspension for a higher fine. The committee's co–chairmen, George Oliver and Peter Orthwein resigned, and the officiating umpires, Roy Barry and Benny Gutierrez, refused to umpire the game.[15] Such lack of support for the officials and the disciplinary body of the Palm Beach Polo Club, at the time the largest in Florida, was abysmal.

The umpires have a profound impact on the outcome of polo games. There are numerous instances during a game when the umpires can decide to give one player the benefit of the doubt in calling a foul or in showing a yellow or red flag. What the players want most is consistency. Nevertheless, the often idiosyncratic, and with the benefit of hindsight, blatantly wrong decisions by officials have as great an impact on the outcome of a match as the players' performance on the field.

It has been argued that television replays will solve the problem. Polo is a most difficult game to umpire; even experts reviewing images often disagree whether a particular play was or was not a foul. However, it should be applied to all levels of play, which makes it impracticable at present. The experience with replays in Argentina, although reducing the uncertainty of close calls, also causes lengthy delays in the flow of the game, that may be excellent opportunities for commercial advertisements, but are annoying to the paying spectators.

One of the attractions of the ancient game of polo is that it is played around the world at all levels with the same primitive tools: a ball, goalposts, a ground marked with some lines. The notoriously erratic performance of the umpires provides an entertainment facet, contributing to amusement, excitement, and at times outrage among spectators and players alike.

Changes in the Rules

In this day of globalization in the game of polo it is difficult for players and umpires to obey and apply the rules of the games in different countries. The failure of the major polo associations to reach a reasonable accord and unify the rules of the games is hard to believe.

In the United States, there are changes to the rules and their interpretation on a yearly basis. While it is true that rules and regulations must change from time to time in order to adapt to changes in tactics, there is also something of value in stabilization of the rules for a period of time, so players and spectators adjust to the new formats.

On the other hand, some rules are changed with disregard for common sense. For example, in America Penalty 2, a 30-yard shot at goal is not allowed to be defended, making it the most boring play during a match. However, a 40-yard penalty shot may be defended.

The risk of injury has been advanced as the rationale for not allowing a 30-yard shot to be blocked. It does not make sense that a ten-yard difference will have a significant outcome when a player or pony is hit by a ball. It is far more dangerous for a player to stand still 30 yards in front of an opponent about to hit a 60-yard penalty, than to be a moving target in a 30-yard attempt at goal. Perhaps either Penalty 2 or Penalty 3 should be done away with, as suggested by 9-goaler Julian Hipwood.

Another rule that merits a second look is changing ends after a goal is scored. Occasionally, it is forgotten by a player or an official; however, it is a source of puzzlement to newcomers to the game. In no other major sport are ends changed after a score.

Some other rule changes have been proposed and tried in exhibition games. The most egregious was the institution of a two-point allowance for a goal scored from a minimum distance. It was tried at a charade event on the former site of the venerable Hurlingham Club ground in Fulham. A D ring was painted 45 yards from the goals; any successful shot from outside the D counted for two points, producing a slugfest among the heavy hitters. The matches attracted enough attention to be the main story in England's *Polo Times*,[16] a reflection on the deadly fear of boredom which afflicts our, at times, aimless society.

A variation was tried at International Polo Club Palm Beach on the occasion of the annual match to benefit the Polo Players' Support Group, a worthy organization headed by Canadian player David Offen. In this event, any goal scored from 60 yards outside the goalposts counted for two points. Informal conversations at game's end failed to elicit much support for such practice.

In reviewing time-honored rules and regulations, a sense of balance must be achieved between temporary measures that have ossified into unsatisfactory permanence and real change for improving the continuity of polo.

Safety

In 1983, outgoing U.S.P.A. chairman William Sinclaire characterized the state of safety in polo a "deplorable situation" at the Annual Meeting in San Antonio on 20 October 1983.[17] Bill Sinclaire cited faster play, an increase in the number of players, added pressures, and younger, more aggressive players as reasons, and he urged all U.S.P.A. members to quell the growing danger.

Not much has changed in the polo scene since that strong condemnation by the then U.S. Polo Association's chairman. The fact of the matter is that polo has always been a dangerous game, a thought that is not always present in the players and spectators' minds. The history of modern polo is littered with reports of polo players killed on the field of play, from Robert Darley at Phoenix Park in Dublin in 1877 to Tracy Mactaggart on the Outback grounds in Wellington in 2009.

Safety on the polo grounds is addressed by several rules of the game. Head injury is probably the leading cause of death. Rule 4, Equipment, notes that the U.S.P.A. has developed standards by which different helmets can be evaluated in terms of how much protection they afford. Research should be continued towards head protection matching the standards set by the National Football League.

Players are also encouraged to wear face and eye protection at all times during play.[18] Argentine player and veterinarian Eduardo Amaya has developed an eye protector for ponies that is available on the market.

Deborah Spark, Sugar Erskine's sister-in-law, warming up a pony prior to a game at International Polo Club Palm Beach (Museum of Polo, Alex Pacheco photograph).

Regarding mounts, a pony blind in one eye is not allowed on the polo field. A pony showing vice, or not under control, must be removed from the field of play. Pony abuse is controlled by prohibitions of slash whipping, overwhipping and heavy whipping, and by forbidding a player to strike a mount with any part of his mallet.[19]

Dangerous riding, a preventable cause of accidents, is covered in Rule 26. What constitutes a dangerous ride-off is left to the umpire's discretion. Other instances of dangerous riding include blind-siding, zigzagging in front of another player, riding across or over a mount's fore or hind legs, and intimidation, that is, riding at an opponent in such a manner to intimidate and cause the opponent to pull out or miss his stroke.

Strict adherence by the players and strict umpiring regarding these rules will certainly decrease the incidence of ghastly accidents involving both mount and rider. The players bear a major responsibility in helping making polo a safe game. One hundred years ago Cameron Forbes wrote in his *As to Polo*: "The first care of every player should be to make the game absolutely safe by avoiding committing fouls, which are usually, *per se*, dangerous riding."[20]

Sportsmanship

Sportsmanship is an unwritten, time-honored rule of civilized conduct. There are two factors that combine to launch an attack, perhaps unwillingly and unintended, against pure amateurism and its attendant high value in sportsmanship. One is the obsession with winning in all sports and the other the decreased value of good manners on the fields of play.

The ideals of sportsmanship go back a long time in America. Those ideals did exist and they were most often enforced informally and without hesitation by the dire prospect of ostracism. Failure to adhere to time-honored attitudes of honor, honesty and good manners were taken far more seriously in those days than they are today.

The American amateur sporting spirit was deeply rooted in unwritten codes of honor and decency. The sportsmen's code was, and remains, an ideal and not a description of actual behavior. President Theodore Roosevelt stepped in to quell the brutalities of football in the days that the genteel tradition was still in vogue. At the same time, many of the leading colleges in the nation were breaking up with football rivals who, so they thought, were violating the codes of honor and gentlemanly behavior. The U.S. Military and Naval academies did not play between 1893 and 1899, Harvard and Yale between 1894 and 1897, Princeton broke with Harvard and also with Pennsylvania.

Professor David Brogan once mentioned that in America, being a good loser is not as good as being a winner, good or bad. John Tunis echoed that sentiment years ago when he wrote, "One might as well expect Bannister or Chataway to run a six-minute mile as expect an American to regard a loser with anything but pity mixed with contempt."[21]

Robin Uihlein, president of the Sarasota Polo Club in Florida, adheres to the Hap Sharp's school of polo sportsmanship: "If you do anything to disrupt everyone's enjoyment of the game, you hit the road."[22]

In the same issue of *Polo* magazine, founding editor Ami Shinitzky took an opposing view. In his article "Our Obsession with Sportsmanship," Shinitzky equals a polo game with a circus cage full of tigers. "Of course, the tigers need to be orderly, and safety considerations are paramount, but they are also allowed to remain tigers—that is what the show is all about."[23] However, the comparison is hardly valid. Polo players are not animals nor respond tamely to the crack of a whip. They are intelligent people who play mostly for fun and their own pleasure.

Mauricio Devrient-Kidd, a good player as well as an umpire, once mentioned how lucky he was for being paid to do something that gives him great pleasure.[24] The game of polo is a most dangerous pastime, and at times deadly. Sportsmanship, which includes respect for others, is the first defense in the prevention of polo accidents. There is absolutely nothing wrong with sportsmanship.

The universities, those privileged institutions, bear a heavy responsibility for the decline of sportsmanship in the United States. Theodore Roosevelt always emphasized the duties rather than the rights of privilege. The American colleges, many of which are pre–professional treadmills for the major professional sports, have in a sense betrayed their main reason for existence, education. The percentage of students to graduate after being drafted by professional teams is abysmally low.

This betrayal of sport by the American colleges has been a factor in generating an educational mess. What is sarcastically referred to as an athletic scholarship is offered to gifted athletes in football, basketball, baseball and many other sports. But rumors abound that in some colleges, where the supervision of the athletic department is not what it ought to be, scholarships are also awarded to scholars.

Of course, collegiate polo is immune to this chaos because it is not a varsity sport. The Polo Training Foundation must be commended for its support of interscholastic and intercollegiate polo. University polo should be one of the major sources of future players. These men and women of promise, not yet of performance, must be mentored and supported; they are the future of polo in America.

In the 1980s, the author visited Stewart Iglehart at his home in Florida by the Atlantic Ocean. The leaves of autumn had not taken away any of his skill, energy and charm, sterling qualities that would have made him a polo star at any time and in any place. Iglehart spoke at length about his career and his strong feelings on diverse matters such as the deleterious effect on the evolution of the game brought about by the institution of a handicap limit in the U.S. Open Championship, and the decline of sportsmanship on the polo grounds.

Many years after his retirement, Stewart Iglehart was deservedly an iconic figure, still the best-known and most influential voice in polo, and if the tone of his voice was indeed a little nostalgic then polo today is not quite as wholesome as it was in his heyday.

However, not everything is lost. Lt. Col. Steven E. Walsh on polo:

> Early in my playing career I had the opportunity to play in England with a player of more than 40 years of experience. He reminded me that unlike most other sports played in the world, polo, a game played by ladies and gentlemen, was a game of invitation. As long as you acted as a gentleman, both on and off the field you will always be invited to and welcome to participate. Only if we remember the conduct expected from this game of invitation can we expect our great sport to prosper and flourish.[25]

Colophon

While researching and attempting to reconstruct the history of American polo from Foxhall Keene down to Adam Snow and other players who have striven to retain their own dignity and well-being in the midst of administrative chaos, it became apparent that a number of approaches were needed. In any discussion of this wonderful game there has to be room for dewy-eyed nostalgia. But hard-headed realism and objectivity are called for as well. These qualities are all here. The book recalls golden moments and initial endeavors, but also makes clear that it is high time for things to get better. Now more than ever polo in these United States has to find and show its true character.

The game of polo is meant to make us glad. This objective applies to players, administrators, officials and spectators alike. As far as the top players are concerned, in these days it is also meant to make them wealthy. However, although huge payments have changed the status of the polo professional, the men who earn more in a month than many of the fans take home in a year still find pleasure in the game. It could not be otherwise.

Appendix 1.
Rules of the California Polo Club, 1876

1st. The goals shall be 200 yards apart, or according to the number of runs to be made.

2nd. The ball shall be three and one-half inches in diameter, the sticks not to exceed three and one-half feet in length.

3rd. Sticks may be hooked and taken from an opponent but no stick can be hooked either under or in front of a horse.

4th. Any player catching an opponent's arm or horse, or holding his stick in front of an opponent's horse in order to prevent the horse's advance, or hitting an opponent's horse to drive him over the ball, shall be declared to be out of the game.

5th. If it can be shown to the umpire that a run has been won by a foul, it shall be the duty of the umpire to declare it a dead run.

6th. Two decisions of foul runs shall score one run against the offending side.

7th. In case a ball is hit beyond the goal but outside the flags, the ball shall be put on the line through which it should have passed and both sides behind the goal, the party defending the goal shall be entitled to a hit-off.

8th. In case the ball passes outside the side limits, the ball shall be placed in the center of the course opposite where it left the course, which each party on their respective sides facing the ball, and shall be started by the umpire.

9th. The game shall be started by the umpire, either by word or dropping the flag. The opposing parties to face each other thirty yards from the ball, the two starters to step to the front of their respective sides, and to advance at the signal.

10th. Any party losing his stick must either dismount to recover the stick or pick it up from his horse. Any party receiving his stick either from a fellow player or from a spectator, shall have a foul scored against him, or by order from the umpire, shall throw his stick to the ground and recover it himself.

Appendix 2.
Clubs Affiliated to the
Polo Association, 1890–1900

	Elected	Resigned
Country Club of Westchester	June 6, 1890	June 6, 1912
Essex County Country Club	June 6, 1890	April 18, 1899
Reelected	June 14, 1905	January 10, 1917
Meadow Brook Club	June 6, 1890	
Changed name to Meadowbrook	1976	
Morris County Country Club	June 6, 1890	March 4, 1895
Reelected	March 6, 1895	
Changed name to Whippany River	March 30, 1904	May 22, 1911
Philadelphia Polo Club	June 6, 1890	1931
Reelected	August 1938	World War II
Rockaway Hunting Club	June 6, 1890	1932
Westchester Polo Club	June 6, 1890	World War II
Oyster Bay Polo Club	June 18, 1890	March 12, 1895
Myopia Hunt Club	August 6, 1890	World War II
Reelected	July 1959	
Harvard Polo Club	August 6, 1890	March 8, 1897
Hingham Polo Club	August 12, 1890	February 3, 1897
Tuxedo Polo Club	February 24, 1891	March 12, 1895
The Country Club of Brookline	March 1, 1892	April 15, 1902
Country Club of St. Louis	March 21, 1893	World War II
Reelected	September 1947	
Monmouth County Polo Club	June 6, 1893	
Changed name to Southampton	August 31, 1897	February 13, 1912
Reelected as Monmouth Co.	Dec. 14, 1919	1949
Dedham Polo Club	May 23, 1894	
Joined with Norfolk Country Club	May 26, 1910	March 1931
Reelected	March 1936	World War II
Buffalo Country Club	September 5, 1894	January 21, 1919
Reelected	February 28, 1922	1932
Chicago Polo Club	March 4, 1895	March 9, 1897
Lowell Country Club	March 4, 1895	
Changed name to Vesper	August 27, 1895	July 1, 1896
Devon Polo Club	March 6, 1895	January 21, 1919
Point Judith Country Club	July 22, 1895	1932
Genesee Valley Polo Club	September 9, 1895	March 3, 1897
Washington Polo Club	April 6, 1896	1924
Evanston Country Club	June 3, 1896	February 10, 1899
Riding and Driving Club	June 3, 1896	November 30, 1899

	Elected	*Resigned*
Staten Island Polo Club	March 3, 1897	September 29, 1904
Onwentsia Club	March 3, 1897	1935
Jacksonville Polo Club	December 4, 1898	April 17, 1900
Somerset County Polo Club	February 10, 1899	April 21, 1908
Lakewood Polo Club	April 12, 1899	January 21, 1919
Aiken Polo Club	October 24, 1899	
Saratoga Polo Club	October 24, 1899	September 27, 1910
Camden Country Club	April 17, 1900	2002
Squadron A Polo Club	April 17, 1900	February 10, 1920
Great Neck Polo Club	October 17, 1900	World War II

Appendix 3.
Henry L. Herbert's
1888 Handicap List

Forty-two players were handicapped in 1888, as follows:

Meadow Brook		Rockaway	
Hitchcock, Thomas	5	Keene, Foxhall P.	5
Belmont, Augustus, Jr.	4	Cowdin, John E.	4
Sands, Samuel S.	4	Cheever, John D.	2
Thorn, William K	4	La Montagne, René	2
Bird, Oliver W.	3	Turnure, Lawrence	2
Kernochan, James L.	3	Collier, Peter F.	1
Winthrop, Robert D.	3	Burrill, Middleton S.	0
Mortimer, Stanley	2	Clark, Farley	0
Roosevelt, Elliot	2	La Montagne, Edward	0
Winthrop, Egerton	2	Tower, A. Clifford	0
Zborowski, Eliot	2		
Richardson, H.B.	1	Essex County	
Carroll, Charles	0	Farr, T. Powers	1
Ripley, Sidney D.	0	Pfizer, Emile	1
		Robinson, Douglas	1
Pelham		Tucker, W.W.	1
Havemeyer, Theodore	2	Dallett, John	0
Potter, Edward C.	2	Heckscher, Charles A.	0
Waterbury, James M.	2	Knoedler, Charles L.	0
Potter, Howard N.	1	Lee, Charles H.	0
Cooley, James C.	0	Pfizer, Charles	0
Hunter, A.	0	Sedgwick, Robert	0
Story, Marion	0		
Watson, Francis A.	0		

Source: *The New York Herald*, "Growth of Polo Realized from First Handicap List — Only Forty-Two Players Were Named in Herbert's Original Ratings in 1888 — More Than 2,500 Are Included in the 1917 Compilations."
Clipping in Mr. William A Hazard's scrapbook; author's collection.

Appendix 4.
Players' Handicaps
in 1888, 1890 and 1891

	1888	1890	1891
Foxhall Keene	5	5	10
Thomas Hitchcock	5	3	7
John Cowdin	4	4	8
William Thorn, Jr.	4	3	5
Oliver Bird	3	3	6
Winthrop Rutherfurd	3	3	6
Robert Winthrop	3	2	5
August Belmont, Jr.	2	3	6
Edward Potter	2	3	6
John Cheever	2	2	4
Stanley Mortimer	2	*	4
T. Powers Farr	1	3	6
Douglas Robinson	1	3	6
Francis Appleton	1	1	5
René La Montagne	1	2	4
William Lord	1	2	4
Theodore Havemeyer	1	2	3
Farley Clark	0	2	4
John Dallet, Jr.	0	2	4
Edward La Montagne	0	2	4
Charles Carroll	0	1	3
Augustus P. Gardner	0	†	3

*Stanley Mortimer not listed in July 1890.
†Myopia not affiliated until August 1890.

Sources: Casper W. Whitney, *Polo in America*, Harper's Weekly, 572.
Minutes of the Polo Association, 10 July 1890.
Polo Association 1891 Year Book.

Appendix 5.
Winners of Major Championships,
1890–1921

Polo Association Cups

1890   at Newport. **Meadow Brook**. Augustus Belmont, Jr., Thomas Hitchcock, Oliver W. Bird, Roger D. Winthrop.

1891   at Cedarhurst. **Rockaway**. John D. Cheever, John E. Cowdin, Foxhall P. Keene, Winthrop Rutherford.

1892   at Myopia. **Harvard**. Columbus C. Baldwin, Robert G. Shaw, II, James B. Eustis, Jr., Rodolphe L. Agassiz.

1893   at Meadow Brook. **Independence** (Morris County). George L. Day, Thomas Hitchcock, George W.P. Eustis, Benjamin Nicoll.

1894   at Westchester. **Meadow Brook**. George L. Day, Thomas Hitchcock, Harry P. Whitney, Benjamin Nicoll.

1895   at Brookline. **Country Club of Brookline**. Walter S. Hobart, Robert W. Williams, William H. Goodwin, Frank Blackwood Fay.

1896   at Buffalo. **Meadow Brook 2nd**. William C. Eustis, Harry K. Vingut, Charles Raoul-Duval, Maurice Raoul-Duval.

1897   at Bala. **Philadelphia C.C.**. Joshua B. Lippincott, Jr., Mitchell G. Rosengarten, Jr., Albert E. Kennedy, John F. McFadden.

1898   at Dedham. **Dedham 2nd**. Alfred R. Weld, Elton Clark, William H. Goodwin, Joshua Crane, Jr.

Championship Cup and Added Cups

Later (1895) known as Senior Championship

1895   at Prospect Park, Brooklyn. **Myopia**. Augustus Peabody Gardner, Robert G. Shaw, II, Rodolphe L. Agassiz, Frank Blackwood Fay.

1896   at Prospect Park. **Rockaway**. Joseph S. Stevens, John E. Cowdin, Foxhall P. Keene, George P. Eustis.

1897   at Prospect Park. **Meadow Brook**. William C. Eustis, Thomas Hitchcock, Harry Payne Whitney, Benjamin Nicoll.

1898   at Prospect Park **Meadow Brook**. William C. Eustis, Thomas Hitchcock, Columbus C. Baldwin, Harry P. Whitney.

1899   **Westchester Polo Club**, by default. James M. Waterbury, Jr., John E. Cowdin, Foxhall P. Keene, Lawrence Waterbury.

1900   at Prospect Park **Dedham**. Allan Forbes, Edward M. Weld, William H. Goodwin, Joshua Crane, Jr.

1901   at The Country Club, Brookline. **Lakewood.** C. Randolph Snowden, James M. Waterbury, Jr., Foxhall P. Keene, Lawrence Waterbury.

1902   at Saratoga Springs. Not awarded. (L. Waterbury declared ineligible after the event). **Lakewood.** F. Hervey A. Lyle, John E. Cowdin, James M. Waterbury, Jr., Lawrence Waterbury.

1903   at Bala. **C.C. of Westchester 1st.** John E. Cowdin, James M. Waterbury, Jr., Harry P. Whitney, Lawrence Waterbury.

1904   at Point Judith C.C. **Myopia 1st.** Maxwell Norman, Robert G. Shaw, II, Rodolphe L. Agassiz, Devereux Milburn.

1905   Rockaway withdrew, at Van Cortland Park. No other entries.

1906   at Newport. **Meadow Brook 1st.** Eugene S. Reynal, James M. Waterbury, Jr., Lawrence Waterbury, Robert L. Beeckman.

1907   at Onwentsia. **Rockaway 1st.** John A. Rawlins, René La Montagne, Jr., Foxhall P. Keene, Daniel Chauncey, Jr.

1908   Not Played. No teams.

1909   at Narragansett Pier. **Meadow Brook.** John S. Phipps, James M. Waterbury, Jr., Lawrence Waterbury, Devereux Milburn.

1910   at Narragansett Pier. **Meadow Brook.** John S. Phipps, James M. Waterbury, Jr., Malcolm Stevenson, Devereux Milburn.

1911   at Narragansett Pier. **Meadow Brook.** John A. Rawlins, James M. Waterbury, Jr., Malcolm Stevenson, Devereux Milburn.

1912   at Narragansett Pier. **Meadow Brook.** Eugene S. Reynal, James M. Waterbury, Jr., Foxhall P. Keene, Lawrence Waterbury.

1913   at Narragansett Pier. **Cooperstown.** Frank S. von Stade, Charles C. Rumsey, C. Perry Beadleston, Malcolm Stevenson

1914   at Narragansett Pier. **Bryn Mawr,** by default of Meadow Brook and Cooperstown. John W. Converse, Alfred M. Collins, Mitchell G. Rosengarten, Jr., Alexander Brown.

1915   at Narragansett Pier. **Meadow Brook.** Raymond Belmont, James M. Waterbury, Jr., Malcolm Stevenson, Devereux Milburn

1916   at Narragansett Pier. **Great Neck.** Thomas Hitchcock, Jr., J. Watson Webb, Malcolm Stevenson, Louis E. Stoddard.

1917   Not played. World War I.

1918   Not played. World War I.

1919   at Bala. **Rockaway,** by default of the Philadelphia C.C. Charles C. Rumsey, Earle W. Hopping, Malcolm Stevenson, Thomas Hitchcock, Jr.

1920   at Westbury, N.Y. **Meadow Brook.** Charles C. Rumsey, Thomas Hitchcock, Jr., J. Watson Webb, Devereux Milburn.

1921   at Bala. **Rockaway.** Louis E. Stoddard, Thomas Hitchcock, Jr., Malcolm Stevenson, J. Cheever Cowdin.

Appendix 6.
Winners of the
U.S. Open Championship

Players in preliminary matches are shown in brackets.

1904   at Van Cortlandt Park, NY. **Wanderers:** Charles Randolph Snowden, John E. Cowdin, James M. Waterbury, Jr., Lawrence Waterbury.

1910   at Narragansett Pier, RI. **Ranelagh:** Riversdale N. Grenfell, Francis O. Grenfell, George, Earl of Rocksavage, Frederick A. Gill. [Also played: Lord Hugh Grosvenor]

1912   at Narragansett Pier. **Cooperstown:** Frank S. von Stade, Sr., Charles C. Rumsey, Courtney Perry Beadleston, Malcolm Stevenson.

1913   at Narragansett Pier. **Cooperstown:** Frank S. von Stade, Sr., Charles C. Rumsey, C. Perry Beadleston, Malcolm Stevenson.

1914   at Narragansett Pier. **Meadow Brook Magpies:** Norcross L. Tilney, James Watson Webb, William Goadby Loew, Howard Phipps.

1916   at Narragansett Pier and Westbury, NY. **Meadow Brook:** Howard Phipps, Charles C. Rumsey, W. Goadby Loew, Devereux Milburn. [Also played: Frank S. von Stade, James M. Waterbury, Jr.]

1919   at Bala, PA. **Meadow Brook:** Frederick H. Prince, Jr., J. Watson Webb, Frank von Stade, Sr., Devereux Milburn.

1920   at Westbury. **Meadow Brook:** Frank von Stade, Sr., J. Watson Webb, Robert E. Strawbridge, Sr., Devereux Milburn.

1921   at Bala. **Great Neck:** Louis E. Stoddard, Rodman Wanamaker, II, J. Watson Webb, Robert E. Strawbridge, Jr.

1922   at Rumson, NJ. **Argentine Polo Federation:** John B. Miles, John D. Nelson, David B. Miles, Lewis L. Lacey.

1923   at Westbury. **Meadow Brook:** Raymond Belmont, Thomas Hitchcock, Jr., Robert E. Strawbridge, Jr., Devereux Milburn. [Also played: W. Averell Harriman, R. Penn Smith, Jr.]

1924   at Westbury. **Midwick:** Edgar G. Miller, Eric L. Pedley, Arthur P. Perkins, Carleton F. Burke.

1925   at Westbury. **Orange County:** W. Averell Harriman, James Watson Webb, Malcolm Stevenson, John Cheever Cowdin.

1926   at Westbury. **Hurricanes:** Stephen Sanford, Eric L. Pedley, Charles T.I. Roark, Robert E. Strawbridge, Jr.

1927   at Westbury. **Sands Point:** William Averell Harriman, Thomas Hitchcock, Jr., J. Cheever Cowdin, Louis E. Stoddard.

1928   at Westbury. **Meadow Brook:** Cornelius V. Whitney, F. Winston C. Guest, John B. Miles, Malcolm Stevenson.

1929   at Westbury. **Hurricanes:** Stephen Sanford, Charles T.I. Roark, J. Watson Webb, Robert E. Strawbridge, Jr.

1930   at Westbury. **Hurricanes:** Stephen Sanford, Eric L. Pedley, Charles T.I. Roark, Robert E. Strawbridge, Jr.

1931   at Westbury. **Santa Paula:** Andrés Gazzotti, Juan J. Reynal, José C. Reynal, Manuel Andrada. [Also played: Alfredo J. Harrington]

1932   at Westbury. **Templeton:** Michael G. Phipps, F. Winston C. Guest, D. Stewart B. Iglehart, Raymond R. Guest.

1933   at Westbury. **Aurora:** Seymour H. Knox, Jr., James P. Mills, Elbridge T. Gerry, Elmer J. Boeseke, Jr.

1934   at Westbury. **Templeton:** Michael G. Phipps, F. Winston C. Guest, D. Stewart B. Iglehart, Raymond R. Guest.

1935   at Westbury. **Greentree:** George H. Bostwick, Jr., Thomas Hitchcock, Jr., Gerald M. Balding, John H. Whitney.

1936   at Westbury. **Greentree:** George H. Bostwick, Jr., Thomas Hitchcock, Jr., Gerald M. Balding, John H. Whitney.

1937   at Westbury. **Old Westbury:** Michael G. Phipps, Cecil C. Smith, D. Stewart B. Iglehart, Cornelius V. Whitney.

1938   at Westbury. **Old Westbury:** Michael G. Phipps, Cecil C. Smith, D. Stewart B. Iglehart, Cornelius V. Whitney. [Also played: Ivor Balding]

1939   at Westbury. **Bostwick Field:** George H. Bostwick, Jr., Robert L. Gerry, Jr., Elbridge T. Gerry, Eric H. Tyrrell-Martin.

1940   at Westbury. **Aknusti:** Gerard S. Smith, Robert L. Gerry, Jr., Elbridge T. Gerry, Alan L. Corey, Jr.

1941   at Westbury. **Gulf Stream:** John H.A. Phipps, Michael G. Phipps, Charles S. von Stade, Alan L. Corey, Jr.

1946   at Westbury. **Mexico.** Gabriel Gracida, Guillermo Gracida, Sr., Alejandro Gracida, José Gracida.

1947   at Westbury. **Old Westbury:** Clarence Combs, Jr., Pedro Silvero, D. Stewart B. Iglehart, George K. Oliver, Jr.

1948   at Westbury. **Hurricanes:** James Larry Sheerin, Peter Perkins, Cecil C. Smith, Stephen Sanford.

1949   at Westbury. **Hurricanes:** J. Larry Sheerin, Roberto L. Cavanagh, Cecil C. Smith, Stephen Sanford.

1950   at Westbury. **Bostwick Field:** George H. Bostwick, Jr., George K. Oliver, Jr., Alan L. Corey, Jr., Devereux Milburn, Jr.

1951   at Westbury. **Milwaukee:** Pedro Silvero, Peter Perkins, George K. Oliver, Jr., Robert A. Uihlein, Jr.

1952   at Beverly Hills, CA. **Beverly Hills:** Robert Fletcher, Tony Veen, C. Robertson Skene, Carlton Beal.

1953   at Westbury. **Meadow Brook:** Henry Lewis, III, Philip L.B. Iglehart, Alan L. Corey, Jr., George H. Bostwick, Jr.

1954   at Oak Brook, Hinsdale, IL. **C.C.C.–Meadow Brook:** Andrew D. Beveridge, George H. Bostwick, Jr., Alan L. Corey, Jr., Harold L. Barry.

1955   at Oak Brook. **C.C.C.:** Andrew D. Beveridge, William R. Linfoot, Paul W. Barry, Harold L. Barry.

1956   at Oak Brook. **Brandywine:** George Raworth Williams, Walter Ray Harrington, Jr., Clarence Combs, Jr., William A. Mayer.

1957   at Oak Brook. **Detroit–C.C.C.:** Andrew D. Beveridge, Robert D. Beveridge, George K. Oliver, Jr., Harold L. Barry.

1958   at Oak Brook. **Dallas:** G. Raworth Williams, William R. Linfoot, C. Robertson Skene, Luis Ramos.

1959   at Oak Brook. **Circle F:** Delmar W. Carroll, W. Ray Harrington, Jr., William A Mayer, Russell Firestone.

1960   at Oak Brook. **Oak Brook–C.C.C.**: Andrew D. Beveridge, Wayne Brown, Cecil C. Smith, Harold L. Barry.

1961   at Oak Brook. **Milwaukee**: Guillermo Gracida, Sr., Julio Muller, George K. Oliver, Jr., Robert A. Uihlein, Jr.

1962   at Oak Brook. **Santa Barbara**: Ronald P. Tongg, William R. Linfoot, C. Robertson Skene, Roy M. Barry, Jr.

1963   at Oak Brook. **Tulsa**: John T. Oxley, W. Ray Harrington, Jr., Harold L. Barry, Robert D. Beveridge.

1964   at Oak Brook. **Concar–Oak Brook**: Leslie L. Linfoot, Charles W. Smith, Julio Muller, Jack Murphy.

1965   at Oak Brook. **Oak Brook–Santa Barbara**: Ronald P. Tongg, Charles W. Smith, William R. Linfoot, Jack Murphy.

1966   at Santa Barbara, CA. **Tulsa**: John T. Oxley, W. Ray Harrington, Jr., Harold L. Barry, Jack Murphy.

1967   at Oak Brook. **Bunntyco–Oak Brook**: Delmar W. Carroll, W. Ray Harrington, Jr., Jack Murphy, Richard B. Bunn.

1968   at Memphis, TN. **Midland**: George H. Landreth, W. Ray Harrington, Jr., Roy M. Barry, Jr., Harold A. Barry.

1969   at Oak Brook. **Tulsa–Green Hill**: James R. Sharp, Thomas Wayman, W. Ray Harrington, Jr., William G. Atkinson. [Also played: Gastón R. Dorignac]

1970   at Oak Brook: **Tulsa**: James R. Sharp, Reuben Evans, Harold L. Barry, Harold A. Barry.

1971   at Oak Brook: **Oak Brook**: Hugo Dalmar, Jr., Charles W. Smith, Allan D. Scherer, Robert D. Beveridge.

1972   at Oak Brook. **Milwaukee**: William T. Ylvisaker, Thomas Wayman, Bennie Gutierrez, Robert A. Uihlein, III.

1973   at Oak Brook. **Oak Brook**: Hugo Dalmar, Jr., William G. Atkinson, Charles W. Smith, Robert D. Beveridge.

1974   at Oak Brook. **Milwaukee**: Delmar W. Carroll, Thomas Wayman, Harold A. Barry, Robert A. Uihlein, III.

1975   at Oak Brook. **Milwaukee**: Robert A. Uihlein, III, Thomas Wayman, Harold A. Barry, James I. Uihlein.

1976   at Oak Brook. **Willow Bend**: William S. Farish, III, Charles W. Smith, Roy M. Barry, Jr., Norman Brinker.

1977   at Oak Brook. **Retama**: William C. Linfoot, Guillermo Gracida, Jr., Harold A. Barry, Stephen M. Gose.

1978   at Oak Brook. **Abercrombie & Kent**: Geoffrey J.W. Kent, David Wigdhal, Antonio Herrera, Stuart T. Mackenzie.

1979   at Retama, San Antonio, TX. **Retama**: William C. Linfoot, Guillermo Gracida, Jr., Harold A. Barry, Stephen M. Gose.

1980   at Retama. **Southern Hills**: Seth W. Herndon, Jr., Steven Jake Sieber, Thomas Wayman, Rubén Gracida. [Also played: Julian B. Hipwood, Owen R. Rinehart]

1981   at Retama. **Rolex A & K**: Geoffrey J.W. Kent, Joel R. Baker, Antonio Herrera, Stuart T. Mackenzie.

1982   at Retama. **Retama**: Rubén Gracida, Carlos Gracida, Guillermo Gracida, Jr., Stephen M. Gose.

1983   at Retama. **Fort Lauderdale**: John C. Oxley, Fortunato Gómez Romero, Bart Evans, Rubén Gracida.

1984   at Retama. **Retama**: Thomas H. Gose, Carlos Gracida, Guillermo Gracida, Jr., Stephen M. Gose.

1985   at Retama. **Carter Ranch**: Preston M. Carter, Jr., Carlos Gracida, Guillermo Gracida, Jr., Pablo Rincón Gallardo.

1986   at Retama. **Retama II**: Michael V. Azzaro, Thomas Wayman, Owen R. Rinehart, Thomas H. Gose.

1987   at Eldorado, Indio, CA.. **Aloha:** Robert Fell, Carlos Gracida, Guillermo Gracida, Jr., Warren C. Scherer.

1988   at Indio. **Les Diables Bleus:** Ted Moore, Carlos Gracida, Guillermo Gracida, Jr., Guy Wildenstein.

1989   at Horse Park, Lexington, KY. **Les Diables Bleus:** Alejandro Agote, Juan I. Merlos, Guillermo Gracida, Jr., Guy Wildenstein.

1990   at Lexington. **Les Diables Bleus:** Sebastián Merlos, Juan I. Merlos, Guillermo Gracida, Jr., Julio R. Arellano [Also played: Guy Wildenstein]

1991   at Lexington. **Grant's Farm Manor:** William K. Busch, Michael V. Azzaro, Carlos Gracida, Andrew Busch.

1992   at Indio. **Hanalei Bay:** Julio R. Arellano, Carlos Gracida, Guillermo Gracida, Jr., Ronald Bonaguidi.

1993   at Indio. **Gehache:** Rubén Gracida, Michael V. Azzaro, Guillermo Gracida, Jr., Glen Holden, Sr.

1994   at Bethpage, NY. **Aspen:** Eugene H. Kneece, III, Carlos Gracida, Guillermo Gracida, Jr., Douglas Matthews.

1995   at Bethpage. **Outback:** Julio R. Arellano, Sebastián Merlos, Guillermo Gracida, Jr., John Timothy Gannon.

1996   at Palm Beach Polo, Wellington, FL. **Outback:** Valerio Aguilar, Michael V. Azzaro, Guillermo Gracida, Jr., J. Timothy Gannon. [Also played: Jeffrey W. Blake]

1997   at Wellington. **Isla Carroll:** Martín Estrada, Michael V. Azzaro, Guillermo Gracida, Jr., John B. Goodman.

1998   at Wellington. **Escue:** Nicolás E. Roldán, Sebastián Merlos, Juan I. Merlos, Stuart Erskine.

1999   at Wellington. **Outback:** J. Timothy Gannon, Jeffrey W. Blake, Adolfo Cambiaso, Bartolomé Castagnola.

2000   at Wellington. **Outback:** Sunny Hale, Bartolomé Castagnola, Adolfo Cambiaso, Philip O. Heatley.

2001   at Wellington. **Outback:** Santiago Chavanne, Fabio Diniz, Adolfo Cambiaso, Christopher T. Gannon.

2002   at Royal Palm, Boca Raton, FL. **Coca-Cola:** Gillian E. Johnston, Adam Snow, Miguel Novillo Astrada, Thomas J. Biddle, Jr.

2003   at Royal Palm, Boca Raton. **C-Spear:** Thomas B. Boyle, III, Matías G. Magrini, Carlos Gracida, Jeffrey S. Hall.

2004   at International P.C., Wellington. **Isla Carroll:** Stuart Erskine, Francisco Bensadón, Guillermo Gracida, Jr., John B. Goodman.

2005   at Wellington. **White Birch:** Julio F. Gracida, Lucas A. Criado, Mariano M. Aguerre, Delmar C. Walton. [Also played: Peter M. Brant, Martín Ravina]

2006   at Wellington. **Las Mojitas:** Camilo Bautista, Adam Snow, Eduardo Novillo Astrada, Jr., Ignacio Novillo Astrada.

2007   at Wellington. **Crab Orchard:** David Stirling, Matías G. Magrini, Adolfo Cambiaso, George W. Rawlings.

2008   at Wellington. **Crab Orchard:** Jeffrey W. Blake, Ignacio Heguy, Adolfo Cambiaso, George W. Rawlings.

2009   at Wellington. **Audi:** Marc C. Ganzi, Facundo Pieres, Gonzalo Pieres, Jr., Nicolás Pieres.

2010   at Wellington. **Crab Orchard:** Hilario Ulloa, Julio R. Arellano, Adolfo Cambiaso, George W. Rawlings

Appendix 7.
Winners of the U.S.
Women's Polo Association
Open Championship

1937   **Riviera**: Louise Tracy, Dorothy Rogers, Audrey Scott, Ruth Cropp.
1938   **Santa Barbara**: Louise Tracy, Rose Donnelly, Ann Jackson, Willametta Keck.
1939   **Las Amigas**: Joan Baker, Wrenn Tevis, Louise Tracy, Dorothy Rogers.
1940   **Pogonip**: Audrey Scott, Wilma Kann, Elaine McInerney, Dorothy Wheeler.

Chapter Notes

Chapter 1

1. Oliver Carlson, *The Man Who Made News* (New York: Duell, Sloan & Pierce, 1942), 383.

2. Don C. Seitz, *The James Gordon Bennetts* (Indianapolis: Bobbs-Merrill, 1928), 217.

3. Although architect Stanford White has often been credited with the Casino's design, situated on Bellevue Avenue, in reality it was Charles McKim — from the same architectural firm — who was responsible for the plans. The name, Newport Casino, did not imply that gambling took place on the premises. In this particular case the word "casino" derives from the Italian word "cascina," that is, "little summer house."

4. Maj. Henry A. Candy (1842–1911) was educated at Rugby School — where the game of rugby football originated — and purchased a commission into the 9th Lancers in 1864; he retired as a captain in 1870. Joined the Warwickshire Yeomanshire in 1874 and resigned in 1884. His portrait, painted in 1873 by Louis William Desanges, was offered for sale with a tag of 8,900 pounds.

5. Pierre Tucoo-Chala, *Histoire de Pau* (Toulouse: Privat, 1989), 222.

6. Seitz, 217.

7. Lord Montagu of Beaulieu, *The Gordon Bennett Races* (London: Cassell, 1963), 7.

8. F. Gray Griswold, "How the Matches Began," *Polo*, September 1930, 31. The players' correct names are Henry Ridgeway and Raoul de Brinquant.

9. "Shinney on Horseback," *The San Francisco Call*, 4 April 1895, 5. Mr. Henry Ridgeway, M. Raoul de Brinquant and M. Hennessy are mentioned among some of the earliest polo players in Pau.

10. Rosecliff was the site for some scenes of the 1974 film *The Great Gatsby*. The polo scenes in the film were also taken in Newport, with members of the Fairfield County Hunt Club team participating as players.

11. *The New York Times*, 4 September 1906, 4.

12. Michael Capuzzo, *Close to Shore* (New York: Random House, 2001), 20.

13. Griswold, 31.

14. Peter Vischer, *Horse and Horseman*, June 1939, 21.

15. E. Willard Roby, "The Beginnings of American Polo," *Outing*, Vol. 40, 318.

16. Lawrence Timson, "Polo," *Outing*, July 1891, 330.

17. Clarence D. Levey, *Torrence-Clendennin Episode and the Melville Letters* (New York: private printing, 1892), 101.

18. *Appleton Dictionary of New York* (New York: D. Appleton, 1883), 178.

19. Peter Vischer, "Beginnings of Polo," *Polo*, July 1929, 5.

20. *Daily Graphic*, 20 May 1876. "It is built of wood, in the Queen Anne gothic style, being made by four 'bays,' one on each side. In one of these, in the ballroom, is a large old-fashioned fireplace, 8 feet wide and 7 feet high, decorated with tiles. The entrance to the building is on the north side, and on the south side there is a large piazza, from which the game can be seen by the guests of the club. On the left of the large entrance hall is the dining-room, and on the right is the ball-room. It is lighted by two large bay windows, is finished in panels with gilt mouldings, and hung with cretonne. Thus decorated and finished, the ball-room is a very handsome room. In the second story are dressing rooms, and in the basement a complete kitchen. The cost of the building was about $20,000."

21. *Appleton*, 178.

22. *Newport Daily News*, 11 July 1876.

23. *The New York Times*, "Striking the Polo Ball; Six Good Bouts on the Improved Manhattan Grounds," 26 September 1880, 12.

24. Roby, 318.

25. Subsequently, the facility was leased out to the New York Giants baseball team. When the Giants moved uptown to new premises around 1890, they renamed the field "Polo Grounds," although no polo was played at this location. The author thanks Mr. Dennis J. Amato for this information.

26. Griffith Borgeson, "The Zborowski Saga" (*Automobile Quarterly*, Volume 22 # 2, 1984), 146.

27. Griswold, 31.

28. Sir Foster George Ross-of-Bladensburg, *A History of the Coldstream Guards* (London: Innes, 1896), 473.

29. Information provided by Debra Gracy, 8 November 2007. Further information supplied by Debbie on 11 September 2009. "In Southwest Texas (Boerne) is the famous Balcones Ranch (owned by Capt. Turquand). It is a monument to a class who helped to give Texas her peculiar reputation. Balcones Ranch was improved by a wealthy Englishman who came out from the old country with a pocketful of money and his head full of ideas of a good time. He put on the raw land the usual improvements and then he added a race track, a polo ground and various diverting institutions. While the money lasted, the fun was fast and furious for everybody who chose to come. But the end of a check book and of a fast life was reached together." Ms. Gracy is restoring the Phillip Manor, one of the oldest buildings in Texas, where several of the polo players lodged and met as a

clubhouse. Phillip Manor's bar is named Capt. Turquand's Saloon in honor of the 1883 Boerne Polo Club.
    30. *London Gazette*, 21 July 1871, p. 3264.
    31. Lawrence M. Woods, *British Gentlemen in the
Wild West* (New York: Free Press, 1989), 127.
    32. *San Antonio Light*, Wednesday, 24 October, 1883.
    33. Dennis J. Amato, "Early California Polo," *Polo*,
April 1996, 35. The author is grateful to Mr. Amato for
calling his attention to this pamphlet and providing a
photocopy of the program.
    34. *History of Santa Monica Bay Cities*, Ingersoll's
Century Histories (Los Angeles: Ingersoll, 1908), 307.
    35. J.A. Edmonds, "California's Rise in Polo," *Polo*,
January 1930, 9.
    36. Ingersoll, 307.
    37. J.B. Macnahan, "Polo in the West," *Outing*, Sep-
tember 1895, 475.
    38. *Outing*, September 1895, 471.
    39. J.C. Cooley, "Polo Notes," *The Sportsman*, Janu-
ary 1927, 43.

Chapter 2

    1. John Elliott Cowdin, "Polo in America," *The
Book of Sport*, William Patten, editor (New York: J.F.
Taylor, 1901), 140.
    2. F. Gray Griswold, *The International Polo Cup*
(New York: Dutton's, 1928), 11.
    3. Alden Hatch and Foxhall Keene, *Full Tilt* (New
York: Derrydale, 1938), 129.
    4. John Hanlon, "A Posh Game in a Posh Town,"
Sports Illustrated, 22 September 1969, 125.
    5. *The New York Times*, 26 August 1886, 2.
    6. For a detailed description of the first game, see
Cowdin, "Polo in America," 144.
    7. "The First Matches in America," *International
Polo*, Arthur W. Coaten, editor (London: Vaughn, 1912),
10.
    8. Ibid., 10.
    9. E.D. Miller, *Fifty Years of Sport* (New York: Dut-
ton, no date [1925]), 67.
    10. J.C. Cooley, "A Champion of America, *Polo*, June
1930, 23.
    11. "International Polo," *Outing*, June 1911, 380.
    12. Griswold, *International Polo*, 12.
    13. Nigel à Brassard, *A Glorious Victory, a Glorious
Defeat* (Chippenham: Antony Rowe, 2001), 19.
    14. Ibid., 20.
    15. *The Westchester Cup Commemorative Program*
(Lake Worth, FL: Museum of Polo and Hall of Fame,
2009), 48.
    16. Nigel à Brassard, "The Westchester Trophy: A
Tiffany Design," in *The Westchester Cup Commemorative
Program* (Lake Worth, FL: Museum of Polo, 2009), 46.
    17. J.C. Cooley, "Post and Paddock," *Polo*, September
1935, 18.

Chapter 3

    1. Dennis J. Amato, "The Whitneys and Saratoga
Polo" (*Eastern Horse World*, Vol. 9, No. 16), 38.
    2. "Played Polo into Night," *The New York Times*, 5
August 1902, 6.
    3. Addison Geary, *Mallet and Hounds* (Buffalo, NY:
private printing, 1931), 8.
    4. J. Blan Van Urk, *The Story of American Foxhunt-
ing* (New York: Derrydale, 1941), 187.
    5. Allan Forbes, *Early Myopia* (No place: private
printing, 1942), 65.

    6. *The Harvard Polo Club 1883–1905* (Cambridge:
University Press, 1905), [5].
    7. Amos Tuck French, *Harvard Polo Club 1883–1885*
(New Rochelle, NY: Knickerbocker, 1930), 11.
    8. Quoted in French, *Harvard Polo*, 11.
    9. Louis Dembitz Brandeis (1856–1941), graduated
from Harvard Law School with the highest average in
the school's history. Nominated to the Supreme Court
in 1916, Brandeis became one of the most influential jus-
tices, with an unswerving advocacy of freedom of speech
and the right to privacy.
    10. George von Lengerke Meyer [(1858–1918) was
Secretary of the Navy in the William Howard Taft pres-
idency and Postmaster General, 1907–1909, where he
implemented the first stamp vending machines and the
first coil stamps; ambassador to Russia and to Italy during the William McKinley and Theodore Roosevelt ad-
ministrations.
    11. "Author Escaped" E. and O. E. *Not a History of
the Dedham Polo Club* (Boston: Walton, 1907), 10.
    12. Ibid., 11.
    13. Allan Forbes, *Sport in Norfolk County* (Boston:
Houghton Mifflin, 1938), 14.
    14. Ibid., 45.
    15. Allan Forbes, *Early Myopia* (No place: private
printing, 1942), 60.
    16. Ibid., 64.
    17. George Custis, "Aiken Memories," *Polo*, April
1935, 29.
    18. Harry Worcester Smith, *Life and Sport in Aiken*
(New York: Derrydale, 1935), 84.
    19. Alderman Duncan, "Fifty Years of Polo," *Polo*,
May 1932, 17.
    20. Betty Babcock, "The Lure of Aiken," *Polo*, March
1932, 15.
    21. John H. Daniels, *Nothing Could Be Finer* (Cam-
den, SC: Culler, 1996), 12.
    22. Ibid., 14.
    23. Ibid., 40.
    24. Ibid., 28.
    25. Curtis Harnack, *Gentlemen on the Prairie* (Ames:
Iowa State University, 1985), 138.
    26. J. B. Macmahan, "Polo in the West," *Outing*, Au-
gust 1895, 384.
    27. Harmack, 138.
    28. Ibid., *St. Louis Republic*, quoted in the *Le Mars
Globe*.
    29. Harmack, 208.
    30. Ibid., 208. Interview with Mr. Curtis Harnack,
1953.
    31. The author is indebted to Mr. Stephen A. Orth-
wein, Sr., for his loan of material regarding the St. Louis
Country Club. Personal communication, 22 September
2009.
    32. Allerton Seward Cushing, Ph.D. (1867–1930) was
the author of *Chemistry and Civilization*, among other
scientific works. Dr. Cushman was Director of the Institute of Industrial Research in Washington, D.C., and
during World War I served as a Lt. Col. in the Ordnance
Department.
    33. A full report of the match was published in the
St. Louis Globe-Democrat, 22 October 1893, Vol. 19, No.
158.
    34. W. R. Pride, *The History of Fort Riley* (Topeka,
KS: Capper, 1936), 323.
    35. Macmahan, "Polo in the West," 391.
    36. Hobart Chatfield Taylor's granduncle, Wayne
Chatfield, was an immensely wealthy Cincinnatian.
When Mr. Wayne Chatfield died he left his money to

his grandnephew, on condition that the legatees add Chatfield to his last name. Hobart Chatfield Taylor thereupon became Hobart Chatfield Chatfield-Taylor.

37. F. Harland Rohm, "Onwentsia, Midwestern Pioneer," *Polo*, October 1927, 21.

38. J.B. Macmahan, "Polo in the West," *Outing*, August 1895, 391.

39. Marshall Sprague, *The Grizzlies* (No place: Cheyenne Mountain Country Club, 1983), 83.

40. Ibid., 10.

41. Ibid., 20.

42. Ibid., 54. There is a polo link between polo in Colorado and Meadow Brook Club. John George Milburn named one of his sons Devereux — the 10-goal superstar — after Horace Devereux's grandfather.

43. The influence of British investors in the Far West is described in Curtis Harnack's *Gentlemen of the Prairies* and in Lawrence M. Woods' *British Gentlemen in the Wild West*. There is also interesting information in *Gone to Texas*, edited by Thomas Hughes, the author of the famous *School Days at Rugby* and its sequel, *Tom Brown at Oxford*.

44. J.B. Macmahan, "Polo in the West," *Outing*, Sept. 1895, 472.

45. Bucky King, *Big Horn Polo* (Sheridan, WY: Still Sailing, 1987), 2.

46. Ibid., 6.

Chapter 4

1. Polo Association 1890 *Year Book*, 20.

2. The story of the Rockaway Hunting Club is told by Dr. Benjamin Allison in *The Rockaway Hunting Club*, privately printed by the club in 1952.

3. Dennis J. Amato, "Foxhall Keene: A Life of Pure Delight," in *Profiles in Polo*, Horace A. Laffaye, editor (Jefferson, NC: McFarland, 2007), 33.

4. Beverly Rae Kimes, "The Countrified Gordon Bennett Races," *Automobile Quarterly*, Vol. 4, #3, 332.

5. Alden Hatch and Foxhall Keene, *Full Tilt* (New York: Derrydale, 1938), 160.

6. Ibid., 166. Keene confuses the driver's name and nationality. Ferenc Szisz (1873–1944) was a Hungarian who drove for the Renault factory. Szisz achieved fame as the winner of the first French Grand Prix, at Le Mans in 1906.

7. J.C. Cooley, "A Champion of America," *Polo*, June 1930, 23.

8. J.C. Cooley, "Post and Paddock," *Horse and Horseman*, September 1936, 38.

9. Allison, 135.

10. Newell Bent, *American Polo* (New York: Macmillan, 1929), 33.

11. Robert F. Kelley, "Meadow Brook, the Heart of American Polo," *Polo*, June 1927, 12.

12. Jane P. Alles, *The History of Philadelphia Country Club* (Wilmington, DE: Kaumagraph, 1965), 6.

13. The Challenge Cup was donated by Edward de Veaux Morrell (1863–1917) who was born in Newport, Rhode Island, and graduated from the University of Pennsylvania in 1885 having studied Law. A passionate horseman, he was active in the National Guard of Pennsylvania where he was Colonel of the Third Regiment, later promoted to Brigadier General and Commander of the First Brigade. Elected to the United States Congress, he served from 1900 to 1907, and for the rest of his life carried out philanthropic work for his adopted city of Philadelphia.

14. Alles, 44.

15. Caspar W. Whitney, "Evolution of the Country Club," *Harper's New Monthly Magazine*, Vol. 90 (Dec. 1894), 30.

16. *The New York Times*, 1 October 1922, 130.

17. Dennis J. Amato, "Long Island Polo: Past & Present," *Long Island Forum*, Summer 1992, Vol. LIV, N0.3, 20.

18. John R. Tunis, *The American Way in Sport* (New York: Duell, Sloan & Pearce, 1958), 31. John Roberts Tunis (1889–1975) was a Harvard-educated (Class of 1911) sports writer and novelist.

19. *Acts and resolves of the General Assembly of the state of Rhode Island and Providence Plantations*, November session, 1904 (Providence, RI: Freeman, 1905), 179.

20. Charles L.A. Heiser, Brown University Class of 1890, was one of the founders and president of the Maryland Horse Breeders' Association. In his early years in Providence he played polo at Rumford P.C. and was a leader in promoting outdoor sports at the Agawam Hunt Club. Mr. Heiser was the owner of Snow Hill Farm, in Glyndon, Maryland; he built a steeplechase course which became the venue for the Maryland Hunt Cup Steeplechase. In his memory, The Charles L. A. Heiser Handicap for three-year olds was run for the first time on 10 November 1936, at the Pimlico racetrack.

21. Allan Forbes, "A Review of the Polo Season of 1903," *Outing*, April 1904, 245.

22. "Author Escaped," E. and O. E. *Not a History of the Dedham Polo Club* (Boston: Walton, 1907), 75.

23. *Polo Association Year Book* (New York: private printing, 1891), 33.

Chapter 5

1. Polo Association *Minutes*, 10 July 1890. Original document in the National Museum of Polo and Hall of Fame, in Lake Worth, Florida. The author is grateful to Mr. George J. DuPont, Jr., the Museum's Director, for giving permission to research the documents.

2. Polo Association *Minutes*, 8 October 1897.

3. His obituary in the *New York Times* read: "Columbus Calvert Baldwin died Oct. 24, 1899, of typhoid, at his home in New York City. He was 26 years old, the son of the late Christopher C. Baldwin. Immediately after graduation he entered the banking house of Blair & Co., New York. In outdoors sports he excelled in daring feats of horsemanship and in polo. He was a member of the famous Meadow Brook team, and was accounted one of the best players in this country. His playing was thoroughly sportsmanlike, in the best sense of the term, not only brilliantly, but uniformly clean and manly." *Harvard Graduates Magazine* (Boston, Vol. 8, 1899–1900), 410.

4. Allan Forbes, *Sport in Norfolk County* (Boston: Houghton Mifflin, 1938), 56.

5. The gorgeous silver trophy, emblematic of the oldest polo competition in America, resides in a special box in the Museum of Polo and Hall of Fame. The mounted polo player atop the lid appears to have been modeled after a bronze by Alexander Pope. It is said it represents James Gordon Bennett on his pony Sultan.

6. Minutes of the Polo Association, 21 November 1902. "At a meeting held at Madison Square Garden, New York City, Friday, Nov. 21st, 1902, it was noted that owing to the fact that the Lakewood team was found ineligible after winning the Championship, and the other two teams having withdrawn, the Championship of 1902 be not awarded." Polo Association *Year Book* 1903, page 127.

7. *The New York Times*, "Polo Clubs in Dispute," 22 July 1904, 7.

8. "Daniel Chauncey, Jr. Dies of a Polo Blow," *New York Times*, 9 June 1909, 3.

9. Joseph B. Thomas (1879–1955), a 5-goal polo player, yachtsman, architect, financier and author, graduated from Yale University, where he played polo and was a champion hurdler. Thomas took the Junior Championship and, while playing in England, the Novices' Cup at the Ranelagh Club. An authority on fox hunting, Thomas was M.F.H of the Piedmont Hunt and had a pack of foxhounds on his estate "Huntlands" in Middleburg, Virginia. His opus magnus is *Hounds and Hunting Through the Ages*. The leather-bound limited edition, published by the Derrydale Press, is a rare and expensive find.

10. *The New York Times*, "Championship Polo at Van Cortlandt," 21 September 1905, 6.

11. Polo Association 1905 *Year Book*, 169.

12. Personal communication from Mr. George J. DuPont, Jr.

13. Polo Association 1919 *Year Book*, "Chairman's Report," 116.

Chapter 6

1. Halden and Keene, 131.

2. Ibid., 134.

3. Perry R. Duis, *Challenging Chicago: Coping with Everyday Life 1937–1920* (Chicago: University of Illinois, 1998), 308.

4. Hurlingham Polo Association 2009 *Year Book*, 338.

5. *The Field*, 7 June 1902, 861.

6. The oldest rules of polo, those of the Silchar Club in Assam, specified that when a defending team hit the ball behind their own backline, a free shot from the intersection of the back and side lines was awarded to the attacking team, just as in hockey and soccer. This is the origin of the term "corner" in Argentina referring to what in the United States is called a "safety."

7. *Country Life*, 28 June 1902, 851.

8. *Baily's Magazine*, "Our Van," March 1902, 239.

9. For a biographical study of Harry P. Whitney, see Nigel à Brassard, "Harry Payne Whitney: 'Total Polo,'" in *Profiles in Polo* (Jefferson, NC: McFarland, 2007), 42.

10. Halden and Keene, 136.

11. Ibid., 144.

12. à Brassard, 45.

13. Halden and Keene, 143.

14. A. W. Coaten, editor, *International Polo Matches* (London: Vaughn, 1912), 54.

15. Henry Holmes, "The English Team in America, 1911," in Coaten, *International Polo*, 60.

16. Ibid., 63.

17. J.C. Cooley, "1927, an International Year in Polo," *The Sportsman*, February 1927, 70.

18. Polo Association 1919 *Year Book*, "Chairman's Report," 121.

Chapter 7

1. Bill Mallon, *The 1900 Olympic Games* (Jefferson, NC: McFarland, 1998), 142.

2. Mallon, ibid, 144.

3. David Wallechinsky, *The Complete Book of the Olympics* (New York: Penguin, 1988), 592.

4. Colonel N. E. Margetts, "The Trip of the American Forces in Germany Polo Team to England," *Field Artillery Journal*, July-August 1920, 435.

5. *Time*, 9 August 1943.

6. Norman Cinnamond, *El Polo* (Barcelona: Librería Catalonia, no date), 183.

7. Bill Mallon and Anthony Th. Bijkerk, *The 1920 Olympic Games* (Jefferson, NC: McFarland, 2003), 221–222.

8. Nelson W. Aldrich, Jr., *Tommy Hitchcock — An American Hero* (Gaithersburg, MD (?): Fleet Street, 1984). 167.

9. Wallechinsky, 593.

10. Ibid., 592.

11. Ibid., 364.

12. Mallon and Bijkerk, 149.

13. Wallechinsky, 249.

14. Ibid., 240.

15. Allen Guttmann, *The Olympics — A History of the Modern Games* (Champaign: University of Illinois, 2002), 85.

16. Wallechinsky, 245

Chapter 8

1. For a full-scale biography of Tommy Hitchcock, see Nelson W. Aldrich, Jr., *Tommy Hitchcock: An American Hero* (Gaithersburg, MD (?): Fleet Street, 1984). A shorter biography is "Tommy Hitchcock Jr.: The Best of America was in His Veins," by Nigel à Brassard, in *Profiles in Polo — The Players Who Changed the Game*, Horace A. Laffaye, editor (Jefferson, NC: McFarland, 2007), 108.

2. The U.S.P.A. Year Books until 2008 wrongly list Rockaway as the 1920 winner, and Meadow Brook as the 1921 winner of the Senior Championship. The reverse is the correct result.

3. W.F. Pride, *History of Fort Riley* (Topeka, KS: Capper, 1926), 326.

4. Stephen Henry Velie, Sr., was a partner of the plow manufacturer John Deere and married his daughter Emma. Tom Velie shot himself in Great Neck, Long Island, in 1920. Mr. Velie had been in a morose state since returning from France, where he was shell-shocked and gassed while a captain in the Artillery.

5. *The New York Times*, "Polo Surprise at the Pier," 10 August 1912, 5.

6. H.L. FitzPatrick, *American Polo* (New York: American Sports, 1904), 43.

7. Carrie Westlake Whitney, *Kansas City, Missouri: Its history and Its people 1808–1908*, Volume 1 (Chicago: Clarke, 1908), 232.

8. "The Cavalry School Polo Tournament," *Spalding Polo Guide* 1921, 56.

9. Pride, op. cit., 332.

10. Josephine G. Munson, "Humboldt Cowboys Helped Foster Polo Play in Area," Kansas Historical Society, *Museum Musings*, 22 November 1987.

11. Pride, *Fort Riley*, 328.

12. Ibid., 329.

13. Ibid., 331.

14. "Watching Polo in St. Louis," quoted in *Polo*, October 1928, 29.

15. Personal communication from Mr. Stephen A. Orthwein, Sr., 22 September 2009.

16. James F. Healey, *St. Louis Country Club — A Legacy of Sports*, "The Polo Crowd" (Ladue: St. Louis Country Club, 2009), 293.

17. Ernest Grove Cullum's (1883–1956) *Selection and Training of the Polo Pony* is one of the most comprehensive works on the subject.

18. For a biographical study of Ernest Marland, see

John J. Mathews, *E.W. Marland: Life and Death of an Oilman* (Norman: University of Oklahoma, 1951).

19. Orville Volkmann, *55 Years of Polo in Minnesota: 1922–1977* (No place: private printing, 1979) [1].

20. Ibid., [3].

21. Fort Snelling, originally Fort St. Anthony, was named after Col. Josiah Snelling (1783–1828), who while in command of the 5th Infantry Regiment changed the local landscape while enforcing the United States law and policies, putting an end to British control of the profitable fur trade in the area.

22. Arthur Inkersley, "Polo," *Western Field* (Vol. 10, No. 2, 1907), 133.

23. *Des Moines Tribune*, 5 September 1922.

24. Fred Daley, *Polo Is a Four Letter Word* (Honolulu, HI: Topgallant, 1986), 12.

25. U.S.P.A. *Year Book*, 1920–2009.

26. Lewis P. Lapham, one of the founders of Texaco and the man who built Waveny House, spent summers there with his family for many years. The Lapham family gave the town of New Canaan most of the estate land in 1967 and sold Waveny House and its surrounding 300 acres to the Town for $1,500,000.

27. Fredericksburg in Gillespie County was founded in 1846 by Baron Otfried Hans von Meusenbach. The town is also known as the home of Texas German, a dialect spoken by the first generations of settlers who initially refused to learn the English language.

28. In the early 1920s, Marland and his associates controlled about 10 percent of the world's oil reserves, similar to Saudi Arabia's holdings today.

29. John Joseph Mathews, *Life and Death of an Oilman* (Norman: University of Oklahoma Press, 1951), 103.

30. Bucky King, *Big Horn Polo* (Sheridan, WY: Still Sailing, 1987), 19.

31. The Fort D.A. Russell — now Francis E. Warren Air Force Base — was established in 1867 for protection of the workers engaged in the construction of the Union Pacific Railroad. It was named after David Allen Russell, a Union general killed during the Civil War in the battle of Opequon, near Winchester, Virginia.

Chapter 9

1. Ernest A. Rovelstad, "A Vast Establishment Rises at Chicago," *Polo*, July 1928, 14.

2. Gates Mills is a village located in the Chagrin Valley founded in 1826 by Holsey Gates, who bought 130 acres of Chagrin River land to secure a good water supply for his sawmill. The good location and abundant water supply led to the construction of several more mills, which gave the area its name.

3. J. Blan van Urk, *The Horse, the Valley and the Chagrin Valley Hunt* (New York: Ellis, 1947), 125.

4. Ibid., 135.

5. C. Robert Boyd, *A History of the Carranor Hunt and Polo Club 1921–2002* (Perrysburg, OH: private printing, 2003), 5.

6. *Spalding Polo Guide* (New York: American Sports, 1921), 73.

7. Vivian M. Baulch, "When Detroit Rode the Polo Ponies," *The Detroit News*, 5 May 2000.

8. Dennis J. Amato, "Early Florida Polo: Starbuck's Orlando Play," *Polo Players' Edition*, March 2007, 64.

9. Murdo Morrison, "Polo in Florida," *Polo*, January 1932, 38.

10. *Polo at Pinehurst, N.C.*, The Albertype Co.,

Brooklyn, N.Y. Hand-Colored. Pinehurst, NC: E.L. Merrow, circa 1905–1915.

11. Quoted in Addison Geary, *Mallet and Hounds* (Buffalo, NY: private printing, 1931), 125.

12. Ibid., 131.

13. Seymour H. Knox, *Polo Tales and Other Tales* (No place, private printing, no date), 14. Gen. Harold Child Bickford was commissioned as a 2nd Lieutenant into the 6th Dragoon Guards from the Active Militia of Canada in 1897. He resigned in 1910, when he was a Major.

15. George Bahto, *The Evangelist of Golf* (Chelsea, MI: Clock Tower, 2002), 147.

16. Charles B. Macdonald, *Scotland's Gift — Golf* (Stratford, CT: Classics of Golf, 1985), 225.

17. A sampling of Piping Rock's initial members is listed below. It gives a good indication of the type of membership the club had when it opened:

Charles Blair Macdonald, one of the best known personalities in American golf; Charles H. Sabin, cofounder of the National Golf Links and prominent banker; Devereux Emmett, amateur golfer and gifted architect; Theodore Havemeyer, from a polo playing family and the U.S. Golf Association's first president; and Howard F. Whitney, secretary of the U.S.G.A.

The world of finance was represented by J. P. Morgan, Jr.; Benjamin Strong, Jr., president of the Federal Reserve Bank of New York; Percy Chubb, co-founder of the insurance company; Mortimer L. Schiff, banker and early leader of the Boy Scouts.

The arts and letters counted Louis C. Tiffany, famous for his stained glass; Frank N. Doubleday, from the giant publishing company; and Condé Nast, the celebrated fashion magazine publisher.

Captains of industry included William L. Harkness, from Standard Oil; Charles H. Pratt, Frederic B. Pratt, George D. Pratt and Harold I. Pratt, Standard Oil heirs and philanthropists; and Henry Phipps, from Carnegie Steel.

Politicians and philanthropists included Theodore Roosevelt, listed as an Honorary Member; William Averell Harriman, future New York Governor, F.D.R.'s trusted advisor and Ambassador to Russia; Payne Whitney, patron of the New York Public Library; Alfred G. Vanderbilt, who would die as a passenger on the *Lusitania* when it was torpedoed and sunk by the German U-29 submarine off the Old Head of Kinsale on the coast of Ireland, while steaming towards Liverpool; Cornelius Vanderbilt; William Vincent Astor; and William W. Aldrich, future ambassador to Great Britain.

18. Peggie Phipps Boegner and Richard Gachot, *Halcyon Days* (New York: Abrams, 1986), 258.

19. Dennis J. Amato, "Long Island Polo: Past and Present," *Long Island Forum*, Vol. LIV, No. 3, Summer 1992, 20.

20. Jane P. Alles, *The History of the Philadelphia Country Club* (Wilmington, DE: private printing, 1965), 39.

21. Edward Weeks, *Myopia* (Hamilton, MA: private printing, 1976), 61.

22. I am indebted to the late Mr. Thomas B. Glynn, a gentleman polo player endowed with an incredible recall, for his reminiscences of polo at the Fairfield County Hunt Club.

23. Winston Churchill was a novelist from St. Louis who settled in Cornish. He decided to buy land at once, and in 1898 purchased from Leonard Spaulding and John Freeman some five hundred acres of woodland and valley mowings. Mr. Churchill wrote several novels: *The Crisis*, *The Crossing*, *Coniston*, and *A Modern Chronicle*. Cornish became an artistic and literary colony.

24. Bent, *American Polo*, 51.

25. Charles Adams Platt (1861–1933) was a prominent landscape gardener and architect. Throughout his life, Platt maintained his house and garden in Cornish, and an office and residence in Manhattan.

26. In 2002, the author was shown the putative site of the polo grounds. This was quite possibly the correct place, because it was the only level ground for miles around.

27. Bent, *American Polo*, 76.

28. Henry Mayer Halff (1874–1934) was a rancher and breeder in Texas. He attended Staunton Military Academy, Virginia, and Eastman Business College, Poughkeepsie. Halff owned the Quien Sabe (Who knows?) Ranch, where he had 3,000 top Hereford cattle. Halff also imported Belgian stallions to improve his draft horses and purchased thoroughbred stallions to breed with local mares, producing wiry horses used as polo ponies. His polo teams competed at Fort Bliss, Aiken, Newport and Dedham. The ponies were trained on the H.M. Halff Polo Farm in Midland, Texas.

29. "Virginia Poloists Win," *The New York Times*, 25 March 1913, 14.

Chapter 10

1. Until 2008, the U.S.P.A. Year Books indicated Robert E. Strawbridge, Jr., as one of the winners of the 1920 Open Championship. Actually, it was his father, Robert E. Strawbridge, Sr., who was on the winning Meadow Brook team. Bobby Strawbridge played on the Bryn Mawr squad, which was defeated in the semifinal game by his father's team. This mistake was corrected in the 2009 edition. The error first appeared in the 1923 *Year Book,* which was the first time the book carried the list of winners from previous years.

2. Peter Vischer, "The Hurricanes, Open Champions," *Polo*, October 1929, 23.

3. Ibid., 25.

4. The day before those words were written, the author watched a 12-goal championship game at Gulfstream Polo Club in which nine fouls were called in the first period.

5. "The Open Championship," *Polo*, October 1930, 49.

Chapter 11

1. For a comprehensive history of the 1921 Westchester Cup, see Nigel à Brassard, *A Glorious Victory, a Glorious Defeat.*

2. Founded in 1921, the Federación Argentina de Polo had the support of the majority of polo players in Argentina. Among the shakers and movers were Francisco Ceballos, Miguel Martínez de Hoz, Jack and Luis Nelson, Carlos Rodríguez Egaña and Alejandro Villegas. Their main demands included elections by the club's delegates and statutes and rules of the game in Spanish. A compromise was reached in September 1923, when the Asociación Argentina de Polo was founded.

3. Frank S. Butterworth, "Polo Notes and Comment," *The Sportsman*, November 1927, 69.

4. United States Polo Association, *Argentina vs. United States*, 1928 Official Program, 49.

5. "The Editor takes the Floor," *The Sportsman*, November 1928, 21.

6. Personal letter from Mr. John D. Nelson, courtesy of John P. Nelson.

7. "International Trial Matches," *The Polo Monthly*, May 1930, 119.

8. U.S. Polo Association 1931 *Year Book*, "International Polo," 24.

9. "America Keeps the Cup," *Polo*, October 1930, 35.

10. Robert F. Kelley, "You Better Look Out for Us!" *The Sportsman*, August 1932, 46.

11. Robert F. Kelley, "British Done in U.S. Polo?" *The Sportsman*, June 1932, 6.

12. Although James P. Mills, "U.S. Wins in Argentina," *Polo*, December 1932, page 14, names Mike Phipps in the Number 3 position, a photograph of the scoreboard at Palermo following the final match shows Phipps, Guest, Boeseke, Post as the Meadow Brook team. See Seymour H. Knox, *To B.A. and Back* (Buffalo, NY: private printing, 1933), 73.

13. J. C. Rathborne, "The Copas [sic] de Las Americas," *The Sportsman*, January 1933, 22.

14. The original vase is 10 feet high and was found at the bottom of Lake Tivoli, near the Roman Emperor Hadrian's villa. It was purchased by Sir William Hamilton, British consul in Naples, who gave the vase to his nephew, the Earl of Warwick. It stood at Warwick Castle — hence the name — until 1979.

15. Peter Vischer, "The International Polo Matches," *Horse & Horseman*, July 1936, 18.

16. Peter Vischer, "Whom to Play?" *Horse & Horseman*, January 1937, 34.

17. Peter Vischer, "Argentina's Brilliant Victory," *Horse & Horseman*, November 1936, 20.

18. Peter Vischer, "American Triumph," *Country Life*, July 1939, 17.

19. U.S. Polo Association 1940 *Year Book*, 24.

20. Personal communication from Bob Skene, Santa Barbara, November 1978.

21. U.S. Polo Association, 1940 *Year Book*, 25.

22. U.S. Polo Association, 1942 *Year Book*, 24.

23. U.S. Polo Association, 1949 *Year Book*, 18.

Chapter 12

1. These two tours are described in detail by Mr. Knox in *Aurora in England* and in *Polo Tales and Other Tales.*

2. "Polo in California," *Polo*, January 1932, 36.

3. Australian Reginald Leslie "Snowy" Baker (1884–1953) was an actor who excelled at many sports. He competed in the 1908 Olympic Games in London in boxing, diving and swimming, and took the silver medal in the middleweight class in boxing. Baker represented Australia in rugby and water polo, and was highly proficient in cricket, track and field, equestrian events, including polo, and rowing. After moving to California, Baker was already a matinee idol for his silent movie performances. In Hollywood, he coached Greta Garbo, Elizabeth Taylor, Shirley Temple, Douglas Fairbanks and Rudolph Valentino in fencing, riding and swimming. Baker is considered Australia's best all-around athlete ever.

4. "Ex-Immigrant Buys Midwick Polo Field," *Lodi News-Sentinel*, 5 July 1941, 5.

5. Vivian M. Baluch, "When Detroit Rode the Polo Ponies," *The Detroit News*, May 5, 2000.

6. John F. Ivory, Sr., who died in 1971 at the age of 83, had made his fortune with the John F. Ivory Moving and Storage Co. His father, a saddler in Queenstown, Ireland, moved to Norwich, N.Y., where he taught his son to ride horses.

7. Edward Weeks, *Myopia* (Hamilton, MA: private printing, 1976), 63.

8. "Waterbury Cup," *Horse and Horseman*, October 1936, 37.

9. Polo Scene, "Mural of the Story," *Polo Players' Edition*, December 2009, 19.

10. "Northwest Polo," *Horse & Horseman*, November 1937, 36.

11. Blair Calvert, *Cecil Smith: Mr. Polo* (Midland, TX: Prentis, 1990), 100.

12. "Legends Lost, Two Hall of Famers Remembered," *Polo*, March 1994, 41.

13. Robert F. Kelley, "New Champions of the West," *The Sportsman*, September 1933, 30.

14. Personal communication from Heriberto Duggan.

15. Robert F. Kelley, "Race Horse Polo," *The Sportsman*, October 1933, 66.

16. Arthur W. Little, Jr., "Polo from the Near-side," *Country Life*, October 1938, 57.

17. Nelson W. Aldrich, Jr., *Tommy Hitchcock — An American Hero* (Gaithersburg, MD (?): Fleet Street, 1984), 234.

18. Peter Vischer, "A New Leader for American Polo," *Horse and Horseman*, Feb. 1936, 21.

Chapter 13

1. Robert F. Kelley, "Sportsmen from the Pampas," *The Sportsman*, October 1931, 43.

2. Robert F. Kelley, "Come On, Let's Go, Let's Go!" *The Sportsman*, August 1931, 53.

3. Peter Vischer, "Winston Guest's Templeton Wins the Open Championship Tournament," *Polo*, October 1932, 14.

4. Peter Vischer, "Seymour Knox's Aurora Side Wins the Title in a Stirring Match with Greentree," *Polo*, October 1933, 16.

5. Peter Vischer, "Greentree Wins the Open," *Polo*, October 1935, 35.

6. J. C. Cooley, "Shot Heard 'round the World — The Championship depends on a single shot, made by a single player, at the critical moment," *Horse & Horseman*, October 1936, 20.

7. The Whitneys, Jock and Sonny, were the big polo sponsors of the 1930s. John "Jock" Hay Whitney (1904–1982) was the son of William Payne Whitney, better known as Payne. Cornelius Vanderbilt Whitney (1899–1992) was Harry Payne Whitney's son. Harry Payne (1872–1930) and William Payne (1876–1927) were sons of William Collins Whitney (1841–1904), who started polo in Saratoga.

8. Lt. Charles Skiddy von Stade was killed in Germany in the final days of the war, when his Jeep ran over a mine. In his memory, based on von Stade's letters to his wife, Richard Danielpour composed *Elegies*, a work scored for orchestra, mezzo-soprano, and baritone. Frederica von Stade, his posthumous daughter, a talented mezzo-soprano, realized a personal and professional dream performing in *Elegies* at Carnegie Hall.

Chapter 14

1. Lt. Gen. Robert Lee Bullard (1861–1947) was in command of the 2nd Army, American Expeditionary Forces in France during World War I.

2. Polo Association *Year Book*, 1923.

3. *Time*, 16 June 1924.

4. *The New York Times*, "Games for Princeton Polo Team," 4 April 1903, 6.

5. *The New York Times*, "Activity in College Athletics," 3 May 1903, 15.

6. Polo Association *Year Book*, 1904, 80.

7. R.P. McGrann, "Polo at Princeton," *Princeton Alumni Weekly*, Vol. 22, No. 10, 7 Dec. 1921, 222.

8. John R. Townsend (1862–1923), a stockbroker, was Master of Hounds of the Orange County Hunt Club. He was a director of the National Horse Show Association and a leading advocate of indoor polo and was instrumental in bringing the English team to America.

9. Crocker Snow, Jr., "Polo: The Fat Years," in *Myopia — A Centennial Chronicle*, edited by Edward Weeks (Hamilton, MA: private printing, 1975), 58.

10. *The New York Times*, "Yale Polo Team Beaten," 11 June 1903, 6.

11. Winston Guest's full name was Frederick Winston Churchill Guest. Almost invariably he is referred to as Winston F.C. Guest.

12. Valentine Del Vecchio, *Beneath the Dome of PMI* (Santa Barbara, CA: Reference Desk, 1997),

13. "The Possibility of Polo at Cornell University," *Polo*, June 1929, 10.

14. Stephen J. Roberts, *An Autobiographical History of Collegiate Polo and its Players at Cornell University 1919–1972 and Beyond* (No place, private printing, no date [1997]), 18.

15. V.M.I. Archives on line photographs database: Photos number 2515, 2921 and 2015.

16. Peter Vischer, "Polo at the Western Colleges," *Polo*, May 1929, 14.

17. Ibid., 14.

18. Bent, *American Polo*, 97.

19. "College Women in Polo — Show Skill in Playing Match at Central Riding Academy," *The New York Times*, 21 January 1915, Part 2, 10.

Chapter 15

1. Robert F. Kelley, "West Point's Contribution to Polo," *Polo*, March 1928, 7.

2. Gen. Robert Lee Bullard was born in 1861. Gen. Bullard donated a polo bronze as the trophy for the Inter-Collegiate Polo Championship, illustrated in the 1926 U.S.P.A. *Year Book*, page 55.

3. J.B. Macmahan, "Polo in the West," *Outing*, September 1895, 474.

4. Col. Edward Buchanan Cassatt (1869–1922) attended Haverford College, the French École Militaire at St. Cyr, and the U.S. Military Academy at West Point. His father was Alexander Cassatt, president of the Pennsylvania Railroad, and his mother was Lois Buchanan, a niece of U.S. president James Buchanan. Col. Cassatt served in both the Spanish-American War and the American-Philippines War. In 1906, he inherited Chesterbrook Farm in Berwyn, Pennsylvania where his father had bred thoroughbred race horses. The most successful runner for Alexander Cassatt was The Bard, a winner of the 1886 Preakness. Not to be outdone, Col. Edward Cassatt became successful with Layminister, a thoroughbred horse that won the Preakness in 1910.

5. Col. James Lockett (b. Georgia 1855) was Superintendent of Sequoia National Park, aide to Gen. Arthur MacArthur in the Philippines, and Commandant of the Mounted Riding School in Fort Riley. Fought in the punitive expedition to Mexico; retired in 1919 after 44 years in the service. Camp Lockett, near San Diego, was named after him.

6. Brig. Gen. Robert Alexander Brown (1859–19XX), born in Pennsylvania, U.S.M.A. class of 1885, saw extensive service during World War I.

7. Lt. Col. Gordon Voorhies was born in 1868 in

Kentucky into a military family — his great-grandfather Maj. Peter Gordon Voorhies had served in the 1912 War — and graduated from the U.S.M.A. in 1891. Assigned to the 25th Infantry, in 1892 transferred to the 4th Cavalry, just in time to start his polo career. Capt. Voorhies resigned from the service in 1897. He volunteered for the Spanish-American War and also served in World War I. Voorhies married into the Burrell family of Portland, Oregon; he devoted his energies to running the big Eden Valley Orchards, owned by his wife's family.

8. Fort Walla Walla (place of many waters) was built by the Hudson's Bay Company in 1818 and manned by French-Canadian fur trappers. It was abandoned in 1911.

9. Fort Riley was named to honor Maj. Gen. Bennett C. Riley, who had led the first military escort along the Santa Fe Trail in 1829.

10. Quoted in Pride, *Fort Riley*, 325.

11. Fort Leavenworth, named after Col. Henry Leavenworth who established the fort in 1827.

12. Established in 1879, Fort Assinniboine got its name from the Assinniboine people. Fort Grant after Gen. Ulysses S. Grant; Fort Robinson was named in honor of Lt. Levi H. Robinson, who was killed by Indians in 1873, while collecting wood.

13. Fort Niobara, established in 1880, was located on the margins of the Niobara River, four miles east of the present town of Valentine, Nebraska.

14. Polo Association *Year Book* 1904, 7.

15. Polo Association *Year Book* 1908, 7.

16. Lt. Adair was killed in battle at Carrizal, Mexico, on 21 June 1916.

17. Fort Ethan Allen, located in Colchester, Vermont, has a long and fascinating history. Named after Revolutionary War hero Ethan Allen, the Fort was in active military use from 1894 until 1961 when it was decommissioned.

18. 1912 Polo Association *Year Book*, 96.

19. John H. Daniels, *Nothing Could Be Finer* (Camden, SC: Culler, 1996), 62.

20. Fort Oglethorpe named after James Oglethorpe, founder of Georgia.

21. Brig. Gen. Albert J. Myer, who commanded the Signals School for Army and Navy officers.

22. In addition to the 1922 championship team the following players were on the other winning teams: majors Harry D. Chamberlin, Karl C. Greenwald, John K. Herr, and Charles C. Smith; captains Charles H. Gerhardt, George E. Huthsteiner, Peter P. Rodes, Joseph S. Tate, and Candler A. Wilkinson; lieutenants Homer W. Kiefer, Morton McD. Jones, Charles N. McFarland, George W. Read, Jr., and John A. Smith, Jr.

23. Fort Bliss was named after Lt. Col. William W. S. Bliss, Army Assistant Adjutant General during the Mexican War.

24. **Winners of the Twelve Goal Championship**: 1925 — Fort Bliss: Capt. Delmar S. Wood, Maj. Harry D. Chamberlin, Capt. Lucien K. Truscott, Capt. George H. Huthsteiner. 1926 — Fort Leavenworth: Capt. Candler A. Wilkinson, Capt. Charles C. Smith, Maj. Ira P. Swift, Maj. John K. Brown. 1927 — Fort Bliss, Lt. Earl F. Tompson, Capt. Chester E. Davis, Maj. John K. Brown, Capt. George E. Huthsteiner. 1928 — Fort Riley: Capt. Vaughn M. Cannon, Capt. Carleton Burgess, Capt. Lucian K. Truscott, Jr., Capt. James C. Short. 1930 —(Eastern Division)Fort Sam Houston: Capt. C. P. Chapman, Lt. Harry Cullins, Capt. William H. Craig, Capt. John A. Smith, Jr. 1930 —(Western Division) Fort Sill: Lt. Albert R. S. Barden, Lt. James W. Clyburn, Maj. Horace L.

McBride, Maj. Joseph M. Swing. 1933 — Fort Sheridan: Lt. George S. Smith, Capt. Candler A. Wilkinson, Capt. Chester E. Davis, Lt. Lawrence G. Smith. 1936 — Fort Myer: Lt. George R. Grunert, Capt. Donald H. Galloway, Capt. John H. Stadler, Jr., Lt. Harry W. Johnson. **Winners of the Twelve Goal Inter-Circuit Tournament**: 1925 — Fort Bliss: Capt. Delmar S. Wood, Maj. Harry D. Chamberlin, Capt. Lucian K. Truscott, Jr., Capt. George H. Huthsteiner. 1926 — Fort Leavenworth: Capt. Candler A. Wilkinson, Capt. Charles C. Smith, Maj. Ira P. Swift, Maj. John K. Brown. 1930 —(Western Division) Fort Sill: Lt. Albert R. S. Barden, Lt. James W. Clyburn, Maj. Horace L. McBride, Maj. Joseph M. Swing. 1933 — Fort Sheridan: Lt. George S. Smith, Capt. Candler A. Wilkinson, Capt. Chester E. Davis, Lt. Lawrence G. Smith. 1935 — Fort Sheridan: Capt. Edwin C. Greiner, Maj. Candler A. Wilkinson, Lt. Col. Harry D. Chamberlin, Capt. Lawrence G. Smith. 1938 — Field Artillery School: Capt. Arthur E. Solem, Capt. John A. Smith, Jr., Lt. Duff W. Sudduth, Lt. Edwin A. Walker.

25. Newell Bent, *American Polo* (New York: Macmillan, 1929), 132.

26. Mitchel Field was named in 1918 after Maj. John Purroy Mitchel (1979–1918), a reformer Mayor of New York City from 1914 to 1917, who volunteered for the Air Corps after being defeated in his bid for reelection. Maj. Mitchel was killed while flying in a training accident. The airfield is wrongly often named Mitchell Field, with the thought that it was named after aviation pioneer — and polo player — Gen. Billy Mitchell.

27. Sir Richard Loudon McCreery (1898–1967) had a distinguished career in World War II, ending as Commander-in-Chief, British Army of the Rhine. His brother Walter, an officer in the 12th Lancers, played polo in California during his leaves of absence.

28. Maj. Willis D. Crittenberger, "Polo in the American Army," *Polo*, June 1927, 32.

29. Col. W.V. Morris, "The Army Polo Team in Argentina," *The Field Artillery Journal*, March-April 1931, 214.

30. Wesley J. White, "The Army Four in Argentina," *The Sportsman*, February 1931, 45.

31. Lucian K. Truscott, Jr., *The Twilight of the U.S. Cavalry* (Lawrence: University of Kansas, 1989), 189.

32. Truscott, 190.

33. F.S. Aitzazuddin, *Year Book of Pakistan Polo* (Lahore: Habib, 1974), 80.

34. "Back in the Saddle Again," *Polo*, December 1992, 9.

Chapter 16

1. Unidentified newspaper clipping in W. Russell G. Corey, *Alan Corey: 9-Goals* (No place: private printing, 2009), 113.

2. Alex M. Robb, *The Sanfords of Amsterdam* (New York: William-Frederick, 1969), 184.

3. CCC stood for Commercial Contracting Corporation, A.D. Beveridge's firm based in Detroit.

4. Seymour H. Knox, *Aurora at Oak Brook* (No place: private printing, 1956), 27.

5. James F. Healy, *St. Louis Country Club: A Legacy of Sports* (Ladue: St. Louis C.C., 2009), 300.

6. Crocker Snow, Jr., "Polo: The Postwar Revival," in Edward Weeks, *Myopia — A Centennial Chronicle* (Hamilton, MA: private printing, 1975), 108.

7. John H. Daniels, *Nothing Could Be Finer* (Camden, SC: Culler, 1996), 168.

8. Personal communication from S.K. Johnston, Jr., 25 February 2010.

Chapter 17

1. U.S. Polo Association 1950 *Year Book*, 20.
2. Don Juan Manuel, "Campeones de América," *El Gráfico*, 15 December 1950, 54.
3. "New York Team in Bogota," U.S. Polo Association 1954 *Year Book*, 23.
4. J.R.C. Gannon, "Introduction," Hurlingham Polo Association 1970 *Year Book*, 1.
5. Francisco E. Dorignac, personal communication, 14 July 2006.
6. Northrup R. Knox, *To B.A. Once More* (Buffalo, NY: private printing, no date), 3.
7. Ibid., 37.
8. J.G., "Introduction," Hurlingham Polo Association 1972 *Year Book*, 3.

Chapter 18

1. "Women Play Polo," *The New York Times*, 9 March 1901, 3.
2. "Nannie Langhorne Shaw Soon to Wed Waldorf Astor," *Spartanburg Daily Herald*, 10 March 1906, 3.
3. "Women Play Polo: Miss Eleanor Sears and Sister Players Cause Sensation at Narragansett Pier," *The New York Times*, 14 August 1910, Part 2, 1.
4. "Women Polo Players Put Up Fast Game," *The New York Times*, 4 August 1912, x 3.
5. Edwin P. Hoyt, *The Whitneys* (New York: Weybright & Talley, 1976), 222.
6. "Women Play Good Polo," *New York Evening Post*, 1913, clipping in William Hazzard's scrap book, private collection.
7. "Women as Polo Stars," *The New York Times*, 2 July 1913, 7.
8. "Society Women Play Polo," *The New York Times*," 20 August 1916, xx1. Miss Sears' correct name was Eleonora Randolph Sears.
9. "Formation of Feminine Teams Is Planned for Boston Tourney," *The New York Times*, 3 September 1920, 16.
10. For a full biography of Eleonora Sears, consult Peggy Miller Franck, *Prides Crossing* (Beverly, MA: Commonwealth, 2009).
11. *Riviera Chukker*, Vol. II, 21 March 1937, 3.
12. U.S.P.A. 1925 *Year Book*, 117; U.S.P.A. 1926 *Year Book*, 150.
13. Joan Gilbert Martin and Colleen McInerney-Maegher, *Pogonip* (Santa Cruz, CA: Otter B, 2007), 43. Colleen McInerney played polo in California in the 1930s.
14. *Riviera Chukker*, op. cit., 2.
15. David E. Outerbridge, *Champion in a Man's World* (Chelsea, MI: Sleeping Bear, 1998), 122. The brassie, an obsolete golf club, was fairly similar to a number two wood, with a brass sole, hence the name.
16. "Polo in the Pacific Coast Circuit," U.S.P.A. 1932 *Year Book*, 37.
17. "Alice in Pololand," *Country Life*, Jan. 1935, 72.
18. *Polo*, June 1935, 36.
19. Dennis J. Amato, "Women's Polo in America," *A Brief History of Scholastic, Collegiate and Women's Polo in America* (No place: private printing, no date). Reprinted in *1994 Interscholastic and Intercollegiate Polo Program*.
20. Marshall Sprague, *The Grizzlies: A History of the Cheyenne Mountain Country Club* (No place: The Club, 1983), 62.
21. Suzanne Dabney Taylor, "Women Who Play Polo," *Polo*, December 1930, 20.
22. T.J. Randolph Nicholas, "Women's Polo to the Fore," *Polo*, June 1929, 15.
23. "Women's Polo," *Polo*, July 1935, 10.
24. Louise Treadwell Tracy, "Women and Polo," *Polo*, June 1935, 36.
25. Original letter in the Museum of Polo and Hall of Fame archives.
26. Minutes of the U.S. Polo Association, 21 October 1936, page 5.
27. James F. Healy, *St. Louis Country Club: A Legacy of Sports* (Ladue: St. Louis Country Club, 2009), 298.
28. The story was told to the author by Mr. Steve Orthwein, who declined to divulge the suitor's name. Perhaps, as a good lawyer, he was aware of the potential hazards of self-incrimination. Further research uncovered Josephine's real identity: Joe Carpenter, polo player and club member.
29. *The New York Times*, 5 May 2003, B 8.
30. U.S.P.A. 1972 *Year Book*, "Handicaps," 130.
31. Andrea Galliher, "When the Walls Came Tumbling Down," *Polo*, December 1992, 17.
32. Sue Sally Hale, "First All-Girl Polo Tournament," *Polo News*, February 1976, 35.
33. *Westchester Cup 2009 Official Program*, 39.
34. Suzanne Dabney Taylor, "Women Who Play Polo," *Polo*, December 1930, 20.

Chapter 19

1. Robert A. Granniss, "Indoor Polo's Beginnings," *Polo*, April 1932, 16.
2. "Polo as Indoor Game; Two Teams Give Amusing Exhibition in Durland's Academy," *The New York Times*, 3 March 1904, 6.
3. "News from the Out of Doors," *Outing*, Vol. 56, 1910, 126.
4. "Officers and Executive Committees Since Organization," 1935 *Official Manual*, Indoor Polo Association of America, 4.
5. Indoor Polo Association, *Constitution, By-Laws and Playing Rules*, 1922, [3].
6. Indoor Polo Association, *Constitution, By-Laws and Playing Rules* (New York: American Sports, 1923), [12–13].
7. "Indoor Polo, as Played in the United States," *Polo*, April 1929, 18.
8. A.G. Blaisdell, "A Short Article on Indoor Polo," *Indoor Polo Association of the U.S. of A.* (New York: American Sports, 1924), 13.
9. "The First International," 1923–1924 *Official Annual*, I.P.A., 10.
10. John R. Townsend (1862–1923), the donor of three important indoor polo trophies, had a successful career as a stockbroker on Wall Street, which allowed him to engage in foxhunting in three countries, England, Ireland and the United States. At the time of his death, he was M.F.H. of the Orange County Hunt and a director of the National Horse Show. Townsend played outdoors polo in the 1890s at the Genesee Valley Polo Club.
11. "1934: Ladies Polo," *Polo Players' Edition*, September 2009, 62.
12. Tim Sayles, "The Star-Spangled Apex of Arena Polo," *Polo*, March 1987, 38.
13. "Pro Polo in L.A. Thrives Despite Center's Troubles," *Polo*, December 1984/January 1985, 76.
14. Samantha Hamilton, "Down and Out in L.A." *Polo*, April 1990, 38.

Chapter 20

1. A photograph of the Willis Hartman Trophy appears in *Polo*, October 1987, 39.
2. "National Open Championship," U.S.P.A. 1976 *Year Book*, 104.
3. Bill Phillips, "Visiting Argentine Team brings International Touch to Brandywine," *Polo Newsletter*, September 1974, 10.
4. Al Ullman, "Polo on Long Island," *Polo News*, September 1974, 9.
5. Horace A. Laffaye, "Argentine Team Visits the Northeast," *Polo News*, December 1974, 17.
6. "Argentines at Santa Barbara," *Polo News*, October-November 1975, 38.
7. F. S. Aitzazuddin, *Year Book of Pakistan Polo* (Lahore: Habib, 1974), 79.
8. Ibid., 85.
9. Crocker Snow, Jr., "Polo: The Postwar Revival," in Edward Weeks, *Myopia* (Hamilton, MA: private printing, 1976), 114.
10. U.S.P.A. 1980 *Year Book*, 170. Jack Van Dell, Thomas Monaco, Gary McMullen and Neil Raymond played for Myopia; David Clark, William Sawyer, Peter Rizzo and George Haas represented Fairfield.
11. "Polo on the Prairie," *The Iowan*, Spring 1974, 10.

Chapter 21

1. Ami Shinitzky, "Viva Mexico!" *Polo*, December 1976, 13.
2. "Mexico Dominates Camacho Cup," *Polo*, 30.
3. Ami Shinitzky, "Who Was Minding the Store?" *Polo*, January-February 1980, 43.
4. Personal communication from Alberto P. Heguy.
5. Ami Shinitzky, "Cool Head Latin: Gonzalo Tanoira," *Polo*, January-February 1977, 14.
6. Personal communication from Juan Carlos Harriott.
7. Jim Willis, "A Learning Experience," *Polo*, August 1984, 28.
8. Ibid., 29.
9. William Loyd, quoted in "A Crowning Achievement," *Polo*, October 1897, 17.
10. The Pegasus Triumphant Trophy is a copy of a polo prize produced by Louis Cartier in Paris in 1925, the year the Art Deco Movement received much publicity at the Exhibition of Decorative Arts. The silver replica presented on International Day was created in 1984.
11. Marty LeGrand, "The Westchester Cup," *Polo*, September 1988, 33.
12. United States Polo Association, 2009 *Year Book*, 185.
13. A copy of the deed of gift and conditions for the Westchester Cup is in "America Polo Cup," *The Polo Annual* (London: Cox, 1913), 180.
14. Crocker Snow, Jr., "Worth the Wait," *Polo*, October 1992, 40.
15. Dennis J. Amato, "The Westchester Cup: A Past Renewed," *The Westchester Cup Commemorative Program* (Lake Worth, FL: Museum of Polo, 2009), 25.
16. Peter Rizzo, "R-e-s-p-e-c-t," *Polo Player's Edition*, September 1997, 25.
17. Judith Bannister, *English Silver Hallmarks* (London: Foulsham, 1995), 96. Wakelin and Taylor were the successors to Parker and Wakelin, who had supplied the Richmond Race Cup in 1763.
18. "Numero Uno — Argentina Unseats USA in the Third World Championship," *Polo*, August 1992, 23.

19. Gwen Rizzo, "Polo Maximus," *Polo Players' Edition*, November 1998, 20.
20. The venues and results of the F.I.P. World Championships are as follows:

Year	Place	Gold	Silver	Bronze
1987	Buenos Aires	Argentina	Mexico	Brazil
1989	Berlin	U.S.A.	England	Argentina
1992	Santiago de Chile	Argentina	Chile	England
1995	St. Moritz	Brazil	Argentina	Mexico
1998	Santa Barbara	Argentina	Brazil	England
2001	Melbourne	Brazil	Australia	England
2004	Chantilly	Brazil	England	Chile
2008	Mexico City	Chile	Brazil	Mexico

21. Gabriel Ellison and Kim Fraser, *Harmony of Hooves* (No place: The Natal Witness, 1999), 165.
22. Julie Thomas, "Maui's Tour of New Zealand," *Polo*, May 1982, 15.
23. Chris Ashton, *Geebung — The Story of Australian Polo* (Sydney: Hamilton, 1993), 227–228.
24. Quoted in Donald C. McKenzie and John R. McKenzie, *Polo in South Africa* (Pietermaritzburg: Teeanem, 1999), 302.

Chapter 22

1. Data provided by Elizabeth C. Day, Director of Membership and Handicaps, U.S. Polo Association, 18 March 2010.
2. Ami Shinitzy, "1976 Open & Polo Week," *Polo*, October-November 1976, [25].
3. U.S.P.A. 1976 *Year Book*, 49.
4. Editorial, "A Matter of Principle," *Polo*, October-November 1976, 11.
5. "The Goal That Cost Fairfield the Game," *Polo*, October-November 1976, 44.
6. Shinitzky, "1976 Open," 24.
7. Stephanie M. Burns, "1980 Southern Hills' Year for the Open," *Polo*, December 1980, 25.
8. Ami Shinitzky, "Rolex A&K 1981 U.S. Champions," *Polo*, November 1981, 26.
9. Leslie Bates, "A New Era for the U.S. Open," *Polo*, August 1988, 24.
10. Richard I. G. Jones, Jr., "Black and Blue, but Mostly Bleu," *Polo*, December 1989, 27.
11. Peter J. Rizzo, "Escue Wins U.S. Open," *Polo Players' Edition*, May 1998, 29.
12. Peter Chew, "Fine Line from the Argentine," *Classic*, December 1977/January 1978, 68.
13. Ami Shinitzky, "USA–Texas has it, or, Weekends were made for...," *Polo*, June 1979, 25.
14. "Personally Speaking — The World Cup and the Cup of the Americas," *Polo*, June 1979, 45.
15. "Personally Speaking: The High Goal Dilemma — High Stakes Are Challenging the Game's Integrity," *Polo*, June/July 1990, 9.
16. *Polo*, August 1990, 7. Letters. "In your June/July issue, the Personally Speaking column entitled "The High Goal Dilemma," contained an error in reporting on this year's World Cup final. As a member of the Michelob team, I would like it known that I never conferred with my teammates, nor did I receive any money to allow White Birch to come to the field as a 31-goal team.
Charles S. Bostwick
Gilbertsville, New York
Editor's Note: We stand by our report, but extend our apologies to Mr. Bostwick for incorrectly implying he was a party to the agreement."

17. Marty LeGrand, "T Stands for Trouble," *Polo*, June/July 1994, 5.

18. "The Troubling Case of Ignacio Heguy, *Polo*, June/July 1994, 12.

19. The author is indebted to Robert Mountford for information about polo clubs in New Jersey and Pennsylvania.

20. The Morris Field was named in memory of Col. Wyllis Virlan Morris who was the non-playing captain of the 1930 U.S. Army team in Argentina. Col. Morris was killed the following year during a polo match at Meadow Brook.

21. Horace A. Laffaye, "Timeless Traditions," *PQ International*, Winter 2007, 30.

Chapter 23

1. The nine contributors, all respected journalists and authors, are Nigel à Brassard, Dennis Amato, Sebastián Amaya, Chris Ashton, Yolanda Carslaw, Roger Chatterton-Newman, Sarah Eakin, Lady Susan Reeve, and Peter Rizzo.

2. Fort Stotsenburg, north of Manila, was named in honor of Col. John M. Stotsenburg, in command of the Nebraska Volunteers, killed in the Philippines during the Spanish-American war. The military camp was later transformed into Clark Air Force field.

3. *A Manual of Polo* (Fort Stotsenburg, Philippine Islands: private printing, 1910), [1].

4. Ibid., 3.

5. Ibid., 4.

Chapter 24

1. "Foxhall Keene," *The Sportsman*, March 1929, 36. "Mrs. Hitchcock," May 1929, 40. "Devereux Milburn," July 1929, 38. "T. Hitchcock, Sr.," August 1929, 32. "J. Watson Webb," December 1929, 38.

2. Burlington Gallery catalog, London, 1990, 16.

3. Ron Heron, *The Sporting Art of Cecil Aldin* (London: Sportsman's, 1990), 86.

4. Several of these pictures are illustrated in Armour's autobiography, *Bridle and Brush*. The painting of the 1913 Westchester Cup appears in the 2009 Official Program published by the National Museum of Polo, page 4.

5. Illustrations in the magazine *Polo*, June 1983, 27.

6. Del Carroll's ponies are reproduced in *Classic*, December 1976, 81. Frivolity is illustrated in *Polo*, July 1977, 12.

7. Bellows.

8. For a detailed narrative of Paul Brown's career, see M.L. Biscotti, *Paul Brown*, Lanham, Derrydale, 2001.

9. *Polo*, November 1989, 31.

10. F. Turner Reuter, Jr., *Animal & Sporting Artists in America* (Middleburg, VA: National Sporting Library, 2008), 255.

11. H. Jeremy Chisholm, "Rediscovering Joseph Golinkin, *Polo*, December 1979, 25.

12. Sally Mitchell, *The Dictionary of British Sporting Artists* (Woodbridge, Suffolk: Antiques Collector's Club, 1985), 270.

13. This painting is reproduced in color in Mary Ann Wingfield, *Sport and the Artist* (Woodbridge, Suffolk: Antique Collector's Club, 1988), 290.

14. *The Shot from the Grey Pony* is illustrated in J.N.P. Watson, *The World of Polo* (Topsfield, MA: Salem, 1986), 61.

15. Reference to this match is made in *The Polo Monthly*, August 1921.

16. Marty LeGrand, "Hidden Treasures," *Polo*, October 1988, 50.

17. A.J. Munnings, *The Second Burst* (London: Museum Press, 1950), 170.

18. *Polo* appears in an advertisement in page 4, December 1982 issue. *Prince Charles* is shown in the June 1983 issue, page 3.

19. Illustrated in *Polo*, October 1979, 18.

20. The author is grateful to Mr. F. Turner Reuter, Jr., for his identification of player and ponies in this painting. Personal communication, 28 May 2010.

21. An illustration of *The Old Polo Grounds* appears in *Polo*, October 1986, 26. Claude B. Prescott (1870–1932) was a painter and illustrator. Mary Ann Wingfield, *A Dictionary of Sporting Artists 1650–1990* (Woodbridge, Suffolk: Antique Collector's Club), 228.

22. The original painting is in a private collection. Two hundred and fifty prints were issued, to benefit the Polo Training Foundation. An illustration of *Tail Shot* appears in *Polo*, December 1976, 20.

23. *Outing*, Vol. 18, August 1891.

24. The mounted version is illustrated in *Polo*, November 1992, 34.

25. James Mackay, *The Animaliers* (New York: Dutton, 1973), 157.

26. Illustrated in *Polo*, October 1987, 29.

27. For a short biography of Charles Rumsey, see Dennis J. Amato and Lynda Anderson, "Poloist and Artist," *Polo Players' Edition*, November 2004, 28.

28. Peggy Miller Franck, *Prides Crossing* (Beverly, MA: Commonwealth, 2009), 126.

20. "Tradition," *Polo Players' Edition*, November 2006, 29.

30. *A Master Stroke*, oil on canvas, is illustrated in *Polo*, November 1991, 34.

31. U.S.P.A. 1923 *Year Book*, 153.

32. *Polo Players' Edition*, November 2000, 20.

33. *Polo*, August 1930, 12.

Chapter 25

1. U.S.P.A.1951 *Year Book*, "Member Clubs," 5.

2. U.S.P.A. 2009 *Year Book*, "Active, Affiliate and Inactive Clubs," 23.

3. The Spreckels Cup was presented in 1909 by the Coronado Country Club in memory of sugar magnates Adolph and John Spreckels.

4. The Perry Trophy was designed by Oscar L. Lantz and presented to the club in 1905 by Mrs. Marsden Perry.

5. U.S.P.A. 2009 *Year Book*, "Florida Circuit," 11.

6. Gwen Rizzo, "Open Present," *Polo Players' Edition*, June 2004, 26.

7. Gwen Rizzo, "Broken Curse," *Polo Players' Edition*, June 2005, 34.

8. Personal communication from S.K. Johnston, Jr.

9. Gwen Rizzo, "Peak Performance," *Polo Players' Edition*, June 2006, 36.

10. Gwen Rizzo, "Golden Ticket," *Polo Players' Edition*, May 2007, 36.

11. Rule 11c. "Enforcement of Rules. The USPA will enforce all of its rules in any USPA tournament. Member clubs are strongly recommended to adhere to these rules in all other clubs events." 2007 U.S.P.A. *Year Book*, 89.

12. Letter from Mr. Jack L. Sheldon to Mr. Guillermo Gracida, *The Morning Line*, 24 March 2007, 2.

13. Stephen A. Orthwein, "Welcome from the Chairman," in *The 2009 Westchester Cup Official Program*, Horace A. Laffaye, editor (Wellington: The National Museum of Polo and Hall of Fame, 2009), 8.

14. Alex Webbe, "Red, White and Green," *Polo Players' Edition*, May 2009, 34.

Chapter 26

1. Chris Ashton, "Polo Reflections," *Polo Players' Edition*, 2010, 14.

2. Marty LeGrand, "Editorial," *Polo*, March 1994, 5.

3. Gwen Rizzo, "All-wheel Drive — Audi Quad Dominates California Season," *Polo Players' Edition*, 30.

4. Editorial, "U.S.P.A. Who?" *Polo*, December 1976, [11].

5. E. Digby Baltzell, *Sporting Gentlemen* (New York: Free Press, 1995), 33.

6. Ibid., 390.

7. Personal communication from Dr. Alberto Pedro Heguy.

8. 2009 U.S.P.A. *Year Book*, vi.

9. 2009 H.P.A. *Year Book*, 64.

10. J.C. Coolidge, *Polo*, March 1934, 14.

11. Statement issued by Keith Kane, Director of Equine Protection for the Humane Society of the United States on April 23, 2009:

While we still await conclusive results of toxicology tests, The Humane Society of the United States extends its condolences to those affected by the tragic deaths of the Polo ponies of the Lechuza Caracas team at the U.S. Open Polo Championship in Wellington, Fla. last Sunday. While news reports suggest that this may have been a case of accidental overdose of a toxic substance, this does not lessen the grief of those who cared for and loved these animals, and the American public. This tragedy has brought to light the absence of drug policies and regulation within the sport of polo. There are no prohibitions or testing requirements for the use of drugs or other performance-enhancing substances. The HSUS calls on the authorities involved to continue to vigorously pursue this investigation and for the polo industry to use this tragedy as a catalyst to begin implementing reforms to ensure that policies are enacted and enforced

that will ensure better protection for the horses in its care.

12. *Ellenhorn's Medical Toxicology* (Baltimore: William & Wilkins, 1997), 1607–1609; *Haddad and Winchester's Clinical Management of Poisoning and Drug Overdose* (Philadelphia: Saunders Elsevier, 2007), 1164.

13. "There Will Be Blood," Peter J. Rizzo, *Polo Players' Edition*, December 2009, 19.

14. Daniel Wallace, "Umpire Abuse: Getting Tough Isn't Enough," *Polo*, September 1991, 14.

15. Marty LeGrand, "A Gentleman's Game? Bad Behavior Turns Polo into a Battlefield," *Polo*, March 1994, 38.

16. James Mullan, "Simple but Effective: Polo Gets a Makeover," *Polo Times*, July 2009, 28.

17. The Polo Report, "No Willful Intent in Sieber's Death," *Polo*, December 1984/January 1985, 78.

18. U.S.P.A. 2009 Yearbook, 89.

19. "Slash whipping" is defined as loud and repeated strokes. "Overwhipping" occurs when three or more strokes are used, or whipping when the mount is laboring. "Heavy whipping" is defined as hitting the mount following a missed play.

20. W. Cameron Forbes, *As to Polo* (Dedham Polo & Country Club: private printing, 1911), 3.

21. Prof. Sir David William Brogan (1900–1974) was a Scot professor at Cambridge University. John R. Tunis, *The American Way in Sports* (New York: Duell, Sloan & Pierce, 1958), 151. Roger Bannister and Chris Chataway were famous athletes in the 1950s. Roger Bannister, later Sir Roger, is a distinguished neurologist and was the first man to run one mile in less than four minutes. His friend Chris Chataway, later Sir Christopher, was one of Bannister's pacers during the historic run, while studying at Oxford University.

22. Marty LeGrand, "A Gentleman's Game? Bad Behavior Turns Polo into a Battlefield," *Polo*, March 1994, 59.

23. Ami Shinitzky, "Our Obsession with Sportsmanship," *Polo*, March 1994, 12.

24. Personal communication from Mauricio Devrient-Kidd, February 2010.

25. Steven E. Walsh, "An Inviting Game," *Polo Players' Edition*, May 1998, 12.

Bibliography

à Brassard, Nigel. *A Glorious Victory, a Glorious Defeat*. Chippenham: Antony Rowe, 2001.

_____. *Tommy Hitchcock — A Tribute*. Cirencester: Letter Press, 2003.

"Addison Geary" [Addison Geary Smith]. *Mallet and Hounds*. Buffalo, NY: private printing, 1931.

Aldrich, Nelson W., Jr. *Tommy Hitchcock: An American Hero*. Gaithersburg, MD(?): Fleet Street, 1984.

Aitzazuddin, F.S. *Year Book of Pakistan Polo*. Lahore: Habib Press, 1974.

Alles, Jane P. *The History of the Philadelphia Country Club*. Wilmington, DE: private printing, 1965.

Allison, Benjamin R. *The Rockaway Hunting Club*. Brattleboro, VT: private printing, 1952.

Appleton Dictionary of New York. New York: D. Appleton, 1883.

Armour, G.D. *Bridle and Brush*. New York: Scribner's, 1937.

Ashton, Chris. *Geebung — The Story of Australian Polo*. Sydney: Hamilton, 1993.

Asociación Argentina de Polo. *Campeonato Argentino Abierto de Polo*. Buenos Aires: A.A. de Polo, 1993.

"Author Escaped" E. and O.E. *Not a History of the Dedham Polo Club*. Boston: Walton, 1907.

Ayer, Neil R. *Wind Over Willowdale*. Beverly, MA: Memoirs Unlimited, 1991.

Bahto, George. *The Evangelist of Golf*. Chelsea, MI: Clock Tower, 2002.

Baltzell, E. Digby. *Sporting Gentlemen*. New York: Free Press, 1995.

Bannister, Judith. *English Silver Hallmarks*. London: Foulsham, 1995.

Barnes, Simon. *The Meaning of Sport*. London: Short Books, 2006.

Beal, Carl. *Into Polo*. Midland, TX: Prentis, 1993.

Bent, Newell. *American Polo*. New York: Macmillan, 1929.

Biscotti, M.L. *Paul Brown*. Lanham, MD: Derrydale Press, 2001.

Board, John. *Year with Horses*. London: Hodder & Stoughton, 1954.

Boegner, Peggie Phipps, and Richard Gachot. *Halcyon Days*. New York: Abrams, 1986.

Boyd, C. Robert. *A History of Carranor Hunt and Polo Club 1921–2002*. Perrysburg, OH: private printing, 2003.

Brooks Brothers. *Polo*. New York: private printing, 1927.

Brown, J. [James] Moray. *Polo*. London: Vinton, 1895.

Brown, Paul. *Good Luck and Bad*. New York: Scribner's, 1940.

_____. *Polo*. New York: Scribner's, 1949.

_____. *Spills and Thrills*. New York: Scribner's, 1933.

_____. *Ups and Downs*. New York: Scribner's, 1936.

Buchan, John. *Francis and Riversdale Grenfell*. London: Nelson, 1920.

Calvert, Blair. *Cecil Smith: Mr. Polo*. Midland, TX: Prentis, 1990.

Ceballos, Francisco. *El polo en la Argentina*. Banfield: Dirección General de Remonta, 1968.

Capuzzo, Michael. *Close to the Shore*. New York: Random House, 2001.

Chaine, Federico. *Los Heguy*. Buenos Aires: Imprenta de los Buenos Ayres, 2001.

Chartier, Jean-Luc A. *Polo de France*. Paris: Média France, 1988.

Christensen, Karen, Allen Guttmann and Gertrude Pfister. *International Encyclopedia of Women Sports*. New York: Macmillan, 2001.

Clendenning, Iris. *The History of the Montreal Polo Club*. Les Cèdres, Quebec: private printing, 1987.

Coaten, A.W. [Arthur Wells], editor. *International Polo*. London: S.B. Vaughn, 1912.

Corey, W. Russell G. *Alan Corey: 9-Goals*. No place: private printing, 2009.

Courage Exhibition of National Trophies. *Sporting Glory*, London: Sporting Trophies Exhibition, 1992.

Cowley, Guillermo, and Alexandra de Wankowicz. *A Season of Polo*. Palm Beach, FL: Citigroup, 2002.

Cullum, [Ernest] Grove. *Selection and Training of the Polo Pony*. New York: Scribner's, 1934.

Cullum, George Washington. *Biographical Register of the Officers and Graduates of the U.S. Military Academy*. Several editions, 1891–1940.

Dale, T.F. [Thomas Francis]. *The Game of Polo*. Westminster: Constable, 1897.

_____. *Polo at Home and Abroad*. London: London & Counties, 1915.

_____. *Polo — Past and Present*. London: Country Life, 1905.

_____. *Riding and Polo Ponies*. London: Unwin, 1899.

Daniels, John H. [Hancock]. *Nothing Could Be Finer*. Camden, SC: John Culler, 1996.

Del Vecchio, Valentine. *Beneath the Dome of PMI*. Santa Barbara, CA: Reference Desk, 1997.

Devereux, W.B., Jr. *Position and Team Play in Polo*. New York: Brooks Bros., MCMXIV [sic] [1924].

Disston, Harry. *Beginning Polo*. South Brunswick, NJ: A.S. Barnes, 1973.

Drybrough, T.B. *Polo*. London: Vinton, 1898.

Ellison, Gabriel, and Kim Fraser. *Harmony of Hooves*. No place: The Natal Witness, 1999.

Ferguson, Ronald. *The Galloping Major*. London: Macmillan, 1994.

FitzPatrick, H.L. *Equestrian Polo*. New York: American Sports, 1904.

Forbes, Allan. *Early Myopia*. No place: private printing, 1942.

_____. *Sport in Norfolk County*. Boston: Houghton Mifflin, 1938.

Forbes, W. Cameron. *As to Polo*. No place: Manila Polo Club, 1911.

14th U.S. Cavalry. *A Manual of Polo*. Camp Stotsenburg, Philippine Islands: private printing, 1910.

Franck, Peggy Miller. *Prides Crossing: The Unbridled Life and Impatient Times of Eleonora Sears*. Beverly, MA: Commonwealth, 2009.

Freeman, William S. *History of Plymouth County, Iowa*. Indianapolis: Bowen, 1917.

French, Amos Tuck. *Harvard Polo Club*. New York: Knickerbocker, 1930.

Griswold, Frank Gray. *The International Polo Cup*. New York: Dutton's, 1928.

_____. *Sport on Land and Water*. Norwood, MA: Plimpton Press, 1913.

Halpin, Warren T. *Hoofbeats*. Philadelphia: Lippincott, 1938.

Harnack, Curtis. *Gentlemen on the Prairie*. Ames: Iowa State University, 1985.

Hatch, Alden, and Foxhall Keene. *Full Tilt*. New York: Derrydale, 1938.

Healy, James F. *St. Louis Country Club: A Legacy of Sports*. Ladue: St. Louis Country Club, 2009.

Heron, Roy. *The Sporting Art of Cecil Aldin*. London: Sportsman's Press, 1990.

Hoyt, Edwin. *The Whitneys*. New York: Weybright & Talley, 1976.

Ira, Luning Bonifacio. *Manila Polo Club*. No place: private printing, 1984.

Kelly, Robert F. *The Year Book of the Horse 1934*. New York: Dodd, Mead, 1935.

Kendall, Paul Green. *Polo Ponies*. New York: Derrydale Press, 1933.

King, Bucky. *Big Horn Polo*. Sheridan, WY: Still Sailing, 1987.

Knox, Northrup R. *To B.A. and Back, Again*. Buffalo, NY: private printing, no date. [1967]

_____. *To B.A. Once More*. No place: private printing, no date. [1970]

Knox, Seymour H. *Aurora at Oak Brook*. No place: private printing, no date. [1969]

_____. *Aurora in England*. Buffalo: private printing, 1934.

_____. *To B.A. and Back*. Buffalo: private printing, 1933.

Laffaye, Horace A. *The Evolution of Polo*. Jefferson, NC: McFarland, 2009.

_____. *The Polo Encyclopedia*. Jefferson, NC: McFarland, 2004.

_____. *El polo internacional argentino*. Buenos Aires: Edición del Autor, 1988.

_____, ed. *Profiles in Polo: The Players Who Changed the Game*. Jefferson, NC: McFarland, 2007.

Layton, Elizabeth Y. *The Golden Mallet*. Kauai, HI: Grey Lady, 2003.

Levey, Clarence D. *Torrence-Clendennin Episode and the Melville Letters*. New York: private printing, 1892.

Levinson, David, and Karen Christensen. *Encyclopedia of World Sport*. Santa Barbara, CA: ABC-Clio, 1996.

Lubash, Robert D. *Polo Wisdom*. No place: Jostens, 2003.

Macdonald, Charles B. *Scotland's Gift — Golf*. Stratford, CT: Classics of Golf, 1985.

Mallon, Bill. *The 1900 Olympic Games*. Jefferson, NC: McFarland, 2000.

_____, and Anthony Th. Bijkerk. *The 1920 Olympic Games*. Jefferson, NC: McFarland, 2000.

Mackay, James. *The Animaliers*. New York: Dutton, 1973.

Matthews, John J. *E.W. Marland: Life and Death of an Oilman*. Norman: University of Oklahoma, 1951.

Martin, Joan Gilbert, and Colleen McInerney-Meagher. *Pogonip*. Santa Cruz, CA: Otter B Books, 2007.

McKenzie, Donald C., and John R. McKenzie. *A History of Polo in South Africa*. Dargle: private printing, 1999.

McMichael, E.H. *Polo on the China Pony*. Shanghai: Mercantile, 1931.

Melvill, T.P. *Ponies and Women*. London: Jarrolds, 1932.

Milburn, Frank. *The Emperor of Games*. New York: Knopf, 1994.

Miller, E.D. *Fifty Years of Sport*. New York: Dutton, no date. [1925]

_____. *Modern Polo*. London: Thacker, 1896.

Mitchell, Sally. *The Dictionary of British Sporting Artists*. Woodbridge, Suffolk: Antiques Collector's Club, 1985.

Montagu of Beaulieu, Lord. *The Gordon Bennett Races*. London: Cassell, 1963.

Munnings, A.J. *The Second Burst*. London: Museum Press, 1950.

Outerbridge, David E. *Champion in a Man's World— The Biography of Marion Hollins*. Chelsea, MI: Sleeping Bear, 1998.

Patten, William. *The Book of Sport*. New York: J.F. Taylor, 1901.

Piping Rock Club. No place: private printing, 1914.

Prescott, Lucian K., Jr. *The Twilight of the U.S. Cavalry*. Lawrence: University of Kansas, 1989.

Pride, W.F. *History of Fort Riley*. Topeka, KS: Capper, 1926.

Rees, Tony. *The Galloping Game*. Cochrane, Alberta, Canada: Western Heritage, 2000.

Reuter, F. Turner, Jr. *Animal & Sporting Artists in America*. Middleburg, VA: National Sporting Library, 2008.

Robb, Alex M. *The Sanfords of Amsterdam*. New York: William-Frederick, 1969.

Roberts, S.J. *An Autobiographical History of Collegiate Polo and Its Players at Cornell University, 1919–1972 and Beyond*. No place: Private printing, no date [1997].

Rodríguez Egaña, Carlos. *Manual de Polo*. Buenos Aires: Buttafoco, 1923.

Ross-of-Bladensburg, Sir Foster George. *A History of the Coldstream Guards*. London: Innes, 1896.

Roy, Frederic. *Your Polo Game*. West Palm Beach, FL: Stadium Polo, 1993.

Seitz, Don C. *The James Gordon Bennetts*. Indianapolis: Bobbs-Merrill, 1928.

Shackleford, Geoff. *The Riviera Country Club*. No place: private printing, 1995.

Shinitzky, Ami, and Don Follmer. *The Endless Chukker*. Gaithersburg, MD: Polo, 1978.

Smith, Harry Worcester Smith. *Life and Sport in Aiken*. New York: Derrydale, 1935.

Spencer, Herbert. *Chakkar— Polo Around the World*. New York: Drake, 1971.

"The Sportsman." *Polo and Coaching*. London: Sports & Sportsmen, no date. [1923]

Sprague, Marshall. *Newport in the Rockies*. Denver: Sage, 1961.

_____. *The Grizzlies— A History: The Cheyenne Mountain Country Club*. No place: The Club, 1983.

Stock, Alphons. *Polo: International Sport*. London: Universal Bridge of Trade, no date. [1930]

Tucoo-Chala, Pierre. *Histoire de Pau*. Toulouse: Privat, 1989.

Tunis, John R. *The American Way in Sports*. New York: Duell, Sloan & Pierce, 1958.

U.S. Military Academy. *List of Cadets from Origin till June 30, 1937*. West Point, NY: U.S. Military Academy, 1937.

Van Der Zee, Jacob. *The British in Iowa*. Iowa City: Historical Society of Iowa, 1922.

Van Urk, J. Blan. *The Horse, the Valley and the Chagrin Valley Hunt*. New York: Ellis, 1947.

_____. *The Story of American Foxhunting*. New York: Derrydale, 1941.

Viana, Marqués de. *De la posición y forma de jugar un team en el polo*. Madrid: Lacau, 1928.

Villavieja, Marqués de. *Life has Been Good*. London: Chatto & Windus, 1938.

Vischer, Peter, editor. *Horse and Horseman*. New York: Arco, 1975.

Volkmann, Orv. *55 Years of Polo in Minnesota: 1922–1977*. No place: private printing, 1979.

Wallechinsky, David. *The Complete Book of the Olympics*. New York: Penguin, 1988.

Watson, J.N.P. *The World of Polo*. Topsfield, MA: Salem, 1986.

Weeks, Edward. *Myopia*. Hamilton, MA: private printing, 1976.

Weir, Robert, and J. Moray Brown. *Riding— Polo*. London: Longmans, Green, 1891.

White, Wesley J. *Guide for Polo Umpires*. New York: U.S.P.A., 1929.

Whitney, Carrie Westlake. *Kansas City, Missouri: Its history and Its people 1808–1908*. Chicago: Clarke, 1908.

Wilson, Hamish. *Polo in New Zealand 1956–1976*. Auckland: Viking, 1976.

Winants, Peter. *The Sporting Art of Franklin B. Voss*. Lexington, KY: Eclipse, 2005.

Wingfield, Mary Ann. *A Dictionary of Sporting Artists 1650–1990*. Woodbridge, Suffolk: Antique Collector's Club, 1992.

_____. *Sport and the Artist*. Woodbridge, Suffolk: Antique Collector's Club, 1988.

Woods, Lawrence M. *British Gentlemen in the Wild West*. New York: Free Press, 1989.

Annuals and Year Books

Asociación Argentina de Polo. *Centauros*. Buenos Aires, 2002–2006.

_____. *Libro Anual*. Buenos Aires, 1924–1980.

The Horseman's Year. London, 1952–1960.

Hurlingham Polo Association Year Book. London, Billingshurst, Midhurst, Kirtlington and Little Coxwell: H.P.A., 1951–2007.

The Polo Association Year Book. New York: The Association, 1890–1922.

The Polo Year Book. London, 1928–1937.

Simmonds, L.V.L., and E.D. Miller. *The Polo Annual*. London: 1913.

Spalding's Polo Guide. New York: 1921–1923.

U.S. Polo Association Year Book. New York, Oak Brook, and Lexington: 1923–2008.

Bibliography

Magazines and Newspapers

Automobile Quarterly. Kutztown: 1962–2009.
Baily's Magazine of Sports and Pastimes. London: 1875–1915.
El Caballo. Buenos Aires: 1949–1989.
Centauros. Buenos Aires: 1955–1983.
The Field Artillery Journal. 1921–1931.
Galveston Daily News. 1876–1883.
El Gráfico. Buenos Aires: 1924–2007.
Harper's New Monthly Magazine.
Horse and Horseman. New York: 1936–1938.
International Journal of Sport. London: 2001–2003.
Journal of Field Artillery. 1911–1946.
The Le Mars Sentinel. Le Mars: 1878–1887.
The London Gazette. London: 1845–2007.
Outing Magazine. 1891–1923.

Polo. New York: 1927–1936.
Polo. Gaithersburg and Wellington: 1972–1996.
Polo & Campo. Buenos Aires. 1933–1939.
Polo & Equitación. Buenos Aires. 1924–1932.
The Polo Magazine: 1977–1979.
The Polo Monthly. London: 1909–1939.
Polo Players Diary. London: 1910.
Polo Players' Edition. Wellington: 1997–2008.
Polo Players Guide. London. 1910–1912.
Polo Quarterly International. 1992–2008.
Polo Times. North Leigh, Oxfordshire. 1993–2008.
Riviera Chukker. 1936–1939.
San Antonio Light. 1883.
Sidelines. Wellington: 1974–2007.
Spalding Polo Guide. New York: 1921.
Sports Illustrated. New York: 1969.
Western Field. San Francisco: 1907.

Index

Numbers in *bold italics* indicate pages with illustrations.